Land Legislation in
Mandate Palestine

Land Legislation in Mandate Palestine

VOLUME 5

OFFICIAL REPORTS AND MEMORANDA, PART I

Editor: Martin Bunton

an imprint of

CAMBRIDGE UNIVERSITY PRESS

Cambridge, New York, Melbourne, Madrid, Cape Town, Singapore, São Paulo

Cambridge University Press
The Edinburgh Building, Cambridge CB2 2RU, UK

Published in the United States of America by Cambridge University Press,
New York

www.cambridge.org
Information on this title: www.archiveeditions.co.uk

© Copyright in this edition including research, selection of documents, arrangement, contents lists and descriptions: Cambridge Archive Editions Ltd 2009

Cambridge Archive Editions is an imprint of Cambridge University Press.

Facsimiles of original documents including Crown copyright material are published under licence from The National Archives, London, England. Images may be used only for purposes of research, private study or education. Applications for any other use should be made to The National Archives Image Library, Kew, Richmond, Surrey TW9 4DU. Infringement of the above condition may result in legal action.

Subject to statutory exception and to the provisions of relevant collective licensing agreements, no reproduction of other parts of the work may take place without written permission of Cambridge University Press.

Spry Collection: Documents reprinted with permission from Middle East Centre Archive, St. Antony's College, Oxford and under licence from The National Archives as described above.

Every reasonable effort has been made to contact all copyright holders; in the event of any omission please contact the publisher.

First published 2009

Printed and bound by CPI Group (UK) Ltd, Croydon, CR0 4YY

British Library Cataloguing in Publication Data
Land Legislation in Mandate Palestine.
  1. Land tenure–Law and legislation–Palestine–History–
  20th century. 2. Land tenure–Law and legislation–
  Palestine–History–20th century–Sources. 3. Palestine–
  Politics and government–1917-1948.
  I. Bunton, Martin P.
  346.5'6940432-dc22

ISBN-13:   978-1-84097-260-3 (set) (hardback)
           978-1-84097-262-7 (volume 5)

Land Legislation in Mandate Palestine

CONTENTS

VOLUME 5:

OFFICIAL REPORTS AND MEMORANDA, PART I

Section 1: Memoranda on Land Law and Tenure, 1918–1925   1

1.01 Col. French, Acting Chief Political Officer, Egyptian Expeditionary Force, Cairo, to Secretary of State for Foreign Affairs, London, 25 July 1919, regarding promulgation of a new land transfer ordinance, and enclosing copies of a draft ordinance and a memorandum by Lt. Col. N. Bentwick, Senior Judicial Officer, Jerusalem [FO 371/ 4226]

1.02 Draft of 1919 land transfer ordinance, with notes on same by Dr. Ch.Weizmann, Mr. C.C. Garbett, Sir E. Bonham-Carter and Lt. Col. E.B. Howell [FO 371/5138]   13

1.03 'Note on Land Law' by Judge G.W. Williamson, 1919 [MECA, Spry Collection, 1/1]   25

1.04 Minute dated 10 February 1922 from H.G. Samuel, High Commissioner, Jerusalem, forwarding 'The Land Settlement Commission's Report'; letter from N. Bentwich to Major Abramson, 19 April 1920, commissioning the report; letter from A. Abramson and colleagues, 31 May 1921, covering the completed report [CO 733/18]   35

1.05 Sir E. Dowson, Kent, to Under Secretary of State, Colonial Office, London, 21 August 1924, regarding the efforts of the British to resolve the tangle of real rights to land in the wake of destruction of evidence which had existed under Ottoman rule [CO 733/85]   91

1.06 Lord Plumer, High Commissioner for Palestine, Jerusalem, to L.S. Amery, Secretary of State for the Colonies, 21 September 1924, with observations on the standardization of measures of land, and enclosing a draft ordinance to provide for the introduction of a standard measure of land, and an explanatory note by N. Bentwich, Attorney General; a letter from Sir E. Dowson, 20 November 1924; L.S. Amery response to draft ordinance, 10 November 1925 [CO 733/97]   97

1.07 N. Bentwich, Attorney General, Jerusalem, to J.N. Stubbs, Director of Lands, Jerusalem, 7 November 1924, enclosing memorandum written by Stubbs entitled 'Notes on Land Law in Palestine,' [MECA, Spry Collection, 1/4, 1/6 pp. 1-26] — 111

1.08 Sir E. Dowson, Jerusalem, to Chief Secretary, Jerusalem, 12 March 1925, regarding the interpretation of Ottoman law and the definition of government title to forest land [CO 733/97] — 143

1.09 'Preliminary Study of Land Tenure in Palestine, November 1925,' by Sir E. Dowson, Kent [CO 733/109]; extract of private letter from Lord Plumer to Sir J. Shuckburgh, 20 November 1925, regarding report by Dowson [CO 733/109]; Sir E. Dowson, 5 December 1925 covering 'Report on the Land System in Palestine, December 1925' [CO 733/109] — 151

Section 2: Memoranda on Credit, 1918-1930

2.01 Maj. Gen. A.W. Money, Chief Administrator Occupied Enemy Administration, (South), Jerusalem, to General Staff, Cairo, 9 May 1919, regarding the urgent provision of agricultural loans and enclosing a copy of proposals [FO 371/4226] — 267

2.02 G. Clayton, Officer Administering the Government, Jerusalem, to J.C. Thomas, Secretary of State for the Colonies, London, 3 July 1924, enclosing report on agricultural loans [CO 733/70] — 277

2.03 J. Chancellor, High Commissioner for Palestine, Jerusalem, to Lord Passfield, Secretary of State for the Colonies, London, 11 January 1930, regarding the establishment of an agricultural bank in Palestine, and enclosing the report of the commission tasked to consider establishment of agricultural bank, letter dated 22 November 1929; Colonial Office memorandum 'Land titles in Palestine' [CO 733/184] — 319

Section 3: Memoranda on Land Taxation, 1922-1926

3.01 W. Churchill, Secretary of State for the Colonies, London, to H. Samuel, High Commissioner for Palestine, Jerusalem, 22 August 1922, draft letter regarding a system of land taxation based on survey; H. Samuel, Jerusalem, to W. Churchill, London, 31 March 1922, enclosing 'Report of the Tithes Commission' [CO 733/20] — 351

3.02 Memorandum, dated December 1923, covering 'Notes on land-tax, cadastral survey and land settlement in Palestine', by Sir E. Dowson, Kent [CO 814/60] — 491

3.03 Lord Plumer, High Commissioner for Palestine, Jerusalem, to L.S. Amery, Secretary of State for the Colonies, London, 10 September 1925, with enclosure and an extract from a memorandum by Sir E. Dowson regarding payment of land transaction fees, 10 April 1925; L.S. Amery to Lord Plumer, 5 October 1925, regarding same [CO 733/97] — 557

3.04 G.B. Symes, Officer Administering the Government, Jerusalem, to L.S. Amery, Secretary of State for the Colonies, London, 6 October 1926, enclosing letter from W.J. Johnson, Chairman, Land Committee, 26 July 1926, and majority and minority reports by the 'Average Tithe Committee', and also forwarding observations by district commissioners J.E.F. Campbell and A. Abramson [CO 733/117] — 569

Section 4: Memoranda and Reports on Land Survey, 1925–1946

4.01 Sir E. Dowson, Jerusalem, to Treasurer, Government of Palestine, Jerusalem, 25 February 1925, enclosing memorandum and survey and land settlement estimates 1925–1926; observations and notes on same by H.C. Ley, Director of Surveys [CO 733/92] — 603

4.02 C.H. Ley, 'Note on the Technical System of the Survey of Palestine, January 1927' (Government of Palestine, February 1927) — 663

4.03 Sir E.M. Dowson, Kent, to Sir J.E. Shuckburgh, London, 4 August 1927, regarding appointment of Survey Officer in Trans Jordan [CO 733/140/7] — 675

4.04 C.H. Ley, Survey of Palestine, 'The Structure and Procedure of Cadastral Survey in Palestine' (Government of Palestine, 1931) — 683

4.05 Department of Surveys, 'Report for the years 1940–1946 (with supplement for 1947–1948)'. [Maps reproduced in facsimile in the Map Box.] [CO 814/40] — 745

Section 1: Memoranda on Land Law and Tenure, 1918–1925

1.01

GENERAL HEADQUARTERS
EGYPTIAN EXPEDITIONARY FORCE.

25th July 1919.

My Lord,

With reference to your Lordship's telegram No. 218 of July 9th, I have the honour to attach two copies of the Land Ordinance in question.

Copies of this Ordinance were circulated to all Zones of Enemy Territory Occupied by the Egyptian Expeditionary Force.

The Chief Administrators have now been informed that no steps are to be taken by them to put this Ordinance into force, pending the receipt of further orders.

I attach also copies of correspondence received by the General Staff from Chief Administrators on this subject.

I have the honour to be,
My Lord
Your Lordship's Obedient humble Servant,

C. French.
COLONEL.
Acting Chief Political Officer.
Egyptian Expeditionary Force.

To His Britannic Majesty's
Secretary of State for Foreign Affairs.
The Foreign Office.
LONDON.

101.

ORDINANCE

WHEREAS it is expedient to permit certain transactions in immovable property and to re-establish the Land Registry Offices.

IT IS HEREBY ORDERED as follow :-

1. This Ordinance applies to all immovable property the subject of the Land Law of 7 Ramadan 1274, as well as to mulk land, all forms of wakf land and every other form of immovable property, and shall be substituted as far as it applies for the Proclamation of 18-11-18 concerning immovable property.

2. The expression "disposition" in this Ordinance means a sale, mortgage, gift, dedication of wakf of every discription and any other disposition of immovable property, and includes a transfer or other disposition of a mortgage and also a lease for a term of more than three years.

3. No disposition of immovable property will be valid until the provisions of this Ordinance have been complied with.

4. Any person wishing to make a disposition of immovable property must first obtain the written consent of the O.E.T.A.
In order to obtain this consent, a petition must be presented to the Military Governor of the district in which the land is situated, setting out the terms of the agreement intended to be made and applying for his consent to a disposition in accordance with the agreement. The petition must contain an application for registration of a deed to be executed for the purpose of carrying into effect the terms of the agreement. The petition may also include a clause fixing the damages to be paid by either party who refuses to complete the disposition if it is approved.

5. If the application for registration is made by an agent or nominee on behalf of a principal, the agent or nominee shall make full disclosure in his petition of the principal for whom he is acting, and the immovable property disposed of shall be registered in the name of the principal.
If at any time it appears in a Judicial proceeding that immovable property has been registered under this Ordinance otherwise than in accordance with the foregoing provision, the Court shall inquire into the case and make a report to the Chief Administrator, who may impose upon any of the parties concerned such penalties by way of fine or forfeiture of the property in whole or in part as he may think fit.

6. When the person acquiring the immovable property is permanently resident in Palestine the consent of the Administration will be given through the Military Governor of the district in which the land is situated, provided that the disposition complies with both the following conditions :-
   (a) That the area of the immovable property does not exceed 200 donums. (dunums.)
   (b) That the value of the immovable property does not exceed £E.1000.

7. The Military Governor shall withhold his consent in the case of agricultural land unless he is satisfied that the person acquiring the land intends himself to cultivate it. He shall also withhold his consent in the case of a disposition of any immovable property if he is of opinion that the person acquiring the immovable property is obtaining an excessive amount thereof in any particular neighbourhood.

8. Excepting the cases complying with the conditions set out in section 6 hereof, all dispositions shall be referred to the Chief Administrator for his consent, which he may give or withhold in his absolute discretion.

9. After the consent of the Administration has been obtained a deed shall be executed in the form prescribed by Rules made in accordance with sec: 15 hereof and the deed shall be regiestered in the Land Registry.

10. No mortgage shall be accepted for registration unless it complies with the terms of the Provisional Law for the mortgage of immovable property of 16 Rabia Tani 1331 and the amendments of the said law.

11. Every disposition to which the written consent of the Administration has not been obtained shall be null and void, provided that any person that has paid money in respect of a disposition which is null and void may recover the same by action in the Courts.

12. If any person is a party to any disposition of immovable property which has not received the consent of the Administration and either enters into possession or permits the other party to enter into possession of the immovable property, whether by himself or any person on his behalf, he shall be liable on conviction by a Court of 1st Instance to payment of a fine not exceeding one fourth of the value of the Immovable property.

13. When any immovable property passes by operation of a will or by inheritance, the legatees or heir, as the case may be, shall be jointly and severally responsible for the registration of the immovable property in the name of the legatees or heirs within a year of the death. The registration shall be made upon the certificate of a competent Court stating that the person or persons requiring registration are entitled as legatees or heirs or upon a certificate signed by the Mukhtar or Imam and two notables.
 If registration does not take place within one year of the death, an additional registration fee of 5 per cent of the value of the immovable property shall be levied by way of a fine for each year or part of a year during which there has been default.

14. The provisions of the Proclamation of 24 June 1918 preventing the Courts from giving a decision as to ownership of land and from ordering the sale of immovable property in execution of a judgement or in satisfaction of a mortgage shall be cancelled. The highest bidder for any immovable property so sold must apply for the consent of the Administration in manner laid down by this Ordinance, and the property shall not be registered in his name until that consent has been obtained. If the consent is withheld the Land Registry shall forthwith be notified and the property shall again be put up to auction 15 days after the notification. At this auction all bids shall be recorded and any bidder shall be deemed to have made an irrevocable offer to buy the property. The property shall be sold to the highest bidder who can obtain the consent of the Administration.

15. The Senior Judicial Officer may with the sanction of the Chief Administrator re-establish a Land Registry Office in such places as may seem desirable and may appoint such number of registrars and assistant registrars as may be necessary.

 The general superintendence and control over all land Registry Offices shall be vested in the Senior Judicial Officer who, with the sanction of the Chief Administrator, may from time to time make rules as to any of the following matters :-

(a) The organization, procedure and business of the Land Registration Offices.
(b) The function and duties of the Registrar and other officials of the Land Registry Office.
(c) The mode in which the Register is to be kept.
(d) The forms to be used for deeds and documents.
(e) The requirements for attestation and official verification of the execution of deeds.
(f) The fees payable for or in connection with registration.
(g) Any other matter or thing, whether similar or not to those above mentioned, in respect of which it may be expedient to make rules for the purpose of carrying this Ordinance into effect.

This Ordinance shall be called " The Transfer of Land Ordinance 1919".

FROM :- O.E.T.A. WEST.

TO :- GENSTET.

5/6/19.

Urgent SG/1368. After examination of ordinance 101 on transfer of lands we have no observations to make.

FROM :- OEAT NORTH.

TO   :- GENSTET.

2447   8/6/19.

    I have received regulations ralating to land transactions. I am in complete agreement with the proposal, the application of which appears to me to be useful.

==

37/50/6981.

G.S.(O.E.T) G.H.Q.

Mount Carmel.

     I forward herewith certain criticisms and questions put forward by the Chief Administrator on the subject of the proposed Law Transfer Ordinance.

(Sgd) W. CLAYTON.
Major.
A. P. O.

DAMASCUS.
28/6/1919.

No. 6326
/1846.

TO :-
H.E., D.C.P.O.

Reference your letter of 14/6/19 No. 37/50/6643 we beg to say that we have informed the offices concerned about the copies of the Law of 1919 dealing in the transfer land ordinance draft.

The Land Registry Office gave its suggestions on Art. 1st as follows:-

If the Law of property dated Ramadan 7th, 1274, were the one in action as far as the immovable property of all kinds and description and all kinds of Wakf are concerned, are the transfer laws and the free use of the land and the Turkish Wakf Laws to be annulled I wonder? Are the real Wakfs for the generation(seed) as well as the Mursad Wakfs to follow the registration Department or not? The last Transfer Law is still wider than that dated Ramadan 7th. 1274. What about the transferred property of those who died before this law was published? Do they follow the last Turkish Law dated Rabeah Awel 27th, 329 or the law dated Ramadan 9th. 1274?

The Land Registry Office gave its suggestions on the Art. 15th as follows :-

From this Art it is understood that the Registrations Departments are closed whereas they are not. They still continue their work according to the Turkish Law, relying on the decision of the Arab Civil Council of State dated 13 November 1918, under No. 199: besides this it is understood from the same Art, the necessity of binding the Registration Departments to the Director of the Judical Court, although the former had been quite independent in its work and the Judical Court has nothing to do with it as far as taking action is concerned.

The Land Registry Office said they have got many instructions and orders which would explain the Laws. Will all those instructions remain in force or will they be annulled after this law is published? I beg to refer all this to H.E., C. in C. that he may consider the said suggestions, and issue his orders as to what should be done in this respect.

Damascus
25/6/1919.

(Sgd) RIKABY.
Military Gove

G.S.(O.E.T.) G.H.Q.
MOUNT CARMEL.

Reference your GS/ET/259 of 5/7/19.

The remarks of the Land Registry of O.E.T.(E) on Art 1 of the Ordinance are, I think, based on a misapprehension. The reference to the Law of Ramadan 1274 is intended only to define the kinds of immovable property subject to the registrations provisions and does not affect in any way the application of later Ottoman Laws as to the disposition of immovable property. The rights in immovable property will be determined according to the Ottoman Law as it was at the time of the Occupation. It is clearly expressed that all forms of wakf land are subject to the provisions of the Ordinance, and therefore will have to be dealt with through the Registration Department. The purport of the last part of the question on Art.1 is not clear. If the question refers to the Law of Succession to be applied to the property of those who died before the publication of the law of 1329, that is a difficult matter of law which the Courts will determine. This Ordinance does not affect matters of substantive law at all, but only the provisions as to registration.

As regards the remarks on Art. 15 of the Draft Ordinance, the position in O.E.T(S) is that the Land Registries have been closed since the Occupation, and therefore have now to be re-established. The position is apparently different in O.E.T.(E); and some change will therefore be required in the wording of the clause of the Proclamation to be issued there. I agree that detailed modifications of this kind will have to be made in the Proclamations for the different territories. The arrangement by which the Senior Judicial Officer in O.E.T.(S) is constituted the head of the Land Registry Department is one which need not be followed in the other Administrations. In the Ottoman System, the Land Registry was a

2.

perfectly separate department from the Law Courts, and it maybe convenient in other territories to continue this separation, whereas in this territory a combination of the two is desirable. The instructions received by the Land Registry Offices from the Ottoman Government explaining Laws will remain valid so far as they are not inconsistent with anything in this Ordinance, or any other Ordinances and Public Notices issued by O.E.T.A. or so far as they are not found to be unreasonable in themselves.

(Sgd) N.BENTWICK.
Lt. Col.
a/Senior Judical Officer.

Law Courts,
Jerusalem.
10/7/1919.

1.02

EASTERN.

TURKEY.

Eastern: Turkey.
Registry Number: E1368/131/44
FROM India Office (Communicated by)

Received 11th March, 1920

Last Paper.

E1080

(Print.)

(How disposed of.)
P.U.T. Mar. 17th.

(Action completed.) (Index.)

Next Paper.

E1505

Land Transactions in Palestine.

Printed copy of draft Ordinance, with notes by Dr. Weizmann, Mr. Garbett, Sir E. Bonham-Carter, and Lieutenant Colonel E.B. Howell.

(Minutes.)

Q / 3 Copies to W.O.
2 / F.O.T. O. G Sec 13th

We have suggested minor changes in the Ordinance.

D.G. Osborne.
16/3.

ORDINANCE.

WHEREAS it is expedient to permit certain transactions in immovable property and to re-establish the Land Registry Offices:

IT IS HEREBY ORDERED as follows:—

1. This Ordinance applies to all immovable property the subject of the Land Law of 7 Ramadan 1274, as well as to mulk land, all forms of wakf land and every other other form of immovable property, and shall be substituted as far as it applies for the Proclamation of 18th November 1918 concerning immovable property.

2. The expression " disposition " in this Ordinance means a sale, mortgage, gift, dedication of wakf of every description and any other disposition of immovable property, and includes a transfer or other disposition of a mortgage and also a lease for a term of more than three years.

3. No disposition of immovable property will be valid until the provisions of this Ordinance have been complied with.

4. Any person wishing to make a disposition of immovable property must first obtain the written consent of the Occupied Enemy Territory Administration.
In order to obtain this consent, a petition must be presented to the Military Governor of the district in which the land is situated, setting out the terms of the agreement intended to be made and applying for his consent to a disposition in accordance with the agreement. The petition must contain an application for registration of a deed to be executed for the purpose of carrying into effect the terms of the agreement. The petition may also include a clause fixing the damages to be paid by either party who refuses to complete the disposition if it is approved.

5. If the application for registration is made by an agent or nominee on behalf of a principal, the agent or nominee shall make full disclosure in his petition of the principal for whom he is acting, and the immovable property disposed of shall be registered in the name of the principal.
If at any time it appears in a Judicial proceeding that immovable property has been registered under this Ordinance otherwise than in accordance with the foregoing provision, the Court shall inquire into the case and make a report to the Chief Administrator, who may impose upon any of the parties concerned such penalties by way of fine or forfeiture of the property in whole or in part as he may think fit.

6. When the person acquiring the immovable property is permanently resident in Palestine the consent of the Administration will be given through the Military Governor of the district in which the land is situated, provided that the disposition complies with both the following conditions:—
(a) That the area of the immovable property does not exceed 200 donums.
(b) That the value of the immovable property does not exceed £E.1,000.

7. The Military Governor shall withhold his consent in the case of agricultural land unless he is satisfied that the person acquiring the land intends himself to cultivate it. He shall also withhold his consent in the case of a disposition of any immovable property if he is of opinion that the person acquiring the immovable property is obtaining an excessive amount thereof in any particular neighbourhood.

8. Excepting the cases complying with the conditions set out in section 6 hereof, all dispositions shall be referred to the Chief Administrator for his consent, which he may give or withhold in his absolute discretion.

9. After the consent of the Administration has been obtained a deed shall be executed in the form prescribed by Rules made in accordance with section 15 hereof and the deed shall be registered in the Land Registry.

10. No mortgage shall be accepted for registration unless it complies with the terms of the Provisional Law for the mortgage of immovable property of 16 Rabia Tani 1331, and the amendments of the said law.

11. Every disposition to which the written consent of the Administration has not been obtained shall be null and void, provided that any person that has paid

money in respect of a disposition which is null and void may recover the same by action in the Courts.

12. If any person is a party to any disposition of immovable property which has not received the consent of the Administration and either enters into possession or permits the other party to enter into possession of the immovable property, whether by himself or any person on his behalf, he shall be liable on conviction by a Court of First Instance to payment of a fine not exceeding one-fourth of the value of the immovable property.

13. When any immovable property passes by operation of a will or by inheritance, the legatees or heir, as the case may be, shall be jointly or severally responsible for the registration of the immovable property in the name of the legatees or heirs within a year of the death. The registration shall be made upon the certificate of a competent Court stating that the person or persons requiring registration are entitled as legatees or heirs or upon a certificate signed by the Mukhtar or Imam and two notables.

If registration does not take place within one year of the death, an additional registration fee of 5 per cent. of the value of the immovable property shall be levied by way of a fine for each year or part of a year during which there has been default.

14. The provisions of the Proclamation of 24th June 1918 preventing the Courts from giving a decision as to ownership of land and from ordering the sale of immovable property in execution of a judgment or in satisfaction of a mortgage shall be cancelled. The highest bidder for any immovable property so sold must apply for the consent of the Administration in manner laid down by this Ordinance, and the property shall not be registered in his name until that consent has been obtained. If the consent is withheld the Land Registry shall forthwith be notified and the property shall again be put up to auction 15 days after the notification. At this auction all bids shall be recorded and any bidder shall be deemed to have made an irrevocable offer to buy the property. The property shall be sold to the highest bidder who can obtain the consent of the Administration.

15. The Senior Judicial Officer may with the sanction of the Chief Administrator re-establish a Land Registry Office in such places as may seem desirable and may appoint such number of registrars and assistant registrars as may be necessary.

The general superintendence and control over all Land Registry Offices shall be vested in the Senior Judicial Officer, who, with the sanction of the Chief Administrator, may from time to time make rules as to any of the following matters :—

(a) The organisation, procedure and business of the Land Registration Offices.
(b) The function and duties of the Registrar and other officials of the Land Registry Office.
(c) The mode in which the Register is to be kept.
(d) The forms to be used for deeds and documents.
(e) The requirements for attestation and official verification of the execution of deeds.
(f) The fees payable for or in connection with registration.
(g) Any other matter or thing, whether similar or not to those above mentioned, in respect of which it may be expedient to make rules for the purpose of carrying this Ordinance into effect.

This Ordinance shall be called " The Transfer of Land Ordinance, 1919."

2.—Note by Dr. Weizmann, dated 6th September 1919.

I have carefully considered the proposed Ordinance regulating sales and transactions of immovable property in Palestine, upon which you advised me in your letter of 18th August that Lord Curzon desired to have my views.

Realising the inconveniences occasioned by the absolute prohibition of all transaction in land, the Zionist Organisation appreciates the need of a relaxation of the present restrictions. It also appreciates the intention of His Majesty's Government, as expressed in the proposed Ordinance, to prevent indiscriminate dealings in land for speculative purposes.

I cannot but view with concern, however, the relaxation of the restrictions regarding the dedication of wakf and the transfer of property by way of gift. The

3

economic life of the country does not require at the present moment the opening of the cadastres, either for the making of gifts or the dedication of wakfs. If the restrictions regarding the creation of new wakfs are removed, it is likely that a considerable part of the land of the country will be made wakf, not in order to promote charitable or religious purposes so much as to remove the land from the effective control of the Government and to frustrate needed reforms. You are aware that the dedication of property to wakf does not necessarily deprive the donor and his family of valuable interests therein. Whatever land policy may be adopted in the future, the situation should not certainly be prejudiced unnecessarily before the mandate is issued. The Ordinance ought, therefore, it is submitted, to be modified so as to expressly exclude the dedication of wakf and transfer by way of gift.

I presume that under the proposed Ordinance no objection will be raised to the purchase of land for settlement purposes by Jewish bodies, such as the Jewish National Fund, the Jewish Colonisation Association, the Palestine Land Development Company, and other bodies approved by the Zionist Organisation, of the public purposes and *bona fides* of which the Government is satisfied.

In view of the possible issuance of the mandate within the next few months, and in order to avoid the accusation of surprise on the part of any elements of the community, it is suggested that the Ordinance be not made effective before 1st January 1920.

C. H. WEIZMANN.

3.—Note by Mr. C. C. Garbett, C.I.E., I.C.S., dated 1st October 1919.

1. The draft Ordinance consists of two parts : the first, regulations regarding the disposition of immovable property ; the second, the establishment of Land Registration Offices. It is proposed, apparently, to institute both *pari passu*. If Mesopotamian experience may be considered a guide, it would be wise to defer the regulations permitting land tranfers until it is certain that the Land Registration Offices are working well. It will probably be found in Palestine, as elsewhere in Turkey, that the best of title deeds contain inconsistencies and inaccuracies, that many title deeds are of doubtful validity, and that there are areas for which no proper deeds exist. If transfers such as are contemplated are to be permitted with the approval of the Administration, the Administration must take every precaution against being a party to fraudulent claims and fraudulent transfers, otherwise it will be laying up for the future inhabitants of Palestine an unlimited extent of disastrous litigation, and incurring for itself a very grave odium.

2. The way the problem was faced in the Baghdad Vilayet was that the Registration Offices were opened primarily for the registration of title in town properties only. The towns were divided into Mohallas, and the inhabitants of each Mohalla were invited to attend the Registration Offices at a specified time, bringing their original deeds together with copies. These copies they were invited to prepare on forms which were issued by the Administration ; or, if they chose, certified copies were made for them at a slight cost. These originals and copies were presented to a Committee at which the Mukhtar of their quarter and at least two notables sat. In this way the more obvious frauds were avoided. After registration had been completed, the public were allowed to make transfers. A similar system was to be extended gradually to the districts and agricultural land.

It is to be remembered that the only final proof of title in Turkey are title deeds registered at the head office at Constantinople. During the war local offices suffered damage, and the head office was of course cut off. Transfers in land were therefore deliberately reduced in Baghdad to a minimum until such time as the records at Constantinople would be available for the settlement of disputes.

It is suggested, therefore, that if the Ordinance is to be promulgated, effect should be given first to that portion which deals with the opening of Registration Offices.

3.—(a) As to the text itself, it is observed that the restrictions regarding the sale of land to foreigners, which are enforced in Mesopotamia, find no place in this draft.

Under the Turkish law of Jemadi-ul-awal of 1284 A.H., foreigners were permitted to acquire land in Turkey provided that they forewent all benefits otherwise accruing to them from capitulations or other treaties. In other, words a foreigner prepared to submit to Ottoman Law was permitted to acquire land.

A

4

(b) Para. 4 of the Ordinance.
It is suggested that petitions of the nature described should be signed by both parties and prefaced by a statement on oath that neither party knows of any impediment to the title of the transfers.

(c) Para. 8. It is suggested that some rules for the guidance of the Chief Administrator should be drafted. Under the Ordinance as it stands, the Chief Administrator has apparently absolute authority to give or withhold sanction to sales or other dispositions of any land up to any extent. The provision restricting military Governors does not obtain in his case, and accordingly bodies such as the Jewish National Fund, the Jewish Colonisation Association, &c., hope immediately to make purchases. Not only is it suggested that rules for the guidance of the Chief Administrator should be drawn up, but in view of the large increase in work publication of the Ordnance will probably involve, the Chief Administrator should perhaps have power to depute the function of giving sanction. This will be the more easy if rules for his guidance have previous authoritative approval.

(d) Para. 15. The proposal that Land Registration Offices should be under the general supervision of the Senior Judicial Officer was at one time made in Mesopotamia also. But it was urged that, under Turkish Land Law, Tapu (*i.e.*, registration) offices combined the function of registration with that of supervision over Government lands. The Tapu office is the custodian of Government rights, and it is through Tapu officials that suits to uphold these rights are brought—and squatters sued. It was, therefore, deemed inappropriate that the Tapu office should be under the Senior Judicial Officer, whose duty it was ultimately to decide such claims. The point may be worth consideration in Palestine.

4. Waqf. Broadly speaking two types of auqaf are recognised: the one religious, and the other secular. Secular auqaf would be described in English law as fees in tail with remainder to a charitable object. Property so dedicated was liable to a limited degree of supervision by the waqf department. In Mesopotamia it is subject to taxation in the same way as any other land, but, as Dr. Weizmann points out, the very slight sanctity such land acquires is not infrequently exploited for secular interests to the embarrassment of Government.

The history of real property in England (and particularly the Statutes of Mortmain) show that both the dedication of estates to religious purposes and the limitations resulting from permanent entail are considered contrary to the interests of the community. The Ottoman Government passed in March 1914 an enactment the effect of which appears to have been to restrict the acquisition of reality by waqf. It would be retrograde to make such dedications easier under our administration.

For these reasons I would subscribe to Dr. Weizmann's suggestions that the Ordinance should not apply to dispositions of waqf land, a matter which could be deferred without hardship to the establishment of the future Government of Palestine.

C. C. GARBETT.

4.—Note by Sir Edgar Bonham-Carter, K.C.M.G., C.I.E., Judicial Secretary, Baghdad, dated 5th January 1920.

1. I gather that the objects of the proposed Palestine Land Ordinance are—

(a) To check speculation in land and the formation of large estates and to enable the Government to prevent the acquisition of land by undesirable persons;

(b) To provide for the reopening of the Land Registry Office.

The proposed Ordinance appears to me suitable to effect these objects, though I have a few amendments to suggest. But before discussing the provisions of the Ordinance it may be useful to deal with a few preliminary points.

2. A registry of land title has been in existence in the Ottoman Empire for many years, the Land Registry Office being known as the Tapu Land Registry. Unregistered sales and mortgages of land are invalid. The purchaser under an unregistered sale or agreement for sale cannot obtain specific performance of the contract or damages for non-fulfilment of the contract against a vendor who refuses to carry out the sale; he can, however, in the event of the sale being avoided, obtain the return of any purchase money paid by him.

3. Although the Turkish land registry system has considerable merits, in practice it suffered from serious defects. The principal defects of the system, as it operated in Mesopotamia, are the following:—

(a) Notwithstanding the risks involved in non-registration, large numbers of properties, and specially of small house properties, are not registered. Waqf properties have rarely been registered.

(b) As the land registry officials were neither honest nor accurate, and as no cadastrial maps existed, fraudulent deeds are not rare, and erroneous deeds are common. Generally speaking the boundaries and areas of agricultural lands shown in title deeds are of little value, if boundaries are disputed.

(c) In modern system of title registration, registration confers an absolute title except in case of fraud. A *bonâ fide* purchaser for value obtains by registration a good title against everyone. This is not so under the Turkish system, nor is it desirable that it should be so until the registers are much more accurate than at present. For instance, if on the death of an owner some only of his heirs get registered as entitled to the whole property, and they subsequently by a registered deed sell the property to a purchaser, the excluded heirs can recover their shares from the purchaser though he was ignorant of the defects in his title.

4. In Mesopotamia the situation was further complicated by the destruction of the Turks on their retirement of most of the registers.

5. Before allowing dealings in land, it was necessary in Mesopotamia to reconstitute the land registers. The registration in towns was sufficiently accurate to enable the register to be reconstituted by means of the Turkish title deeds in the hands of the owners and photographic maps taken by aeroplane. But in agricultural districts the title deeds are very unreliable, and before dealings can be safely permitted a general demarcation and registration of properties must be undertaken. I understand that the land registers in Syria are much more reliable than in Mesopotamia. Hence the land registries can probably be reopened to dealings without the preliminary of a general re-registration. But before dealings in any particular property are permitted it will be necessary to hold a careful examination of the title of the property.

To put the land registry in a satisfactory condition a cadastral survey, accompanied by the demarcation of all properties, and their re-registration, will, I imagine, eventually be necessary, but presumably the re-opening of the Land Registry Office need not await these measures. The need for some such measures were recognised by the Turks, and by the Provisional Law of 11 Rabi Awal, 1331, provision was made to demarcate and register all lands within the Ottoman Empire. The law, however, was not in fact carried into effect in Mesopotamia, nor, I understand, in Syria.

6. The proposed Ordinance vests in the Chief Administrator the power to refuse sanction to a dealing with land without giving any reason. Questions may arise as to whether this is in accordance with Turkish Law and Treaties.

I am informed that the Turkish Government occasionally refused to allow transactions in land on the ground that the persons acquiring the land was undesirable, though that might not be given as the ostensible reason. The law on the subject is not altogether clear, but I am advised that the Government had this power as regards "miri" land, but not as regards "mulk" land.

The Law of 13 Sefer, 1284 (16th June 1867) granted to foreigners the same right of acquiring and holding lands as Ottoman subjects, on the condition that as regards such lands they were liable to the same laws and regulations as Ottoman subjects. This law was issued after negotiations with the Powers and received the assent of all the chief Powers. Hence the right of a foreigner to hold land in Turkey is secured by treaty. It follows that no greater restrictions can be placed on the acquisition of land by foreigners than is placed on the acquisition of land by Ottoman subjects. The proposed Ordinance rightly makes no distinction between foreigners and Ottoman subjects.

7. According to the Mohammedan Law of Pre-emption, if an owner of mulk land sells it the owners of contiguous properties have the right within a certain period to buy out the purchaser at the price he has agreed to with the original owner. Similarly, if an owner of "miri land" within a village alienates it to a stranger, the

inhabitants of the village, subject to certain conditions, have the right to buy out the purchaser at the price he has agreed to. The proposed Ordinance makes no reference to pre-emption or to the analogous right with regard to "miri" land, although by means of them an owner may be able, by adding estate to estate to defeat the object of the Ordinance. I presume it is intended not to interfere with the right. This, I think, is wise. The right of pre-emption is extremely inconvenient, and it would probably be to the advantage of the community to abolish it, or at least to restrict it. But the right is one derived from the religious law, and is one to which Mohammedans attach considerable importance, especially in the case of town property. It would seem advisable not to interfere with pre-emption until it can be dealt with by a legislative body on which the inhabitants are represented.

8. Corporations are restricted under Ottoman Law from holding land. By the Provisional Law of the 22 Rabi al Awwal, 1331, uncommercial associations and Turkish commercial companies were authorised to hold land provided they were empowered to do so in their deeds of constitution as sanctioned by the Government. Charitable institutions and Ottoman communities were also authorised to hold town lands. Foreign companies and corporations are not authorised to hold land. Until the passing of the above law the custom was for companies and corporations who could not hold land in their own names to vest it in the name of a nominee; but this arrangement is expressly prohibited by the 3rd section of the above-mentioned law.

The practice of registering land in the name of a nominee was also prohibited by the Provisional Law of the 5th Jamad II. Awwal, 1331.

The law as it stands, therefore, prevents a foreign company from holding land either in its own name or that of a nominee. Amendment is necessary.

9. Turning to the provisions of the proposed Ordinance, the only general criticism I have to make is on the question of penalties. It is always open to objection to penalise acts which are not themselves wrong. Under systems of registration with which I am acquainted the only penalty for non-registration of transactions is that the transaction is void, and this was the rule under Turkish Law. It is true, however, that in the past the fact that transactions carried out outside the Land Registry were void was not sufficient to prevent such transactions. And I agree, therefore, that under conditions existing in Palestine the penalties imposed by section 5 and section 12 are probably necessary, if it is desired to strictly enforce the policy laid down by the Proclamation, leaving it to the authorities concerned to remit the penalties in cases when non-registration is due to ignorance and the transaction is one to which consent would have been granted if applied for.

The penalty imposed by section 13 on heirs and legatees who fail to register within a year appears to me undesirable, and I suggest its omission.

The increased registration fee charged in case the devolution is not registered within a year will in some cases be unjust and will be unpopular.

It must be remembered that in Mohammedan countries the class of landowners (including owners of houses) is a very large one and includes the most ignorant and conservative classes, and that the majority are illiterate; also, under Mohammedan law, the heirs are usually numerous, often very numerous, and the shares of individuals are often very small. Heirs are often absent or minors or women. It will be impossible for them in many cases to apply within a year, and even when possible they often will not do so.

It is also relevant that any form of taxation of successions is extremely unpopular in Mohammedan countries. Any proposal for such taxation is always met by the argument that you are taxing the widow and the orphan. Popular feeling in Syria, unless it is different to what it is in Egypt and Mesopotamia, will be strongly opposed to this clause.

10. Going through the Ordinance section by section, I have the following observations to submit:—

Section 2.—The definition of disposition would include a devise by will. I suggest that a devise should be excluded.

Section 4.—While the first paragraph includes all disposition, the wording of the second paragraph is not applicable to a proposed gift nor to an endowment of waqf. A verbal amendment is required.

7

The title of the person who wishes to make the disposition must be examined either before consent is given to the transaction or that consent must be given subject to the title being in order. Some amendment of the Ordinance is necessary to make this clear.

Section 5.—If a penalty is to be imposed on registration of land in the name of an agent for an undisclosed principal, it is not clear why the penalty is limited to the case when the fact of such registration has been disclosed in a judicial proceeding. The fact would ordinarily be detected by the Land Registry Office in connection with subsequent dealings with the land, and not in the course of a judicial proceeding.

Section 6 and Section 9.—Some words are required to make it clear that consent to the transaction will only be given and the deed will only be registered if the title is in order.

Section 10.—The effect of this section is to exclude the customary form of mortgage by "bey il wefa." This is the only form used in Mesopotamia and is probably the usual form in Syria. The form of mortgage authorised by the Provisional Law referred to in the section is more in accordance with modern ideas and is sounder economically. But the "bey il wefa" is more in accord with Mohammedan sentiment. One form of "bey il wefa" allows a mortgage without payment of interest, the mortgagee going into possession of the property and such possession taking the place of interest. This satisfies the Mohammedan objection against charging or paying interest, and should not, I consider, be prohibited, notwithstanding the objections to it on economic grounds.

Section 14.—Under the Provisional Law as to mortgages, when repayment of a mortgage debt is overdue the Land Registry Office, upon the application of the mortgagee, enforces the mortgage by sale by auction. No application to the Court is necessary.

Some amendment of the section seems necessary to cover such a case.

Section 15.—I suggest adding after sub-paragraph (*f*), as an additional sub-paragraph, "the appointment of attorneys."

Under Turkish procedure, the parties must attend the Registry Office either personally or by duly appointed attorney, and sign the register.

15. With regard to Mr. Weizmann's objections to the effect of the Ordinance on the creation of awqaf and gifts, it is to be remarked that under the provisions of the Ordinance waqfs can only be created and gifts can only be made after the consent of the Chief Administrator has been obtained. Mr. Weizmann's fears that the Ordinance will lead to creation of awqaf and gifts, with the intention of defeating its purpose, appear therefore to be unfounded.

Having regard to the religious issues involved, the Ordinance, in my opinion, goes as far as is advisable in restricting the creation of waqf and gifts. Indeed, unless there is real reason to apprehend that the removal of restrictions will lead to the creation of awqaf with the object of defeating the purpose of the Ordinance, it appears to me that it would be preferable at the present time to place no restriction on the creation of awqaf. According to the practice followed by the Courts in Mesopotamia, a waqf can only be created by declaration before a qadhi. If the same rule exists in Syria, the Administration can keep themselves informed of all awqaf created, and provisions to restrict the creating of awqaf might be postponed until it was proved that Mr. Weizmann's fears are well founded.

16. With regard to the views expressed by Mr. Garbett and Colonel Howell that it is preferable for the Land Registry Office to be under the Chief Revenue Authority rather than the Chief Legal Authority, I will only say that, while under existing conditions I have no objection to the Land Registry Office in this country being under the Revenue authorities, I have seen no reason to alter the opinion which I have previously expressed, namely, that the business of a Register of Title is essentially legal and is most suitably placed under the supervision of a legal authority.

E. BONHAM CARTER.

8

5.—Note by Lieut.-Col. E. B. Howell, C.S.I., C.I.E., I.C.S., dated 5th December 1919.

The Secretary of State has asked for your views and those of Mr. Bonham Carter and/or other Mesopotamian experts on the draft Land Ordinance which the Palestine Administration has referred to him. Presumably comment is invited in the light of knowledge acquired by experience in Mesopotamia. The first point which I have to make is, therefore, that, to judge from the indications which the Ordinance and other enclosures to the Secretary of State's letter afford, conditions here offer one feature of similarity to those obtaining in Palestine, but otherwise seem to be fundamentally different. The Turks themselves recognised the peculiarity of 'Iraq in respect of land tenures—*vide* the Circular from the Ministry of Tapu, dated 5th Safar 1310, a translation of which is given on page 12 of the Translation of Turkish Laws printed at Baghdad under No. 2363, dated 9th April 1919.

The feature of similarity lies in the fact that both in 'Iraq and Palestine, as also no doubt elsewhere, the Turkish Government attempted, using the Tapu Department as its instrument, to maintain a complete and systematic registry of title, and to record all private rights in immovable property, without taking the trouble to provide the necessary safeguards in the shape of survey maps, well-ordered registers, records and reasonable departmental efficiency of routine. Here, moreover, except in Mosul, such record as existed was destroyed or thrown into confusion by the war, whereas in Palestine events, as in Mosul, seem to have moved too quickly to enable the Turks to add to our difficulties by the deliberate destruction or removal of their records. The Palestine Ordinance is silent as to whether a would-be vendor of land has to produce his title-deeds or not, and there is no information on record here to show whether, at present, an owner of immovable property in Palestine who has lost his deeds can get new ones or not. If the production of deeds is a *sine quâ non*, and no machinery exists for the issue of new deeds, the relaxation of restriction which the Ordinance purports to effect may be more apparent than real. If production is not necessary there is clearly a wide opening for fraud and much trouble brewing for the future Registrar. If machinery for renewal does exist, it would be interesting to know how the procedure compares with that used by the Turks and the modifications of their system which we have introduced here.

It is believed that in Palestine the efficiency of the Turkish Tapu Department was considerably more respectable than here. Nevertheless, in so far as there, too, it seems to have fallen short of a reasonable standard, and suffered to some extent by the war, the problems are the same. Here in Mesopotamia (except in Mosul) the administration set up by us met this difficulty at the beginning by prohibiting all transfers of immovable property, and then, as it evolved order out of chaos, by relaxing this prohibition in respect first of urban properties, and then of garden lands in suburban and certain riverain areas. Beyond this point we have not yet advanced, and transfer of agricultural lands still cannot be registered, although it is hoped that the inception of settlement operations in the Baghdad and Hillah Divisions will soon extend the activities of the Tapu Department to agricultural lands also in those areas.

The same difficulty seems to have been met in the same obvious manner in Palestine. But clearly the difficulty there cannot have been so acute as here, or the way to the re-opening of transactions in immovable properties could not have been so speedily cleared.

Curiously enough as it might seem, the closure of transfers of agricultural lands in this country, which has now lasted for more than four years in some parts, has caused practically no public inconvenience. The reason for this is the complete divorce that existed here between the actual and the theoretical position. A comparatively small portion of the country is even claimed by persons who take their stand upon legal documents (Tapu Sanads). Of these a fair proportion have never, or not for a long time, held actual possession. Even before our arrival they were already well accustomed merely to receive some sort of annual payment from the persons in actual possession, enough to keep them quiet, and make the best of that. Naturally there is no lively traffic in such precarious rights as these. Nevertheless, many landowners and occupants do exercise the usual rights of such persons. Such are usually prosperous, and by no means anxious to part with their lands. Landowners, and garden owners, and house owners alike, in defiance or oblivion of the law, have always been very careless about registration and the renewal of deeds. Registration was only theoretically compulsory under the Turks, and one of our chief difficulties here, even in urban areas, has been to get the people to produce their deeds for registration. This apathy seems due partly to a natural distrust engendered

9

by the inefficiency of the Tapu Department in Turkish times, partly to the fact that registration and renewal involve the payment of a certain, if small, fee. The combination of doubtful benefit and certain expense makes no appeal to the Arab.

In each of the three divisions of Mosul, Erbil and Kirkuk a reformed Tapu Office deals with urban properties. Outside the towns in Erbil and Kirkuk, there is little land registered in Tapu, and all that we are attempting to do is to keep an informal record of such transactions in non-urban land as are reported, with details of price, &c., but without any guarantee.

Difficulties such as those indicated above, which we are taking steps to meet in our own way, do not, I believe, confront the administration in Palestine. There the Turkish Tapu Department, though inefficient, did more or less maintain an actual record of marketable rights, and the administration has had to give way to the necessities of those who own land and desire or are constrained to sell it. It has, however, sets its face against the transfer of large properties, a transaction which is less likely to arise from necessity than the sale of small plots by the peasantry, and is especially eager to check speculative purchase. For these purposes the Ordinance seems well enough adapted, but I think Mr. Garbett's advice sound. He urges the administration in Palestine to satisfy itself that the registration offices are really in working order before the attempt to work them is made.

The point which Mr. Garbett deals with in para. 3 (d) of his note is, I think, of very great importance. There is no need to elaborate the argument as set forth there, but we can say, with the experience of four years behind us, that the system whereby the Tapu Department is supervised by the Chief Revenue Authority has worked well in Mesopotamia on the whole, and that there is now no serious demand that Tapu should be under the management of the Senior Judicial Officer.

As to waqf lands, it may be inferred that in Palestine many Moslem landowners, through fear of the Zionist movement, would seek to protect themselves by making their lands "dhurriyah" or waqf in reversion. Here there is no such fear and no such tendency. Nor have we had any inconvenience here from bequests of immovable property to waqf, which we would desire to respect, but which we might be unable to register. No such bequests in respect of agricultural land or gardens have, as a matter of fact, come to notice. I attribute this partly to the fact that waqf here is very adequately endowed already, partly to the supreme lack of confidence which that Department inspired in a country largely Shia', where it was most partially administered for the benefit of Sunnis, and partly to the paucity of lands held in mulk right, which alone are capable of being made the subject of a bequest.

A few remarks as to the checking of speculative traffic in lands, and the acquisition of rights by foreigners, in Mesopotamia, may be offered. Presumably the Palestine administration considers that its powers to withhold sanction to proposed transfers will enable it to deal with both these. Probably this will be found adequate, and the omission of all attempt to fetter discretion is, at this stage, wise, though some general declaration of principle will before long, I think, be forced upon them.

I consider that in respect of those two objects, our policy, declared in the Civil Commissioner's Notification of the 20th November 1917, 24th February 1918, and the General Officer Commanding's Proclamation of the 30th July 1919, has been completely successful.

It may be noted that the measures referred to in the preceding paragraph restrict rights conferred by the Turkish law. If Mr. Weizmann's views are to be carried out it will be necessary to widen certain provisions of the Turkish law. Formerly no private corporate body could hold real property as a body, and though the law of 16th February 1328 makes certain concessions in this respect, it restricted the ownership of real property by agricultural companies to "Ottoman companies the shareholders in which are Ottoman subjects." Unless, therefore, the shareholders in the various companies mentioned by Mr. Weizmann are all Ottoman subjects, it would appear that special legislation will be necessary to enable them to acquire agricultural land.

E. B. HOWELL.

1.03

ST ANTONY'S COLLEGE
MIDDLE EAST LIBRARY
PRIVATE PAPERS

NOTES ON LAND LAW

Land Law.
----

1. The land law of the Ottoman Empire is very complicated and in this note it is possible to give only a very general idea of the principal rules, which are scattered in different sources.

The Law of MIRI is principally found in a special land code. The law of WAKF is contained in the Moslem Religious Law, "the Shari".

A number of the new laws were made in the years immediately preceding the WAR and introduce large changes in the system of land holding. Finally consideration has to be paid to the Proclamations and Ordinances issued by O.E.T.A. A Proclamation of December 1918 forbade all dealing in the land other than leases for a period not exceeding 3 years and an Ordinance is about to be issued which authorizes dealings subject to strict control of the Administration. All sales and mortgages and leases for a period of 10 years or more must be approved by the Military Governor of the district or the Chief Administrator and no dealing in land will be legal which does not pass through the Land Registry.

2. Kinds of Land.

Land in the Turkish Empire is divided into 5 classes:-

1. Mulk, property over which the holder excises a complete right or ownership, with powers of disposition by will up to one third.

2. Miri, property over which the state has a right of ownership but over which a right of usufruct is conferred on private persons. The holder has a right to use the property and enjoy or dispose of its fruits. In practice he has approximately the same rights as the holder of Mulk, except that he cannot dispose of it by will, and it is subject to forfeiture in certain circumstances with possible rights of re-purchase. (See below (13)).

3. Wakf, mortmain property; land devised for some religious or charitable object.
Wakf may be either Mulk or Miri.
Wakf or Mulk is the only true Wakf. It is governed by the rules of the Sharia, and the land law does not apply to it.
Wakf or Miri exists where the revenues of Miri property have been dedicated by the Sultan or by his permission for religious or charitable foundations. The Land Law concerning Miri applies to this form of Wakf.

4. Metrouke. - property which forms part of the Public Domain made over to the public use such as the public roads, or pastures which are used in common by the inhabitants of the village, etc.

5. Mevat, waste land owned by the state not possessed by any one, and not forming part of the lands of the Public Domain.

Registration of Land.

3. By a Turkish Law of 1820-1904 all land was required to be registered in the Government registry "the Tapu" and the holder received a deed called the "Kushen". Land Registries have been established in all the Kazas of Palestine but a considerable amount of land has not yet been registered. The land registers were

- 2 -

carried away from a number of the Kazas by the Turks prior to the occupation. They have now been recovered and the registries are being re-established under a new system. ~The registration is of deeds and not of title i.e. the documents affecting any dealing with the land must be files in the Registry but no guarantee of the registered title is given. The present title deeds and the registers will require very close scrutiny. The registry offices were notorious for their corruption, and the disappearance of the registers for a long period, in some cases nearly 2 years, will have given an opportunity for falsification. The deeds and registers seldom give the size of the holding clearly and the recorded area is often less than half the actual area in order to evade payment of land taxes. The boundaries of a holding and not its area are binding in a deed of transfer, but the boundaries also are frequently defined so vaguely as to be almost useless. In the Turkish times there was a multiplicity of boundary disputes, many of them collusive, and it is certain that the Administration will have to deal with many cases of this kind. A surveyor will always be employed in new transactions to fix the boundaries and the area of the land transferred.

New registers will be started for each village so that it will be possible gradually to build up a more trustworthy record on the land holding.

Land is frequently registered in the name of a person who is not the real owner. The Ottoman law prohibited foreign subjects and foreign corporations and associations from holding land. When these persons and corporations required land they had it registered in the name of an individual Ottoman subject who held it on trust. The trust and no legal sanction but as a practice was respected. The land of most of the Jewish villages and the big charitable orders is registered in this way in the names of Ottoman individuals.

Illegal contracts of transfer.

4.   The courts were forbidden to hear any action based on a contract of sale which had not passed through the registry. A year was given to the holders of deeds which had not been made through the registry in which to have them registered.

If an irregular contract was made hereafter and the property transferred to the purchasers, the vendor could claim its restitution; and if the vendor refused to deliver the property, the purchaser would only have a right to claim restitution of the price. These rights to obtain restitution of the price would remain against his heirs in the event of the death of the vendor. By the operation of the Law of 5th Jamad Awal 1331 Art.16 this right against the heirs of the vendor exists also in case of Miri land. If the vendor leaves no heirs, the state is the heir and an action would be against it for the price.

The purchaser who obtains possession of the property transferred by irregular contract obtains a good title over the property after 15 years uninterrupted possession in the case of Mulk, and 10 years in the case of Miri and the vendors right to reclaim the property ceases.

The purchaser by an irregular contract who has obtained possession of the property has no civil remedy against a trespasser; but if the vendor has a Kushan he may give the purchaser a procreation and the Civil Courts will protect the purchaser. The purchaser can bring a penal action against a trespasser, especially if force has been used, without the intervention of the vendor.

In some parts of the country, however, e.g. round Bearsheba and Jericho, land has not been registered and private unregistered contracts are the rule. The holder could prove his title to these lands by private deeds and receipts, and payment of taxes would also be some evidence of title. Deeds and evidence of this kind, however, will require to be very closely scrutinised contracts of transfer since the time of the occupation are likewise invalid in virtue of both the Ottoman Law requiring registration for a valid transfer and of the Proclamation of December 1918. But if the parties to a contract of this kind desire to carry out these terms it may be treated as a fresh transaction and considered on its merits.

Lease.

5. The contract of lease of Mulk and Miri land is valid by the present Ottoman Law in whatever form it may be made. If the contract is made before a Public Notary, it has the force of an official instrument, that is to say, the signatures of the parties have not to be proved and the contents of the document cannot be upset by the evidence of oral witness. Further, on termination of the lease the Executive Office will proceed to ejectment without an order of the Court.

The term of the lease is not limited by the Ottoman Law. If no period is mentioned in the contract it will be taken to be that for which the rent is paid i.e. if rent is paid annually it will be for one year. A special agreement may be made in the contract that buildings and plantations made by the lessee may belong to him, but if there is not such an agreement they belong to the lesser. An option to purchase contained in a contract of lease has no binding effect as a contract of sale; but it may be enforced only by way of giving damages for breach.

Mortgages.

6. Prior to 1912 the transfer of land by the way of security was carried out by the way of contract of 'vente a remers', that is to say, a contract of sale giving the vendor the right to recover his land after a certain period stated in the contract on repayment of the price to the purchaser.

The formalities were the same as in sale. The old Kushan was handed over to the Tapou Office which issued to both parties a 'Senad Mudayana' or record of security. When the vendor repaid the price to the purchaser he received back his old Kushan.

A private contract had no value.

If the vendor did not repay the price at the time fixed in the contract, the purchaser could go to the Tapou Office and ask that the property be put up to auction. He obtained payment out of the price received.

By law of 1912 a regular system of mortgage was established by which the borrower gives his land in security to his creditor without requiring to enter into a contract of sale. Two copies of the contracts are made and signed by parties. The borrower's Kushan is handed over to the Tapou Office and both parties receive a 'Senad Mudayana'. The Tapou Office make the same enquiries as in sale.

The creditor can obtain sale by auction of the property on application to the Tapou Office without recourse to the Court.

The rights of the parties on the death of either of them pass to their heirs.

A second mortgage may be made subject to the first, that is to say, the new creditor can only receive payment of his debt from the proceeds of the sale after the debt of the first creditor has been paid in full.

If there is a lease with a prior date to that of the mortgage, the rights of the lease prevail over the rights of the mortgage who will be unable to have the land sold until the terms of the lease are expired, unless the lessee is a party to the mortgage and agrees to waive his rights.

A mortgagee can assign the mortgage debt with the consent of the debtor and a debtor can transfer property mortgaged with consent of mortgagee.

All mortgages made henceforth will be according to the form prescribed by the Law of 1912 subject to some modifications which are embodied in an Ordinance that is now being issued.

Execution of Immovables.

7. The execution creditor searches the Tapou Office for property belonging to the judgement debtor, then goes to the Execution Officer of the Court who notifies the debtor and the Tapou Office of the execution. After 3 days he announces that he will receive offers for the purchase of the debtor's property which will be transferred to the person making the highest offer. Each bidder must deposit 10% of the price he offers. The bidding to continue for a period of 30 days. During these 30 days the sale must be announced at least 3 times by public crier. Any one who wishes to bid goes to the Execution Office and makes his bid and deposits his 10%.

After this period of 30 days, there may be a notification by the public crier that there will be a further period of 15 days in which further offers will be received provided that they are more than 5% of the highest price already offered.

After the second period the property is awarded to the highest bidder and notification is given to the debtor and he is allowed 3 days in which to make payment, failing which the property will be transferred to the highest bidder.

If the price offered is much below the true value of the property the Execution Officer may delay the decision as to whom the property is to be awarded and give notice of further period of 30 days in which offers will be received.

On failure of the debtor to make payment the property will be transferred to the highest bidder, but if he fails to complete this payment of the price he offered, his 10% will be forfeited and property transferred to the second highest bidder.

The procedure is under the control of the President of the First Instance Court and any application in regard to it will be made to him, e.g. by a person who claims to have a right over the property seized and wishes to claim it.

Persons having rights prior to the commencement of the execution procedure, e.g. a lessee, their rights are preserved. All dealings which are subsequent to execution procedure, e.g. a lease, are only good till the execution is completed.

If there are several creditors and the price received is not sufficient to pay them all in full, they share pro rata. Certain debts, however, are privileged.

If the judgement on which a creditor, other than the execution creditor, bases his claim was given by consent or on the refusal of the debtor to take the oath it must be prior in date to the commencement of the execution proceedings to enable him to take part in the division.

-5-

On completion of payment by the purchaser of the property the subject of the execution, the execution creditor notifies the Tapou Office, whereupon the registration of the property in the name of the judgment debtor is expunged and the name of the purchaser is registered as owner and a Kushan in issued to him.

Execution of immovables has hitherto been prohibited in the Occupied Territory by the Proclamation of June the 24th 1918, but the prohibition will be withdrawn by the new Ordinance. The purchaser however of the land sold in execution will need to be approved by the Administration in the same way as the purchaser of land or disposed of by voluntary sale.

Pre-emption.

8. The Land Law gives the rights to some persons to buy land in preference to others, and this right may be exercised in some circumstances even if the land has been disposed of to another. In the case of Mulk the right is enjoyed by the neighbour of the vendor and must be exercised within a month of disposition if notice has been given to him of the intended sale. If no notice has been given, he may exercise the right any time. In the case of Miri the co-sharer or co-holder has the right of pre-emption of the share of the joint holding. If one person owns the land and another owns trees or building on it the latter can claim to purchase the land within 10 years of the disposition A resident in the district who is in need of land may pre-empt within one year a holding which has been disposed of to a person residing outside the district in which the land is situated.

Succession.

9. The holder of Miri land cannot dispose if it by will, but the land passes to his heirs, who are determined, by a special law of 1912. A holder of Mulk may only dispose, by will, of 1/3. the remaining 2/3 go to the heirs who are determined by the Sharia Law. In default of heirs both Miri and Mulk land escheat to the State.

The heirs of Miri are divided into 3 classes:-
A. Children and grandchildren.
B. Parents and their children and grandchildren
C. Grandparents and their children and grandchildren.

The grandchildren only inherit the share of their father and mother when the latter is dead. The shares of males and females are equal. The share of the widow or widower is as follows:-
    In the presence of class A. heirs - ? of estate.
      "   "   "   "   " B " - ? "   "
      "   "   "   "   " C "   ? "   "
Plus the share of any grandparent who died without heir. Parents succeed to one-sixth of the estate in presence of children and their grandchildren.

In default of the above heirs the land escheats, but the following persons in the order stated are entitled to take over the holding on payment of Tapou dues:-
A. The Shari heirs within a period of 10 years.
B. The co-sharers and co-holders with 5 years.

C. Resident in the neighbourhood within 1 year.
D. A stranger owning Mulk trees and buildings on the land, may purchase at the market price within 10 years. Soldiers of 6 years' service are exempt from the payment of dues on an area up to 3 damans and soldiers in the reserve up to 2½ damans.

Wills must always be proved in the Court of Personal Status of the Testator.

i.e. The will of a Moslem Ottoman will be proved by the Mehkemeh Shari
The will of a non Moslem Ottoman subject by the Court of his Religious Community.
The will of a foreign subject by the Court of 1st Instance.
The Tapou will register a Kushan for any of these.

Any disputes in regard to the succession of immovables if the parties are Ottoman subjects, whether they are Moslem or not, will be decided by the Mehkemeh Shari according to the Moslem Law.

The intestate succession of foreigners is regulated by Moslam Law and foreigners can only dispose by will of 1/3 of his Mulk property.

Partition.

10. Partition of land held in joint ownership may be affected by consent of all the parties through the land registry office. Disputes must be settled by the Courts. The special law of 1332 - 1914 - gives the details of the procedure for partition.

Wakf.

11. Only Mulk land can be constituted Wakf. The party constituting the Wakf makes a declaration before the Kadi of the Shari Court who issues an Alan or certificate. The law provides that this certificate should be sent to the Tapou Office but in practice it was generally often given to the party constituting the Wakf. But by the new Ordinance all constitutions of Wakf must pass through the Registry and must be approved of by the Administration in the same way as sales of land. Wakf property cannot be disposed of except by exchange of lease; and except with the special consent of the Kadi, leasing may not be for more than 8 years in the case of agricultural land and one year in the case of buildings.

Mevat Land.

12. Mevat land is land owned by the State, the possession of which has not yet been granted to a private individual. On obtaining authorisation a private person may enter into possession of Mevat Land, and if he cultivates it for three years, the Tapou Office will give him a Kushan without any payment. The holder then acquires a right similar to that enjoyed by a holder of Miri Land who has a Kushan.

If he occupies the land without previous authorisation and cultivates it, the Tapou Office may issue a Kushan on payment of a fee.

The Tapou Office appears to be the authority which decides whose possession is to be protected before the 3 years are completed.

Mahloul.

13. Mahloul is Miri and Miri Wakf land which has been allowed to lie wasted or uncultivated by its owner for three consecutive years.

The Tapou notify the holder of such land that it is claimed by the state and brings an action to have it declared Mahloul. If it is declared Mahloul the Tapou invites the owner to pay its value and resume his usufruct. On his failure to do so the property is put up to auction.

Special registers were kept by the Tapou of all Mahloul land.

Miri land which escheats to the State is treated as Mahloul.

1.04

1922   **PALESTINE**

FROM: H. C. Samuel Desp. 78
DATE: 10 Feb.
Rec'd/Reg'd: 1 MAR 22
No. 9614

FOR CIRCULATION:
Mr. Mills 7/4
Major ——— 7/4 at once
Mr. ———
Mr. Grindle
Sir H. Lambert
Sir H. Read
Sir J. Masterton Smith
Mr. Ward
Mr. Churchill

SUBJECT: Land Settlement Commission's Report

Fwds. 3 copies.

Previous Paper
HCr. 7979
In C.O.

MINUTES

I have been sitting on this Report and digesting it slowly. I think on the whole that it augurs badly for Jewish settlement. The report was completed some time ago and it has been found necessary to go very slowly on some of the recommendations. The only thing I can suggest at present is that continuous efforts be made to complete demarcation of village lands and individual holdings.

? Shortest.
6.4.22.

Subsequent Paper

GOVERNMENT OF PALESTINE
LEGAL SECRETARY'S OFFICE.
JERUSALEM.

August 19th 1920.

Major Abramson.

587

The High Commissioner has been pleased to appoint you as Chairman of a Commission to inquire into land settlement in Palestine. The members of the Commission will be Faidi Eff. el Alami and Mr. Kalvarisky.

The Commission will, in the first place, ascertain the area and nature of the various kinds of lands which are at the disposal of the Government. The Turkish Government kept records of the Mudawara Land or Jiftlik land but no proper check appears to have been preserved of the Mahlul and Mawat land. The Commission will consider and report upon what steps should be taken to obtain an accurate record of these areas, and to make the best disposition of them in the interests of the country.

The Commission will also report upon the lands in the country which are available for closer settlement, that is the more intensive cultivation of the soil by a larger agricultural population. The Commission will report to the High Commissioner on the measures which should be taken by the Government to secure the greater productivity of the country. At the same time it will make recommendations as to the measures to be taken to protect the interests of the persons who are tenants or occupants of Government lands.

The Commission will advise also on the measures to be taken to prevent private land owners selling land which is now cultivated by tenants, without making arrangements to protect the interests of their tenants.

The Commission will also be required to

- 2 -

Major Abramson

588

act as an advisory body to the High Commissioner upon any questions concerning settlement of land, including proposals for the disposition of parts of Government lands.

                                                   (Sgd) N.Bentwich.
                                                    <u>LEGAL SECRETARY</u>

Your Excellency,   589

    During the period Aug.15 - Nov.15 two members of the Commission visited Nablus, Haifa, Jaffa and Beersheba Districts to examine the tenure of certain lands for which applications were received for development leases; preliminary discussions were held on recommendations to be submitted in due course to Y.E. and progress was made on collecting and collating records of State Property.

    In view of the absence in Europe of the third Member, Mr. Kalvarisky, the work was mainly of a preparatory nature.

    On November 15 Mr. Kalvarisky arrived since which date full meetings were regularly held.

    The Land Commission visited every District in Palestine and held meetings in Haifa, Acre, Nazareth, Tiberias, Beisan, Jenin, Tulkeram, Nablus, Jaffa, Jericho, Hebron, Beersheba and Gaza.

    The meetings were attended by Land owners, villagers, Jewish Colonists and Bedu and were representative of all classes interested in Agriculture and in the agricultural development of the Country.

    In addition to certain recommendations referred to in the attached report, recommendations were submitted to Y.E. on

    The Wady Farah Settlement Scheme.

    The J.C.A. Development Scheme of State Lands, and Sand Dunes between Athlit and Caesarea.

    The sale of the Tob Alti lands at Acre.

    The Disposal of the Ard es Sirr estate Beersheba.

    The 'Bassa' Property North of Jaffa Development Scheme.

    The Sand Dunes dispute South of Jaffa.

    The Tel-Aviv Bathing Establishment Scheme.

    The Latin Patriarch's Agricultural Settlement Scheme for Orphans.

    The Disposal of the Municipal Lands Beersheba.

On the termination of the main work of the Land Commission we have the honour to submit our General Report to Y.E. with recommendations on the steps which would appear to be desirable to be taken by the Government to secure the greater productivity of the Country, its closer settlement and the best disposition of State lands (Aradi Mudawara, Aradi Mahlul, and Aradi Mewat) in the interests of cultivators and of the general public.

      We have the honour to be
        Excellency
      Your obedient Servants

M. Kalvarisky	A. Abramson	Faidi el Alami
MEMBER	CHAIRMAN	MEMBER.

Jerusalem May 31. 1921.

ARADI MUDAWARA

591

Particulars of Aradi Mudawara and of Aradi Mahlul are not compiled in any general Register but are kept separately for each District in District Registers.

We have however obtained particulars from those Registers from which we have compiled a General Register in the Land Department.

The total area of Aradi Mudawara as ascertained and registered is 857566 dounoms and consists of :-

```
Cultivable land          804779 dounoms.
Marshes                   40242    "
Pasturage                  9900    "
Gardens and Orchards       2645    "
```

The State also owns 340 shops, houses, mills and other buildings. 4 lighthouses and about 680 dounoms of Quarries.

ARADI MAHLUL

The area of Aradi Mahlul as ascertained is 87233 dounoms and is composed of :-

```
Cultivable land          85193 dounoms.
Marshes                   2000    "
Gardens                     40    "
```

Since the outbreak of the Great War very little land which escheated to the State through failure of heirs was declared as such and no steps were taken to enforce the " Right of Tapou " on lands which had been left uncultivated.

The Land Commission therefore proposed that an Ordinance be promulgated calling on all persons to declare lands which had reverted to the State and which persons may have taken possession of wrongly.

This Y.E. approved and the following "Mahlul Land Ordinance 1920" was published :-

2

"Whereas by the Land Code Miri Land reverts to the Government on failure of heirs of the holder or non-cultivation during 3 years, and

"Whereas as a result of the Cadastral Survey all lands which through failure of heirs or non-cultivation during 3 years will become known in due course, but it is necessary that the Administration obtain forthwith a complete record of all such lands.

"Notice is hereby given as follows :-

"1. Every person who at any time previous to the issue of this Ordinance has taken possession of any land which owing to failure of heirs or non-cultivation became Mahlul is required to inform the Administration within 3 months of the date of this Ordinance.

"No action will be taken against any person who has held such lands and who complies with the requirements of this article. The Administration will in a proper case lease the land to the person who has possessed it.

"The right of inheritance will be determined according to the Provisional Law of the 3rd of Rabi'El-Awal 1331 relating to the inheritance of immovable property.

"2. Every Mukhtar of a town, village or mazraa is required to inform the Administration within 3 months of all Mahlul lands of which at any time previous to the issue of this Ordinance illegal possession was taken, stating the names of the persons who have so taken possession.

"3. Any person who having taken possession of Mahlul lands fails to inform the Administration will be liable to a fine of £.E.50 or imprisonment not exceeding 3 months or both these penalties.

"Any Mukhtar who having reason to know of such illegal possession fails to inform the Administration in accordance with Art. 2 will be liable to a fine of £.E.25 or imprisonment not exceeding one month or both these penalties.

-3-

"4. This Ordinance shall be known as ' The Mahlul 593
"Land Ordinance 1920 ². "

Mahlul Land is of two kinds :-

1) Land which escheats to the State through failure of heirs.

2) Miri land which is left uncultivated for 3 years and is therefore subject to " Right of Tapou " for which the owner refuses however to pay the Tapou Value.

No declarations have been made as yet. As a result, however, of the activities of the State Land Demarcation Commission (SEE Page 10) and of the Land Department Inspectors, cases of illegal holdings will come to light and the penalties prescribed in the Mahlul Land Ordinance will probably act as an incentive to others to declare Mahlul Property.

RENTAL.

Most of the Aradi Mudawara and Aradi Mahlul are held on an indefinite tenure and generally speaking on the basis of 10% on the yield plus tithes. In Haifa and Acre Districts, however, the rental is sold by auction each year, in addition to which the usual tithe is paid.

Buildings are leased for one or more years.

The rental from State Property in 1919/20 was :-

Beersheba	£.E. 414.
Nablus	" 1273.
Gaza	" 1893.
Galilee	" 15014.
Haifa	" 1684.
Jaffa	" 397.
Jerusalem	" 1926.
Total	£.E.22601.

ARADI MEWAT.

It is not possible to state with any degree of certainty the area of Mewat Land.

-4-

594

The area of Western Palestine is given roughly as 22000 square kilometres.

Turkish Statistics previous to 1914 give the area of the country exclusive of Beersheba District as 14,853,400 dounoms. Beersheba District is said to be about one third of the total extent of Western Palestine.

It is estimated by Agriculturalists that about 20% of the total area is ordinarily under cultivation in any given year.

About 15% more is easily cultivable by the present existing cultivators, leaving roughly 14,000 square kilometres uncultivated; of this however a percentage must be deducted for pasturage.

The area required for extensive pasturage can be roughly estimated at 1,153,000 dounoms or 1,059 square kilometres which is roughly 5% of the total area of the country. This is arrived at as follows :-

A census of animals was made in 1909/10 in the Lewa of Jerusalem. It was estimated that the animals in the Lewa of Jerusalem were roughly 40% of the total number in Palestine.

Animals	Jerusalem Inc. Hebron	Acre & Nablus Lewas: estimated at 60% of total in country: J'rm. Representing 40% of total.	Palestine Total
Stallions	30		
Mares	1904		
Geldings & Colts	3483		
Mules	2392		
	7809	11700	19500
Donkeys	20442	30560	51000
Bulls	5335		
Cows	15366		
Oxen	26904		
Calves	2280		
Buffaloes	225		
	50110	75000	125000

Sheep	189594	284400	474000
Goats	95409	143100	238500
Camels	17290	26600	43290
Pigs	790	1150	1920

According to Prof.D.Tamaro (see Trattato completo di Agricultura ad uso d.agrico. Italiani, Milano 1912 page 669) the following area of pasturage would be required per head :-

Cow	2-3 years old requires	0,25 - 0,35	hectare of pasture ground
Ox	2-3 " " "	0,25 - 0,30	" " " "
Bullock	1-2 " " "	0,15 - 0,25	" " " "
Calf	0,5-1 " " "	0,10 - 0,15	" " " "
Horse	1 " " "	0,25 - 0,30	" " " "
"	2 " " "	0,35 - 0,40	" " " "
"	3 " " "	0,40 - 0,45	" " " "
10 Sheep		0,35 - 0,40	" " " "
10 Pigs		0,30 - 0,40	" " " "

Thus for
19500	horses	on an average of 0,35 hectare per head	6500	hectare
51000	donkeys	equal to 10200 Horses	3570	"
125000	cattle	on an average of 0,25 " " "	31250	"
474000	sheep	on an average of 0,30 " " "	14220	"
238500	goats	on an average of 0,30 " " "	7155	"
43290	camels	(as horses)	15150	"
1920	pigs	on an average of 0,30 " " "	675	"
		Total	78520	hectare
		or dounoms	863500.	

Taking, however the maximum areas the requirements would be :-

Horses	8775 hectares
Cattle	43730 "
Goats	9540 "
Pigs	740 "
Donkeys	4590 "
Sheep	15960 "
Camels	19480 "

Total 105845 hectares = Dounoms 1,153,000 or 1,059 sq. kilometres.

The Mewat area would therefore be roughly 60% of the total area of the Country. Much of this is in the South and South-East of Palestine and the sand dunes on the Coast. A large proportion is of no use for agricultural purposes for in the S. & S.E. the rainfall is slight and uncertain and the nature of the ground is stated to be unsuitable even for dry farming, besides which the absence of roads, the distance from centres of habitation would preclude the possibility of any attempts for many years to cultivate these areas.

Of the remainder, a large percentage is rocky and hilly and is only suitable for afforestation.

Another method to arrive at the percentage of Mewat land would be based on the estimated requirements of the agricultural population of the country.

A rough census of the inhabitants of the villages and tribes gives a round total of 400,000 souls.

This, at say 5 persons per family would give a total of 80,000 families.

From our enquiries in the various Districts it would appear that the average area which a family possessing a yoke of oxen can cultivate under Summer and Winter Crops in any given year and which would be sufficient for their maintenance including wastage for roads, buildings and pasturage is 150 dounoms.

80,000 families by 150 dounoms each would be 12,000,000 dounoms or about 11,000 sq.kilometres. The area of Palestine being about 22,000 sq.kilometres would leave about 11,000 sq.kilometres Mewat or about 50% of the total area of the Country.

A third method to arrive at a rough percentage of the area which is not required by the present population of the country and which is not cultivated and which could therefore be considered as Mewat would be by taking the yield of any given year as a basis.

In 1919/20 the total yield of the country, but exclusive of Beersheba is stated by the Revenue Department to have been :-

Wheat	45,702,232	Kilos.
Barley	25,739,521	"
Sesame	984,644	"
Durrah	15,271,060	"
Legumes (Lentils, Kursennah, Peas, Turmos, Beans, Julbaneh, Hilbeh, Lubieh)	8,175,888	"

-7-

Fruit and Olives	18,676,273 Kilos
Grapes	5,622,896 "
Vegetables (Onions, Garlic; Tomatoes, Egg-plant; Bamia, Turnips; Potatoes, Lubieh; Cucumber, Fakus; Radish, Marrows; Locust, Squash; Pepper and Chillies; Cabbage and Cauliflower; Kulkas, Carrots; Beetroots, Pumpkins; Lifet, etc, etc.)	3,437,980 "

Cultivators and landowners whom we interrogated generally agreed that the average yield per dounom of each of the above varieties could be estimated at :-

Wheat	75 Kilos
Barley	110 "
Sesame	40 "
Durra	40 "
Legumes	80 "
Fruit & Olives (Exclusive grapes)	300 "
Grapes	600 "
Vegetables	500 "

Based on the total yield and on the estimated yield per dounom the cultivated area would be arrived at as follows :-

	Total yield		Estimated yield per dounom		
Wheat	45,702,232 Kilos	÷	75 Kilos	=	609,363 dounoms
Barley	25,739,521 "	÷	110 "	=	233,995 "
Sesame	984,644 "	÷	40 "	=	24,616 "
Durra	15,271,060 "	÷	40 "	=	381,776 "
Legumes	8,175,888 "	÷	80 "	=	102,198 "
Fruit & Olives	18,676,273 "	÷	300 "	=	62,254 "
Grapes	5,622,896 "	÷	600 "	=	9,371 "
Vegetables	3,437,980 "	÷	500 "	=	6,876 "
			Total		1,430,449 dounoms.

Beersheba District should be separately estimated as the yield per dounom is less in that District than in other parts of Palestine owing to the scanty rainfall and different rotations of sowing.

8.

1919/20 was a particularly poor year in Beersheba. In 1920/21, however the yield was more satisfactory and, based on tithe estimations, was :-

    Wheat   4,364,160 Kilos.
    Barley 20,924,736   "
    Durra   1,223,504   "
    Melons 1,238,016   2

The yield per dounom is estimated at :-

    Wheat   45 Kilos.
    Barley 48 "
    Durra   40 "
    Melons 500 "

Based on the total yield and on the estimated yield per dounom, the cultivated area would be :-

Wheat	4,364,160 Kilos	÷	45 Kilos	=	96,981	dounoms.
Barley	20,924,736 "	÷	48 "	=	435,932	"
Durra	1,223,504 "	÷	40 "	=	30,587	"
Melons	1,238,016 "	÷	500 "	=	2,476	"
					565,976	"

It is considered, however, that the tithes that year were underestimated by about 25%; add therefore the area which would have been cultivated with the 25% underestimated tithes)   141,494 "

                   Total   707,470 dounoms.

Notwithstanding this seemingly satisfactory yield, we ascertained that there was a scarcity of seed, animals, etc. in 1920/21. It is said that this has now been made good and that therefore twice as much land is under cultivation this year in Beersheba or 1,414,940 d in all.

The system of fallow rotations varies in different parts of the country, but particularly so in Beersheba, some lands there being cultivated with barley one year, wheat the next, fallow the third and summer crops the fourth.

In the Azazmeh areas there is even more diversity of rotation owing to the more varied nature of the soil.

Some follow the four year rotation as described above, others cultivate for five years and then leave fallow the next two, three or

9.

four years; others again cultivate two years and leave fallow the third, while in the areas N.W., N. and N.E. where the rainfall is more or less regular the land is cultivated each year.

Taking an all round average of one year cultivation and one year fallow the cultivable area would be roughly double the area cultivated.

```
Palestine (excl. of Beersheba) area cultivated   1,430,449 dounoms
Beersheba                       do       do      1,414,940    "
                                                 2,845,389    "
    to allow for fallow rotation    x                2
                                                 5,690,778    "
                                    or           5,223 sq. Kilometres.
plus grazing area for the whole )                1,059   "        "
                        country  )               6,282   "        "
```

or about 28% of the area of the country. A substantial percentage must however be added for spaces occupied by cities, Villages, Settlements, Roads, etc, etc. The remainder could be considered "Mewat".

At least 50% of this remainder must be considered uncultivable as it is either in the South or South-East of the Country or is on the Coast and consists of sand dunes or is rocky and hilly country which would be chiefly suitable for afforestation.

TO ASCERTAIN THE TRUE AREA OF
MEWAT AND MAHLUL.

In order to ascertain the correct areas of Mewat and Mahlul land we suggested the appointing of Demarcation Commissions, which H.E. approved.

A difficulty which arose was to determine what lands should be considered Mewat.

Art. 103 of the Ottoman Land Code states :-

" The expression dead land (mewat) means vacant
" (khali) land such as mountains, rocky places, stony fields, pernallik
" and grazing ground which is not in the possession of anyone by
" title deed nor assigned ab antiquo to the use of inhabitants of a

10.

"town or village and lies at such a distance from towns or villages
"from which a human voice cannot be heard at the nearest inhabited
"place."

This was considered vague and it was generally agreed that in the interests of the Public a more accurate definition of Mewat land was necessary.

We suggested therefore that the method adopted in Cyprus should be followed and that all uncultivated land for which no title deed was held and which was one and a half miles from the outside houses of villages should be considered Mewat.

As for the towns, lands which had never been cultivated or for which no title deeds were held should be considered Mewat.

Land for which title deeds are held but which are not cultivated would be considered subject to Right of Tapou if they were uncultivated for three years or longer.

It was felt, however that owing to the war during which certain persons were in Military Service and therefore unable to cultivate and for other valid reasons resulting from the war, besides those valid reasons laid down in Art. 68 of the Ottoman Land Laws, it would be necessary to make allowances. Instructions as approved by Y.E. were therefore given to the Demarcation Commissions to accept valid reasons for non-cultivation, but to warn those title holders that if the land is not under cultivation during the next sowing season Tapou Tights would be enforced. The general instructions prepared for the Demarcation Commissions are as follows :-

" 1. The Commission will consist of a member of the Department
" of Lands, a Forestry Official and a District Official.

" 2. The following State Lands will be demarcated :-

11.

a) Mewat Lands.
b) Mahlul Lands.
c) Lands Subject to the Right of Tapou (Mustehiki Tapou)
d) Any other State Lands.

" 3. Mewat Lands are vacant lands for which no title is
" held and which are not allotted to the inhabitants of any place or
" village and which lie so far from the last point of the house of a
" place or village that the voice of a man calling from those points
" cannot be heard. This distance may be taken at about a mile and
" a half.

" 4. Instances will be found in which land has been set
" aside as " Metroukeh " for grazing without the boundaries or exact
" location being defined. Where the exact area of Metroukeh has not
" been already delimited the Commission with the representatives of
" the village will select a plot of the given area out of the unculti-
" vated land and this piece will, after approval by the Director of
" Lands, be the village Metroukeh grazing area and the remaining
" uncultivated land will be State Land. The village should be asked
" to produce the documents under which it claims the land as
" " Metroukeh ".

" 5. With regard to villages which have no Metroukeh allotted
" to them, the Commission, with the Village Representatives, will
" agree upon the necessary area required for grazing and will select
" a plot from the uncultivated lands near the village to be set aside
" as the common village lands. After the consent of the Department
" of Lands has been obtained to the allotment of Metroukeh, the
" remainder of the waste will be demarcated as State Land.

" 6. With regard to towns, all lands within a Municipal
" or a town planning area for which no title is held and which have
" never been cultivated will be regarded as State land and will be
" demarcated accordingly.

" 7. Mahlul lands are lands which through failure of heirs

12.

" or non-cultivation for 3 years reverted to the State and became
" State Domains.

" 8. All Mahlul Lands will be demarcated as State Lands
" (see Ordinance No. 186 of the 1st of October 1920, Official Gazette
" No. 31.)

" 9. In accordance with the provisions of Art. 2 of Ordinance
" No.186 every District Governor should have a list of Mahlul lands
" which have been declared in his District. A copy of this list should
" be obtained from the District Governor.

"10. Commissions when visiting villages should make full
" enquiries as to whether any persons have taken possession of Mahlul
" Lands and have failed to inform the Administration before the
" 15th of February 1921. All such cases together with a short note
" of the evidence and the names of the witnesses and the Mukhtars
" of the village should be immediately reported to the Department of
" Lands.

"11. Lands subject to the Right of Tapou (Mustehiki Tapou)
" are lands which have not been cultivated for 3 consecutive years,
" and which the occupant may again take up on payment of Tapou value.
" The Commissions should assess the value of such land and make a
" recommendation to the Director of Lands as to the Bedl Misl to be
" charged.

"12. All areas (other than Mulk) which have been unculti-
" vated for 3 consecutive years will be demarcated as State lands and
" cairns will be erected on all such lands as have no natural or well
" defined boundaries.

"13. When a claimant to Mustehiki Tapou land gives satis-
" factory reasons for non-cultivation such as those which are set out
" in Art. 68 of the Ottoman Land Laws, or pleads disabilities arising
" from the War or the difficulty of obtaining agricultural loans, that
" land should not be demarcated but a full report of the circumstances

13.

" should be made to the Department of Lands who may give instructions
" to the Commission to warn the claimants that after the next' year's
" sowing season, the right of tapou will be enforced if the land is
" still uncultivated.

" 14. A report should be made on each plot demarcated as
" State lands showing :-

" a) Town or Village and number of allotment.
" b) Approximate area.
" c) Name of Land.
" d) Nature of Land.
" e) Situation and boundaries.

" Similar reports will be furnished in respect of all
" private lands which are to be declared forest areas. This list will
" be sent to the Director of the Lands Department who will then forward
" a copy in Arabic or Hebrew to the Mukhtar of the village or settle-
" ment and one in English and Arabic or Hebrew to the Governor of the
" District. Notice of any land demarcated as State Domains and which
" may be within an area claimed by two villages will be sent to each
" of the disputing villages.

" 15. Any person objecting to the demarcation of areas as
" State Domains will send in his claim to the Director of Lands
" Department, Jerusalem, within three months of the date of the list
" being sent to the village. When any person objects to the demarcation
" the Commission will make a full note upon the report of such land
" stating the reason for which it was demarcated and source from which
" they obtained their information and the names of any persons who
" may be able to give evidence in support of the Commission's
" demarcation. The grounds of the claimants objections will also be
" noted.

" 16. The claim will be heard and decided by the Land
" Settlement Court, the objector to be the plaintiff and the Govern-
" ment the defendant. In the event of the objector being successful
" in his claim, the Court will make such order as seems just for
" payment of costs by the Government.

14.   604

" 17. The Director of Agriculture will state which of the lands " demarcated are to be declared forest areas.

" 18. All areas decided by the Land Settlement Court to be State " Domains and all areas with regard to the demarcation of which there may have been no objection will then be registered as Government " Property and will be available for leasing or other disposition by " the Department of Lands.

" 19. After areas are declared State Domains, soil values will be " taken by the Department of Agriculture for valuation of the land for " cultivation, rental or other purposes.

" 20. Should any member of the Demarcation Commission not be " able to proceed at any time on demarcation work he will be authorised, " subject to the approval of the Director of his Department, to delegate " a substitute."

AUTHORITY TO CONTROL
GOVERNMENT PROPERTY.

We recommended to Y.E. to add to the Advisory functions of the Land Commission the Executive functions of a Land Department to register and control all State Properties, to effect leases, to inspect cultivation etc. This Y.E. approved and the Land Department was opened on the first of April.

The Land Commission and Land Department combined consists of :-

```
A Director.
An Asst. Director.
An Inspector for Northern Palestine.
An Inspector for Southern Palestine.
Two Typists and
Three General Clerks.
```

The two Inspectors are also members of the Demarcation Commission referred to above.

When all State Lands have been demarcated, registered, divided into plots and numbered and when systems of tenure and

15.

leasing have been decided on, the functions of the Land Commission would be terminated. The Land Department could then be merged into the Land Registry Department.

TENURE AND CONDITIONS OF LEASING.

The Land Commission recommended the non-alienation of State Property. This Y.E. approved.

We suggest long leases but the period of the lease should be governed by circumstances. Natural difficulties in certain areas and the expenditure which is likely to be involved in developing property must also be considered.

Marshes and rocky lands or sand dunes the clearing of which would entail heavy expenditure would require long period leases.

Ordinary agricultural land should be leased on annual or short leases.

In order to encourage development non-renewal compensation must be agreed to be paid on permanent improvements such as buildings, trees, soil values etc.

AMENDMENT OF ART. 103 OF LAND CODE.

It was obvious that if state lands could no longer be alienated Art. 103 of the Ottoman Land Code would need to be amended to enable the State to control lands hitherto Mewat and which according to that Art. could be revived without permission from the Official and could be alienated from the State on payment of Bedl Misl.

We therefore recommended the following Ordinance which was approved by Y.E.

" Whereas it is expedient to amend the provisions
" of Art. 103 of the Ottoman Land Law
" BE IT ENACTED BY THE HIGH COMMISSIONER FOR PALESTINE, AFTER
" CONSULTATION WITH THE ADVISORY COUNCIL AS FOLLOWS :-

16.

"(a) The following shall be substituted for the last paragraph of the said article 103:

"Any person who without obtaining the consent of the Administration breaks up or cultivates any Waste land shall obtain no right to a title deed for such land and further will be liable to be prosecuted for trespass.

"(B) Any person who had already cultivated such Waste land without obtaining authorisation shall notify the Registrar of the Land Registry within two months of the publication of this Ordinance and apply for title deed."

With reference to clause (B) of this Ordinance, as a number of persons had already revived Mewat lands without obtaining authorisation it was necessary to appoint Commissions in each District to inspect those revived areas and to recommend the grant of title deeds in valid cases.

The instructions given to these Commissions as approved by Y/E. were as follows :-

"1. The Mewat Land Ordinance in Official Gazette No.38 of 1.3.21. provides that any person already cultivating Mewat land shall notify the Registrar of the Land Registry within two months of the publication of the Ordinance and apply for the issue of a title deed.

"2. Commissions consisting of the local Land Registration Officer, A Representative of the Lands Department and a Representative of the District Governor's Staff are being appointed to inspect the areas for which it is desired to obtain a Kushan.

"3. The Commission will consider only such applications as are received by the Registrar of the Land Registry up to and including the 1st day of May 1921 and no other applications will be considered.

"4. The Commission will proceed to and inspect each plot. "Care will be taken to ascertain that the plot was actually being

17.

" cultivated before the 1st of March, the date of publication of the
" Ordinance. The Commission will guard against instances where persons
" have planted trees upon Mewat Land since that date, or have made any
" other efforts to give the impression that the land was being culti-
" vated, where in fact, it was not being cultivated.

" 5. The Commission will supply the following particulars
" of each plot :-
" a) Name of applicant.
" b) Situation.
" c) Area (Note 1600 sq,pics = 1 dounom).
" d) Boundaries.
" e) Period for which cultivated and nature of culti-
"   vation. Whether trees or cereals, and if former
"   the number of trees and other full particulars
"   of the cultivation.

" f) If the applicant is claiming on behalf of the heirs
"   of a deceased person the name of such deceased
"   person will be given.

" g) The Commission will record its opinion as to
"   whether the applicant was bona fide cultivating
"   the land for which he applies prior to 1.3.21.
"   An odd tree does not constitute cultivation.

" 6. This report will be signed by all members of the
" Commission and handed to the District Governor who will forward it
" with his remarks to the Director of Lands, Lazarist Convent, Jerusalem;

" Any member of the Commission may record his dissent from
" the finding of the remaining members, stating his reasons.

" 7. The Commission will keep the District Governor fully
" informed of its movements.

" 8. In case any doubt arises as to whether any land is
" being actually cultivated or not the Agricultural Assistant should
" be called in.

" 9. Where Government Transport is not available attention
" will be paid to Treasury instructions that the cheapest transport is
" to be hired and that vouchers supporting the payment must be attached
" to Travelling Allowance Claim.

18.

LEASES.

AGRICULTURAL LAND.

Agricultural lands held on an annual tenure should be leased on the basis of a percentage on the yield. This we consider necessary because of the variableness of the rainfall, the risk of destruction of crops by pests etc. and because it is the system which has generally prevailed hitherto in the country.

BUILDING LAND.

Land leased to individuals for building purposes would have to be on a long tenure and it is recommended that the basis of the rental be a percentage on the unimproved capital value of the land.

AFFORESTATION

Areas leased for afforestation to be on a long tenure and should pay a nominal rent only until the trees are ready for felling, after which a percentage should be paid on the felling yield.

QUARRIES

Licences should be issued for a definite number of cubic metres of stone, allowing for wastage. In addition to the fee for the licence a charge should be made, payable in advance, of say 10% on the estimated value per metre of the stone to be quarried.

DEVELOPMENT

Lands leased for development and settlement purposes to be on a long tenure and either free of rent or on a nominal rent charge for an initial period during which drainage and other constructional works would be carried out.

Rental should also be fixed for a succeeding stated number of years, at the end of which the land would be re-assessed for rental, having regard, however, to the capital expenditure incurred, and similarly at the end of each rental-assessment period.

Clauses, however, should be inserted in the contract of lease to provide for non-renewal compensations for permanent improvements

19.

such as drainage works, buildings, trees, soil values, etc. etc.

As far as possible vacant land should be leased in small plots and in preference to persons with agricultural experience.

A man who has agricultural experience even if he were in possession of a moderate capital only, would be better able to improve his land than an inexperienced persons with a large capital.

It is difficult to suggest the area to which individual leases should be limited but they should not exceed an extent which having regard to the nature and quality of the land, would provide for the maintenance of the lessee and his family in a reasonable state of comfort.

TO MAKE MORE PRODUCTIVE LARGE AREAS HELD BY INDIVIDUAL OWNERS.

It has proved impossible to obtain particulars from the Land Registries of the areas held in individual private ownership.

A number of townspeople and others also own shares in village communal lands (Mesha'a).

Village lands are all registered in the names of a few of the headmen and there is therefore no record of the areas of the individual shareholders.

We have, however, made exhaustive enquiries in each district and it is estimated that about 1,200,000 dounoms are owned by 350 individuals not including shares owned in village areas nor owners of small registered plots.

These figures do not include lands owned in common by villagers (Mesha'a), nor areas owned by Jewish Settlers.

It will be easily apparent even to a casual observer that much of the land owned or claimed by individuals and even lands owned by villages or Jewish Colonies are left uncultivated. One argument

20.

to be deduced from this would be that generally speaking the fellah has as much land as he can cultivate although in a few cases certain villages are badly off in that respect.

We are of opinion that every encouragement should be given to landowners to sell their excess areas and that there should be no restriction on sales.

With regard to the fear that the fellah will alienate all his land if the 300 dounom restriction in the Land Transfer Ordinance is removed, we are of opinion that as he is dependent on his cultivation as his means of livelihood having no other regular method of supporting himself and his family and as he is an intelligent person and a keen agriculturalist he is not likely to part with all his lands.

In pre war days he was not as happily circumstanced as he is to-day. He suffered under disabilities and was the object of exactions which no longer prevail.

Before the Occupation he was obliged to part with some of his land to purchase food for himself or seed for sowing.

The altered condition of the villager is best instanced by the fact that whereas some years ago he was usually the borrower and the townsman the lender, the position is reversed and it is rather the townsman who to-day applies to the fellah for a loan.

It should also be borne in mind that the Government has advanced about £.E.300,000 to peasants and to other agriculturalists and when Credit Banks are opened these will also be available for the occasional hard pressed fellah to apply to for financial assistance.

The Land Transfer Ordinance has restricted land sales and in consequence has shackled the free flow of money.

The Ordinance is also objected to on religious ground by many Moslems, and the majority of the inhabitants of Palestine are

21.

Moslems.

The Sharieh Law states " A possessor may dispose of his " possession as he pleases," and the Land Transfer Ordinance is in direct contradiction to this.

We recommend therefore a revision of the Land Transfer Ordinance, removing the restriction on sales.

In addition, however, to the enforcement of the " Right of Tapou," it is necessary to introduce some method whereby land which is habitually left uncultivated will be made productive.

In certain newer countries, the Government reserves to itself the right to resume areas which, while well-watered and arable, are ised for grazing only, or lands which the extension of their Railway Systems has brought within about 15 miles of the railway, etc.

The Government resumes the possession of these areas which are then cut up into small plots and leased at say 4% of the value of the land plus the costs of resumption.

Palestine, however, is not a new country neither is it an extensive one and the agricultural population has always been accustomed to extensive cultivation. Many years will elapse before the fellah realises the benefit of intensive cultivation for stock breeding in preference to his present system of extensive grazing.

Grazing areas are not at present defined neither are they registered. In our instructions to the Demarcation Commissions provision has been made to remedy this.

We recommend therefore that after the demarcation and registration of " Metroukeh " areas in each village for grazing is completed uncultivated land in future should be taxed each year and the " Right of Tapou " be also enforced after the third year of non-cultivation.

The Mustehiki Tapou law should be amended.
Art. 68 of the Land Code states :-

22.

Except for one of the following reasons, duly established, namely :-

" (1) Resting the soil for one or two years, or even more
" if owing to its exceptional nature and situation it is
" requisite;
" (2) Obligation to leave land which has been flooded
" uncultivated for a time after the water has subsided
" in order that it may become cultivable;
" (3) Imprisonment of the possessor as a prisoner of war;
" land which has not been cultivated, either directly by
" the possessor, or indirectly by being leased or loaned,
" and remains unproductive for three years consecutively
" become subject to the right of tapou, whether the
" possessor wishes to recover the land, it shall be given
" to him on payment of its tapou value. If he does not
" claim it it shall be put up to auction and adjudged to
" the highest bidder.

According to the Article the State and the Country generally lose revenue and produce for three years before action can be taken to protect public interests. One natural consequence is the high cost of living.

If, however, persons owning land are compelled to pay tithes thereon each year whether they cultivate or not, the tithes on uncultivated areas being based dounom for dounom on those collected on the nearest cultivated land and in addition the Right of Tapou is applied at the end of the third year, landowners will either cultivate if it is within their power to do so or will sell their excess areas. More grain will be produced and the cost of living reduced.

UNDIVIDED VILLAGE LAND (MESHA'A)

One of the most important measures for the improvement of cultivation and one of the most popular in our opinion would be the dividing of Mesha'a land.

Fellaheen all over the country have expressed themselves in favour of it and in reply to our remark that the Provisional Law Relating to the Partition of Immovable Property 1332 gave them the necessary power to divide, they said that the attitude of the peasant was such that unless he was obliged to do so he would not divide although he

23.

realises the benefit of individual holdings and will welcome them.

On 23.9.20. we submitted to Y.E. a proposal for the compulsory dividing of Mesha'a land and strongly recommended the acceptance thereof. On 15.3.21 we submitted the following amended memorandum :-

" 1. Article 3 of the above Law states that Immovable
" property may be partitioned by agreement of the Co-owner.

" 2. It is generally acknowledged that the reason why Village
" Mesha'a lands bear such poor crops, why very few trees are planted
" each year and why these lands have not been improved hitherto is
" because the villager has a different plot allotted to him each year
" and it is not worth his while to spend money or energy on improvements
" which would benefit some other person the following year.

" Since our recommendations were first submitted (23.9.20)
" the Land Commission has visited every district in the Country and in
" reply to the question whether the partition of Village Mesha'a lands
" should be made compulsory, a wide spread and practically unanimous
" wish has been expressed by Villagers and townspeople owning shares in
" Village lands in favour of compulsory partitioning.

" If transfer fees are charged when partitioning is made
" the measure would not be a popular one. It is suggested that only
" the cost of the Kushan be collected as the increased yield from the
" improvements which will result from partitioning will produce a
" corresponding and permanent increase of tithes.

" It is reported that the Jaffa Chamber of Agriculture
" discussed the partitioning of Village Mesha'a land and the members
" agreed that the first step to be adopted for the general improvement
" of Agriculture and for the progress of Palestinian agriculture was the
" partitioning of these lands.

" 3. It is suggested therefore that an additional clause be
" added to the " Provisional Law relating to the partition of

24.   614

" Immovable Property 1332", to the effect that immovable property
" belonging in common to Villages (known as Mesha'a land) will be
" partitioned compulsorily and each villager or other individual who
" at present owns a share in Communal land will have his individual
" plot for which he will hold a title deed.

" 4.   The method of partitioning will be as stated in Art.5
" of the above-mentioned Law.

" Rocky and good land will be partitioned each separately
" among Hamoulehs, Families and Individuals so that each would obtain
" a section of good and of bad land.

" Where this is impossible Clause 2 of Art.5 of the
" above-mentioned Law will be applied.

" 5.   When partitioning has been completed lists will be
" published in each village and a stated period will be allowed for
" legal objections to be made, which will be decided by the Land
" Courts. At the expiration of the period Kushans will be issued.

" The Kushans will state the approximate area, if
" possible, in dounoms, and where there happen to be natural, well-
" defined and known boundaries such as wadies, hills, brooks, roads
" etc., these will be stated. Where there are no such well defined
" boundaries, cairns will be erected and shallow trenches dug and the
" names of the owners of the holdings on each point of the compass
" will be inserted in the Kushan.

" Any person removing the cairns or destroying the
" trenches will be liable to prosecution by the Crown.

" When the survey of the country is complete the actual
" area will be inserted on the Kushans.

" 6.   Only cultivable land will be partitioned.

" 7.   A partitioning Committee will be formed in each
" District and will be composed of the Registrar (because of his
" knowledge of the Land Laws) a Representative appointed by the
" District Governor, and one from each Hamouleh of the Village.

25.

" The expenses of the officials will be a charge on the village.

" 8. The District Governor will inform the village that
" within a period not exceeding 4 months from date of his advice, the
" partitioning will be made.

" Mukhtars must send lists to the District Governor
" within 4 weeks signed by themselves and the Elders and stating:-

  a) Number and names of Hamoulehs.

  b) Names and number of families in each Hamouleh.

  c) Individuals in each family, including women, entitled to Mesha'a land and names of minors, absentees and persons of unsound mind with names of guardians.

" In cases where minors, absentees etc., have no guard-
" ians the Sheri Court will be instructed by the District Governor to
" nominate guardians.

  d) Shares in each Village area.

" The lists will include all Hamoulehs, families and
" individuals who have cultivating shares in the Mesha'a land stating
" the number of shares each possesses.

" 9. A penalty of a fine or imprisonment or both will be
" inflicted if Mukhtars and Elders knowingly send incorrect lists.

"10. Immediately the lists are received copies will be sent
" by the District Governor to each village and eight weeks will be
" allowed for individuals to send claims to the Governorate if a) their
" names have been omitted from the lists, or b) if they consider that
" they are entitled to larger shares than are stated in the Mukhtar's
" list.

" During the remaining 4 weeks before date of partition-
" ing the Committee will examine the claims and add to the list those
" individuals whose claims have been made good.

" The Tabou Registers need not necessarily be considered
" when examining the lists as the custom hitherto appears to have been
" to register all Mesha'a lands in the names of two or three chiefs of
" principal Hamoulehs.

26.

" 11.   On the date of partitioning the Committee will
" proceed to the village and will partition the land by lot in the
" manner set forth in Art.5 of the above-mentioned law.

" Excessive sub-division should be avoided. Land
" being of different qualities the tendency will be to divide it into
" small plots. This will be agriculturally detrimental to the Country.
" Some means should be found to establish a uniform minimum holding
" capable of supporting the cultivator in a reasonable state of comfort
" and which would be of sufficient extent to enable him to obtain
" agricultural loans thereon from a Credit Bank.

" It may be found advisable in certain cases to
" divide into family plots only and to leave it to individual members
" of the family to apply for further partitioning. (See Art.I of Law
" "so that no share shall lose the benefit before partition" and
" Art.15 of Ottoman Land Laws, ' If any land possessed in individual
" shares by several persons is capable of being divided, that is to
" say if each portion can yield separately as much produce 'as if it
" continued to form part of the whole --- shares shall be parcelled
" out").

" In many cases it will be found that villagers
" have already sold portions of Sahems to individuals who may or may
" not be inhabitants of that particular village.

" Such portions will be partitioned similarly by
" lot and the individuals concerned will receive Title Deeds.

" Villagers who may have purchased or otherwise
" legally acquired extra sahams or shares and who also originally are
" entitled to a sahem or share to participate in proportion to the
" extent of both their original and acquired shares.

" 12.   The land will be first partitioned by lot among
" Hamoulehs. Hamouleh plots will be then partitioned by lot among
" families. Family plots will be then partitioned by lot among

27.

" individuals.

" <u>Note.</u> It may be found that portions of Sahems belonging
" to women, poor people, minors, absentees or persons of unsound
" mind have been illegally sold by individuals without the knowledge
" or consent of the owner.

" The Courts will hear any case brought forward at
" any time by persons whose property or shares had been illegally
" disposed of by others.

" It will also be found that in certain villages
" Mesha'a lands have already been partitioned among Hamoulehs. In
" such cases the Hamouleh plots will be partitioned to a) Families
" b) Individuals.

" In the case of villages which will be found to
" have already partitioned their lands among Hamoulehs, families and
" individuals lists of such partitioned shares will be published in
" the village and a stated period will be allowed for legal objections
" to be made. At the expiration of that period Kushans will be issued.

" 13.   It will be necessary for the Committee first to
" establish the boundaries of each village.

" This should not be difficult as these are generally
" known and acknowledged.

" In cases of disputed boundaries the Committee will
" investigate and decide.

" 14.   Orchards, vineyards or gardens if already parti-
" tioned will be registered in actual owners' names. If still Mesha'a
" they will be partitioned by lot.

" In the case of vineyards, orchards and gardens
" already found to be partitioned the courts will hear cases brought
" by persons illegally excluded from their share."

28.

ARAB LANDS BEERSHEBA ETC.
=============================

The Arabs of Beersh[eba]
they have no Mesha'a land. The tribes have fair[ly]
areas over which they roam and which they cultivate, [and graze]
animals on.

Each tribal section has its land which is div[ided among]
families or individuals.

Definite particulars, however, are not available for [it as]
very little Arab owned land is registered.

The Arab has objected to registration because in the [first]
place his women would inherit property on the death of their par[en]t
or husbands.

In the event of a person dying his daughters who may be
married to members of other tribes would inherit part of his pr[operty]
which would then be alienated from the tribe which originally [owned]
it.

If the tribe into whose possession it has come attem[pted]
to cultivate it, the original owners would object with the resu[lt that]
the District would immediately be the centre of disturbances.

Another objection is that registration fees and then W[aqf]
would have to be paid.

Apart from the natural disinclination of the Bedu to pay
taxes at all he objects to do so on the ground that he enjoys little
if any Administrative benefits. There are few tribal schools and no
hospitals; he is dependent on himself for the security of his family
and possessions. There are no public roads connecting up the tribal
areas and as Sheikh Courts have been instituted he does not require the
ordinary protection of the Law.

It is not unlikely, however, that the second reason for
non-registration weighs more with the Arab than the first, for any
women who elects to institute proceedings in the Religious Courts and

[Original page damaged.]

29.

in whose favour judgement is given would be assisted by the Law to secure her rights whether of land or anything else.

It is also beginning to be realised that registration of property does carry with it certain priviliges. At present an Arab cannot obtain a loan from a Bank on his land as he cannot produce a title deed. He is therefore compelled to apply to private individuals who not only charge a high rate of interest but also hold and cultivate the mortgaged land keeping all the proceeds until the debt has been liquidated.

We recommend therefore that all Arabs be compelled to register but that no registration fee be charged on first registration except cost of the title deed and that so long as the land remains in the possession of the original holder it shall not be subject to Werko.

All sales, however, to be subject to the usual transfer fees and land sold to be then subject to Werko.

As these lands have never been registered and as the rotation of cultivation varies so that in some cases cultivable areas are not cultivated for more than three successive years a difficulty arises as to which lands can be considered the possession of the tribes for registration purposes.

We recommend that the areas which should be recognised as Arab property which must be registered as such be those which they have cultivated during the last ten years according to 2, 3, or more years' rotation of Summer and Winter crops and fallow plus 5% of the total area of the District, in proportion to each tribal area, for grazing purposes.

We further recommend that there should be compulsory registration of lands in Beersheba District of cases which are decided by the Land Settlement Court. It is suggested also that the Cadastral Survey of Beersheba District be held back until the

30.

registration of lands in that District has been completed.

G R A Z I N G " METROUKEH "

                                                           Many years will elapse before the fellah realizes the economic value of intensive cultivation for feeding in preference to extensive grazing on uncultivated land.

It has always been the custom to graze animals on extens areas and Art.98 of the Land Code states that " so much assigned land " as has been left and assigned as such Ab Antiquo is deemed to be " pasturing ground. Delimitations subsequently made are of no " validity."

We discovered, however, an investigation that although certain villages have Metroukeh land registered as such for grazing, the majority of villages do not enjoy that legal privilege.

Even those villages which have registered Metroukeh land, the particular plots are no. specified but it is stated simply that so many dounoms of the village area are " Metroukeh "; in other words, provided that those inhabitants leave uncultivated only the Metroukeh registered number of dounoms, the ' Right of Tapou ' cannot be applied to them.

It is imperative that until the fellah acquires a preference for, and the habit of, sowing fodder for his animals, Metroukeh grazing areas should be delimited within stated boundaries and registered as such for each village.

In order to have a basis for determining the grazing area of each village we recommend the adoption of the estimates of Prof Domenico Tamaro referred to on page 5.

It should be comparatively easy to ascertain the number of animals in each village and the necessary area, with boundaries having been agreed upon and selected, it should be registered as such. Certain considerations however, should not be lost sight of.

31.

Some villages possess only a limited number of dounoms of land and are obliged to send their animals some distance away to graze as they require the whole of their area for cultivation. Others again cultivate little or no land but subsist chiefly on dairy produce and on the raising of sheep and goats etc. for consumption.

We recommend therefore the inclusion of Clauses 4 and 5 of the Instructions to the State Land Demarcation Commissions as specified on page 10.

In some parts, particularly in the South, where fallow rotations are the rule it would not appear to be necessary to reserve any pasturage area, for the flocks and herds would graze on the land left fallow. These people would in any event keep their animals close to the camps and to the areas under cultivation and as these would be the areas nearest to those which are being cultivated at that particular time there would not appear to be any necessity to delimit additional ' Metroukeh ' land for them.

They might, however, object to be singled out for treatment apparently less generous than that meted out to others.

For such Districts also we therefore suggest adding to each registered tribal area an additional 5% on the whole area of the District in proportion to the number of dounoms of cultivable land registered for each tribe.

W A K F.
========

There are three classes of Wakf which would be affected by proposals for the closer settlement of the Country.

<u>AUKAF MASBUTA.</u> These were originally ordinary Miri lands the cultivating rights of which were owned by villages or individuals, the " Raqabe " remaining vested in the State.

32.   622

This was subsequently purchased for the benefit of a Mosque, the tithes, transfer fees etc. therefrom being collected for the beneficiary.

When the Tapou was first started title deeds were issued in favour of the cultivator but the documents were endorsed with the name of the Mosque or charitable object which happened to be the Beneficiary.

Some years ago the Turkish Government stopped the collection of tithes by the beneficiary and arranged for their collection by the Revenue Department. The expenses of the Mosque or charitable object were thenceforward met by the Government.

At present the tithes, transfer fees etc. are credited to the General Wakf Council which is now responsible for the necessary expenditure on behalf of the beneficiary.

These lands like ordinary Miri lands would be available by purchase for purposes of closer settlement, provided that the General Wakf Council is guaranteed the revenues accruing from their cultivation and improvement.

AWKAF MUNDARASSE.   These were lands given to Mosques, etc. in fulfilment of vows.

When the Education Department was re-organised the Turkish Government decided that such Mosques etc. which had been the beneficiaries of these vows but which had fallen into ruin or disuse no longer required the proceeds of its lands which were henceforth to be credited to Education and they were registered in the name of the Maaref.

The revenue from these properties could be substantially increased if the Department of Education could properly control and lease them. To do this satisfactorily would however require a special staff and the expenditure incurred might more than swallow up the increased revenue.

33.

It is therefore suggested that these lands be sold for purposes for closer settlement and the proceeds credited to the Department of Education.

The tithes and transfer fees etc. therefrom would then accrue to the State.

AWKAF SABEET.

These are held by Hijjeh and cannot be sold but may be exchanged by permission of the Cadi for property which produces larger revenue.

These would be available by exchange (Istibdel) for closer settlement and we recommend that the STATE should at least encourage if not insist on, the exchange in cases where undoubted benefit would accrue to the Wakf.

In addition to the above, there are several large areas in Palestine which are claimed by certain Wakfs, but the Metwallies are not in possession of Hijjeh or other title.

These were probably originally Mewat or possibly Mahlul lands which were acquired by some means not known now.

    The Wakf Nebi Rubin, near Jaffa.
    Wakf el Bustani.
    Wakf el Ridwann.
    Ard es Sidreh near Ramleh.
    Ard es Sammra Jericho.

are said to be such.

We recommend the appointment of a Commission to examine the position of these properties.

Hijjehs to be granted for such as have been held so long as to give the Wakf a prescriptive title.

Those lands which have not been held so long as to entitle the Wakf to prescription to be sold by the State for purposes of closer settlement but the proceeds of the sale to be credited to the General Wakf Council.

34.

EXTENSION OF WAKFS.

It is many years since the Turkish Government discontinued the sale of the " Raqaba " for the benefit of religious objects.

There can therefore be no longer any extension of Awkaf Masbuta.

We recommend, however, that Miri lands which may be included in the new town limits by the Town Planning Commissions and which will probably therefore become Mulk should under no circumstances be allowed to be made Wakf.

Mulk land i.e. land within the old town limits and which may now be made Wakf should require Government sanction in future before they can be alienated for the benefit of a Wakf.

RIGHTS OF PRESENT TENANTS AND OCCUPANTS.

Cultivators who might possibly be considered as having customary rights are :-

a) Persons who refused or ommitted to register their lands when the Tapou was first opened.

b) Persons who because of their failure to pay tithes or other taxes lost their lands to the Turkish Government who sold them to individuals or attached them as State Domains and leased them to the original owners.

These cultivators did not part with their lands willingly but by force of circumstances.

c) Persons who voluntarily and with their full knowledge and consent sold their lands to private individuals but continued to cultivate them as tenants of the purchasers.

We must differentiate between lands attached by the Government and lands sold by their owners to individuals and again with

35.

regard to lands attached by the Government it will be necessary to make a distinction between the areas sold by the Government and areas which the Government permitted the original owners or claimants to continue to cultivate on payment of a rental of 10% on the gross yield.

The Land Commission has not been able to ascertain definitely the reason why large areas were attached by the State and either sold to individuals like Sursock, Butros etc. or allowed the original owners and claimants to cultivate them on payment of 10% on the yield as rental.

In certain cases persons may have refused or may have omitted to register their areas and for this or for some other reason not known now the Government may have considered their title to the land not clear.

In other cases persons may have been unable to pay tithes or taxes and so lost their lands to the State.

Others again were tithe farmers and were unable to pay the tithes which they had guaranteed and in consequence the Government attached their lands.

Still others mortgaged their property to the Agricultural Bank and not having repaid the loan their lands were sold.

For the purposes of our recommendations we will divide these lands into three classes.

a) Lands attached by the Government and then sold to individuals but the original owners continued to cultivate as tenants of the purchaser.

b) Lands attached by the Government and registered as State Domains but still cultivated by the original owners or claimants.

c) Land sold by the owners themselves to individuals.

36.

CLASS A.

The Land Commission is not a legal body and cannot therefore advise on the legal title of the cultivators.

If the Legal Secretary is of opinion that the mere fact of a person having continued to cultivate as tenant for a number of years land which originally belonged to that person, constitutes a right to that person, then in the event of the land being re-sold by the person who purchased it from the State, provision should first be made for the cultivator to be assured, as tenant of the new purchaser, of an area sufficient, by intensive cultivation, for the maintenance of his family and if a house was provided for him by the first purchaser, he must be assured of accommodation by the next owner.

Such persons, however, should not have the right to sub-let their areas without the consent of the owner and provision should be made to safeguard the interests of the owner in the event of the tenant omitting to cultivate or in the event of any action by him which would be prejudicial to the interests of the owner.

In any case if cultivators are evicted they would be entitled to compensation for permanent improvements affected by them.

CLASS B.

We are of opinion that the Government should ensure to these cultivators the tenancy in perpetuity of areas sufficient for their maintenance and we recommended to Y.E. a system of tenure for the lands in Beisan District which should apply to similar Government lands in other parts of the Country.

The recommendation which we submitted for Y.E. approval was the following :-

" With a view to securing to cultivators and their children
" such tenancy rights as they may have on Government lands in Beisan,

37.

" the Ghor and Semakh and in order that cultivators may feel that it
" is in their own interest to develop the lands they will hold, the
" Government of Palestine will make arrangements with the above
" mentioned cultivators, the terms of which will be as follows :-

" 1. Persons who have acquired cultivating tenancy right
" either by purchase, by succession, or by permission of the Ottoman
" Government for not less than ten years, will keep such areas as
" they have cultivated within the last two years under summer and
" winter crops.

" 2. Such areas as are cultivated in common (Mesha'a) by
" villagers or Arabs will be partitioned.

" 3. Leases must be accepted by all persons referred to in
" clauses 1 and 2. The leases will be personal and will be subject
" to any future Government law of expropriation.

" 4. CONDITIONS:-

"(a) Tithes or such taxation as may be substituted by any
" future legislation.

"(b) Rental 10% on gross yield of crops or the equivalent
" in money at the option of the Government.

" The rental will be subject to increased assessment in the
" event of any improvements carried out by the Government or by
" concessionaries from the Government.

"(c) At the end of the initial period of lease the Lessee
" will have the first refusal of a renewal.

"(d) On the death of the Lessee the lease will be trans-
" ferred to his children or grandchildren who will cultivate in common
" unless the area can be divided into plots of not less than 100 dounoms.
" Any heir may, however, dispose of his share to another heir.

"(e) The Lessee shall follow any instructions of the
" Government concerning the cultivation. Failure to obey these

" instructions or to cultivate any area for two successive years will
" involve a forfeiture of the lease without any compensation.

"(f) Within two years of signing of lease, lessees must
" clear their areas of all scrub, thorns, stones, sidr, etc., and if
" irrigable must be properly canalized to prevent the formation of
" swamps, or lease will be forfeited without compensation. Failure
" to preserve these improvements will also entail forfeiture of lease.
" The decision of the Department of Agriculture on these points will
" be final.

"(g) Sub-leasing will not be permitted. The Lessee must
" cultivate his area himself and with his family (if he has any). The
" lessee must continuously reside on the land. He may employ labourers
" but must provide suitable accommodation for them.. The names of such
" labourers must be sent to the Government and no person who owns or
" cultivates more than 50 dounoms of land elsewhere, or who is not
" an inhabitant of Palestine may be employed by the lessee as a labourer.
" Should the area be greater than he and his family can cultivate, he
" may with the permission of the Government assign his tenancy right
" to the excess, but only in plots not exceeding 100 dounoms to any one
" family. The Government will refuse permission to the assignment to
" any person who owns or cultivates more than 50 dounoms of land else-
" where or who is not an inhabitant of Palestine. The assignee must
" become the lessee of the Government on the same terms as those of the
" transferor.

" The question of the pasturage is an extremely
" difficult one.
" NOTE. Art. 98 of the Ottoman Land Law and the note in Young's
" Corp de Droit Ottoman Vol.VI page 72, preclude persons from using
" Jiftlik - and Aradi Mudawara are Jiftlik - for grazing purposes.

" It will also be apparent that if the Government is to provide
" grazing land much of the portion hitherto uncultivated will be re-

39.

" quired for grazing. You will not have much land free for settlement
" and intensive cultivation on State Property.

" It is said that from 10 to 12 dounoms of uncultivated land
" would be required for extensive grazing <u>per animal</u> and this clearly
" would not be permitted on any Government Jiftlik. On the other
" hand the Mamours of State Domains under the Ottoman Government
" allowed both Villagers and Bedu to use both dry and swampy land for
" grazing, whether the land was cultivable or not.

" To sumarily disallow this would be a harsh measure and
" even if legally defensible would be inexpedient.

" Three alternatives are apparent :

" a)   Cultivators to be informed that they must sow a
" sufficient number of dounoms of the land leased to them with food
" for their flocks and herds.

" b)   It may be found that the area cultivated by each
" village or tribe in the aggregate would work out between 200 and
" 300 dounoms per family. It is presumed and indeed has been so
" stated by certain people in different parts of the country that
" 150 dounoms are sufficient for the maintenance of a family of
" 5 persons. The village to be informed that an area in the village
" land equal to the total surplus on the above basis must be reserved
" and may be left uncultivated for grazing the animals they at
" present possess.

" Any annual increase of sheep, goats or cattle they
" would then naturally have to dispose of. This would bring more
" meat into the markets and tend to reduce prices.

" c)   An area of hitherto uncultivated land to be
" reserved for each village for grazing purposes. The Department of
" Agriculture to estimate what area will be required for the flocks and
" herds the villages at present possess or take the estimate of
" Prof. Tamaro referred to on page 5 of this report as a basis.

40.

"Any annual increase of sheep, goats or cattle they would then naturally have to dispose of. This would bring more meat into the markets and tend to reduce prices.

"The suggestion in (a) could be made to apply only for fresh settlers as the present cultivators are not accustomed to and would not understand intensive cultivation for stock breeding.

"The immediate effect of suggestion (b) would be to reduce the yield of crops and consequently of tithes and rental but would be conpensated for gradually as lands which have hitherto not been cultivated are leased to fresh settlers.

"Suggestion (c) would naturally be preferred by the present cultivators but might not be equally acceptable to the Government in view of the desire to settle more people on the land.

"We recommend suggestion (b) as worthy of consideration."

CLASS C.

While the Government is free to do what it likes with its own property it is a question if it can dictate to individuals regarding the disposal of their property.

Persons who of their own free will sold their lands to others even if they continued to cultivate as tenants of the purchasers would not appear to have any rights except compensation for permanent improvements which they may have effected while cultivating as tenants.

OTHER TENANTS & OCCUPANTS.

We are doubtful of the legal rights of other ordinary tenants and make the following suggestion with all reserve :-

The Land Transfer Ordinance should be amended and the protection of tenants and occupants should be provided for by res-

41.

trictions on the purchaser.

The Ordinance should state that the Government will only give permission for sales if it is satisfied that provision has been made by the purchaser in the deed of sale for Tenants or Occupants of long date who have themselves personally (not with hired labourers) cultivated the identical area for say more than 10 years and who have not more than 50 dounoms of land per family elsewhere or who have no means of livelihood elsewhere and who can be alienated from their means of livelihood against their will.

TAX FARMERS.

With regard to lands of tax farmers or their guarantors which were attached by the Ottoman Treasury, re recommended to Y.E. that the original owners should have the opportunity to resume their areas on payment of the sum due from them together with 6% interest per annum. If, however, the land was attached by the Treasury and was leased to and cultivated by the original owner he should pay only the sum originally due from him without interest.

This recommendation Y.E. approved and the following Public Notice was issued :-

" Notice is hereby given that lands of tax farmers
" or their guarantors which were attached by the Ottoman Trea-
" sury since the year 1327 for failure to pay sums due to the
" Treasury and which are still registered in the name of the
" Treasury may be redeemed provided that the former owner or
" his representatives pay to the District Governor within one
" year of the date of this notice the amount owing to the
" Treasury together with 6% interest per annum for every year
" that the land has been attached.

" If, however, the land has been in the possession
" of the Treasury since the attachment and has been leased to
" the former owner, the sum payable shall be that with which the
" land was charged, and no interest shall be added. If the
" lands attached have been sold by the Treasury, the right of
" redemption will not apply."

42.

CLOSER SETTLEMENT

632

In a previous chapter we stated that the area of Western Palestine is estimated at about 22,000 square kilometres.

From particulars obtained a few years ago by the Department of Agriculture the Ottoman Government estimated the areas of the Districts at :-

Safed	Dounoms	536,100
Acre	"	952,300
Nazareth	"	429,800
Tiberias	"	582,500
Haifa	"	981,400
Jenin	"	1,573,900
Tulkeram	"	781,600
Nablus	"	850,300
Selfit	"	573,900
Jaffa	"	1,115,100
Jerusalem	"	2,076,400
Hebron	"	2,507,600
Gaza	"	1,892,500
Total Dounoms	=	14,853,400 or

13,654 square kilometres.

The area of Beersheba District alone is estimated at about 8000 square kilometres making a round total of 22,000 square kilometres for the whole of Western Palestine.

It is estimated by the Zionist Commission and other Colonization Societies that about 20% of the whole area is under cultivation in any given year. This is to a certain extent confirmed by the yield for the year 1920/21 as given by the Department of Revenue divided by the average number of kilos yield per dounom as stated on pages 6, 7, and 8 of this report.

The system of leaving sections of cultivable land fallow is not so general as would appear at first sight except in the District of Beersheba and in the State lands of Beisan.

In other parts, lack of water, uncertain rainfall, scanty population, losses both of animals and money during the war are probably some of the reasons why more land has not been under regular cultivation but in justice to the programme of closer

43.

settlement it must be admitted that the area actually cultivated appears to be sufficient for the needs of the present agricultural population. The fellah to-day is better off than he has ever been before and not only so as a matter of comparison but he is sufficiently well off to pay his tithes and taxes, he has sufficient food and clothing for the year and he has usually two years reserve at least for seed.

There has hitherto been no cadastral survey of the country neither are there figures available of the total cultivable area, but even a casual observer must realize that large areas are quite uncultivable because of the nature of the soil, the scanty rainfall, the absence of springs etc.

All alomg the coast from Gaza Northward the sands are steadily encroaching on the cultivable land and thousands of dounoms previously planted with trees and cereals are now rolling wastes of sand dunes.

The serious attention of the Government is invited to this wastage.

Experiments are already being made by the Department of Agriculture to plant the edges of the dunes with castor oil and other trees with a view to combating the advance of the sands.

The inhabitants of Jaffa and some of the Jewish Settlements along the coast are also engaged in this important work.

Every encouragement should be given to these pioneers.

Large areas on the Eastern frontier are equally uncultivable particularly from the Wady Farah Southwards. The Eastern part of the Jerusalem and Hebron Districts and the Eastern, South-Eastern and Southern parts of Beersheba are particularly so.

One need not be a pessimist to estimate that almost 30% of the area of Palestine is absolutely barren and another 20% will remain so unless planting the sand dunes can be successfully accom-

44.

plished and extensive irrigation schemes are found to be economically possible.

To come down to facts we are informed that 50% of the area of the country can be considered free for closer settlement but not necessarily agriculturally possible.

The present agricultural population of Palestine is estimated at about 500,000 souls.

It should be borne in mind that Industries are comparatively speaking, non-existent and that therefore the large majority of the population of the Country is more or less directly dependent on agriculture.

There has hitherto been no proper census taken of the population but a very moderate estimate at say 5 persons to a family would give about 100,000 families and these, at 150 dounoms of land each, which is the average area stated by persons in different parts of Palestine as sufficient for the maintenance of a family in a reasonable state of comfort, would require 15,000,000 dounoms or about 14,000 square kilometres or 63% of the total area of Palestine. Add the estimate of 30% as absolutely barren land = 93% of the total extent of the country.

At first sight therefore there would not appear to be any land available for fresh settlers but there are factors which must be considered as bearing on this point.

The first and most important is that extensive cultivation and extensive grazing is the method adopted all over the country.

If intensive cultivation were introduced both for cereal growing and for stock breeding fully a third less of the area would be sufficient for the ordinary needs of the present agricultural population.

Another point to be borne in mind is that there are areas of so called " Mewat " land which while cultivable have not hitherto

45.

...n cultivated and again large areas of Marshes (which are also ...trimental to the health of the population) are either absolutely ...ste or are only used for grazing a few herds of cattle on.

In the general interest of public health and in order not to leave large surfaces of agricultural land unutilized all owners of marshes should be compelled by law to drain and cultivate them within a stated period, failing which they should revert to the State.

State owned marshes should also be drained and planted with trees or with cereals either by the State or preferably by the private enterprise of new settlers on long leases.

The crying need of the country is undoubtedly intensive cultivation but it will be many years before the fellah will be an agricultural expert and before he can be brought to realize its benefit.

Closer settlement must necessarily be a slow and lengthy process and can only be brought about by the education of the fellah. There should be experimental stations in each District and Agricultural Schools should be opened for the villagers.

Of the land not hitherto cultivated but portions of which may be found to be cultivable, a certain proportion is far from centres of habitation with no roads and no easy means of disposal of produce or purchase of necessaries.

The good will of the population must be taken into account as also the state of public security in outlying parts.

The areas where land might be considered as now available for new settlements are chiefly tropical in climate and where the rainfall is scanty and uncertain.

New settlers from Europe, America or Canada would have climatic and other almost insurmountable difficulties to contend with and unless they are monied men or are financially supported, two successive rainless years at the commencement of their enterprise

[Original page damaged.]

46.

would ruin them.

Closer settlement should be promoted by encouraging sales of private owned land as well as by leases to new settlers of State-owned property.

It would, however, not be a hardship on, or a deterrent to, new settlement schemes to suspend for some years concessions of Certain State-owned areas or areas which may be considered as State owned after the Beersheba and other Arabs have been allowed to register in their names sufficient land for their tribal requirements.

The condition of public security in say the South, the East and South-East of Beersheba District and the absence of roads as well as the distance from centres of settled habitation would in any case preclude at present the possibility of introducing new settlers there.

If Arabs and others, however, sell their excess land to new settlers they admit strangers by that fact into their areas and their exclusiveness and shyness of the stranger will be gradually overcome.

They will slowly but surely realize the benefit of settled habits and of economic and agricultural intercourse with experienced farmers.

New settlers will build hospitals, schools and other institutions of public utility.

Exclusiveness by new settlers should be avoided and the fellah and Arab will be quick to realize the benefit of the stranger in his neighbourhood.

Such state owned areas as may how be or may in time become available for new settlers should be cut into plots and leased by small holdings in groups. The size of the holdings must necessarily vary and will be subject to the nature of the soil. Intensive cultivation by new settlers must be insisted on.

47.

Ordinary agricultural land should be leased in family holdings not exceeding 100 dounoms in extent. Near towns, however, with market facilities and rapid means of conveyance of produce 5 to 10 dounoms holdings are considered ample.

A policy of small isolated holdings might perhaps be considered by certain people preferable from an agricultural point of view but that would only be possible where public security is assured and where there are easy and rapid means of communication.

Isolated holdings, however, have the disadvantage that schools, hospitals and other public institutions would be some distance away.

Groups of small holdings are therefore advocated because of additional security and because schools and hospitals could be more economically built and maintained and becuase living would be cheaper when many families are grouped in settlements.

The State should exercise its prerogative to dictate as to the width of roads in settlements so that the main arterial or other public high ways can be easily connected up with those of the settlements.

To encourage applicants and to encourage lessees to improve their holdings, leases should be of not less than 50 years' duration and should provide for compensation for buildings, permanent improvements, trees, soil values etc. to be paid in the event of non-renewal of the lease by the State.

Plans of buildings should be submitted for the approval of the Department of Public Health and of the Central Town Planning Commission.

Would-be tenants whose programmes include the improving of the land, the draining of marshes and for afforestation and which entail heavy expenditure should be granted longer leases and provision should be made in all agreements that the lessee must keep down all

48.

weeds which the State may declare to be noxious weeds.

If possible, leases should provide for no extensive grazing at all and the State should insist on intensive cultivation for stock breeding.

When the fellah learns to appreciate and is able and willing to adopt intensive cultivation, areas which are now Metroukhh for grazing purposes should be divided by the State among the Villagers for planting with trees or with cereals.

ADDITIONAL RECOMMENDATIONS.
============================

MORTGAGED PROPERTY.

The law preventing Mortgagees from taking possession of property when asking advances should be strictly enforced as it is noticed that this practice still prevails notwithstanding the provisional Law of Mortgage of Rabi Tani 1331.

REGISTRATION OF SUCCESSION.

Registration of succession as required by the Land Transfer Ordinance should be rigidly enforced as otherwise it will be impossible to know who are the actual owners of land and the extent of the areas held by them.

LAW OF INHERITANCE.

We remarked on page 28 that one of the reasons the Arabs of Beersheba District have refused hitherto to register their land is because in that event the Ottoman Law of Inheritance would apply and their women would inherit. If their daughters happen to marry out of the tribe, any land inherited by them would go out of the tribe also and inter-tribal quarrels and feuds would probably result.

Certain persons have expressed the opinion that the individual should enjoy a certain amount of liberty in the disposal

49.

of his Miri land.

It is suggested that the Government should consider a law permitting individuals to bequeath as they wish 2/3 of their Miri land. The Ottoman Law of Inheritance to apply to the remaining third.

All wills to be valid must, however, be registered with the Government.

In the event of a person dying intestate the Ottoman Law of Inheritance to apply to all his property.

1.05

Wrotham Heath.
Kent.
21 August 1924.

Under Secretary of State,
Colonial Office.

Sir,

I return herewith the papers sent under cover of your 34648/24 of the 18th. It is with extreme diffidence that I express any opinion on this matter, as I had no opportunity during my five days in Palestine last November to learn anything at first hand about the Land courts. I am in consequence ignorant as to their exact scope and function, and more particularly if they deal solely with disputes concerning real rights, or if they also deal with offences arising out of the former and with agrarian crime generally. The observations which follow are on the first assumption.

The position of affairs in Palestine, as I see it, is that when we took over its administration such records of ownership and other real rights as had existed under Ottoman rule had been destroyed so as to embarrass us; that this, added to the confusion and havoc resulting from the war, left us as a legacy a chaotic state of affairs which only a thorough and systematic investigation and settlement of all real rights from one end of the country to the other could bring into order; that, for reasons which are not material, we have never faced the problem resolutely as a whole or embarked upon it competently-. We have had a so-called cadastral survey in half-hearted operation which was no cadastral survey in reality; we have had a so-called system of land-registration which was little more than a re-entry of paper data; we have had, as I understand it, a series of Land Courts which have endeavoured to do justice in such specific cases of dispute as have been submitted to them, with which they are grievously in arrear.

Each of these three efforts to resolve the tangle of real rights in Palestine has pursued an independent path with the very natural result that after some six years occupation of the country a systematic investigation and settlement of real rights has still to be planned.

It appears to me that owing to cadastral survey and land registration having so far not contributed anything to the solution of the problem, resort has increasingly been had to the Land Courts for the settlement of individual disputes; and it may, I think, be anticipated with confidence that the measure of this resort is only determined by the capacity of the Land Courts to deal with cases. If any finality or any equilibrium was to be attained in this way a solution of the main problem might be sought by strengthening the Land Courts until they could deal with every uncertain real right throughout the country, and basing a settlement of the country thereon. Actually no such case-made settlement is practicable, and it would in my opinion be a most undesirable policy to encourage resort to litigation for the settlement of disputes concerning real rights by increasing the capacity of the Land courts.

If, as I imagine, the Land Courts are perambulatory courts making a practice of always visiting the actual sites concerning which disputes have arisen, they must do very valuable work within the limits assigned to them: but they cannot escape the handicap of considering a few pieces of the village mosaic detached from the whole, and they have not the means of defining the portions of land which their judgments concern so that they can be incontestably differentiated at any later date from neighbouring areas in spite of changes in the physical features of the terrain.

It is, in my opinion, only possible to conduct a thorough and universal settlement of real rights by a systematic combined sweep of cadastral survey, investigation *in situ* with the co-operation of the villagers, and registration of the results parcel by parcel, and village by village throughout Palestine. If my recommendations in this sense are in principle approved, as I understand, what course is to be adopted when in the course of the far more thorough scrutiny they will provide previous discordant judgments of the Land Courts are encountered? And moreover what is to be done when the judgments of the Land Court are found to be irreconcilable with, or impossible to locate on the actual terrain as under existing circumstances can hardly fail frequently to be the case? It was no part of my conception that for three years to come there should be two agencies separately investigating real rights throughout Palestine; and whatever else is doubtful it is at least clear that this would be most undesirable. Apart from the discrepant and irreconcilable results that would follow, the resources of the country are not such as to permit of any such waste of effort. British and Palestinian judges with experience of the operation of the laws governing the ownership and disposal of real property will be needed to supply the judicial element in the Land Settlement Commissions, and you will remember that it appears likely that twelve of these commissions will be needed if the already protracted settlement is not to be further unreasonably delayed. And it is judicial officers with experience gained in Palestine itself with knowledge of, and preferably known to, the Palestinian people that are needed.

Whatever difficulties the embodying of judgments of the Land Courts in the complete village mosaic may entail, I presume that all cases actually entered for trial by the Land Courts must to be given judgment; and I do not know how far it would be possible to facilitate such judgments being accurately referred to the sites with which they deal, given assistance from the survey. But I suggest that it would be of considerable advantage if measures could be studied whereby the present jurisdiction of the Land Courts could be terminated, and their functions, in so far as they concern the investigation and settlement of real rights, transferred to the proposed Land Settlement Commissions, if and when they are constituted.

It is therefore briefly my opinion, in the incomplete light of the question that I possess, that the problem of the congestion of the Land Courts is unlikely to be remedied by the engagement of a further Land Court judge, and that the only real remedy lies in the removal of the conditions which breed the litigation in question. The difficulty of dealing with existing arrears, and with the disputes that that will arise throughout the country pending and in advance of cadastral survey, settlement and registration of title, are unfortunately inescapable; but will, I hope, yield with patience and goodwill to the united efforts of all concerned. They should not in any case be allowed to dominate the situation.

I have the honour to be, Sir,

Your obedient servant

Ernest M. Dowson

1.06

PALESTINE.

DESPATCH NO. 1128

REFERENCE NO. Adm. 2/13.

GOVERNMENT OFFICES,
JERUSALEM.

21st September, 1925.

Sir,

I have the honour to submit the draft of an Ordinance to provide for the introduction in Palestine of a standard measure of land, with an Explanatory Note by the Attorney General.

2. A uniform system of measurement is essential to a proper land settlement and cadastral survey. It will also simplify land transactions, which are now confused by the existence of variable units. The dunum has been calculated for the purpose of the assessment of the Tobacco Land Tax as the equivalent of 900 square metres and by the Beisan Demarcation Committee as the equivalent of 919.0324 square metres: in the suspended Ottoman Law of 1869 for the introduction of the metric system it was given the equivalence of 918.667 square metres.

3. Legislation of the kind was proposed by Sir Ernest Dowson, in a letter of which a copy is attached, and he recommended that the change should be made as soon as possible and in advance of the general introduction of the metric system of weights and measures. This larger question is engaging my attention. In the meantime, I agree with Sir Ernest Dowson that the introduction of a standard measure of land should not be delayed.

4. I shall be grateful, therefore, for your early approval of the draft Ordinance.

I have the honour to be, Sir,
Your most obedient, humble servant,

HIGH COMMISSIONER.

The Right Honourable L.C.M.S. Amery, P.C., M.P.,
His Majesty's Principal Secretary of State for the Colonies.

1925   **PALESTINE**

From		Date
H. Commr. Plumer	1128	21 Sept.

For Circulation:—
Mr. [struck]
Mr. [struck]
Maj. [struck]
Asst. U.S. of S.
....
....
Permt. U.S. of S.
Parlt. U.S. of S.
Secretary of State.

Previous Paper
B/trade
17872/22.

10 Nov. 25.
14/9/27 (minute) —

Minuted 15/3 —
Copy covers, B/Trade

Subsequent Paper
44212/27.

Standard measure of land.

Submits alterns. on the subject, and encloses draft of Standard Measure of Surface Ordce. with an explanatory note by Atty-Genl. and copy letter from Sir E Dowson. Requests early approval.

MINUTES

It is worth notice that while action on Sir E Dowson's letter has been delayed in Palestine for 10 months we are now told that "the introduction of a standard measure of land should not be delayed" & are asked for early approval of the draft Ordinance.

I agree that it is desirable to introduce a standard measure of land in Palestine and the present is a particularly appropriate time for its introduction since, following on the forthcoming enactment of the Correction of Land Registers Ordinance, there will be considerable increase in land registration in Palestine.

As regards the draft Ordinance:—
I should omit the second para of the preamble.

G.L.M.

Clause 2

Clause 2. I doubt whether the terms "metre" &c. are anywhere defined in the law of Palestine & if they are not so defined it might be as well to have a definition here. See below.

Clause 3. I should omit "to the exclusion of measures of area of any other system" and for the remainder of the clause substitute:—

"and the area of any land concerning which any right, disposition or contract is hereafter recorded in the register of — — — shall be expressed therein in terms of the standard measure." G.L.?

Clause 4. Most of this seems to me to be unnecessary. In order to validate transactions re land here must be registered and under cl. 3 of the Ordce. registration will, after its enactment, be recorded in terms of the standard measure.

I think therefore that cl. 4 can be confined to providing that nothing in the Ordce. shall affect the validity of any contract re land existing at the date on which the Ordce. came into force. G.L.?

Subject to the above enactment may be approved.   J.H.(?)
                                                    7.10.45

The main point is clause 2. Until Pal. has got a standard 'metre', by which measures in use can be checked it is useless for them to legislate for higher units of measurement; it is like building a house on air. ~~I am disposed~~ Pal. are beginning to think about a Weights & Measures Ordce & we recently sent them Colonial precedents. H.M.G. have a standard metre laid up with other Imperial Measures; I think

...the correct course would probably be to declare this standard metre to be the standard for Pal., & possibly to provide for the Pal. Govt itself to keep a reproduction of this standard metre.

? point out that this Ordce cannot be passed in advance of the Weights & Measures Ordce, make the suggestion above for fixing the standard Pal. metre, add the observations of detail above & say that the Ordce can be put in final form ready for promulgation as soon as the W. & M. Ordce is passed.

G. L. M-Cawson
29/10/25

I agree. If a standard is officially & legally adopted, its use will become general in the ordinary course of things & it is unnecessary & may lead to trouble to exclude other systems or modes of measuring.

A.B.
30/10

As proposed,
G.L.M.
6/11

DRAFT ORDINANCE TO PROVIDE FOR THE INTRODUCTION
OF A STANDARD MEASURE OF LAND.

WHEREAS the surface measures of land now in use in Palestine are different in various parts of the country, and it is desirable to introduce a uniform measure;

AND WHEREAS by an Ottoman Law dated 14/26 September, 1869, the metric system was introduced into the Ottoman Empire, but its compulsory application was from time to time postponed; and pending the general adoption of the metric system, the application of the metric measurement of the surface of land is desirable;

BE IT ENACTED ....

Short Title. 1. This Ordinance may be cited as the Standard Measure of Surface Ordinance, 1925.

Standard Measure. 2. The standard measure of land shall be the standard Dunum consisting of 1000 square metres.

Standard measure to be exclusively used by Government and in Government Registers. 3. From the date at which this Ordinance comes into force the standard dunum and the square metre shall be used for the purpose of all transactions in land entered into by a Department of the Government or a Municipality or other local authority, (to the exclusion of measures of area of any other system; and any disposition of land or contract concerning land which shall be recorded in the registers of the Government or the Municipality or such authority shall be recorded according to the standard measure.

Reservation for existing titles and contracts. 4. Nothing in this Ordinance shall affect any right of property in land or any contract concerning land which is defined according to dunums that are not standard dunums, or according to any other existing measure of area; provided that where after the date of this Ordinance any disposition of land so defined is made, the area affected shall be expressed in any register or record of the
Government/

- 2 -

Government or Municipality or local authority
according to the standard measure.

Explanatory Note.

On the recommendation of Sir Ernest Dowson, it has been decided that the measure of the dunum which is firmly established throughout the country shall be retained; but the area, which to-day varies according to particular local custom and has received a different value in transactions affecting the Government, shall be standardised at 1000 square metres, so that the dunum may fit in with the metric system.

Section 2:

The equivalence of 1000 square metres will make the dunum one-tenth part of a hectare; but no reference to "are" is made because that would be likely to confuse people.

Section 3:

The use of the standard dunum will not be made compulsory for private persons, but by its adoption in all Government transaction and records, it is contemplated that the standard dunum will within a short time come into general use.

Section 4:

It is necessary to safeguard existing contracts and agreements which are expressed in customary dunums. More particularly, the agreement made in December, 1921, between the Government and the cultivators of the Ghor lands provides for the transfer to the cultivators of lands at a rate of so many piastres per dunum. There is no intention of interfering with that arrangement, but the number of customary dunums transferred will be converted in the registers into the equivalent number of standard dunums.

C O P Y.

Reference No.L.S./27.

Sir Ernest Dowson's Office,
Mount Zion Building,
Jerusalem.

20th November, 1924.

A/Chief Secretary.

Subject: Standardisation of the Dunum.

In the course of the notes I furnished to you last December, I referred to the importance of standardising the dunum, if it was to be continued in use for purposes of land survey and registration, and suggested that the standard value should be fixed at 1000 square metres. The suggestion was not original as it had previously been recommended by the Weights and Measures Commission. I am not aware as to what action is contemplated in regard to the recommendations of that Commission, but I suggest that the question of the standardisation of the dunum is a matter which can be and should be dealt with separately and without delay. Considerable inconvenience and misunderstanding is bound to arise if there are various units of area throughout Palestine consecrated under the same term. I understand that in the recent land distribution at Beisan the survey were forced to adopt a dunum of 919.0324 square metres, and that the areas quoted to people in that district have been based on this value.

Similarly, I understand that in distributions of Mesha' land that are being effected or in contemplation, this or other values of the dunum have to be adopted in the absence of any order standardising the dunum at 1000 square metres.

I suggest that it is obviously desirable, if the dunum is to be standardised, that this should be done as promptly as possible before further inconsistencies are introduced or, alternatively, if it is not intended to perpetuate the use of this unit of area officially, that the Survey should be instructed accordingly and advised to record areas in metric measures.

Should standardisation be carried out, it would appear to be advisable that the standard dunum of 1000 square metres should, for some time to come, be known as the standard or national dunum in distinction to other varieties in use.

This would further help to explain to the people of Beisan and other areas whose land areas would be different in the new unit how the change had come about.

(Signed) Ernest M. Dowson.

H.Cr./44810/1925 Palestine

Mr. Lloyd 9/11/25
Mr.
Mr.
Mr. Strachey.
Sir J. Shuckburgh.
Sir C. Davis.
Sir G. Grindle.
S. Wilson
Sir J. Masterton Smith.
Mr. Ormsby-Gore.
Mr. Amery.

DRAFT.

PALESTINE
No. 1513

H.Cr. Plumer.

Downing Street,

November, 1925.

My Lord,

I have the honour to acknowledge the receipt of Your Lordship's despatch No.1128 of the 21st September submitting the draft of an Ordinance to provide for the introduction in Palestine of a standard measure of land.

2. I agree that it is desirable to introduce such a standard measure in Palestine, and that, as there is certain to be considerable business in land registration during the next few years, it is particularly desirable that such a standard measure should be established at the earliest possible date. I am, however, advised that it is not possible to enact such an Ordinance as that which you forward, until a standard metre has been fixed for Palestine by the Weights and Measures Ordinance which, I gather,

is

is under consideration. As H.M.G. have a standard metre laid up with other Imperial Measures, it appears that it would be best for it to be declared in any Weights and Measures Ordinance enacted for Palestine that this standard metre is to be the standard for Palestine; it might also be desirable to provide for the Government of Palestine itself to keep a reproduction of this standard metre.

3. Coming now to questions of detail, I am advised that the second preamble of the draft Ordinance should be omitted.

4. In Clause 3, the words "to the exclusion of measures of area of any other system" should be omitted, and the following should be substituted for the remainder of that Clause:- "and the area of any land concerning which any right, disposition or contract shall be recorded in the registers of the Government or the Municipality or such authority shall be expressed therein in terms of the standard measure".

5. I

5. I am advised that any transactions in land must be registered in order to establish their validity, and as, under Clause 3 of the present Ordinance, registration will, ~~after its enactment,~~ be recorded in terms of the standard measure. Clause 4 can be confined to providing that nothing in the Ordinance shall affect the validity of any right, contract etc. in the land existing at the date on which the Ordinance comes into force.

6. I would suggest that the draft Ordinance should be amended in the light of the foregoing observations, and should be put in a final form ready for promulgation as soon as a Weights and Measures Ordinance has been passed establishing a standard metre for Palestine.

I have, etc.,

(Sgd.) L. S. AMERY.

1.07

Telegrams: LEGALITY, Jerusalem.

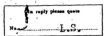

No. ......L.S.......

GOVERNMENT OF PALESTINE

~~LEGAL SECRETARY'S OFFICE~~
ATTORNEY GENERAL'S OFFICE
JERUSALEM

November 7, 1924.

Director of
Lands.

    I have read your note on the Land Law and I consider it is clear and concise. I have only a few observations to make.

    P.2. The remarks that occur about wills of miri property being invalid and jurisdiction in regard to wills should be transferred to the section on succession at p.24.

    P.5. Does the third category of mulk land which you mention exist at all in Palestine?

    P.8. You should, I think, explain the general character of true Wakf, that is, Wakf where the land itself has been dedicated to God so as to be taken out of ownership or disposition. You remark on p.10 that only mulk can be created true Wakf, and that provision should come on p.8.

    P.10. Similarly you should make it clear that in the case of untrue Wakf the land itself is not dedicated to the religious purpose, but only the revenues or tithes of the land.

Correct

    P.11. It is not correct to state that a Wakf may be constituted before the Civil Courts. The Charitable Trusts Ordinance, to which reference should be made, allows the constitution of a charitable trust before the Civil Courts, but that institution corresponds rather with the idea of the English trust than that of the Moslem Wakf.

    The paragraph that follows that the constitution of a Wakf is invalid unless registered in the Tabou applies to all Wakfs and not only to the Charitable Trusts constituted before a Civil Court. You should give the reference also to the Ottoman Law to the same effect which was affirmed in the Land Transfer Ordinance.

    P.15. Expropriation: You should, I think, refer to the two laws of expropriation:

-2-

(1) The law of expropriation for the State dated 1879, amended by the Law of the 30th April,1914 (17th Nisan 1330) and

(2) The law to which you do refer of expropriation by Municipalities.
You should also mention the Ordinance concerning expropriation passed this year which provides that while the procedure is to follow that of the second law the purposes of expropriation prescribed by the first law still hold good.

P.16. I think the statement of the present system of registration of land under the Land Transfer Ordinance as amended should be expanded so as to give a general idea of the present system in its working.

P.18. Similarly, I think the provisions of the Correction of Land Registers Ordinance should be set out more fully and a reference should be made to the later Ordinances of 1921 and 1922 which continued and modified the original Ordinance.

P.20. You do not explain sufficiently what the Mashna system is, and your remarks should be expanded in this respect.

P.23. In the second paragraph concerning Non-Moslems, line 4, read "of" for "for." It should also be more clearly explained that jurisdiction with regard to the succession of Non-Moslems is within the concurrent jurisdiction of the District Courts and Religious Courts. The position is that if all the heirs agree matters are dealt with by a Religious Court, but if any heir requires the matter to be transferred to the District Court and makes application the Civil Court obtains the jurisdiction.

P.24. As pointed out above, the remarks on p.2 concerning succession should be transferred here.

P.26. The limitation of the rate of interest to 9% is not prescribed under the Usurious Loans Ordinance,1922, but under an Ottoman Law of 1304. The Ordinance to which you refer deals only with evidence admissible in actions for recovery of money lent.

P.35. You should, I think, refer to the law dealing with the special tax payable by corporate bodies and to the Public Notice which was issued applying that law in Palestine.

ATTORNEY GENERAL

NOTES ON LAND LAW
IN PALESTINE

Notes on Land Law in Palestine.

General

Immovable property in Palestine is governed by the Ottoman Laws in force on November 1st 1914. Since the occupation of the country by Allied troops 1917-1918 these laws have been amended by local legislation but they still remain the guiding authority under which all matters relating to immovable property are considered and administered by the Government and in the Courts. Ottoman Laws enacted after November 1st 1914 are not in force in Palestine unless expressly declared to be so (Order-in-Council Art.46).

Categories

Immovable property in Palestine is divided into 5 main categories: (a) Mulk (b) Miri (c) Wakf (d) Metroukeh and (e) Mewat.

Mulk

1. Mulk approximates very closely to the English form of freehold, the holder exercising complete rights of ownership. In the case of Moslem owners freedom of disposition is restricted by the Islamic doctrine that a Moslem cannot bequeath by will more than 1/3 of his mulk property. The remaining 2/3 devolves on the heirs of the deceased owner according to Sharia Law. A bequest to an heir is invalid unless with the consent of the remaining heirs. If there are no heirs the holder can bequeath all his mulk property to a stranger. If the will is for more than 1/3 of the Mulk property of the deceased it is valid only for 1/3 and the heirs are at liberty to claim

-2-

the return of surplus. Non Moslems may bequeath the whole of their mulk.

The validity of the Wills of Moslems and the determination of the heirs are matters within the jurisdiction of the Moslem Courts, provided that in the case of Miri the division complies with the terms of the Law of Inheritance 1331. (Palestine Order-in-Council Section 51. Succession Ordinance 1923 Section 4).

Mulk is not governed by the Land Code but is subject to the Sheria Law and the Mejelle (Land Code Art.2).

Mulk land is of 4 kinds:-

(a) Building sites which were within towns or villages at the date of coming into force of the Ottoman Land Code 1274, and areas not exceeding 1/2 Donum situated on the confines of towns or villages which are considered as appurtenant to dwelling houses. (Art.2 Land Code). There is a general principle of Ottoman Law that Miri land can be converted into Mulk only by a special Imperial Order of the Sultan.

Under the Ottoman regime land which was once Miri could never become Mulk unless by special Mulkname of the Sultan. The conversion of Miri to Mulk now requires the express permission of the High Commissioner. Building sites which are Miri and have become included in a town by the

-3-

growth or extension of the town do not become Mulk by the mere fact of such inclusion within the ~~village or~~ town limits. [village → village]

Mulk lands of this category are limited to those building sites which were within towns or villages or appurtenant to the dwellings thereof prior to the promulgation of the Ottoman Land Code (21.4.1858 or 7 Ramadan 1274).

"Land registered as Miri can never be converted into Mulk" (Haji Costandi v. Principal Forest Officer C.L.R. III. 155.)

"No one can turn Miri into Mulk without the express permission of the Sultan". (Haji Kyriako v. Principal Forest Officer C.L.R. III. 100).

(b) [~~The second category of Mulk land is~~] Land separated from Miri land and made Mulk by a Mulkname of the Sultan.

(c) [~~The third category is tithe-paying~~] (ushur) land which ~~was distributed at the time of the conquest~~ among the victors (Moslems) and given in full ownership...

(d) [~~the fourth kind of Mulk land is tribute~~] paying land which at the time of the conquest was left and confirmed in the possession of the non-Moslem inhabitants. There is little, if any,

-4-

of the ~~last two~~ categories in Palestine.

There is now in Law no practical or legal difference between the various divisions of Mulk.

Miri   2. Miri land is property over which the right of occupation or usufruct is enjoyed by private individuals provided that such enjoyment has been granted by the State. The rakaba or absolute ownership remains vested in the Government but the grant has in perpetuity provided that certain conditions, the chief of which is continuous cultivation, are complied with. (Land Code Art.3). The holder has the right to use of the property as he may think fit provided he cultivates it. Nevertheless if cultivation - and consequently tithe - is rendered impossible by building, a ground rental will be imposed in lieu of tithe (Law of Disposition 1331 Art.5)

Prior to 1331 considerable restrictions were imposed on the use of Miri. The soil could not be used for brick making. The planting of vineyards or orchards and the erection of houses or farm building or enclosures was prohibited unless with the consent of the Government. The Law of Disposition 1331, conferred on the holder power to use the land for any purpose he wished provided that he registered any buildings, trees or other fixtures added to the land. An annual tax (Bedl Usher) is levied if the purpose for which the land is used prevents the collection of tithe (Art.5).

Freedom of disposition (subject to the consent of and registration in the Tabo) is permitted provided that the land is not bequeathed by will or constituted wakf (Art.8).

If Miri remains uncultivated for 3 consecutive years without lawful excuse as, for instance, the absence of the holder on military service, it reverts to the State. (Land Code Art.68). The possessor may, however, redeem it on payment of Bedl Misl i.e. the unimproved capital value. Such value should be "fixed by impartial experts who know the extent, boundaries and value of the land according to its productive capacity and situation" (Land Code Art.59). On the death of the holder it devolves upon his heirs in accordance with the Law of Inheritance 1331 and in the event of failure of heirs it reverts to the State. The determination of the heirs and the individual distribution of Miri among them are matters for the Civil Courts or for the Religious Courts constituted under the Succession Ordinance 1923.

Wakf

3. Wakf or Mevkoufeh lands are mortmained property. Land which has been dedicated to some religious or charitable objects or as a family trust or settlement. They are derived either from

-6-

Mulk or Miri.

Under the Ottoman Law all wakfs were constituted before the Sheria Court and were divided into two main classes:

(1) Wakf Sahih (= true wakf)
(2) Wakf Gheir Sahih (= untrue wakf)

The person/responsible for the immediate administration of the wakf - the trustee - was called the Mutawelli.

True Wakf

[In category (1) the land] is dedicated to a (land) pious object and thus taken out of ownership or disposition. It is subdivided into (a) Wakf Mazbuta which [was] administered directly by the Wakf authorities; (b) Wakf Mulhaka, which was administered by the Mutawelli under the supervision - rarely exercised - of the Wakf Department; and (c) Wakf Mustesna which was administered by the Mutawelli free from any supervision or control by the authorities.

Wakf Zurri i.e., private family endowment, is also a special category of true wakf. Wakf Mussakafat (= built upon) and Mustaghilat (= worked, planted) are true wakf but when converted into Ijaratein are subject to the Nizami law. Only Mulk can be created true wakf. (Law of Disposition 1331 Art. 8).

—7—

True wakfs may be let on Ijare Wahedi, i.e., single rent, for periods not exceeding one year in the case of buildings or three years in the case of agricultural lands. The Kadi may consent to a longer lease (Law of Lease 1331 Art.7).

Ijaratein Where wakf property falls into a state of dilapidation and no funds are available for its repair the Kadi may authorise the lease in perpetuity of the property on terms requiring, in addition to an annual rent, the payment in advance of a sufficiently large sum to effect the necessary repairs. Hence Wakf Ijaratein (two rents). Subject to the consent of the Kadi the Lessee, who enjoys a form of limited ownership subject only to the annual rental charge, may sell, lease, mortgage or otherwise dispose of his interest in the property, subject always to the Hikr or annual rent. Except as Ijaratein true wakf can never be sold or encumbered, but it may, with the consent of the Kadi be exchanged.

True Wakf is governed by the Religious Law and the conditions laid down by the founder but it is not subject to the Land Code.

Untrue wakf Wayf ghir sahih (2), untrue wakf, the land itself is not dedicated to any pious object but only the revenues or tithes of the land. It is derived from Miri land and the dedication was by the Sultan or by others with Imperial sanction.

-8-

The Nizami (civil) laws apply to this wakf and it is subject to all the provisions of the Land Code (Art.4). The constitution of this form of wakf, commonly referred to as Tahsisat, is now prohibited (Law of Disposition 133/Art. 8). Although the law required the registration in the Tabu of all wakfiehs - deeds of dedication - they were in practice rarely registered and most wakfs are evidenced by Hojeh Sharia registered in the Sheria Court.

Questions as to whether land is or is not wakf is one for the Civil Courts (in re Ainkarem. Court of Appeal).

Note: Draft Ordinance published in Official Gazette No.144 of 1st May 1924 page 642 is intended to give legislative effect to that decision but the Ordinance has not yet been promulgated as a law.

Constitution of Wakfs.

Wakfs may now be constituted before the appropriate Religious Courts. Those Courts also enjoy exclusive jurisdiction in questions concerning the internal administration of wakfs of members of their respective communities. (Article 52-54 Palestine Order-inCouncil).

Where there are no duly constituted Religious Courts a wakf may be constituted before the Civil Courts.

-9-

The consitution is invalid unless registered in the Tabo.(Instructions as to Title Deeds for Mevkoufeh Land 6 Rejeh 1292. Order No.64 Deftar Khakani 12.8.1331. Land Transfer Ordinance 1920 Art.2).The Charitable Trusts Ordinance 1924 provides means for the endowment of Religious and Charitable trusts before the Civil Courts in accordance with English practice.

Wakf may be expropriated for public purposes. (The Law of Expropriation of 21st Kanun Tani 1329).

Metroukeh
4. Metroukeh land (a) Metroukeh comprises land left for the use of the public such as roads etc, and
(b) land left and assigned to the inhabitants of a village or town or to several villages and towns grouped together such as communal pastures, places of worship, markets etc.(Land Code Art.5).

Metroukeh land cannot be held individually by a kushan, nor can it be bought, sold, inherited, planted or built upon(Land Code Articles 91-102). Custom and usage ab antiquo are taking into consideration in determining Metroukeh. The raqabeh 9 legal estate - remains with the State as in the case of Miri.

For Metroukeh rights in water see Mejelle Articles 1234 ff.

Mewat
5. Mewat land is dead waste land which has not been left or assigned to the inhabitants of a town or village and is not held by kushan. It is so far from a town or village that a loud voice of a person calling from the nearest inhabited spot cannot be heard there (Land Code Art.3).

This has been interpreted by Judicial decision as being about 1½ miles.

A person reviving and cultivating Mewat land <u>with permission</u> is entitled to the issue of a kushan free. If the land is cultivated <u>without permission</u> "there shall be exacted from the occupant payment of the Tabu value" (Land Code Art.103).

It will be noted from this Article that there is no prescription in regard to Mewat cultivated without permission "The cultivation of Mewat without permission does not give the cultivator a right to be registered. Mewat being vested in the Sultan no prescriptive title can be acquired to it by unauthorised cultivation". (Haji Kyriako v. P.F.O. C.L.R. III. 87.). Even where the officials of the Government have for a long period of years had knowledge of and acquiesced in the cultivation the Government may still claim the land on the ground that no permission was given for the cultivation (Kyriako v. P.F.O. C.L.R. III.102).

The Mewat Land Ordinance 1921 constitutes it an offence to break up or cultivate Mewat land without permission after the date of the Ordinance - February 16th,1921.

Where, under that Ordinance, a person made application for a kushan for land already broken up, commissions composed of three members

-11-

constituted under The Public Notice for Demarcation of State Lands (Official Gazette of 1.12.1921) inspected the area claimed, and where continuous occupation and cultivation for ten years was established, the Government, as a concession, granted a free title. Where the occupation or cultivation was for less than 10 years Bedl Misl was collected. Such applications - and the concession - were limited to a period of two months following the date of the Ordinance.

Persons who have cultivated Mewat land without permission and who did not apply under that Ordinance may be granted kushans on payment of Bedl Misl. The Bedl Misl must be paid within three months. (Above Public Notice).

Expropriation   All immovable property, including wakf, may be compulsorily acquired for (a) the purposes of public utility. (The Municipal Law of Expropriation 21st Kanun Tani 1329. Law of Expropriation for Public Purposes 24th Tishrin Tani 1295). By Ordinance No.5, 1924 the former law is applied in Palestine. (Official Gazette No.110).
For the needs of the Army (Acquisition of Land for the Army Ordinance 1920), (c) the purpose of carrying into effect any scheme of town planning (Town Planning Ordinance 1921) or (d) for the preservation or excavation of Antiquities (Antiquities Ordinance 1920).

-12-

Registration

Prior to the introduction of the Ottoman Land Code 1274 (1858) titles to Mulk land and buildings were registered in the Sheria Court, but no form of registration of Miri land existed. Since that time all titles have been granted by the State through the Land Registry and no person can legally hold immovable property which is not registered (Article 1 of Regulations for Tabu Sanads 1276. Fisher p.51). Land Registry Offices existed in all the 13 kazas into which Palestine was divided under the Ottoman regime, but notwithstanding the law making registration compulsory a considerable amount of the land has not yet been registered.

The registration was of deeds and not of title. The Ottoman registration and records are still in use and are prima face valid. The system now being followed is one of registration of title; that is, of separate units of land but is defective because of lack of survey and the possible difficulty of defining the location and boundaries of some of the units so registered. Although no guarantee of title is given (Land Transfer Ordinance Article 9) the greatest care has been exercised to ensure the validity of all registrations effected.

-13-

Title deeds are valid and executory and the Courts may give judgment on them without further proof. They may be set aside only by the judgment of a Court. (Law of Disposition 1331 Art.3).

The policy of the Courts has always been to maintain an existing registration except where the registered owners consent or where the weight of evidence is overwhelmingly strong.

Owing to religious and political disabilities imposed by the Turkish authorities on non Moslem and non Ottoman subjects, most of the land in Palestine belonging to non Ottoman religious and charitable Institutions or persons, was registered in the name of a NAM MUSTAAR, that is a prete nom who was an Ottoman subject. Under Art.4 of the Law of Disposition 1331, correction of such registration was permitted within a period of two years but advantage was not taken of that provision. The Correction of the Land Registers Ordinance 1920 reenacted the above provision for a period of 1 year from the date of the Ordinance. Further extensions were granted by The Correction of the Land Registers Ordinance Amendment Ordinances 1921 and 1922. The Ordinance expired on 10.7.24. Most of the land held by Nam Mustaar has now been registered in the names of the real owners. Orders made under that Ordinance are final and non appealable judgments of a competent court and cannot now be set aside or varied.

-14-

Preemption	Preemption - A preferential right to acquire an adjoining property - applies only to Mulk land and is dealt with under Articles 941 to 1044 of the Mejelle. The application of this principle of law will rarely come up for consideration. A claim to preemption must be made immediately the sale has been brought to the notice of the claimant. "Immediately" has been held to be a reasonable time having regard to the distance of the claimant from the property and all other circumstances of the case (Nicolaides v. Yosif C.L.R.II, 93.). A sale must be complete and the vendor fully divested of his ownership before a claim for preemption can be preferred (Mejelle Art.1026). It does not apply in the case of partition between co-owners. *Pre-emption is applicable only to mulk land (Land Code Art 46)*
Priority	Priority is applicable to Miri land, *and is, in effect, the same as pre-emption, though the procedure is different.* In the event of the sale of shares by a co-owner to any person other than a co-owner the latter has the right to claim the transfer of the area at any time within 5 years on payment of its value at the time of the claim. ~~(Article 41 of~~ (Land Code *Art 41*)

The owner of Mulk trees or buildings growing or standing upon Miri land belonging to another has the prior right to purchase the land, if he so desires.

In the event of a sale contrary to this provision the owner of the trees and buildings shall have the right to purchase the land at any time within 10 years. (Land Code Art 44)
In the event of a person selling property in a village to a purchaser not an inhabitant of the village, the villagers will have the right to acquire it any time within 1 year (Land Code Art 45).

In the event of the sale of trees planted or buildings erected on Miri the vendor (if he is also the owner of the land) is bound to transfer the land also to the purchaser. (Land Code Art 49)

Trees planted on Miri do not pass with the land unless specifically mentioned in the Deed of sale (Land Code Art 48)

Partition

Partition.

Much of the agricultural land in Palestine is held on the Meshaa system. In some villages the land is recorded in the names of the heads of the leading families inhabiting the village at the date of the original registration, whilst in others it is recorded in the names of the whole of the inhabitants of the village at that time.

In the former case the villagers usually have definite and known plots which they occupy

-16-

without any form of rotation, whilst in the latter it is customary for ~~farmers~~ cultivators to shift from plot to plot either at the direction of the Mukhtar or in accordance with lots drawn by the villagers. There is thus neither certainty of tenure nor continuity of occupation.

Partition of land into individual ownership is dealt with by the Law of Partition of the 14th Muharram 1332. It may be voluntary by agreement of the co-owners or compulsory by order of the Magistrate. It must be carried out on the ground. (Article 6 of the Law of Partition). (See also Articles 1147 to 1152 of the Mejelle). But in neither case is the law effective because of the difficulty in the first instance, of ascertaining and obtaining the consent of the whole of the co-owners, and, in the second instance, the difficulty of citing them as parties to the action.

Where a private partition has been made more than 10 years ago and the parties have remained in undisputed possession for that period, the ~~parties~~ occupants have a right to be registered as the owners of the areas which they took under the partition and the existing registration should be set aside, in accordance with Article 3 of the Law of Disposition of 1331. (See also Kyriako v. Kyriako C.L.R. III. 145 *as to the interpretation of Article 17 of the Land Code*)

-17-

Guardians for minors and administrators for absent persons may be appointed by the District Court or the appropriate Religious Court in the case of Palestinians, or by the District Court or the officiating Consul in the case of Foreigners.
(See regulations as to Consular jurisidiction Official Gazette No.80).

Preemption does not apply in the case of partition (Mejelle Art.1027).

Succession, Moslems.

Succession Moslems.

Moslem succession to mulk is governed entirely by the Islamic Doctrine. To miri it is governed by the Law of Inheritance of 1331.

The issue of certificates of Succession is exclusively within the jurisdiction of the Sheria Court.

These certificates should be accepted without question or further proof provided the division of miri is in accordance with the Law of Inheritance of 1331. *In the case of moslems who are foreigners or members of other than the Sunni rite the High Commr may so on request, constitute a special court*

Non-Moslems

Non-Moslems *(succession to immovable pr. 4)*

Prior to the date of The Succession Ordinance 1923 the issue of Certificates of Succession was a matter exclusively for the Sheria Courts except for Nationals of those Powers which enjoyed capitulatory rights within the Ottoman Empire.

-18-

The succession to the estates of non-Moslems & other matters of personal status (See Order in Council 1922 51 ff.) is now within the concurrent jurisdiction of the District Courts and the religious Courts, Where all the heirs agree, a certificate of Succession showing the heirs and the division of the estate may be given by the Religious Court of the Community of which the deceased was a member provided that such community is "a community" within the meaning of the Succession Ordinance 1923.

The division of Mulk may be in accordance with the law of the particular community but the division of Miri must be in accordance with the Law of Inheritance of 1331. All wills are invalid in so far as they affect Miri.

A certificate of inheritance issued by a non Moslem Religious Court must contain a statement that the heirs named in the certificate are the whole of the heirs of the deceased and that such heirs consented to the jurisdiction of the Religious Court. In the case of foreigners the District Court alone is com competent provided that where the deceased was a member of a Religious Community having a Court the District Court may refer the matter to the Court of such community.

In the case of non Moslems a minor may be presumed to be a person under the age of 18 years (Section 20 of Succession Ordinance 1923).

-19-

Mortgages.

The law governing Mortgages of Immovable Property is set out in the Law of Mortgage of Ist Rabi Tani 1331.

Prior to that date, mortgages were usually made by Bei Bil Wafa i.e. a contract of sale having the same formalities as an ordinary sale, and the Mortgagee (purchaser) entered into possession and the practice was that the Mortgagee gave an unofficial sanad undertaking to return the property to the Mortgagor when the mortgage debt was repaid.

The Law of 1331 made such mortgages illegal and the mortgagor now has the right to remain in possession of the mortgaged property.

All mortgages must now conform to that law as amended by the Mortgage Law Amendment Ordinance 1920.

Buildings and other improvements effected on mortgage land whether prior or subsequent to the date of the mortgage are included in the mortgage(Sec.5). The rate of interest may not exceed 9% (Law of Interest 1304, Usurious Loans Ordinance 1922).

Mortgaged property may be sold subject to the consent of the Mortgagee. If leased, the consent of the Lessee must be obtained to any mortgage otherwise the mortgage cannot be foreclosed until the expiration of the lease. A mortgagee may, with the consent of the mortgagor, transfer the mortgage. Where the mortgage is made payable to "order" such consent is not necessary.

-20

All mortgages are invalid unless registered in the Tabo(Transfer of Land Ordinance 1920 Sec3.). Land cannot be sold in satisfaction of a mortgage except by order of the District Court(Land Transfer Amendment Ordinance No.2,1922.).

Leases.

The law governing leases is the Provisional Law of Lease of Immovable Property of 28 Jamad Awal 1299 (See also Art.484 to 543 of the Mejelle).

The contract of lease must be in writing. If for a period of more than three years or containing any cluase by which it may be extended to a period exceeding three years it must be registered in the Tabo.

A lease for a period of less than three years made beflore a Notary Public has the force of an official document and the contents of the document cannot be altered by oral evidence.

Leases of wakf land for a period of more than three years must have the consent of the Sheria Court.

Leases within Municipal areas must be registered with the Municipality.

-21-

Prescription. Prescription is of two kinds:

First: Acquistive prescription, which is a means of acquiring rights or property by possession.
Secondly: Extinctive prescription by which certain rights - usually the right to bring an action - are extinguished or lost. Great care should be exercised to distinguish between these two forms of prescription. The Ottoman Civil Law (The Mejelle) deals only with extinctive prescription - that form which results in the loss of rights and which is usually referred to in English Law as "Limitation of Actions" and in Turkish law as "Maërur El Zaman".

In the Mejelle this prescription is dealt with in the chapter concerning Actions. (Book XIV Table II Articles 1660-1675).

Under the Mejelle no action can be heard after the expiration of (a) 15 years in the case of ownership, inheritance or other interest in dedicated property (Mevkoufeh) (b) 36 years in the case of the "Raqabe" of immovable property or of true wakf, and (c) 10 years in the case of Miri land. This latter must be registered (Land Code Art.20).

With regard to the first kind of prescription Acquistive - no provision whatever exists in the Mejelle. The means of *acquiring* ownership are, according to Art.1248 of the Mejelle limited to three:

-22-

(a) Transfer by the owner to another by way of sale or gift.
(b) Succession.
(c) Occupation of a thing common by nature; water, air etc.

Acquistive prescription is unknown to the Ottoman Civil Law(Mejelle) as a means of acquiring ownership. It is recognised only by the Ottoman Land Code which contains special provisions as to the acquisition of land by possession and cultivation. This form of prescription is referred to in Ottoman Law as "Hak El Karar".

Under Arts.20 and 78 of the Land Code land may, in certain circumstances, be acquired by continuous possession and cultivation. The provisions of Art.20 refer only to land held by title deed. Prescription under either Art.20 or 78 of the Land Law must, to be effective, have been conferred by continuous adverse enjoyment of the land for a period exceeding 10 years without dispute. As regards State land possession alone is not sufficient. It is necessary to prove two elements:

(a) Possession (b) Cultivation (Land Code Art.78).

-23-

If in either case the possessor admits that he took possession of the land arbitrarily and without right his possession is not taken into consideration and he acquires no right thereby. It would appear that actual admission is required.

As Art. 20 refers only to land held by Title Deed it does not apply to unregistered land.

A person claiming to have acquired land under Article 78 of the Land Code must establish that he acquired possession by sale or succession or transfer from some persons entitled to transfer. (Article 8 of the Law of Tabu Sanads of 7th Shewal 1276, Fisher p.53). Ruling by Court of Cassation No.125 p.281, Translation of Ottoman Laws p.12).

In this case also his possession must have been undisputed and there must not be any admission that he acquired the possession arbitrarily or without right. The article also refers only to land held by title deed and it does not refer to Metroukeh as the latter cannot be held by kushan for exclusive enjoyment (Land Code Art.95).

Prescription is ineffective where it is interrupted by the occupant giving up possession or ceasing to cultivate the land or by the institution of an action in Court by a claimant to the land.

-24-

Neither form of Prescription runs against persons subject to incapacity i.e. minority, unsoundness of mind, duress or absence on a journey (Muddeth-i Safer). (The Mejelleh Art.1663 and 1664 Land Code Art.20).

The Land Code recognises certain forms of extinctive prescription - Mêŕur el Zaman. Thus, the right of the State to demand the removal of trees planted without permission on State land is prescribed or lost after 3 years (Land Code Art.25).

The right of a co-owner to claim priority over an undivided share lapses after the expiry of five years. This right is not suspended by the incapacity of a party. (Land Code Art.41). The right of the owner of trees and buildings on Miri land to claim the land lapses after the expiry of 10 years (Land Code Art.44).

The right of heirs or absentees to claim that land should not become subject to the right of Tabu (Mustahiki Tabu) lapses after the expiration of three years (Land Code Arts.74 and 75).

The right of persons who have inherited Mulk trees or buildings on Miri land to claim the land if it has escheated to the State is extinguished after the expiry of 10 years.

-25-

The right of inhabitants to priority over escheated land within their village expires after one year. (Art. 59 and 66 of the Land Code).

Where a person occupies land by loan or on lease i.e., with the permission of the owner, the occupant acquires no rights, irrespective of the period of his occupation (Land Code Art. 23).

Corporate Bodies.

The Law of 22nd Rabi Awal 1331 relating to the Right of Corporate Bodies to Acquire Immovable Property, governs the acquisition of lands by these bodies.

Corporate bodies may acquire in Palestine such property as is needed for their enterprise, plant and works provided that their constitutions permit them to acquire and hold immovable property. Such bodies must be in possession of a certificate of Incorporation either from the Registrar of Companies in accordance with the Companies Ordinance 1920, the Cooperative Societies Ordinance 1921, or the Credit Banks Ordinance 1922 or of a certificate of registration issued by the District Governor in accordance with the Ottoman Law for the Registration of Societies and Clubs of August 3rd 1325 as amended by Public Notice No. 131 of 26th August 1919.

-26-

A special tax is payable by corporate bodies on properties owned by them in lieu of the normal succession dues (Public Notice Official Gazette No.84 of 1.2.23.). Any corporate body desiring to acquire more property than is needed for its enterprise or works must be in a possession of a certificate of public utility issued by the High Commissioner, under ~~Article 8 of the~~ (Companies Ordinance 1920 Art 8) Any corporation acquiring immovable property must obtain the consent of the Director of Lands ~~under Article 8 of the~~ (Transfer of Land Ordinance 1920 Art 8)

Companies and Banks (presumably also other Corporate Bodies) authorised to trade in Palestine may become mortgagees of any immovable property. (Article 2 of the Law of Mortgage of 25th February 1328 as amended by the Mortgage Law Amendment Ordinance 1920. Land Transfer Ordinance 1920 Art.8).

1.08

COPY.

No.L.S./50.

Mount Zion Building,
Jerusalem.

12th March, 1925.

Chief Secretary.

    I have the honour to forward herewith a covering letter, an explanatory note and an amended draft Forest Ordinance, which the Director of Agriculture and Forests asked me to pass on to you with my own observations. The amendments in the form of slips attached to the draft must not be overlooked.

    The conference mentioned by the Director of Agriculture and Forests was held on Mount Carmel, on Monday, 16th February. It was attended by Mr. Sawer himself, and by Messrs. Tear, Masson, Nathan, Muhammad Ragheb, Weizmann and Grasovsky of his Department, by Major Ley, Director of Surveys, and by Mr. Stubbs, Director of Lands, with Amin Effendi Risk and Mr. Doukhan of that Department.

    2. The importance of fostering the development of forest growth throughout the wide stretches of barren hillside at present characteristic of so considerable a proportion of Palestine is not likely to be contested. Even the present financial return from such growth is appreciable and every acre protected will add its increasing quota annually. On financial grounds alone the State cannot afford to neglect the income derivable from the utmost possible development of its areas of potential national forest. The gradual establishment of forest growth on the denuded hillsides will also increasingly check the violence and volume of the surface discharge of the rainfall, and thereby both restrict further denudation and nourish the subterranean accumulation which feeds the water springs.

    It will also produce humus and general promote soil formation and thereby further stimulate the growth of forest produce in the first place and provide the basis for its subsequent replacement in due time by horticulture if, and as, occasion arises.

    3. The principal obstacles to the development of national forest throughout the areas in question during the last five years appear to have been (a) suspicion that Government was really aiming at establishing State ownership with a view to subsequent alienation; (b) claims of villagers that areas affected were communal areas for grazing and for the collection of forest produce; (c) private claims to ownership.

    4. The conference agreed that the determination of the limits of national ownership would be both better and more economically performed during the course of, and by whatever organisations were charged with, the proposed Land Settlement. It also favoured a policy of State protection of woodland growth in areas of potential national forests rather than one of immediate determination of the limits of national ownership, provided that the claims of the nation to such ownership could be reasonably safeguarded against encroachment and the recognition of dubious competing claims pending systematic survey and settlement.

On/

-2-

On the above grounds and subject to the safeguard mentioned it was agreed that the provision for the immediate determination of areas of State Forest contained in the 1920 Forest Ordinance (Articles 9 - 13) and in the 1924 amended draft (Articles 7 - 12) would be advantageously abandoned.

5. The fact that the few areas that have so far been administered have been protected and have not been alienated, has, I understand, already gone some way to mitigate the suspicions of villagers as to the Government's motives, while the benefit of protection has not gone unnoticed. It is evident that such reassurance will be further promoted if claims of national ownership can be left to be decided later at the same time and by the same agencies as other claims. Among such claims will be those of villagers themselves to communal rights and privileges.

6. In practice there seems little doubt that, exercised with sympathy and discretion the protection of potential forest areas can, and should, be effected not only without detriment, but with positive benefit, to the inhabitants of adjoining villages.

Generous recognition of existing beneficial practices, such as the gathering of fuel and the provision of timber, as it becomes available, for implements and building, is proposed, subject only to such regularisation as the prevention of abuse requires. Provision for grazing of village flocks is intended to be made in consultation with the District Officer.

7. The goat is the chief enemy to the es-establishment of national forests in Palestine, and if such forests are to be established grazing must be controlled. With improved methods of farming and the growth of fodder crops both the goat and the need to pasture flocks itinerantly on the hillsides may disappear; but in the meantime it fortunately seems that provision for such flocks and protection for nascent forest can be effectively reconciled. In this connection the extract from a recent report on Australian forestry published by the Australian Government which is annexed to this note is of interest.

8. The one serious difficulty of adopting the above line of policy is to safeguard the areas in question in the interval before settlement. It is reasonable to anticipate that settlement will tend to be latest in the areas in which the most important tracts of potential national forest are situated, because those are the areas of minimum cultivation and population. In these areas settlement may readily be deferred for five to ten years. During this time forests will be developing and the property becoming valuable.

9. Operative encroachment, by which I mean the occupation and cultivation of land on the woodland fringes, can probably be sufficiently controlled by the forest wardens and if fruitful and limited to such fringes may be advisedly regularised. Well authenticated and genuine private ownership must also be cheerfully admitted and occasions no ground for anxiety. The real danger lies in recognition being accorded by the Land Registry or the Courts to wide claims of ownership based upon

dubious/

dubious Ottoman Qushans (title deeds), in the lengthy interval that may occur before settlement takes place in the locality.

The conference agreed that past experience showed that the danger was a real one and resided principally if not exclusively in the interpretation commonly accorded to Article 47 of the Ottoman Land Code.(*)

10. I understand that this Article has been frequently held to require that in the interpretation of all Qushans regard must be solely given to the alleged definition of boundaries however vague this may be and to whatever extent it may conflict with other factors, with the consequence that large private claims to ownership of natural forest and other woodland have regularly received favourable judgment which would not have been secured on an unfettered investigation of ground and document.

11. It is believed that numerous Qushans exist which may be similarly interpreted and that considerable areas of national property are in danger of alienation thereby. It was therefore held by the conference that the just safeguarding of national title to potential forest lands required fuller latitude in the interpretation of these documents than Article 47 of the Ottoman Land Code is at present understood to permit.

The means whereby such fuller latitude could be properly secured was not fully discussed by the conference, but an article in slip form attached to the accompanying new draft Ordinance provides for the exercise of equitable discretion in the interpretation of Qushans on which private claims to natural forest or other wildland are based. Whether this is a sufficient and proper way to secure the fuller latitude postulated is a matter for consideration by the Law officers, and the article has been inserted in this form in the draft so that such consideration should not be overlooked. As various provisions of Ottoman Law indicate that in principle natural forest and wild land cannot be properly alienated from the State, it would seem in keeping with the spirit of that law to subject to special scrutiny Qushans purporting to have alienated such land.

12. It is further to be observed that Article 47 forms part of the chapter in the law expressly dealing with the transfer of MIRI land and would therefore seem only applicable to that tenure of land, and that it is laid down in the article itself that exclusive consideration shall be given to boundaries only when these have been pointed out and fixed. (°)

If proof established *in situ* of compliance with the last stipulation is exacted before exclusive interpretation of a Qushan by the alleged boundaries recited in it is permitted, the danger of the article should be greatly reduced.

13./

(*). Of 7 Ramazan 1274 (21st April 1858). See Young "Corps de Droit Ottoman" (1906) VI. 58, or Fisher "Ottoman Land Law" (1919) p.18.

(°). Young. "Mais s'il agit du transfert des terraine dont on aura indiqué et determiné les limites ...."
Fisher. "In the case of land sold with boundaries definitely fixed and indicated..........."

-4-

13. No attempt can be made here to discuss the ambiguities of the existing Ottoman Law and the defects of existing Land Registration, but one example of the combined operation of these factors should perhaps be given in connection with the above conclusion. It is admitted that it was a common, if not the usual, practice under Ottoman rule for officials of the Land Registry to issue title deeds to land without such land being visited at all, the descriptions purporting to locate the area being supplied by the party applying for registration. Even in the absence of intentional fraud such descriptions were bound in the majority of cases to be vague on account of the lack both of the means and of the knowledge to be precise. This result was further fostered by the vicious official conception that every parcel of land is in essence always a rectangular figure with the sides conveniently oriented. It appears to have commonly followed that an applicant, when interrogated as to the boundaries of a piece of land that he wished to register, stated four salient features that he represented to lie respectively to the north, to the south, to the east and to the west of it, and that these were recorded as the boundaries of land acquired by him without any assurance that such features, even if their existence was correctly stated, defined the limits of such land or were even contiguous to it.

14. The absurdity of this is illustrated, if illustration be needed, by the following abstract of three title deeds which purport to have been granted in respect of three different pieces of land. The three pieces of land supposed to be defined are stated to be in the same village but situated in three localities of it, viz: <u>Geziret Genadi</u>, <u>Geziret Gedua</u> and <u>Jedar Tahtani</u>. The areas are given as 12, 12 and 15 dunoms respectively; the land tax references as 16184, 16183 and 16182; the sale prices as P.4500, 4500 and 6300; the official estimates of value as P.7950, 7950 and 10600, and the boundaries of all three are stated to be: East, <u>Ghassir Hajjar</u>; South, <u>Rumuh to owner</u>; West, <u>Ard el Abdi</u>; North, <u>Mugharat Foka</u> (sic).

Now these four boundaries may have been ignorantly given and accepted, in the manner explained, as defining in turn three separate pieces of land: or they may refer to two pieces one of which was twice registered and pays tax twice, or to one piece which was three times registered and pays tax three times.

Apart from the insufficiency of the description to enable one piece of land to be located with any pretence of certainty or precision, there is thus added some doubt as to whether one, two or three properties are purported to be defined. If only one of the three had been recorded it would have appeared no more ridiculous than the normal run of Ottoman Qushans to which Article 47 has, I understand, been commonly held to apply. The absurdity and inequity of admitting, without severe scrutiny, documents so inherently meaningless and so irresponsibly drawn as justification for the surrender of national property because they carry the name of title deeds need not be laboured.

15. While the example given primarily demonstrates the impropriety of relying upon the alleged boundaries recited in a Qushan without critical investigation on the ground, it will be appreciated that the normal Ottoman Qushan may be unreliable in any or all of its features and that these equally

call/

-5-

call for careful investigation before such Qushan is admitted as admissible evidence of rights over any piece of immovable property. Nor must such care be confined to the Ottoman Qushans for although the existing Land Registry is both painstaking and careful it is rarely in the power of any one at present to issue reliable documents affecting real rights in Palestine.

16. If a policy of simple protection and management of areas of potential national forest can be effectively carried out it is greatly to be preferred to an immediate attempt to define the limits of State ownership and village rights and privileges within such areas. Any sporadic investigation of rights and privileges in advance of regular settlement has evident and serious disadvantages. Such a patchwork settlement cannot be thorough; and it will distract and squander the effort of the Survey and Settlement parties. And if settlement initially takes the form of assertion of State ownership to the above areas it will tend to quicken the suspicions of villagers as to the motive which impels Government to accord priority of consideration to rock and moor rather than to cultivated holdings. This will be liable in turn to arouse adverse prejudice to the settlement operations as a whole. But serious as these objections are it would be better to face them than further to postpone systematic afforestation.

17. Execution of the policy recommended will depend upon co-operation between the Department of Agriculture and Forests, the District Officers and the villagers, and, as has been seen, its success or failure may have an important bearing upon the success of Land Settlement also. At present there is a tendency for District Officers to regard, from the standpoint of the villagers themselves, any assertion of State control over these uncultivated woodland tracts as an unjustifiable imposition upon the established rights of villagers both to usufruct of, and dominion over, these areas. The ability and readiness thus to see with the eyes of the villagers themselves must be recognised as the secret of the confidence and sympathy between District Officers and people. And although District Officers will doubtless do their best to carry out the forest policy of Government if so instructed, whatever their own views about it may be: that policy is unlikely to attain success, if these officers have not been satisfied at least of its reasonableness and justification. They must not be expected to enforce the law in spirit as well as letter, still less to overcome the prejudices and win the assistance of cillagers, unless they feel themselves justly impelled to do so. On these grounds I am of opinion that no pains should be spared in the first place to explain the policy of Government to District Officers and win their adherence to it, and in the second regularly to consult with, and utilise, them in its execution. The senior staff of the Department of Agriculture and Forests is much too small to enable it effectively to supervise the protection and management of all areas of potential forest throughout Palestine. If it is to be done, it can, I think, only be done by a combination of inspection and technical supervision by the Departmental officers and administrative control by District agencies. The responsibility of the latter and the necessity for their participation in the national duty of afforestation would doubtless be made clear.

18./

18. The general control and management of grazing and forestry throughout Palestine in the manner suggested will necessitate a large increase in the numbers of the forest wardens: if afforestation is to be achieved, a considerable increase of expenditure on this and other accounts is unavoidable; and it should rapidly result in, if it cannot actually be accompanied by, a considerably larger increase in revenue.

In the last connection it may be advisable to enact in the Ordinance that revenue derived from forest land that has been controlled and managed by the State is not recoverable by persons subsequently adjudged to own the land, and also that a competent Court may fix a redemption price to be paid for the value of the produce standing on such land before it is handed over.

It may well be that land that is redeemed from neglect by care and expenditure on the part of the State may be claimed and adjudged private property after it has thus acquired value: and that in this event a Court may judge that in addition to the accrued revenue at least a proportion of the capital sunk in its development should be repaid to the national purse.

19. It was suggested earlier that villagers were apt to regard themselves as having a right to both the current usufruct of, and the dominion over, contiguous areas of wild hillside and moor. Private rights apart, the forest policy recommended by the conference provisionally admits such usufruct but denies dominium, pending a reconsideration of both in detail during settlement. As the policy is likely to become crystallised in operation during the next decade, if it is successfully put into operation, it is desirable to consider how far it is justifiable before it is adopted.

The advisability, if not the equity, of recognising usufruct to the existing degree is not contested: but there are partisans both of the view of national and of communal dominium. The point requires fuller and more competent consideration but *prima facie* communal dominium can only be claimed on the ground that an area is "matruké" appears intrinsically to be a category of State Domain and to confer on the affected villages certain rights of usufruct but none of dominium. And if this prove not to be so the higher right remains of the nation as a whole to assume control and develop these neglected areas in the general as well as the particular interest.

There accordingly appear good grounds for concluding that the policy recommended is one that will both meet immediate needs and tend towards the establishment of a just and sound solution in the long run.

(Sgd) ERNEST M. DOWSON.

1.09

PRELIMINARY STUDY of LAND TENURE in PALESTINE.

§§ 1 - 4. Origin, object and limitation of Memorandum. Page 1.
§§ 5 - 7. General basis of land law. Page 9.
§§ 8 - 14. The five regular categories of land. Page 13.
§§ 15 - 20. Mahlul land (Escheat), Prescription, Expropriation, Mortgage, Lease, Corporate bodies. Page 25.
§§ 21 - 25. Customary tenures. Mudawara or Jiftlik and Mesha'. Page 33.
§§ 26 - 34. Succession and subdivision of land. Page 42.
§§ 35 - 38. Concluding Observations. Page 58.

TABLE I. showing alienation of land held in Mesha'. Page 36.

TABLE II. showing extreme theoretical subdivision of land registered. Page 52.

Paragraphs of general interest

1 & opening of 2	pp. 1 & 2
opening of 3	p. 4
opening of 4	p. 6
6	p. 11
31, opening & end of 32	pp. 47 - 51
35	pp. 58 & 59
37 & 38	pp. 61 - 65

CORRIGENDA.

Page	line				
8	9	for	"text"	read	"texts".
12	8	"	"Naquq"	"	"Haquq".
19	18	"	"musafagat"	"	"musafaqat".
21	2 from bottom	"	"inscrits"	"	"inscrit".
27	5	"	"Cassatun"	"	"Cassation".
30	11	"	"Rejah"	"	"Rejab".
38	21	"	"of the"	"	"if the".
43	4	"	"Rah-el-Awal"	"	"Rabi-el-Awal".
59	4 from bottom	insert "as" after "defined".			
83	1	for	"but"	read	"and".

N.B. In connection with §§ 21-25 the references to the Mesha' system in India mentioned on pp.120 and 121 of "India as I knew it" by Sir Michael O'Dwyer are of great interest. Also those on pp. 37, 52-58, 91-99 dealing with land-revenue settlement.

PRELIMINARY STUDY OF LAND TENURE IN PALESTINE.

Origin, object and limitations of Memorandum.

In the notes which I furnished in December 1923 on land-tax, cadastral survey and land settlement in Palestine, I said that a simplification and modification of the land law would be a necessary precursor to the establishment of a secure and economic land tenure, and that no assured progress could be made with cadastral survey and settlement until the necessary legislation had been workedout in detail and was in force.

A new land law, I added, need not and should not be revolutionary; it is primarily needed to simplify existing practice so that it is made as easy as possible for simple people who possess, part with, or acquire real rights to understand without expert intervention where they stand. So far as possible familiar forms would doubtless be retained and familiar names be perpetuated.

I ranked the drafting of the new laws and the regulations for effecting settlement as the most urgent needs and ventured to suggest that the drafting of the necessary legislation should be taken up. No action was taken on this and my other proposals, because I was asked to come out again to Palestine last winter and go more fully myself into all the questions at issue than was at all possible during my five day visit in November 1923.

2. It remains my opinion that an attempt to review, as a comprehensive whole, the land tenure of Palestine as it exists in law and in practice to-day, must precede any properly considered endeavour to carry out a national settlement of land rights, to make registration of such rights simple and effective, and generally (to borrow the words of the Mandate) "to introduce a land system appropriate to the needs of the country." This is all the more necessary because the absence of any unified code or

explanatory collection of land laws makes it at present
virtually impossible to get and keep acquainted with
these laws unless it can be made into a special study.

When I was asked to visit Palestine again last winter
I hoped that it would be found possible for someone qualified by real knowledge and experience of the working of
the law to satisfy this need; and it may not be out of
place to repeat what I said in writing to the Civil Secretary a year ago (30th September, 1924) on the subject, as
it explains my standpoint and the genesis of the present
Memorandum.

It appears most necessary, I said, if questions of real
rights are to be threshed out authoritatively and registered
throughout Palestine, that the difficulty in obtaining copies
of the Land Law of the country should be put an end to as soon
as possible. Everyone who has to deal with the work
of settlement even indirectly should be able readily to obtain
and retain a record of all the legislation under which existing rights over immovables have been acquired. In addition to
the written law there is presumably also a considerable
body of custom and usage - perhaps different in different
parts of the country - which also should be known.

To reprint all the legislation under which existing real
rights may have been acquired in Palestine would probably take
some time and would be expensive, particularly as it might
involve a considerable amount of translation if it was to
appear in English, the language in which it would seem to
be most needed. Moreover it is probable that a great deal of
the full text of such legislation would rarely be needed for
reference, even if it all in actual practice governs, or has
governed, the acquisition of rights still existant.

The above considerations lead me to suggest the great
service that would be rendered by the compilation of a

- 2 -

reliable and authoritative digest in English of the legislation that has at various periods governed the acquisition of real rights in Palestine. The dates on which alteration came into force would have to be made very clear, since the validity of a claim may turn on this factor. Full references to the complete body of law on which the digest was based would also be required, so that the actual original text of the relevant law or laws could be readily referred to in cases of doubt or when the digest was insufficient.

In addition to this digest of actual legislation it would probably be of great utility to compile an accompanying record of prevalent custom and usage, which possibly differs in different parts of the country. Any land settlement that is to conform as closely as possible to equity, as this presents itself to the mind of the people of Palestine, must of course pay careful regard to prevalent custom and usage. While nothing but chaos can be expected if the settlement parties have not full knowledge of the legislation that has been in force during the period in which all existing real rights have been acquired, and do not pay the most careful regard to it, it is an equitable and not a legal settlement that must be aimed at if the nearest approach to what the people themselves will consider a just settlement is to be obtained. It will probably be generally agreed that this is not only the proper criterion by which the merit of the settlement should ultimately be primarily gauged, but also the factor which will preponderantly determine its stability and political and administrative success.

In response to this suggestion the Director of Lands prepared for me some extremely useful "Notes on Land Law in Palestine". Invaluable as these notes have been to me in the preparation of this Memorandum, they fall far short of the comprehensive review needed. This did not materialize simply because there was no one with the requisite knowledge and experience free enough to undertake it.

3. I have therefore been constrained most reluctantly to make a preliminary and provisional essay myself. I have found this task beset with almost incredible obstacles for the outside investigator, firstly because of the entire absence of reliable statistical information of even the crudest character in regard to the distribution of the land according either to the recognized legal categories or to any other administrative, fiscal or economic subdivisions, and secondly because of the insuperable difficulty in obtaining in any complete form the text of the laws, public orders, regulations and instructions that are, or have been, in force.

When I first visited Palestine in November 1923 a private copy of Ongley's translation of the Ottoman Land Code[+] was temporarily borrowed for me and supplemented by a scratch collection of post-Occupation proclamations, ordinances, etc. When preparing for my second visit a precious copy of Young's Corps de Droit Ottoman[x] was secured for a short time for me from the Foreign Office. During and since my second visit the same difficulty has been experienced in obtaining standard translations or a complete collection of the Ottoman texts. I was fortunate enough to be able to buy a copy of Young in Jerusalem, and to be given two copies of Fisher[++] annotated by the Lands Department; but I have never again seen a copy of Ongley, while the Crown Agents for the Colonies have only with the greatest difficulty been able to

---

[+?] Correct reference.

[x] *Corps de Droit Ottoman.* George Young, 7 Vols. Clarendon Press, 1905.

[++] *Ottoman Land Laws.* Stanley Fisher. Oxford Univ. Press, 1919.

- 4 -

to secure me a battered copy of Grigsby's translation of the Majellé[+] and have failed to find a copy of that by C. R. Tyzer and Demetriades which I understand is much better.

The latest Ottoman law given in Fisher is dated 1883 (25 Rabi-el-akner 1300), and the latest in Young relating to land 1901. Fisher gives notice of nine provisional laws concerning land, published in 1913 (1331); while translations of fifteen laws, provisional laws, orders &c. published between 1859 (1276) and 1914 (1332) are contained in a pamphlet issued by the Iraq Government in April 1919.[x]

That pre-war Ottoman law as applied and practised in Palestine should baffle full and precise presentation in English and French is perhaps not to be wondered at; but the lack of any complete and authoritative collection of all Orders-in-Council, Proclamations, Ordinances, Public Orders &c., which have been published in Palestine since the British Occupation, in virtue of which the Ottoman laws still operate, or have been displaced or amended, is a matter for much greater regret. Such a publication issued with historical and explanatory notes made while the actors were still on the scene or for the most part available would have been, and would still be, invaluable.

My own investigation has been greatly hampered and delayed by the extreme difficulty there has been in discovering and obtaining even the bare texts of such papers; and there still exist three important gaps in my collection which it has not yet been found possible to fill.[++]

I understand that the scarcity has arisen through lack of facilities to keep type standing or stereotype it, and from a desire to minimize the cost of printing. I venture to suggest that if the main expense of the administration, executive and judicial, of a law is justified, the relatively trifling cost

[+]The Medjellé or Ottoman Civil Code translated by W.E. Grigsby. Herbert Clarke, Nicosia, 1895.

[x]Translations of Turkish Laws. S.G.P.Bd.0.4.19.

[++]Ordinances, &c. published in the periods Jan-March 1921, July-Dec.1921 and July-Dec.1922.

of keeping it and any subsidiary instruments in print should be included; if only because it may well be considered an elementary obligation of any civilized government to keep at least the text of its current laws and public regulations within the reach of all. But it must also, I think, be recognised that both the economical and the effective administration of law are difficult to secure without understanding and co-operation on the part of the public, and that these cannot be expected if the text of current laws and regulations are so difficult to obtain.

4. I am very conscious of the imperfections of the accompanying study of Palestine land tenure. For reasons that have been cited it has cost me a most disproportionate amount of time and labour, and is bound to be inaccurate and incomplete: while from its very nature it must, I am afraid, also prove tedious and wearisome to read.

It is, however, in my judgment work that had to be done by someone, at least in the broad outline attempted, before I could justly complete, my general report.

The barren results of the persevering efforts made during the last seven years to put the land tenure of Palestine on to a sound footing are an emphatic warning against any repetition of insufficiently considered, as they are against any repetition of sectional, attempts to achieve reform in a matter which penetrates so deeply into the social, economic and religious structure of the whole country. A continuance of failure for either of the above reasons would now be inexcusable, and until the broad outlines of both existing land tenure and land taxation had been fairly thoroughly explored, there still remained a risk that some fundamental consideration had escaped attention.

This cannot I think be the case now if the accompanying paper may be submitted to the early correction, criticism and amendment of those who have shaped post-war policy and legislation on the general subject, who have less superficial acquaintance with Ottoman law as applied in Palestine; who have taken a leading part in its administration, executive and judicial, and who have knowledge and experience of the results of these at first hand.

I would, however, venture to ask that, so far as possible, correction, criticism and constructive comment should be referred to the numbered paragraphs of this memorandum, so as to facilitate assimilation of such help, and that they should be directed with a view to the ultimate objectives. These objectives in the present connection appear to me briefly to be the simplification of the land tenure with provision for better economic development and the reconciliation of its statutory expression with current needs and practice.

Land Registration although an organic part of land tenure in Palestine is intentionally omitted from review in this memorandum, both because it should, and can be, made to conform to any real needs and effective provisions and because it will be more conveniently considered separately in due course.

Some other aspects of land tenure are also omitted from immediate consideration primarily because I cannot at this stage afford to devote proper attention to them: but with one exception they are either matters which have already received sufficient preliminary consideration for the present purpose or do not appear to possess unusual features. In the former class is the very important subject of the restoration, preservation and management of woods and forests. In the second are the laws and regulations governing sales, gifts, options, etc.

The exception is the question of water rights and obligations, one of great if still largely undeveloped importance. The existing body of law deals with this question quite inadequately and it calls for most careful and farsighted consideration and legislation.

In a country which lacks rain for so many months each year the definition and registration of water rights, where they occur, is as important as the definition and registration of rights over the land; while if research and enterprise are successfully harnessed, it can hardly be doubted that the area of irrigable or partly irrigable land in Palestine will increase very greatly during the next twenty-five years.

General Basis of the Land Law.

The Palestine Order in Council of 10th August 1923 constitutes the supreme authority for the laws now in force in Palestine. As copies of this Order are scanty it may be advisable to quote in extenso Article 46 which defines the law to be applied by the Civil Courts. It is, however, necessary to bear in mind that the jurisdiction exercised by the various Religious Courts in matters of personal status reacts upon the operation of land tenure in certain important respects, and also that provision is made in the Order in Council for application of tribal custom in tribal areas. It is the civil law nevertheless which primarily governs the tenure of immovable property, and the civil law to be applied is defined by Article 46, which runs as follows:-

"The jurisdiction of the Civil Courts shall be exercised in conformity with the Ottoman Law in force in Palestine on November 1st., 1914, and such later Ottoman Laws as have been or may be declared to be in force by Public Notice, and such Orders in Council, Ordinances and regulations as are in force in Palestine at the date of the commencement of this Order, or may hereafter be applied or enacted; and subject thereto and so far as the same shall not extend or apply, shall be exercised in conformity with the substance of the common law, and the doctrines of equity in force in England, and with the powers vested in and according to the procedure and practice observed by or before Courts of Justice and Justices of the Peace in England, according to their respective jurisdictions and authorities at that date, save in so far as the said powers, procedure and practice may have been or may hereafter be modified, amended or replaced by any other provisions. Provided always that the said common law and doctrines of equity shall be in force in Palestine so far only as the circumstances of Palestine and its inhabitants and the limits of His Majesty's jurisdiction permit and subject to such qualification as local circumstances render necessary."

It must, however, be noted that the term Ottoman Law in force in Palestine on November 1st., 1914 is unavoidably loose, for in addition to uncertainties in laws having unquestionable legal force there appear to have been in operation, on trial or under consideration certain provisional laws throughout various parts of the Ottoman Empire, besides numerous administrative orders having, or accorded, the force of law. An explanation which appears in a preliminary note to translations of such provisional laws issued by the Iraq Government on the 9th.April, 1919 is of interest in this connection.

"A provisional law (it is explained) is a law which has not received formal ratification from the General Assembly at Constantinople. Laws were promulgated and put into force provisionally before receiving such ratification, and it has in the majority of cases not been possible to trace any notice of the fact that they have been ratified. It is assumed that they have the force of law in the absence of information to the contrary. The orders, circulars and instructions issued by various Ministers and published in the Dastur or the Jeridat-el-aaliya appear to have been binding on the Courts."[+]

This explanation was issued in the early years of the establishment of the post-war government in Iraq, four years before the Palestine and Iraq Orders in Council now in force, and is an indication of the confusion which prevailed between legally enacted law, unratified legislation and administrative orders when these countries were occupied. This confusion was aggravated by the complexities, uncertainties and contradictions of the main body of the law, by the incompetence, if not corruption, of the agents who administered it, and by the concurrent toleration of important practices unknown, if not running counter, to it. It is the

---

[+]Extract from Preliminary Note in "Translations of Turkish Laws," Government Press Bagdad, 9th.April, 1919.

resulting amalgam which the term Ottoman law in force in Palestine on November 1st., 1914 presumably represents.

6. The adoption of Ottoman law as it actually existed and was applied was clearly inevitable when Ottoman territory was initially taken over; nor is its replacement now by an extraneous land code likely to commend itself to any prudent and experienced person as the means of introducing beneficial and assimilable reform. As elsewhere, law and practice in the Near East have developed to a large extent in direct response to local needs and conditions, however imperfect such response may have been; and it is evidently by perfection of such development that improvement will be most successfully pursued, if only because of the extreme difficulty of re-orienting the view point of the mass of the population on a matter of such close and widespread concern as the land. But while the spirit and fundamental concepts of Ottoman law should, on this showing, remain the basis of Palestinian land tenure, the statutory expression of such tenure must be purged of inconsistencies and of moribund provisions, be reconciled with reasonable and well established practice, assimilate where it can lessons derived from the experience of others, and above all be clarified and simplified if it is indeed to constitute the foundation of a land system appropriate to the needs of the country and, ceasing primarily to be a quarry for justiciable conundrums, ensure the simple definition and secure holding of rights to own or use land.

7. The specific Ottoman land law is contained in the Land Code promulgated on the 7th. Ramazan 1274 (21st. April 1858),[+] supplemented, amended and explained by decrees, regulations,

---
[+] Young, op. cit. Vol. vi, p.44.
Fisher, op.cit. p.1.

instructions, vizirial letters, &c. Now the civil law of the Ottoman Empire, although largely the outcome of impact with Europe, had to be grafted upon, and administered in reconciliation with, Ottoman common law which was the Muslim religious law. It having been found in the early days of the growth of the Civil Law that conflicts of jurisdiction and jurisprudence occurred between the Religious and the Civil Courts (Mekhema sheria and Mejlis temiz Naquq) a Commission was constituted to bridge the gulf by drawing up a code based on the religious law, but designed to meet more modern needs and to provide a basis for the settlement of questions which arose daily in civil dealings.+

The compilation known as the Majellé or somewhat ambiguously as the Ottoman Civil Code, resulted, and was promulgated in sixteen books by successive Imperial Irades between 1287 and 1293 A.H. (1870-76). The Majellé is succinctly defined as a collection in the form of a code of those principles of the Religious law to be applied by the Civil Courts to what may be termed ordinary civil rights and obligations.^{x}

It therefore appears that the Majellé constitutes an integral, if not a dominant, part of the Ottoman civil law in force in Palestine on November 1st., 1914, that the Ottoman land law should be read in the light of the Majellé and that where the former is silent the latter should be referred to. There are moreover numerous direct references to immovable property scattered throughout the Majellé and every book, except possibly III. and IV., contains sections of importance in connection with such property.

+.....la redaction d'un Code, basé sur la Droit Sacré, approprié aux besoins de l'epoque actuelle et suffisant pour resoudre les questions qui surgissent journallement dans les transactions." Report of the Commission 18 Zu el: Qi'da 1286 (1 Ap.1589).Young op.cit. vol.vi., p.172.

^{x}J.B.Barron. Mohammedan Waqfs in Palestine p.43,March 1922. Greek Convent Press, Jerusalem.

No marked change occurred in the spirit of the Ottoman land law after the issue of the Land Code until the years 1331 and 1332 A.H. (1913-14 A.D.) following the Turkish revolution, the deposition of the Sultan Abdel Hamed II., and the subsequent wars in the Balkans and with Italy. In these two years the Ottoman legislators became very active, and numerous laws relating to immovable property were issued substantially modifying the holding and disposition of rights over immovable property. The important series of provisional Ottoman laws published in English translation in 1919 by the 'Iraq Government as noted above, belong to this period.

8. <u>The five regular categories of land.</u>

The Ottoman Land code divides land into five classes termed respectively Mulk, Miri, Mevqufé, Metruke and Mewat.

Mulk generally is defined as anything that can be owned whether a definite object or its produce.[+] Mulk lands (arazi memluke) are those of which the "raqaba" is vested in the possessor.[x] The word raqaba, strictly meaning "subjection", is translated "pleine propriété" and "dominium plenum" in Young, "legal ownership" in Fisher, and is defined by Barron[++] as the power to grant or dispose of land unconditionally. The term is explained by Belin[xx] as meaning, when applied to living things, the nape of the neck on which a yoke is fixed. Savvas Pasha[+++] says it is the chain or ring that a slave wore round his neck, which has become a legal term for "la nue propriété". In any case it appears that, as the result of having the raqaba invested in him, an owner of mulk land has the most complete form of ownership of land known to Ottoman law.[xxx] In effect mulk corresponds

-----

[+] Majellé Art.125 v. Young vi,187, Grigsby 17.

[x] Art.2, Land Code.

[++] Op.cit.pp.15 and 16.

[xx] Young, vi.48 footnote.

[+++] [xxx] Fisher, p.2. footnote.

closely to English freehold tenure or fee simple.

The creation of mulk land in four ways is recognised, viz.: (i) Sites (for houses) which were within towns (koura) and villages (kassaba) at the date of the coming into force of the Land Code, with their curtilages and small enclosures used in connection with habitation or industry,[+] (ii) State land validly converted into mulk according to the provisions of Religious Law, (iii) and (iv) Land distributed at the time of the original Muslim conquest in full legal ownership (i.e. with the raqaba) among the victors or confirmed in such ownership to the conquered subject to obligation to pay tithe[x] or tribute[++] respectively. I understand there is little, if any, land in Palestine which can be claimed as mulk on either of the last two grounds. Finally to be validly held as mulk immovable property must be registered in the Land Registry.[xx]

Mulk tenure is essentially an exceptional assimilation to immovable property of the absolute ownership of movable goods; and immovable property registered as Mulk is considered as analogous to such goods and governed by the Muslim Religious Law and not by the Civil Law. In particular immovable mulk property devolves by inheritance under the Religious Law, and the provisions of that law with regard to dedication, pledge, mortgage, gift and pre-emption are applicable to it.

[+] cf. Sir Thomas Haycraft. Ottoman Land Law in Cyprus, Law Quarterly Review, No. xcv. July 1908. "By way of entering upon a classification of land we may begin with the town or village, and we there find land which more nearly resembles freehold than any other category of land under the Ottoman system. The sites of buildings with their curtilages and small enclosures used in connection with habitation or industry are Mulk lands, and these are regarded by the law in much the same light as personal property".....

[x] Ushr.

[++] Kharaj, which was of two kinds — kharaj-i-mukassemé (proportional tribute) assessed at a tenth to a half of the produce, and kharaj-i-muvazzaf (fixed tribute) paid annually.

[xx] Law of 28 Rejab 1821 (10 Sept. 1874).

It should be noted that mulk tenure may be acquired of buildings standing or of trees growing on State Land, on mulk land the property of others,[+] or on mevqufe or waqf land. In cases where the land is waqf, but the buildings or trees on it are mulk (and thus at the absolute disposal of the possessor) the owner is entitled to the use of the site so long as the fixtures exist. He rents the site from the waqf for an equitable annual rate, and the mutawali (or administrator of the waqf) has no power to dispossess him so long as this fixed annual rental (mukata) is duly paid.[x] All such mulk rights have however to be registered to be valid.

Minerals are also the mulk property of the owner (holder of the raqaba) of the soil in which they occur.[++] Crops are the mulk property of the cultivator[xx] regardless of whether the raqaba or ownership of the land is vested in him.

It will have been noted that mulk ownership of land has to be specifically created. Normally land throughout the Ottoman Empire is the property of the State. Miri lands (Arazi miri or State lands) comprise such land of every variety[+++] of which the raqaba is vested in the Treasury and the usufructuary possession (tasarruf) is granted out permanently, so long as it is properly exercised, so that the land shall be made productive and the Treasury obtain a

---

[+] Arts.28, 50, 81 Land Code.

[x] Young, vi, 116. Fisher p.64. Barron p.41.

[++] v. Art.107 Land Code.

[xx] v. Art .1248 Majelle and Art.80 Land Code.

[+++] "Les champs, lieux de campement et de parcours d'été et d'hiver, les forêts et autres domaines dont le Gouvernement donnait la jouissance." Young, vi, 46. "Arable fields, meadows, summer and winter pasturing grounds, woodland and the like, the enjoyment of which is granted by the Government." Fisher, p.2.

- 15 -

tithe or other share in its productivity. This unfructuary possession is throughout the law treated as a personal right; but the law always speaks of the State as the owner+ of the land and does not recognise any other right in or over it save this right of usufructuary possession, which may be assigned by permission of the proper representatives of the State, and may pass by inheritance, but which escheats to the State on the failure of heirs or other proper claimants[x] or upon failure to cultivate or otherwise make the land productive. The usufructuary (mutesarrif) is not a proprietor but a sort of lessee and his rights must be registered to be valid.[++] Miri may thus be described as registered heritable leasehold of State land.[xx] [+++]

The production of title from land that would otherwise be idle having been a dominant motive with the State, the rights granted under the Miri tenure were originally restricted to cultivation by the actual usufructuary. Without express authority miri land could not be leased or lent or mortgaged; its subsoil could not be dug up to make bricks or tiles; buildings could not be erected upon it; it could not be utilized unproductively as a threshing floor; even vines and fruit trees could not be planted upon it.[xxx]

+ e.g. Art.3. Land Code.
Art.1. Tapu Law.
In this connection it may be useful to note the caution recorded by Fisher (footnote p.15) against the use by the legislator of the words sale, vendor and purchaser in respect of transfer of miri rights, and the analogous caution in the interpretation of the words "owners, ownership and own" entered as a translator's note on p.8 of "Translations of Turkish Laws" issued by the Iraq Government.

[x] v. Arts 59 et seq. Land Code.

++ v. Arts.8-11 dealing with initial registration, Arts.14,21, 22 Tapu Law and Art.1 of the Regulations as to Title Deeds of 7 Shaban 1276 (Fisher 7.61).

xx v. Fisher p.3 footnotes.

+++ Cf. Haycraft, op.cit. "We must come to that mass of land which is used for Agricultural purposes and which is known as Mirie or State land. This is not held in absolute ownership by cultivators. It is a huge State domain granted by a sort of perpetual lease to occupiers of the surface."

xxx v. Arts.9 Land Code.
Arts.25-30 Law of Registration of miri property (Tapu Law). Arts.12,31,34,25 Land Code.

A provisional law of 5 Jamad-el-Awal 1331 (13 February 1913) regulating the right to dispose of immovable property was designed to absolve formally registered holders of miri land from these restrictions, provided dealings or action of the nature indicated were in turn formally registered, and an annual tax in lieu of tithe (bedl'usnr) was paid when necessary.[+]

Under Ottoman law miri land could only be converted into mulk by special Imperial Order of the Sultan and could not be dedicated to any purpose (as waqf) by the holder until the legal ownership (raqaba) was, or thus became, vested in him.[x] This authority has now devolved upon the High Commissioner.[++]

10. Mevqufe (arazo mevqufe) waqf or "dedicated" lands are lands which have been devoted to (a) some religious or (b) charitable purpose or (c) under cover of the former effectively as a family trust or settlement. Muslim jurists recognise these three classes and group the first two under the general term charitable institutions (muassasati khairiya).[xx]

The dedication of a thing as waqf can only be rightfully made by a person who is legally capable of constituting a transfer of the ownership. It follows that such dedication is properly confined to mulk property and cannot be made by a declared debtor or anyone under any other legal inhibition to dispose of his property. Mulk property legally dedicated is known as waqf sahih or true waqf. Property so dedicated is still in principle mulk, of which the raqaba is irrevocably and inalienably vested in God. As such it continues to be governed by the religious law and by the conditions laid down by the founder, but is removed from human ownership and disposition.

True waqf is subdivided into (1) waqf mazbuta (fixed or held fast) which is the most regular form administered directly by the

---

[+] v.Art.5, op. cit.

[x] v.Art.121 Land Code. Also v.Art.8 of provisional law of 5 Jamad el Awal previously cited.

[++] ? reference.

[xx] v. Barron, op. cit. p.11.

waqf authorities, (ii) **waqf mulhaqa** (appended or attached) ministered by an administrator or trustee (mutawali) theoretically under the supervision of the waqf authorities, and (iii) waqf muteena (exceptional) administered by a mutewali without control.[+]

Private family trust (waqf zurri) constituted from mulk land (under cover of a religious object) is also true waqf.

Normally true waqf can only be leased for short periods, but when the dedicated property falls into dilapidation the religious court can authorise its lease in perpetuity on terms requiring in addition to the annual rent the payment in advance of a capital sum to effect the necessary repairs. This practice is called ijaratein (two rents). Subject to the consent of the religious court such a lessee, who virtually enjoys a limited ownership subject to the annual rent charge (Meku), can sell, lease or otherwise dispose of his property. For such transactions land subjected to ijaratein comes under the Civil Land Law. Except as ijaratein true waqf cannot be sold or encumbered otherwise than provided by the constituent waqfia or deed of dedication. It may, however, be exchanged with the approval of the religious court for other property which then takes its place as the foundation of the waqf.

11. There are very few true waqfs in Palestine;[x] but there is a second class of waqf known as **waqf gher sahih** (untrue) or **takhsissat** (assigned) waqf, constituted from miri land which is of great importance. As Miri or State land could not be dedicated to any purpose an assignment or appropriation (takhsissa) from its production in some form or another (e.g. assignment of tithe) was substituted by special act of dedication by the Sultan or with his permission.

[+] Barron says (p.17 op.cit.) that true waqf did not come under the administration of the Ottoman Ministry of Waqf: (also p.22), that the revenues of mulhaga waqfs are left or ceded by private persons partly for the benefit of religion partly for the benefit of some person named or succession of persons, and that such waqfs are also known in Palestine as "private waqfs". Later (p.34.) he says that the dedication of property as a family settlement (mulnaqa) is not recognised by Anglo-Indian law.

[x] Barron, op. cit. p.17.

The assignment of tithe in this way forms the outstanding feature of religious endowments in Palestine, and in 1923 represented 55% of their gross receipts and 2% of the total tithe assessment for Palestine (Cis-Jordan).+ The making of further taknsissat or untrue waqf was forbidden by Article 8 of the Ottoman provisional law of the 5 Jamad-el-Awal 1331 (12 April 1913)× which I understand has the force of law in Palestine.

The raqaba of miri land dedicated as untrue waqf remains vested in the Treasury. It is governed by Book II. of the Land Code under a common heading, and generally in common, with miri. In the case of untrue waqf however the transfer, succession and acquisition (tapu-i-misl) fees are paid to the waqf concerned instead of to the State.xx

None the less in some cases of untrue waqf the provisions of the civil land law with regard to transfer and succession do not appear to be applied; and the land is cultivated and managed by the waqf authorities either directly or by leasing.+++

The terms musafagat (roofed) and mustaghilat (worked i.e. cultivated) appear to be applied to both true and untrue waqfs.xxx

12.   Under Ottoman law the validity of the deed of dedication of a waqf must be proved to the Religious Court during the lifetime of the dedicator if by gift, or after his death if by will. The constitution of the waqf is invalid unless registered in the Land Registry.++++ Waqfs may be expropriated for public purposes.xxxx

---

+Barron op.cit. pp.18 and 59.

xTranslations of Turkish Laws, p.5.

++Translated "Domaine public: erazii mirie ve mekoufe" by Young (vi.43) and "State Land" by Fisher (p.6).

xx .v.Art.4. Land Code.

+++.v.Barron op.cit.p.16 subdivision of Taknsissat waqf land. It is not clear under what authority or to what extent this exception is made.

xxx v. definition of these terms. Fisher p.59.

++++Law of 9 Rabi-el-Awal 1293 (5 April 1876) Registration of immovable waqf property.
Instructions as to title deeds for Mevquf6 land 6 Rejab 1282.
? Order No.84 Daftar khaqani (Imperial Book) 12.8.1331.
Art.2. Land Transfer Ordinance.

xxxx   ? The Law of Expropriation 21 Jomad-el-Awal 1286 (15 May 1879).

? The Law of Expropriation of 21 Kanun-el-Tani 1338.

Nor was the power of creating waqfs confined to Muslims. Non-Muslims might create religious endowments within the same limitations as Muslims.[+] Under Articles 52–54 of the Palestine Order in Council true waqfs (as religious endowments) may now be constituted before the appropriate Christian and Jewish Religious Courts. These Courts and the Muslim Religious Court also enjoy exclusive jurisdiction over the internal administration of waqfs affecting their respective communities. When there is no appropriate religious court a true waqf may be constituted before the Civil Courts. The "Charitable Trusts Ordinance 1924" provides for the endowment of religious and charitable trusts in accordance with English practice before the Civil Courts.

Although the law requires the registration of all waqfias (deeds of dedication) in the Land Registry, this was rarely complied with; and such evidence of the intention to constitute waqfs as exists is generally in the form of hoja sheria (deeds registered in the religious court). Judgment was given by the Court of Appeal (in re Ainkarem) that the decision as to whether property is or is not waqf rests with the Civil Courts. A Draft Ordinance published (as a bill) in the Official Gazette of the Palestine Government No. 144 of 1 May 1924, and probably promulgated since, gives legislative effect to this judgment.

It broadly appears on review that the constitution of waqf – whether true or untrue – does not really introduce a change in the underlying and essential tenure of the land dealt with. True waqf is constituted from and essentially remains mulk administered in trust for a special purpose, while untrue or takhsissat waqf is constituted from and essentially remains miri the usufruct of which is administered similarly in trust in whole or in part. The prohibition of the creation of further untrue waqf in future will further simplify the position.

[+] v. Barron op. cit. Appendix III. "Note on Non-Moslem Waqfs."

13. Metruke lands are lands "left" for the use of the public. They are considered[+] as divided into (i) those assigned for use of the general public (manmie), such as public highways, and (ii) those assigned for the use of a particular community (murefeké), such as communal pasture (mer'a) communal woodland (baltalik), village threshing floors, places of worship, etc.[x]

The chief characteristic of metruke lands is that the raqaba is inalienably vested in the State in the public or communal interest. Thus no transfer of ownership is allowed and no exercise or recognition of possession permitted.[++]

Matruké land must be registered to be legally valid as such, and although assignment for a public or communal purpose from time immemorial seems to be recognised as the justification for registration initially, no prescriptive acquisition of communal rights by lapse of time not immemorial is admitted.[xx] The existence of pastures within the confines of villages which have been used from time immemorial as such but have not been assigned as, and are not, matruke, appears to be recognised by Articles 24 and 105 of the Land Code. The existence of miri threshing floors is also recognised by Article 34.

[+] Art.5 Land Code.

[x] Cf. Haycraft op.cit. "that land which is left apart for public uses and is called Metrouké. Such includes roads and public places, public threshing floors, the beds of rivers, and according to the Land Code, pastures assigned to villages. It is doubtful however whether in Cyprus there exist, strictly speaking, any Metrouké pastures, although doubtless there are grazing rights enjoyed by villages ab antiquo over Mevat lands."

[++] Land Code, Book II., Chap.I. Particularly Arts.95 and 97. v. also Art.13 Tapu Law.

[xx] Art.95,98 and 102.Land Code. An explanatory footnote in Young (vi.72) says "Par consequent les habitants des communes ne peuvent acquérir par l'usucapion au nom de leur commune aucun droit de paturage sur les terres domaniales non inscrits au Defter-Khané, comme destinées à l'usage des communes."

- 21 -

No encroachment upon the use of communal matruké by other communities is allowed, nor is the erection of buildings or the planting of trees upon, nor the ploughing up and cultivation of, land of public or communal utility permitted.[+]

Any fees levied for the use of matruké land[x] are due to the Treasury, as representing the State in whom the raqaba is vested.

14. Mewat or "dead lands" (Arazi mewat) are described generally as comprising unoccupied (khali) land such as hills, rocky and stony places (kinach), scrub woodland (pernallik) and grazing grounds (otlak) which are not held by anyone by title deed, have not been assigned from time immemorial to a village as communal pasture (mera) or felling ground (baltalik) and are sufficiently remote from the nearest village for the voice of a loud speaking man not to be heard.[++][xx] This distance is defined as a mile and a half.[+++]

[+] v. Arts. 91-94, 97 and 101 Land Code.

[x] e.g. Dues for winter and summer pasture (kishlak and yaylak). v. Arts. 24 and 101 Land Code.

[++] v. Majelle. Art.1270 et seq. and Land Code Arts. 8 and 103 et seq.

[xx] Cf. Haycraft op cit. "that land which is uncultivated and unappropriated, waste land of mountains, swamps and stony places, wild heaths and moorlands. This is known as Mevat, or dead land, and is the property of the Crown. Without permission it may not be built upon or cultivated. When, however, Mevat land is cultivated by permission of the government, it becomes Mirie and falls permanently into that category.

[+++] A table of equivalence in Young gives the Turkish mile as equal to 1895 metres (vi. 370).

Anyone who has need of mewat land can with the leave of the Government cultivate it subject to the raqaba remaining vested in the State. The provisions of the Civil Law which apply to cultivated miri land also apply to such reclaimed mewat land.[+] If subsequently neglected for three years the usufructuary right escheats to the State but can be redeemed on payment of the Tapu value.[x]

No prescriptive right is acquired by cultivation of Mewat land without permission: and even when the Government have for long known and acquiesced in such cultivation it may apparently at its discretion evict or exact payment of the Land Registry value of the land.

The Mewat Lands Ordinance was published on 18th.February 1921 with a view to checking the acquisition of such land by unauthorized squatting. It reaffirmed that no prescriptive rights were acquired by unauthorized cultivation, declared such cultivation a trespass, and required any person who was so cultivating to apply for a title deed within two months.

Under a subsequent Public Notice for the Demarcation of State Lands a small commission examined applications made under the Ordinance, and when satisfied granted miri title at their discretion gratuitously or on payment of bedl misl. Persons who ignored the Ordinance may, however, also be granted a title deed on payment of bedl misl which seems very unsatisfactory.[++]

[+] "Les dispositions de la loi civile en vigueur pour les terres miri ensemencées (mezroua) sont egalement applipables aux terres mevat defrichées." Translation of Article 103 Land Code. Young, vi.74.

[x] Tapu-i-misl, v.815.

[++] Official Gazette, 1st. December 1921.

- 23 -

In point of fact the Ordinance closely resembles the Mahlul Land Ordinance, referred to a little later, in having been an endeavour to induce squatters on public land to report their usurpations themselves as the Government was not in a position to discover them.

Doubtless in both cases a number of squatters were bluffed and a number thought it to their advantage to regularize their positions: but until the Government itself knows the location and extent of its property it is not capable of enforcing either ordinance and illicit seizures of public land must be expected to continue.

Jebal Moubahi or hill lands that have not passed into the possession of anyone and have not been assigned from time immemorial as communal woodland, are dealt with in the Land Code under the heading of, and in the same chapter as Mewat. Anyone can cut wood for fuel, or for buildings on such hill land, and wood cut or herbage gathered there is not titheable. Ownership of such hill land cannot be alienated, possession of it must not be granted or recognized, and occupation of it is not permitted.[+]

[+] Art.104 Land Code.
Art.13 Tapu Law.

Mahlul land (Escheat).

15. Miri land is said to become mahlul (vacant, unpossessed) when the usufructuary possession (tasarruf) escheats owing to the land having been left unproductive through failure of heirs or persistent neglect. In such event the land becomes subject to the right of Tapu or of acquisition of the escheated usufructuary possession from the Land Registry on payment of a sum known as the Tapu or Land Registry value.[+] The escheat may, however, be redeemed by the original usufructuary himself (mutasarrif) before it passes elsewhere, by an equal payment then called bedl misl.[x] When the escheat is not redeemed privileged consideration may be granted to applicants claiming its reversion on grounds of contingent[++] or neighbouring rights.[xx]

Rights in untrue waqf which lapse through failure of heirs under the provisional Ottoman law of 3 Rabi'-el-Awal 1331 (11th. February 1911)[+++] escheat to the Waqf authorities.[xxx]

Mulk immovable property of persons who die intestate without heirs escheats to the State and is assimilated to mahlul or vacant State land.[++++]

[+] Tapu-i-misl or Land Registry value at which the land is assessed under Article 59 of the Land Code by competent and impartial assessors.

[x] Equivalent value, i.e. equivalent to the Tapu-i-misl.

[++] e.g. Owners of mulk trees or buildings situated on the land, partners in the estate etc.

[xx] v. Chapter IV. Land Code on the escheat of miri land generally.

[+++] Translations of Turkish Laws, p.4.

[xxx] v. Barron op cit. p.83.

[++++] v. Art.15. Law of title deeds for mulk of 28 Regab 1291 (10th. Sept.1874) also Article 8. Law of possessory titles of 10 Rab-el-akhin 1293 (Fisher p.77).

On 1st October 1920 an Ordinance entitled the "Mahlul Land Ordinance" was issued which announced that all miri land that had become mahlul would become known in due course as a result of the (then projected) cadastral survey, and in anticipation of this required both village authorities and the parties concerned to report the illegal occupation of all such land within three months. If the cadastral survey had been suitably conducted it would, as expected, have led to the progressive discovery of all the abandoned or illegally occupied State Domain characterised under the term mahlul. Conducted as it has been, without any authoritative settlement of rights, the survey has not been in a position to fulfil this perfectly reasonable anticipation, and the Ordinance thus deprived of its real ultimate sanction of inevitable discovery has been generally ignored.

Prescription.

18. The extinction, on the one side, and the acquisition, on the other, of rights over mulk immovable property by prescription is governed by Book XIV., Articles 1660 et seq. of the Majellé. Actions claiming mulk property as true waqf are admitted for a term of thirty-six (lunar) years but not after. Actions claiming part of the Public Domain (presumably of any category) as the mulk property of another party are admitted for a term of ten years. Actions which do not concern either true waqf or the public domain are admitted for a term of fifteen years.[+]

[+] Cf. Haycraft. op cit. "Possessory titles may be obtained on proof of occupation of Mirie land for ten, or Mulk for fifteen years, provided the original occupation is not admittedly wrongful. In computing time the possession of a deceased occupier and that of his heir or heirs may be joined. A common case of such grant is when the claimant or his ancestor was a purchaser without a legal transfer in the first instance, but a mere trespasser may vindicate his right to be registered on proving his possession for the required period and resolutely refusing to admit that his original occupation was wrongful. But minority, unsoundness of mind, or absence from Cyprus may prevent the time of prescription running against the legal owner so long as such disability exists."

- 26 -

The extinction and acquisition of rights over miri and untrue waqf land appeared to be primarily governed by Articles 78 and 20 of the Land Code as interpreted by Article 8 of the Regulations as to Title deeds of 7 Sha'ban 1276 (1859 A.D.), and a ruling of the Ottoman Court of Cassatun.[+]

Anyone who can prove a right of usufructuary possession of miri or untrue waqf land acquired by succession, purchase or transfer from some party entitled to transfer, and has continuously occupied and cultivated such land for ten years without dispute acquires the right prescriptively, even if he held no title deed. And anyone who has occupied and cultivated such land for ten years without dispute and cannot prove rightful possession originally may acquire such possession by payment of the Land Registry value (Tapu-i-misl). Failing regularization of the ten years occupancy by registration the prescriptive claims lapse in both cases.

If any party having rights over miri (or untrue waqf land) allow such land to be occupied by another party for ten years without claim or valid excuse, no suit for the restoration of such rights is allowed unless the occupant admits that he took possession of the land wrongfully.

It, therefore, appears that while rights over miri may be extinguished by undisputed adverse possession for ten years by a third party no purely prescriptive acquisition of rights over immovable State property is recognized at all.[x]

[+] v. Land Code Arts 20-23 and 78, 79, and Regulations mentioned.

v. Young, pp.50-52 and 87, Fisher pp. 8-11, and Translations of Turkish Laws, pp.11 and 12, regarding the right of occupancy in the case of Miri and Waqf lands.

[x] v. also the "Mahlul Land Ordinance 1920" and the "Mewat Lands Ordinance 1921."

Expropriation for public purposes.

17. Rights over any immovable property, including true waqf, may be expropriated for purposes of public utility: but owing to my not having been able to get hold of the text of some of the relevant documents and to ambiguous citation of dates, I am not clear as to the powers now vested in government and the procedure followed in this connection.

Young, who published in 1905, only gives the text of the Ottoman law of 21 Jemad-el-Awal 1296 (15 May, 1879) on the subject,[+] and references to Article 1216 of the Majellé and Article 278 of the Ottoman Commercial Code of 18 Ramazan 1266 (1850).

On 20 May 1919 the Chief Administrator of Occupied Enemy Territory (South Palestine) issued a Public Notice under martial law applying the Ottoman Law of Expropriation of 21 December 1329, when it was necessary to expropriate land for a public purpose, subject to minor adjustments. The 21 December 1329 presumably corresponds to 21 December 1911 A.D. and to about 30 Zu'l Hegga 1329 A.H.[x]

Provision was subsequently made under the "Antiquities Ordinance", published in October 1920, for the expropriation of historical sites; under the "Acquisition of Land for the Army Ordinance", published on 21 September 1920 for the expropriation of any land required for the permanent use of the Army; and under the "Town Planning Ordinance 1921"[x] for the expropriation of any land needed for town planning schemes.

On 13th February 1924 the "Expropriation of Land Ordinance" No.5 of that year was issued. It took cognizance of

---

[+] Young, vi.130.

[x] No copy of text so far available.

the Public Notice mentioned above but excluded from its restriction the purposes for which land might be expropriated outside Municipal areas; and it maintained in force Section 1 of the Ottoman Law of Expropriation of 21 Jamad-el-Awal 1296 as amended by the law of the 17 Nisan 1330[+] with regard to the purposes of such expropriation. Subject to the provisions of the "Acquisition of Land for the Army Ordinance" and the "Town Planning Ordinance" it prescribed the application of the Ottoman Law of the 7th. Rabi-el-Awal 1332 (circa 3rd. February 1914) as amended by the said Public Notice to expropriation for all purposes.

As the only Ottoman law mentioned in this Public Notice is that cited as dated 21st. December 1329[x] there appears to be some ambiguity here. From the notes of the Director of Lands I conclude that the reference in both cases is to the Ottoman Municipal Law of Expropriation of 21 Kanun Tani 1329. He also refers to the Law of Expropriation for public purposes of 24 Tishrin Tani 1295[+] as being in force.

18. **Mortgage.**

Prior to 1913 the Ottoman codes appear to have recognised the pawn or pledge both of mulk property and of rights over miri and waqf land, but not mortgage. Book V. of the Majelle treats of pawn or pledge (rehin) and Articles 711 and 724 instance the pledging of (mulk) land.[++] When it

---

[+] No copy of text so far available.

[x] Both in "Proclamations etc. issued by O.E.T.A. (South)" p.33 (Oriental Advertising Co., Cairo, 1920) and in "Ordinances, etc. issued by the Military Authorities and the Government of Palestine prior to January 1921", p.97. (Goldberg's Press, Jerusalem.)

[++] v. also Art.18 law of registration of mulk immovable property of 28 Rejab 1291 (10th. Sept. 1874).

- 29 -

was desired to utilize rights over miri or waqf land as security for a debt the system of transfer or sale with right of redemption (feragh bil wafa or bei bil wafa) were commonly resorted to.[+]

On 1 Rabi'-el-Tani 1331 (10th. March 1913) the Ottoman Government published a provisional law for the mortgage of immovable property[x]. This law is applied in Palestine subject to the provisions of the "Transfer of Land Ordinance 1920", of the Transfer of Land Amendment Ordinance 1921,[++] of the Mortgage Law Amendment Ordinance 1920, and of the Ottoman Law of the 9th. Rejah 1304 (3rd. April 1887) fixing the maximum legal rate of interest at 9%.[xx] The "Usurious Loans (evidence) Ordinance 1923" was designed to facilitate convictions under the last named.

The Land Transfer Ordinance provides that a mortgage is not valid until the provisions of that Ordinance are complied with. These provisions require the previous consent of the Administration to the mortgage; the execution of a deed in accordance with prescribed rules, and the registration of such deed: but no mortgage may be registered that does not comply with the terms of the provisional Ottoman law mentioned above as duly amended.

[+] v. Art.116-119 Land Code.
Art.25-30 Tapu Law.

[x] Translation of Turkish Laws, p.5.

[++] Cited as the "Transfer of Land Amendment Ordinance, No.2., 1921", apparently erroneously as I am advised there was only one.

[xx] Young, iv. 38. Translations of Turkish Laws, p.3.

The "Mortgage Law Amendment Ordinance 1920" requires any person who wishes to make immovable property security for a debt to do so in accordance with the provisions of the Land Transfer Ordinance. This implicitly prohibits resort to the customary methods of transfer or sale with right of redemption mentioned above. The motives which caused this prohibition are explained in a "Note on the law of mortgage" which was published with the Mortgage Law Amendment Ordinance.

19. Leases.

The lease of immovable mulk property appears to be governed by Book II. of the Majellé more particularly Articles 484-543. The lease of rights over miri (and presumably untrue waqf) by the holder and by the State are both recognized in the Land Code.[+] The Imperial Iradé of 28 Jamad-el-Awal 1299 (17th. April 1882) on the leasing of immovable property as amended by the Ottoman provisional law of 18 Rabi-el-Awal 1332 (14th.February 1914) is applied to govern leases of such rights. Leases of property within Municipal areas must be registered with the municipality.

20. Corporate bodies.

Under Article 8 of the "Transfer of Land Ordinance 1920" the acquisition and holding of rights over immovable property by corporate bodies is governed by the provisional Ottoman law of 22 Rabi'-el-Awal 1331 (2nd.March 1913) on the subject, which appears from Article 5 to have applied to mulk as well as to other rights. Such bodies, other than Departments of State and Municipalities, must be in possession of a certificate of incorporation either from the Registrar of Companies in accordance with the Companies Ordinance, the Co-operative

----

[+] v. Arts. 8 and 78 Land Code.

Societies Ordinance, the Credit Banks Ordinance[+] or a certificate of registration issued by the District Governor in accordance with the Ottoman Law of 3rd.August 1325[x] requiring the notification of political and philanthropic societies and clubs to Government.

Corporate bodies desiring to acquire or deal otherwise with immovable property must obtain the consent of the Director of Lands under the "Transfer of Land Ordinance 1920" and the "Transfer of Land Amendment Ordinance 1921."

A special tax is payable by corporate bodies on properties owned by them in lieu of the normal succession dues.[++]

[+] So far as I have been able to trace them in the publications available the dates of these three Ordinances are 1921, 1920 and 1920 respectively, but as references cited to me give the dates as 1920, 1921 and 1922 there may be some mistake in the former dates.

[x] So cited in Public Notice of 26th.August 1919 by the Chief Administrator applying and amending the said law.
? 3 August 1325 = 3rd.August 1907 = 23 Jemad-el-Akhera 1325.

[++] v.Public Notice Official Gazette No.84 of 1st.February 1923 (unverified reference).

21. **Customary tenures, Mudawara or Jiftlik and Mesha'.**

Having briefly reviewed the five forms of legally recognised land tenure it is necessary to consider two current developments which occur widely and where they occur mask, and even tend to extinguish, the underlying basic land tenure. These are the existence of landed estates known as Mudawara or Jiftlik lands previously in the possession of the Sultan, and of the system of holding and working land known as Mesha'.

Mudawara lands are, I understand, lands originally in private possession which were "turned over" to the possession of the sovereign, in this connection Abdel Hamid II. It seems that at one time this Sultan was keen on being a good farmer and landlord, and that the peasantry in various parts of Palestine recognising the better regime then prevailing on the Sultan's private estates applied that the land they held and cultivated on miri tenure should be thus "turned over" to him.

Jiftlik or chiftlik in law means a tract of land requiring a yoke of oxen to work it, which is cultivated and harvested every year. Ordinarily it means the whole outfit or plant of a farm, the land, the buildings, the stock, the implements etc. It has thence in Palestine come in specific use to mean the landed estates farmed by the Sultan.

The Turkish Constitutional Government established in 1908 treated all such estates as simple domain of the State and leased them out to cultivators subject to the payment of an annual rent equivalent to 10% of the gross production paid in addition to the regular tithe and other taxes. Since the British Occupation the Palestine Government has normally done the same although in the Beisan District, as noted elsewhere, a special agreement is being carried out which transfers (or retransfers) on miri tenure a large estate of this

- 33 -

character[+] to established tenant cultivators.

I do not know whether any of the Sultan's personal estates can be shown to have been mulk, but in the absence of properly constituted change of tenure at the time the estates "turned over" at the request of the peasants no doubt retained their miri character. But this point seems merely of historical interest now, since all personal rights previously possessed by the Sultan in any of these estates have lapsed to the State and the raqaba must at present vest in it absolutely whether such estate was previously owned by the Sultan as mulk or simply exploited as miri. And it is emphasised in the Beisan Agreement beyond any risk of ambiguity that the land that is being distributed to tenant cultivators thereunder is transferred on miri tenure, which is the point of practical importance.

22. The Mesha system was the subject of enquiry by a strong Commission who in 1923 submitted an admirable report on it to Government. The essence of this system, to adapt the definition of the Commission, is that land possessed by a corporate body, usually a village, is temporarily partitioned for purposes of cultivation among the individual members of that body subject to the condition that fresh partitions shall be made at regular intervals.

The constitution of the parent body or the basis on which the land is periodically divided varies. Thus sometimes the shares (sahm, asham) are held by the heirs of long bygone holders the origin of whose rights have been forgotten. In other cases village clans (hamuli, hamail) share the mesha' and subdivide it again among their members: in others the mesha' shares are periodically re-apportioned among the males

----
[+] which was managed from Beisan and covered twenty-two villages or tribal groups. v. Schedule to the Agreement published in the Official Gazette, No.59 of 15th, January 1922.

of the community at the moment (Zakur): in others the shares are divided among the holders of plough oxen; and there are yet further varieties. Moreover it is customary for the tenant cultivation of the State lands previously in the private possession of the Sultan, which have just been mentioned, to be periodically re-allotted for cultivation on the mesha' principle.

It is unnecessary here to enter into the periods or systems of allotment which also vary widely; but it may be as well to note that the term mesha' is also loosely used to denote the co-operative holding and working of fractional shares under the ordinary laws of inheritance or partnership. This is a fundamentally different thing and the application of the term mesha' to it is confusing.

The Commission after an investigation, as evidently sympathetic as painstaking, recommended unanimously and strongly that land held under the mesha' system should be permanently partitioned, or in other words that the system should be gradually abolished. The Government were not entirely satisfied and the question was one of these that I was particularly asked to consider. I expressed in December,1923 and now confirm my entire agreement with the Commission. There is no doubt that the system is a most, probably the most, serious handicap on the economic development of the country and the improvement of the position of the peasantry. There is also no doubt that the few advantages claimed for it – stimulation of co-operation, and a tendency to prevent alienation of the land and subjection of the villagers to outsiders – are illusory. The mesha' system is in no sense co-operative; while there is ample evidence to show that it has not prevented the alienation of village land. The accompanying table embodying information on this subject supplied by the Governor of the Southern

– 35 –

TABLE I. showing alienation of land held in Mesha' in the Southern District.

Information supplied by the Governor, December, 1924.

Village	Approx. Share held by absentee landlords.	Village	Approx. Share held by absentee landlords.
Julis	2/3	Burair	1/20.
Sawafir Gharbi	1/15	Hulaiqat	Little.
Sawafir Sharqi	1/15	Kaukaba	"
" Shamali	1/15	Beit Tima	-
Bait Daras	1/20	Barbara	1/4
Batani Gharbi	1/4	Majdal	Little.
" Sharqi	1/5	Ne'lia	1/4
Burka	3/4	Khussas	1/4
Yasur	1/2	Jora	1/2
Katra Islam	1/20	Hamama	Little.
Maghar	1/5	Jaldiyeh	1/4
Bashit	Very little.	Bait Affa	-
Yebna	" "	Ibdis	-
Masmiya Kabira	--	Iraq Sudan	1/20
Masmiya Saghira	--	Keratiyeh	-
Kustina	1/2	Hatta	1/30
Tal Turmus	1/20	Jseir	1/4
Ba'lin	1/20	Faluja	1/10
Summail	1/5	Araq Manshieh	1/20
Nazleh	1/20	Sukrair	-
Bait Lahia	1/3	Rafah	-
Herbia	1/10	Khan Yunes	-
Dair Seneid	Little.	Deir Balah	1/10
Bait Hanun	1/4	Muharraqa	State Domain.
Dumra	1/3	Kaufakha	-
Beni Seila	-	Huj	1/10
Abasan	-	Jabalia	1/4
Jiyeh	1/3	Esdud	1/8
Nejd	1/10		
Sumsum	1/4		

District alone appears conclusive on this point. It shows that the mesha' shares originally held entirely by members of local communities have been largely bought up by absentee landlords throughout a wide area. And I understand that when this occurs the original shareholders commonly become the employees of the purchasers and largely at their mercy, since there is no obligation to employ them, while refusal to accept the absentee landlord's terms usually involves the previous landowner being driven to casual labour and perhaps having to leave his village. Instances from other districts could also be given. The mesha' system is thus demonstrated as no protection against the alienation by the peasantry of their land: on the contrary it is, I think, clear that it facilitates rather than prevents such alienation owing to the severe handicap it imposes upon decent cultivation and upon the development of personal ties with the land, and to the hand to mouth existence thereby fostered. The constant redivision of mesha' is also a fruitful and even present cause of intrigue and quarrel (fasad) and consequent public insecurity in the villages concerned.

23. But it is self evident that shifting occupation of land and good husbandry are incompatible. A temporary occupant will aim at extracting all he can from the land and will put nothing into it. He will exploit and impoverish it but will not develop it. He cannot effect permanent improvements, such as the erection of buildings and fences, the planting of trees etc., as he himself will move before he gets a return from them and has little prospect of being compensated for his outlay by his successor.

When mesha' land is permanently partitioned and passes definitely into a man's possession he can take longer views and is naturally stimulated to do all he can to increase

- 37 -

its productivity. The permanent allotment of mesha' does not, of course, either invariably or at once convert bad husbandmen into good, but it introduces conditions previously lacking without which good husbandry cannot reasonably be expected.

The Mesha' Commission while careful to point out the speculative nature of any attempt to estimate the amount of land held and worked on the mesha' system, owing to the lack of all reliable statistics, deduced from special enquiries that more than half of the cultivable land in Palestine (Cis Jordan) was mesha'.

It is in any case certain that the prevalence of the mesha' system is widespread, that it constitutes a handicap of the gravest kind on the economic development of the land, and that its supposed social and protective advantages are illusory. I am also satisfied that its abolition is widely desired by the people, that the progressive elements among them look to Government, but cannot themselves as a rule supply the initiative to carry it out, and that the conversion of those who doubt or hesitate can be safely left to time and the experience of their neighbours of the general policy of partition is adopted and patiently and considerately pursued.

Such partition would form a natural and regular part of a national settlement of title and other rights and will be considered later in connection with it.

24. As already emphasized even when statistics relating to the land in Palestine can be compiled they are so unreliable that it is useless to seek evidence from them as to the increase in productivity that may be expected after mesha' land has been partitioned. Devoid therefore of weight on this account and because the cases reported are too few it is yet interesting to find that the average tithe paid on

nine plots in the Ramleh District is returned as having been 15 piastres per donum when the land was mesha' and 108 piastres per donum last year after it had been partitioned.

And while no body of reliable statistical evidence on the subject is likely as yet to be found, there are a considerable number of competent and trustworthy observers who concur that the economic development to be expected to follow permanent partition of mesha' is ocularly demonstrated as a rule to have occurred when such a partition has already been effected. It is, however, upon intelligent consideration of the whole range of agricultural development generally and the inherent factors of the case that the decision of the Government must really be based.

I venture to suggest that the grounds for judgment on a matter of public policy are rarely so clear and compelling, and that the responsibility incurred by continued acquiescence in a system which is a palpable drag upon the economic establishment of a great mass of the Palestinian peasantry and upon the financial position of the State is inescapable and more open to misconstruction than the most ill judged attempts to reform it.

But there now exists a considerable body of information and experience which should enable partition to be carried out with knowledge and good judgment if it is patiently conducted as part of the general settlement of all rights. Moreover in mitigation of the fears of doubters it may be remembered that the absence of proof of mulk rights, which are exceptional, the raqaba or real ownership of all land in Palestine is vested in the State, that the State has a definite right to intervene if possession is abused or ineffective, and that the reinforcement of such right to the extent necessary to secure the partition of mesha' would be quite in accord with existing principles and need not be in the least drastic.

25. Joint ownership is dealt with in Book X. of the Majelle and partition of property so held in Articles 1114 to 1191. falling within that book: but presumably this properly applies to mulk property personal and real. Under the Land Code miri land held in shares shall be partitioned by lot in accordance with the provisions of the Religious Law[+] or in any other equitable manner, if demanded by one or more of the co-possessors provided that subdivision is not carried out to an uneconomic degree.[x] A law issued provisionally by Imperial Irade on the 14 Muharram 1332 (13th. December 1913)[++] was intended further to facilitate the partition of land held in common under tenure. Under both the Majelle and the provisional law partition may be effected either voluntarily or compulsorily by a magistrate's order. Under neither alternative is the existing law effective because of the difficulty in the first case of securing agreement among all the shareholders and in the second of citing them as parties to the action.

New legislation consequently appears necessary to enable land held jointly in mesha' or otherwise to be permanently partitioned when desirable. Such legislation should embody effective means to partition jointly held immovable property upon the application of any shareholder and also secure power to Government to order such partition in the case of miri or other State land if this be considered advisable in the public interest. Such measures should sufficiently remedy the present impotence of the law while conforming in spirit fully to

[+] v. Art.1151 Majelle.
[x] Arts.15-18 Land Code.
[++] Translations of Turkish Laws, p.9.

the general underlying conceptions of the Ottoman Land Code and of the provisional law of partition.

Although it is essential for Government to secure and have in reserve power to order the permanent partition of land held in mesha', there should be little if any need actually to exercise this power if such partition is made part of the general land settlement and is conducted with knowledge, consideration and judgment. Given patience the benefits of partition will come home to all but the most narrow-minded or recalcitrant, while those who favour the maintenance of an undesirable system from interested motives will find public opinion increasingly concentrating against them as the fruits of partition appear and develop.

28. <u>Succession and sub-division of land</u>.

The laws governing the succession to or inheritance of rights over immovable property, and the administration of these laws are factors of the first importance in the operation of any system of land tenure. The character and administration of such laws in Palestine must, therefore, be briefly reviewed.

Following the normal differentiation the regular position under Ottoman law appears broadly to have been that succession to mulk property, movable and immovable, was governed entirely by Muslim Religious Law administered by the Mekhema Shar'ia or Muslim Religious Courts, while succession to rights over miri or untrue waqf property[+], of which the raqaba is vested in the State, was governed by the Civil Law administered by the Civil Courts.

Inheritance ab intestat is a fundamental basis of Ottoman succession, the distribution of inheritance of mulk and other rights being respectively defined minutely although differently by the Religious and the Civil Law. Testamentary disposition is restricted to a third of the testator's mulk property and must not be in favour of any legal heir.[x] Testamentary disposition of miri and untrue waqf rights is invalid. Inheritance of such rights was required to be wholly and strictly in accordance with the table of succession laid down by the civil law, with reversion to the State as ultimate owner in the event of failure of heirs.

[+]"Arazi miri ve mevqufé" rendered by Young as "Domaine public"", and by Fisher as "State Land". True waqf which is essentially mulk and regulated by Religious Law and was apparently not even administered by the Ottoman Ministry of Waqfs (v.Barron op.cit. p.17) is evidently not included in this term.

[x]v. Young I. 307 inter alia.

Prior to 1913 succession to miri and untrue waqf rights was governed by the laws of 17 Moharrem 1284 (May 1867) and 4 Rejab 1292 (August 1875) on the subject.[+] On the 3 Rah el Awal 1331 (11th. February 1913) a new provisional law regulating the inheritance of such rights was published.[x] On 23rd. of Zu'l Qi'da 1332 (14th. October 1914) a provisional law purporting to regulate the respective provinces of the Religious and Civil Courts was published, which also appears relevant.[++]

Under Ottoman rule the succession of Christians and foreigners to mulk property seems broadly to have been governed by the laws of the particular communities or nations concerned as administered by their respective ecclesiastical or consular courts.[xx] The acquisition of mulk rights over immovable property in Ottoman territory by foreigners was doubtless difficult, but appears to have not infrequently been obtained through wives or relations who passed as Ottoman subjects, through the practice of dummy nominees (nam mustaar), or through carelessness, inadvertence or favour.

The succession of Christians and foreigners to miri and untrue waqf rights appears to have been strictly governed by the Ottoman Civil Laws on the subject for the time being[+++]

[+] v. Young I. pp.318 et seq.

[x] v. Translations of Turkish Laws, p.4., and Fisher, p.78, where the law is differently dated.

[++] v. Translations of Turkish Laws, p.1.

[xx] v. Young, p.321 et seq.

[+++] "La succession proprement dite n'existe que pour les immeubles 'mulk' qui font seuls partie du 'tereke' avec les meubles, etc. Les immeubles 'vakoufs' et 'miri' sont réglés par des dispositions spéciales applicables a tout sujet Ottoman ainsi qu'aux étrangers." Young I. 326.

- 43 -

which have just been mentioned.

27. By the Palestine Order in Council of 10th. August 1922 it was laid down that, subject to certain limitations, jurisdiction in matters of personal status should be exercised by the Courts of various religious communities. The definition of personal status for the purpose included guardianship, inhibition from dealing with property, successions, wills and legacies and the administration of the property of absent persons.+

In application and extension of the above the "Succession Ordinance 1923" was published on 8th. of March of that year. The object of this Ordinance as defined in the preamble is "to make provision for the succession on death to persons in cases where the Courts of the Religious Communities do not exercise such jurisdiction and otherwise to provide for the succession to persons dying possessed of immovable or movable property in Palestine."

Exclusive jurisdiction under the Ordinance rests with the Civil District Courts in all matters relating to the succession to, and the confirmation of wills of, Palestinians; provided that they are not at their deaths either Muslims or members of certain specified religious communities (Art.1.).[x]

+v. Order in Council Arts. 51 et seq.

[x] As specified in a schedule annexed to the Ordinance these were the Eastern (Orthodox), the Latin (Catholic), the Gregorian Armenian, the Armenian (Catholic), the Syrian (Catholic), the Chaldean (Uniate) and the Jewish communities. To these the Greek Catholic Melkite community was added by Order dated 10th. August 1923.

Under Article 51 of the Order in Council mentioned inclusive jurisdiction in matters of personal status shall, subject to certain limitations, be exercised by the Courts of the religious communities established and exercising jurisdiction at the date of that Order. Under Article 1 of the Succession Ordinance the communities authorized to exercise this privilege are, or may from time to time be, specified by the High Commissioner. The latter suggests power to extend the privilege, while the Order-in-Council seems definitely to limit it to communities actually exercising it on 10th.August 1922.

Exclusive jurisdiction in matters relating to succession of those who at the time of their deaths are (Sunni) Muslims was conferred on the Muslim Religious Courts (Art.4). Concurrent jurisdiction was conferred on the Civil District Court and the Religious Courts of any of the specified communities in regard to succession of any person who died a member of such community (Art.1.iii). When all the heirs agree any of the specified religious courts may grant a certificate of succession in the case of a member of that particular community.

28. The succession to mulk property of deceased Muslims, therefore, continues as previously to be governed by Muslim Religious Law administered by the Muslim Religious Courts.

The succession to the mulk property (inter alia) of a deceased Palestinian who at death was not a member of one of the specified religious communities (nor a Muslim) is, subject to any testamentary disposition made by the deceased, governed by a translation of the relevant articles of the Ottoman provisional law of 3 Rabi-el-Awal 1331 relating to the inheritance of immovable property, which is annexed as Schedule II. to the Ordinance (Art.2.ii.)

The succession to the mulk property of a deceased member of one of the specified religious communities is governed by the testamentary dispositions of the deceased, subject to any restrictions upon the power of such disposition and any devotion of such property to beneficial ends imposed by the law of that particular community. In default of testamentary disposition, or in so far as it is inadequate, the provisions of Schedule II. operate (Art.9).

If this schedule is consulted it will be seen that the provisional Ottoman law related only to the inheritance of miri and untrue waqf property.† By the Ordinance it was also applied to mulk property under the conditions and to the extent mentioned.

All succession to miri and untrue waqf rights is determined exclusively by the provisions of the said Schedule II., and all Courts having jurisdiction in matters of succession must conform thereto (Art.19). All wills purporting to dispose of such rights are invalid.

29. In thus treating immovable property other than mulk as subject entirely to the Civil law of the State on the matter, and requiring general and uniform compliance therewith from everyone, the Succession Ordinance maintains the consistent fundamental differentiation of Ottoman law between mulk property, which is the holder's own to do as he will with subject to the dictates of the moral code as embodied in religious law, and miri or State property of which usufructuary rights alone are conditionally acquired and may be transmitted to others.

I also understand the Ordinance to place the administration of the civil law of succession to miri rights within the jurisdiction of the various religious courts to exactly the same degree as succession to mulk property which is governed either exclusively or largely by the religious law of the various communities. This is presumably in conformity with Article 51 of the Order in Council.

The Ottoman provisional law regulating the respective provinces of the Religious and Civil Courts referred to a few pages earlier places the "possession, transfer and partition

---

†Article 1 reads: "On the death of a person, the Miri and Waqf land held by him are transferred to a person or persons according to the following degrees . . ." Article 7 and last of the schedule: "The provisions of the foregoing articles apply also to (untrue) waqf musaqqafat and mustaghilat ......"

of immovable property" within the jurisdiction of the Civil Courts and the hearing of "suits to decide the shares of heirs to movable and immovable property in accordance with the laws pertaining thereto and the Shara' procedure" within that of the Religious Courts. This line of demarcation would seem difficult to observe strictly.

30. In the case of foreigners who are not Muslims, jurisdiction in matters of succession lies exclusively with the Civil District Court (Art.1.ii),, but this Court may under certain conditions and limitations refer some questions to an appropriate Religious Court (Art.3).

Succession to foreigners who are Sunni Muslims lies within the jurisdiction of the regular Muslim Religious Court. A special Muslim Court may be constituted to deal with succession to foreigners who are Muslims of other rites (Art.4.ii).

Succession to mulk property of foreigners (other than Muslims) is distributed in accordance with the national law of the deceased subject to certain limitations (Art.2.iii). Succession to miri or untrue waqf rights held by foreigners, whether Muslims or otherwise, is in conformity with Schedule II. to the Ordinance as in all other cases. (Art.19).

The term foreigner is defined in Article 59 of the Order-in-Council of 10th. August 1922.

31. The legal determination of succession of rights to immovable property has hitherto been attended by too much difficulty, delay and expense to have been generally effected. This cause alone would have been sufficient to produce the widespread confusion in, and lack of authoritative knowledge of, such rights prevalent in Palestine. In the absence of effective, prompt and reasonably cheap means of determining such succession authoritatively the most intelligent, careful

and systematic attempt to register rights over immovable property is bound to fail. At present it is notorious that persons long dead continue widely to figure in the Land Register as existing holders of rights because the subsequent passage of the rights held in the past by them has never been authoritatively determined.

If a reliable and authoritative record of rights to immovable property in Palestine, with its attendant security of tenure, liquidation of the capital value of the land, abolition of litigation and stimulation of economic development is to be successfully established, the procedure for granting certificates of succession upon the decease of holders must as far as possible be made automatic, inescapable, prompt, uniform and cheap. There should be no insuperable, or even serious difficulty about this; and if the need is carefully explained and the Government's intentions made clear, the necessary cooperation from the various communities should with patience be won, if only because the members of the communities who do cooperate will be able so much more securely and easily to succeed to, hold and benefit from rights over immovable property acquired by succession.

32. The partition of immovable property upon succession is carried out theoretically and recorded in Palestine at present to an extent which is entirely devoid of sense or practical meaning, as is sufficiently shown by a few examples extracted from the Land Registers given in the accompanying Table II. Fear is expressed that even if the system of Land Registration is placed upon a sound basis, meaningless subdivision of this nature will steadily operate to reduce it again to a farce. The short answer to this is that the Torrens system of Land Registration is amply flexible enough to record without difficulty or confusion all actually operative facts whether in respect

- 48 -

of the subdivision of immovable property or of participation in privileges or rights; but no system can incorporate fairy tales with its facts and yet be a dependable or for long even a comprehensible record. It is evident that the limit of operative partition, whether of land or of its production, is arrived at long before ridiculous fractions such as those given in the accompanying table are reached; and it is the subdivision that is actually effected, not impracticable flights of the imagination, that it should be the function of the Land Register to record.

In Book X. of the Majellé dealing with joint ownership and partition the Ottoman legislator appears to have had a clear appreciation of the necessity of confining partition to practicable and concrete limits. This limitation is of such outstanding importance that a few extracts from the Articles bearing particularly on this point should perhaps be included here.

Joint ownership is the state in which a thing is common property whether from sale, gift, will, succession, or arrangement (Art.1030).

Compulsory joint ownership is that due to causes other than the act of the joint owners: e.g. by involuntary merger or by succession (Art.1084).

Joint ownership may exist either of actual property or of claims (Art.1066). The former is that which pertains to a definite piece of property, such as a flock of sheep owned by two persons (Art.1067); the latter occurs when persons are joint creditors (Art.1068).

Partition is separation into distinct undivided parts. This is effected by measurement of volume, area or weight (Art.1114). The thing to be partitioned must have definite entity (doit être un corps certain) (Art.1123). Partition is not valid if the parts are not separate and distinct (Art.

1148). Lands and building sites are partitioned by measurement, but buildings and trees situated thereon by value (Art.1148).†

If these principles are acted upon there should be no difficulty in recording shareholding and partition, and no danger of regrowth of confusion after a settlement has been effected and a sound system of land registration is in operation.

In Egypt where the majority of the land is in private mulk ownership of Muslims the danger of an impracticable subdivision of land upon repeated succession has not appeared. The property survey of the province of Minufiya now in progress shows almost identically the same subdivision of property as existed twenty-five years ago when the first property survey of the province was made. This province is the most populous, the most fertile and the most closely divided in Egypt, and if an impracticable subdivision has not occurred in this area it need not be feared anywhere: always provided that actually operative and valid subdivision is alone recognised and recorded.

Recent experience of the reform of Land Registration in course of introduction by the Egyptian Government fully confirms this conclusion. In no case has partition in practice been found to have been carried to a stage which rendered it difficult either to record or to operate. Sale, exchange or other arrangement has been found invariably to have taken place before this limit has been reached.

So long as the Land Register remains for the most part an unreliable and incomprehensible record not wedded to fact, the theoretical subdivision of property by ever growing

----

† v. Young I. 317 et seq. and Grigsby op. cit.

fractions may be expected to continue: if the records are
made and kept consonant with fact and become authoritative
in reality as well as in theory no difficulty need be appre-
hended from the continuance of impracticable and fanciful
subdivisions of property.

TABLE II. Showing extreme theoretical subdivision of property registered.

Deed.	Character of property.	Situation	Area in dunums.	Share registered.
1155/23	Miri Olive Orchard	Ramleh	41.	$\frac{2,513,510}{111,476,736}$
1143/23	Mulk land and house	Jaffa	15.	$\frac{440,335}{5,159,184}$
1057/23	Mulk land and courtyard	Jaffa	30.	$\frac{165,990,960}{4,269,957,120}$
1004/23	Miri plain land	Sarafand	400.	$\frac{329,595}{93,123,120}$
930/23	Miri land with shop on it	Jaffa	$\frac{1}{18}$	$\frac{1,040,544}{25,873,528}$
911/23	Mulk house and shop	Ramleh	$\frac{7}{80}$	$\frac{594,544}{5,225,472}$
899/23	House on mulk land	Jaffa	$\frac{1}{9}$	$\frac{3,823,390}{18,083,360}$
887/23	Miri Olive Orchard	Ramleh	26	$\frac{8,781,030,680}{632,073,093,130}$
1269/23	Mulk plain land	Jaffa	$\frac{1}{8}$	$\frac{46,298,235}{49,763,400}$
1324/23	Two rooms mulk	Jaffa	$\frac{1}{5}$	$\frac{732,430}{1,006,020}$
1340/23	Miri plain land	Wad Hunein	400	$\frac{11,979\frac{1}{2}}{3,123,120}$
1481/23	Miri plain land	Ramleh	24	$\frac{16,634,475}{291,133,440}$
1479/23	Mulk Orchard	Jaffa	20	$\frac{11,156,504,328}{32,899,842,560}$
1482/23	Miri plain land	Ramleh	26	$\frac{16,634,475}{291,133,440}$
23/24	Haski Sultan waqf plain land	Yahudiya	5859	$\frac{9,340}{17,852,298}$

33.   A clear distinction must, however, be made between practicable and economic subdivision of rights over land. It is quite practicable to subdivide land to an extent which is most detrimental economically although it can be readily individualized and recorded. This has unquestionably happened to a most serious extent throughout Palestine, and it is one of the factors in the economic situation of the country calling for corrective measures as soon as possible.

In the case of Muslims succession to a deceased person's estate legally involves subdivision each time that it occurs whether by the distribution of mulk property under the Muslim Religious Law or of miri and untrue waqf holdings under Schedule II. of the Succession Ordinance 1922. In the case of other communities mulk property may escape subdivision but miri, as already noted, must follow the common law.

Consistently applied in the absence of adequate compensatory correctives the operation of these laws tend to reduce land throughout the country to masses of minute holdings perfectly capable of individual record but quite incapable of economic cultivation. Among its other evils the mesha' system tends to promote and perpetuate this disastrously excessive subdivision: since in the usual course each shareholder, initially, and each successor to each shareholder subsequently, has a right to and demands an apportionment of his total share throughout every quality and every location of the village lands affected. He must have a portion in the area nearest the village and most remote from the village, in the best arable land and in the worst arable land, in the highland and in the lowland, near the water and far from the water, and in every intermediate stage between these.

Much time and labour is wasted by cultivators in carrying their implements each day from the village to their lands, sometimes an hour or so away. Lack of security is not the determining factor as many cultivators now live out in their vineyards during the summer months. One reason is that in hill country where springs are scarce cultivators must water their animals at the most convenient spring and cannot live far from it. The chief reason, however, I understand, is because individual holdings are so scattered that in practice the village itself is the central site for every cultivator.

As an example of the extent to which such uneconomic subdivision is actually carried may be instanced the case of a Ramallah farmer who is officially reported to hold 300 dunums (circa 68 acres or 28 hectares) distributed in 270 scattered plots.

34. Such extreme and uneconomic subdivision of land is not confined to Palestine. For example in Switzerland, a country to a considerable extent topographically analogous, it is a matter of most serious concern to the Federal Government and is being attacked, as I recommend that it should be in Palestine, in connection with the execution of the cadastral survey and the establishment of registration of title to land. The Swiss are an eminently practical people and the question is of such moment to Palestine that it may be useful to quote some extracts from a communication of the Swiss Federal Council to the Cantonal Governments on the subject:-[†]

"C'est un fait connu du longue date que dans beaucoup des contrées de notre pays le haut degré du morcellement et la désagrégation de la propriété foncière en un grand nombre des petites parcelles de forme peu convenable, ainsi que le defaut de voies de communication, sont les principaux obstacles auxquels se heurte le dévellopement utile de notre agriculture.

[†]Circulaire du conseil fédéral suisse aux gouvernements canton aux concernant l'encouragement des remaniements parcellaires (du 23 mars 1918).

"On ne dira également rien de nouveau en désignant le remaniement parcellaire comme étant le moyen le plus efficace de remédier à tous les défauts de cette nature dont souffre nos terres.

La réunion parcellaire facilite l'exploitation de la terre, il en résulte une grosse économie de travail et de temps; c'est d'elle que dependent l'augmentation de la productivité et l'amelioration du crédit hypothecaire des biens fonds. Elle est donc un des moyens les plus propres à rendre notre agriculture et notre économie nationale plus prospères.

. . . . . .

"Peut-on encore trouver étrange le fait que, dans les endroits des cantons du Valais, du Tessin et autres que souffrent de cet état de (morcellement), des centaines d'hectares de sol fertile ne sont plus cultivés, et que les propriétaires desertent leurs terres, préférant emigrer et gagner leur pain en pays lointain?

"C'est un devoir imperieux de remédier à cette situation désavantageuse, parfois même intenable, en entreprenant des remaniements parcellaires.

"L'occasion se présente actuellement, dans le moment le plus propice, de faire le nécessaire avant de mettre en oeuvre la mensuration cadastrale obligatoire et avant d'etablir le registre foncier.

. . . . . .

"Malgré l'existence de bases légales suffisamment developpées pour permettre l'organisation et l'execution de remaniements parcellaires . . . ces travaux d'amelioration ne progressent que lentement dans beaucoup de contrées de notre pays. Les motifs sont de nature diverse. D'une parte la connaissance des lois y relatives n'est pas encore assez répandue dans le peuple, à cause de leur promulgation récent et, d'autre part, ces lois livrent au hasard la mise en oeuvre des remaniements parcellaires, c'est-à-dire que ces derniers dependent de l'initiative d'une majorité de proprietaires éclairés. Enfin, en maints endroits, on n'est pas encore renseigné comme il le faudrait sur la nature et l'importance de ces entreprises.

"On si l'assainissement de notre propriété foncière ne continue à progresser que dans la mesure actuelle . . . l'état defecteux actuel passera aux prochaines générations, au grand detriment de notre agriculture. Il faut éviter cela.

"La mensuration cadastrale doit servir à dessein les entreprises de réunions parcellaires dans tout le pays, les propager et les favoriser.

. . . . . .

"On peut procéder de différentes manières pour encourager l'execution de remaniements parcellaires. Avant tout, les organes techniques cantonaux devraient s'efforcer de répandre plus de clarté sur le but de ces derniers, en rendent les proprietaires de terrains très morcelés attentifs aux avantages et facilités qu'offre une propriété bien arrondie pour l'exploitation agricole, ainsi qu'aux subsides plus élèves accordés par la Confederation (pour ce remaniement) s'il était impossible d'arriver aux resultats voulus en s'en remettant à la bonne volonté, il y aurait lieu d'envisager l'adoption des prescriptions légales sur l'execution forcée des remaniements parcellaires, comme plusieurs cantons les possedent déja."

It is instructive to note that the Swiss Federal authorities attach so much importance to the grouping of holdings more economically that they propose if necessary to resort to general compulsion to obtain it. The attainment of the same object is of much greater importance to Palestine. Switzerland has other resources, including abundant water power, and if holdings are uneconomic in number, size and distribution, her land tenure is simple and secure. Palestine has no dependable economic resource other than agriculture and this is heavily and gratuitously handicapped by being widely conducted in innumerable scattered and ever shifting plots, occupied on a most uncertain and insecure tenure. On the other hand the difficulties in the way of reform are probably considerably less in Palestine, if it is recognized from the outset that it must be pursued very gradually, sympathetically and patiently. The peasantry are fully alive to the need for reform, and frankly look to British administration to bring it about, while at the same time characteristically distrustful of any change that has not commended itself to them by actual experience.

The Government of Palestine is also much better placed than the Swiss Federal Government to deal with the problem, because in Palestine it is considered the function of the Government to take such a lead and because the ownership of the vast mass of the land, although it may be heritably leased, is recognized by long standing law and custom to be vested in the State. The inherent right and duty of the latter to see that the nation's own land is properly developed and to amend the terms of tenure in the general interest is unquestioned, and is unlikely to be challenged, if considerately pursued with equitable regard for admitted rights, as part and parcel of a comprehensive national settlement of rights over the land.

- 57 -

35. **Concluding Observations.**

Apart from its general uneconomic reaction, the most remarkable thing about the current land tenure is the deep breach between existing law and actual practice. This is evidenced by the widespread and accepted disregard of the statutory obligation to register all rights over immovable property. Possibly, but improbably, one person in ten, one waqf in ten have registered their rights: and it might be hazarded with no great risk that, even if so, not a tenth of such tenth is registered in an unassailable way and with clear and unambiguous reference to the property affected.

The breach between law and practice is equally forcibly brought out by the general ignorance and disregard of the five statutory categories into which by law the land of Palestine is divided. Even in official returns I found the five statutory categories confused with each other and with mesha' which is not a legal category at all. Thus mesha' was confused with communal matruké, communal matruké with mewat, mewat with mahlul, and even mesha' mafruz (mesha' that has been partitioned) with mulk. And although mulk and miri are supposed to be clearly differentiated by taxation from the other statutory categories and from each other[+], it was not found possible to compile returns even of the land in these two categories alone.

Another example of the breach between law and practice is afforded by the impracticable and ridiculous subdivisions solemnly registered which have already been illustrated earlier in Table II. Other instances could be given but would be superfluous, as the deep breach between the law and current practice is too palpable to be questioned. Resort is, of course, had to every turn and twist of the land law in litigation or in planning inroads on the public domain: but such uses of the law are no measure of its general value.

[+]By law land tax (worko) is levied annually on mulk land at the rate of ten per thousand of the capital value, on miri at the rate of four per thousand: and tithe is levied on miri and not on mulk.

This breach between law and practice is not because the land tenure is not suitable or practicable, for it is for the most part both or can readily be made so, but because its operation is so largely based upon the statutory classification of the land and the accurate and punctual operation of the Land Registers. The failure of these basic records has reacted heavily upon the working of the whole law of which they constitute an essential part.

This basic record can only be restored now by a systematic land settlement, and only be maintained afterwards by the substitution of a sound system of Land Registration for that purporting now to be in force. It is evidently useless to undertake a settlement unless its fruits are to be maintained, and consequently the new system of Land Registration must be tested, worked out in detail and cast into legislative form as an intrinsic part of the preparations for settlement, which brings us back to the point from which I started. This should present no great difficulty when the ground has been properly cleared and the general policy of carrying out effective reform has been definitely adopted.

Concurrently and in connection with this the remainder of the land law should be carefully recast with a view firstly to simplifying and making it easier to observe and apply, and secondly to facilitate and foster the more economic distribution of holdings. Progress in the last direction must, at best, be very slow and gradual and first: and it will be particularly dependent upon the understanding, sympathy and active assistance of progressive Palestinian opinion.

38. Fundamentally there are two main classes of land in Palestine - Mulk and the Public Domain. With mulk, which may be defined as property that is privately owned whether by individuals, groups or juridical persons, should be classed its derivative true waqf, which may be properly considered to be private property dedicated as a perpetual trust by the owner.

All immovable property that is not mulk or true waqf is Public Domain. In law this is divided into three categories (a) Miri or public domain heritably leased, (b) Metruke or public domain devoted to public service, and (c) Mewat or unused and idle public domain.

There is no place in this classification for public domain that is neither heritably leased, nor in public use, nor idle, as for example State forests and mines, or other public domain directly or indirectly exploited by the State itself. The omission could be readily corrected by widening the Mewat category to include this last class of public domain, and renaming it (for example) free public domain. Mewat Jebal moubahi, and Mahlûl (other than true waqf mahlûl) would all fall under this heading conveniently. There is no advantage in maintaining a subdivision in law between utilized and unutilized free public domain. Indeed the latter should be gradually converted into the former, and no definite demarcation between them is either practicable or desirable.

A greater defect of the existing classification is the grouping together of true and untrue waqf. True waqf, as noted, is simply mulk land vested in perpetual trust and as mulk land continues to be governed by the Religious Law. Untrue or takhsessat waqf is not an affectation of the land at all, but merely the existence of a charge on its production. Land so charged maintains its miri character and continues to be governed by the provisions of the Civil Code applicable to miri land.

Waqf, whether true or untrue, is most conveniently considered, not as a category of land at all, but as a way of dealing with it: but if the retention of the term as a category of land is desired it should be strictly conferred to true waqf. All existing takhsissat waqf rights over miri land can be fully safeguarded by suitably charging the land.

The modification of the existing classification that I should suggest so as to cover the whole ground in the simplest way and with the minimum of change is as follows:-

(i). *Mulk* to be recorded as (true) waqf if so constituted.

(ii). *Miri* to be recorded as charged with a taksissat or untrue waqf appropriation when this is so.

(iii). *Matruke*. The character of the public municipal or communal use to which the land is devoted to be always recorded.

(iv). *Free Public Domain*, which it is the duty of the Government to render as productive or useful as possible in one way or another.

87. Public Domain cultivated by private enterprise under the miri tenure constitutes by far the most important part of the capital wealth of the country. The terms of miri tenure require careful revision so that, while its essential features are preserved, the utmost encouragement is given to the holders to develop the land to the greatest possible economic advantage. From the national standpoint miri tenure has three advantages over mulk. It is governed by the civil law, it cannot be converted into waqf, and if the land is not cultivated or developed its tenure is forfeited.

The wide extent and enormous economic importance, actual and potential, of the public domain make the questions of its location, custody and management of such great practical importance in the working of the land tenure in Palestine that they must be briefly touched on before conclusion. In my Note of December 1923 I suggested that, judging from the experience of Egypt, the delay in carrying out a land settlement might be expected to result in the loss to the nation of a vast aggregate area of public domain. This anticipation was emphatically

- 61 -

endorsed by the Director of Lands who at the time of writing was involved in 80 actions against encroachments or illegal claims on the public domain of which he had knowledge. These are, of course, a small proportion of the whole.[+]

When I wrote I was in a position to understand miri tenure broadly, but I had not grasped the limited extent of mulk and the specific safeguards against its creation. As I understand it now encroachment upon the public domain throughout the countryside cannot result in the loss of public ownership: but at most in the establishment of some prescriptive claim to miri tenure. Although such unregulated growth of claims to miri tenure may and do operate greatly to the public disadvantage, as for example when they intrude in a haphazard way into areas of State forest and hamper their protection and economic development, they must probably for the time being be leniently regarded in general since they can only be established when the land has been actually developed and cultivated for a considerable period, there is no loss of ultimate public ownership, and in the absence of some proof of initial right an acquisition fee has to be paid.[x]

It seems that only in towns can land be claimed as mulk property in the absence of documentary proof of its specific creation by constituted authority as such[++]; and if this is correct it is only in areas that are, or are included, within town limits that there is any real risk of loss of public ownership through failure to define and defend it in time. But the financial importance of even this more limited risk none the less seems to be great, particularly as the urban areas have tended to extend widely during the last few years

----
[+] v. Letter No.G.336 of 3 April 1924 from the Director of Lands to the Chief Secretary.

[x] v. §16 of this memorandum.

[++] v. Arts 1.ii and 121 Land Code and §9 of this Memorandum.

but are the most valuable. Thus I am advised that the loss of such public ownership in Haifa, of a character for the most part financially liquid and realizable, is to be assessed at a very high figure. In view of Palestine's heavy capital obligations it is clearly advisable to close the door as promptly as possible to such illicit drains on her capital resources. This suggests the advisability of pressing forward land settlement in the principal towns at as early a date as possible.

It is I know argued that the loss of public domain is really no bad thing since, however illegitimately, it results in the transfer of land from the paralysing hold of the State to hands in which it will fructify. The basis of the argument is weak since there is probably as much neglected land in private as in public hands in Palestine: nor if called upon to explain losses of public domain could the Government seriously claim that it wittingly condoned theft of public domain in a larger public interest.

The public domain is, of course, just as much a part of the assets of the nation as the Government's buildings, plant and stores, and even as the very funds in the Treasury. Laxity in safeguarding the public domain is only more defensible than laxity in safeguarding these other assets to the extent that it is unavoidably more difficult. It is perfectly true that land may be developed to greater advantage in private hands: but the same may be held of other public property, for example the State Railways. In both cases there are open and legitimate means of bringing such a transfer about if it was judged to be desirable without entailing any surreptitious sacrifice of the capital value of the property.

The location and establishment of the limits of the public domain, of all categories, must await systematic settlement, but after settlement its custody should be automatically secured under the operation of systematic Land Registration. The management of the public domain will probably be most successfully conducted by a combination of local administration with central specialist supervision, financial and technical: but in any case - and this is the point of immediate relevance - such management should be entirely separated from that of the Land Registries.

This separation should be effected if only because the task of bringing the management of the public domain up to the desired standard and the task of placing and keeping the registration of rights over land on a reliable footing will each demand exclusive attention and a prolonged effort.

But, as previously emphasized, it is in any case essential in the public interest that the two functions should be kept entirely separate. The service that manages the public domain represents the State in its capacity as landowner and landlord. As such it will be its duty, both during and after settlement, to maintain the nation's rights and claims as a whole, against the conflicting rights and counter-claims of private parties. This duty cannot be combined either fairly or effectively with that of impartially enquiring into and disinterestedly recording rights without regard as to whether they pertain to this or that body or person.

And even if by a miracle the two roles could be associated without subordination of either duty, it would never be credited, especially when sectional feeling was aroused over some transaction or series of transactions as is bound sometimes to occur particularly in Palestine. It is necessary on the one side that the Government's Land Agent shall be able to uphold the nation's rights as a whole against all comers singlemindedly and wholeheartedly: on the other that the Land Registry shall be entirely disinterested and impartial and be recognized as such.

38. In conclusion it may be repeated that, although the introduction of "a land system appropriate to the needs of the country" will necessarily be a slow and difficult task calling for much hard work and patience especially in the initial years, the objective is not only attainable but sure, if upon this occasion all attractive short cuts are firmly excluded and it is finally accepted: (a) that a real and abiding reform must be founded upon a complementary survey and a thorough settlement conducted on the ground village by village; (b) that such survey and settlement must be kept up to date when made; that this involves (c) the replacement of the present procedure of land registration by a system that will work and (d) the concurrent recasting of the present land law.

Other essential points are (e) that the law shall come down to earth so that practice and the law, and particularly the actual and theoretical classification of land, may conform; (f) that the formalities for succession to rights over immovable property are made easy and prompt; (g) that every possible effort is made to bring about the better distribution of holdings and better economy in the use of land generally; and finally (h) that the keeping of the Land Registers is entirely separated from the management of the Public Domain.

Extract of private letter from Lord Plumer to Sir J. Shuckburgh, of 20th November, 1925.

Agriculture and a Land Policy are the crying needs here.

At all turns I am met with the response "it all depends on Sir E. Dowson's report".

When we shall get it - the report - Goodness only knows.

Can you do anything to hasten?

Wrotham,
Kent.
5. December, 1925.

Under-Secretary of State,
Colonial Office.

Sir,

<u>Covering memorandum to report on the Land
system in Palestine.</u>

I have the honour to forward herewith the report of my mission to Palestine last winter in pursuance of your 40464/1924 of the 28th.August 1924 and other letters and conversations. I have taken great pains to make my report as concise as the intricacy of the subject permitted, so as to present the salient features of the problem clearly: but I can readily amplify it in any direction desired.

The variety of questions regarding which an expression of my opinion has been asked appear to me to be best described as general reform of the land system in Palestine, which consorts with the objective outlined in the second paragraph of Article 11 of the Mandate. And the main point that I feel obliged to stress throughout is the necessity to treat all the inter-related issues covered by this term as fundamentally one compound problem.

I trust it will be convenient both to the Secretary of State and the High Commissioner if, in the form of this covering memorandum, I recapitulate the elements of the complex problem under consideration and amplify my report in one or two particulars which I feel should not be ignored, but are better mentioned here than in the report itself.

Before proceeding I should like to add that the necessity for both concise presentation and statement make it rarely possible to explain, even when I realize them properly myself, the grounds which appeared in advance to justify lines of action which have since proved disappointing. It is evident that this complex problem looks very different now regarded in retrospect as a whole, than it did when approached from half a dozen different angles in the midst of initially establishing the elements of order and good government in the country. It is proverbially easy to be wise after the event: and when I criticize I do so not to disparage, but because I must do so to present the lessons of experience. The same necessity for brevity and to focus on defects makes it impossible to pay a just tribute to the vast amount of admirable work that has been done by every branch of the service to improve current administration and practice.

I have several times suggested that the first step needed is a thorough review of land tenure as it exists in law and in practice in Palestine to-day. Not only is a decision required on various points of policy or principle in connection with land tenure before reform can be usefully embarked upon, but there are also reconciliations between law and custom to be made, and uncertainties, omissions and anomalies to be remedied. I have recently submitted a preliminary note on this land tenure in the hope of initiating such a review.

The following weaknesses which demand attention in any constructive programme of reform have been discussed in the above note, and are only recorded here for the sake of completeness:

(a) Widespread prevalence of the mesha' system, or practice of periodically re-apportioning agricultural land.

(b) Difficulty, expense and delay in obtaining certificates of succession.

(c) Uneconomic subdivision and distribution of holdings.

A few additional words on the miri tenure may, however, be useful. It may be remembered that privately owned freehold (mulk) is exceptional in Palestine and that the mass of agricultural land falls into the miri category, i.e. owned by the State and held by cultivators on a transferable cultivating tenure. The normal development might be expected to be the conversion of such land into freehold on suitable terms, and this may in due course commend itself as the proper policy: but caution should I think be exercised to safeguard all existing rights of the State until the full implications of any change are clear and have been weighed. Thus it is to be borne in mind that tithe is payable on miri but not on mulk; that miri is governed by the civil law regardless of race or creed, and thus in great measure escapes the complications of the multiple religious jurisdictions extant in Palestine; that miri land cannot be converted into waqf and thus can be kept in the hands of the people; and finally that (at least in theory and in law) rights over miri land escheat to the State if they are not productively exercised.

The elements of the main problem to be faced may be summarized as follows:-

(i) The working of the Ottoman land code and of the Ottoman land tax (werko) depend upon the working of the Land Registers.

(ii) It was recognized before the war by the Turks that the existing land registers and tax records were useless, and must be entirely replaced by new ones built up on the foundation of a systematic land settlement and valuation of immovable property. The table given as Appendix I. to my report illustrates the unreliability of the existing records.

(iii) The position deteriorated further during the war; and in 1918 was found to be so bad that all dispositions of land were forbidden by proclamation under martial law until such time as it was found possible to re-establish and re-organize the Land Registries.

- 3 -

(iv) Continuous efforts have been made ever since to put Land Registration on to a sound basis and to deal with the various evil consequences of the long standing failure.

(v) In spite of much good work done in administrative and judicial alleviations of the situation, the failure of the Land and Land Tax Registers to function properly is essentially as complete as it was under the Turks: and no effective measure of reform has yet been initiated.

(vi) The reasons for this are that the problem has never been considered in any thorough manner and its attack has been conducted piecemeal by sections of the public service working without concert or constructive objective.

(vii) This is illustrated by the fact that although the cadastral survey was initiated in the neighbourhood of Gaza in February 1921 for the purpose of providing a reliable technical basis for the registration of rights over land not only has this work never been used, but all this time the surveys which have been used by the Land Registries for purposes of land registration have continued to be carried out independently under the direction of these offices, while the Courts dealing with land cases have even had recourse to unlicensed surveyors upon whose untrustworthy maps judgments have been given and registered.

The more direct evil consequences of the failure of the Land Registries to function may be summarized as follows:-

(a) General ignorance and insecurity of legal rights over land, which foster land theft and encroachment, breed litigation and violence, discourage enterprise and development.

- 4 -

(b) General inability of the State to locate, protect, dispose of, or develop the enormous tracts of public estate. This is illustrated by the continuous difficulty encountered by Government in reforesting such tracts.

(c) The necessity to maintain special courts and procedure for dealing with land cases.

(d) The impracticability of applying the Ottoman land tax and tax on roofed property in the absence of the necessary records; with consequent dependence upon the tithe and resulting disturbance of the equable incidence of taxation between townsman and agriculturalist.

(e) The absence of any secure basis for agricultural credit and the consequent perpetuation of local usury and debt enslavement.

If these and other prevailing defects are to be remedied the reform must be planned and executed as a united whole. So far the establishment of reliable land and tax registers, the location and development of the public estate, the introduction of simpler and more economical taxation, the restoration of conditions which will permit of land cases being heard by the regular procedure of law and justice, the provision of good agricultural credit, the abandonment of uneconomic local practices have for the most part been treated as separate questions, instead of a compound of closely inter-related problems which must be attacked as a connected whole.

In my report I have outlined what appear to me to be fundamental objections to the maintenance of the tithe as applied in Palestine. I should perhaps also here recall that the Committee set up in November 1921 to consider and advise on the working of the tithe recommended that the cadastral survey should be pressed forward with all speed with a view to the adoption of taxation on land instead of on yearly produce.*

It also appears that nearly fifty years ago the Turkish Government recognized the desirability of replacing the tithe entirely by a land tax: but never succeeded in carrying out the requisite measures.† Last winter Reuter announced that the abolition of the tithe had been effected by the present Turkish Government. The announcement of the abolition of the tithe by the Government from which we inherited it, coming after several years local discussion of the same question, naturally created considerable impression in Palestine.

It would be interesting to know the real facts: but whether the announcement is true or false it accentuated interest in the question and I think adds to the desirability of deciding without further delay whether the tithe is in due course to be abolished or further attempts are to be made to amend it.

A brief reference to the Ottoman land tax is also necessary here. As stated this tax has fallen into neglect owing to the failure of the registers. By law it should be re-assessed every five years and its individual incidence always be on record. Actually, I understand, it has never been reassessed since its establishment in 1886, although arbitrary all round increases were imposed once or twice by the Turks. I also understand that, apart from levies on recent buildings and transactions, liability for payment is now commonly severed from traceable connection with the property on which it purports to have been originally levied. The general situation, therefore, appears to be one which permits of no defence if challenged, and which calls for the initiation of early measures to bring the assessment and collection of this tax

----

*Commission's report.   Summary of recommendations, § 100, p.121.

†Young. Corps de droit ottoman V., p.306 et seq.

into accord with law, irrespective of any decision come to concerning the future of the tithe.

Now no effective measures can be taken either to amend the administration of the tithe and land tax or to replace the former by the latter until there is some suitable basis of survey to work on. If at all possible something much more rapid than an authoritative property survey is needed: for it would be deplorable if all fiscal reform had to await the necessarily slow march of determination of property rights. I have, therefore, recommended that an advance skeleton survey should be carried out as quickly as possible, which could most usefully combine a provisional basis for fiscal reform with valuable preparation for any land settlement to follow.

The aggregate effect of the conditions that have been previously outlined is to impose a formidable economic handicap both on the Government and on the great mass of rural cultivators, on top of the natural difficulties of rocky soil and uncertain rainfall. The man-made difficulties can be steadily lessened and ultimately, for the most part, removed if they are sensibly and patiently attacked: but there is no royal road or short cut by which this end can be attained. It must be based, as the Turks appear to have recognized, upon a systematic land settlement and valuation of property conducted steadily throughout Palestine. But it is useless to attempt such a land settlement until the Land Code has been revised and the measures for carrying out and maintaining the settlement have been threshed out and actually tested in practice. As I suggested last spring the work now being done under the Beisan Agreement provides an admirable field for testing and developing the details of land settlement and for training staff in its execution. It also provides valuable experience in the permanent distribution of land held in mesha' shares.

If such distribution of mesha' shares is to be generally taken up it will be most easily and economically carried out at the same time as land settlement, as also any more advantageous regrouping of holdings that may be desired by the holders.

The executive direction of the general scheme of reform is a matter about which it is useless to attempt to advise ex cathedra, as it must be primarily determined by the views of the Government both as to personalities and methods. The primary requirements are that piecemeal operations shall cease and the general planning, direction and financial control of reform shall be exercised from the capital and in regular liaison with the Central Government. Subject to this central command being effective the fullest detailed responsibility - both administrative and financial - should devolve upon those charged with the execution of the various branches of the work.

Initially at least (since they have to be entirely organized and developed ab ovo) the most difficult parts of the work will be the valuation of property for purposes of fiscal assessment and the field investigation and adjudication of claims to ownership or other rights over land. The successful discharge of these functions will demand an exceptional combination of local knowledge and influence, acumen, energy, acquaintance with the law and judicial mindedness, which by general consent is only to be found in a few specified District Officers. In India, where the closely similar operation of revenue settlement has been in regular operation for many years and long familiar to the people, the necessity for the highest qualities in a Settlement Officer is recognized. In Palestine the task will have all the added difficulties of a novel proceeding.

The composition and procedure of the land settlement commissions can be considered later when the general policy has been more fully decided; but I think it is desirable to stress here

- 8 -

that the service of the best men must not be grudged to this branch of the work if it is to be successful, and that such service should be made attractive as it will be extremely exacting and difficult.

10. Consideration must also be given to the necessity of securing the co-operation of the population in the execution of reform. No one will question the necessity: but there may be different views as to the course to be followed: for it is as well to recognize at the outset that there will be considerable divergences of interest and viewpoint. In the Jewish Colonies the demand for effective land registration and less primitive taxation is strong and criticism of the existing state of affairs caustic: but this will not prevent them from demanding the best of both worlds when the time comes. There is, however, homogeneity of interest in favour of reform in each colony; and if it is made clear that no local modifications of the general obligations and conditions can be entertained the Jewish colonies may I think be relied upon to do their part.

On the other hand among the native born Palestinian population there are considerable divergences of interest. Thus landowners who have acquired wide possessions by lending usuriously to and squeezing out mesha' or other small holders, by piracy of public land or other doubtful practices which present conditions permit, may be expected to oppose on most plausible grounds reform of such conditions and any payment of land tax on wide acres which they can now withhold from cultivation and taxation simultaneously. Again village headmen may object to losing licit and illicit tithe powers and perquisites, or the opportunities the mesha' system offers of picking the eyes out of the village lands. And the inhabitants of villages adjoining stretches of public estate may continue to obstruct measures for the protection and development of such estate (more particularly reforestation) as

- 9 -

curtailing the destructive licence of the goatherd and wood cutter. The waqf authorities may also hesitate to welcome the strict definition of waqf estate and obligations. In short various vested interests which have grown up under the prevailing uncertainty and insecurity of rights may be expected at the outset to oppose measures which affect them.

Reform is mainly in the interest of the nation at large and of the mass of small rural cultivators in particular. But the latter's ingrained suspicion of the motives of any Government is accentuated by the everlasting Jewish bugbear, and they are necessarily open to the plausible misrepresentations of interested fellow Palestinians. They are also disappointed that British rule has not done more to relieve their own particular disabilities; and they are the least vocal part of the population. They are at the same time, like most peasants, extremely shrewd as to which side their bread is buttered; and, from the frank way I have heard them talk, they seem to possess considerable independence of mind and to combine a healthy trust of their British District Officers with distrust of all more remote authority.

My conclusions are that criticism of our failure so far to introduce any real amelioration of the Turkish land system must be expected to grow the longer it continues: that whatever steps we take at first will meet with more opposition than help but should be steadfastly, although not inelastically, pursued: and that if a sensible and well tested scheme is put into operation in the villages by selected British District Officers who address themselves in the first place to win, no matter how slowly, the confidence and co-operation of the villagers concerned, success will only be a matter of time and patience.

The actual putting into motion of reform should be preceded by the publication of a clear and simple statement of the Government's policy and procedure, in the preparation and issue of which local leaders and organizations should be consulted. When the cards are on the table opposition must be expected to some measures or features of any scheme: but I think that with patience and consideration general good will and co-operation cannot readily be withheld.

It is, however, essential that all temptation to win co-operation by tampering with the efficacy of the programme or by subordinating the general interest to particularistic influences of any sort should be resisted. A sound and equitable programme of reform steadily persevered in will win its way in time: while an easier or more rapid start will be much too dearly purchased by permanent defects or inequalities for which we shall moreover be ultimately held to be responsible.

I venture to think, in concluding this covering memorandum and presenting my report, that my main obligation is to emphasize the need for the adoption of some considered policy in regard to the land system as a whole and to putting land registration and land taxation on to a sound footing in particular. Ever since 1919 an unceasing succession of expressions of opinion on this or that aspect of the problem have been sought both from external specialists and internal commissions: but the problem never seems to have been adequately considered in all its bearings by the Government itself and certainly no constructive policy has so far been adopted and put into action.

     I have the honour to be, Sir,
      Your obedient servant,

        Ernest. M. Dowson

Report on

The land system in Palestine

December 1925

REPORT ON

THE LAND SYSTEM IN PALESTINE.

December, 1925.

C O N T E N T S.

		Page.
1.	Preamble	1.
2.	Economic importance of reform	3.
3.	Dependence of land code and land taxation upon registration of rights over land	5.
4.	Failure of Ottoman registration	6.
5.	Reopening of Land Registers, 1920	7.
6.	Cadastral survey operations, 1921-25	10.
7.	Evil consequences of failure of registration	10.
8.	Objectionable character of the tithe as a system of taxation	12.
9.	Uneconomic holding of land	15.
10.	Ineffective pursuit of reform to date	15.
11.	Main lesson of failure	17.
12.	Objectives of reform	18.
13.	Land settlement	19.
14.	Fiscal survey	20.
15.	Beisan agreement	22.
16.	Colony records	23.
17.	System of land registration	24.
18.	Financial provision	25.
Appendix I. Table illustrating unreliability of existing registers		27.
Appendix II. Tax incidence on urban and rural taxpayers		28.
Appendix III. Defects of personal basis of record of rights		30.

CORRIGENDA.

Page	line		
6	at bottom	for "settlement-survey .... records - and" read "settlement (i.e. survey ... records) and".	
9	15	for "on"	read "as".
14	9	for "musafaqat"	read "musaqafat".
18	21	for "the judgment" read "judgments".	
21	2	for "(i) and (ii)" read "(i) and (iii)".	
23	5	insert "a" before "sound".	
	footnote	insert "13" after "§"	
25	3 from bottom.	for "sound" read "second".	

THE LAND SYSTEM IN PALESTINE.

Preamble:

Two years ago I was invited to visit Palestine and report on the complex series of inter-related questions which have been summed up under the above heading. I was in Palestine five days and submitted my report a month later. In due course I was asked to go out again last winter and go more fully into the whole problem with a view to the execution of my proposals. On this occasion I spent four months in Palestine and accumulated a considerable mass of material which I have since attempted to digest.

The present report embodies my conclusions in their baldest and most concise form. The complicated nature of the problem and its various deep-seated reactions upon the economic, social and even religious, life of the people and their political contentment make any concise presentation of the question only possible in the barest and boldest outline. Almost every one of the sections of this report required lengthy and detailed exposition in the first place, and will require it again if action is to follow; their presentation here is the fruit of repeated and perhaps in some cases misleading compression. And there are also many important aspects of the problem which have necessarily been entirely omitted from consideration here. But I conceive my primary business to be the clear presentation of the salient facts of the situation without extenuation, and more particularly to remove the terminological fog which appears to have obscured the fact that no advantage has yet been reaped from the establishment of the cadastral survey in 1921.

If (1) the basic causes of the consistent failure to date to effect constructive improvements in (as distinct from administrative and judicial alleviations of) the land system are admitted, and (11) the ambiguities, weaknesses and lacunae of the existing jumble of Ottoman statute law, religious law, provisional law, regulations, &c.,

and of superimposed British proclamation, ordinance and order are analysed, the foundation for the establishment of the desired reform of the land system will for the first time have been cleared. When this has been done the details of constructive proposals can be usefully worked out and tried. This report is an attempt to outline the basic causes of past failure, the evil consequences of acquiescing in it, and measures for steadily reversing it. In my recent preliminary study of land tenure in Palestine I endeavoured to provide a lay basis for the concurrent consideration of the actual working of existing land law and current practice.

The necessity to curtail the present report to the outstanding facts of the situation has made it impossible for me to emphasize the vast amount of excellent work that has also been done. By its nature, as an investigation of a particular failure, my enquiry is primarily directed to the past with a view to diagnosing and establishing mistakes, so that the lessons to be derived from them may be usefully applied in the future. While such an analysis is an essential preliminary to a more successful constructive effort, it does not provide an equitable basis for passing judgment. It is notoriously difficult even in a judicial summing up justly to re-appraise a situation as it unfolded itself to the actors under difficult and complicated conditions; it is manifestly impossible and unfair to do so on the basis of an investigation which of set purpose must explore errors and accept successes.

My proposals for the ultimate establishment of reform differ in no important particular from those that I made in December 1923: but they are derived from a much clearer view of the whole problem and they are based on much fuller knowledge. I now also appreciate that there will be need for a considerably longer preparatory period, a slower initiation of reform than I then realised. Happily, however, preparation can to a large extent take the form of work which is both immediately needed and can be subsequently absorbed (v. §§. 14-16).

That there are no errors of statement I cannot hope. Not only have I found it impossible yet to assimilate my information fully; but, in spite of the utmost goodwill, that information itself contains gaps which may be important. I am none the less satisfied that both the criticisms and the proposals made are sound, and more particularly that reform of the land system must be treated as a primary concern of the Central Government and be dealt with as a united whole if it is to be attained economically or even at all.

Economic importance of reform:

It will generally be conceded that the economic prosperity of Palestine, and its resultant the financial prosperity of the Government, is bound up with the much better agricultural development of the land. Admitting that the high hopes based upon the commercial possibilities of the Dead Sea salts and other mineral deposits and commercial enterprises are not unreasonable, they are dwarfed by the sober, and ascertainable prospects of unspectacular agricultural development both in economic importance to the country as a whole and in bringing well-being and contentment to the mass of the population who live on, and by, the land.

Palestine, both cis and trans Jordan, grows, and can grow in far greater quantities, excellent fruit, olives and tobacco, and in the plains and across Jordan cereals and other crops. Now almost denuded of trees she can produce a steadily increasing volume of marketable wood and later of timber. She can develop with no serious difficulty her flocks and herds and export both meat and hides.

And in conjunction with these great possibilities of agricultural production, Palestine has at her very doors in direct rail and easy sea connection with herself a wealthy neighbour with eighteen times her own population who has need of all these things and produces hardly one. Added to this solid initial advantage, Palestine is situated close to the entrance of the Suez Canal on the highway of the World's commerce which also has need of every product mentioned. It is not of course to be expected that Palestine can rival the great natural wealth of Egypt, but there is no reason why the next decade or two should not see a re-establishment of her ancient reputation as a land flowing with milk and honey, as striking as, if necessarily on a more modest scale than, the corresponding economic revival wrought by Lord Cromer in her one-time sister vilayet.

The master key to economic success in Palestine is to be found, not in the development of material resources (e.g. harbours and communications) although these aids are needed, not in the adoption of more scientific methods of cultivation, although these will establish and accentuate success as they are locally tested and assimilated, not even in the better conservation and use of the rainfall, which is probably the most important physical problem; but, as it was in Egypt and as it is everywhere else, in stimulating the individual enterprise of the mass of the population. It is the man behind the gun that counts most in economics as in war.

In this connection it is I think important to remember that although the introduction of cotton cultivation and the extension of irrigation set the scale of Egypt's economic revival the fundamental transformation was the classic conversion of the downtrodden, dispirited, fellahin into a well-nourished peasantry, whose industry was stimulated by being protected from exaction, by being taxed not only lightly but definitely and individually, whose personal and economic liberty was a matter of primary concern throughout, and whose increase in numbers was made possible by the increased means of subsistence that resulted from the general economic reform set in motion.

- 4 -

The contribution that Jewish and other immigrants are making, and can make, to an economic revival of Palestine, are well known; but it is apt, I think, to be too readily assumed that the Palestinian Arab (as he is misleadingly termed) is by nature incurably listless and idle. Under present conditions he may excusably be both; but I have now seen quite enough of him to be satisfied that, given mutatis mutandis the same economic liberty and stimulus, he will work as effectively as the Egyptian. The immigrant colonies also suffer from the economic disabilities imposed by the consequences of a broken-down land system and are not lacking in pungent criticisms of their survival; but they are better organised, better financially backed and more vocal than the native peasantry.

It is I believe proverbially said by the Arab that the grass refuses to grow where the hoof of the Turkish horseman has pressed. In effect, the justice of the gibe can hardly be denied, although the result seems, at least in this case, to have been due to administrative failure rather than ignorance or apathy. The consequences of this administrative failure are still deeply impressed on the land system of Palestine and limit in half-a-dozen serious ways (v. §§.7-9) the healthy economic and political effects of increasing security and good government generally.

Dependence of Ottoman land code and land taxation upon registration of rights over land:

It is desirable at the outset to recognise that the operation of the Ottoman Land Code and of the Ottoman taxation of land and buildings depends upon the punctual and reliable working of Land Registers in which all rights to own, use or dispose of land and buildings have by law to be recorded. No such rights, private or corporate, are valid unless they are so recorded; and only persons so recorded as owners or possessors of land and buildings are rightfully liable for the taxes imposed on such property. The classification of land into the

- 5 -

five statutory categories+ also depends upon the due and punctual working of the Land Registers. Different chapters of the Land Code apply to the different categories of land, and the classification of a piece of land must be known before it is possible to apply the relevant provisions of the law to it.

The expedient of a statutory record of such rights is of course common, both throughout Europe and elsewhere; and at least in no country in which rights rapidly become obscure, permanent boundaries are absent and encroachment is commonly practised can injustice and confusion be avoided, litigation be kept down, or taxation of land and buildings be equitably, unvexatiously and economically applied if such a record is not maintained. In theory and in law these needs were recognised and even elaborately provided for by the Ottoman legislator. In fact a practical system of land registration was never worked out and put into operation; so that the machinery of the Ottoman Land Code and of the taxation of land and buildings has also failed for the most part to function.

Failure of Ottoman registration:

This failure was recognised by the Turks themselves, as is shown by the issue in 1908 of a new law for the taxation of roofed property and in 1913 of a new provisional law of survey and registration of immovable property. The former provided de novo for the registration of the owners or possessors of roofed property and for the valuation of such property as a basis for the new tax, although in theory and pre-existing law both already stood recorded. The latter provided for an entirely new land settlement (survey, investigation of all rights and re-writing of all records) and fiscal valuation of all immovable property, village by village throughout the Ottoman

----
+These in English dress may be described as:
(i) freehold (mulk).
(ii) transferable cultivating tenure of public land (miri)
(iii) land governed by a permanent trust (waqf).
(iv) land of public utility (matruki).
(v) unused public land (mewat).

thus. Thus prior to the outbreak of the war the Ottoman Government had publicly accepted the necessity of scrapping all its existing records and had provisionally enacted a comprehensive law providing for a completely new land settlement, the registration of all rights over land and buildings thus defined, and a valuation of all such property for fiscal reasons.

The situation thus accepted in 1913 by the Turks themselves as only redeemable by an entirely new land settlement, naturally deteriorated further during the war; and after the British Occupation affairs were in such a tangle that a Proclamation* was issued saying that time was required to re-establish and re-organise the Land Registries and prohibiting all dispositions of immovable property until this had been done. Drastic as the proclamation sounds it was in effect nothing more than a formal announcement that the lawful methods of disposing of land and buildings were unable to function. This, as already pointed out, was no new thing, and the bulk of people doubtless merely continued to acquire and dispose of such property as before, without regard to previous law or the proclamation. The chief interest of the proclamation now lies in the evidence it affords that the British authorities found the Turkish land system entirely broken down when they took over the administration.

Re-opening of Land Registries, 1920.

In 1919 the Director of Land Registries in the Sudan and the Director of the Cadastral Survey in Egypt came to Palestine to advise Government on the underlying problem. In the official report issued next year† it was said (i) that the chief weakness of the (existing) system lay in the fact that there was no cadastral or other survey, so that land could not be correctly described by reference either to area

---

* Dated 18th. November, 1918.

† **Report on Palestine Administration,** July 1920-December 1921, p. 109 et seq.

or boundaries, and (ii) that the recommendations of the Director of Land Registries in the Sudan were accepted in principle and that the re-organisation of the thirteen Turkish (Land Registry) Offices had been undertaken. No copy of the recommendations mentioned could be found for me last winter; but I was advised that actually it had been found impracticable to use the new forms that had been drawn up by the Director of the Sudan Registries.

The point is of less importance than it may seem; for although an abandonment of the existing forms and methods is necessary if intelligible records are to be kept, no change of system or methods however sound, is of the slightest good if the accumulated confusion of the existing records is not straightened out. No attempt was, or has yet been, made to do this.

However in 1920 the Land Registries were re-opened by authority of the "Transfer of Land Ordinance 1920" under the direction of an officer who had previously been Registrar General of Lands in Cyprus. The ordinance contained no provision either for clearing up past confusion or for amending the system of record, but contented itself with stating in the preamble that the Land Registries had been re-established and that a Land Settlement Court was shortly to be set up. The policy that inspired the ordinance was explained in a contemporary note published with it, and may be summarised as an attempt to exercise administratively a beneficent control over all land transactions in Palestine.

Probably it was hoped that the projected Land Settlement Court would co-operate with the Cadastral Survey (the commencement of which in February 1921 was concurrently announced)*to clear up the legacy of past confusion, and that the administrative control intended to be exercised by the Land Registries over all new land transactions would restrict the growth of further confusion. Actually the exercise of a

----

*op. cit. p.113.

beneficent administrative control over all land transactions is an impracticable ideal; while the Land Settlement Court appears never to have been formed. For the latter must not, I take it, be confused with the Land Courts set up in April 1921* with jurisdiction to hear actions regarding ownership in lieu of the regular courts,† which were debarred by the existing confusion from doing so. In any case the Land Courts have been too occupied with current litigation to co-operate in any land settlement work.

As already noted the chief weakness of the existing system of Land Registration was officially diagnosed as the absence of cadastral survey; and in February 1921 such a survey was started, with a view to remedying this defect. Unfortunately no measures were taken to lay down a common plan or policy, or even to ensure that the Departments of Survey and of Land Registries should work together. More strangely still it was announced at the same time as the commencement of the cadastral survey, that "with a view to preventing future boundary disputes and to enable registration to be reasonably accurate, the Department (of Land Registries would itself undertake) survey of properties which are the subject of transactions at a nominal fee."** The Land Registry surveyors are now borne on the budget of the Survey Department but this is little more than a camouflage: they continue under the orders of the Land Registries and the Survey rarely sees and is not responsible for their work. In short the creation of the Survey Department four years ago to remedy the chief weakness of the existing system of Land Registration has left that system virtually untouched. If the Survey was abolished to-morrow the procedure of Land Registration would not be affected.

----

*Under the Land Courts Ordinance 1921.

†v. Report on Palestine Administration. July 1920-December 1921, p.90.

**Ibid, p.111.

Cadastral Survey Operations:

Just as the Land Registries have conducted their own survey operations; so have the Survey conducted their own investigations of title. The cadastral survey of Palestine was begun in February 1921 in the neighbourhood of Gaza. It began and has continued as a departmental operation. In respect of property limits it has throughout been based solely upon enquiries regarding ownership and other rights made at varying times during the course of survey by the survey parties themselves. However sound at the moment these conclusions may intrinsically have been, they possessed no validity (since the Survey had neither the experience nor the authority to decide property rights) and no lasting value.

If the survey work had been promptly followed up by, and made to conform to, an authoritative settlement of property rights, and if the Land Registers had been written up on the basis thus provided, solid progress might by now have been made.

Actually no attempt seems to have been made to turn the work to useful account at all. Even the map work remains unpublished, and thus generally unavailable for use by other departments or the public. In short the cadastral survey initiated four years ago has hitherto been and so far promises to remain, a sterile technical undertaking from which neither the land system in particular, nor the country in general has benefitted.

Evil consequences of failure of Registration:

The more obvious evil consequences of the confusion and uncertainty induced by the long-standing failure of the Land Registries to function should now be briefly analysed. They are:

(a) The reaction upon enterprise and public peace.

The general insecurity of rights acts as a deterrent to enterprise and industry in working up the land and to sinking capital in its development, encourages encroachments and land piracy, breeds quarrels within, and between villages, and fosters litigation.

(b) The prevention of the productive utilization of the national estate.

The Government is at present ordinarily unable to locate, protect, develop, or dispose of public land in the interest of the nation at large, or can only do so with extreme difficulty. This is illustrated by the volume of litigation in which the Government is always engaged in the defence of public land, by its inability to state what, if any, public land exists justly available for colonization by immigrants, and by the unceasing obstacles encountered in endeavouring to reforest Palestine and stay the destructive movement of the coastal sand dunes.

(c) The necessity to maintain special Land Courts.

Owing to the impossibility of applying the Land Code under existing conditions actions concerning the ownership of land and buildings and other real rights cannot be heard by the regular courts or be decided by the regular procedure of law and justice.

(d) The serious repercussion upon the lawful and proper taxation of immovable property.

As the record of property units and property holders has ceased to function the due and legal apportionment by Government of the existing taxes among the individuals legally liable is for the most part impracticable. This has led to a neglect of the Ottoman land tax (werko), little short of abandonment, and to Government in practice levying the tithe as a gross tax on village communities and leaving its unit cash apportionment and collection to village headmen or other leading members of the community. Neglect of the land tax and concentration on the tithe also has fostered the uneven incidence of taxation between urban and rural taxpayers.*

(e) The absence of the security needed for agricultural credit.

So long as rights to own, use and dispose of immovable property are undefined and insecure there is no foundation upon which cheap,

----

*v. Appendix II.

simple and reputable means of providing the credit needed by cultivators can be based. In the absence of good credit machinery the local moneylender and his debt-slavery of the cultivator with all its attendant evils is bound to continue; and these evils tend to be aggravated rather than mitigated by anti-usurious enactments.

No agricultural community can do without credit. Credit cannot be supplied on good terms on bad security. Articifial attempts to regulate credit tend to put up its price and thus to defeat their own purpose. Given good security, good credit will follow; and it is only good credit that will rescue the cultivator from the usurer.

8. Objectionable character of the tithe as a system of taxation:

Neglect of the land tax with consequent undue dependence upon the tithe and disturbance of the balance of taxation between town and country has been mentioned as one of the outcomes of the failure of the land records. But attention must also be called to some objectionable features of the tithe itself as a fiscal measure for employment by a modern civilised central Government.

Attractive in theory, in sober fact to attempt the equitable assessment of the yield, quality, condition and marketable value of every crop of every cultivator throughout Palestine, and the collection of the ever-varying contributions justly, unvexatiously and economically, from the rightful persons in the absence of all reliable records is a task beyond the powers of any Government. In practice the operation of the tithe also commonly involves three particularly objectionable features:

 (a) the enforced transport of field crops to a central village site and their retention there until agreement has been reached as to the amount to be paid. This may interfere with both agricultural and marketing arrangements and offers undesirable opportunities of coercion.

 (b) the employment as primary estimators of the quantity, quality and condition of crops of locally recruited temporary officials whose freedom from bias, fear, favour, cupidity and grudge cannot be reasonably expected.

(c) the utilization of village headmen (or other leading members of the community), who may be doubly interested personally,[*] as the agents for the apportionment of the gross cash tax payment among, and its collection from, the individual members of the community concerned. When it is remembered that these individuals are commonly illiterate and likely to suffer if they complain (even successfully) against the leading members of their own community, that the sums asked from them are never the same twice running, are readily susceptible of plausible modification up or down the scale, and are continuously falling due on one crop or another throughout the year,[†] the opportunity that the tithe offers for peculation, oppression and general abuse is evident and has been officially recognized.[**]

---

[*] As receivers of Government commission and as tithe-payers themselves.

[†]
First vegetable crop,	End February, March.
Winter Crop assessment	Mid April, May.
Almonds, figs, second vegetable crop	June.
Summer crops	End June, July.
Melons and Grapes	End July.
Oranges	End October, beginning Nov.
Olives	November, December.

[**] Report on Palestine Administration, July 1920-December 1921, p.10.

- 13 -

In brief there seems no room for doubt that the unceasing [valu]ation of the whole agricultural production of a country with the [deg]ree of individual accuracy which the theoretical elasticity of [the] tithe demands, is an impracticable undertaking, making indefensible inroads upon the time and energies of all concerned and [li]able to the gravest abuse.

The long period valuation[*] of the land and buildings already [re]quired by law for the purpose of the other two statutory taxes on immovable property (werko and musaqqafat) is not only a far less [on]erous undertaking, but one whose proper and equitable performance [can] be readily and effectively controlled. Such a valuation reduced [to] a common period (e.g. ten years) is all that is needed for the [tax]ation of immovable property and there appears to be no justification either for maintaining two parallel systems of valuation or for [pr]eferring the one which is more troublesome to both sides, more [co]stly and more liable to abuse.

The mass of cultivators would be much better off if they were [re]lieved of the unending inquisition and interference entailed by [t]ithing operations, were left at liberty to harvest, thresh, store, use or realise on their crops as their own judgment or needs dictated, [a]nd were required to pay a definite sum upon an official demand at a [d]efinite date and against an official receipt to a regular agent [o]f the Central Government. The country on its side would be spared [t]he heavy cost - indirect and direct -, the extensive field for oppression and abuse, and the unceasing dislocation of work and administration associated with the tithe.

Under a regular land tax the maintenance by absentee landlords [of] large tracts of land untilled would not go unpunished as at pre[se]nt; while provision could readily be made for remission of taxation

----

[*] i.e. five-yearly and ten-yearly.

in case of serious failure of crops, or pending their maturity, as is done elsewhere.

9. Uneconomic holding of land:

The widespread uneconomic subdivision and distribution of holdings and the prevalence of the mesha' system (or the practice of periodically re-apportioning agricultural land) are also serious handicaps upon the agricultural development of Palestine.*
And although the existence of these two evils is not due to the failure of the Land Registries to function, their perpetuation has probably been greatly assisted thereby; and their remedy should be included among the main objectives of any reform of the land system.

10. Ineffective pursuit of reform to date:

Since the British Occupation the remedy of the evils mentioned has been a matter of continuous concern to the Administration. Among important Commissions of Enquiry that have been set up to deal with them may be mentioned the Land Commission appointed in 1920 and still I believe in being in an advisory capacity, the Sand Dunes Afforestation Commission, the Athlit Marshes Enquiry Commission, the Tithes Commission, the Committee on the Taxation of Agriculturalists, the Committee on Agricultural Loans, the Committee that reported on the Mesha' system, and numerous commissions concerned with the definition and settlement of State land such as the Mahlul and Mewat Commissions, the Forest Demarcation Commissions and the Beisan Commission.

Legislation and orders connected with the establishment or conduct of the Land Registries, the Surveys and the Land Courts are too numerous to be cited: but among attempts to deal with the second of the specific evils mentioned (§.5) are the "Mahlul" and "Mewat" Ordinances, the various Forest Ordinances, the Sand

----
*v.§.22 (p.34) et seq. and §.33 (p.53) et seq. of my preliminary study of land tenure in Palestine.

Drift Ordinance, and with the fifth the Agricultural Loans Ordinance, the Credit Bank Ordinance and the Usurious Loans Ordinance. The provisions of the Forest Ordinance issued in 1920 proved virtually impotent in respect of the definition and protection of the boundaries of the public land concerned, and their effective amendment has continued ever since to be the subject of consideration. In addition to legislation, public orders, &c., unceasing efforts have been made by every branch of the administration to alleviate the effect of the evils mentioned both in the regular course of their duties and by personal interest and influence. Yet for the most part the ill consequences of the defects in the land system remain deep rooted and are no nearer eradication than they were in 1918.

This is not due to any lack of appreciation of the underlying necessity to establish the record of rights over land on a secure, orderly and lawful footing. As early as 1919 (as already noted) Mr. Williamson, Director of Land Registries in the Sudan, and Mr. Sheppard, (then) Director of the Cadastral Survey in Egypt came to Palestine and made recommendations on the subject to Government. In 1920 **firstly** the **Land Commission** was appointed,* secondly, Mr. Ongley, previously Registrar General of lands in Cyprus, was nominated Director of the Land Registries in Palestine and re-opened these Registries, and, thirdly, Mr. Quinlan of the Sudan Survey came to Palestine to advise on the conduct of a cadastral survey. In February 1921 the cadastral survey was started under the direction of the present Director of Surveys, who had been selected in England for the purpose. During 1922 and 1923 Col. Newcombe, who was in command of the British Boundary Commission, and the Surveyor General of Bombay, who was passing

----

*v. Official Gazette No.26 of 1 September 1920, for the Land Commission's terms of reference.

through Palestine, were in turn asked to examine and give their opinions on the technical methods employed. In November of the latter year I was asked to visit Palestine on my way home from Egypt and advise on the whole question, which I did the following month. Last winter (1924-25) I was asked to go out again and re-examine the problem more fully.

The fact that Government has thought it necessary during the last seven years continuously to seek specialist assistance on land registration and survey, indicates sufficiently their dissatisfaction with the progress made with the solution of the problem. They have the fullest justification for such dissatisfaction.

Broadly speaking the results achieved to date are that certain legislative amendments of the Ottoman Land Laws have been made, the current administration of the Land Registries has been purged and improved, a Survey Department has been established and the foundation for a national property survey laid: but that nothing of a constructive nature has either been planned or effected towards substituting order for the chaos in which the land system was left by the Turk, and which even he had recognised before the war to be intolerable.

Main lesson of failure:

The principal lesson to be learnt from past experience is the necessity for thoroughly considered and concerted action, if land tenure and taxation are to be put on a satisfactory footing. To continue to pursue reform without having examined its basis, on no comprehensive plan, and through the agency of the unco-ordinated efforts of sections of the public service whose views are focussed on their own departmental fields, is to continue to expend money and effort to no useful purpose.

The problem is a major issue, deeply affecting the well-being of the mass of the population and touching their social and religious life. Its solution calls for the earnest attention of the Central Government itself, not only in digesting reports but in the detailed planning and execution of reform, at least until the difficult corners have been turned and the confidence of the people in our ability to remedy the evils of the current situation has been established, as it can only be established, by actually making land tenure simple and secure and land tax simple and unvexatious in some corner of Palestine. Such exercise by Government itself of general direction and unifying control of reform is perfectly compatible with its decentralized execution. But decentralized execution of a properly planned comprehensive scheme of reform is a radically different thing from the disconnected sectional efforts which have hitherto held the field.

Space here does not permit of a discussion as to the best means of enabling the Central Government to combine adequate general command with an effective measure of freedom to executive units; nor is such a discussion probably useful at this stage. If the governing principles are accepted their translation into action will depend more on the men in charge than on abstract measures.

12. **Objectives of Reform**:

A scheme for constructive reform of the land system should, in my opinion, embrace:

(a) The establishment of the Land Registers de facto as well as de jure as the authoritative record (subject to the judgments of the regular courts) of all rights to own, use or dispose of immovable property.

(b) The valuation of all immovable property for fiscal purposes.

(c) Provision for the permanent apportionment of land held on the mesha' system.

(d) Provision for facilitating the grant of certificates of succession.

(e) Provisions to facilitate and stimulate the more economic subdivision of land and distribution of holdings.

(f) The re-drafting, as necessary, and codification of the Land Law and the review of all fiscal legislation affecting immovable property.

- 18 -

13. Land Settlement:

It has already been noted that before the war the Turks had recognised that the existing Land Registers were useless and must be made up entirely afresh. This still remains to be done. It can only be done if rights over immovable property in Palestine are put on a clear and stable basis by an investigation and settlement of all claims to own, or exercise rights over, immovable property, which is methodically conducted and recorded village by village and town by town progressively throughout the whole country. Such an investigation, settlement and record necessitates (i) an enquiry into and an authoritative adjudication of all such claims accompanied by (ii) an exact location of the positions and limits of the consequent property units. The results of the combined operation must (iii) be put on record in a form which will enable them to be of use for permanent reference. Throughout these discussions I have used, and shall continue to use, the term Land Settlement to denote this compound process of (i) definition of property rights, (ii) survey of properties and (iii) joint record, which is required.

The strongest emphasis must be laid on the complementary nature of the two parts of the operation (i. and ii.) and that their united objective is the creation of an intelligible and reliable record, (iii) for subsequent use. A caution should also be given against allowing the use of labels such as "cadastral survey", "settlement", "demarcation" and the like, to hypnotize the mind and block intelligent consideration of the actual processes so labelled. These warnings may appear trite and obvious; but a dispassionate consideration of the actual value, as measured by the use made, of the one-sided operations conducted in Southern Palestine since February 1921 under the designation of cadastral survey will show that they are not superfluous.

Land Settlement must be a slow process, especially at the start, as all arrangements for its conduct have still to be made except on the survey side; and it will only be a further waste of money and effort to push on before matters have been properly planned and prepared. Fortunately there are several pieces of immediately useful work which will fully occupy attention in the meantime, and will both pave the way for, and fall into place, in an ultimate general scheme.

I proceed to consider three of these. A fourth which cannot be usefully considered at this stage or in this report is co-operation of the Survey in advance of Land Settlement with the Land Registries and the Land Courts to define land that is the subject of a registered transaction or judgment.

Fiscal Survey:

The first of the pieces of work mentioned is the execution of a combined programme of survey and valuation of land and buildings for fiscal purposes. Measures for conducting the necessary valuation would require arrangement, but should present no serious difficulty; and such a valuation could be reviewed, and amended, as information and experience was gained. A fiscal survey of the nature suggested is an infinitely less serious undertaking than Land Settlement and could be pushed forward without the detailed consideration, preparation and trial that the latter must receive before it is launched, if it is to be successful.

The taxation of land and buildings cannot be put on to a completely sound footing until the foundation exists for the compilation of a trustworthy tax-roll of such property. Such a tax-roll should comprise methodical returns (i) of all taxable units of immovable property, (ii) of the taxable value of such properties, and (iii) of the persons legally liable (in virtue of ownership or other rights) for the taxation levied thereon.

Authoritative, and therefore reliable, determination of (i) and (iii) can only be provided in the process of Land Settlement, which must necessarily be slow; but there is commonly no great difficulty in determining the limits of house property and the occupiers if not the owners of such property. Therefore in urban areas the execution of a fiscal survey in advance of land settlement should prove feasible. In Jerusalem and Jaffa the technical basis is, at least for the most part, already available. The value of such an early fiscal survey of urban areas will be apparent.

In rural areas assessment of land for fiscal purposes can best be effected irrespective of property boundaries, by including all contiguous land of closely equal value in blocks of convenient size and shape. Each block can then be assessed in turn, and all land follow the assessment of the block in which it is situated.

The expedient of constituting blocks of land of approximately equal value is familiar to the people and has long been used by them as an equitable basis for the apportionment of mesha' and other shares. Its adoption also as an equitable basis for assessment of land tax is therefore an obvious move, which will be readily understood; and it is one that cannot be easily bettered for simplicity of operation. Moreover some such systematic subdivision of villages will in any case be required in due course for purposes of land settlement and subsequent record; and if it could be carried out rapidly it would greatly facilitate the difficult task of defining ahead of any such settlement land which is the subject of a registered transaction in the meantime.

In rural areas a fiscal survey would require to locate and adjust village boundaries, to demarcate on the ground and indicate on the map the limits of the blocks mentioned and such topographical detail as appeared desirable. It would provide in the shortest possible time the basis now lacking for a concrete, as opposed to an abstract consideration, of the replacement of the present amalgam of tithe and semi-abandoned Turkish land tax by one simple fiscal instrument for the taxation of immovable property; for as soon as the fiscal survey was sufficiently advanced in a few representative districts a comparison could be made between the yield of the tithe and that of varying rates of land tax. And at any subsequent time judged desirable the tithe could be abandoned and a regular land tax substituted in any district of which the fiscal survey had been completed. Pending the passage of Land Settlement and the compilation of a tax-roll of individuals, the blocks of land mentioned would be the Government's effective taxation units in each village. And, however imperfect the levy of a definite sum on each of such subdivisions would be, compared with the individual assessment which should follow Land Settlement, it would none the less be an enormous advance on present practice.

The substitution of a fiscal survey on the lines proposed for the present cadastral operations would enable the expenditure on the Survey to be turned to useful account with the shortest possible delay in a manner which would at the same time provide invaluable preparation for Land Settlement work later; and it would enable a large measure of effective fiscal reform to be thoroughly investigated and initiated without waiting for the slower march of such settlement.

15. Beisan Agreement:

The second piece of such work that I have in view has been in progress for some time and affords the only instance brought to my notice in which the complementary operations of (i) definition of rights and (ii) property survey have been associated. Much criticized as the Beisan Agreement is, and open to criticism as some details of the consequent operations are, it has resulted in the one piece of work of the nature of genuine Land Settlement* yet done in Palestine. The most serious fault to be found with it is that although it afforded an opportunity for establishing and maintaining the Land Registers of an extensive district on a sound basis, this opportunity has not been taken advantage of; and if matters are left as they are the confusion and uncertainty of rights temporarily banished here at considerable cost of money and effort will steadily recur.

This should be prevented by somewhat recasting the field operations and radically recasting the Land Registers used. If this is done the work can be made of permanent value and will immediately provide an incomparable field for testing the local application, and familiarizing existing staff in the use of a workable system of record.

16. **Colony Records**:

The third piece of immediately and permanently useful work consists in taking over the Land Registers of various Colonies, for the most part Jewish, who have long complained with considerable justification that their own Land Registers though reliable and comprehensible are legally invalid, while the Government's Registers though legally valid are unreliable and incomprehensible. As the matter has already been the subject of considerable discussion no useful purpose will be served by re-examining it here. It is sufficient to say that the representations of the Colonies are for the most part justified, and should be met, and that the examination and transfer of their records provides Government with another, if more restricted opportunity, for combining the execution of a long needed piece of work with useful preparation for the future.

---
*i.e. Land Settlement in the technical sense defined in §.13 as distinct from colonisation.

System of Land Registration.

I have not made any reference in the course of this report to the system which I recommend should be substituted for the present methods of recording rights over land, as I understand from the observations made by both the Director of Land Registries and the Director of Surveys on the report I furnished two years ago, that they have both been aiming at the adoption of the Torrens system. This is also indicated in an authoritatively based review of the question recently published.[*] There is not, I think, really any reasonable alternative. The system of registration of title to land, initiated in Australia in 1857 and associated with the name of Sir Robert Torrens, now so widely and successfully applied, when brought down to bed rock is simply authoritative record of rights over land systematically based upon permanent cadastral or property survey. In a long settled country utilizing surnames and possessing a large proportion of stable boundaries, carefully kept personal records are workable, if troublesome; in more primitive countries a property survey provides the only feasible basis for constructing and maintaining a reliable and intelligible record of rights over immovable property,[+] or even a purely fiscal register.

In the report I furnished two years ago I made some cursory suggestions for the adoption of the Torrens system in Palestine. As I recommended verbally last spring, these and other details should be provisionally worked out and tested in actual application at Beisan and in connection with the Colony records before they are formally adopted. Before land settlement is actually initiated they should have been well tested and embodied in legislation and regulation.

----

[*] *Palestine of the Mandate*, W.B.Worsfold, pp.66-69.

[+] v. Appendix III. for French experience of the defects of a personal basis of record.

Financial provision:

No consideration has so far been given in this report to the financial aspects of the question. The funds annually available may affect the degree of efficiency, and must determine the rate of execution of reform; but past failure has not been occasioned by deficient, nor can future success be ensured by abundant, financial provision. During the past seven years a considerable sum in the aggregate has been expended by the various public services concerned without constructive result, which employed in the execution of a connected scheme might by now have provided Palestine with a considerable instalment of permanent reform. The important thing is to minimize such useless or dead end expenditure and turn it to productive account.

The first financial decision needed is that initially estimates, and ultimately actual expenditure incurred, shall be scrutinized in relation to the results foreshadowed or obtained. To enable this to be done all financial provision for effecting reform in the land system should be considered as a whole, preferably brought under one main budgetary and accounting head, and administered in its broad features by an officer of, or in regular touch with the Central Government, if not by the Treasury itself. This is perfectly compatible with all reasonable executive requirements, indeed it should be accompanied by the removal of various current restrictions on departmental initiative and judgment which merely foster ineffective use of public funds. A simple statement of such expenditure and of the results obtained for it, should be prepared and seriously examined each month. In this statement a clear discrimination should be observed between work (a) that is preparatory, incomplete or so far unused, (b) that which has merely contributed to the maintenance of the status quo, and (c) that which has effected some definite advance or improvement.

The second financial decision needed is that proper balance shall be instituted and maintained between the various branches of the work. Thus it is useless to expand the survey field parties

- 85 -

if no provision is made for reproducing the maps they make. It is also useless to maintain an organization for carrying out the technical side of land settlement if complementary provision is not made for definition of rights and valuation of property. In practice this suggests three reasonable, though not of course equally desirable, courses: (a) additional financial provision so as to enable the existing deficiencies in balance to be made up, (b) redistribution of current provision with the same object, and (c) abandonment of all attempts to reform the land system and restriction of the survey to ordinary topographical mapping.

That the long-standing attempt to effect reform in the Ottoman land system should be abandoned is not, however, I imagine, to be contemplated. The principal aim should therefore I think be to pursue a financial policy which will secure cumulative improvement of the land system, so that the existing confusion with all its attendant evils is steadily cleared up and order and security of rights progressively substituted. The difficulty of putting the main work of reform on to sound lines now is naturally much greater than it would have been seven, or even five years ago; and greater than I anticipated two years ago. It must consequently proceed on slower and more modest lines at first. This need not make for ultimate delay. Well begun is half ended: and if reform is now sensibly planned, conducted and persevered in for a few years until its fruits begin to show it will increasingly provide its own justification for expansion and accelerated completion.

APPENDIX I.

COMPARATIVE TABLE of Areas of certain properties as recorded in the Land and the Tax Register and as determined by recent measurement.

The information in the following table, supplied by the Director of Land Registries, illustrates characteristic discrepancies in the areas of thirty random properties as recorded in the Land Register and the Land Tax Register (Werko) respectively, and as determined by the Land Registry Surveyors. It should be noted as an accompanying anomaly that the dunum, which is the primary unit of area employed, has never been standardised and possesses no legal value.

On the doubtful assumption that throughout the units are comparable, and the relations of pic to dunum constant, (1600 square pics = 1 dunum) the Land Register entry varies from half to ninety-seven times the measured area, the Land Tax entry varies from a sixteenth to fourteen times the measured area, the Tax Entry varies from a thirtieth to twice the Land Register entry.

Property	Area in dunums and square pics according to						Entries expressed % of measured area.	
	Land Reg.		Tax Reg.		Measurement		Land Reg.	Tax Register
1	31	0	3	0	5	130	610	60
2	2	0	0	900	0	348	1100	260
3	1	0	0	200	0	244	670	82
4	15	0	8	800	6	726	230	130
5	25	0	2	100	2	664	1010	87
6	60	0	51	0	37	40	160	138
7	25	0	0	-1200	1	744	1670	52
8	27	0	1	-1200	26	626	101	6
9	25	0	1	0	0	1459	2800	110
10	1	0	0	-1200	0	1090	160	110
11	1	800	0	75	0	104	2400	75
12	28	0	-	-	6	302	450	-
13	15	0	1	800	2	634	625	63
14	108	0	42	800	11	190	700	375
15	31	0	-	-	-	-	-	-
16	29	0	2	400	5	648	538	42
17	1	0	1	200	1	1426	53	60
18	37	0	-	-	5	482	700	-
19	76	800	12	-	9	1202	780	193
20	2	0	0	600	0	626	530	100
21	42	0	12	0	25	652	166	47
22a	13	0	6	0	1	2	1300	600
22b	13	0	6	0	3	766	370	170
23	25	0	48	0	16	382	154	295
24	4	0	0	400	0	666	960	60
25a	45	0	48	0	3	1027	1240	1320
25b	45	0	48	0	6	301	785	770
25c	45	0	48	0	20	529	230	225
26	28	0	48	0	3	612	830	1410
27	20	0	25	800	10	548	194	245

APPENDIX II.
Incidence of taxation on urban and rural taxpayers.

An attempt to investigate the incidence of taxation between the urban and the rural taxpayer was recently made (March 1935) by the Palestine Treasury for the guidance of the Committee originally constituted in June 1933 to enquire into the taxation of the non-agricultural population.

While emphasizing the caution with which all figures must be regarded the conclusion was reached that the average taxation of an agricultural family was just under ten per cent. (10%) of its income and that of a non-agricultural family at just over six and a half per cent. (6½%). As municipal taxation, for which townsmen get a special return, appears to be included the discrepancy between the average incidence of national taxation on the two classes would seem to be even greater.

Of the conclusions expressed the following are of particular relevance:-

"The tax burden of the agriculturalist has been aggravated of late by the rapid fall in prices and the slower downward movement in cost of production......The change from the (Ottoman) method of collection of tithe in kind is also a hardship, as the cultivator in order to pay tithe in cash is compelled to dispose of part of his crops at a time when the market is most unfavourable. This is particularly hard on the small cultivator and 80% of the cultivators are small holders. The greater portion of their produce is for domestic use, and in pre-war days such exchanges as did take place were usually transacted by way of barter. - There is ample evidence .... of the unequal distribution of direct taxation between the agricultural and the non-agricultural population."

And again: "while the results of (the comparisons given) are very general and their utility limited they indicate that the minimum of subsistence is very much lower for the rural than for the urban population; that taxation is greater for the villager than for the townsman in relation to income; and that the incidence of taxation is relatively lighter on higher incomes...... Apart from the point of view of fiscal administration the attitude of the community towards the question of taxation has of late been somewhat critical. To some extent, the economic position has been exploited for ulterior objects by people of different political views but in the main criticism is justified."

APPENDIX III.

Defects of personal basis for record of rights over land.

The failure of a personal basis for record of rights over land, even in France, is forcibly expressed in the following quotation from M. Paul Gide, the well-known French economist:-

"Vous voulez savoir la situation de tel domaine, vous demandez au conservateur s'il est hypothéqué (aliéné ou grevé d'un droit réel.) Il vous repond: je ne connais pas les immeubles, je ne connais que les propriétaires. Vous citez alors le nom du propriétaire actuel: Jean Berhard; le conservateur trouve une demi-douzaine de Jean Bernard qui sont tous grevés d'hypothèques. Il vous délivre un etat portant toutes les hypothèques de ces homonymes. Par contre, si vous omettez ou si vous designez mal les noms de propriétaires, le conservateur ne fait pas de recherches au nom de ces personnes, et vous risquez d'ignorer les hypothèques (ou les alionations et droits réels) qu'ils ont consentis. Ajoutez que dans les actes, et par consequent dans les transcriptions, le signalement de l'immeuble estplus souvent donné par les noms des propriétaires voisins; quand les voisins ont changé, on ne sait plus de quel immeuble il s'agit."

The impracticability of such a basis of record in a country in which surnames are rarely used is brought out in the following extract from a report of M. Paul Cambon written in 1885 when Resident General of France in Tunis and President of the Commission on Registration of Title to Land there:

"Les indigènes n'ont ni etat civil ni nom patronymique. Dans la practique, les indigènes se reconnaissent par un prénom auquel vient s'ajouter le prenom du père, Mustapha fils de Mohammed par exemple; comme le nombre de ces prénoms est assez limité, il en résulte que beaucoup d'indigènes portent des appelations identiques. Si l'on songe qu'en France la similitude de certains noms plus fréquemment utilisés est déjà une source de difficultés et de complications pour la tenue de nos registres hypothécaires, on se rendra aisément compte des impossibilités d'un pareil système en pays musulman."

Section 2: Memoranda on Credit, 1918–1930

2.01

Copy.
No.8065/FR.

Headquarters,
Occupied Enemy Territory Administration(South)
Jerusalem.

9th May, 1919.

General Staff,
G.H.Q.

      Under the Turkish regime a regular system existed for the grant of loans to cultivators and others for agricultural improvements. This system was however entirely broken up by the war: the registers were dispersed and the funds available were either appropriated by the enemy before retreat, or if left, seized by the army as booty. The result has been a considerable set-back to the agricultural prosperity of the country, and consequently to the development of its revenues.

      During the later months of last year this Administration attempted to deal with the most urgent cases with the scanty means at its disposal, and short term loans were granted in the Jaffa district to save the orange crop and in other districts to resuscitate cultivation that had been completely destroyed by the military operations. This however did not by any means meet the requirements of the case, or enable me to satisfy the needs of the people to the same extent as was done by the Turks. To do this, a much larger sum than was at my disposal was necessary, and loans for a much longer period than was warranted by the political circumstances of a temporary military administration were called for. The urgency of an additional provision was pressed by the Military Governors of the districts and remarked by Major-General Sir Walter Lawrence, whose exceptional experience of these matters made his advice particularly valuable, with the result that, subject to the approval of the Commander-in-Chief, arrangements have now been made with the official bank, i.e. the Anglo-Egyptian Bank Limited, for the grant of loans for a period up to five years on the guarantee of a mortgage of the immovable property of the borrowers given through this Administration, which thus undertakes no risk in the matter beyond the unlikely contingency of a depreciation of land values. It is not anticipated that more than £70,000 or £80,000 will be actually required, but powers are proposed to borrow up to £500,000. The interest charged is $6\frac{1}{2}$%, i.e. 6% for the bank and $\frac{1}{2}$% for administrative expenses, which is less than that for similar loans to India and elsewhere.

      A copy of the terms on which it is proposed to operate the loan and which have been provisionally accepted both by the Anglo-Egyptian Bank and by myself is attached for information.

(Sgd:) A.W. Money,

Major-General,
Chief Administrator.

W.
Encl.

AGRICULTURAL LOANS O.E.T.A. SOUTH.

With a view to the improvement of Agriculture in the Occupied Enemy Territory South, the Anglo-Egyptian Bank Ltd. engages with the Chief Administrator, O.E.T. South to grant loans to cultivators through the O.E.T.A. South on the following terms :-

A. **Between the Administration and the Cultivator :**

(1) Loans are granted to genuine cultivators for the purpose of agricultural improvements. The interest charged on such loans is $6\frac{1}{2}\%$.

(2) The term "improvement" means any work which adds to the produce or to the capital or letting value of the land, and includes the following :-

   (a) The purchase of agricultural implements or stock.

   (b) The construction of works for the supply or distribution of water for the purpose of agriculture.

   (c) The preparation of land for irrigation.

   (d) The reclamation, clearance, enclosure or permanent improvement of land for agricultural purposes.

   (e) Planting and sowing.

(3) Applications for loans will be made to Military Governors on form 'A' attached.

   The applicant will record in column 4 full details as to the nature of the proposed improvement.

   The Military Governor, or a British officer on his behalf, will ascertain by personal examination that the projected improvement will yield a return to the cultivator sufficient to justify the loan applied for.

(4)(a) The security demanded will be a mortgage of immovable property only, which must be of sufficient value to cover the loan granted with interest and charges thereon, after allowing for a margin of 25%.

   The greatest care will be exercised in regard to the title of the mortgagor.

   All mortgages must be made in accordance with the Ottoman Provisional Law for Mortgage of Immovable Property of 2nd March 1331.

   The mortgagor must produce a certificate signed by the Mukhtar and two notables stating that he is the owner of the land offered as security and that there are no encumbrances on it other than those specified. If within a municipal area he must also produce a certificate from the municipality stating whether the property has been leased and if so for what period.

   (b) All mortgages must be registered at the office of the Land Registry or in the Military Governor's office pending the establishment of a registry, and may be renewable every six months up to a period of five years at the option of the Administration. If the borrower chose he may give notice of redeeming the whole amount

before

before the expiry of the period of the loan.

All registration fees in connection with the registration of mortgages are remitted.

(c) When a loan is made to the members of a village community, or to any other persons, on such terms that all of them are jointly and severally bound for the repayment of the whole amount, a statement showing the portion of that amount which each is bound to contribute and signed by each, must be delivered to the District Revenue Department countersigned by a British Officer.

(d) The dwelling-house and agricultural implements of the mortgagor will be admitted as security.

(5) (a) Loans to agriculturists who cultivate state domains or are tenants, require not less than two guarantors who will give as security a mortgage of their own immovable property.

(b) A person having no right to effect permanent improvements, e.g. a tenant, must before applying for loans first obtain the consent in writing, attested by two witnesses, of the landlord personally.

(6) Every loan granted will be repayable by such instalments as may be decided on by the Administration extending over a period of not more than five years from the date of the granting of the loan, or when the loan is advanced in instalments, from the date of the granting of the first instalment paid to the borrower by the Administration.

(7) The interest at the rate of $6\frac{1}{2}\%$ per annum will be collected with the instalments by the District Revenue Department.

The law relating to the collection of arrears of taxation shall apply to the collection of the interest and instalments.

(8) On the completion of enquiry and the verification of security, the Military Governors will forward the application (Forms A. and B.) to this Headquarters with his recommendation for approval.

(9) Periodical reports by the Agricultural Assistant should be made to Military Governors of all improvements on work carried out by cultivators.

(10) The following forms are attached :-

Form A. Application form.
" B. Particulars of security, etc.
" C. Agreement (retained by Military Governor).
" D. Register ("   "   "   "   ).

B. <u>Between the Administration and the Bank</u>:-

(11) The Administration guarantees the loans and interest and their repayment to the Bank on the dates due.

(12) The Bank will not itself ordinarily accept land mortgages, but while allowing this form of security as between the Administration and the borrower, will accept the former in case of foreclosure to dispose of the land by sale to repay the Bank.

(13)

(13) No loans will be for a longer period than five years except in special cases at the request of the Administration.

(14) The Bank will make the loans to the Administration at the rate of six per cent per annum and the Administration shall make itself responsible for the punctual payment of the instalments. Postponement shall only be allowed in special cases on the recommendation of the Administration, and interest at the rate of 9% shall be due on all unpaid instalments.

(15) The Bank shall furnish the Administration with a quarterly statement of outstanding (a) Capital, (b) Interest.

(16) The Administration shall furnish the Bank with a quarterly statement of collections of (a) Capital, (b) Interest.

(17) The total amount to be advanced by the Anglo-Egyptian Bank will not exceed £500,000 unless by special agreement.

(18) In the event of the present British Administration being handed over to that of any other Government the debts due under this scheme and guaranteed by the British Administration to the Anglo-Egyptian Bank will remain guaranteed in all respects as to principal, interest and maturity, by the British Government.

On behalf of the Occupied Enemy Territory Administration South.

(Sgd:) V. Gabriel,

Lieut. Colonel,
Financial Adviser.

AGRICULTURAL LOANS.

Form of Application.

FORM "A".

    Serial No............

    Date ....

    Name, residence etc. of Applicant.

    Amount of loan required.

    Security offered.

    Nature and details of proposed improvement.

    Situation of Land to be improved.

    Applicant's rights in land.

    Proposed dates of repayment.

AGRICULTURAL LOANS.

Particulars of Security etc.

FORM 'B'.

Serial No............
Date   ....

I. Situation and area of the land to be improved.

II. Status of applicant, whether proprietor or tenant. If a tenant, and the landlord's consent is required to any improvement, whether the landlord consents in writing.

III. Security:
    (a) If the land itself or an interest therein, the value of the land, or the nature and value of the interest, as the case may be.

    (b) If property other than the land itself or an interest therein, the nature of the property, the pre-existing encumbrances (if any) thereon, and its value.

    (c) If the property other than the property of the borrower, the names of the guarantors (vide para. 5 (a)) and the nature of the property with pre-existing encumbrances (if any) thereon, and its value.

    (d) If the property is within a municipal area, whether the property has been leased and if so for what period (vide para. 4 (a)).

IV. The improvement :
    (1) Its estimated utility and value.
    (2) Objections, if any, of third parties.
    (3) Date on which it will bring in to yield profit.

V. Repayment :
    (1) Suitable date for first instalment with reference to IV (3).

    (2) Proposed instalments, and dates on which repayable.

IV. Date or dates on which the loan or instalments of it should be received by the applicant.

DEED OF MORTGAGE FOR AGRICULTURAL LOANS.

Serial No........

FORM "C".

    District.
    Village or Town.
    Borrower.
    Amount of Loan.

        This deed made the   day of   1919 between   on behalf of Administration of the O.E.T. (South) hereinafter called the Mortgagee of the one part and   cultivator of   hereinafter called the Mortgagor of the other part witnesses as follows :

    (1)   The Mortgagee has agreed to lend to the Mortgagor and the Mortgagor has agreed to receive and hereby acknowledges the receipt of the sum of L.E.   Mills.   which loan is for a period of   years from

    (2)   The Mortgagor undertakes to repay to the Mortgagee the said sum of L.E.   Mills.   together with interest yearly at the rate of   % at the office of the Military Govt. by instalments as set out in Schedule I. hereto.

    (3)   The Mortgagor hereby mortgages the property described in Schedule II. hereto in addition to the land for the benefit of which the loan is granted as security for the payment of the said sum of L.E.   Mills.   and interest according to the instalments shown in Schedule I.

    (4)   The Mortgagor undertakes to use the loan advanced for the purpose of :

        (a)   (Here describe the improvements to be effected) for the benefit of (here describe the land to be benefited).

        (b)   The loan shall be applied solely to the purpose specified above, and if it shall be proved to the satisfaction of the Military Governor of   that any part of the loan has been misapplied, the whole amount of the loan shall at once be deemed to become due together with such interest as may have accrued due thereon, as well as costs (if any).

        (c)   Unless (here enter any condition as to the period or periods appointed for commencing or completing the work or improvements) has been commenced by (date) or completed by (date)   (as the case may be) the loan shall be held to have been misapplied.

    (5)   If the Mortgagor fails to pay any of the instalments when they fall due, the Mortgagee shall have the right to call on him at once for the payment of the whole sum and any interest that may be due thereon.

    (6)   In default of the payment of the sum due the Mortgagee shall have the right to apply to the Court for the sale of the property mortgaged in the manner laid down by the 'Provisional Law for the mortgage of Immovable property of 16 Rabi Tani 1331' as amended.

FORM 'C'

SCHEDULE I.

	Principle. L.E. M.	Interest. L.E. M.	Costs. L.E. M.	Total. L.E. M.	Date of payment
1st Instalment.					
2nd Instalment.					
3rd Instalment.					
4th Instalment.					
5th Instalment.					

SCHEDULE II.

Nature of tenure.

Description of property.

Area.

Boundaries.

I understand and agree to the aforesaid terms and conditions.

Signed or sealed by ....

In the presence of ....

Signed or sealed by ....

In the presence of ....

This deed was registered under No.   on the   day of in the Land Registry of the District of   and the register of   Town or village No.

                                        Registrar of Lands

                                        District of

2.02

PALESTINE.

CONFIDENTIAL.

Reference No. Adm.2/813.

GOVERNMENT HOUSE,
JERUSALEM.

3rd July, 1924.

Sir,

I have the honour to refer to your predecessor's despatch Confidential of the 10th December, 1923, and to transmit a copy of a summary of Agricultural Loans as on 31st March, 1924.

2. The attention of the District Governors has been directed to the large balances outstanding and they have been instructed to make every effort to collect the arrears as soon as the crops now being harvested are available for sale.

3. I transmit, for purpose of comparison with the summary now provided, copies of the documents attached to the Treasurer's letter of the 25th of October, together with a copy of the report of the Committee appointed to investigate the question of Agricultural Loans, which were requested in the second paragraph of the despatch under reference.

4/

Right Honourable J.H.Thomas, P.C., M.P.,
His Majesty's Principal Secretary of State
    for the Colonies.

- 2 -

4. The delay in furnishing the statement of the difference of interest in respect of arrears payable to the Bank has been due to the fact that this statement could only be prepared from the books of the local branch of the Bank, and that its compilation was found to involve considerable difficulties. The Manager of the Jerusalem Branch of the Anglo-Egyptian Bank, however, is disposed to agree that the rate of six per cent, only, should apply to loans obtained from the Bank by Government, and that the rate of nine per cent, quoted in clause 14 of the Agreement of 20th April, 1919, applies only as between cultivators and the Government; he has sought the authority of the Head Office to enter into an agreement with the Treasury here to that effect. The presentation of the statement, therefore, is no longer a matter of urgency and possibly will not be necessary at all in the event of the proposed agreement being concluded.

                    I have the honour to be,

                            Sir,

                        Your most obedient,

                              humble servant,

Gilbert Clayton

OFFICER ADMINISTERING THE GOVERNMENT.

SUMMARY OF AGRICULTURAL LOANS
AS AT 30.9.1923.

Total Loans Issued	Total Repayments	Balances Outstanding	Instalments Due	Repayments of Due Instalments	Repayments of Instalments before Due Date	Arrears of Due Instalments	Arrears of Interest	Total Arrears	% of Arrears of Instalments due at 30.9.23
£. T/ms	£. T/ms	£. T/ms	£. T/ms	£. T/ms	£. T/ms	£. T/ms	£. T/ms	£. T/ms	
20,762,000	7,268,000	13,494,000	12,218,500	7,169,000	109,000	5,169,500	66,711	5,236,211	41.9
9,815,000	2,328,300	7,486,700	7,667,000	2,328,300	–	5,338,700	19,272	5,357,972	69.0
4,097,000	2,947,000	1,150,000	2,889,000	2,889,000	50,000	–	–	–	–
1,707,170	785,000	922,170	1,575,170	785,000	–	790,170	72,497	861.637	50.1
153,294,157	51,892,130	101,402,027	94,994,000	45,213,130	6,079,000	39,160,967	6,929,433	45,090,400	48.4
55,666,760	30,914,639	24,752,121	40,329,420	30,779,330	155,000	9,540,829	711,130	10,251,959	23.7
13,728,000	6,115,500	7,612,500	6,882,000	6,007,500	48,000	816,500	76,705	917,205	11.0
20,639,500	16,254,500	4,385,965	19,015,000	16,856,635	–	1,721,465	6,957	1,854,452	9.0
44,676,647	21,276,090	23,400,557	24,547,000	20,925,000	315,000	3,554,015	33,070	3,917,085	14.6
30,379,838	16,346,749	14,031,092	19,718,100	16,135,749	215,000	3,564,390	427,556	4,012,926	15.2
36,158,000	15,571,480	20,587,550	16,172,000	15,225,300	346,450	607,500	159,195	1,116,895	5.8
15,336,000	7,676,063	7,157,017	11,499,000	7,854,063	24,000	3,44,917	23,935	3,907,852	31.7
35,542,810	18,234,465	17,304,345	21,856,000	18,766,465	150,000	2,837,871	420,471	3,258,262	13.2
29,834,500	13,738,871	16,095,129	16,495,000	13,222,471	543,900	3,272,632	290,410	3,562,942	19.3
47,123,000	14,287,765	32,835,235	28,975,075	14,002,765	287,000	14,974,310	1,577,243	16,551,553	31.7
16,972,000	6,969,950	10,002,050	15,728,000	6,808,950	61,000	8,919,050	273,925	7,192,975	42.7
15,577,000	7,594,411	7,961,589	12,468,411	7,594,411	–	4,873,925	253,145	5,122,070	32.1
561,211,000	241,197,438	320,773,944	309,534,000	256,136,166	9,371,550	107,169,351	12,317,647	119,085,798	31.5

(Sgd.) B. S. DAVIS
TREASURER

Treasury,
Khartoum,
4th October, 1923.

[Copy is poor in original file, this and following 2 pages.]

SUMMARY OF AGRICULTURAL LOANS
as at 31st March 1924

District	Total Loans Issued	Total Repayments	Balance Outstanding	Instalments Due	Repayments of Due Instalments	Instalments paid before date	Arrears of Due Instalments	Arrears of Interest	Total Arrears	% of Arrears of Instalments Due at 31.3.24
	L£.m/ms	L£.m/ms	L£.m/ms	L£.m/ms	L£.m/ms	L£.m/ms	L£.m/ms	L£.m/ms	L£.m/ms	
...alem	20,782.000	10,937.500	9,824.500	18,272.000	10,904.000	33.500	7,368.000	408.490	7,776.490	40.3
...llah	9,815.000	3,784.800	6,030.200	8,961.000	3,784.800	-	5,176.200	297.983	5,474.183	57.7
...lehem	4,097.000	3,626.000	471.000	3,619.000	3,619.000	7.000	-	-	-	-
...cho	1,707.170	1,117.975	589.195	1,707.170	1,117.975	-	589.195	49.920	639.115	34.5
...h ...:	153,284.157	67,094.550	86,199.607	104,014.157	61,780.550	1,314.000	42,233.607	5,174.183	47,407.790	46.6
	65,666.760	36,523.849	29,142.911	49,501.359	36,193.849	330.000	13,307.510	800.032	14,107.542	26.9
...ababa	13,728.000	8,242.500	5,485.500	9,066.500	8,230.500	12.000	828.000	20.345	848.345	9.1
...on ...:	20,839.500	18,071.762	2,767.718	18,298.000	18,070.032	1.750	227.968	2.968	230.936	1.2
...in	44,678.647	27,894.588	16,784.059	39,443.202	27,860.588	34.000	5,582.614	340.590	5,923.204	13.7
...urm	30,379.638	19,876.654	10,503.184	23,799.838	19,710.654	166.000	4,089.184	339.606	4,428.790	17.1
...in	36,159.000	18,677.450	17,481.550	25,448.000	18,574.450	103.000	6,873.550	663.811	7,537.361	27
...an ...:	16,086.000	9,989.274	5,096.726	11,501.098	9,871.274	63.000	1,630.724	128.310	1,759.034	14.2
...fa	36,242.810	25,151.430	11,091.380	28,946.609	25,091.430	60.000	3,855.379	592.923	4,448.302	13.3
...r	29,834.500	18,482.856	11,351.644	24,814.616	18,063.856	419.000	6,750.960	347.978	7,098.938	27.2
...areth	47,123.000	16,340.585	30,782.415	33,781.580	16,212.585	28.000	17,468.995	1,853.381	19,322.376	51.7
...erias	16,972.000	8,286.701	8,685.299	14,404.000	8,272.701	14.000	6,121.299	337.610	6,458.909	42.5
...a?	15,576.000	9,837.121	5,738.879	12,523.000	9,837.121	-	2,685.679	136.267	2,822.146	21.4
	561,311.382	303,885.615	258,025.767	422,088.429	297,295.365	6,500.250	124,773.064	11,494.417	136,287.481	29.5

The Treasury,
Jerusalem.
5th June, 1924.

(Signed) S. S. DAVIS
TREASURER.

ANALYSIS OF ARREARS AT 30TH SEPTEMBER, 1923, IN RESPECT OF INSTALMENTS AND INTEREST PAYMENT IN THE PARTICULAR YEARS.

96

	Arrears Due 1920-21			Arrears Due 1921-22			Arrears Due 1922-23			Arrears Due (1st April to 30 September) (1923-24)			Grand Total		
	Principal	Interest	Total	Principal	Interest	Total	Principal	Interest	Total	Principal	Interest	Total	Principal	Interest	Total
	LE.m/ms	LE.m/ms	LE.m/ms	LE.m/ms	LE.m/ms	LE.m/ms	LE.m/ms	LE.m/ms	LE.m/ms	LE.m/ms	LE.m/ms	LE.m/ms	LE.m/ms	LE.m/ms	LE.m/ms
[illegible]	191.500	88.358	279.858	1417.000	176.253	1593.253	2441.000	212.100	2653.100	110.000	-	110.000	6159.500	476.711	5636.211
[illegible]	1149.000	157.782	1306.782	1754.000	131.475	1885.475	2435.700	60.065	2495.765	-	-	-	5338.700	349.272	5687.972
[illegible]	-	-	-	-	-	-	-	-	-	-	-	-	-	-	-
[illegible]	-	33.465	33.465	55.000	35.047	90.047	655.170	2.925	658.095	80.000	-	80.000	790.170	71.427	861.597
[illegible]	1405.005	243.153	1648.158	5418.060	1731.950	7150.010	16618.950	2152.360	18771.320	15739.052	1731.950	17471.002	39180.967	5859.433	45040.400
[illegible]	56.000	13.000	69.000	505.000	76.155	581.155	2682.828	315.357	2998.185	6306.001	346.668	6652.669	9549.829	751.180	10301.009
[illegible]	-	2.800	2.800	20.000	1.300	21.300	80.000	3.900	83.900	718.500	90.905	809.405	818.500	98.705	917.205
[illegible]	10.000	0.650	10.650	40.345	-	40.345	333.120	-	333.120	1378.000	92.317	1470.317	1761.465	92.967	1854.432
[illegible]	133.825	21.905	155.330	446.000	37.400	483.400	2302.890	187.685	2490.575	701.500	86.620	788.120	3584.015	333.670	3917.685
[illegible]	188.000	75.725	263.725	503.000	103.935	606.935	1902.390	131.628	2034.018	991.000	117.250	1108.250	3584.390	428.538	4012.928
[illegible]	-	-	-	425.000	54.275	479.275	462.500	100.620	563.120	60.000	14.300	74.300	947.500	169.195	1116.695
[illegible]	-	-	-	94.822	27.950	122.772	918.045	73.300	991.345	2632.050	160.735	2792.885	3644.917	263.035	3907.952
[illegible]	-	-	-	-	-	-	288.331	227.348	515.679	2579.540	193.043	2772.583	2867.871	420.391	3288.262
[illegible]	-	-	-	390.734	96.356	487.090	2882.098	194.154	3076.252	-	-	-	3272.832	290.510	3563.342
[illegible]	[illegible]	4.680	42.680	2514.730	308.854	2823.584	5968.580	748.944	6717.524	6453.000	514.865	6967.865	14974.310	1577.343	16551.653
[illegible]	-	-	-	829.322	81.185	910.507	3422.728	219.660	3642.388	2567.000	76.480	2643.480	6819.050	377.325	7196.375
[illegible]	-	3.829	3.829	62.795	30.225	93.020	1500.440	138.476	1638.916	3310.700	135.795	3446.495	4873.935	308.135	5182.070
[illegible]	[illegible]	[illegible]	3816.037	14475.806	2802.360	17268.168	45894.870	4768.542	50663.212	43626.343	3562.038	47188.381	107167.951	11867.847	[illegible]

The Treasury,
Jerusalem.
24th October, 1923.

(Signed) S. S. DAVIS
TREASURER.

SUMMARY OF AGRICULTURAL LOANS

at the end of March, June and September, 1923.

Particulars	At 31st March, 1923. £E.	At 30th June, 1923. £E.	At 30th Sept., 1923. £E.
Total Loans Issued.........	554,289	561,751	561,911
Total Repayments...........	191,117	203,690	241,137
Outstanding................	363,172	358,061	320,774
Instalments Due............	279,578	289,936	339,334
Payments of Instalments Due...................	183,310	194,544	232,166
Payments of Instalments before Due Date.......	7,806	9,145	8,971
Arrears of Instalments.....	96,268	95,392	107,168
Arrears of Interest........	11,412	12,084	11,867
Total Arrears.......£E.	107,680	107,476	119,035

(Signed) S. S. DAVIS

<u>TREASURER.</u>

Treasury,
Jerusalem.
October, 1923.

STATEMENT SHOWING THE TOTAL LOANS ISSUED AND REPAYMENTS DURING EACH FINANCIAL YEAR.

Year	Loans Issued	Repayments
	£E. m/ms	£E. m/ms
1919 - 20	151,762.750	6,945. -
1920 - 21	195,642.997	32,466.033
1921 - 22	119,846.135	72,197.903
1922 - 23	87,037.500	79,507.985
1923 - 24 (1st April to 30th September)	7,622. -	50,020.517
Total £E.	561,911.882	241,137.438
Balance outstanding £E.		320,773.944

(Signed) S. S. DAVIS
TREASURER.

Treasury,
Jerusalem.
th October, 1923.

--oo-- A G R I C U L T U R A L   L O A N S. --oo--

P R E L I M I N A R Y.

CLASSIFICATION OF AGRICULTURAL LOANS.

The Palestine Government has followed the practice of the previous Military Administration in dividing Agricultural Loans, for the purpose of issue, into two main classes. The period allowed for the repayment of loans not exceeding £60 may extend to three years; that for the repayment of larger loans may extend to five. The two classes have therefore been officially designated Long Term and Short Term Loans.

In the financial year 1922-23 the classification was modified by sub-division. The full classification of Agricultural Loans at the present time is therefore as follows:-

A. LOANS EXCEEDING £60 (LONG TERM LOANS).

(1) Period.
The period for repayment may extend to five years.

(2) Security.
The security must be a mortgage on immovable property.

(3) Sanctioning Authority.

(a) Loans exceeding £300.
The sanction of the Treasurer and subsequently of the Chief Secretary is necessary.

(b) Loans not exceeding £300.
Sanction may be given, within the limits of the sum allotted to him for the purpose, by the District Governor.

- 2 -

B. LOANS NOT EXCEEDING £60 (SHORT TERM LOANS).

(1) Period.

The period for repayment may extend to three years.

(2) Sanctioning Authority.

Sanction may be given, within the limits allotted to him for the purpose, by the District Governor.

(3) Security.

(a) For Loans exceeding £20.

The security must be a mortgage on immovable property.

(b) For Loans not exceeding £20.

Subject to certain collateral guarantees, the security of the crops may be accepted.

It is thus clear that the real criterion for determining the sanctioning authority, the period for repayment and the form of security is the amount of the loan and that the classification might be made more aptly into Large and Small Loans.

PRESENT SYSTEM OF AGRICULTURAL LOANS.

I. METHOD OF ISSUE.

A Committee is usually formed in each Sub-District, of which the Sub-District Governor is President and the Assistant Inspector of Revenue, the Agricultural Inspector or Agricultural Assistant, and the Land Registrar are members, to deal with all applications for Agricultural Loans. The number of applications for Long Term Loans is usually small, but the applications for Short Term Loans usually amount to several thousand. The procedure may be divided into four stages.

First/

- 3 -

FIRST STAGE (PRELIMINARY).

(1) <u>Application.</u>

The cultivator desiring a loan submits a written application for a loan of a certain amount, stating the purpose for which he requires it and offering the requisite security.

(2) <u>Rejection for previous Indebtedness.</u>

The application is passed to the local Revenue Department for scrutiny, and if the applicant is already in debt to the Government for a loan, it is forthwith rejected. Further, in some districts, if the applicant owes arrears of taxes or tithes, his application is similarly rejected. In other districts an application is not rejected on this score unless the arrears are considerable. In other districts again, such arrears are not considered at all.

SECOND STAGE (INVESTIGATION).

Applications not disqualified under the terms of the previous section are then further examined.

A. <u>Long Term Loans.</u>

(1) <u>Examination of Title.</u>

(a) <u>Property to be improved.</u>

The local Land Registrar verifies the applicant's title to the property to be improved.

(b) <u>Security.</u>

He similarly verifies the title to the property offered as security.

(2) <u>Inspection of Properties.</u>

(a) <u>Property to be improved.</u>

The property to be improved is inspected

by a/

- 4 -

by a representative of the Agricultural Department. When the amount of the loan applied for exceeds £300, the inspection is made by the Agricultural Inspector of the Circle concerned; when it does not exceed £300, it is inspected by the Agricultural Assistant. The inspecting official reports on the desirability, the practicability and the probable cost of the proposed improvements.

(b) Security.

The same official inspects the property offered as security and reports whether in his opinion a mortgage on it would provide adequate security for the loan.

B. Short Term Loans.

(1) Examination of Title, or Guarantee.
 (a) When a mortgage is required, the procedure is the same as for Long Term Loans.
 (b) If not, the necessary bond and guarantees are examined to ascertain that they are in proper order.

(2) Inspection of Properties.

Owing to the numbers involved, the inspection of individual properties is not always practicable.

THIRD STAGE (SELECTION).

At the end of the first two stages, a certain number of applications have been disqualified, but the funds available are never sufficient to permit of granting all the remaining applications. The Committee is therefore obliged to select those to which preference is to be given and to consider the amount to be granted to each.

1/

- 5 -

1. Selection.

 A. Long Term Loans.

 The principal factor in determining which loans shall be granted is the recommendation of the Agricultural Inspector or the Agricultural Assistant.

 B. Short Term Loans.

 The methods adopted usually comprise two stages: In the former, attention is paid to villages or sub-tribes; in the latter, it is paid to individuals. For the sake of brevity the term "village" will be considered to include "sub-tribe".

 (1) Village (or Sub-Tribe).

 (a) Usually out of the total sum available for a Sub-District a fixed sum is allotted to each village in accordance with its population or its special needs.

 As a development of this system, it may happen that the total sum available is allotted to certain villages and that no allotment is made to others. If any village does not utilise the full amount of its allotment, the surplus is re-allotted to other villages.

 (b) Sometimes a list of villages is drawn up in the order of their need for loans as estimated by the Committee, and all applications from a village higher on the list have preference over any application from villages lower on the list.

N.B./

- 6 -

<u>N.B.</u> In estimating the needs of a village, the Committee considers the state of its crops, the ravages of pests, the damages caused by drought or fire and any special circumstances.

2. <u>Individuals.</u>

(a) If the method of allotment to villages has been adopted, it is usually necessary to make a further selection among individual applicants.

(1) As a rule, the Committee depends mainly on the recommendations of the Mukhtar and the Elders of each village but supplements them with information from any other available source. One Sub-District Governor dispenses altogether with the recommendations of Mukhtars and Elders and relies on secret information from individuals in each village whom he trusts.

(2) Another method is to take the applicants in the order of application, on the principle of "First come, first served".

(3) Yet another method is to select applicants by lot, applications from each village being drawn haphazard till the allotment has been exhausted.

(b) If an order of preference has been drawn up no further selection is necessary. The exhaustion of the available funds automatically limits the issue of loans.

3. <u>Amounts Granted.</u>

Unless either the amount allotted to a village is sufficient to pay all eligible appli-
applicants/

- 7 -

applicants the amounts for which they have respectively applied or an order of preference has been adopted, another difficulty is to determine the amount of the loan to be granted to each eligible applicant.

   (1) One system is to grant the full amount applied for to applicants selected by one of the three methods described (in section B 2) above.

   (2) Another system is to reduce each amount applied for in the proportion of the village allotment to the total amount applied for in that village. E.g. If £250 has been allotted to a village and the total which it is desired to grant amounts to £1000, each eligible applicant receives one quarter of the sum he applied for.

   (3) On one occasion loans were granted in accordance with the amount of tithe paid by each eligible applicant in the previous two years. E.g. A man who had paid £60 in tithe might be granted a loan of £40, while one who had paid £10 in tithe might be granted £15.

FOURTH STAGE (APPROVAL).

   There remains the final approval.

A. Long Term Agricultural Loans.

   All applications for Long Term Agricultural Loans are usually forwarded by the Sub-District Committee with its comments and recommendations to the District Governor.

   (1) Loans exceeding £300.

      After examination of these applications, the

District/

- 8 -

District Governor forwards those he himself recommends to the Treasurer. After further examination, the Treasurer either approves or refuses the loans recommended. In the former event, he almost invariably makes a large reduction from the amount recommended. Final approval rests with the Chief Secretary.

(2) Loans not exceeding £300.

The District Governor himself sanctions those loans of which he approves for such amounts as he sees fit.

B. Short Term Loans.

The District Governor usually delegates to Sub-District Governors authority to sanction on his behalf Short Term Loans up to the amount allotted to the Sub-District. The Sub-District Governor, therefore, sanctions the loans recommended by his local Committee.

II. CONDITIONS FOR LOANS.

The conditions on which loans are granted may be summed up as follows:-

(1) Security.

A. Loans exceeding £20.

The security must be a mortgage on immovable property. A mortgage on a share of Musha' land less than one quarter of the whole is rarely accepted.

B. Loans not exceeding £20.

The borrower is required to enter into a bond to refund the loan at the time or the times appointed. The borrower is also required to produce two guarantors

certified/

- 9 -

certified by the Mukhtar to be owners of immovable property, men of standing, and able to refund the loan in the event of default by the borrower.

In some places a direct guarantee from the Mukhtar is accepted instead of guarantees from two other individuals. The bond, the guarantees and the certificate must be registered by the Public Notary.

(2) Period.

A. Long Term Loans.

The period for repayment may not exceed five years.

B. Short Term Loans.

The period for repayment may not exceed three years.

(3) Repayment.

The loan is repayable in annual instalments, the first being payable at the end of the first year, or, in some Districts, with the first instalment of Winter Tithes.

(4) Interest.

Interest is ordinarily at the rate of $6\frac{1}{2}\%$, but on arrears overdue the rate is increased to 9%. The interest for the first year is paid in advance.

(5) Penal Clause.

If the loan is spent for any purpose other than that for which it was granted; or if the improvements are not effected within the specified, or within a reasonable, time; the Government may demand immediate repayment of the loan and the

interest/

- 10 -

interest in full, and in default of such payment may foreclose the mortgage or come upon the guarantors as the case may be.

III. SUBSEQUENT CONTROL OF LOANS.

Administrative Officials and Officials of the Department of Agriculture do what they can to control the use made of loans issued. The control of Long Term Loans is in some degree effective, but, owing to the large number of loans, the amount of detail involved and the great opportunities for fraud, the control of Short Term Loans is quite ineffective. Consequently money granted in Agricultural Loans is frequently devoted to other purposes.

(1) Some borrowers waste it on unproductive expenditure, such as the purchase of luxuries, or the celebration of marriages.

(2) Others devote it to paying Government tithes and taxes.

(3) Others again devote it to paying off loans to Banks or to private money-lenders.

(4) If one man is unable to obtain a loan for himself he sometimes arranges with another man to obtain it for him. The latter doubtless receives a consideration for his altruism.

(5) Many borrowers lend out the money received for Agricultural Loans in smaller sums at exorbitant rates of interest. Sometimes the sums thus lent are lent again at still higher rates of interest. Though Long Term Loans naturally offer most scope for this practice, it extends even to Short Term Loans.

IV/

- 11 -

IV. RECOVERY OF LOANS.

Twenty days before each instalment falls due, the Revenue Department sends a notice to the borrower concerned.

Should he fail to pay, a warning is sent that unless he pays within ten days, legal action will be taken against him.

If the warning is ineffectual, in theory, the Revenue Department has recourse to the Courts. In some places it has been arranged that the papers shall be passed direct to the Execution Officer.

In practice, partly through leniency, partly owing to the vast amount of clerical work involved, partly owing to the paucity of Execution Officers, legal seizure has comparatively rarely been made. Consequently, large amounts of arrears are due from many borrowers.

CRITICISM OF PRESENT SYSTEM.

I. METHOD OF ISSUE.

FIRST STAGE.

The Committee emphasized the importance of requiring from the applicant a detailed statement of the improvements he proposed to make together with an estimate of the cost of each item.

SECOND STAGE.

The Committee had no comments to offer.

THIRD STAGE.

A. <u>Long Term Loans</u>.

The Committee considered the existing system to be satisfactory.

B/

- 12 -

B. Short Term Loans.

The Committee recognised that none of the methods of selection and of determining the amounts to be granted were satisfactory. The recommendations of Mukhtars and Elders are hardly likely to be impartial, and to obtain information by other means was becoming with the decrease of Staff increasingly difficult. On the whole the method of taking applications in the order in which they were received and granting the full sum applied for seemed to be the least objectionable.

FOURTH STAGE.

The Committee was of opinion that the Local Authorities were in a better position than the Treasurer to judge the merits of an application. The Committee, therefore, considered that the District Governor should, within the limits of the sum allotted to his District, be empowered to sanction both Long Term and Short Term Loans, and for small loans, say, up to £50, should delegate his powers to Sub-District Governors. This system would have the further advantage of avoiding much delay. To minimise the risk of bad debts in the absence of direct Treasury supervision (and also, as will appear later, for other reasons), it was thought desirable that the amount of a loan should not exceed one quarter of the value of the security offered. It was also thought that a maximum of £500 should be fixed for loans.

II. CONDITIONS.

(1) /

- 13 -

(1) Security.

  (a) Loans above £20.

    The Committee was of opinion that Musha' Land should be partitioned before it could be accepted as security.

  (b) Loans not exceeding £20.

    It was pointed out that the cost of registration by the Public Notary of loans not exceeding £20 consumed an appreciable portion of the loan. The Committee, therefore, decided to recommend that registration by the Public Notary should be abolished or, alternatively, if for legal reasons it was necessary, that it should be effected without fee.

(2) & (3) Period and repayment.

    The Committee commented also on the period allowed for repayment and the conditions of repayment. It was thought that for certain purposes a period of five years was too short, and that payment of the first instalment at the end of one year was inequitable. If the loan were devoted to ordinary crops, the present conditions were satisfactory; but many kinds of tree did not yield any produce for a number of years, and until the borrower received some return for his outlay, it was impossible for him to repay any instalments of his loan. The Committee, therefore, considered that the conditions of repayment for each loan should be fixed on its individual merits.

III./

- 14 -

III. CONTROL.

The Committee was strongly of opinion that most of the disadvantages attached to the present system of Agricultural Loans were due to the inadequacy of the subsequent control, as a result of which loans were very frequently misapplied.

Sometimes the money was devoted to unproductive expenditure and, therefore, instead of helping the cultivator, tended to pauperise him and to increase his indebtedness. To recover the sums due to it, the Government was then obliged to resort to seizure, and this naturally caused discontent. Sometimes the money was lent out again at exorbitant rates of interest. In this event, the issue of loans not only facilitated a most objectionable practice, but also afforded to other cultivators greater opportunities of accumulating a hopeless burden of debt and thereby defeated its own object.

It was, therefore, most important to control the use to which loans were put and rigidly to enforce the penal clause when they were misapplied.

PRECAUTIONS.

The Committee, therefore, proceeded to discuss possible methods of facilitating control and the machinery for putting these methods into effect.

A. METHODS.

(1) Village Responsibility.

It was proposed that the details of the disbursements which a borrower/ had named in his application/

- 15 -

application should be posted in each village and that the whole village should be responsible for seeing that the loan was really spent for these purposes. If any default was discovered, the whole village would be penalised by being refused any agricultural loans for one or more years.

The Committee felt that this precaution would probably be ineffective, as the notables would band together to conceal any default from the Government while the smaller men would not dare to expose it. Further it was felt that the innocent would unduly suffer for the guilty. The proposal was, therefore, rejected.

(2) Certificate from Borrower.

It was next proposed that each borrower should within a fixed period forward to the Local Committee a certificate that he had actually disbursed the loan in the manner shown in his application. As small loans were always expended promptly, the period should not exceed one year.

Many objections were pointed out to this proposal. The certificate in itself was worthless; verification of each item was impracticable; the possibilities of fraud were enormous. For example, it was not practicable to verify repairs to ploughs, wages paid to weeders, etc.; nor was it possible to ensure that the recipient of a loan did not borrow some one else's

animals/

- 16 -

animals for the purpose of the inspection. Even if branding was introduced, villagers were quite capable of keeping a few branded cattle for inspection purposes.

(3) Control by Village Committees.

It was then suggested that an Agricultural Loan Committee should be formed in each village (as is done at present in one Sub-District); and that the Local Committee should forward to these Village Committees lists of the expenditure which each borrower in their village proposed to make. The four or five members of each Village Committee would be required to certify at the appointed time that the loan had been properly expended and they would be personally liable to the penalties of the Ottoman Code if they rendered a false certificate. The Committee finally agreed that a combination of the last two suggestions was the best system that could be recommended. The majority of the Committee was of opinion that the introduction of this system would lead to a considerable improvement in control, but would still leave much to be desired. The minority considered that the improvement would be so small as to be almost negligible.

(4) Tree Loans.

Another suggestion made was that loans should be granted only for the purpose of planting trees. The advantage of this system was that control would be comparatively easy. After some discussion the majority of the

Committee/

- 17 -

Committee was opposed to so severe a limitation. It was thought desirable, however, that, in order to encourage tree-planting, one of the conditions of every loan should be that the borrower must plant 10 trees for every £1 of loan granted. It was explained that this would normally involve no expenditure but only a little trouble in obtaining plants from the various forest areas (ahrash). As some lands were not suitable for tree-planting the Local Committee should be empowered to remit this condition if adequate reason were shown.

Applications for tree loans should be submitted in September, examined in October, and issued in November; planting should take place in January and February and inspection in April.

B. MACHINERY.

It was thought that, as the Agricultural Department was mainly responsible for the issue of Long Term Loans, it should also be responsible for the control of them; but it was admitted by the majority that the Department had not time nor staff to devote to such control. Certain members, however, desired to record their opinion that a Department spending £42,000 per annum ought to be able to find time and staff for this purpose.

As regards Short Term Loans, certain members contended that if administrative officials could find time to attend to the Tithe Estimation in summer, they could also

find/

- 18 -

find time to attend to the control of loans in winter.

The majority of the Committee was, however, of the opinion that there were so many details to be supervised, not only in winter but throughout the year, and so many possibilities of fraud, that ordinary administrative officials could not exercise adequate control.

It was, therefore, suggested that a special Department should be created to deal with the issue, control and recovery of loans, with a Senior Official and a clerk in each Sub-District, and that the interest on loans should be increased from $6\frac{1}{2}\%$ to 8% or 9% to defray the cost. However, after long discussion it was agreed that the establishment of a new Department would probably be impracticable at a time of financial stress and that in any case an Agricultural Bank would perform the required work more efficiently. In the end the Committee was unanimously of opinion that the establishment of an Agricultural Bank with adequate capital was the only satisfactory solution of the problem.

ISSUE IN KIND.

The Committee next discussed the question of issuing loans in kind instead of in money.

I. ARRANGEMENTS FOR ISSUE.

    A. Government Depots.

One arrangement for dealing with issue in kind would be to establish Government depots. This arrangement would, however, be open to numerous objections:-

(1) /

- 19 -

(1) The expense of the initial outlay and of the subsequent management would be heavy.

(2) There would be danger of loss while the grain, live stock, etc., was awaiting distribution.

(3) The fellah could buy his requirements cheaper elsewhere.

(4) Consequently he would suspect the Government of profiteering.

(5) (a) If the Government stocks were standardised, prices might be lower than elsewhere; but the fellah would probably not like the particular standard selected. For example, he utterly refuses a new type of grain seed which experiment has shown to yield from 15% to 60% more than the usual seed.

(b) If the stocks were not standardised the cost of keeping a large assortment of agricultural commodities would be prohibitive.

B. <u>Purchase by Government Officials as required.</u>

An alternative method would be for a Government official, perhaps of the Agricultural Department, to buy things as they were required. As he would buy only things of good quality, the standard of grain, live stock, etc., would thus be raised. However, to do this successfully, the official would have to study the market carefully and devote a long time to

each/

- 20 -

each operation. A case was quoted where the "Agronome" of a Jewish Colony spent over a year in buying live stock for forty persons. Another objection to this arrangement is that it involves the entry of the Government into the market in the capacity of a merchant or dealer.

C. **Purchase by Borrower under Government Supervision.**

A third course would be for a Government official to accompany each borrower while he made his purchases. Under this system the hope of introducing commodities of a better class would be lost. Above all, in view of the vast number of loans issued each year, the system would be so cumbrous as to be impossible.

II. POSSIBILITIES OF FRAUD.

Various possibilities of fraud were next pointed out.

A. **Sale of Supplies issued.**

The fellah might sell the supplies issued to him as a loan and devote to wrong purposes the amount thus obtained.

It was suggested that this danger might be obviated by stamping all live stock, implements, etc., issued. However, certain villagers were quite capable of keeping a few branded cattle for inspection purposes.

B. **Theft, Poisoning, etc.**

Next, the supplies issued might be stolen, live stock might be poisoned and so on. The Government would then lose its security.

Further/

- 21 -

Further, a mock theft might be arranged in order to defraud the Government.

III. OTHER DIFFICULTIES.

There remained the fact that money instead of kind was sometimes essential.

A. A borrower might need to make a number of petty disbursements, e.g., for repair of ploughs, which could not possibly be arranged through the Government.

B. Money was also necessary for paying wages to weeders or other labourers, and for rendering assistance to so-called "partners".

After full discussion of the question, the Committee was almost unanimously of opinion that the issue of loans, whether Long Term or Short Term, in kind was neither practicable nor desirable.

IV. RECOVERY OF LOANS.

The Committee was of opinion that all instalments should be promptly collected and that legal action should be taken immediately against defaulters. The Government was now beginning to follow this rule, but had not done so in the past. Consequently debtors were being called upon to pay all at once the arrears due for several years. It was argued that the object of agricultural loans was to benefit the cultivator, and that the present severity defeated that object. The Committee was of opinion that the existence of these arrears was partly attributable to the undue leniency displayed by the Government and, therefore, considered that certain concessions should be made to debtors.

After considerable discussion the Committee

proposed/

- 22 -

proposed that

(a) as a general principle for the future, foreclosure (and similar penalties) should be rigidly enforced against defaulters.

(b) but that as a special concession for the past, in view of the partial responsibility of the Government for the default, only one year's arrears should be demanded in each twelve months from any debtor.

In detail, it was proposed that a notice should be published in the Official Gazette to the effect that, at a date three months later than the date of the notice, every debtor who owed arrears of agricultural loans would be called upon to pay one instalment of his loan together with the interest up to date; that a year after this date (i.e. 15 months after the original notice), he would be called upon to pay the second instalment together with interest up to date; and so forth. If he failed to pay any of the amounts thus demanded, foreclosure would be made without delay.

The effect of the proposal would be to alter the repayment dates of all loans on which arrears were due on the date named in the Gazette and to leave all other loan contracts as they were.

It was then suggested that if concessions were granted to those who had not paid at all, say, for three years, some concessions should also be made to those who had paid regularly in the past but were in difficulties over the impending instalment. The majority of the Committee, however, was of the opinion that a graduated scale of concessions would be hopelessly complicated;

that/

that complete equality of treatment was impossible; and that the only practicable distinction was between the past for which the Government was partly responsible and the future when every one would have fair warning of what he had to expect.

Certain members were of opinion that the difficulty of collecting arrears was due entirely to the present poverty of the cultivators, which they were inclined to attribute to the importation of Australian flour. They, therefore, considered that the Government had shown not an undue but a proper leniency in not pressing the recovery of arrears. They were naturally in favour of the proposed concessions, but they also agreed that greater severity in taking legal action was necessary in the future.

The Committee was further of opinion that the sum available for Agricultural Loans in each District and Sub-District should be fixed for a term of years. Fresh loans could then only be granted as funds became available from the repayment of previous loans. It would thus be to the general interest to see that borrowers paid their instalments at the proper time. It would be necessary, however, that the sums allotted should be generous and that the transition to the new system should not be too abrupt.

To secure that the repayment of instalments should not be too heavy a burden on a borrower and to minimise the hardship if legal seizure should become necessary. The Committee considered that the amount of a loan should never exceed one quarter of the security offered.

Benefit/

- 24 -

BENEFIT OF LOANS.

After discussing the details connected with the issue of Agricultural Loans, the Committee came to the more general questions of the need for loans and of the benefits derived from them.

(1) <u>Comparison between 1920 and to-day.</u>

As a preliminary measure, the Committee discussed whether the need for Agricultural Loans was as great at the present time as it had been in the past.

(a) <u>Luxuries.</u>

It was suggested that the expenditure by cultivators on luxuries had increased. The Committee as a whole, however, dismissed the suggestion.

(b) <u>Cattle.</u>

It was pointed out that the number of cattle had enormously increased since the Occupation. The reply was that at that time practically all cattle had been carried off and that, therefore, the comparison should rather be made with pre-war figures. It was also pointed out that the great decrease in the price of live stock had facilitated purchase.

(c) <u>Landowner and Labourer.</u>

The Committee agreed that the condition of the labourer, who was now paid as much as ₤15 a day, had greatly improved, but that the condition of the landowner who had to pay these high

wages/

- 25 -

wages was proportionately worse.

(d) <u>Decrease in Monetary Value of Tithe.</u>

It was pointed out that, whatever the tithe yield by weight might have been, its monetary value had steadily decreased. Even leaving aside the exceptional year 1920-21 when the Tithe Assessment had amounted to £492,859, Tithe had decreased from £270,559 in 1919-20 to £231,811 in 1922-23. It was maintained that the general fall in prices did not compensate this fall in the monetary value of tithe, which indicated a corresponding fall in the monetary value of the crops. The Committee refused to accept a suggestion that it was unsafe to argue from Tithe figures, as market prices were artificially lowered till the redemption price was fixed.

As a result of the discussion, a majority of the Committee was of opinion that the need for agricultural loans was effectively as great to day as in 1920.

(2) <u>Need for Loans at present.</u>

It was argued that poverty is general throughout the country at present. As there is no Agricultural Bank, cultivators are obliged to borrow from money-lenders at exorbitant rates of interest the money they require for cattle, seed, implements or improvements.

(a) <u>Cattle.</u>

For the sake of cheapness, cultivators are in the habit of buying inferior cattle,

which/

- 26 -

which, therefore, have to be renewed every three or four years. Sometimes the cattle are so feeble that they die immediately after the ploughing is finished. Other cattle die from disease or as the result of drought or inadequate pasturage.

Milch cows are also required, at any rate in some Districts. A small number of wealthy persons have many cattle. The rest have few or none.

Thus there is a continual demand for cattle.

(b) <u>Seed.</u>

Cultivators almost invariably have to buy seed for one or more crops. In one year it may be wheat, in another barley; in a third kersenneh. The shortage of seed is of course greater after a bad season.

(c) <u>Implements.</u>

It is constantly necessary to buy new implements or to repair old ones.

(d) <u>Improvements to Land.</u>

Enterprising cultivators need funds to effect improvements on their land. It is said that many donums of land have been opened up recently, but that the owners have been compelled to obtain the necessary funds from money-lenders.

After consideration of these points, <u>a majority of the Committee was of opinion that loans were necessary at the present time.</u>

(3) /

- 27 -

(3) <u>Benefit under present system.</u>

The Committee was agreed that even with the proposed improvements the system of Agricultural Loans would be far from satisfactory, but it was unable to come to any agreement on the question whether the issue of loans by the Government should consequently be discontinued.

The majority held that as Palestine was an agricultural country and its prosperity depended almost entirely on agriculture, it was essential at all costs to render financial assistance to the cultivator. They further held that, though many borrowers had doubtless misapplied the loans granted to them, a great many others had made good use of them. In any case only a small section of the population had as yet benefited by Agricultural Loans and a large proportion still needed the benefit derived from them.

The minority took the view that, as no means of adequate control could be found under the existing system, the issue of Agricultural Loans, by pauperising the inhabitants and promoting usury, merely defeated its own object. They believed that these objections were inherent in any system of issue by the Government and that they could only be overcome by the establishment of an Agricultural Bank working with a technically qualified Staff on business lines. They were also inclined to believe that if the Government once took the decisive step of

discontinuing/

- 28 -

discontinuing the issue of loans, the need for an Agricultural Bank would become so pressing that still further efforts would be concentrated on securing the speedy establishment of such a Bank.

As the point on which this divergence of opinion appeared was so fundamental, it seemed necessary to embody both opinions in the final recommendations of the Committee.

FINAL RECOMMENDATIONS.

I. The Committee unanimously recommended, as the only satisfactory method of solving the problem of Agricultural Loans, the establishment of an Agricultural Bank with adequate capital to undertake all the kinds of business usually undertaken by such Bank.

II. The Committee also unanimously recommended that, if the Government continued to issue Agricultural Loans, the following modifications should be introduced into the present system:-

(1) That the loan capital for the whole country should be fixed; and that from this fixed capital allotments should be made to each Sub-District. Thus fresh loans would be available only as instalments were repaid.

(2) That no loan exceeding £500 should be granted.

(3) That each District Governor should have full power to grant loans of any amount up to £500 and for any period up to ten years, provided that he did not at any time exceed the allotment made to his District; and that District Governors should delegate to Sub-District Governors, acting

in/

- 29 -

in consultation with the Local Committees, authority to grant loans up to £60 for any period up to three years, provided that they did not exceed the allotment made to their respective Sub-Districts.

(4) That the period of each loan from £20 to £500 should be fixed in accordance with its special needs.

(5) That the amount of a loan should not exceed one quarter of the value of the security offered.

(6) That Musha' Land must be partitioned before it can be accepted as security.

(7) That the agreements and guarantees for loans not exceeding £20 should not be required to be registered with the Public Notary; or that, if for legal reasons registration is necessary, the fees shall be remitted.

(8) That in selecting from eligible applicants those to whom loans exceeding £60 are to be given, the District Governor and the Local Committee should be guided mainly by the Agricultural Department.

(9) That in selecting from eligible applicants those to whom loans not exceeding £60 are to be given, the Local Committee should, in default of special reasons to the contrary, be guided by the date of application.

(10) That loans shall be issued as heretofore in money and not in kind.

(11) /

- 30 -

(11) That, unless the Local Committee is satisfied that there are reasons for exemption, a loan should be granted only if the intending borrower undertakes to plant ten trees for each £1 of loan granted.

(12) That applications for loans should be submitted in September, examined in October and issued in November.

(13) That, as a partial precaution against fraud,

(a) borrowers shall fill in on a printed form a list of the items on which they propose to spend the loan together with the approximate cost of each item;

(b) at the end of a fixed period borrowers shall sign a statement on the same form to the effect that they have actually spent the loans on the items shown;

(c) an agricultural Committee including the Mukhtar(s) and several Notables shall be formed in each village to certify that the statements made by borrowers are correct; and that if they render a false certificate they shall be liable to the usual penalties of the Law.

(14) That only one instalment of arrears now due should be claimed in each twelve months (as explained above in pp. 21 - 22).

The Committee was unable to agree whether or not to recommend that the Government should continue to issue Agricultural Loans, if for lack of funds or for any other reason the establishment of an Agricul-

Agricultural/

- 31 -

Agricultural Bank was at present impossible.

A. The Majority recommended that, until an Agricultural Bank was fully established, the Government should continue to issue Agricultural Loans.

B. The Minority recommended that, whether an Agricultural Bank could be established in the immediate future or not, the Government should discontinue the issue of Agricultural Loans.

Signatures of Majority.   Signatures of Minority.

(Signed) Amin Abdulhadi.   (Signed) R.E.H.Crosbie, (Chairman).
" Suleiman A.Toukan.   " G.G.Masson.
" C.F.Reading.   F.Aylmer Harris.
  A.Bril.
  A.Rizk.

Mr. Anton Gelat was absent from the final Meeting, but was in agreement with the majority.

2.03

PALESTINE.

**GOVERNMENT OFFICES,
JERUSALEM.**

Despatch No. 21
Reference No. 5643/29.

11 January, 1930.

My Lord,

I have the honour to inform Your Lordship that I have had under consideration the question of establishing an Agricultural Bank in Palestine and Village Cooperative Credit Societies.

2. Three months ago I appointed a Committee consisting of the Treasurer as Chairman and the Commissioner of Lands and Director of Agriculture and Forests as members to study and to make recommendations upon these matters: and I transmit a copy of their Report.

Enclosure I.
Enclosure II.

I also enclose a copy of a booklet by Mr. H. Viteles which is referred to in paragraph 34 of the Report.

The question of establishing an Agricultural Bank in Palestine has been the subject of serious consideration by successive Secretaries of State and High Commissioners since 1920.

It is admitted by all who are acquainted with Palestine that the introduction of capital is indispensable if agriculture is to be developed; and that credit facilities must be given to <u>individual agriculturists</u> throughout the country in order to enable them to improve their methods. The greater part of the cultivation by Arabs is conducted on primitive lines; and those agriculturists who wish

to/

The Right Hon'ble LORD PASSFIELD, P.C.,
His Majesty's Principal Secretary of State
for the Colonies.

-2-

to improve the standard of their cultivation are forced to borrow the necessary money from usurers at high rates of interest, with all the risk that that entails, or from the commercial banks from which they can obtain short term loans only. They thus experience great difficulty in undertaking agricultural improvements involving capital expenditure.

3. The Ottoman Government recognised the necessity for an Agricultural Bank; and, as Your Lordship will observe from paragraph 3 of the Report, the establishment of the Ottoman Agricultural Bank was sanctioned by the Law of the 28th August, 1898. The capital of that Bank was obtained partly from the assets and the accrued interest thereon of the <u>Caisses d'Utilité Publique</u> which were succeeded by the Agricultural Bank and partly from an additional 10% (reduced to one-twentieth in 1905) on the tithe which was to be payable until the capital of the Bank reached Turkish Pounds 10,000,000.

The Military and Civil Administrations continued to collect the addition on the tithe imposed for the purposes of the Bank; but credited the proceeds to general revenue and not to the Agricultural Bank which was put into liquidation at the conclusion of the War.

4. In 1921 Sir Herbert Samuel considered the question whether such additional tithe should be utilised for purposes of the administration of the country or should be earmarked for the purposes of an agricultural bank.

On/

-3-

On this point the Attorney-General in November, 1921, advised that Government were at liberty either to collect the additional tithe and pay it to a Government Agricultural Bank or to maintain the tithe at the rate which was in force at the time and pay the whole proceeds into general revenue. The additional tithe, approximating £P.76,500, was in fact collected and paid into general revenue.

5. The Military Administration, in order to enable cultivators to obtain seed, live-stock and agricultural implements and to develop agriculture following a long period of hostilities, poverty and distress, arranged with the Anglo-Egyptian Bank to make advances to the Administration for loans to cultivators in amounts not exceeding in the aggregate £.500,000; and the Civil Government, recognising that it was under a moral obligation to obtain some means for providing agricultural credit for cultivators, continued the arrangement until the year 1923 when loans to cultivators were suspended owing to the financial needs of the Government and the reluctance of the Bank to make further advances without the guarantee of His Majesty's Government.

6. Since 1923, apart from loans which had been granted in consequence of the distress occasioned by drought and locust invasions, no agricultural credits have been made available by Government.

It is to the interest of the country that credit facilities which were accorded by the Turkish Government should be continued by this Government in

order/

-4-

order to promote the welfare of the people and
the development of the agricultural resources of
the country.

7. It was at one time hoped that the capital for
an Agricultural Bank would be obtained by allocating
a portion of the Palestine Loan for that purpose. That
hope has not been fulfilled, because the whole of the
Palestine Loan has been allocated to other purposes.
This Government has at the present time therefore no
funds at its disposal for the capital of an Agricultural
Bank.

8. I accordingly set up the Committee to which I
have referred above in order to ascertain what measures
could be devised for obtaining the necessary capital.
The Committee advise that it is possible to establish
an Agricultural Bank on the basis of a minimum capital
of £P. 500,000, and at the same time to provide for the
management of the Bank without imposing an unduly heavy
burden on the cultivator.

9. I have discussed the possibility of establishing
a Bank on the lines proposed in the Report with Mr. A.
Barnes and Mr. A.P.S. Clark of Barclays Bank (Dominion,
Colonial and Overseas).

Mr. Barnes in criticism expressed the view that
Government in issuing short term loans such as are
proposed might compete with Barclays Bank who at present
issue such loans to the amount of approximately £P. 40,000
to £P. 45,000 per annum in the Northern District of
Palestine. He also suggested that it might be undesir-

able/

-5-

able for political reasons for Government to place itself in a position in which it might be compelled to enforce payment through the Courts. No objection was raised by Mr. Barnes to the issue of long term loans by the proposed Bank since Barclays Bank does not undertake the business of a Mortgage Bank and does not therefore make long term loans secured by mortgages.

In regard to long term loans, therefore, no question of competition with Barclays Bank arises.

10. In regard to short term loans, Mr. Barnes suggested that in order to avoid competition it might be possible for Barclays Bank to make loans to in-dividual cultivators at the request of and on the guarantee by the Government. I understand that the Bank will be prepared to pay (say) 1% of the interest to Government to meet possible losses; but as the suggestion by Mr. Barnes was only tentative it will be necessary to await definite proposals by Barclays Bank which can then be considered in point of detail and with a view to minimising as far as possible the cost or loss which would devolve upon Government.

I do not attach much weight to the suggestion that politically it might be undesirable for Government to place itself in a position in which it might be obliged to have recourse to the Courts to enforce payment. If loans were issued by the Bank at the request of Government it is certain that every borrower in the country would believe that pressure or leniency by the Bank would be exercised at the will of Government; and the ultimate effect, therefore,

of/

-6-

of adopting his suggestion would be identical with the effect that would follow recourse by Government to the Courts in order to recover debts incurred towards the Government directly.

11. I have considered the Report of the Committee in Executive Council and I am satisfied that the measures proposed are prudent and practicable and will supply a deeply felt want of the agricultural population.

I therefore hope that Your Lordship will approve means of affording credit facilities to cultivators on the lines proposed by the Committee or subject to such modifications as may be desirable after consultation with Barclays Bank; and to this end, I would request that Your Lordship be so good as to ascertain from the Crown Agents the prospects of a loan issue by the Government of Palestine for the purpose of an Agricultural Bank and as to the possibility of enlisting financial support by Commercial Banks.

12. I directed the Treasurer to submit copies of the Report of the Committee to the Commission of Inquiry when he gave evidence before them and I propose to cause copies of the Report to be sent to Barclays Bank for their detailed observations, Mr. Barnes's remarks having been based on a general discussion of the proposals and not on a detailed examination of them.

13. I understand that an Agricultural Bank has

been/

been established in Kenya for long term loans and I have requested the Government of Kenya to supply me with information in regard to its establishment and working.

    I have the honour to be,
      My Lord,
      Your Lordship's most obedient,
        humble servant,

J. R. Chancellor.
HIGH COMMISSIONER
FOR PALESTINE.

458/7748.   THE TREASURY,
                         JERUSALEM.

                         22nd November, 1929.

Sir,

   We have the honour to refer to your letter No.5643/29 of the 20th September on the subject of the early establishment of an Agricultural Bank in Palestine and appointing us as a Committee to consider in broad outline the means for putting the proposal into effect, and to consider also the question of establishing village co-operative credit societies.

   2.   As a preliminary we propose to outline the measures taken by the Ottoman Government to accord facilities to cultivators by the establishment of an Agricultural Bank, and the steps taken by the Occupied Enemy Territory Administration (South), and subsequently by the civil administration, to grant and facilitate loans to cultivators.

                Ottoman Agricultural Bank.

   3.   The establishment of the Ottoman Agricultural Bank was sanctioned by the Law of the 20th August, 1898 (see Young Vol.V page 343). The capital of the Bank was obtained from the following sources:-

                                              (1) /

The Chief Secretary,
   - The Government of Palestine.

- 2 -

(1) The assets, and the accruing interest thereon, of the Caisses d'Utilité Publique, which were succeeded by the Agricultural Bank;

(2) An additional tenth (reduced to one-twentieth in 1905) on the tithe until the capital of the Bank reached £T.10,000,000.

After the occupation the military and civil administrations continued to collect the charge of ½ per centum additional to the tithe and credited the receipts to general revenue. The tithe was restored to 10 per centum by the Tithes Reduction Ordinance, 1925.

4. Some thirteen agencies of the Bank operated in Palestine and were accommodated in the Government Offices. The object of the Bank was to grant loans for agricultural purposes, secured by mortgages on immovable property or other suitable security. It will be seen in a foot-note in Young (Volume V, page 347) that long term loans were subsequently issued to persons who were still debtors to the Caisses d'Utilité Publique, in order to avoid recourse to usurers although the law prohibited loans to such persons, and that debts to usurers were liquidated by the bank on the transfer of the

mortgages /

- 3 -

mortgages. Loans were issued at an initial charge of 1 per centum for administrative expenses, and interest at 6 per centum per annum was charged.

5. As the records of the Bank were for the most part removed before the British occupation, it has only been possible, by means of reconstructing accounts from other documentary evidence, partially to ascertain the outstanding liabilities in regard to loans made to cultivators in Palestine. Any cash assets were removed before the occupation or seized as loot.

6. At the 30th September last the sum of £P.20,512, had been paid over to the Treasurer as shown in the Statement of Assets and Liabilities of the Palestine Government; and the outstanding local assets as ascertained by the Official Liquidator are stated to approximate £P.86,000, as under:-

Loans	£P.	£P.
Secured by Mortgage	66,000	
Secured by Guarantors	5,000	71,000
Bank Property		15,000
		£P. 86,000

We are not in a position to estimate the amount which will ultimately be collected.

Agricultural /

- 4 -

Agricultural Loans to cultivators during the period of 1919-1923.

7. In the terms of an Agreement dated the 18th June, 1919, between the Financial Adviser on behalf of the Occupied Enemy Territory Administration (South) and the Anglo-Egyptian Bank, Limited, the Bank undertook to advance to the Administration for loans to cultivators amounts not exceeding in the aggregate, unless by special agreement, £E.500,000. The rate of interest paid by the Administration to the Bank was 6 per centum per annum, and the rate charged to the cultivators was 6½ per centum on instalments paid on due dates and 9 per centum in respect of overdue instalments.

8. The arrangement entered into by the military administration was continued by the civil administration until the year 1923 when loans to cultivators were suspended owing to financial necessity and the reluctance of the Bank to make further advances without the guarantee of His Majesty's Government.

9. It will be seen from Appendix I that during the period 1919-1923 loans in Egyptian currency to the equivalent of £P.576,319 were made to cultivators, of which £P.527,727 has been repaid at the 30th September last, leaving a balance of £P.48,591

outstanding /

outstanding at that date.

10. The repayments by the cultivators were transferred periodically through the Treasury to the Anglo-Egyptian Bank, and in January, 1928, the balance then outstanding was repaid to the Bank from surplus balances. It was economical to adopt this course since the interest then obtainable on surplus balances held by the Crown Agents approximated only 4 per centum.

11. A summary of the loans to cultivators and repayments is given in Appendix II. The outstanding loans t the 30th September last amounted to £P. 45,116. The loans were required to enable cultivators to obtain seed, live-stock and agricultural implements following a long period of hostilities, poverty and distress; and, in the circumstances, loans in many cases were given in the earlier days of the Administration without adequate security.

12. It is not practicable at present to forecast what portion of the outstanding balance will ultimately have to be written-off as irrecoverable; but it is not unreasonable to assume that the bad debts will not exceed 4 per centum of the total loans issued. There can be no doubt, however,

that /

- 6 -

that the loss eventually sustained by Government will have been more than compensated directly from the increased tithes obtained from the cultivators by reason of the facilities afforded.

Loans to cultivators in Beersheba District.

13. In the year 1927 in consequence of the severe drought in the Beersheba sub-district, Lord Plumer obtained the sanction of the Secretary of State to make advances to cultivators for the purchase of seed and the replacement of livestock. The total advances made amounted to £P. 19,944, as under, and are being repaid in instalments with interest at the rate of 6½ per centum:-

Period	Loans issued £P.	Repayments £P.
1927	19,979	-
1928	15	7,960
1st January to 30th September, 1929		2,657
	19,994	10,617
Balance at 30th September, 1929.	-	9,377
	19,994	19,994

The arrears at the 30th September last approximated to £P.4,400.

Seed Loans.

14. Later, in the year 1928, the Secretary of State's approval was sought for the issue of seed

loans /

- 7 -

loans to farmers in the Northern District as a measure of relief necessitated by crop failure. These advances, amounting to £P.19,366, as under, consist of small amounts rarely exceeding £P.10, and are mainly repayable before the end of the current financial year with interest at 5 per centum per annum:-

	£P.
Loans issued to cultivators	19,366
Repayments at 30th September, 1929	65
	£P. 19,301

Projected Agricultural Bank.

15. It was the intention of Sir Herbert Samuel to establish an Agricultural Bank in Palestine and to this end provision was originally made in the draft Palestine Loan Schedule. It became necessary, however, for financial reasons, to eliminate the provision from the draft schedule before any scheme for constituting and operating the Bank had been considered.

Enquiries by Agricultural Bank of Egypt.

16. Steps had also been taken in the year 1923 to induce the Agricultural Bank of Egypt to extend its business to Palestine. The Bank was favourably inclined to consider the proposal and sent a

representative /

- 8 -

representative to Jerusalem to study relevant questions on the spot. It was proposed that Government should facilitate the Bank by collecting instalments when due from the cultivators through the district administrative staff; but mainly owing to the insecurity of titles to land, and the consequent risks involved, the Bank was unable to proceed further.

Recommendations by Committee.

17. It will have been seen that the available balance of the Ottoman Agricultural Bank, namely £P.20,512, is inadequate, though it may serve as a nucleus, for the establishment of an Agricultural Bank; and we are advised by the Treasurer that there are no available Government balances from which further loans to cultivators can be made.

18. The Banks in Palestine provide to some extent short term loans to cultivators in localities where branches of the Banks exist, but only in exceptional cases grant long term loans as they are opposed in principle to locking up their available funds.

19. It has been reported that a company styled "Misr - Palestine Bank Limited" with an initial share capital of £P.50,000 is likely shortly to be

established /

- 9 -

established in Palestine for the purpose of carrying on banking business including all businesses and enterprises relating to agriculture. Although loans to cultivators may form a part of the operations of the concern such facilities will only to a very limited extent contribute to the needs of the cultivators.

20. It will be realised, therefore, that since commercial Banks do not adequately meet the requirements of agriculturists for short term loans and only in exceptional cases for land development by means of long term loans, the establishment of an Agricultural Bank by Government is of importance to the country. We are of opinion, however, that such a Bank operating independently of the Treasury would present difficulties in regard to financial control and its administration would be more costly.

21. We consider that the operations of the Bank should be conducted strictly in accordance with regulations to be approved by the Secretary of State, under a local Committee of management comprising the Treasurer, the Commissioner of Lands, and the Director of Agriculture, or officers acting for them. The Committee would determine, after

consultation /

consultation with District Commissioners, the allocation of the loan issues as between the several districts in Palestine for the various categories of loans to which we will refer later.

22. We also consider that for purposes of economy the accounts and records of the concern should be kept by the Treasurer and his Sub-Accountants and the issues of loans, after investigation of applications by the Department of Agriculture, should be effected by the District Administrative staff, who would also collect the instalments payable and interest thereon as in the case of agricultural loans hitherto issued. It will be necessary to employ additional staff, but we do not anticipate that the cost will exceed one-half per centum of the capital to be employed.

23. The only practicable means of securing the capital necessary to meet the present needs of cultivators is by way of a loan, preferably by the issue of bonds redeemable in forty years by the establishment of a sinking fund of 1.1/6 per centum for the purpose.

24. Mr. A.P.S. Clark, the local Manager of Barclays Bank (Dominion, Colonial and Overseas),

with /

- 11 -

with whom we have discussed the question informs us that by the issue of bonds the Banks might be induced to subscribe to the capital of a Government Agricultural Bank since the bonds would constitute a marketable security. It will, therefore, not entail on the part of the Banks indefinitely locking-up their available funds as would be the case if they participated otherwise in the undertaking.

25. We have broadly outlined in Appendix III the categories of loans and maxima amounts which we consider should be issued; but it will be necessary to amplify them in point of detail. The proposals are designed, at the outset, to assist the smaller land-owners and tenant-cultivators who constitute the large majority of cultivators and who have not the same facilities for obtaining credit as the larger land-owners. We also recommend that long term loans be granted to small land-owners who experience at present difficulties in raising money and, in consequence, often cultivate relatively unproductive crops failing available capital for development. These loans, which would be mainly devoted to the planting of citrous groves, olives, etc., and for improvements, would be secured on first mortgage.

26. /

- 12 -

26. It will be observed from Appendices IV and V that the greater portion of agricultural loans issued in the past have been for comparatively small amounts and for short periods, and we have taken these facts into consideration in formulating our recommendations. Mr. Clark, with whom we have discussed the proposals, is satisfied that they will not operate prejudicially to the interests of the principal commercial Banks.

27. It is difficult to forecast at present the amount of capital which might usefully be employed by agriculturists in Palestine; but we consider that the facilities to be granted should be based, in the first instance, on a minimum capital of £P.500,000, and the issue of loans in the first year of amounts not exceeding in the aggregate £P.100,000. The situation should be reviewed annually in the light of experience gained.

28. In order to preserve intact the loan capital and to provide for the issue of subsequent loans from instalments repaid, it is of paramount importance that loans should only be issued to agriculturists within their capacity to repay at due dates and thus obviate recourse to usurers for

the /

- 13 -

the purpose of meeting obligations.

29. The wish has been expressed in the Press that loans should be made to cultivators to extricate them from their indebtedness to usurers. Apart from the indefiniteness of these liabilities we do not consider that any useful purpose would be served by the issue of loans for this specific object as in all probability persons already ininvolved would again be driven to the usurer in order to meet their liabilities to the Bank when due. The suppression of usury cannot be achieved by direct action, but will be accelerated by the grant of the proposed credit facilities and by debtors seeking redress in the Courts.

30. In determining the rate of interest at which money may be lent it will be necessary to take into consideration the rate of interest which will have to be paid in respect of the loan to be contracted. At the moment the Bank of England rate is 5½ per centum, and it is unlikely that the required capital can be obtained at a lower rate of interest. To this must be added a charge (say) 1 per centum for bad debts and 1.1/6 per dentum for the sinking fund. These charges, exclusive of administration charges, amount to 7.2/3 per centum.

31 /

- 14 -

31. It is desirable to keep the rate of interest as low as possible, but it does not appear practicable to charge less than 8 per centum, and even on this basis the yield on the total capital of the concern would not amount to 8 per centum since the receipts from the temporary investment of unemployed capital would not yield as much.

32½ It should be mentioned that the Banks usually charge 9 per centum on similar loans. The proposed rate of 8 per centum cannot be compared with the charge of 6 per centum on similar loans by the former Government without taking into consideration the fact that the Ottoman Government imposed a charge of one-tenth of the tithe on the cultivator and a single administrative charge of one per centum of the amount of the loans issued. These charges were probably more advantageous to the Ottoman Agricultural Bank than an interest charge of 8 per centum.

33. Should our proposals be approved in principle, it will be necessary to seek the advice of the Crown Agents, through the Secretary of State, in regard to the prospects of a loan issue by the Government of Palestine for the purpose of an Agricultural Bank, and to enlist financial support by the Banks.

34. /

- 15 -

34. As regards the question of the establishment of village co-operative credit societies, it will be seen from Mr. Viteles's book (page 29) on the Jewish Co-operative Movement in Palestine, that there are some 60 agricultural co-operative societies operating in Palestine. There are, however, no similar Arab institutions; and we understand that an attempt to organise an Arab co-operative society on behalf of the tobacco growers in the Northern District proved abortive.

35. We do not consider that co-operative credit societies can be successfully established and operated by Arabs without direction. Even with such assistance development along these lines is likely to be of slow growth as the majority of the felaheen are not in a position to provide any capital and those who may be able to do so require education in the principles involved.

36. We nevertheless consider that, as mutual credit societies have proved very beneficial to cultivators elsewhere and also in Palestine so far as they have been instituted and developed under expert guidance, every encouragement should be given to fostering similar institutions in Arab villages and that someone of experience should be

appointed /

- 16 -

appointed actively to interest cultivators in the co-operative movement.

37. As a further inducement it might be considered at a later stage whether loans might not be made to co-operative societies at a somewhat lower rate than loans to individual cultivators since there should be less risk of bad debts; but we are disinclined to recommend that loans be granted to any co-operative credit society until such time as effective control of the operations of such societies be established and exercised, as it is an admitted fact that some of the local concerns have contravened their own rules.

      (Sgd) S.S. Davis.
       Treasurer.
      (Sgd) A. Abramson.
      Commissioner of Lands.
      (Sgd) E.R. Sawer.
      Director of Agriculture.

APPENDIX I.

AGRICULTURAL LOANS TO CULTIVATORS.

Period.	Loans Issued	Recoveries
	£E. m/ms.	£E. m/ms
Year 1919 - 1920	181,762.750	6,945.000
" 1920 - 1921	195,642.997	32,466.033
" 1921 - 1922	119,846.135	72,197.903
" 1922 - 1923	87,037.500	79,507.985
" 1923 - 1924	7,622.000	112,768.694
" 1924 - 1925		101,094.450
" 1925 - 1926		56,171.205
" 1926 - 1927		25,249.639
Total in Egyptian Currency	561,911.382	486,500.909.
	£P. mils	£P. mils.
Total converted into Palestine Currency	576,319.366	498,975.292
1st April to 31st December, 1927		13,945.937
1st January to 31st December, 1928		11,451.176
1st January to 30th September, 1929	-	6,355.443
	576,319.366	527,727.848
Balance outstanding at 30th September, 1929		48,591.518
£P.	576,319.366	576,319.366

LAND TITLES IN PALESTINE.

1. The following extracts from the Report on Palestine Administration - July 1920 to December 1921 gave a general indication of the land registration system obtaining in Palestine under the Ottoman regime and the manner in which that system was administered.

"Following the passing of the Ottoman Land Code of 1274 A.H. (1858), the Turkish authorities established a primitive system of registration of title throughout various parts of the Ottoman Empire. The chief weakness of the system lay in the fact that there was no cadastral or other survey, so that land could not be correctly described by reference either to area or boundaries; hence the multiplicity of boundary disputes existent to-day. Thirteen offices working under this system were established in Palestine prior to the Occupation."

x   x   x   x   x   x   x   x   x   x

"Under the Ottoman régime the Land Registry had been a source of corruption. Lands were registered frequently at a fourth or less part of the real area - thus avoiding payment of Land Tax. Others were registered under assumed names to avoid liability for military service. Every form of deceit was resorted to in order to defeat the law and evade taxation"

x   x   x   x   x   x   x   x   x   x

"Under the Ottoman régime registration of property was nominally compulsory, but was rarely
enforced

enforced." Hence much of the land is unregistered and is held in virtue of privately drawn contracts of a primitive nature. In yet more cases the Turkish registers do not show the actual state of the property, which in many instances has passed through numerous hands by private sale; and the heirs of vendors now dispute the sales made by their deceased ancestors. Added to this are the complications arising from unregistered successions and illegal transactions, so that practically all applications for registration in the name of the present holders are contested. Many disputes are amicably settled by the officials of the Department, and the remainder are referred to the Land Courts mentioned above. "

2. On the Occupation of Palestine by the British Forces it was found that the Turkish authorities had removed many of the registers and records. Most of the missing registers were subsequently recovered, and the land registries were re-opened in October 1920. The Transfer of Land Ordinance, which was enacted in 1920 provided for the registration of all land transactions, including changes in title on the death of the owner.

3. In view of the deficiencies of the Turkish system, and the general insecurity of tenure arising out of that system and the unsatisfactory manner in which it had been

administered,

administered, it was decided to introduce a new system of registration of land. Accordingly in May 1928 there was enacted an Ordinance to provide for the settlement of land and the registration of titles thereon. Settlement Officers appointed in pursuance of that Ordinance started their labours in July 1928. The first year of the scheme was necessarily one of experiments. By the end of 1928, however, the settlement parties had decided the boundary disputes between 9 settlement villages and 17 neighbouring villages, recorded 6,798 claims of which 3,105 were investigated and 2,665 decided, and demarcated 160 blocks covering 77,951 dunams.

Apart from the steps which have been taken under the land settlement scheme referred to in the preceding paragraph to obtain an efficient registration system and to give security of title, a Commission was appointed in 1922 to register lands allocated under the terms of the Beisan Lands Agreement and to issue title deeds to transferees. The principal object of that agreement was to secure permanent settlement on the area covered by the agreement of those persons who were cultivators of the lands. By the end of 1927 the Commission had investigated 3,956 claims and settled 2,862, surveyed approximately 167,000 dunams of which 74,258 were irrigable and allotted 107,000 dunams. During 1928 the Commission parcelled and assigned to transferees 21,000 dunams of irrigable land.

It would appear that the persons holding
titled

titles to agricultural land which would be acceptable by a Bank or other reputable credit institution as security for a loan are restricted to -

(a) Persons registered as owners of land in the new registers opened in connection with the land settlement scheme.

(b) Persons to whom land has been assigned by the Bdisan Lands Commission.

(c) Persons registered as owners of land in the existing registers in accordance with the provisions of the Land Transfer Ordinance, that is land registered on transfer or on the death of the owner.

The titles held by persons in category (c) would presumably be subject to revision by Settlement Officers when settlement and registration of rights is carried out in the area in which their land is situated.

As regards category (a) no information is available as to whether any of the new registers are yet in existence and whether any titles have been registered therein, but it is unlikely that there is an appreciable number of Arab owners falling within this category at the moment. Mr. Abramson, the Commissioner of Lands, in his evidence before the Commission of Enquiry expressed the view that with 8 settlement parties working it would take about 12 years to complete the scheme of land settlement in Palestine. I believe there are at present only

only three settlement parties working. The persons falling under category (b) would form a relatively small proportion of the Arab land owners in Palestine, while persons (or institutions) under category (c) are likely to be mainly Jewish. It would seem that at the moment the majority of Arab owners of agricultural land are not in possession of titles to their property which would be acceptable by a bank or other credit institution as security for a loan.

Section 3: Memoranda on Land Taxation, 1922–1926

3.01

22 August 1922.

Sir;

 I have etc to inform you that the report of the Tithes Commission forwarded with your despatch No:198 of the 31st March has received my careful consideration. I agree in principle that it would be wise to substitute for the present arrangement with regard to tithes a system of land taxation based upon survey and in so far as the recommendations of the Committee aim at carrying out this change by degrees I am in entire sympathy with them. The detailed recommendations for improving the present system which are set out in the summary appear to me generally suitable for the purpose in view, the only question which appears to require any comment being that of the relationship between the headquarters of your administration and the district administrations in relation to the estimation, control, inspection and collection of tithes. I am not altogether in agreement with the definition given by the Committee of the alternatives which present themselves for defining this relationship. It appears to me that while so technical a matter as the estimation of tithes cannot suitably be left entirely in the hands of district authorities, who might, if their results were not co-ordinated, at headquarters, arrive at different assessments for identical conditions in the various districts, it is essential that the responsibility, not only for the actual collection, but for the final assessment should be recognised as being the responsibility of the District Governors. The collection

DRAFT.

Sir H. Samuel.
Jerusalem.
 No: 908

MINUTE.

Major Young.
Mr.
Mr.
Mr. Davis.
Sir G. Grindle.
Sir H. Read.
Sir J. Masterton Smith.
Mr. Wood.
Mr. Churchill.

DRAFT.

MINUTE.

Mr.
Mr.
Mr.
Mr. *Davis.*
Sir *G. Grindle.*
Sir *H. Read.*
Sir *J. Masterton Smith.*
Mr. *Wood.*
Mr. *Churchill.*

collection of revenue is the most important function of a district officer, and any system which may result in the people of the country deriving the impression that this vital element in their social condition is not the immediate concern of the local representative of your administration would, in my opinion, tend very greatly to reduce his authority and influence in the district. I understand that the question whether the revenue collected in a district should figure in the budget of the district or in a general revenue budget is at present engaging your attention and the ultimate decision as to the respective functions of the head quarters of your administration and of the District Governors must depend to some extent upon the conclusion eventually arrived at. But this should only affect the question whether the revenue collecting staff is organised in the first place under a central department or decentralized under the District Governors. It should not affect the principle which I have outlined above that the actual operations of collection of revenue should be recognised as the responsibility of the District Governors. I should be glad to learn in due course what comments are offered by the District Governors on the report of the Commission, and to consider your proposals for the organization and control of collection of revenue.

(Signed) WINSTON S. CHURCHILL

PALESTINE.

Despatch No. 198
Reference No. Adm.825.

GOVERNMENT HOUSE,
JERUSALEM.

31st March, 1922.

Sir,

I have the honour to transmit a copy of the Report of the Committee which I appointed to consider the present system of Estimation and Collection of Tithes and which was presided over by Mr. L.H.W. Nott, Governor of Gaza District.

A copy of the terms of reference of the Committee is enclosed.

2. I have invited the opinion of Governors on the recommendations made in this Report and contemplate introducing a number of improvements, in pursuance thereof, before the Tithe Estimation for this year is carried out, but I am not of the opinion that it would be practicable to give effect at present to the larger reforms proposed by the Committee.

3. I should be grateful if I might receive your observations on the recommendations that are contained in the Report.

I have the honour to be,
Sir,
Your most obedient, humble servant,

Herbert Samuel
HIGH COMMISSIONER.

The Right Honble. Winston S. Churchill,
P.C., M.P.,
His Majesty's Principal Secretary of State
for the Colonies,
Whitehall. LONDON. S.W.1.

APPENDIX (A)

TERMS OF REFERENCE

I appoint:

Mr. L.H.W. Nott	...	Governor, Gaza District
Mr. J.B. Barron, O.B.E., M.C.		Director of Revenue & Customs.
Mr. A. Sifri	...	Asst. Inspector of Revenue, Phoenicia.
M.B. Tayan Eff.	...	Wady Hawareth - Tulkeram.
Mr. B. Dinovitch	...	Petah Tikvah, J a f f a.
Saleh Mohamed Eff.	...	Biet Wazan. Samaria.

to be a Committee to consider and report upon the present system of estimation and collection of tithes, and to recommend what changes, if any, are desirable.

And I further appoint Mr. L.H.W. Nott to be the Chairman of the Committee and Taufic Farah to be the Secretary.

(signed) Herbert Samuel
         High Commissioner.

November 22nd 1921.

REPORT OF THE TITHES COMMISSION

PALESTINE

CONTENTS.

Section 1. Page 1. Preliminary:
    Terms of reference.
    Meetings of the Committee.
    Evidence, how taken and other particulars.

Section 2. " 4. History of Tithes.
    Hebrew legislation.
    Roman period.
    Arab and recent periods.

Section 3. " 8. The tenure of land:
    Mulk Land.
    Miri Land.
    Wakf Land.

Section 4. " 10. Factors influencing taxation:
    Conditions of agriculture in Palestine.
    Means of communication and transport.

Section 3. " 13. The system of tithes, methods of assessment and collection described.
    Under the Turkish Government.
    Under the Military Administration.
    Under the Palestine Government.

Section 6. " 22. Criticisms on the present system:
    A. Difficulties from the view point of the Government.
    Estimators & estimation of crops.
    Inspection and Control.
    Collection of tithes.
    Difficulties of weights and measures.

Section 6 " 38. B. The opinion & suggestions of the public:
    the advantages and disadvantages of tithes as a system of taxation.
    Estimation of Tithes.
    Estimation of standing crops and on threshing floors compared.
    Delays caused by estimation.
    Constitution of the estimating Committee.
    Qualification of estimators.
    Appointment of selection committee.
    The representatives of the cultivators.
    Inspectors or inspecting commissions.
    The Committee's opinion & recommendation.

    " 54. C. Report on the collection of tithes at Cyprus.
    The opinion of the Committee on the collection in kind in Palestine

-2-.

Section 6 Page 62. D. The redemption of the tithes:
　　　　　　　　　　The opinion of the public.
　　　　　　　　　　The Committee's opinion and recommendation.

　　　　　"　65.　 E. The agency used for the collection of tithes:
　　　　　　　　　　Mukhtars as compared with Tax Collectors.
　　　　　　　　　　The recommendation of the Committee.

Section 7 Page 69.　The different classes of tithes lands:-
　　　　　　　　　　Wakf Lands.
　　　　　　　　　　Lands exempted from tithe.
　　　　　　　　　　Products exempted from tithe.

Section 8　"　74.　Communal Difficulties.
　　　　　　　　　　Jewish Colonies.
　　　　　　　　　　Ecclesiastical Institutions.
　　　　　　　　　　Revenue from Wakf Lands.
　　　　　　　　　　Immunity from tithe.

Section 9, "　78.　Experimental system.
　　　　　　　　　　Compounding.
　　　　　　　　　　Olives tithed at the oil press
　　　　　　　　　　Measurement of cereal crops on the land.
　　　　　　　　　　The Tathleeth and Takhmees systems.
　　　　　　　　　　The opinion of the Committee.

Section 10. "　84.　Land Tax :-
　　　　　　　　　A. The opinion of the public.
　　　　　　　　　　Considerations on the adoption of a
　　　　　　　　　　land tax.
　　　　　　　　　　Proposed scheme on land tax.
　　　　　　　　　　Land tax on orange groves.
　　　　　　　　　　Tolkowsky's scheme.
　　　　　　　　　　Explanatory remarks.
　　　　　　　　　　Difficulties involved.
　　　　　　　　　　Recommendations on orange groves.
　　　　　　　　　　Vineyards.
　　　　　　　　　　Vegetables land.

　　　　　　　"　109.　B. A tax on olive trees in lieu of tithing.

Section 11 Page 114.　Financial consideration.
　　　　　　　　　　Emoluments of estimators.
　　　　　　　　　　Difficulties in presenting a financial
　　　　　　　　　　　statement.
　　　　　　　　　　Cost of new proposal on change in estimation.
　　　　　　　　　　　procedure.
　　　　　　　　　　Savings and increased revenue.
　　　　　　　　　　Transport considerations.

Section 12. "　119.　Land Survey:
　　　　　　　　　　The need of a rapid land survey.
　　　　　　　　　　The need of immediate division of
　　　　　　　　　　　Masha land.

Section 13. "　121.　SUMMARY.
　　　　　　　　　　Recommendation & proposals.
　　　　　　　　　　Acknowledgement of assistance.

SECTION I.

PRELIMINARY.

Terms of Reference.

I. The Committee was appointed under orders contained in the terms of reference printed in appendix A. dated 22nd. November 1921, and signed by His Excellency the High Commissioner. These terms were previously referred to the Advisory Council on November /. 1921.

Meeting of the Committee.

2. II. A Sub-Committee met at Jerusalem on the 25th of November 1921 and determined upon the Committee's mode of investigation with a view to covering the field as rapidly and in as economical a manner as possible. They reviewed the evidence previously taken by the Chairman both at Jerusalem and Gaza, and by a sub-committee in the Jewish Colonies of the Jaffa District. They sanctioned the sending out of a questionaire in English, Arabic and Hebrew as a guide to witnesses to confine their evidence to matters covered by the terms of reference, and they arranged a tour in the various districts nominating sub-committees to undertake this work. The tour of these ~~Tithes~~ Committees is to be found in appendix B.

The Committee met at the Governorate Haifa on the 6th and 8th of December 1921. All the members were present with the exception of Mr. Barron who was unable to attend owing to

/duty

2.

duty in Jerusalem. They confirmed the arrangements of the sub-committee previously held in Jerusalem and considered in detail both the answers to the questionaire, and the oral evidence given by witnesses from Jerusalem, Hebron, Jaffa, Nablus, Tiberias, Nazareth, Bisan and Haifa.

A third meeting took place in Jerusalem on the 12th, 13th, and 14th of January 1922, when the whole evidence was reviewed and the headings of the report determined upon.

The final meeting was held at Jerusalem on the 27th of Feb? when the final draft of the report was approved of and signed by all the members.

Publicity.

3. In order to give members of the public an opportunity of giving evidence, a statement was sent to the newspapers printed in the official languages informing them of the tour of the Committee. The Governors of Districts were also requested to prepare a list of witnesses considered qualified to place criticisms and suggestions on tithing matters before the Committee.

It is satisfactory to record that by these means 203 witnesses were examined. They represent the opinion of every district and section of the public.

/It.

Evidence.

4. It was found impossible to prepare a verbatim report of the evidence taken as this would have entailed the employment of a considerable staff of experts. Where, however, important matters are touched the actual words of the witnesses are given, so that had it even been possible to obtain the necessary staff the Committee are of the opinion that no better result proportional to the extra labour involved, would have been obtained.

As witnesses were examined notes of their evidence were made. These notes have been collected in files and are to be found " in toto " at the office of the Director of Revenue. The Committee has been at pains not only to investigate the suitability and imperfections of the law as now operated, but the divergencies which occur in the various districts with a view to improvement and uniformity.

estionaire.

5. The care with which the questionaire sent out, has been answered and the desire manifested by the witnesses examined orally to state their views fully and with frankness, showed the appreciation of the public concerning the enquiry.

nges.

6. The latter part of the terms of reference, referring to changes to be recommended if necessary has been interpreted by the public

/and

4.
and by the Committee in its broadest sense. This will be seen from the extracts of the evidence given and from the recommendations set forth.

List of witnesses.

7. A list of witnesses giving their occupations and the districts from which they were called is recorded in appendix C.

SECTION. II.

History of Tithes.

8. The origin of tithes is undoubtedly religious. Sacrificial gifts were given in kind to propitiate the deity, or as thanks-offering for the produce of land, or for the increase of flocks. These were gradually regulated as can be seen by the Hebrew legislation of first fruits and firstlings. Ex.22: 29. followed by laws on tithes of corn and wine and oil. (Deut.12:6 & 11 and 14; 22 & 23. and Levit. 27 etc.) Later its essential religious character was lost and tithes became a common form of tax upon production for civil as well as sacred purposes. In the west generally its religious character has been retained. In the Roman Empire it took the form of a 10th part of the profits of lands, the stock on farms and the industry of the people and was alloted to the clergy for their maintenance. The Council of Tours 567 A.D., recommended that the custom of giving these tithes to the clergy should be maintained.

5.

The Council of Macon on 585 transformed this into an order. In 778 Charlemagne made a law to the same effect dividing the revenue from tithes into four parts, one to maintain the edifice of the Church, the second to support the poor, the third the bishop and the fourth the parochial clergy. In England this law was observed and strengthened by Offa in 794 and by Ethelwolf and others later. Tithes are of three kinds:-

(i) Proedial, or those from the soil itself such as corn, hay, fruits and wood etc.

(ii) "mixed" those consisting from natural products but improved and preserved by attention and care of men such as the increase of flocks, herds, milk and eggs, ~~and~~

. (iii) "personal" such as arise from the profits of personal industry, in the pursuit of trade, profession etc.

Originally all lands in Great Britain were tithed except Crown and Church lands. But at the Reformation this exemption was retained on all lands and properties alienated from the Church or from monastaries and handed over to noblemen and other laymen. A payment of a capital sum was generally taken in lieu of tithes. Various measures of commutation have since been added owing to the dislike of the tax. The law now allows any tithe to be redeemed on 17 years purchase.

/The

6.

The special home of the tithing system is the East. Tithes were exacted on agricultural products and flocks by Hebrew Kings, I.Sam.8: 15.and 17. and on imports by the Kings of Babylon. The revenues of Strapas were derived from the fruits of the soil.

In Moslem states, the tithes form an important element in the fiscal system. The Arabs before the rise of Islam, paid tithes on fruits and cereals in two rates, one on produce grown on irrigated lands, and the second on those watered by rain or streams only, where no elaborate irrigation works existed. The Tithe was not mentioned by name in the Coran but the verse in the Anaam Sura referring to trees and plantations which reads:- "Eat from their fruits when they bear fruits and give their right at the day of their harvest." is said to refer to it.

The Al Hadeeth (Traditional religious books) mentions tithes in the following words:- "What is watered by buckets or by wheels should be half tithed.

At the time of the Caliphate Abdul Malik, the land was surveyed and a fixed tax was placed on land whether cultivated or not. Several of the poorer cultivators forsook their properties as a result and settled in the cities.

/The.

7.

The Caliphates themselves controlled the collection of taxes up to the time of the Abbasieh dynasty, when a special department was created for the control of Poll-taxes. The land was then divided into four classes, and taxes levied on cultivated lands only:-

1. Land which the Moslems undertook to improve.

2. Lands whose owners embraced Islam.

3. Lands conquered by Moslems.

4. Lands owned by non Moslems and with whose owners a treaty of reconciliation was made.

Lands in the first three categories were liable to tithes, the fourth had a tribute tax placed on it even if its owners became Moslems. The amount of tribute levied depended upon the produce of the land concerned. It was not less than 1/5 and not more than 1/2 of the amount of the produce.

The Turks at the first adopted the Arab taxes. The Sultan Mahmud il Fateh paid the revenue from tithes to his Princes, Miniters and to support the public intitutions. In 1241 A.H. (1825) a new law was promulgated ordering all tithes to be paid to the Treasury.

In 1858 the land laws were again changed, throughout Turkey, and the law framed by Said Pasha

/was

8.

was sanctioned by the Sublime Porte, and put into force. The Sheria law forbidding the farming out of tributes was changed by the Abbasieh dynasty. Later as will be seen in Section 13. the contracting out of the collection of tithes became the general method.

SECTION. III.

The Tenure of the Land.

9. Land in Palestine is divided into the following classes:-

1. <u>Mulk Land</u>. This corresponds in the principle to the British freehold land and entails full ownership. It includes firstly sites for houses within the limits of a town or village and areas not exceeding ½ a dunum on the confines of towns, appurtenant to houses. Secondly, land separated from State lands and made Mulk in accordance with the terms of the Sharia Law. Thirdly, tithe-paying land given in reward for war service. A fourth division, existing in Turkish Law namely, tribute paying land, does not appear to exist in Palestine.

2. <u>Miri Land</u>. Property of which the ownership is vested in the State but over which a right of possession is conferred upon the cultivator. The occupant can not dispose of it by gift or will, but is otherwise free to deal with it. In the event of the land

/remaining

9.

remaining uncultivated for three consecutive years it reverts to the State. Most of the land in Palestine is of this class. Lands popularly called Mashaa, fall under this head. This term is used for property held in common between persons in share.

3. <u>Wakf Lands.</u> Lands separated from the State and dedicated. The possessors can dispose of this land under certain conditions. The right of the original commitments to which the land is subject, must be reserved. Wakfs lands of all kinds are included under this term, that is, properties dedicated to religious orders and institutions or families. Such can not be sold, but can be exchanged or leased in accordance with the terms of the Sharia Law. These properties are of four kinds:-

  A. Mundarisa. Wakf for which no records exist but which are traditionally set apart for the benefit of certain institutions.

  B. Mazbouta. Wakfs land registered in the Wkf Department, and administered by that Department.

  C. Mulhaka. Wakfs administered by the Mutawalli, under the control of the Wakf Department.

  D. Mustathna. Wakfs of which the whole produce goes to the beneficee and which are administered by the Mutawalli independent of any supervision.

p. 10.

4. **Matrouka Land.** Land which is assigned to the use of the public, or the inhabitants of a particular village. Practically all village grazing lands are of this class. Matrouka land cannot be cultivated and cannot be held by individuals.

5. **Mawat.** State land which is uncultivated and unoccupied lying outside the range of the human voice from outskirt of a village or town.

Two further local and merely popular terms used by the fallaheen to describe land are:-

A. Mudawarra. Land formerly the property of the Sultan, but confiscated by the Government, and vested in the Treasury.

B. Jiftlik. In Law this term means a tract of land such as needs one yoke of oxen to work it and which is cultivated and harvested every year. Its extend varies from 70 to 130 dunoms. In Palestine it is a term popularly applied to land formerly owned by the Sultan.

SECTION IV.

Conditions of Agriculture.

10.
1. The agriculture of Palestine is for the most part of a primitive nature. It is effected to a large extend by the configuration of the land which can briefly be described as being made up of maritime plain, lowland hills,

/a

a mountainous region and the deep Jordan Valley. Each of these divisions has its own peculiar problem. Common to all is the absence of an adequate or regulated water supply. The land has but one large river, the Jordan, from which by the adoption of modern skill and enterprise much is expected in the future. The Kishon and the Ouja are two other streams which run through the plains to the Mediterranean and both of which provide possibilities for irrigation. The principal products are diverse in the extreme. Probably in few countries in the world are such a large number of important agricultural crops produced. Before the war there was a large export of these which even with the backward state of agriculture were regarded by foreign purchasers as of high grade quality. This diversity is the result of climatic consideration due to the physical configuration described above.[1] The chief cereal products are, wheat, barley, maize, (durrah) Kursenneh and sesame. Large crops of beans, peas and lentiles are also grown. Olives are cultivated in every district except Beersheba. Among the fruits, grapes and figs are valuable, whilst oranges have reached a high state of perfection in Jaffa and its neighbourhood.

/Vegetables.

---

[1]. The export of barley to England, maize to Italy sesame oil to France, olive oil to Egypt, oranges to England, Egypt and Russia are cases in point.

12.

Vegetables are cultivated in the vicinity of towns and in the Jordan valley. (2) Tobacco is chiefly cultivated in the north more particularly in the sub districts or Acre and Safed. Among the minor products may be mentioned Jilbaneh, melons, lemons and almonds etc.

Means of Communication and Transport.

13. The means of communications between villages is poor. In the mountains access to certain of them entails painful climbing. Heavy loads are difficult either to take up or down the so called paths. In the plains the cottony nature of the soil render the tracks difficult of use during the winter. On low lying tracks travel is impossible after rain owing to the many swamps and undrained areas of land existing between villages. The need of a rapid construction of roads, the making of culverts and drawing up of new laws for the upkeep of the narrow but workable village tracks is of paramount importance to the developement of agriculture, in the country Miles of light railway material exist and with but comparatively small capital outlay could be used to open out valuable stretches of country. For instance, a light railway line from Gaza to Beersheba with extension to the Gaza port

/and

---

2). The cultivation of tobacco is subject to a special land tax and not to tithe-Vide Official Gazette No.43 dated 11th May 1921.

13.

and the reopening of the old line from Beersheba to Ludd would increase in a remarkable manner the value of possibly the most productive agricultural land in Palestine.

SECTION. V.

The System of Tithing. Methods of collection described.

The System in practice under the Tukish Government.

12. In appendix W will be found an English translation of the Ottoman Law on Tithing taken from Young's Corps de droit Ottoman Vol.V. page 310-341.

Tithes were collected from the yield of the soil. They were not collected on wood used as fuel. This commodity was specially dealt with by the Forest Law.

Perishable vegetables, except those which could be pickled were exempted from tithes.

Tithes were paid in kind or in money after measurement or weighing on the threshing floor. Estimation had not been resorted to for over 25 years prior to the war, but was reintroduced as an emergency measure then. When tithes were paid in kind the cultivators were obliged by law to carry the produce to a depot situated not more than one hours transport free of charge, a tariff being fixed for a greater distance.

14.

In practice they were never paid for this transport however far away the depot was from the village threshing floor.

Tithing was carried out by one of the two following systems:-

1. By farming out the tithes to contractors.

2. Direct collection in kind by the Government.

The contracting out of the collection of Tithes.

13. Under the first system the collections of tithes were leased out yearly, except on olives which was for periods of two years, for a price payable by the contractor in money. These contracts were secured by auction. No member of the Government nor any official was allowed to deal with any tithe contract. It was generally forbidden to lease a district or number of villages in bulk, each having to be dealt with separately. A list of persons intending to bid for leases, was submitted to Governors at least a week before the auction took place, for the purpose of examining the position and character of those desiring to tender. Guarantees were required from intending contractors that they possessed property up to the value of 50% of the price they were prepared to pay for the tithes of any one or more separate villages. The Government in case of failure on

/the

15.

the part of the contractors could destrain on the properties, mentioned on the guarantee forms. A village could tender for its own tithes. After the leasing the contractor was required to commence assessment and the collection either personally or through an agent within three days of a notice from the cultivators that their crops were ready for tithing. Failing assessment in the period stated the villagers were by law allowed to thresh and the contractors ~~was~~ obliged to accept the declaration of the cultivators as to the quantity of the grain or their produce. This time limit was never adhered to, but was extended to weeks, the contractors making various excuses to prolong their operations in order to force the fallaheen to agree to their excessive demands.

The amount of tithes in money was demanded from the contractor in equal instalments on the first day of the months July to January following the harvest. In event of default the securities offered were seized. The contractors were protected in the matter of non payment of dues from cultivators by recourse to the execution officer through an appeal to the Governor.

Tithes on various products other than cereals, were collected in special ways. The tithes on olives were collected after the olives had been transported to the press, mill or store. Vineyards and fruit trees were estimated by weight per dunum.

Direct Government collection.

14. XIV. In the event of no contractor offering or an adequate price being unobtained, the Government collected the tithes direct, (See para 18). The assessments were made either by measurement, or by estimation of grain after winnowing on the threshing floor, and in other parts of the Turkish Empire, but not in Palestine, by the following method:-

System of counting sheaves or loads.

15. XV. Sheaves of grain or loads were counted on the field before removal to the threshing floor. A certain number of shieves, thus counted were threshed and winnowed and the quantity of grain collected was taken as a basis in the levying of the tithe. The number of carts, camel or other loads of produce previously counted on the field was checked on being brought to floor. From the assessment arrived at, the tithe was collected.

Cereals were measured by a *keleh* measure on the threshing floor. The Turks endeavoured to introduce a standard capacity measure but failed.

Use of Gendarmes.

16. XVI. Gendarmes were freely used in all processes of tithing operation, as guards on the threshing floors, and when grain was in transport and also for the apprehension of all persons contravening the law of tithes..

Contractors and their ...

17. Contractors were generally drawn from the richer classes of the community. There were but few chances for the poorer merchants to successfully compete. Even when a village contractor obtained a lease, he was put forward by the influential notables who secured the profit. The tithe collected was generally in excess of the regular tax. Breaches committed by the contractors in the tithes regulations were never looked into by the Government officials who favoured the contractors in every case. In the event of a cultivator venturing to make a complaint, he laid himself open to an accusation of having stolen or concealed certain portions of the crops. False witnesses were always obtainable. The average tax collected by the contractor amounted to not less than from 18 to 20% of the produce. The excess was claimed to cover the wage of guards and assessors and transport expanses etc. Cultivators moreover were obliged to arrange accommodation for the contractor and his servants, to supply them with food and to give forage to their horses for the whole period of the tithing process which lasted for 3 months. These expenses and the additional percentage added to the tithe were in contravention to the Law.

18.

The assessment and collection of tithes under the Military Administration with a history of changes. The procedure as carried on with the improvement made yearly down to the present time officially stated by the Department of Revenue.

18.

Alternative Turkish item.

XVIII. Under the Ottoman Government tithes were, as has already been fully explained, usually farmed out, a system which lent itself to oppressive irregularities. In cases where the tenders for farming the tax were low or unsatisfactory the collection was undertaken by the Administration under the provision of Articles 26-72 of the Law of 24 May 1287 (1872). 3)
By this method an estimator was nominated by each group of four or five villages, control being exercised by agents appointed by the authorities of a kaza and a further supersision being provided by the vilayet authorities. The methods of estimation, ~~the fixing of the price of tithes collected in kind~~ and, the regulations for the transport and distribution of grain were similar to those already discussed. After a portion of the cereals had been assigned for the use of the troops, the remainder was sold by public auction against cash payments, or against drafts at short date guaranteed by reputable persons.

---

3). This method was carried out during the war period from 1915 until the occupation only.

19.

Proclamation by Commander-in-Chief.

XIX. This, then, was the system which the British Army found in vogue in Palestine. Southern Palestine was occupied in December 1917 and by a Proclamation dated 7th May 1918, the Commander-in-Chief reinstated "all taxes in force under the Turkish Government prior to the entry of Turkey into the present war", and they "will be collected with effect from the first day of March 1918". [4].

20.

Instructions issued to Military Governors.

XX. Instructions were issued for the assessment and collection of the "Winter" tithe at the rate of 12.5% of the produce. The term "winter" tithe is applied to the grain, etc. planted during the winter months and harvested in June and July, the terms "summer" tithe being applied to the crops planted in the late spring and harvested in September, October and November. The instructions issued differ materially in many particulars from the Turkish:-

1. The tithe is collected not in kind but in money.
2. it is assessed in kilos.
3. the redemption price is fixed by the Military Governor assisted by a committee appointed by him.

---

[4]. A previous notice to the same effect had been issued by the Acting Administrator, O.E.T. Lt.Col. A.C. Parker, dated 27th February 1918.

20.

4. the list of prices fixed is posted in each village, a statement of assessment being kept by the Mukhtar.

5. appeals against assessment or against the redemption price are heard by a special committee appointed by the Governor whose decision is final. Such appeals must be lodged within <u>six days</u> from the publication of the redemption price.

Estimation, how carried out.

21. The estimation of crops was carried out in some instances by assessing the standing crops and in others on the threshing floors, no specific orders being issued on this point. The system of estimation was as follows:-

A district was divided into a number of circles or zones to each of which was appointed a salaried person to carry out the assessment assisted by the Mukhtars of the village concerned. Control was exercised by the officials of the Governor's staff, who usually settled disputes upon the spot. During the first years estimations this system on the whole worked well as the prestige of British officers was sufficient to ensure an approximate estimation

Method adopted in Gaza.

22. In the District of Gaza the crops were assessed standing in the fields the methods here adopted being different to elsewhere. A schedule

/was

21. demanded from each village giving the name of the cultivator and the number of dunum planted with the kinds of cereal. The mukhtar then added an approximate estimation of the yield of the crops by weight, which was handed in to the Governor. A second estimation was then taken just before the crops were cut by a salaried assessor, who was often the mukhtar of a neighbouring village. In cases of discrepancy of dispute a British Official adjudicated the matter on the spot.

Redemption Price.

23. The fixing of the redemption price was done locally in each District by the Military Governor, subject to the approval of the Controller of Revenue, the Public being notified by Public Notice posted at the Governorate and distributed among villages. The market price of the crop was taken as a standard the actual redemption price being fixed a little below this figure. As a consequence prices varied in each District to the inconvenience of cultivators whose arable lands extended into, or were situated in other districts. In Beersheba (5) were special conditions prevailed owing to an

---

(5). It was customary for the Turks to accept a composition for the tithe in Beersheba based upon the statement of the Sheikh of Tribes. It was usually accepted in money and never approached the true value of the tithe.

22.

assessment not having been carried out before, the redemption price was fixed by the Mufti of Jerusalem. Generally it may be stated that during the first year of our occupation the cultivators were the gainers as all cereals rapidly rose in price, and naturally it was to the benefit of the cultivator to settle his tithe in money and not in kind when the sale of grain was a highly lucrative operation.

Collection.

24. The collection of the redemption price is not made from each individual grower, but from the mukhtar who signs an agreement or "promissory Note" see Appendix K. whereby he undertakes to collect the entire amount due from his village against a rebate of 2% of the amount collected. The amount may be settled in three monthly and equal instalments. Arrears due after this period are subject to nine per cent interest (6).

The "Promissory Notes" signed by mukhtars are subject to the proportional stamp fees as set out in Art.11. of the Ottoman Stamp Law of 1906. They were presumably recoverable from the cultivator though no instructions appear to have been issued to that effect.

---

(6). See Regulations for the collection of taxes and payment of tithes Art.16 Appendix E.

23.

Improvements in 1919.

The system followed in 1919 was in general similar to that of the previous year excepting that in certain instances the methods employed were improved upon as a result of the experience gained. The area over which the tithe was collected was also doubled by the occupation of the Sanjaks of Nablus and Acre in September 1918. By Public Notice dated 15th of November 1918 the arrears of tithes due to the Ottoman Government for that year were cancelled "in view of the hardship suffered by Agriculturists on account of the war". (7).

The instructions dated 3.4.1919 (8) issued under the signature of the Chief Revenue Officer systematised the method of assessment, control and collection. The improvements on the previous year's methods may be summarised as follows:

a). Each District is divided into circles for purposes of estimation. The "number in all cases is to be the lowest consistent with efficiency".

---

(7). The Turks in the year 1917-1918 requisitioned grain in kind, in some instances as much as 37½% being forcibly seized against payment in paper money. This requisition was an addition to the 12½% tithe.

(8). Letter No.7037/FR dated 3.4.19. These instructions formed the basis of all subsequent instructions until the issue of the Tithe Regulations published in the Official Gazette No.41 dated 15.4.21 (see Appendix E).

24.

b). The assessment is made by the method of estimation on the threshing floor.

c). Each estimating commission consists of one non-official estimator, assisted by two elders nominated by the inhabitants. The Commission is accompanied by a clerk, who, in most instances, was an official of the local Revenue Office. Military Governors were also informed that the commission "will be appointed by you in consulation, if you think fit, with the Administrative Council of the District". (9).

d). To ensure the protection of the crops and to prevent theft or hiding of grain a mounted guard who is to be either "a tax collector or gendarme", will guard the threshing floors which are to be registered.

e. The District Finance Inspector (Asst.Inspector of Revenue) and the Mudir Il Mal (Chief Clerk of the local Revenue Office) were required to check personally on the spot "as large a proportion as possible of the work of each commission".

It was further provided that the details of the assessment of a village would

---

(9). This suggestion would appear to have been impossible as the Administrative Council were never convened by the British Military authorities, the Military Governor representing the Council in his own person by virtue of office.

25.

on completion be entered in a special Register (Revenue Book 20.A.) which had to be approved and signed by the Commission and elders. In case of disagreement the produce "will be divided by the cultivators into a certain number of small stacks. The Commission is then to single out any one of these small stacks and have it threshed on the spot. The weight of grain yielded by this stack, will be used as a basis of calculation for the whole quantity, and the amount of tithe thus arrived at will be final".

tion Prices

Supplementary instructions were issued which laid down that the redemption prices should be fixed by the Revenue Directorate after consulation with the Military Governor concerned (10). These instructions were subsequently modified during 1920, whereby the redemption prices of wheat, barley, kursenneh, lentils, beans (ful) durrah and sesame were fixed by the Directorate. The object of this was to rectify the anomalous position of cultivators having cultivated areas in two or more districts subject to

---

10). Letter No.3480/FR of 27.6.1919.

26.

separate prices (11).

---

(11). These instructions are contained in letter No.7766/FR dated 2.6.1920. The fixing of the redemption prices is a matter requiring expert knowledge. The following considerations are involved:-
a. Transport facilities and prices.
b. Tendency of market prices to rise or fall during the months in which the instalments are due.
c. Relative population and production returns
d. Accessibility of markets.
e. Methods of estimation i.e. whether on threshing floors or on standing crops.

The collection of money was also to be made in three instalments as follows:-

One fifth   payable during the 1st month
Two fifths   "   "   "   2nd   "
Two fifths   "   "   "   3rd   "

27.

SECTION VI (A).

Criticisms on the present methods.
The view point of the Government.

DIFFICULTIES OF TITHES OPERATIONS.

The views of the Directorate based on the experiences gained since the Military occupation.

28. Without entering into a discussion of the merits or otherwise of assessing crops on the threshing floor or standing in the fields, or the respective methods of farming out tithe as against direct collection, the period reviewed in the previous sections has presented problems and difficulties that are no less important to day than formerly.

[margin: ience of District & Control sion.]

29. The instructions issued from the Directorate are often difficult to apply in districts and Sub-Districts where the revenue staffs available are comparatively untrained in the technicalities of tithe operations. Inexperience must, therefore be counted as a grave defect of the system. The adjudication of tithe disputes, the necessity for which is frequent from the nature of any estimation based upon guess-work, rests in the first instance upon the control commission and in the last resort upon the British Officials of the Governors Staff.

/In

28.

In certain districts inspectors from the Directorate have operated as control commission with satisfactory financial results ~~in many instances~~, although the cultivators dislike the interference of officials unknown to them. There has, ~~however~~ also, been a certain amount of friction between the Governor as administrative head of a district and the Directorate inspector as representing the executive power of his Department. The line of demarcation has never officially been laid down, and in the nebulous state of a Military Administration these differences of opinion were always easily adjusted, but the transformation of the Government into a civil body makes the settlement of the question one of importance.

(12) In a circular to Military Governors the following paragraph appears. " The Chief Administrator wishes to impress on you the importance of these estimations, and I am to ask that during the estimating season, you will use your best endeavour by frequent touring and inspection on your own part and that of the British Officers of your staff to secure a good result." Further it was pointed out that, "the work of the commissions would have been better

/done

---

(12) Letter No.7037/FR dated April 2nd.1920.

29.

done if a greater degree of control had been exercised by the superior officers of the District." There can be no doubt that the prestige of senior officers carries great weight with cultivators, and the adjudication of disputes without loss of time is an important and very urgent reform, the more so as the assessment and collection of tithe is to the cultivator the most important feature of his year after the planting season is over. It is also the one period of the year when he is brought into the closest touch with Government officials and he looks to and expects the senior officials of his District to give an unbaised opinion on tithe matters.

30. The local influence exerted upon an estimator when assessing in his own district, not necessarily in his own village, is immense. In 1921 the system was instituted of sending estimators from other Districts, but very obvious disadvantages are attached to this method such as are ignorance of localities being assessed, the differences between the weight and quantity of grain of mountain and plain planted areas and the variation in

/rainfall

30.

rainfall which affects the quantity of the grain. (13). Again the salary of estimators (14). who have to work continuously from 30-50 days cannot be considered as adequate to obtain the services of the best and most reliable class of man. Complaints involving these difficulties have been numerous for the past three years.

ration of Assessment.

31. Mention is frequently made of the delay in estimating and of controlling the assessment of crops once they have been placed on threshing floor. The estimator is faced with the fact that different kinds of cereals do not mature at the same date so that frequent visits have to be made, to each village involving loss of valuable time. In the mountains barley matures at the end of May, wheat in June and July, kursenneh in July and so on, while a difference scale of periods is observable in the plains. A solution may be found in increasing the number of circles.

---

(13). A comparison of the assessment of the two districts of Beersheba and Galilee where variations of rainfall play a more prominent part that in other districts is as follows:-

	Beersheba. £E.	Galilee. £E.
1921-22.	44.758.	39.405.
1920-21.	42.714.	61.753.
1919-20.	1.557.	36.588.

(14) This was fixed in 1921 at £E.35 per seasonal assessment and the controller at £E.40.

32. While the remarks advanced in the last paragraph may be taken to add weight to the argument for assessing crops standing, there can also be no doubt that much grain is lost between harvesting and its removal to the threshing floors. It is customary in large areas for labourers to be employed receiving their salary in kind. Under the farming out system a percentage was added by the contractors to make up for the loss of grain in this manner and the percentage was often increased to guard against the introduction of foreign matter into the stacks. These difficulties remain and have become accentuated by the Directorate cancelling the use of paid guards and placing the responsibility for guarding grain upon the Mukhtar who is incapable and often unwilling to impose his full authority upon cultivators with whom he must live on terms of friendship. In addition there must always be present ordinary cases of theft and concealment of crops.

Threshing floors and stacks.

33. There exists no offical list of threshing floors authorised to be used for the stacking of grain. Though custom has sanctioned use yet there may be many such floors belonging to one village widely separated from each other. The stacks when made up are of any size and shape each

/different

32.

different and bearing no relation to the amount of grain involved. A stack of wheat is about one third heavier than a stack of barley of the same size, a kursenneh stack again may be from two to three fifths heavier than a barley stack. Similarly these crops would offer different gross weights in the plains than those of the cooler and more humid climates of the hills.

Fruit Crops.

34. In the estimation of fruits and vegetables the system of estimation is more cumbersome than in the case of cereals. For cereals there are certain rough and ready calculations with which all cultivators are acquainted, used by them in the ordinary way of business to arrive at an approximate area of the yield. In the case of fruits and vegetables no such calculation can be of assistance as climatic considerations, windfalls and crop deseases play a large part in the actual yield obtained. There are, too, different qualities of fruit giving large variations in yield. All these considerations must technically be taken into consideration by an estimator who is often unable to read and write, and who perchance may be a cereal expert but have no knowledge of fruit.

/There

Entertainment and
Other Expenses.

33.

35. There is, of course, always present the grievance that the wealthy man's crops are underestimated to the disadvantage of the fellah. But no less important is the difficulty of preventing the estimator from accepting freely the hospitality of the community whose crops he is about to assess. Indeed in some cases this system has developed into a veritable unofficial tax upon the resources of a village regarded by the commission as a privilege sanctioned by tradition. Where a large village is concerned having much arable land no inconsiderable expense is incurred by the inhabitants who may be unofficially called upon to provide hospitality for the commission and their riding animals. To these expenses must be added the amount payable under the Ottoman Stamp Law of 1906 and Public Notice No.78 for the affixing of stamps on promissory notes. It may be asked how the Mukhtar partition these payments among his community and whether any abuse may be prevalent in this respect. (15)

---

(15) Letter No.7766/4/Rev dated 23.3.21 lays down the duty payable on Revenue Form No.11.

H.J.Z. Stamps Duty, item 24 Documents of Security or Guarantee-1 per mille with a minimum charge of PT.2 and a maximum of PT.25.

/ O.P.D.A. Stamps.

Collection of Redemption price.

36. The collection of the redemption price through a Mukhtar who undertakes to collect the tithe from each individual tax-payer is an ideal one for the Department of Revenue. The costs of collection are almost negligible, the promptness with which the instalments are paid is a noticeable feature in comparison with other taxes and a minimum of clerical work is involved. Yet collection from the individual by a Mukhtar is fraught with very obvious dangers. In the majority of cases it may be stated that no receipt is given on even expected, though on the whole Mukhtars have not abused their positions in this respect. But there is little or no safeguard for the cultivators. It is true that a Mukhtar must post in each village the tithe in kilos due from each cultivator and although instructions have frequently been issued to this effect in practice it is not often done. This safeguard even if carefully carried out is not very real one since the majority of the fellaheen are unable to read.

(15 cont)
O.P.D.A. Stamps Duty: Art.9, item 22, Documents of Security or Guarantee- for any amount over £E.400, PT.25. for any amount under £E.400 proportionate duty is charged.

35.

Further he must make himself acquainted with the redemption prices and then calculate the amount payable by ascertaining the weight in kilos from the posted list. This leads to another aspect which involves considerable confusion.

Weight & Measures used.

37. The Government standard is a kilogram. Estimators are acquainted with this weight, but more often than not the cultivator calculates the tithe due by him not in kilos but in a local measure. These measures vary from district to district and even from village to village so that the commissions must be capable of converting the equivalent weight or measure into kilogrammes, when discussing the yield of produce with the representatives of the village. Again an estimator or cultivator who is used to hill measures may have no knowledge of those in use in village of the plains. Weights and measures though of the same nomenclature often bear no relation to each other, thus a keleh in Beersheba is different from a keleh in Galilee, a mid in Jenin differs from a mid in Acre and so forth. A jarrah of oil in Southern Palestine

/is

36.

is not used as a measure in Northern Palestine. Olives are measured in Galilee by capacity measure, elsewhere by weight. There are no Government sets of weight and measures for tithe commissions to use on the threshing floor when taking a shishna or weighing a stack after threshing has taken place. A table of weights and measures is given in Appendix D.

Defaulting tax-payers.

38. As has already been stated a Mukhtar assumes the responsibility for the collection of the tithe in money. In the case of a tax-payer who refuses to accept his liability the Revenue Officials hold the Mukhtar primarily responsible, and may, therefore, proceed against him in Court. A promissory note is registered at the office of the Notary Public free of charge.(16). In accordance with the Tithe Law, tithe may be collected by direct reference to the Execution Officer of the Courts. This involves seizure of crops by the Department of Revenue who are required to produce an official document of contract showing that it has been registered before a Notary Public, together with two copies of a petition requesting that seizure be laid on the property of the contractor.

---

(16). The necessity for the registration of promissory notes was long a matter of dispute. in 1920 certain Mukhtars of Nablus refused signature and as a result registration has since been insisted upon. Letter No.7766/4/Rev of 9.6.21.

37.

If the contract has not been registered recourse must be made to the Courts before action can be taken. (17). By this decision then, the crops of a mukhtar are liable for seizure. He in turn may take action against individual defaulters. The Department submits all cases of recovery of taxes to the Attorney General, the Public Prosecutor undertaking actions on behalf of the Government.

In practice it has been found that the prestige of the Governor is generally sufficient to ensure payment. Pressure may also be applied to the individual tax-payer, on behalf of the mukhtars through similar means. But the existance of the legal remedy outlined above is detrimental to a mukhtars interests who bear a heavy financial responsibility and may be involved in the payment of costs for any action taken by the Public Prosecutor. (18).

---

(17). Decision of Legal Secretary dated January 31st.1921. Revenue letter No.3480/13/Rev. dated 4.2.21.

(18). An Ottoman order issued by the Ministry of Finance, states that a Mudir el Mal is entitled to 1% of the arrears collected by way of distraint when documents are registered at the office of the Notary Public,& ½% when application is made to the Courts direct. This has not been applied.

38

SECTION VI. (B).

The opinions and suggestions of the Public.

Advantages & disadvantages of tithes as a system of taxation.

39. Tithes are the most important and most ancient of the taxes ruling in the East. They are sanctioned both by age and by sacred Law. The cultivators are accustomed to the tax and look upon its payment as a sacred duty. It is a levy upon actual produce which varies with the profit enjoyed by the owner. The replacement by a fixed annual tax would in the eyes of many of the ignorant fallaheen seem a retrograde and impious move. This point is expressed briefly as follows:-

" What could be more just than a tax which is yearly based on actual results, and what more unjust than to take a fixed sum as a tax, the same in bad as in good years."

Against the above must be placed the opinion of all progressive cultivators and the many disadvantages of the system. It entails hardship on growers owing to the necessary delay caused by weighing, measurement or estimation of the crops and to the danger

/of

39.

of loss of crops by theft, fire or vermin. The farmer is unable to deal with his harvest until tithing has been carried out. He may thus lose the opportunity of making good prices for early crops. The system militates against improvement in agriculture as generally the less intensification and developement carried out, the less in proportion are the dues payable. Energy initiative ~~from~~ and enterprise are not encouraged thereby. An extract from evidence given by a witness is recorded to illustrate these points:-

Witness ~~No.18~~ Jaffa.

"I am not satisfied with the present system of tithes in principle, because it hinders intensification of agriculture and therefore the developement of the country."

From the Government point of view, tithes are difficult of assessment by weighing, measurement or estimation. Whatever method is adopted it is costly. The taking of tithes leads yearly

/differences.

40.

differences between the Government and the cultivators and it fails to produce a steady revenue owing to the fluctuations due to the harvest returns.

Estimation of Tithes.

40. There is but little criticism throughout the country on the principle of the system of estimation as opposed to a system of measurement or of weighing. It is noted, however, that the Cyprus Government looked with so much disfavour on estimation as to do away with tithes on vegetables, and fruit trees which were formerly assessed by this method. Estimation is at best only approximately accurate, it opens the way to fraud and oppression. Nothing can be easier than to give a relatively small underestimation to a friend or to over assess an enemy. The system brings the Government yearly as a bargainer against the cultivators and unseemly wrangles take place between officials and village-estimators. The latter objection is shared but in a lesser degree if measurement or weighing be adopted. From the above remarks it is evident that the adoption of a system by which such annual complaints are avoided, would be politically advantageous.

/The

41.

The Committee has not studied nor prepared evidence sufficient to propose an entirely new system as such would appear to be outside its terms of reference. They point ~~them~~ out the various views expressed in the hope that they may be useful when and if a change of system be determined upon.

Extracts of criticisms and suggestions made which influenced the Committee in their recommendations on this and other matters, are given in ~~appendix~~ section VI. They effect for the most part the details of the working of the system and not the system itself. The system of estimation is generally popular amongst the fallaheen, in comparison to that of contracting out as carried on by the Turks. The cultivators in Jewish Colonies and a few individuals who have had experience and education on modern agricultural lines criticise it severely. These latter as will be seen condemn the system of tithes whether assessed by estimation weighing or measurement and ask for a land tax to be placed on the dunum in lieu thereof.

Estimation on the Threshing Floor and Standing Crops compared.

41.
~~42.~~ Para 12 of the Regulations for the assessment of tithes refers. Appendix E. Estimation on the threshing floor is preferred by a majority of cultivators to that on standing crops. It can generally be said that neither system

/is

42.

is popular and hopes of a speedy change to one of land taxation are entertained. The advantages of each system may be briefly described as follows:-

Advantages of Estimation on the Threshing Floor.
1. Fairly accurate results can be arrived at by experts.
2. In the event of disputes satisfactory assays can be carried out.
3. The crop is transported from the field to the Threshing Floor which adjoins the village before estimation thereby lessening danger of loss from theft, vermin and climatic conditions.

Disadvantages of Estimation on the Threshing Floor.
1. The delay caused by estimation and inspection and the holding up of sales on this account.
2. The danger of loss from fire, and if the delay be lengthened from vermin also.

Advantages of Estimation on Standing Crops.
1. It leaves the grower at liberty to dispose of his crops to an earlier market.

Disadvantages of Estimation on Standing Crop.
1. Difficulty under present conditions of ascertaining the areas assessed.

/ 2.

2. Difficulties of estimating due to the configuration of the land, differences in the quality of the soil in patches especially when dealing with large areas.

3. Generally an absence of knowledge amongst cultivators with this system of assessment (except in Beersheba).

4. The many complaints from agriculturists who state that much loss is incurred in carrying the grain home after assessment in the field.

of the two & difficulties ted therewith.

42. There is considerable differences of opinion from officials on the merits and demerits of the two systems. Those of Galilee and Haifa generally favour and have adopted estimation on standing crops in certain villages in the plains with success. The complaints from the public in these districts have not been more numerous than where estimation has been carried out on the threshing floor. In Beersheba the rule has been to estimate on standing crops. Dissatisfaction was manifested by the Bedwin this year at the assessment made. A Sub-Committee visited Beersheba on the 4th of January, where the Sheikhs were seen as a body and five representatives chosen by the Sheikhs themselves examined. They all declared that the system of estimation on standing crops is preferable to that on the threshing

/floors

44.

Three stated that the present system was better than that adopted by the Turkish Authorities and two gave their opinion that the contracting out of tithes was the best method of all. This latter system was discussed. The three Sheikhs who voted for estimation stated:-

1. That Government taxes are better when estimated as at present and collected by Sheikhs through official channels.
2. That there would be difficulty in preventing abuses, such as the oppression on or favour to individuals which formerly occured, where the contracting out system again adopted.
3. That it would be impossible to get contractors outside the few persons who know the tribes and had influence with them.

The Sheikhs were unanimous in their opinion that the troubles of last harvest were due not to the fact that crops were estimated standing but to the ignorance of the estimators sent them from Jerusalem.
(For evidence see Appendix J.)

45.

The evidence of the British District Inspector supports this view. He writes:-

In my opinion the chief causes of the dissatisfaction evinced by the cultivators of this District against last years estimation was on account of the unsuitable estimators sent by the Department of Revenue The large majority were residents and cultivators of land situated in the hills and when called upon to estimate large plots of more or less flat country, were out of their element.

Choice of system to remain with Governors.

43. After reviewing the evidence, the Committee are of the opinion that Governors of Districts should be left free to decide which of these two systems of estimation they care to adopt.

They recommend that the method of the Sudan Government Appendix G be communicated to the Governors of Beersheba for consideration. The Sheikhs seem to be not desirous of rendering service which involves fatigue or responsibility, but the Committee recomends that they be instructed to render to the local Revenue office a return showing the names of cultivators together with a statement signed

/or

46.

or sealed by each cultivator of the amount of ground he cultivates. The cultivator and not the Sheikh should be responsible for this information. The return should be drawn up during the yearly animal enumeration which is carried out by the Sheikhs during the months of February and March.

Delay Caused by Estimation.

44.

~~52~~. There is a consensus of opinion that much might be done to lessen the serious delays that occurs in estimation. Days and sometimes weeks elapse, after the notification that the crops are on the threshing floor before the arrival of the estimating commission. Efficient control is needed to hasten the commissioners who it is pointed out at present spend a considerable portion of the day enjoying the hospitality of the village whose crops are being estimated. The keeping of a careful record of threshing floors estimated daily, with the hours at which work commenced and finished, together with surprise visits by an inspecting officers would do much to accelerate matters. In the Nablus District and elsewhere an arbitrator has been asked for to accompany the assessment commission and to settle differences on the spot. Appendix H. This it is stated

/would

47.

avoid the delay now incurred owing to the necessity of referring the difference to the Governor and await the arrival of an inspector or inspecting commission.

Constitution of the Estimation Commission.

45. Public opionion is divided upon the number of members that should be appointed on the estimating commission. The majority favour four i.e. two being appointed by the Government and two chosen by the people. This system prevails in Haifa. The Assistant Revenue Officer of that District considers that the few complaints received this year from cultivators is in a measure due to the increase in the personnel of the commission. He pointed out that four accomplish double the work of two, that discussion on differences are thereby shortened, and satisfactory decisions are more speedily arrived at. The Assistant Revenue Officer of Galilee, referring to Government appointed estimators says, " Assessors should proceed to their work in pairs and not singly as at present, one would serve as a check to the other." Appendix J.

Qualification of Estimators.

48. Complaints are general as to the type of estimators employed. It is noticed that many are dismissed for inefficiency or for dishonest practices yearly. This fact tends to confirm the statement of witnesses that :-

1. Inexperienced men are employed.
2. That they are chosen by one individual and not by a committee and thus sufficient care is not exercised in their selection.
3. That mountaineers are sent to estimate in the plain districts and dwellers in the plains to assess the crops of mountainous districts.
4. That cultivators of cereals are sent to estimate fruit and vegetables or crops on which they have no knowledge, and vice versa. Appendix K.

There is also a general feeling that estimators should be chosen from their own districts. Appendix L

Appointment of Selection Committee.

49. A general request is made for the appointment of a district selection committee whose duty it will be to recommend individuals as estimators to the Governor. The Committee should consists, it is asked, of two

/representatives

49.

representatives of the local Revenue Officer, two of the Municipality, two of the local Agricultural Committee, and two independent Agriculturists. The Governor should preside over the Committee. This body would prepare a list of estimators considered qualified and suitable from which the Governor would select and appoint. A list of all appointments should be sent to the Civil Secretary and be publicly announced in the Official Gazette. Appendix L.

The Representatives of the Cultivators.

49. 50. These persons are chosen by the villagers with the approval of the Governor. They are under no bond nor have they any feeling of responsibility for the correct performance of their duties. Reference Para I. of 7766/4/Rev. Appendix E They seek to safeguard the interest of their fellows by bargaining with the Government estimators over the amount of grain found on each threshing floor. Witnesses state they are necessary but that their voice carries little weight. Requests have been made that they should be made responsible for giving correct estimation, and that their estimation should be recorded, and that in the event of gross under estimation they should be made liable to prosecution together with the Government estimators.

/The

50.

The Committee believes that such legislation would tend to reduce the delays and wrangling which occur on threshing floors. They suggest that the names of these estimators be published in the local papers. See para 7. of 7766/4/Rev. Appendix E.

Inspectors of Assessment.

49. Para 5 of the regulations for the assessment of tithes No.7766/4/Rev of the 23.3.20, rules that an Inspector of assessments may be appointed in each district. A large number of complaints have been received regarding the superficial character of the work done by these officials, especially where they have been selected outside of the districts, their arbitrary methods and discourteous manners. The evidence from Nablus suggests that inspectors make cursory tours round the villages, select one or two threshing floors that are obviously underestimated and proceed to place such additions as are required to make that particular floor correct upon a whole village. Most of the other districts make similar complaints. Criticism on their inexperience of these officials is also general. Appendix M

Often the Assistant Revenue Officer of the District has constituted himself the

/inspector

51.

inspector and delegated the inspector appointed under Para.5. as a S/Controller. This would appear irregular. Considerable confusion exists in the public mind between the control and inspection of assessment.

The Committee's opinion and recommendations concerning estimation, estimators, inspections etc.

88. The matter is further complicated by the superinspection of officials of the Revenue Department.

50. The Committee have no hesitation in stating that most of the delay in estimation is due to the differences which arise between the Government and village appointed estimators. They also consider amendments should be made on the selection and appointment of personnel. They recommend that the Law be modified so that the following changes may be brought about:-

1. That a daily log book be provided in which the hour of commencing and finishing work should be recorded together with the number of estimations completed by the Commission.

2. That an arbitrator should always accompany the estimating commission. His duties should be:-

a). To give decisions on the spot when difference arise between the estimators.

b). To report all cases of under-estimation that come under his notice. These he should report and not arbitrate on.

52

3. That an estimating commission consist if financial considerations allow, of four estimators, two appointed by the Government and two by the people, or if this is ruled excessive of one on each side. A clerk for clerical work should be attached to the commission,

4. That estimators be appointed who are:-
a). Agriculturists.
b). From the district itself, or from one in which similar conditions prevail as in the district to which estimators are sent to work.
3. That they be possessed of expert knowledge of the kind of crop they are called upon to estimate.

5. That village estimators should be made responsible jointly with those of the Government ones for their assessments.

6. That Inspectors be chosen from the most experienced of the estimators or from Government Officials with expert knowledge of assessment. At the most, one such official for each District would be sufficient. The work would generally be done by the District Revenue Staff.

7. That the personnel be chosen by the Governor of a district acting on the advice of a selection Committee. The local

/Revenue

53.

Revenue and the Agricultural Officials should be ex-officio members. The Municipality and the District Agricultural Committee and independent agriculturists should be represented. In Districts where special crops such as oranges are cultivated, representation should be given to an association such as the Orange Growers Association of Jaffa.

8. That the estimating Commission be ordered to estimate crops within 15 days of notification of their readiness by the Mukhtars or Sheikhs concerned.

9. That a limit should be stated before the expiration of which an inspector should visit a threshing floor or standing crops after assessment. That in no case should this exceed 7 days after the completion of the original estimation. At the expiration of this period the villagers should be permitted to winnow.

10. That the name of District inspector should for the purposes of estimation and inspection be changed to that of "Controller" and the name Inspector of tithes to be retained for an official inspecting from the Directorate of Revenue. These officials should keep a daily log book showing threshing floors visited with an exact record of work done thereon.

54.

SECTION VI (C).
Collection of Tithes in Kind.

The Cyprus System.

51. The Chairman of the Tithes Committee proceeded to Cyprus on the 13th of December 1921, to investigate the procedure of the assessment and collection of the tithes ruling on the Island. He reports that:-

The assessment of grain crops is made by measuring with a ½ kelo measure (½ bushel) the amount found on the threshing floor. This measurement is carried out by officials such as coldjis (watchmen) under the personal supervision of a Mamour, both of whom are temporary officials. Their duties also include the watching of the threshing floors, the winnowing and the placing of grain in sacks and the sealing of such sacks after they are filled. All materials including the sealing wax are supplied by the cultivators. The mamours are responsible for recording the amount to be taken from each grower on the official forms supplied, and they see that sound sacks only are used for grain delivery. Tithes supervisors appointed from the permanent staff organise the duties, and move about inspecting the work of the mamours and coldjis. They make notes on official forms of their own visits and the work they actually perform.

/One

55.

One supervisor, who is a permanent official, directs the tithing of each District. He moves about freely and has but little clerical work. Under the supervisors are revenue or temporary officers acting as sub-supervisors who are responsible for Nahiehs or sub-Districts. The Treasurer is charged with the general superintendence of the tithes assessment and collection. He selects through his officers the persons nominated for tithe duties by the Commissioners of Districts. All orders to finance officials, permanent or temporary, are transmitted to them by and through the commissioner in whose district they are working, and no changes are made except by order of the commissioner concerned.

Elaborate rules have been framed to prevent irregularities in measurement, collection and storing. The principal ones are as follows:-

Officers charged with actual tithes assessment are not allowed to collect or receive revenue. Mamours and cadjis are forbidden to deal directly or indirectly in produce. Mamours are to hand Koushans to

/farmers

56.

farmers on giving them leave to winnow and all measurement, operations and results are noted thereon and on two other special forms. Copies of these are attached in Appendix N. No grain can be removed from the threshing floor whilst measurement is being carried on. Delays in winnowing have to be reported. All alterations in records, have to be rewritten and initialed. Supervisors are required to keep diaries setting forth the work done such as the number of checkings made on threshing floors and the inspection of Kushans and other documents.

From the above it will be seen that the system is one of measurement and not of estimation. It is said to give satisfaction to the public. The farmer cuts and threshes his crops when he likes, but has to get permission to winnow. It is stated that not more than 24 hours elapses between the application to winnow and the granting of the permission. If this be lengthened beyond three days the law rules that the cultivators can winnow without waiting for the arrival of permission. After winnowing there is never more than 30 hours delay before measurement. After measurement the farmer is obliged to deliver the grain to the nearest Government store within 15 days.

/The

57.

The average cost of the assessment and the collection of grain over a number of years is stated to be approximately 15% of the tithes which are 10% and not 12 and ½% of the produce as in Palestine.

Officials employed and cost of Tithing operations.

52. The following are the officials employed with the salaries of the temporary ones attached.

1. <u>General Oversight</u>.

Treasurer with general oversight of assessment and collection.

2. <u>Estimation and Collection</u>.

6 Commissioners. These direct the operations. They act as final arbitrators in cases of disputes in their Districts.

6 Supervisors (£.300 grade). If an official inferior to this grade is employed he is given salary during his period of duty at this rate.

13. Revenue Officials. 6.permanent and others temporary, £.36 to £.45 per mensem, each over a period of about four months.

81. Mamours - Clerks - at 3/- daily wage.

262. coldjis - watchmen - at 2/ daily wage.

58.

3. Storing of grain and checking and compilation of returns.

Treasurer.
Revenue clerks - permanent staff.
10 Store-keepers - £.7. to £.10 for three to six months.
15. Coldjis, £.5. per mensum.

The cost of assessment, transport etc., and amount of Tithes received for the years 1918 to 1920, inclusive is submitted in £. Sterling.

Year.	Cost of Assess.	Cost of By Rail	Transport by Road.	Cost of Handling of Grain at Store.	Wages-Store keepers & Coldjis.	Other Items. approximately.
1918.	5573	1119.	1768.	180.	1013	200.
1919.	4731	748.	1135.	150.	1013	200.
1920.	6032	801.	1335.	154.	1013	200.

Revenue from Tithes in £.Sterling of Principal Crops Only.

Year.	Wheat.	Barley.	Vetches.	Oats.	TOTAL:
1918.	97895.	50263.	9159.	3484.	150801.
1919.	71263.	38182.	10905.	1772.	122122.
1920.	114737.	39747.	10320.	2959.	167763.

The approximate number of dunums cultivated and production is bushels for the year 920 to 21 for each principal - follows:-

	Dunum.	Bushels.
Wheat.	592996.	2266000.
Barley.	385648.	2274000.
Vetches.	203321.	350000.
Oats.	55642.	197000.

The amount of Tithes derived from each dunum cultivated in 1920 was PT.1322. /2-22.

59

In addition to the recurring expenditure the cost of the erection and repairs of grain stores must be considered. For example the grain store at Nicosia was built in 1907-9 at an original cost of £.1095. It was twice enlarged at a cost of £.537 2nd £.700 respectively. The total amounted to £.2332.

This building could not now be erected under £.5000. There are 10 such large stores in the Island and five smaller ones approximately half the size. At 6% interest these represent without repairs an addition of £3750 a year on cost of collection that is £.300 on each of the ten large stores and approximately £.150 on each on the smaller ones. The total revenue from tithes for 1920 was £.176.000. The tithing collection and storing charges amounted to £.9537 plus interest on capital expenditure. This gives the cost of assessment and collection at a little over 13%.

Tithes on fruit and vegetables.

53.   Fruits - trees and vegetables have not been tithes since 1881.   Certain commodities such as cotton, raisins and silk are taxed at the ports on export and the tax on these has been increased to meet some of the loss incurred from the exemptions above mentioned.   The reason for the exemptions is the determination of the

60

council of the Island to abolish all estimation of crops and to use the system of measurement only. It has, however, been found impracticable to measure the grain in some 20 to 30 villages in the mountains and in these estimation is still resorted to. It should be noted that the exemption from tithes has not increased to any appreciable extent, the amount of vegetable and fruit tree cultivation.

The advantage of measurement by a capacity measure over estimation is apparent. It is a more accurate system and but rarely complaints of irregular assessment are received. It, however, is not so correct as that of weighing in that a clever filler of a measure can increase and decrease the amount in that measurement by some 5% at will. Both measurement and weighing are lengthy in operation. The Cyprus Government considers that the system of measurement of grain on threshing floors is the best available.

Collection in kind advantages and disadvantages.

54. The collection of grain in kind is undoubtedly popular with the cultivators. It is also favoured by the Government. The tithes are in the stores 15 days after tithing is completed and there are no arrears of payments. The cultivators are saved the

/trouble

61.

trouble of selling the grain and are protected against a falling market. Against these advantages are the expense and the danger both of collection and storing and the difficulties of disposal. The bulk of the income in money from tithes can not be handled by the Government, until the grain is sold which is approximately six months after the harvest.

The Cyprus Government has had much difficulty in the disposal of the grain lately and some of the stock from 19-20 is not yet disposed of."

The opinion of the Committee on collection in kind in Palestine.

55. The Committee are of the opinion after reading the Chairman's report (~~see appendix~~) that the introduction of the collection of tithes in kind in Palestine would be attended with grave disadvantages to the Government. They observe that the Cyprus Government is unable to carry out this system in the mountainous region. A large portion of Palestine is included in this category and the transport of grain from many of the mountain villages is difficult. The gravest objections to the system are the cost of collection and the necessity of the outlay of capital expenditure for the provision of stores.

62.

The advantage claimed that the grain is gathered and placed in store some 15 days after assessment and that there are no arrears of tithes is neutralised by the necessity of finding a market for the grain. It has to be delivered to contractors and payment recovered from them. This system and also ~~together with~~ that of collection in money fails to provide a stable revenue as ~~it is~~ they are entirely dependent upon harvest results. By either system the Government is unable to handle the bulk of the money accruing until some six months after assessment.

Section. VI.D.

Redemption of Tithes. 56. Para 13 of 7766/4/rev dated 23.3.21 rules that the District Governor will inform the Directorate of the prices they consider certain titheable crops should be redeemed at. At the same time they are requested to forward the market prices then active. From these prices are fixed by the Directorate. The products dealt with are as follows:-

Wheat.	Oranges, Lemons & Citrons.
Barley.	Grapes. (Lesser & Wine).
Lentiles.	Figs.
Kursenneh.	Melons (Sweet & Water.
Jilbaneh.	
Chick Peas.	Honey. Olives and Olive Oil.
Lupin (Tourmus)	
Beans.	
Durrah.	
Sesame.	

63.

The redemption price of other products are fixed by the Governor who forwards a copy to the Directorate. Requests have been generally received that modifications of these rules may be made. The principal requests are:-

1. That prices be fixed at least two months after the harvest, i.e. at the end of August when the position of the market may be more stable.

2. That in fixing prices outlying villages should be considered in relation to their distance from the railroads and the main roads.

3. That the prices at Haifa and Jaffa should not rule throughout Palestine, but that the cost of transportation charges for grains to these ports should be taken into consideration.

It is suggested that the Public should be more consulted in the fixing of the redemption prices. Consultation with various Chambers of Commerce is considered insufficient as these bodies are made up for the most part of merchants and traders who are only indirectly affected by these prices, while the farmers who are the tithes payers

/are

64.

are seldom represented. It is thought by some that local agricultural Committees should be consulted and by others that special Commissions to deal with redemption prices should be appointed in each District.

Appendix O.

The Committee's opinion and recommendation.

57.
65. The Committee are of the opinion that the Law should be modified to allow the following:-

1. The fixing of the redemption price to be based on or about the price ruling in the market of the capital of a District or Sub-District, at a date not earlier than the end of August, and that in fixing the price the situation of Nablus (Nahiehs) should be considered.

2. That the fixing of these prices should be with Governors of Districts who should be assisted by a local Committee on which the local Agricultural Committee, independent Agriculturists and the Municipality are represented. The local Revenue Officer or Mudir El Mal and the Agricultural Assistant should be ex-officio members.

3. The Directorate of Revenue should cause Governors of Districts to be informed of the market prices ruling throughout Palestine at the periods when redemption prices are being fixed.

65.

Section 6. E

58.

88. Para 1. 8. 10. 14. 15. and 16

Considerations concerning the agency used in the collection of Tithes in Money.

of the Regulations for the assessment of tithes reference (Appendix E.).

The method by which mukhtars and elders of a village are made responsible for the tithes of a community by means of securing their signatures on a promissory note is an ideal one for the Revenue office. There are, however, many complaints from mukhtars that the responsility they are asked to accept is too great. It is doubtful whether the signature of a promissory note does in law compel a mukhtar to assume full respnsibility for the collection of the tithe. The tax is due from individuals and not from a community as a whole. This fact is clearly established by the estimation of the produce of individuals separately and by Para 8 of the regulations referred to above which reads:-

" Each cultivator will be handed a copy of tithe bill No.19 giving full particulars of the amount of tithes due from him."

Further, the tithes are paid to the Mukhtars at irregular times and in different amounts. He is busy collecting from tithe payers for months every year.

/He

66.

He takes what amounts the cultivators care to give him and keeps a rough account of these payments on a special list. He gives no official receipts for amounts received and no record is made of the date of payment. Interest at the rate of 9% is, however, charged by law on overdue accounts. This he usually pays from his pocket, as it is well nigh impossible to apportion it amongst the defaulting tax payers. Again the mukhtars are charged for stamps which have to be placed on the promissory note, see para 14 of the Regulations above quoted, and all collecting expenses must be paid by him. The Government does not concern itself in any of the above. The results of this procedure are:-

1. Certain mukhtars keep large sums of money for weeks, trading with it in grain or loaning it to others, in the meantime.

2. In the event of loss in trading the villagers are called upon in one way or another to make up the loss.

3. Mukhtars are compelled to make a charge on villagers for out of pocket expenses. This opens the door to abuse as these accounts are not open for inspection.

67.

4. The Mukhtars are themselves called upon to defray expenses.
    a) for travelling.
    b) Stamp duties.
    c) Entertaining.

All this compels them to resort to demands in excess of the tax on villagers. The public ~~generally~~ *on the whole* approve of the collection by means of mukhtars. *Appendix. P. 59.*

Recommendation on the Collection of the Tithes.

~~68~~. The Committee consider that on the whole, the work has been well done by ~~them~~ *the mukhtars*. They make the following recommendations:-

1. That the promissory note as such should be abolished.

2. That mukhtars be made by law, temporary tax collectors with written appointments to this effect from the District Governor. That they be guaranteed by their village. That in the event of difficulty of collection from individual cultivators they be empowered to refer lists of defaulters, direct to the Execution Officer for action.

3. That mukhtars be given regular receipt books and that all payments be recorded with date on counterfoil. That each tax payer pay the stamp duty for the receipt given him.

4. , That the regular tax collectors of the district be empowered to examine these books monthly. That all sums collected,

/if

68.

If not previously taken to the Treasury should be taken by them for transmission to the local office.

5. That the amount of tithes due under PT.100, be paid in one instalment, over PT.100, and under PT.500 in two monthly instalments and over PT.500 in three monthly instalments.

6. That mukhtars be better remunerated for their services. It is suggested that this extra cost be paid by other Departments using them or by an increase of fees.

7. There is a request from many that the tithes should be paid in five instalments The Committee are unable to recommend that this be granted, believing that a modification whereby the redemption price is fixed later in the year and based on a consideration of the market price ruling locally at that time will do away with the necessity of prolonging the period for payment.

Collection from Religious Institutions.

60. The Committee are of the opinion that the collection of such tithes should be taken out of the hands of the Mukhtars and be dealt with directly by the Government. See also appendix. P and para 79.

69.

SECTION VII.
Tithes on different classes of property.

Lands that are not revenue producing for the state.

61. The titheable lands of Palestine are not wholly revenue producing land for the State. A considerable portion of the revenue is collected on behalf of Institutions which are only in part associated with the Government.

Wakf Tithes.

62. Tithe is collected from the produce of Miri lands, which included, broadly speaking, lands entailed to Moslem pious and charitable institutions known as "WAKF". The tithe of such properties may even be settled upon families and private persons, so that there exists two categories of wakfs that receive revenues from tithes known as "Mazbutah" and "Mulhaka" Wakfs. The former is administered directly by the Supreme Moslem Sharia Council, and the latter by mutawalis or trustees under the supervisory control of the Council only.

Mazbutah Wakf.

63. The tithes (19) accruing from Mazbutah lands are collected by the Government on

---

(19) The tithe on Wakf lands is technically only 12%, the addition of ½% imposed by the Turks for military equipment was not added to Wakf lands. The Military Administration ruled that 12½% should be collected from all lands chiefly for the sake of convenience and regularity.

70.

behalf of the Supreme Moslem Sharia Council. They constitute approximately *2.75* per cent of the total tithe revenue of Palestine. The local Mamour of Wakfs is instructed to accompany all estimating commissions when the assessment takes place. He is requested to sign the Tithe Register, and he may raise objection to the assessment in which case the point at issue is adjudicated by the control commission. The Government debit the Wakf with the costs of estimation and collection, calculated approximately in 1919 and 1920 at £.E.850.

The collection on account of Wakf was in

	£.E.
1918-19	19,312.
1919-20	~~22,524.~~ *17.322*
1920-21	~~25,844.~~ *27.649*

Mulhaka Wakf.

64.
~~78.~~ The tithe from Mulhaka Wakf Lands being a private or family endowment is assessed and collected by the trustee, the Government commissions merely supervising the estimation.

Educational Wakfs.

65.
~~93.~~ There is one other class of property appertaining to Wakfs. There are lands known as "Educational Wakf Lands" that were formerly wakf property which has reverted to the state by means of escheat. Their revenues are state

/revenues

71

revenue devoted to Moslem education. For the year 1919 and 1920 the income was £E.284 and £E.1292 respectively.

Government Share.

66 From the tithes of mazbutah and mulhaka Wakfs the Government retains 2½% out of the 12½% as the true "ushur" is a tenth only the additional 2½% having been imposed by the Ottoman Government (20).

State Domains.

67 Certain lands included in the category of Miri Lands are the property of the State. They may be termed "Crown Lands" ceded to the Treasury by the Civil List in 1908. These imperial domains were originally the private lands of the Sultan acquired through feudal means or by purchase from subjects. It is customary for such lands to be rented to cultivators or tribes on payment of 10½ of the produce.

---

(20). The tithe is made up of the following rates:-.
    10 true tithe or ushur.
    1½% surtax imposed by the Decree of 7th August 1302(1886) of which by the Law on Finances of 1909/1910 (Art.27) ½% is allocated to the Ottoman Agricultural Bank and 1% to Education.
    ½% surtax imposed by the Decree of 1313 (1897).
    63% surtax, imposed for military equipment in 1316 (1900) A certain Circular dated 19th August 1909 reduced this surtax from 63% to 50% for the sake of convenience.

The total tithe is therefore 12½% or 1/8 of the produce.

72.

This cannot be regarded as a tithe but as a form of rent (21). The Revenue Department includes such lands within its assessment for tithe, the rate being 22½% or 12½% tithe plus 10% rent.

The tithe and {tithe rent} collected of these lands was in,

	12½% £.E.	10% £.E.
1919-20	9,990	10,354
1920-21	19,500	15,244.

EXEMPTION OF PRODUCTS FROM TITHES.

Lands.

68. The produce of lands which are of the mulk category are exempted when enclosed to the extent of less than one dunom. (22). Other mulk lands in vicinity of towns also enjoy immunity from tithe though there does not appear to be any legal ruling on this point. Municipal areas have been regarded in general as the areas over which the tithe is not collected following the precedent set by the Ottoman Goverment.

---

(21). It is noteworthy that Art.14 of the Ottoman Law of Finance of 1910/1911 authorises the Government to find other means for their exploitation than by a rental tithe.

(22). See Art.2 of CH.I. of Tithe Law of 23rd.June 1889.

73

Land not subject to tithe is taxable for land tax at a higher rate, i.e. 10 per mille with additions amounting to 56% of this original tax, than miri lands.

69   Lands which are leased by the Department of Agriculture for the purpose of crop experimentation are also exempted (letter No.7037/Rev. dated 15.6.21.

Exempted products.

The following products have been exempted from tithes:-

a). Kusa, or vegetable marrow, by letter No.7672/Rev dated 22.5.20.

b). Cotton for a period of two years commencing from April 1st.1921, by Public Notice dated February 1921. (Official Gazette No.37).

c). American vines from 10 years from date of plantation. Decree dated 25th September 1920.

d). Prickly Pears when not utilised as a commercial commodity by letter No.7037/12/Rev. dated 1.10.21 (23).

---

(23). There are small local differences, thus radishes are exempted by Ottoman precedent in certain districts.

74.

SECTION. VIII.

Communal Difficulties.

70. The special conditions prevalent in Jewish colonies has necessitated from time to time Jewish Commissions being appointed to the colonies in the Jaffa District. In Phoenicia and Galilee and Gaza, this principle has not been insisted upon. The special difficulty which tithe commissions meet amongst the more advanced agriculturists, who in general are mostly Jews, is that they utilise modern machinery for harvesting etc., and therefore any delay in estimation, or control of estimation, involves the cultivator in serious difficulties in which expensive machinery often hired by one farmer to another stands idle. In addition threshing machines of the latest pattern do this work in places other than regular field on the threshing floors. In this case stacks cannot, therefore, be formed on threshing floors, nor can the ordinary procedure of assessment be carried out.

In certain instances the registers of the local Vaad, or village council, have been produced as evidence of over estimation, and requests have been received to allow these books to be accepted as the basis for calculation of the tithe, subject naturally to

/inspection

75.

inspection. So far owing chiefly to political reasons this system has not been favoured, and the Directorate has maintained the attitude that preferential treatment would be unwise under present conditions. Before such a system could be generally adopted certain guarantees would be required and the form of the register laid down. The subject was discussed in a letter (24) to the Civil Secretary dated 24.6.21 from which the following extracts are quoted.

" The best estimators, irrespective of religion, are chosen in each District and each Commission is allotted a geographical Circle to work through. These Circles in some districts include Jewish Colonies, Christian and Moslem Villages and Moslem Tribes. Any change from geographical to religious grouping will involve increased expenditure, serious difficulties as regards adjustment of estimators and (a very important factor) loss of time.

"The Revenue Department have, indeed, made special arrangements, where possible, for Jewish Estimators to assess the crops of Jewish Colonies and even on occasion, have allowed the Colonies themselves to estimate on the books of the Colonies, subject to Control Commissions

---

(24). Letter No.675/Rev dated 24.6.21 addressed to Civil Secretary.

76.

This was done in Galilee in 1919 and in Jaffa this year at the request of the Colonies."

Requests were also received from the Committees of certain colonies in Phoenicia the comment of the Governor being "important questions of principle and policy seem to be involved, which, if accepted, would constitute a precedent difficult, if not impossible, to apply elsewhere".

It must not, however, be thought that this question has been definitely settled to the disadvantage of the cultivator, as undoubtedly if the necessary safeguards are provided some such system could be installed with advantage.

Ecclesiastical Communities.

77. Certain ecclesiastical communities claim exemption from all tithe under Capitulatory rights confirmed by the Ottoman Government in the Treaty of Mytelene in 1901. An examination of the Treaty does not however, bear out this contention. Lands cultivated by ecclasiastical institutions may be of three kinds:-

1.. Lands attached to and forming part of the building concerned.

2. Lands not so situated, but owned by the institution and situated elsewhere.

3. Lands rented from felaheem and tilled often by a system of a division of produce.

77.

Immunity from tithe is claimed on all three classes though there appears to be adequate grounds only for the exemption of lands attached to and forming part of the institution. The result of this claim is that large portions of cultivable areas are not assessed, and that in the cases of lands which are rented, the Mukhtars are held responsible for the collection of the tithe by the Directorate. These immunities are not claimed by the 'native' churches such as the Orthodox and Armenian Patriarchates, but only by foreign ecclessiastical institutions It is noteworthy in this connection that the Ottoman Public Debt excise duties on wines etc., are payable by all institutions manufacturing wines irrespective of religion or nationality establishing the principle that taxation is applicable to foreign ecclesiastical Institutions.

The right of immunity rests not upon a legal basis but upon the practice of tithe farmers under the Ottoman Government collecting the tithes due not from the institution concerned but from the neighbouring fellaheen by imposing an additional percentage to cover the quota of the convent assessment.

The question assumes increased importance as since the opening of the Land

/Registries

78.

Registries ecclesiastical institutions are enlarging their holdings. (25).

SECTION. IX

EXPERIMENTAL SYSTEMS.

Compounding.

72. On a few occasions experiments have been tried to lighten the vexatious system of estimation particularly as regards fruit crops. The problem as to how fruit crops such as olives, oranges, figs and grapes should be assessed is not easy to solve. Olives for instance may be assessed in kind of fruit or in litres of oil, oranges by boxes containing twelve dozen or by trees, figs and grapes by weight. The question of the percentage to be allowed for windfalls, bad and diseased fruit is a complex and difficult subject. In Ramallah and Nablus the Mukhtars have been allowed to fix the tithe of their village after a preliminary survey by the local Revenue officials. This has been far from successful, in practice from a Government point of view, *for example* Ramallah was assessed for tithes at 150 kilos for olives this year whereas an inspection of the oil passed through the local press showed that the assessment should have been over 2000 kilos.

---

(25) A case has recently been decided by the Court of the 1st Instance, Jeruslem, against the Mukhtar of Bethlehem. The arrears due for the winter tithe 1921 amounted to £E.150 which the Mukhtars stated is entirely due from Convent lands.

79.

Tithe taken on amount of oil produced.

73. In Bethlehem and Beit-Jala for the year 1920 it was arranged that the olive crushing millers of the Sub-District should keep books showing the quantity of oil produced for each grower and that these figures if agreed to by an independent expert, would be accepted by Revenue. It cannot be said that this system worked successfully as no reliable check could be maintained. For olives sold as fruit two per cent was added to the assessment. The Mukhtars found great difficulty in making the tax-payers recognise their individual liabilities and the system was accordingly dropped.

Measurement.

74. A more ambitious reform, however, was considered in 1919. It was based upon the Sudan method by which all cultivated land is measured. A superficial measurement of lands cultivated is first made, small areas of say 4 dunoms and under are estimated by eye, whilst large areas are measured with a pole, chain or other contrivance. Details which include the names of cultivators and the kinds of crop are entered in a special register. On the ripening of crops an estimating commission then examine the grain standing and uncut classifying the crops into three classes for each kind of cereal. This is only done after a (shishna'; or assay, is

/made

80.

made by threshing not less than an area of 2 dunoms for each kind of crop. The commission then makes an assessment entering the quantity for each grower under his class, or classes, i.e. 1st. or 2nd, or 3rd. in accordance with the condition and nature of the crops. A control is exercised by a British Official assisted by two experts who rides round the field seven days after the estimation within which period any complaints should have been lodged.

The above method was actually ordered to be carried out as an experiment in the kazas of Jaffa, Haifa and Beersheba, but the instructions were withdrawn owing to the difficulty of finding persons capable of undertaking measurements. It was also represented that it would not be possible to adopt the system in hilly country, involving the measurement of many dunums. There would, however, appear to be no difficulty in applying this method to the wide and open spaces of Beersheba provided the necessary personnel could be trained - not a very difficult matter. Political considerations also influenced the authorities in cancelling this possible reform [26]

---

[26]. The instructions (letter No.5731/FR.dated 28.2.1919 issued to the Military Governors of Haifa, Jaffa and Beersheba are set out fully in Appendix

Ottoman Experiments.
The Thaleeth System.

75. It is of interest at this stage to mention briefly the two attempts made by the Ottoman Government to institute reforms. In 1895 the triennial method was introduced into the three vilayets of Andrinople, Monastir and Kossovo. The average of three years assessment was taken as a basis which was imposed in toto upon a community of village concerned. The distribution of the amount among the cultivators was made on the percentage of the land tax which a cultivator paid. But as the assessment of the land tax is notoriously unequal and bad, the large land owner escaped payment of tithe, or passed on the tax to the fallah who worked the land on the system of a division of crops. It was abandoned in 1898. Appendix Q

The Takhmees System.

76. The second attempt to remedy the existing system was made in the same vilayet is 1904/05 and is known as the "quinquennial system". The average of five years assessment was taken as the tithe. The percentage of the allotment of the amounts to be paid was made in accordance with the area and productiveness of the land cultivated. These calculations were made by village councils supervised by special commissions appointed to groups of villages. Appendix Q

/Payment

82.

Payment was made in money, and disputes were settled in the last resort by the Administrative Council of the Kaza. The grave objection to this system is that it does not allow of any rebatement on account of the failure of crops through lack of rain or other climatic considerations. In addition, it is difficult to see how without a preliminary survey and without ownership having been established in all cases such a method can be regarded as final. On the other hand it avoids many of the abuses of the existing system and is the first step towards amlagamating the tithe and land tax into a fixed and single tax. (27).

The Ottoman Government afterwards extended this method to the more settled vilayets in Asia Minor. It was not introduced into Palestine.

---

(27). The following figures for the years 1905-1914 inclusive are of interest:-

Vilayet.	Assessment. per annum	Average Collectin per annum.
Monastir.	L.T. 34,700.	L.T. 27,800.
Uskub.	" 18,100.	" 15,200.
Salonica.	" 15,700.	" 13,380.

83

Committee's opinion on the experimental system mentioned.

77. The Committee after considering the system of compounding for fruit crops and olives do not recommend that further trials be made.

The Sudan system of measurement of large areas of land seems capable of producing fairly accurate results and might with advantage be experimented upon in the Beersheba District.

In Appendix R. will be found an answer written by the President Land Courts of the Samaria and Galilee Districts to the questions on the Indian System of "settlement of taxes on land produce" put before him by the Committee. The Committee have been unable to consider adequately the proposals made but are of the opinion that they should be weighed before radical changes of the present system are attempted.

The Tathleeth and Takhmees system were fully put to witnesses. See Appendix Q. The Committee find no wish for these systems and do not recommend their adoption.

The system of estimating olives after crushing at the wine presses presents difficulties.

a). It would be difficult to provide effective control on these presses.

84.

b). Such control would not account for the large amount of olives eaten.

It is estimated tha the consumption is not less than a rotl per head per annum. The subject is further discussed is para 95.

Section X.

Land tax on improved land of which the boundaries are settled.

The opinion of the public.

78. As has been stated the wish of the more scientific agriculturists is for the abolishment of estimation, measurement or weighing as systems by which a tax on produce can be assessed. They ask that a land tax to include the old werko tax should be placed on each dunum instead of the tithe. It is pointed out that it is unnecessary on certain lands to wait for the completion of the cadastral survey before effecting a change as for purely taxing purposes separate surveyed charts of properties and holdings are sufficient. The area cultivated by three plantation and by crops or vegetables can be marked on the charts and calculations made accordingly. It is suggested that owners be given the option to ask for such a tax forwarding with their petition the chart of their property and all information regarding it which the Government may require to enable them to fix a rate. Two views have

85

been put forward:-

a). That the average yields of crops on the land should be calculated and a tax placed upon them yearly fixed in relationship to the ruling market prices.

b). A land tax pure and simple fixed for a term of years.

The first would be more favourably received by agriculturists but has the disadvantage to the Government of yearly fluctuation. The second would provide a steady revenue and provision could be made for abatement in times of famine, locust, plague, pest or other calamity. A scheme put forward by the Revenue Officer of Galilee is a modification of system (a) adopted for lands other than those described as "Improved and with boundaries fixed and otherwise dealt with". It is possible of adoption but needs the laboured cooperation of mukhtars, sheikhs and village elders who might not view with favour so radical a change. The scheme is as follows:-

"In lieu of the present system of estimation, I beg to suggest the following procedure, but in submitting it, I must state that I do not consider it perfect, but it might form the basis of a working system in the near future. and until a cadastral survey of all cultivable land is made which may revolutionise

86.

entirely the present system of taxation:-

1. The Government should appoint expert assessors in permanent civil employment.

2. Lands under cultivation in every village area held by each cultivator will be determined by these assessors before the maturity of the crops every year and divided into three classes in proportion to their productivity.

3. When the crops approach maturity and immediately before the harvest, the assessor will proceed to a village and in a company with a village assessor will assess the average produce per given area (Feddan or dunum) of each kind of product in each of the three classes of land in the village.

Taking this as a basis the tithe of the whole village in kind will be determined. A tithe bill will be issued to each individual cultivator giving the area of land cultivated by him, and the area allotted to each product, the class of productivity of the land and the amount of tithe in kind due by him.

4. In villages where the land is communal (Mushaa) there is no need to state the class of land of each individual cultivator because land of various degrees of richness is parcelled out to every one of them equally,

87.
so that each feddan in the village is made up of several plots of varying richness. It is therefore only necessary to assess the gross produce per feddan.

Requests from Fellaheen.

79. Requests for some such form of assessment in lieu of estimation have been received from the cultivators of Government Land in Beisan and of Mushaa Land in Gaza. Certain cultivators of the Government Lands ask for a small tax on the dunum on all lands whether cultivated or not and assert that such a tax would not harm the small holder who would not even if poor be forced to sell but would be led to lease lands to others in order to secure sufficient for the tax and for his other needs.

Considerations requiring attention if tax land is adopted.

80. In assessing a tax on land in lieu of tithes the following factors should be considered.

1. The productivity of the land.
2. The rotation of crops suitable to the land.
3. Its proximity or remoteness to adequate means of communication either rail road or water, or to market.
4. Whether irrigated or not.

A proposed scheme based on a land tax.

81. The views and figures of the Revenue Officer, Haifa, are here inserted.

He divides lands for taxation purposes into :-

88.

1. Cereal Growing.
2. Lands under vegetable culture.
    a. Under irrigation and
    b. Under dry farming.

In order to enable the Government to impose a tax on land generally, a proper cadastral survey must first take place, but as this cannot be done inthe near future, it is suggested as a start and with a view to encourage and accustom cultivators in general to this method, to begin with these elightened cultivators or associations who possess plans and correct measures of their lands by fixing a land tax on their cultivable lands for a maxiumum of 5 years. Such a tax should not in any way exceed the proportion of tithes actually collected year by year on the rotation basis taking into consideration the fluctuation of prices of cereals and vegetables etc.

Thus taking as an example one dunum of first class good and fertile dark grey clay soil situated on the plain of Sharon the yield will be —

89.

Dry Farming	The average gross produce and price			Tithe
1st Year.	100 Kilos of wheat at	PT.	120.	PT. 15
2nd "	36 " Simsim "		72.	" 9
3rd "	120 " Karsenneh "		96.	" 12
				PT. 36
	or per dunum per annum.			PT. 12

From this amount we should deduct :-

a. Allowances for uncultivated plots through lack of animals, labour or seeds 14 % - 1.6.

b. Allowances for loss sustained by owing to lack of rain or too much rain or siroco, and transport expenses. 20%
2.4   4

This leaves the tax for 1st Class land at PT. 8 per dunum.

Other classes of land are *and rates of tithe*

2nd. Class grey, yellow clay soil above plain level at

3rd. Class Roha and hilly places (clean and not stony) at

4th. Class Roha and hilly stony places and red sandy plots at

5th. Class Lowlands subject to submersion and rocky at

Cereals lands under irrigation.

1st class i.e. dark grey clay soiled
25% above the average dry farm   10

2nd class grey and yellow clay soil   9

90.

Vegetable lands under irrigation within a radius of two kilometers from cities or principal railways stations:
average yield valued at PT. 1000   per dunum   PT. 125

Within a radius of eight Kilometers from towns,
Average yield valued at PT.640   per dunum   PT. 80

Outside of a radius of 8 Kilometers
yield valued at PT. 320   PT. 40

Vegetable lands dependent on rain: Within a radius of 2 Kilometers from cities or railway stations. Average yield valued at PT.800 per dunum   PT. 100

do 8 Kilometers Average yield valued at PT.500 per dunum   PT. 62

Outside of a radius of 8 Kilometers from towns,. Average yield valued at PT.200   per dunum   PT. 25

It will be observed his calculations are worked out on a basis of a tax notexceeding PT.8 per dunum for dry farming and PT.10 for cereals growing and irrigated land.

The Cyprus tithe which average PT.12 a dunum must be compared with this. It is calculated that at PT.8 for dry farming lands and in proportion as above stated for inferior lands, the revenue would not be less than that obtained by the present method of estimation if all Cultivable lands are to be taxed.

9/

If, however, only cultivated lands are to be included, the Cyprus figure will approximately give the necessary revenue return. For evidence on Land Tax see Appendix S.

92

Tax on Orange
Groves in lieu of Tithes.

82 At a meeting of the Orange Growers Association of Jaffa, held at the Governorate on the 27th December 1921 at which the following members were present:-
Mr.Michiel Beyrouti. Said Eff.Abou Khadra.
Mr.Appelaum. Mohamed Eff.Abd.Ul Rahim.
Mr.Alfred Rock. Mr.S.Tolkofsky.
Mr.Antoin Kassar. Mohamed Eff.Habbab and
Mr.Michiel Durkhoum. and Mr.Bul of I.C.A.
the matters enumerated below were discussed with a sub-Committee of the Tithes Committee

1. The impoverished condition of the orange groves owing to the lack of attention during the war and from which they are only now beginning to recover.

2. The increased expenses the owners of orange groves have to bear namely.
    a. Wages for labour.
    b. Cost of fuel.
    c. Cost of building, repairs and extentions.

3. The difficulties attending estimation together with the inaccurate results obtained.

4. The request that all orange land, mulk and miri be placed into a single category, and the tithe rate be halved on irrigated lands, in accordance with the intention of the Turkish Government.

93.

5. A scheme for arriving at a capital valuation for orange groves put forward by Mr.S.Tolkofsky, and the demand for a land tax based on such valuation in lieu of tithe.

6. The statement that vegetables could be brought from Egypt and sold at a cheaper rate than those grown locally owing to the high price of the tithe assessed, together with the difficulties and the expenses on the owners attending the estimation system.

After considering the above matters in detail, the Sub-Committee were of the opinion that the system of the estimation of oranges might with advantage be changed and a tax on the groves per dunum be made in lieu. They attach Mr.Tolkofsky's scheme below as a bases for discussion.

The members of the Orange Growers Association were in agreement with this scheme. (see scheme overleaf.)

The Sub-Committee considered also the statement concerning vegetables. This was further discussed at a full Committee at Jerusalem and the recommendation arrived at are inserted in para 90 entitled Vegetable Lands.

94.

Mr. Tolkofsky's Scheme.

1. There is no market for the sale of orange groves at present there being neither offer nor demand and in consequence no real price can be ascertained by sales.

2. No two orange groves in the country are of equal value, every grove needs separate assessment.

3. The groves have often a value other than commercial. Certain persons are attached to their groves on account of family or sentimental considerations. They would not sell but at a price higher than their proper value. On the other hand no one would under present conditions buy except at a very low price.

To arrive therefore at a valuation for taxation purposes, the following method is suggested.

1. A calculation should be made of the average number of boxes produced by the orange groves in the Jaffa District.

2. The average net profit per box should then be calculated.

3. The number of dunums on which oranges are grown should be ascertained and calculations made multiplying the average number of boxes

/produced

95.

produced by the net profit and dividing by the number of dunums. Thus the nett average profit per dunum would be ascertained.

4. This figure should be capitalised at the present bank rate. This will give the capital value /of a dunum.

5. It will be necessary to modify the value of certain groves on account of the condition of the property, their distance from the market, shipping port or railway siding and such considerations.

The Orange Tithe Return for the Jaffa District is found in Appendix. W.

96

The scheme proposed by Mr. Tolkowsky of Tel-Aviv requires a few explanatory remarks on the general conditions prevalent in the Jaffa District.

Preliminary Remarks.

84. The new method is briefly the imposition of a single tax based upon the productive value of the grove. But to arrive at this value a difficulty is at once encountered as no two groves of equal size have the same value. The lack of purchasing power, the uncertainty of foreign markets, the availability or otherwise of shipping for export purposes all tend to destroy any fixed market value for the purchase of groves. These considerations are not present when dealing purely with agricultural land, since the market is in general constant, establishing an approximate valuation easily ascertainable.

A grove may be said to be a plantation of not less than twenty trees or an area of not less than one dunum. The number of trees to a dunum varies in accordance with the methods of different growers, the American method adopted in new plantations having fewer trees to a dunum than the system in vogue among other owners.

The heavy expenditure necessary to maintain a grove in a high state of productivity varies considerably in relation to the cost of labour employed and the methods of cultivation adopted. As, therefore, the

97.

proposed scheme involves a consideration of annual expenditure these differences must be dealt with.

Orange groves may, in general, be stated to come to maturity about the sixth year when the yield in produce is such as to allow the grower to realise an income sufficient to cover his current expenses on the years labour etc. Form this time onwards until the twenty fifth year a tree is at its most productive period, from the twenty fifth year onward its yield gradually declines in quantity. In practice trees the yield of which have begun to decrease are uprooted and young stock planted in their stead.

There are, then, two periods in the life of productivity of an orange tree:-

1. From planting to the end of the sixth year when the fruit available is inconsiderable.

2. From the sixth year onwards when normal crops are produced.

Under the present conditions mulk lands pay the Werko tax only at an

/increased

98

increased rate, whereas the miri lands pay the werko tax at a lower rate and are in addition subject to tithe on product grown.

Keeping the above remarks in mind the proposed system involves:-.

1. The reduction of the present werko tax on mulk groves from 10 per mille to 4 per mille and thus retaining a general tax of 4 per mille upon both categories of groves, new valuations being made in each case. There will be no loss of revenue from a reduction of the rate upon mulk properties since the new valuation will tend to increase the capital value.

The basis of the new valuation requires consideration. It may be taken on the agricultural capital value of land. No difficulty exists in ascertaining the value since there is a constant market for the conveyance of this kind of land.

2. The abolition of the tithes on miri properties.

3. The substitution of the old taxes by a single tax based upon the <u>nett receipts per dunum</u> obtainable by growers on and from the 7th year, the net receipts being

·99

calculated over a period of three years.

To arrive at the net receipts per dunum, it will be necessary to find the net receipts per box. These can be ascertained by deducting from the gross receipts certain known expenses together with expenses incurred upon the field the average in each case being taken. The whole will then be substracted from the average price per box on the foreign market, thus:- ( ).

1. Average price per box in England. = a
2. Cost of cultivation in the Grove including labour irrigation etc. per box. = x

Expenses from Tree to Market abroad, per box. = y

Therefore $a-(x+y) =$ net revenue per box to the grower

Having obtained the net revenue per box the average number of boxes per dunum can be ascertained, either by taking the average of the district or through utilising the books and evidence of a number of growers checked by the tithe returns. Therefore net average revenue per box multiplied by average yield per dunum, equals average net income per dunum.

(d). The average net income having been ascertained it is suggested that the sum should be capitalised over a period of 20

( ). Mr. Tolkosfsky considers that interest on invested capital up to the 6th year should be also deducted.

100

years, or at five per cent thus:-

Net income.   £E. 10.
Capital Value.   £E. 2,00.   *200.*

e). From the capital value there are certain deduction to be made which may be taken at an approximate percentage for the different areas. These include deduction on account of:-

1. distances of transportation from grove to railhead or port.
2. damages to groves on account of certain adverse circumstances such as military operations, pests etc.

These deductions would be made for the entire period of the fixed tax, and would be re-examined when a new valuation is made.

(f). The tax on the capital value of groves, thus ascertained, will be fixed for a period of five years, when a reassessment will be made every ten years. The actual rate of tax should not for the first five years impose a greater financial burden on the individual miri grower than he at present bears. Thus, by calculation, the rate of percentage of taxation on the capital value could be calculated at present miri land tax plus the average tithe of three years.

/o/

(g). After the twenty fifth year the fixed tax upon groves ceases if the stock has not been renewed.

Difficulties involved.

85. It must be recognised that before a new system of taxation involving a radical change in method is satisfactorily introduced certain difficulties must be overcome. Without going into details there are for example the following:-

1. Any change in the present system may involve the mulk owners in increased taxation. The Werko tax valuation on mulk properties in Jaffa is low, unless the groves were registered just prior to or during the war. There are many groves situated in Jaffa Town itself whose value as building sites is considerable. In many cases the owners consider them as an inconsiderable factor in the value of the land. The following figures which must be regarded as approximate only, are of interest in this connection:-

		Jaffa. £E.	Tulkeram.
(a).	Mulk Properties.		
	Land Tax.	4,413.	
(b).	Miri Properties.		
	Land Tax.	1,648.	38.
	Average Tithe Assessment	7,500.	400.
	TOTAL:	£E.9,146.	£E.438.

102

The average of the tithes in the case of Tulkeram is for three years and in Jaffa for Four years.

2. Among the older groves owners sometimes adopt intercultivation. Vegetables are usually planted, large crops resulting since there is an abundant supply of water at hand for the irrigation of the orange trees. The incidence of the new tax will in every case be borne in the first place by the owner of the land on which the grove is situated. Under present conditions the owner or grower of the particular crop pays tithes.

3. In many cases it will be asserted by owners that there are no net receipts. In support of this statement they will advance the question of their indebtedness to banks, money lenders and the Government, bringing forward they heavy interest charges etc., to show that the net receipts are swallowed up in meeting these obligations contracted to maintain their groves in condition since the British Occupation.

4. Among the expenses incurred will be included the costs of packing materials such as wood, paper, nails etc., An import duty is chargeable on these articles as they are all of foreign origin. This duty is

103

refunded by the Department of Customs, and the percentage of refund must therefore be deducted from the expenses incurred.

Lemon Groves.

86. The scheme proposed is to be applied to Orange Groves. It has been suggested that it may be also applied to Lemon and Mandarin plantations as well but in the case of lemon groves there can be very little doubt that these groves have been maintained since our occupation at an annual loss. In such cases they might be reassessed for purposes of Land Tax on the basis of an agricultural land valuation when miri, or as building sites when mulk.

Further, it is probable that owing to the recent introduction of special machinery and the establishment of factories utilising lemon products the annual value of the lemon groves is likely to increase substantially in the near future. In so far as lemon groves are concerned only the 4 per mille tax might be imposed for a first period of 5 years.

Financial Results. 87.   It will be observed that in considering Mr. Tolkowsky's scheme the proposal has been advanced that the individual assessment of the single tax should not be more for the first five years than the owner and grower at present pay in werku tax and tithe. The Committee concur with this view, and express the opinion that though the amount payable by individuals may be the same the total amount receivable by the Government from miri properties will be more than that at present received, since they are convinced that through defective registration many groves are unregistered while others have been omitted by tithe inspectors from the assessment lists.

Alternative proposals.   88   In the event of it being deemed impossible to change the present system to a <u>tax on land</u>, An alternative has been proposed, which in effect, is a modification of the tithing system. This proposal is as follows :-

    1.   To abolish the present tithe, together with the land taxes on Mulk and Miri.

    2.   To tax Mulk and Miri properties with a single tax based upon the average yield calculated per dunum over a period od five years.

    3.   The fixing of the tax per dunum to be undertaken by a Commission annually.

    In explanation of this method it may be stated that the procedure would in the first place be for the owner or occupier to present to the Revenue officials a boundary survey giving the area of his grove.

105

This map would be accompanied by a statement showing the average yield reckoned in cases of fruit for five years. A check could be obtained by reference to previous tithe statements or by actual inspection. A Commission will then proceed to fix the redemption price per dunum on the basis of the current wholesale market price in Jaffa on the day of the first shipment of oranges to Europe. A reduction for windfalls or extraordinary climatic conditions would be made on a general survey of the fruit producing area.

The Committee are of the opinion that if a change is to be made the entire abolition of any system introducing ~~assessment~~ estimation is essential. They are also of opinion that one land tax on both miri and mulk properties is the only sound and equitable method of ~~showing~~ solving the present difficulty of tithing orange groves.

For total orange production for 1921-22 see Appendix T.

106.

VINEYARDS.

Taxation on vineyards. 89.   By a decree published on the 25th September 1920, vineyards planted with American stock were declared exempt from tithes for a period of 10 years, from the date of planting. The decree is based on an Ottoman Irade dated the 5th of February 1315 (1918 A.D.) There is an export duty of 1% ad valorem on all fruit and other products in addition to tithes.

The present method of estimation cannot be well be defended. 'It is, if properly carried out, laborious and lengthy. It fails in practice to give satisfactory results. The vine produce may be divided into two classes. (1) grapes grown for wine making (2) grapes for dessert. The first category might be estimated at the wine vats with a small percentage added to cover consumption by growers themselves, the second category is difficult of estimation except on the vine.

As the areas of vineyards can easily be ascertained, the boundaries being always clearly defined, the Committee are of the opinion that ~~most of~~ the difficulties of taxing by means of tithes would be removed where a tax on land levied. Here as with the proposed change on orange groves the differences of the two classes of land mulk

They recommend that a special commission be appointed
and miri require consideration (1) to value

107.

The vineyards of owners desiring the proposed change, (2) to consult waqf authorities where necessary and (3) to adjudicate on the differences between mulk and miri lands.

(29.) Decree No.191 published in Official Gazette No.31 of 15.11.20.

arable lands other than one under a land tax

VEGETABLE LANDS.

90. Estimation of vegetable products is possibly the most difficult of tithing operations. It is tedious and suffers in accuracy as all assessments must. It necessitates the sending of several commissions to adjudicate the different crops as they ripen. Many are the complaints raised by the public on the expense and trouble involved by the reason of the varied assessments carried out. In order to avoid these difficulties the committee are of the opinion that reasonably accurate results would accrue by the following system :-

1. All vegetable growers, on lands not otherwise taxed in lieu of tithes, to render quarterly to the Local Revenue Office a statement on an official form giving (a) position of land cultivated with vegetables (b) roughly the area of the same, (the land can be measured by a standard pole measure made by the Government

108.

and paid for by each village or land owner requiring one), (c) the names of the vegetable grown. (d) nature of the soil (e) irrigated or not.

2. A quarterly inspection should be made by a board made up of the following members: (a) Agricultural Assistant. (b) Official of Local Revenue Office. (c) the owner of the ground or a representative of the village or community concerned and a report made on the productively of the lands examined and an estimate of probable results. (d) That the tithes be calculated on this basis subject to powers to adjust the ampunt so arrived at, on petition from the grower, in the event of ultimate failure of harvest from climatic conditions pest, locust or other calamities. On the presentation of such an appeal a special commission will be appointed to inspect the crop. If the appeal is justified, the tithe will be reduced to a correct figure, but if it is held that there are no grounds for complaint the owner will bear the amount of the expenses of the commission. (e) The special commission will be appointed in the same way as other estimating commissions details of which are found in paras 47 and 50 (7).

109

Section X. B.

A TAX ON OLIVES AND FRUIT TREES IN LIEU OF TITHES

proposal to tax trees.

91. The present system of estimating the yield of olives is far from satisfactory. Estimators make the wildest guesses and there can exist no systematic method of inspection and control. The opinion of the country can be ascertained by extracts from the evidence given in Appendix U.

The trees, *both olive and fruit* are scattered over vast tracks of country and the yearly estimation of separate trees is impossible. The number of trees is at present unknown. One witness states that were an estimator to devote 2 minutes to each *olive* tree in the village of Mughar and Saffurieh in the Galilee District it would take him 125 days to complete his work.

It has been suggested that a biennial tax on each tree would be

1. convenient
2. possible
3. popular.

Were this adopted the Government would be in possession of statistical knowledge regarding the progress or decay of olive and fruit tree cultivation. *Appendix U.*

Note - <u>Vines and Oranges are excluded from this section.</u>

110

After the first enumeration a yearly inspection would be an easy matter. All trees taxed should be marked.

For the purpose of taxing, trees should be divided in four categories.

1. The Sapling Age. All trees under the fruit bearing age should be in this class to include the first bearing year.
2. The early years of fruit bearing
3. The fruit bearing age of full productivity.
4. Aged and decaying trees.

Amongst the Fellaheen an olive tree is grafted on the wild stock in its fifth year and bears fruit in small quantities in the 6th and 7th year. Such a tree reaches a full fruit bearing age in its 18th year. The Jewish Colonists plant a tree of Spanish stock which is said to bear in its fifth year and mature in twelve years.

It must, however, be borne in mind that olive trees attain a great age and increases in productivity year by year. In the plains the average age of decay is some 70 years, but in the hills trees attain 100 years and more and still give a full yield of olives.

Any tax placed up on olives trees should be one which would not deter their cultivation.

III.

It is proposed that it be on the following scale :-

From 1 - 9 to ~~I suggest 9 years age~~ years of age no tax
" 9 -18 years of age, taxed on a yield of 32 kilos.
" 18 - Old age taxed on a yield of 48 kilos.

The redemption price would either be fixed for a number of years or better be liable to change year by year according to the market.

On reaching an age when a tree fails to yield its quota of produce, its owner would petition the local Governor or Forestry Department for permission to have it cut down.

The numbering of the trees could be done by a special commission controlled by the Agricultural Department.

The following figures are given to show that this method of taxation would be advantageous to the Government. It would also give the Fallah encouragement to plant trees as

1. he would be free to dispose of his produce without waiting for estimation.
2. he would know on what yield he would be taxed.

The villages of Saffurieh and Kefr Menda in the Galilee District have been selected as examples of villages that cultivate the olive.

112

The result from taxation per tree and of estimation is compared below:-

SAFFURIEH.

	Saffurieh. No.of Trees.	Tax proposed in P.T.	Assessment in £E. biennally.
Sapling Age.	2000.	Nil.	
Lesser productivity.	1000.	5.	50.000.
Greater "	20000.	3.5.	1500.000.
Old Age.	2000.	Nil.	
	25000.		1550.000.

KEFIR MENDA.

	No.of Trees.	Tax proposed in P.T.	Assessment in £E. biennally.
Sapling Age.	200.	Nil.	
Lesser productivity.	Nil.	Nil.	
Greater "	3000.	7.5.	225. 000.
Old Age.	Nil.	Nil.	
	3200.		L.E. 225. 000.

TITHE ESTIMATION IN 1920 & 1921 IN £E.

	1920.	1921	TOTAL
Saffurieh.	1008.	9.	1017.
Kefer Menda.	144.	3.	147.

The totals read £E.1775 and £E.1164 respectively, or a difference of £E.611 in favour of the new method.

1. PROPOSED SYSTEM CALCULATED ON PRESENT REDEMPTION PRICE AND AVERGAE YIELD OF TREE IN THE HEBRON SUB DISTRICT.

Total No trees.	No of bearing trees.	Average biennial yield per tree	Tithe yield. Kilo.	Current redemption price per Kilo.	Total income of tax.
37.000.	25.000.	40 kilos.	5.	2.5 P.T.	£E.3125.

2. SYSTEM OF ESTIMATION CALCULATED WITH THE PRESENT REDEMPTION PRICE.

1919-20. the yield assessed amounted to   9600 kilos.
1920-21.   "   "   "   "   "   502160 "
           The total for the two years = 511760.
12½% of this amount = 63970.Kilos.
Redemption price 2.5.PT.total tithe value =£E.1600.
    Result of proposed system   (1). £E. 3125.
      "   "   present system   (2). " 1600.

    Showing an increase of   £E. 1525.

113

The yield of olives differs in the various districts from an average of some 22 kilos in Gaza to 60 kilos in Acre per fully matured tree on good soil. There may possibly be a necessity for a more elaborate classification of trees taking in soil and situation considerations before fixing the amount of productivity. Local Commissions appointed in the same way as other estimating commissions would be able to do this work.

The system might be extended to all other fruit bearing trees, not planted in enclosed orchards, groves or gardens the owners of which have elected for a tax on the dunum.

Before a change of the system of estimation on olive yields can be made to that of a tax on productive trees, it will be necessary to consult the Wakf authorities as a large number of trees are upon properties held by them. For Example in Hebron twon there are 4430 bearing trees on Wakf Lands. No tithes are at present collected from these neither have they been reckoned in the figures dealing with the new method.

Recommendation.

92. The Committee recommended that the scheme above set out be considered as a basis in altering the law substituting a tax on each tree in lieu of estimation.

114.

Financial Considerations.

Emoluments of Estimators.

93. The present emoluments are £E.1. per day for,
   1. Winter.
   2. Summer.
   3. Fruit Estimations ~~with a limit~~ of £E.35 for each of the above named crops.

Vegetable commissions are paid varying rates in no case exceeding £E.35.

Difficulty in presenting a financial Statement.

94. The Committee find some difficulty in presenting satisfactory ~~financial~~ figures concerning the changes proposed. They are of the opinion that each subject such as:-

1. The optional land tax.
2. The taxing of trees.
3. The valuation of orange groves.
4. The tax on vegetable lands,

requires through financial investigation by experts. The absence of all satisfactory records such as an approximately accurate estimation of lands cultivated and whether with cereals or other products, the differences in statements as to yield from those considered experts. (see Appendix V) makes even a tentative estimation difficult. The figures stated in the section on olive trees are given with all reserve.

They consider from figures supplied that the changes above mentioned will, whilst being satisfactory to the public benefit the

/Government

115.

Government and for the following reasons,

1. There will be no loss of revenue.
2. The incomes from dues will be less fluctuating.
3. The expenses and difficulties will be lessened.

They have had these considerations before them when collecting evidence and preparing the report. They recommend the reduction of estimation as a system of assessment as far as possible and consider any changes that are made should pave the way to its entire removal when a cadastral survey has been completed.

Cost of new proposals.

95. The figures for the change proposed in the number and personnel of,

1. Estimation commissions.
2. Controlling or inspecting commissions are here given as only in these items is there any extra cost involved.

The old System.

```
        1 Estimation at £E. 35.
        1.Clerk.       @     12.
                       £E.   47.
```

The proposed new system. (1).

```
        1. Arbitrator  @ £E.36.      £E.36.
        2. Estimators  @  "  35.      "  70.
        1. Clerk.      @  "  18.      "  18.
                                     £E.124.
```

Alternative. (2).

```
        1. Arbitrator. @ £E.36.      £E. 36.
        1. Estimator.  @  "  35.      "  35.
        1. Clerk.      @  "  18.      "  18.
                                     £E. 89.
```

116

It is calculated that by the new system the number of circles, as has been proved by experience in Phoenicia, can be considerably cut down. In an average season 122 estimating circles will be required as against 171 under the old system. The salaries of 34 controllers at £.40 each will also be saved.

The Old System.

  171 Circles at 47. 8037.
   34 Controllers 40. 1360.
         £E. 9497.
           3

The proposed new system. (1)

  122 Circles at 124. 15128.

Alternative (2).

  122 Circles at 89. 10858

The extra cost will therefore be if (1) be adopted £E.5731 and if (2) £E.1461.

In considering this increase it must be borne in mind that the emoluments of the clerks have been increased from £E.12 to £E.18 and that this £E.6 would probably have to be reckoned together with an increase in the emoluments of the estimators of £E.5 each if the old system be adhered to. To the £E.9497 must therefore be added £E.11. on each of the 171 circles or a total of £E. 1881. The nett extra cost on proposed new system (1) would therefore be £E. 3850 and on (2) there would be a saving of £E. 420.

117

The estimated number of circles district by district if either of the two new proposals are adopted, are:—

	Winter.	Summer.	Orange.	Vegetables.		TOTAL.
Beersheba.	10.	3.				13.
Gaza.	10.	6.	1.	6.	2	23
Jerusalem.	7.	7.		4.		18.
Jaffa.	6.	5.		2.		15
Samaria.	12.	7.		2.		21.
Phoenicia.	8.	4.		2.		14
Galilee.	11.	5.	—	2.		18.
	64.	37.	3.	18.		122.

Savings and increased revenue.

96 The system of taxation on bounded lands groves and gardens will result in a large saving to the Government and also an increased yield of Revenue. If the option suggested is taken up by the public the number of circles above mentioned may be further reduced. The tax proposed on olives trees will likewise lessen the annual expenditure as after the first year the work could be performed by cooperation between the Agricultural and the Revenue Departments and by means of their permanent officials. The Revenue will also be considerably increased. The eighteen circles for vegetable estimation will also be saved by the new proposal on vegetable lands.

118

Transport Considerations.

97 The Committee consider that every facility for travel should be given to inspectors and controllers of tithes estimation during the harvest season. A car should be placed at their disposal in order to facilitate rapid travel and to avoid fatigue. A man tired after a long ride is not in a good condition for settling disputes. Expense can be saved by the fewer travelling allowances required. One example to illustrate the above is given.

An inspector travelling from Haifa to Ixim by car, would spend one hour each way on the journey, by horse the time required each way would be 3 hours. By car he would leave Haifa at 6.a.m. and would commence work at 8. a.m. continuing until noon. He could then work from 2 to 5 p.m. returning to Hafa by 6.30. No travelling allowances would be required. By horse he would require two days to do the same work.

Expense:-

(1) Government Car say PT.200.

(2). Horse or horse and carriage 2 days.   160.

Travelling Allowances 1 night.   100.

PT.260.

119

SECTION. XII.

The Need of rapid Survey.

98. The need of a rapid and correct Survey is urgent. Without it an absolutely indefensible title without dispute as to areas or boundaries is impossible. Nothing tends to encourage improvements and interest in land so much as a sense of security of title.

At the present time a property is described as being bounded on any given side by some physical object, say a road, but there is no indication as to the length of the frontage to that road with the result neighbours are in constant dispute with each other on the question of encroachment. Each threatens the other with an action at law and the consequent feeling of insecurity does not inspire a villager to effect improvements with a threatened action hanging over his head.

Increased productivity is urgently needed to bring down the cost of living, increase the revenue, and rectify the adverse trade balance. It cannot be obtained without security of title and these latter can only be guaranteed by a survey.

120.

Division of the Mashaa Lands.

99. [Mashaa Lands: In the majority of villages in Palestine the village lands are mashaa, that is, they are held in common undivided shares. They are registered in the name of, perhaps four or five notables, although in reality they are the property of all the villagers, possibly some hundreds.

Much of the trouble among villages is due to disputes arising from succession when one of the share holders dies. A villager does not have allotted to him any specific plot of land. He is frequently given a fresh piece every one to three years.

The portion allotted is made by casting of lots amongst all entitled to a share. The result is that a cultivator has neither the interest nor the energy to improve his temporary holding, and the productivity of the soil and the revenue of the Country suffer accordingly.] The division of the Mashaa Lands would appear desirable for the following reasons.

1. It will reduce disputes as to ownership and succession thus removing many of the cause of friction in the villages.

2. It would mean increase production as the owner would appreciate that his occupancy was not of a temporary nature and he would feel justified in improving the land.

(2).

3. It would facilitate the collection of Government Taxes.

4. It would relieve the courts, the Land Registry and the villages from a volume of formality which now surrounds succession in Mashaa Lands.

Section XIII. Summary.

Recommendations

100. The Committee are unanimously of the opinion that a radical change in the system of taxation would be beneficial both to Agriculture and to the Government. They suggest that the cadastral survey of Palestine be pressed forward with all speed with the view to the adoption of taxation on land instead of on the yearly produce. They favour the giving of an option immediately to owners possessing gardens orange groves and even large enclosed areas whether cultivated with trees, fruit, vegetables or cereals enabling them to request for a tax on the dunum in lieu of tithing. They recommend that any person desiring to take up this option should accompany their petitions with a surveyed plan of the area referred to, together with a statement of the crops grown on each portion and showing the number of dunums planted with trees or other permanent form of agriculture. The existence of irrigation works, pumping machines, wells etc. should be marked on the plan which should be prepared by a registered surveyor.

122

They further suggest that a local Committee for the valuation for such grounds be formed in each District and that such Committee be strengthened by the presence of a Government Surveyor and Agricultural expert with permanent appointments and detailed for such work. These Committees would prepare figures showing yields over a number of years and would adjudicate and assess the tax on these results with the added considerations on the rotation of crops, the nature of the soil and the situation of the lands that are to be valued. They are of the opinion that this option will be generally taken up and that its adoption will pave the way to a general approval of land taxation when the cadastral survey has been completed.

As palliatives to the present generally condemned system of estimation the Committee recommend the following:-

1. That the two systems of estimation,

    (a). on standing crops.

    (b). on the threshing floor,

be allowed temporarily to remain.

2. That the Government estimators be more carefully chosen. That in every District a Committee be appointed consisting of representatives of

    a). The members of the local Agricultural Committee.

    b). The agriculturists outside of that Committee.

123

c). The Municipality.

d). One official of each of the local departments of Finance and Agriculture. That the Governor of the District should be president of the Committee. That a list of all persons appointed as estimators be printed with dates of appointments in the Official Gazette. That dismissals in the irregularities be likewise inserted.

3. That the names of these estimators chosen by the villages should be brought before the Committee above mentioned. That on a recommendation by them the Governor should give appointments. That their names be printed in district records and in the local newspapers. That they be brought under responsibility together with the Government estimators, for giving accurate estimations. That in the event of irregular conduct they be liable to punishment and dismissal by the Governor.

4. That any inspectors employed by the Government should have had actual experience in estimation by having acted as an assistant on the field before appointment. That the experts accompanying him should be selected by the local Committee as mentioned above.

124

but that the Reveue Department be empowered to change this expert from one district to another, taking care that he is sent to a district whose agricultural conditions are similar to his own.

5. That the estimation Commission should consist of:- *subject to financial considerations on penalty-ies.*

Two estimators appointed by the Government
Two estimators appointed by the village or colony subject to the approval through the District Committee, of the Governor.
One clerk nominated by the Government.

6. That an official book be handed to the clerk of the estimating Commission on which shall be recorded the hours of commencing and finishing work daily, together with the number of separate floors estimated.

7. That an arbitrator nominated by the Governor from the list of estimators or any other expert whose name has been obtained through a Director of Revenue, accompany each estimation Commission for the purpose of settling differences on the spot, *and giving a final decision*. His further duties should include.

a). Inspection of the clerks returns which should be done whilst at the village.

b). The giving of information of any underestimation he may find to the local Revenue Office.

/25

8. That the processes of reaping and carrying of the grain to the threshing floors be unrestricted, but that Mukhtars be respnsible for notifying when crops of each kind are all on the threshing floor.

9. That Mukhtars obtain from the cultivators the number of dunums they are actually cultivating each year and hand this list together with a personal estimate of the produce of each cultivator to the estimating Commission.

10. That estimation takes place within 15 days after the notification. That before the period has elapsed no harvesting work is to take place. After this period the villagers should be empowered to cut or thresh, the estimating commission accepting the village figure for assessment,

11. That the final inspection should be done by at least two persons, an Inspector or Controller and an expert. and that it be made within seven days of completion of estimation. That transport facilities, cars horse etc., be freely placed at the disposal of the inspector or controller, during this season in order to lessen delay.

12. The the redemption prices be fixed on or about the basis of the market prices ruling at a date not earlier than the end of August, and that they be fixed by districts. For further details see Para 57.

126

13. That a general increase in a village when under estimation is found on certain threshing floors should not be made in an arbitrary manner. As cases of under-estimation should be few if the changes recommended in this report be adopted, the Committee are of the opinion that ~~a senior officer of the staff of the District Governor or Sub-District Governor, should decide personally on such, upon a report from the Inspecting Commission~~.

14. That the collection of monies should be carried out by Mukhtars appointed by Governors, as temporary tax collectors and guaranteed by the village. That stamped receipts for all payments be given by a Mukhtar from an official receipt book perforated with counterfoil, the tax payer paying for the stamps. That permanent tax collectors visit villages monthly and take all monies collected, examining the receipt books of the Mukhtars and checking them before so doing. That the signing of the promissory note be abolished.

15. That tithes be paid monthly in three instalments, if over PT.500, in two, if between 100 and 500 PT. and in one instalment if not exceeding PT.100.

16. That tithes due from institutions, companies or entire communities be paid direct to the Government and not through

127.

a mukhtar or Shiekh.

(16.) That all fruit bearing trees including olives growing in lands without defined boundaries be taxed when of fruit bearing age, except those in lands otherwise taxed. The details are laid down in section X.B. para.

17. That lands on which vegetables are to be planted other than those on which a land tax is fixed, should be notified to the Government quarterly for the purpose of an estimation of area and average yields and that on this should be based the tithes to be paid unless a complaint is made by the owner, on account of severe loss due to damage by blight or other pest, in which case an actual estimation on the field will be made.

18. That all orange and other groves be taxed on the basis of a percentage on a capital value and that the necessarily high rates of expenditure borne by owners in the developement of this industry be considered. for further details see para Recommendations on Orange Groves.

29. That while giving freedom to Governors of Districts to make their own arrangements for the estimation on standing crops or on

129.

on the threshing floors a uniform system of procedure for estimating commissions laid down be adhered to. Such should include regulations on:-

a). The number of members on the estimating commission.

b). The number on the inspecting commission.

c). Orders on methods of assay or Shishne.

d). Uniformity in the keeping of record books for the commissions and inspectors.

e). The appointment of estimators, controllers, inspectors tax collectors and other officials.

20. That a division of the Mashaa Lands be undertaken by the Government at an early date.

21. The Committee are of the opinion that the Government should decide upon the relationship of the Director of Revenue and the District Administration on the subject of estimation, control, inspection and collection of tithes. Either (1) the work should be performed by the Directorate, in which case the final selection, appointment and control of all officials should be with the Department, the local authorities simply passing on serious complaints and only make minor local adjustments, or (2) the whole responsibiliy for the assessment of tithes / revenue should fall upon the

129

District Authorities, the Directorate merely regulating the policy. Definite instructions are needed concerning the relationship of Governors with local Revenue officers and the tax-collecting department represented by the Mudir El Mal.

Decentralisation.   101.   From a general review of the question the Committee while not giving a final view on this subject present the following scheme as worthy of consideration:-

A.   That the Governor of the District be the final authority for all matters connected with:-

1.   The appointment of the personnel of estimating commissions and control commissions.

2.   The local administrative regulations bearing upon the new scheme of tithes and regulations thereto.

3.   And the fixing of redemption prices.

B.   That the authority of the Director of Revenue or the body controlling taxation by tithes be as follows:-

1.   The issuing of all regulations which govern policy.

2.   The supervision of the collection of the tithes.

130.

He may, also, act in a advisory capacity to Governors on any matters for which they are responsible.

The Committee call the attention of the Government to the heavy taxation borne by the producers of Agricultural Crops and suggest that the system of taxation be broadened with a view to giving the farmer relief. Some form of taxation might be devised to bring about a revival of the third form of ancient tithes taxation namely "personal" mentioned in para 8.III. which brought professional men merchants manufacturers and others into the class which paid direct taxes. It may be advanced that the house and land tax cover certain of such individuals. This tax is fixed, however, on a notonously low assessment, and does not in fact effect a tenth of the non tithe paying community.

The Committee are of the opinion also that notwithstanding the difficulties connected with the system of estimation the Government has greatly benefitted by it judging from the financial results over those derived from the system of contracting out as practised by the Turks. Some 80-85 pc of the tithes due yield is collected at a reasonable cost. The expenses of collection are approximately 4 pc. of the tithe revenue of

131

if the salaries of permanent officials be exluded. They find no evidence of general over-assessment but uneven assessment is common and is a serious defect. It is the chief cause of complain and undoubtedly individuals have suffered thereby.

The Committee observe also the intimate relationship between the Government and the supreme Moslem Sheria Council on all questions affecting the change in an existing system of tithes taxation. This fact calls for close cooperation between the two administrations as they have already pointed out in para 63 page 70. the large interest the Sheria Council have in tithing matters.

Thanks of the Committee.

103. In conclusion the Committee desire to express their thanks to the Governors of Districts for their assistance in many ways, notably in calling witnesses to give evidence and giving publicity to the Committee work. The thanks of the Committee are also due to the Departments of Revenue, Land Registry and to the Jaffa Orange Growers Association for assistance on technical matters, to the Treasury and the Jerusalem Governorate for the loan of offices and cars. They desire to place on record their appreciation of the able and painstaking work their Secretary Mr.T.Farah who proved himself well competent to file and deal with the mass of correspondence which the Enquiry called forth.

3.02

1923	PALESTINE	
FROM Dowson, E.M.	DATE - Dec.	
FOR CIRCULATION:- Mr. .... Mr. Clauson 14/5 Mr. .... Mr. Vernon Asst. U.S. of S. Perm¹ U.S. of S. Parl⁹ U.S. of S. Secretary of State.	SUBJECT Report on Lands and Survey Depts. &c. in Palestine. Submits copy of Notes presented to Sir G. Clayton.	
Previous Paper	MINUTES	

236

I fear that I have kept this paper for some considerable time. But we are actually awaiting a despatch from the H.C. on this subject and I think we must continue to wait for his comments.

It may be of some use to summarise what Mr Johnson says.

Palestine is an agricultural country. Through historical causes its economic foundations are rotten. The causes are

(1) The uneconomic & excessive taxation of agriculture and land.

(2) The absence of a systematic cadastral survey and land settlement which should proceed pari passu

(3) The existing chaos of land tenures and rights

To remove these causes
Mr Dawson proposes

A for ① and ③ } a Commission

B for ② a special organisation.

A The Commission sh^d

   I consider the form of
land tax which could
most advantageously
for Government & people
be substituted for
existing taxes directly
levied on land &
livestock

   II prepare draft legislation
     (a) for the simplification
and such modification
of the Land Law as
will be needed
     (b) for the introduction of
compulsory registration
of all real rights
subsequent to systematic
cadastral survey &
settlement.

As regards the personnel
of the Commission he makes

the following suggestions:

287

Mr. Abramson as chairman

Mr. Sheppard, Surveyor-General of Egypt to serve on the Commission. He was a member of a similar Commission in Egypt in 1917-20.

B. The Organisation to execute cadastral survey and land settlement, should comprise

(1) an organisation to conduct the technical operations of survey. This is already in existence but needs strengthening.

(2) an organisation to investigate and settle real rights. This needs creating. It is most important for on it depends the progress of survey. This must be accelerated if our economic purpose is to be achieved.

In order that this organisation(?) should complete its work in 5 years it should be arranged as follows :-

(a) There should be 12 settlement parties directed by British District Officers.

(b) The composition of these Settlement parties requires further consideration

(c) a judicial officer with a knowledge of land law and of its practical operation is necessary: presumably a Palestinian. [I am not certain whether M: Dowson means one such officer for each commission or one for the lot.] v. p. 23.

In order to control the work of the 12 commissions he suggests the appointment of an <u>Inspector-General of Land Settlement Commissions</u> who would be assisted by a suitable senior judicial officer and the District Governor of the district concerned.

For the job of Inspector-Gen
of Land Commissions he
thinks Mr. Rizq would be
a good man.   283
His functions would be:
(1) unifying procedure &
    sharing experience
(2) providing for administrative
    appeal on matters of
    principle.
(3) reviewing the work &
    seeing that it was
    done.

To him might be attached
a few of the officers especially
experienced in the interpretation
of Turkish deeds & other aspects
of the work.

Mr. Strosar points out,
what of course is obviously
true, that under this
scheme the District Officers
would be overworked. I fear
we can only accept this
consequence on their behalf.
But as a practical proposal
he suggests that their work
might be relieved by fixing
the tithes for 5 years.

That certainly would be a relief for them. It should be seriously considered. I believe also the cost of assessing the tithe is pretty heavy. Finance Section will be able to advise on this point. It is certain that the work of the D.O.s will have to be relieved in some way if they are to undertake the supervision of the Settlement Commissions. The M. should give us his practical proposals on this point after consulting the Treasury.

Mr. Dowson goes into much greater detail in explaining his proposals and discusses a number of technical points in connection with apparatus and equipment. He also makes some very serious criticisms of the way in which Land Registration & Survey have been carried on up to the present. These will also require consn. in due course.

In order to carry out this scheme in six years, — one for preparation and five for execution — the sum of not more than half a million spread over the whole period is necessary. The economic situation of Palestine cannot be retrieved without it and therefore the half million is necessary. He compares it to Cromer's famous irrigation million borrowed in the midst of Egyptian bankruptcy.

On this point again we need the considered opinion of the Pal. Government. We need some sort of a detailed estimate.

Finally there can be no doubt that this is a most valuable report and that Mr. Dowson has rendered a great service to Palestine. He has established his main proposition. But we must await the views

Comments on the specific
proposals of M. Dawson.
? Wait for the H.C's despatch
(see 1224 below) S.n.
                  21/2

I too have, I fear, delayed
this.
　We have now asked the
H.C., in reply to his desp.
asking us to agree to the
creation of a second post
of Land Court Judge,
when he is going to let
us have his proposals
on this report.
? still wait.
　　　　　G. L. H.
　　　　　　14/5

Chief Secretary,
    Government of Palestine.

NOTES on Land-Tax, Cadastral Survey and Land Settlement in Palestine.

Sir,

Following my recent visit at the request of your Government to Palestine and discussions held with yourself, the Attorney General and the Treasurer, with the Director of Agriculture and Fisheries, the Director of Lands, the Director of Surveys, with the Governor of (?) Samaria, (Colonel Cox), the Governor of (?) the Southern Province, Mr. Abrahamson, and the Assistant Governor of Jaffa, and visi paid to the Land Registries in Jerusalem and Jaffa, and a fairly full inspection of the work of the Survey of Palest both in the office and the field, I have the honour to sum the following notes on the matters concerning which my ar was more particularly asked.

As the notes are long and detailed I have subdivi them roughly under the above heads for greater ease an convenience of reference.

Paragraphs 2 - 7.	Preliminary considerations.
Paragraphs 8 - 10.	Weakness of existing system of Lan Registration.
Paragraphs 11 - 14.	Revision of land-taxes and amendm of land laws.
Paragraph 15.	Organizations to execute cadastr survey and settlement.
Paragraphs 16 & 17.	Preparatory measures and general of campaign.
Paragraphs 18 - 20.	Procedure of cadastral survey tlement in each village.
Paragraphs 21 et seq.	Additional points and c observations.

[Copy is damaged at right foot this and following page.]

Preliminary Considerations:

2.   The notes are unavoidably long and detailed because the success that has so far been lacking, has been primarily lacking for want of the necessary experience of the sufficiently intricate procedure required for the successful execution of a cadastral survey and land settlement, and th introduction of a simple and water-tight system of subsequent record of real rights under conditions so involved as those obtaining in Palestine. The absence of this special experience is not at all remarkable; it is rare in any part of the world, and its absence was not likely to be appreciated by a very busy administration until the fruits engendered thereby became, as they are becoming, uncomfortably evident.

Fortunately during the last hundred years Egypt has slowly traversed a great part of the ascent from a semi-derelict, over-burdened, ex-Ottoman vilayet to a State with a well-founded self-sufficing economy which it is to be hoped that Palestine is now entering upon. The physical features and conditions of Egypt and of Palestine differ radically, and this blinds the vision to the close parall presented by the problem of the economic rescue of the countries. The difference in physical features and cond tions is naturally a factor of prime importance; but i a factor that is readily allowed for, since it only the methods to be applied and by which economic salve is to be secured, and not the fundamental principles should determine the ends these methods must be moul achieve.

When Mohammed Ali wrested Egypt from the Turk he over a land, which allowing for the difference in natur advantages, was as agriculturally derelict as Palestine is to-day. A conglomeration of land tenures - the complicated heritage of ages - survived, the taxes were of the mediaeval Moslem type, the peasant was a starveling without incentive to improve the land and without hope of improving his own position. Mohammed Ali and his successors regarded Egypt simply as their personal estate, but they had the natural genius to appreciate that the clogging effect of obsolete survivals must be lifted from the land if enterprise was to replace apathy, and its ancient prosperity was to be restored. Although much that was evil and economically deadening persisted till the British Occupation, and even persists to-day, it was none the less the House of Mohammed Ali which cleared away the top layer of accumulated rubbish and carried Egypt up the earlier rungs of the ladder leading to her economic establishment, by simplifying her land tenure and giving Egyptian agriculture a measure of central direction.

3. Always allowing for the difference in natural advantage, Palestine appears economically to be to-day very much where Egypt was when Mohammed Ali became its effective ruler. As in Egypt, so in Palestine, agriculture is the only reliable basis for the establishment of healthy national economy. Assistance may be obtained in the future from the development of mineral resources, but except possibly in respect of the salts accumulated in the Dead Sea, this cannot be depended upon, cannot but be slow, is apt to be disappointing in its return to the State, is exhaustible, and only in the event of a quite exceptional find can it become of anything but secondary importance. While care should obviously be taken to encourage prospecting and to ensure betimes that prospecting and development rights are defined with foresight and are

- 3 -

..corded on terms that secure an equitable return to the State in the event of success, it would be highly imprudent to allow any hopes of mineral development to deflect or delay attention being paid to the one sure breadwinner.

Agriculture is the one sure, and probably the only important national economic asset, and it is by universal admission in a very unhealthy state. The diagnosis of the causes of the sickness afflicting agriculture appear also to be universally admitted and indeed to be indisputable. On the one hand the industry is seriously overtaxed, on the other the survival of uneconomic systems of land tenure and the prevailing uncertainty and insecurity of real rights, discourage enterprise and more particularly the improvement of the land. The country has obvious and great agricultural potentialities; and, if it cannot vie, as it can hardly expect to vie agriculturally with the Nile Delta, the nearness of that Delta provides it with a most valuable and readily accessible market for timber, for stock, for fruit, for tobacco and normally for cereals, products which are either ousted there by cotton cultivation, are produced in insufficient quantities for local needs, or for fiscal reasons in the case of tobacco is a crop not grown at all.

4. The direct taxes paid by agriculture are, I understand three:

    (a) the werku.

    (b) the ushur or tithe.

    (c) the animal tax per capita on sheep and goats.

The werku is theoretically 4 per thousand per annum on the capital value of rural property held in fee simple (mulk). The tithe is 12½% of the actual crop harvested compulsorily commuted into a cash payment before the crop is marketed on the then market price of the estimated quality of the produce. I omitted to note the amount of the animal tax: its incidence depends upon the keeping of the animals in question.

The Director of Agriculture in Appendix X. of his published report dated 16th. March 1922 on the basis of a series of maxima yields and current prices for eight representative crops in the Jaffa district, concludes that the tithe was equivalent in 1921 to an average minimum income tax on the cultivator of 30% and rose in the poorer southern districts of Palestine to 45%. In addition to this werku and animal tax may be paid. It therefore does not seem extravagant to say that cultivators may be called upon to pay to the State an annual contribution equivalent to an income tax with no remissions of 5/- to 10/- in the pound. The assessment by the agents of the State of the quality and quantity of the entire agricultural output of the country is a colossal operation and one which it is quite impossible to conduct efficiently, that is equitably, even apart from the ready openings to abuse it affords. It is naturally extremely costly to collect, and involves perpetual friction between cultivators and the provincial authorities, since assessment commutation and collection of tithe or arrears of tithe on either summer or winter crops is increasing.

At the same time it must be remembered that the tithe is enshrined in the traditions and to an extent, probably to be measured by the degree of relief that would be evident in a change, in the affections of the people. It moreover possesses fully in theory and appreciably in practice a quality of partnership in good fortune and in bad with God and with the State that makes a natural appeal.

The second important disability under which Palestinian agriculture suffers is a widespread uncertainty in regard to real rights and the prevalence of uneconomic systems of land tenure. Such merits as the Turkish system of record of land rights possessed, and they were from the point of view of the people negligible, were to a great extent annihilated by the destruction or removal of the registers by the retreating enemy when the country was occupied by H.M.Forces. An effort has since been made to initiate an improved system, but with the best will in the world it is impossible to do so without a thorough clearance of accumulated rubbish and a rebuilding de novo on simpler and better lines, which means on the basis of a national cadastral survey and settlement of real rights from one end of the country to the other.

It was in this connection that my advice was more particularly asked, and it is in respect of the simplification of historic systems of land tenure transmitted by the Turk, in the establishment of a readily collected, light and equitable land tax, and in the introduction of an effective and easily maintained national record of real rights that the experience of Egypt is of such unique value to her one time sister province.

I have endeavoured in the accompanying notes to mobilize that experience in respect of those aspects of the problem that appeared more particularly to require such assistance towards their solution in Palestine. This has involved a considerable amount of tedious detail and also of omissions that would be of capital importance in any attempt to deal comprehensively and exhaustively with the subject. I believe that it is in this form that the notes are most likely to prove of early and practical assistance, and as they make no pretence to be more than a passing contribution to the solution of a complicated problem they can be readily supplemented or modified either in the light of local knowledge and acquired experience, of the most valuable and extensive experience of kindred problems available in the Survey of Egypt for the asking, or preferably in a close and continuous association of the two.

6. As matters have so far proceeded in Palestine a valuable foundation for the execution of a cadastral survey of the country has been laid, and given the creation of an organisation that can authoritatively investigate and settle rights to land at the same speed, the cadastral survey and settlement of the country may be expected to be finished in about eighteen years time. It must however be realized that at the time of my visit (1-5 November 1923) not only had not a single acre of cadastral survey been done, but it was impossible for it to have been done because no body had so much as been set up by Government either authorised or competent to conduct the investigation and determination of real rights which must be associated with mapping to produce a cadastral survey. It is true that the Survey were endeavouring to execute a complete proprietory survey, and for all I know may have been determining proprietory and other real rights very efficiently, but so long as this work was unauthorised and unrecognized, as it inevitably was, it will require to be done all over again at a later date by recognised and properly constituted authority. If land rights are to be authoritatively investigated and determined as they must be, it is evidently useless and wasteful on the part of the Government and irritating and bewildering to the villagers to investigate and record them unauthoritatively first.

(7)

7. But it is doubtful whether this defect is worth remedying or if it is worth attempting to carry through a cadastral survey and settlement at all if it is to take another eighteen years to complete. Egypt is a naturally productive country which was able to await the leisurely introduction of reform in her systems of land tenure and land taxation. Palestine is not, and all evidence seems to unite in establishing that the handicaps upon Palestinian agriculture must be removed with the least possible delay if it is not to tumble into economic ruin.

With, as will appear, much preparation still to be done I judge that six years - one for preparation and five for execution - is the minimum period within which a cadastral survey and land settlement of the country can be economically completed. In view of the issue dependent upon it this is surely one of those cases when - as in the case of Lord Cromer's famous irrigation million borrowed in the midst of Egyptian bankruptcy - the economic position of the country can only, and therefore should, be retrieved by a guarantee of the necessary further expenditure which is unlikely to exceed an advance of half a million spread over the six years in supplement of provision from current sources. If the funds necessary to complete the work within the next six years are guaranteed a move can be made at once and the work so planned that the good effects of land settlement should begin to yield their economic results in the more productive districts within the first three years, and progressively in those and other districts thereafter. The economic development of the country has been blighted initially by years of Turkish apathy and maladministration and subsequently by war, and its removal has doubtless been postponed by the inevitable political pre-occupations engendered by racial rivalry and consequent unrest. The causes of the blight have been diagnosed and are removable, and it is sound business to see that they are removed with the least possible further delay.

Weakness of existing system of Land Registration:

6. The system of registration of transfers of land now in force is a public-spirited and painstaking effort to purge and record current legitimate transfers of land. It is, I understand, confined to transfers. So far as it is now practicable to examine titles in an isolated manner and almost invariably without reliable indications of the piece of property with which they purport to deal, I gathered the impression that the work is well done; but pursued as it is being pursued it must regretfully be said that the service is rather adding to than assisting to clear away the rubbish which only systematic cadastral survey and investigation in situ of real rights can replace by an equitable and stable settlement. This is partly inevitable if transactions were to be admitted at all to a Government Register in advance of such systematic and comprehensive examination of all existing claims; it is partly avoidable in that the definition of the area purported to be dealt with can at least be unambiguously and accurately recorded. So far is this from being the case at present that the Director of the Land Registries stated with entire frankness that he was unable from the registered information and the isolated plan that commonly accompanies it to locate the piece of land that a registered transaction purported to concern. By re-enquiry from the parties, from the local authorities or from the surveyor who made the plan, the land in question could doubtless usually be traced, but there is no assurance that these witnesses would even agree while it is obviously the duty of the Government when it has registered a transaction to identify in case of dispute the area which was purported to have been dealt with by the transacting parties. It is true that Government disclaims any responsibility

either for the plan it makes or the legality of the transaction it registers; but it accepts a considerable fee for registration which is doubtless paid in the belief that repudiation of responsibility is an official formula and that in spite of it a great if incomplete sanction is assured to a transaction by registration. If either in the ordinary course of events or during the process of cadastral survey and settlement an appreciable number of transactions that have been registered under the present administration have to be upset, an outcry that the Government has been accepting fees under false pretences must be expected, and it would not be devoid of justification. I am not apprehensive of any widespread upset of such newly registered transactions, because I gather that the Land Registries are extremely cautious as to the transactions they admit to the register; but it is as well to recognize that the risk is a real one, both because enquiry into isolated titles may readily prove imperfect when a comprehensive examination of all neighbouring claims is simultaneously undertaken and because the areas purported to have been dealt with may be found irreconcilable either with fact or with better established claims. It may not be without significance to Palestine that in writing of the defective registration system which is now being replaced in Egypt Judge Halton stated "that quite a considerable number of the deeds registered in Egypt are believed to be forgeries," and that "in fact, registration is usually resorted to by the forger, as it gives a spurious appearance of genuineness to a fabricated document." +

It is only fair to the present Director of Land Registries to say that he appreciated that the existing form and procedure was most imperfect but felt that in face of the necessit

+Judge Halton. *Egyptian Civil Codes*, Vol.ii., p.340.

for radical change minor modifications were hardly worth while.

8. It is idle now to enquire whether the Government was well advised to re-institute registration of transactions at all before it could be done properly: there were obvious objections to permitting only occult transactions as there are obvious objections to associating the present administration with a procedure which is extremely defective and therefore more likely to breed litigation than to secure rights, and which if persisted in without correction must result in an inextricable confusion of registered transactions applying to areas which cannot be located, or which are erroneously represented, which overlap or which do not exist.

It must also be recognized that the expenditure of money and effort to somewhat doubtful purpose in the conduct of sporadic registration of land transactions in advance of systematic survey and land settlement, the prosecution of a so-called cadastral survey as an isolated technical operation divorced from authoritative investigation of the real rights, and the absence so far of any measures to undertake such authoritative investigation of real rights at all have inevitably resulted in a most considerable misdirection of effort, misapplication of funds and misuse of time. The experience is not uncommon; most countries similarly placed have done the same owing to similar lack of knowledge and experience of a somewhat unusual kind.

In Egypt twenty years of futile attempts and even abandonment in despair were needed before the cadastral survey recommended by the Commission of Enquiry nominated[+]

[+] By Khedivial Decree of January 27, 1878. See also Milner, *England in Egypt*, Arnold 1899, p.80 et alia.

in 1878 to investigate the finances and administration of the country began to be effectively conducted. The net output of these twenty years was 280,000 feddans of indifferent work; the next eight years saw the completion of the 7,200,000 feddans of rapidly improving work, which comprised the balance of the cultivated area of the country. As a consequence the re-assessment of the Egyptian Land Tax urged by the above Commission of Enquiry had to be progressively postponed and to the great economic detriment of the country could not be brought into effect until from twenty-five to thirty-two years[+] after its immediate introduction had been decided upon. Palestine's experience should be more quickly and more cheaply bought, but it is sad, with the experience of an originally similar ex-Ottoman Valiyat at its door and available for the asking, that Palestine should have had to waste effort, money and time at all.

10. Doubtful as it is whether it would not have been better policy to have concentrated every available man and pound from the first upon systematic cadastral survey and settlement, it is evident that there is no choice now but to proceed with sporadic registration in advance subject to effecting without delay such amendments as are practicable. Of these the most obvious, as well as the most urgent, is to define the areas which registered transactions purport to concern, so that they can be located by the Government itself with certainty and in due course fall without serious error into their places in the cadastral map of the village in which they occur.

At present, isolated and uncontrolled plans are made of such areas by surveyors who are paid off the Survey Budget but are attached to the Land Registries and work

----
[+]For the first and the last province respectively.

without technical control or direction. It is essential that this should be changed immediately, and that the Survey should be responsible for survey work ahead, as well as at the time, of systematic cadastral operations. This will involve co-operation between Survey and the Land Registries to ensure the most economical association of investigation of title and of mapping, and the immediate extension of the survey network of reference points (e.g. second, third and fourth order triangulation) over the country so that in every part of Palestine the plan of an individual parcel of land can be readily tied up to several reference points in its vicinity, and thus constitute an advance piece of cadastral survey which should fall into place among its neighbours when eventually the village in which it lies is systematically settled and mapped. Adequate independent verification of the advance mapping thus needed to accompany advance registration is also essential.

Necessary as it is to ensure that this advance registration shall be conducted with regard to its subsequent absorption it is permissible to hope that these advance operations shall be limited to the minimum strictly advisable, and that as little effort and money as possible shall be diverted from the prime objective of completing as rapidly as possible the systematic cadastral survey and settlement of the country, which can alone provide the basis for the two measures most needed to stimulate a revival of Palestinian agriculture - the establishment of the Palestinian peasantry and colonists with secure tenure on land of their own and the introduction of an equitable, unonerous and economical taxation of land.

Revision of Land Taxes and amendment of Land Laws:

11.   It was suggested in the course of conversation I think with yourself, the Attorney General and the Treasurer that Mr. Abrahamson, previously Chairman of the Land Commission and Director of the Land Department and new Governor of the Southern District, might be released for a time from his administrative duties and appointed Chairman of a Commission to consider the form of land tax which could most advantageously for government and people be substituted for the existing taxes directly levied on land and livestock. I hope it is not impertinent on my part to say that my subsequent discussions with Mr. Abrahamson inspire me with a strong hope that this proposal may take shape: and I would suggest that if so the same Commission should be asked also to prepare draft legislation, (a) for simplification and such modification of the Land Law as will be needed and (6) for the introduction of compulsory registration of all real rights subsequent to systematic cadastral survey and settlement.

The passing of such necessary legislation is an essential precursor of the settlement of the peasantry, as of colonists, in secure and economic tenure on the land; and no assured progress can be made with the cadastral survey and settlement until the laws which are to govern the perpetuation of this national stock-taking of land rights throughout the country have been worked out in detail and are in force. To garner the harvest of economic advantage and increased welfare that should follow systematic cadastral survey and settlement it is essential both that the work shall not be undone and that the land system shall be reviewed and uneconomic survivals, more particularly the mesha' system of land tenure shall be abolished. In view of the unanimous report of the Committee set up to report to Government on this last subject, and the widespread endorsement their opinion appears to receive, comment on my part on this subject is superfluous. It is however interesting to observe that the system used also to be prevalent in Egypt and was swept away by Mohammed Ali.

12. Whatever decision is come to on this particular point it is of the first importance to realize that it will be waste of effort and money, as it will be damaging to the reputation of the administration, merely to interpolate a thorough cadastral survey and settlement between the existing chaos of land tenure and rights and a second descent thereto. And yet this is all that will happen if the new and better road to be travelled is not planned, tested and ready for use immediately cadastral survey and settlement in a village is complete.

Of the system of recording and passing real rights to be enacted there should be no doubt. The Torrens principle of basing record and passage of real rights on the indestructable, immovable and readily definable unit of land instead of on the ephemeral, mobile and indifferently definable unit of humanity who temporarily enjoys rights over it is winning its way surely throughout the world, and neither its superiority nor its simplicity are seriously contested anywhere. Indeed its superiority primarily resides in its simplicity, which enables the unlettered cultivator readily to comprehend and assimilate its working.

A great deal of preparatory work has however still to be done if the cadastral survey and settlement of Palestine is to be intelligibly recorded, and its advantages perpetuated on the Torrens or indeed on any other system of Land Registration. The mapping and determination of the real rights enjoyed over a given village area at a given time presents its own difficulties but it will be both a minor and a useless achievement to carry this work through Palestine unless it is accompanied by the introduction of a procedure which will economically furnish the same results at any subsequent date also.

13. In this matter essential help can be given by the new Surveyor General of Egypt, Mr. Sheppard, and to the best of my belief by no one else anything like so adequately. Mr. Sheppard for the last fifteen or twenty years has devoted himself to the study of systems of Registration of Land in all parts of the world and their application to the conditio[ns] obtaining in Egypt, physically differing from those of Palestine, but as already mentioned closely analogous by reason of religious law and tradition and association with the Ottoman Empire. The application of the Torrens principle of Land Registration to Egypt originally recommended by an International Commission (1904-08) was obstructed by France and Russia, and is only now being put gradually into force on the basis of the recommendations of a second Commission (1917-20) of which the writer was Chairman and Mr. Sheppard a member. In the course both of this Commission's work and of subsequent discussion and application a rich store of experience has been acquired which can very readily be applied mutatis mutandis to the analogous but, I anticipate, in practice far less complicated land questions awaiting solution and settlement in Palestine.

Not only conversation with those principally concerned but the fact that with so much good work and good will so little has been achieved and even so little useful foundation for future achievement laid establishes beyond dispute that competent help must be obtained from elsewhere if the uncoordinated and undirected efforts of the last few years are to obtain that touch of tried professional guidance in devising procedure and drafting legislation and regulation without which success cannot be commanded or even rationally expected.

It would of course be most useful if Mr.Sheppard could actually be asked and allowed to serve on the Commission over which it was suggested that Mr.Abrahamson should preside, but I am afraid that Mr.Sheppard's own duties would in any case prevent this. Failing this course I think the essential assistance could be rendered by Mr.Sheppard if he can pay an initial visit to Palestine if and when the Commission is instituted, can correspond and pay medial and final visits when it is sitting, and can draft for discussion with it, the provisions of the necessary law and the detailed technical regulations for the actual application to Palestine of a system of Registration of Title to Land on the Torrens system. Absolute title could not of course be immediately accorded but the findings of the Cadastral Survey and Settlement Commissions could all be brought on to the Land Book and accorded provisional title subject for a given period (e.g. five years) to upset on appeal. Such appeal might possibly be for a time to the Commissions themselves and subsequently to the Courts and should cover the addition of servitudes, easements and charges that were initially overlooked.

The drafting of the necessary laws and the necessary regulations - which latter should be capable of amendment by experience and should not avoidably fetter the technical operations of the survey or the discretion of the Settlement Commissions - is the most urgent need, as until these have been authoritatively adopted and promulgated there is no final assurance that any given procedure will be either adhered to or binding.

New legislation of a two-fold character is needed: (a) a new land law and (b) a law enacting the system of recording real rights to be put into force at the time of cadastral survey and settlement, and of subsequent passage and subsequent record of such rights.

A new land law need not and should not be revolutionary: it is primarily needed to codify and to simplify existing practice so that it is made as easy as possible for simple people who possess, part with or acquire real rights to understand without expert intervention where they stand. So far as possible familiar forms would doubtless be retained and familiar names be perpetuated. The initial reception of reform is admittedly largely governed by the manner of its presentation; its matter is appreciated more slowly. Dead wood must none the less be lopped away, and obstacles to the growth of the bread and oil of the people must be rooted out, considerately, even gradually, but when their character is clear unwaveringly.

14. While the easing of the burden of taxation in agriculture is undoubtedly a matter of pressing urgency, it is evident that an authoritative definition of real rights and of the persons entitled to them must precede the replacement of the existing tithe by any land tax whose equitable distribution cannot be seriously challenged. The assessment of any land tax, even the re-assessment of the present werku which is already long overdue, involves both a determination of the value of the property and of the person legally liable. The latter can only be authoritatively determined in the process of systematic survey and settlement, the former can be most cheaply and conveniently assessed in conjunction with, or immediately subsequent to, the same operations.

It does not of course follow that immediate relief is impracticable: on the contrary I understand that the Government has already under consideration a proposal to fix the tithe for five years to come on the basis of the average of

- 19 -

the recorded returns of the last five years. If some such measure proves practicable a considerable saving will be effected on the direct costs of tithe assessment and collection, and great relief accorded to the Provincial authorities who without some such relief may well be incapable of co-operating in the simultaneous cadastral settlement of all sub-districts in the manner proposed a little later on.

In the course of conversation a competent authority roughly estimated at L.E.25,000 per annum the direct costs tithe assessment and collection for Palestine as a whole. This was the sum that it was estimated could be saved by reduction of staff and saving of expenses solely caused by annual assessment, commutation and collection of the tithe; it omits from consideration the drain upon the time and attention of the regular provincial staff as also upon those of the cultivator. I understand that the gross revenue from the tithe is now in the neighbourhood of L.E. 200,000 per annum and is unlikely to increase, both because of the return of world-prices towards the pre-war commodity-level and of the unhealthy condition of Palestinian agriculture. In view of the evident need to lighten the burden on the industry without waiting for systematic settlement and assessment the above figures suggested the possibility of accompanying an averaging of the tithe with a reduction in its amount from the present $12\frac{1}{2}\%$ to the regular tenth. The saving in the cost of collection would apparently go far towards covering the difference, and even on fiscal grounds some such measure of immediate relief seems imperative. Care must naturally be taken not to grant too great a reduction in advance of the introduction of a fairer and less wasteful impost, both because a change in system should be accompanied by further relief and because it would be imprudent to lower the ostensible rate of the cultivator's annual contribution to the State until a reliable basis for assessment has been provided for the country as a whole.

A further suggestion made to me which appears worthy of the careful consideration of Government was that any regular tax to be substituted for the tithe should take the form and name of the present <u>werku</u>, which appears in intention to be a land tax imposed in addition to tithe on freehold property (mulk). If these proposals commend themselves upon further consideration on their broad lines to Government it might be politic to accompany the announcement of the averaging and the lowering of the tithe for a given period with a statement that it was also intended to consider the substitution of a universal <u>werku</u> for the tithe as soon as the cadastral survey and settlement of the country was completed, and that it was hoped that this would enable further relief to be accorded.

15. Organizations to execute cadastral survey and settlement:

The organization that will conduct the technical operation of Survey is already in existence, it will need strengthening but it is generally on sound lines and calls for no immediate discussion. The organization or organizations that are to investigate and settle real rights have not yet been decided on and call for early consideration. It was, I am told, at one time proposed that an official to be called a settlement officer should follow the cadastral survey and on the basis of its results and of investigations conducted by himself or under his direction should settle and record real rights village by village at least provisionally. I believe that the appointment of this officer has not been authorized, and it is just as well, for admirable official as the candidate is there is neither need for him nor could he have discharged within any useful period the stupendous task with which he was to be charged, if I have understood the proposal properly.

Concern has been felt at the slow progress of the survey, and the work must unquestionably be greatly accelerated if its economic purpose is to be achieved, but it does not seem to me to have been appreciated that it is the rate at which investigation and settlement of real rights can be conducted that is more likely to govern the speed with which the work as a whole can be completed.

From the information given me, which was produced on the spur of the moment and was admittedly defective, it is probable that twelve settlement parties will be required to be continuously operating if the work is to be completed within five years. Their duties will be of a most responsible and delicate nature, they must be directed by men whose impartiality is above suspicion, who are trusted and carry weight with the villagers, who can speak and should read the language, who have at least a good working knowledge of the land law and the traditions and customs of the people, and who bring to the problem actual knowledge of the countryside and of the personalities with whom they will have to deal. After discussion with Mr.Abrahamson, Mr.Crosbie and Major Ley at Gaza it seems that the British Sub-Governors of Districts are the only persons who both fulfil the above qualifications and exist in the requisite numbers. No doubt they will be overworked especially at first, but there appears to be no feasible alternative. Considerable relief would be afforded them if the proposal to fix the tithe for five years proved admissable, while the Survey's operations would have to be conducted so that maps were supplied steadily in each sub-district and the work of settlement in each sub-district could be spread over the entire five years period. The composition of the Settlement Commissions requires consideration but a judicial officer with a knowledge of land law and of its practical operation would be needed and would presumably be a Palestinian. Some means of unifying procedure, of sharing experience and possibly of providing for administrative appeal on matters of principle would be needed: and perhaps this might be met by the nomination of an experienced senior officer as Inspector General of the Land Settlement Commissions, with a suitable senior Judicial Officer and the Governor of the Province concerned to review the work and see that progress is maintained in each province and to give rulings or decide appeals on matters of principle. If such an Inspector General was nominated the advisability should be considered of attaching to him a few of the officers specially experienced in the interpretation of Turkish deeds or other aspects of the work that the country possesses. These could visit the various sub-districts as needed or render assistance centrally. I happen to have more particularly in mind

Mr. Rizq of the present Land Registry Service who in the course of a morning's conversation gave evidence of valuable knowledge and experience of this branch of the work: but the suggestion does not depend upon this actual application, and I do not pretend to say that it is in this capacity that this official would be most usefully employed.

Preparatory measures and general plan of campaign.

16. Before considering the detailed operation in a village of survey, settlement and valuation it is necessary to review the general plan of campaign to be applied to the country as a whole. Without such general plan and a timetable to be worked to punctual and economical work cannot be expected, and the same waste of effort and funds, which has so far attended much sectionally good work because it has lacked competent national direction will continue.

Moreover if this state of affairs is to give way to rapid and effective and, therefore, economical work, a breathing space of a year will be needed to prepare the way for a comprehensive attack on the country as a whole, to gain experience - so far entirely lacking - of comprehensive investigation and definition of real rights village by village, and to train staff. Annoying as cessation of apparent progress for a year will be it is part of the price that must be paid for past lack of preparation and it will be amply rewarded by the subsequent progress that it will promote, and which it is idle to expect without it. So far the building has lacked both plan and foundation, and both should be provided with the least possible delay if construction is to be continued: if it is not to be continued the economic re-establishment of Palestine under the British Mandate, so far as it is to result from intelligent human endeavour, may as well be abandoned.

17. The more important measures that are required to enable the cadastral survey, settlement and assessment of Palestine to be attacked rapidly and effectively as a whole are:-

(a) The definite determination of the lengths of the northern and southern base lines, of their azimuths and of the geographical positions of their terminals. Connection should also be made with any adequate work in Syria and at least a longitude comparison instituted with Iraq. The cooperation of the Survey of Egypt should be obtained for this work.

(b) The laying down of a standard map sheet system for Palestine on the basis of the above primary positions and those of the second order (principal) national triangulation deduced therefrom.

My hasty view of typical portions of the country led me to conclude that a scale of 1:10,000 (approximately 6 inches to the mile) should be adopted as that of the largest standard national map series. Major Ley had previously come to the same conclusion. For a large part of the country (e.g. forest, waste, marsh, sporadic cultivation) no larger scale is likely to be needed at present; in closely cultivated areas (e.g. orange groves and vegetable gardens) a scale of 1:2000 will probably suffice, while in town areas a scale of 1:1000 or 1:500 may be needed. Maps on any of such larger scales must from the first be made to conform to the standard 1:10,000 map sheet system and be directly referable to their place in it, (e.g. the area depicted on a standard 1:10,000 map being exactly covered by 25 sheets on a scale of 1:2,000 when the latter scale is employed).

(c) Provision for economical reproduction and safe and orderly storage of all national map series.

Measures are already being taken to provide for the reproduction of cadastral maps but the methods to be employed both in the field and in the reproduction office to achieve this end with rapidity and economy are still under consideration. It is evident that these maps must be reproduced in a single colour and it is possible that by suitable arrangements in the field they may be directly reproduced from the field sheets by vandyke or donglagraph thus avoiding the delay, cost and possible introduction of error involved by re-drawing. The 1:100,000 sheets a few of which will cover Palestine should be reproduced in several colours in all three mandatory languages and as well as possible, and this can probably be best and most cheaply done in Egypt.

The safe and orderly storage of the maps - especially the original cadastral maps - is a matter of first class importance. The work embodied in them will cost a lot of money and cover a great many sheets, and it must both be safeguarded against loss or destruction and rendered readily accessible. This will necessitate the provision of a proper map store with economically planned steel shelving. It should be constructed in the first place to house all the map sheets and records which the initial survey and settlement are expected to produce, but planned so that as the development of Palestine proceeds it can be extended pari passu to include the increased extension of the larger scale maps and fuller records that will accompany such development.

(d) Decision as to the national and provincial headquarters of the Survey and Land Registration of Palestine.

Although the location of the national headquarters at the capital has an obvious convenience there are more important considerations which may well outweigh this advantage, as it has done in the case of the British Ordnance Survey and others. The three most important needs to be met are probably (i) the economical provision of the necessary space and buildings that will ultimately be required (ii) the optimum climatic conditions obtainable (iii) ease of protection in case of war or serious internal trouble.

The first consideration probably precludes the capital. An adequate area to embrace all likely future requirements should be earmarked from the outset but permanent building should be limited to permanent needs. The configuration of Jerusalem as well as the value of land and buildings there will probably prevent this need being economically met in the neighbourhood. It is moreover undesirable avoidably to add to congestion at the capital. The climatic conditions needed are maximum sunshine, minimum rainfall, low and small range in humidity, absence of dust. The success with which these conditions are met will reflect itself in the speed and economy of working.

(e) The extension of the survey framework of reference points throughout Palestine so that work can be taken up in any village at any moment.

The advisability has already been urged of extending the framework of reference points so that parcels of land dealt with by registered transaction in advance of cadastral survey can be located. This extension is also required so that systematic work can be begun in every sub-district with the least further delay. The reference points primarily referred to are those of the second, third and fourth order triangulation, which I myself would like to see fortified by systematic traverse. It is no part of my intention here to discuss technical methods which cannot be pronounced on ex cathedra as they depend on local conditions, the idiosyncracies of local staff and the degree of accuracy needed; but I should perhaps say that I have suggested to Major Ley the advisability of considering somewhat greater reliance upon traverse and somewhat lesser utilization of the plane table. The plane table is a rapid and cheap map making instrument admirable within its scope, which to my mind it is risky and uneconomical to extend to the fixation of reference points for cadastral survey of land of any value. Immediate speed and cheapness can doubtless be attained by its use in this way, but only I fear at the cost of unreliable control and excessive repetition of work whenever the area has to be revisited. If traverse work - observation, calculation and plotting alike - is reduced to routine its speed can be greatly increased and its cost lowered, while it has the outstanding advantage of being independently controllable, and if reasonable protection for reference marks is secured, is of permanent value.

(f) Review and demarcation of village boundaries, and laying down of a programme of work in each sub-district.

I am advised that frequently village boundaries include neither completely nor solely the land of the village concerned, and that enclaves of land situated within the geographical boundaries of one village but held and administered under some right by the inhabitants or authorities of another village are common. The existence of such enclaves is a usual outcome in all countries in a primitive administrative stage of the extension of the dominance of individuals, families or clans outside of their own domiciliary territory. The practice fosters group quarrels and is administratively inconvenient and wasteful: and its disappearance and replacement by village areas consisting of completely self contained village units is evidently desirable; and indeed is I think an inevitable accompaniment of national development. Unnecessary complexities involving waste of money and time will however be occasioned if this process of disentangling village areas follows instead of preceding survey and settlement.

I understand that there is not likely to be serious difficulty in carrying out the necessary adjustment of village boundaries in co-operation with the authorities of the villages concerned, and as this is done these boundaries should be demarcated at salient points by suitable marks which can be incorporated in the national framework of survey reference points. Although it is most desirable that enclaves should disappear there may be cases of detached areas of a special character (e.g. forest, lake, grazing ground) over which the inhabitants of a neighbouring village enjoy exclusive rights, the administrative dissociation of which from that village may be impolitic. Such cases are I imagine likely to be rare, and that more commonly rights over special areas of the character suggested are shared by several adjoining villages, and that if these areas cannot be partitioned among such villages, they had better be constituted and administered as a separate unit under State wardenship.

It will doubtless also be appreciated that the general review of village areas may disclose cases of accretions of two or more villages which can advantageously be resolved into their component units, or of isolated hamlets which can advantageously be grouped with a neighbour or neighbours.

As review, definition and demarcation of village boundaries proceeds the resulting boundaries should be sketched on an index diagram of the sub-district concerned, so that gradually a diagram of the village areas and boundaries in each sub-district is constituted. This diagram should show all triangulation points, the sheet lines of the 1:10,000 and of whatever larger scale, if any, is likely to be employed in the sub-district concerned, as well as the course of outstanding topographical features, (e.g. railways, main roads, main water courses, coasts of sea and lakes). Villages should be classified in this diagram according to economic importance, and the progress of cadastral survey and settlement in each sub-district planned so that the best economic return to the State and the nation at large is obtained.

(g) Definition of units of length and area.

I understand that the metric system is in regular use combined with an averaged value of the local unit of area the donum, that falls just short of the 1000 square metres which would adapt it very conveniently to the metric system. The perpetuation of this customary unit of area is admittedly desirable but since its variation in size from district to district necessitated standardization, and any standardization is as arbitrary as any other, that at 1000 square metres appears greatly to be recommended since it will save money in calculation of areas throughout Palestine and will gradually familiarize the population with the use of the metric system. The donum, as the jugum, the acre, and the feddan originally, is I believe a unit of ploughing rather than of area: and I am advised that so far the people, with practical wisdom often lacking in public services which have to deal with the land, are indifferent to units of area used provided the correct boundaries on the ground are preserved.

- 31 -

(h) Determination of language to be employed on maps and in records.

The use of all three official languages on maps and records even if practicable would be extremely costly and greatly retard the work. In practice, moreover, it is impossible to give equal weight to records expressed in three languages. However faithfully translations are made, discrepancies are bound to occur and to require settlement, and the use of three languages would thus tend to re-introduce the ambiguities and uncertainties which it is the object of the work to terminate.

The language at present used is English as this at least avoids preference for either the language of Jew or of Palestinian Moslem over that of the other: but although better than the use of three languages the compromise is neither just nor economic, since it imposes upon the vast majority of the population the keeping of the national records in a language which very few of them understand. There appears to me to be no doubt that maps and records should be kept in Arabic, the language of this vast majority of the population and that minority needs in Hebrew and English should be specially met by special extraordinary editions of maps of areas occupied by Jewish or European colonists or groups, and by Government guaranteed translations of records of rights enjoyed by Jews or Europeans. Actual deeds conveying transfer of rights can and should be given in any one of the three languages chosen by the transacting parties.

(i) Preparation and printing of the necessary forms and registers.

These forms require careful drafting of subsequent disturbing changes and expense owing to insufficient original foresight are to be avoided, and they must be ready in adequate quantities for use in each district if neither the initial work nor its subsequent maintenance to date are to be hampered. The Land Book and Mutation Form could probably be printed in all three mandatory languages without much sacrifice of space, while forms in which this was not practicable could be printed according to need and be available in English and Hebrew, in English and Arabic, and in Arabic and Hebrew.

The loose leaf form of register is essential for orderly control and economical working, not so much in the initial years but increasingly as properties become regrouped. Nothing can entirely preclude the risk of registers being tampered with however bound, but a loose-leaf register the binding of which is locked by a key held by a responsible authority is little less secure than the ordinary glue and cardboard binding: and in both cases ultimate security lies in the publicity accorded to all transactions and in the duplicate records of all authentic dealings that will be independently preserved.

(j) Fixing of fees.

Apart from the voluntary demarcation of properties, which when the resources of the Survey permit should be carried out for proprietors at standard rates covering the cost to the State, the Registration Fee should be the only fee charged. Miniature graphic record on a map of the location, boundaries and area of a unit of real property, and manuscript record on a printed form of the rights enjoyed over it and of the

- 33 -

persons enjoying these rights are complementary halves of one operation which is incomplete without the other. The fees charged for registration as at present practised appear high, but however these fees are assessed they should cover all costs. It is an indefensible and irritating imposition for the State to undertake registration of real rights on a prescribed scale of fees and to make an additional charge for an essential part of the operation.

Registration will necessarily be compulsory in the first place, and doubtless no rights will be recognized then or subsequently that are not recorded on map and in register: as soon as the proceedings are understood there is unlikely to be any reluctance on the part of those whose rights are admitted to pay the necessary fees and thus obtain provisional recognition by the State of such rights, but an exception must evidently be made in the case of these rights which have been previously accorded post-war recognition by the present Registry Offices. If such rights pass the scrutiny of cadastral survey and settlement they must clearly be admitted to map and register without additional charge: while the statutory refund of all fees in the contrary event should be considered.

Procedure of cadastral survey and settlement in a village.

I can now turn to a consideration of the procedure to be adopted in each village for the execution of the cadastral survey, settlement and record of real rights. There are two main stages to be envisaged.

(a) Initial unravelment and provisional settlement and record of real rights.

(b) Subsequent maintenance to date of the provisional record and its ultimate conversion to one of absolute title.

If confusion and continued dissipation of effort is to be avoided it is essential to be clear as to the type of permanent record that is to be obtained and what it is expected to achieve. I assume that the type of record aimed at is one on the Torrens principle adapted to the Land Law and conditions of Palestine and kept by villages, also that it is intended that it shall in due course easily and economically furnish complete and final information regarding the rights enjoyed by any person or corporation - including necessarily the State in its dual capacity as custodian of public utility land of various kinds and as steward of exploitable public domain - over any unit of real estate throughout Palestine. When registration of title is in effective operation throughout the country the Land Book of each village should thus comprise an exhaustive record of all rights over real estate within the area of that village, of their nature and duration as well as of the names of all persons or corporations in enjoyment of those rights. In other words not only must the major right of ownership be recorded but also all minor rights such as lease, servitudes, charges, easements, tax rates. This may appear a formidable requirement: in practice it is a great simplification. The cadastral survey of the village should constitute an exact and exhaustive complementary record of the situation, character and extent of every unit of real estate therein. Land Book and Cadastral Survey are indeed the two fundamental component parts of Registration of Title to land, and it is essential that they should operate conjointly. Theoretically the operations of survey and entry in the Land Book should be conducted simultaneously. As in practice this is not entirely possible it is advisable that entry in the Land Book shall form the last stage since it is the stage which gives publicity to the right recorded or acquired.

18. As cadastral map and land book are component parts of one record they should be initially built up, as well as subsequently maintained, in association: but it is necessary so to arrange this that the technical operations of survey, the investigation of rights and the writing up of the land book shall proceed each at their best pace without hampering each other. After a little experience the most convenient methods of co-operation and the numbers and strength of the co-operating parties required to get through the work most economically and quickly will appear: but it is in the meantime necessary to lay down the procedure on which operations shall be initiated pending gain of such experience. After walking over representative map sheets and terrain at Gaza and discussing the problem first with Major Ley and Messrs.Giles and Miller in the field and subsequently with Major Ley, Mr.Abrahamson and Mr.Crosbie in the office, I suggest the following procedure for these combined operations in each village.

(a) Execution of large scale topographical survey of the village, subdivision of village, and demarcation of important invisible internal boundaries.

This survey should show all topographical features including permanently marked boundaries,

— 36 —

and be mapped on a suitable scale for conversion in due course into a cadastral map of the village. As convenient nomenclatures of unit properties necessitates some intermediate subdivision between the village as a whole and the individual property unit, this subdivision will probably be most conveniently effected in consultation with the village authorities in the course of, or immediately subsequent to, topographical survey. Important invisible internal boundaries, such as blocks of mesha' land should be demarcated if necessary and mapped during this stage of the work. While not essential it will greatly facilitate the work of land valuation for purposes of tax assessment if the subdivisions of the village area mentioned above can be effected so that each subdivision includes land of approximately equal value.* These village subdivisions, for which a suitable local name can doubtless be readily found are termed in Switzerland sections and occasionally sub-sections, in Egypt hods and occasionally qisms. Their size is a matter of convenience apt initially to be determined by the closeness of the subdivision of property holdings and by variations in the quality of the land. Trouble will be saved in the long run if all land that may become closely divided, as prosperity is established and the population increases, is subdivided at the outset into sections that can be permanently maintained. In Egypt the

- 37 -

* But v. para 13 infra

sections vary between 50 and 100 feddans in fully cultivated districts which suggests that in less closely divided Palestine limits of 500 to 1000 donums might suffice.

(b) Investigation of real rights *in situ* by a Settlement Commission, and provisional embodiment of such rights on map and in register.

As soon as the large scale topographical maps of a village are finished they should be passed to the Settlement Commission who will investigate section by section the rights claimed. In the course of investigation all the units of property within the section under consideration will be demarcated at least temporarily, and the demarcation will be transferred to the map by one of the survey parties. All units of property will be consecutively numbered on the map throughout each section, so that any unit of property in Palestine can be unambiguously identified by (i) the name of the village in which it is situate, (ii) the name or number of the section in which it lies and (iii) its own individual reference number therein. This plot number is preserved so long as the physical identity of the plot remains unaltered no matter how often the plot changes hands; if its boundaries change in any way the new plot thus formed is given a new reference number which similarly continues in use so long as the newly formed plot remains unaltered. This procedure has been detailed because its simplicity and effectiveness are unrivalled, and successful working will in practice depend greatly upon such things. Each unit of property will be allotted a page in the Land Book or register which will be suitably designed after existing models to show all relevant particulars. The requisite entries on map and register will be completed for each section as the work progresses, suitable arrangements being made to afford the fullest publicity to the results.

20. After a proper interval for the lodging of appeals to the Commission (e.g. three months from completion of the work in a village) the entries will be accorded provisional title liable only to be upset by the Courts.

After a further period the duration of which must depend upon all legal uncertainties being determined, absolute unopposable title should be accorded to all registered transactions. Recourse must still lie against the State on certain counts for damage occasioned by negligence or error of its agents, but the inviolability of registered title should stand. Experience has demonstrated that the financial risk thereby incurred by the State is negligible, and such as it is can be covered by the registration fee.

Subsequent to cadastral survey and settlement rights must only be permitted to pass upon admission to map and land book, and such admission should only be allowed on the strength of duly authenticated and prescribed public instruments which will be governed by the legislation envisaged earlier.

Additional Points and concluding observations:

31. A matter of great practical importance on which my opinion was asked was the administrative grouping of the Land Department, the Land Registries and the Survey.

By the comprehensive term Land Department I understand is meant the service which is responsible for the custody and use of exploitable State Domain. I omitted to find out whether this service is also responsible for the custody of State Domain reserved for public utility purposes (e.g. roads, railways, public buildings, &c.), but if not the desirability of grouping the responsibility for the custody of the entire State Domain under the same service might be considered. The difference between exploitable public domain and that reserved for public utility purposes is merely one of convenience; land in either category to-day may pass to the other category to-morrow, and such passage should be easy subject to proper safeguards that the capital represented by the two categories combined is never avoidably left idle. I do not mean to suggest that the Department responsible for the custody and management of State Domain as a whole should interfere in the use made by other public services (e.g. the Railways or the Public Works) of areas allotted to them for Departmental requirements, any more than it would interfere in the proper exploitation of a portion of the public domain leased to a private individual or group: but ultimately a single public service should be responsible for all public land, safeguard its boundaries and ensure that it is being utilized either to the best economic advantage or in accordance with authorized arrangements.

The discovery and definition of public domain throughout Palestine is a secondary object of systematic cadastral survey and settlement which alone appears to promise a return to the exchequer for the cost of the work, more direct, quicker, and possibly during the next critical decade even greater in amount, than that which will be indirectly derived from the gradual establishment of a healthy national eocnomy. I was advised by a competent authority that the "mewat" land that would be discovered and defined as State Domain during the progress of cadastral survey was likely to comprise one-third of the area of Palestine, and in addition to this there are the categories of land known as "matruk" and "mahlûl". It therefore appears evident that, even if all the occupied and exploited "merie" land is allowed to be inscribed as "mulk" and all "mera" land is allotted to village or other communities, a large and potentially very valuable public estate yet lies in Palestine both largely unlocated and undeveloped. Experience in Egypt makes this probability almost a certainty; and experience in Egypt emphasizes the need in the public interest to locate and define this potentially valuable national domain with as little delay as possible. During the eventual progress of the cadastral survey throughout Egypt it was abundantly evident that the great delay that had occurred in its prosecution had resulted in an enormous aggregate area of public domain having been lost to the State in the interval. While the permanent retention in the hands of the State of a considerable proportion of the land of the country is of questionable desirability, it is clearly a culpable neglect of national interests to allow hundreds of thousands of acres of public land to be simply stolen. My experience of what occurred in Egypt leads me confidently to hazard the anticipation that the promptest possible execution of cadastral survey and settlement in Palestine will be repaid by the much larger extent of public domain that will be salvaged alone, and that if on the other hand

- 41 -

survey and settlement pursue the leisurely course at present indicated the vast potential estate which justly belongs to the nation at large will shrink to a relatively petty measure. The probability of this forecast being realized one way or the other and its financial importance can be readily assessed on the spot.

Further emphasis need not be laid on the importance of pushing forward the work to completion with the least possible delay, even from the point of view of this secondary objective; nor on the great responsibility that will attach to the service charged with the custody of public domain to see both that the claims of the nation as a whole are justly but as adequately sustained before the Settlement Commissions, as those of private individuals or lesser communities, and that the rapidly accumulating estate that will accrue to its care as the work proceeds is safely taken over, guarded and developed.

It will be appreciated that the discharge of this important function is irreconcilable with any part or lot in the execution of the cadastral survey or settlement itself, and also that the existing association of the charge of public domain with control of what I have called, sporadic advance registration is fundamentally vicious and lays the Government open to obvious criticism. From the apparent lack of complaint so far, it may be assumed that the conflicting rôles of the at present associated services have not yet seriously clashed, which I gather to be due to the cautious policy pursued both in sustaining national rights against others, and in admitting transfers to the register at all. Equitable scrutiny of private rights when in conflict with those of the State may doubtless be achieved by the same public service as is responsible for the defence of the latter; but this association of the functions of judge and advocate must obviously not be perpetuated into the arena in which every land claim must be whole-heartedly presented and single-mindedly judged.

I find it difficult to suggest an immediate escape from this undesirable association of functions that does not merely introduce an inconvenient, and probably in practice an unjustified ephemeral change; and I incline to recommend that no alteration in this respect be made until a Land Settlement Commission has been established in a sub-district. As soon as this can be done sporadic advance registration in that district might be brought under the Commission, who would naturally be very cautious in registering any claims in advance of systematic cadastral survey and investigation. In this way the present association between the control of public domain and the direction of sporadic land registration would gradually dissolve and the work and organisation of the latter become merged in the permanent system that is evolved.

32. The record of real rights on map and in register being component parts of one operation will be most economically and effectively executed under a single control, which control must be that of the Survey because the technical work of survey cannot be stereotyped and must therefore be conducted under trained expert direction, whereas the record of rights in a register can be effected by a competent experienced clerk. That clerk must know the people, the land and the land laws, the entries made by him must be effectively supervised, and he and his administrative chief must apply for and readily obtain legal advice whenever occasion arises; but this position is exactly similar to that of any other

Department of State, e.g. the Public Health Service, which must know and apply the laws or the clauses of all laws bearing on the public health of the nation, and must equally whenever occasion arises apply for and be able readily to obtain legal advice. And if such advice is not asked or not taken when needed or is of too academic a character, these weaknesses, like others, will reveal and correct themselves during the opening years when practice and procedure are accommodating themselves to circumstances.

The preceding observations must be understood to apply to the process of <u>recording</u> real rights by the machinery of cadastral map and register, and not to the procedure that may be enacted to effect and provide authoritative evidence of the creation, transmission or extinction of such rights on which to base alteration of such record. The essential needs to be satisfied in this latter connection are that the act shall be legally initiated by a public deed witnessed by reputable persons who vouch for the identity of the party or parties acting. The resulting authenticated instrument constitutes the authority to alter cadastral map and land book to conform therewith, and the mutation (as it is termed) should have no binding force until the last of these operations is effected.

The procedure for effecting and authorizing the inclusion of mutations on map and in land book in a manner that will most economically combine security, simplicity and despatch under the conditions obtaining in Palestine is, I suggest, a matter for the consideration of the Commission proposed earlier in paragraph 11. As part of this procedure I recommend the use of bi-lingual or tri-lingual[+]

[+]If bi-lingual forms were used, three combinations, viz: Arabic and English, English and Hebrew, Hebrew and Arabic, would be needed.

standard forms for the commoner types of transaction.

It is this branch of the work that will particularly demand the attention of the Attorney General or of a special delegate of his Department in the initial shaping of the necessary legislation, in the drafting of procedure and in maintaining close and sympathetic contact especially during the formative years. In time, and it may be hoped in no great time, after the foundation has been laid by systematic cadastral survey and settlement the entire procedure governing the creation, passage and extinction of real rights and their absolute record on map and in land book will have settled down to a simple routine understood by and operated with the aid of all the people. Trained legal supervision will always be needed, but if the procedure develops, as it might, this can be relied upon to assume a preservative form.

The duplication and dual preservation for an adequate term at national and at local headquarters respectively of the authenticated instruments authorizing the inclusion of mutations on map and in land book is an essential precaution to enable the land book of a village to be reconstructed in case of loss or destruction. No attempt should be made to maintain duplicates of the land book in two places, as not only is the risk of loss too slight to justify the cost and difficulty of such duplication, but it is actually inadvisable on the grounds that it is impossible to maintain two geographically separated registers accurately in facsimile to date or to accord equal authority to them.

23. Few references have been made in the course of these notes to the suggested assessment of land tax, because although the equitable valuation of the land for this purpose is far from an easy matter, the principles that may be expected to govern it and the procedure by which it can be

best effected are either more widely understood or more a matter of local circumstances than the execution of a cadastral survey and settlement, and the introduction of a simple and effective system of national registration of land.

It has already been suggested that the sections into which village areas should be subdivided might be selected so as to include land of closely similar value and thus constitute units for tax-rating also. Convenient as this would be I have upon further consideration concluded that time and effort will be lost in any endeavour to select coincident units for the two purposes, and that as any such coincidence could only be maintained for one assessment period it will be better from the outset to select areas of common valuation without regard to the survey and registration sections. The connection between a property unit and its tax rate will not be so simple, but it will present no difficulty.

Valuation for purposes of land tax should take into account not merely the natural fertility of the land but such factors as proximity and access to markets, transport facilities, irrigation and drainage facilities, climatic conditions, &c., &c., indeed all the conditions that unite under a good government in a peaceful country to determine the market price of agricultural land. As the principal object of the substitution of a land tax for the tithe would be to relieve and stimulate agriculture exemption for an adequate term (e.g. ten years) might be accorded to permanent improvements properly established or notified, although the basic valuation of any parcel of land must allow for and register such with all other determining factors.

The tax rate should be fixed for a period adequate to secure economic stability but not for a period long enough seriously to disturb either its equitable incidence or its basic statutory return to the State. The tax assessment now current in Egypt was fixed for thirty years and in half that period it had become thoroughly bad in both the respects mentioned. Economic revival in Palestine may not be susceptible of such a dramatic metamorphosis as occurred in Egypt, but I have no doubt that if it is brought about, as it certainly can be, ten years will see a marked shifting both of relative and absolute values all over the country.

I therefore recommend if a land tax is introduced that it should be fixed for a period of ten years from its initial coming into force. The subsequent reassessment which will be much simpler should be published some five years in advance so that it can be allowed for betimes in agreements and programmes of all sorts. If this ten year period of currency with a five year notice of change proves in practice a satisfactory compromise between the necessity for periodic re-adjustment and the economic undesirability of change it might be permanently adopted. Alternatively it would be modified as experience dictates. Actual payments of tax will of course be designed so as best to suit the convenience of cultivators, i.e. in suitable proportions of the whole after the normal date of marketing each season's crop.

Any change from an ad valorem tax on the crop grown, which the tithe in essence is, to a fixed annual contribution assessed in proportion to the potentialities of the

- 47 -

land must be expected to meet with opposition from those who have been accustomed to wrap up and bury talents in their care by leaving land undeveloped and uncultivated. It is one of the merits of a land tax that it does not permit such sins against the community to escape unscathed, and that it will steadily operate to force such unprofitable stewards either to discharge, or to relinquish to more faithful hands, their stewardship. The change is admittedly also likely to be accompanied by an inclination on the part of cultivators generally to seek to obtain the best of the old world and of the new by accepting the averaged rate contentedly in good seasons and pressing for remissions in bad. It is probable that this disability will have to be accepted and allowed for at least during the first decade that the land tax is in force, by fixing the rate high enough to cover the estimated maximum of total probable remissions over the decade. During this decade the establishment of a national agricultural insurance fund might be considered which would enable such seasonal risks to be covered at less expense to the cultivator and without reaction upon the annual budget of Government.

United control under the Survey of the complementary cartographical and the documentary records of real rights has been recommended above, as also that fuller study is required both of the legislation needed and of the procedure by which authorization for this public recognition of the creation, transmission or annulment of such rights is to be obtained. The collection of any regular rural land tax or urban property tax would doubtless be most conveniently and cheaply effected by the local authorities; but it will be necessary for some central public service to make the periodic statements of the amounts due from each unit of property, to maintain general financial control of the operation of these taxes, to see that temporary remissions (e.g. for permanent improvements) are not extended beyond their term, to act as a central advisory agency in regard to all questions, and to be responsible that periodic reassessment of all real property, rural and urban and statutory notification of the same is properly and punctually effected. This duty can be most readily and most economically discharged in association with the survey and maintenance of the record of the real rights that are taxed, provision of course being made for the necessary co-operation of other branches of the public service more particularly the local authorities and the Department of Agriculture.

14. It will have been noticed that so far nothing has been said about either registration of real rights or re-assessment of taxation in urban areas. This is because, whatever the need for reform in these respects and I was advised that it was great, neither vitally affects the issues of the economic health or sickness of Palestine. Urban areas will doubtless require to be both geographically and legislatively differentiated from rural, and any consideration of the application of an amended "werku" to the latter should embrace the shape that this should take in the former. Fortunately cadastral diagrams depicting with considerable faithfulness the visible bulk of the patchwork of urban property boundaries can be readily constructed from suitably exposed aeroplane photographs, and if these fall short of the cadastral map on which dimensions and areas are autheritatively recorded, such weaknesses will probably prove to be far outweighed at least for the time being by the gain in cheapness and speed. If investigation of real rights and re-assessment of tax can be

– 49 –

undertaken in urban areas by purely urban authorities, it should be possible for the R.A.F. and the Survey to co-operate in the production of such diagrams, and for the Survey to undertake in due course the writing and custody of the complementary registers with very little additional strain upon the latter's resources. The settlement of rights and reform of taxation in rural and urban areas in close sequence would obviously offer advantages. If, as very possibly, the Survey are not equipped for the production of the suggested cadastral diagrams of urban areas without interfering with other work, the assistance of the Survey of Egypt could be invoked; and if asked soon they could doubtless undertake in co-operation with the R.A.F. the production of these diagrams for any areas required at moderate cost. Such cadastral diagrams of urban areas would also serve as at least the general basis for town planning, and might save on another occasion the irritating delay and the wasteful absorption of the Survey's nascent energies which correspondence on record indicates as having occurred in providing the authorities with a basis for the town planning of Jerusalem.

26. Another point to which no reference has been made, as it is bound to come under the consideration of any body convoked to make recommendations for the application of any change in the method of taxing agriculture, is the probability that special treatment will have to be accorded to certain areas e.g. the Beersheba District. I am also myself unaware as to whether any reaction on the methods of taxing the cis-Jordan valley lands is likely to be occasioned by those in force in Transjordania. I understand that the latter term explicitly applies to an area east of Jordan which is integrally part of Palestine and included as such in the British

mandate, but is for convenience separately and tribally administered, by the Emir Abdalla as Arab deputy of the British High Commissioner. If I am correct I would urge that the utmost care be taken, particularly while the affairs of the world and consequently also those of Palestine, are in their present unstable state, not to give any pledges to the inhabitants of these desert fringes of Palestine of any perpetual, or even long term, differentiation between the fiscal and land tenure systems of these frontier districts and those of the body of the country. While the perpetuation of such differentiation for a long time to come, or even for ever, may be both just and politic, it is evident that even the broad lines upon which the stabilization of the world and of Palestine itself is likely to take place will not be clear for at least a decade, and past experience has sufficiently demonstrated the unfairness to governed and governors of binding the unknown future with pledges given, as there can for some time be no assurance they are not given, in the light of a transitory phase, and under fluctuating conditions.

If it is the intention of the British Government and People, having set their hand to the plough as mandatories of the civilized world, to establish "The Land of Three Faiths" as a stable and self-sufficing political entity, it appears essential that it shall embrace these eastern and southern desert marches, and that nothing shall prevent their ultimate absorption into one homogeneous State, if the political and economic development of the land gradually extends to them as given health at the heart may be naturally expected.

It is a fallacy to assume, as is frequently assumed, that people are nomadic or preserve a tribal organization

- 51 -

of engrained character. Nomadism is a stage in the development of human communities which lingers under conditions which handicap further advance, and although engrained habit and tribal tradition yield slowly by our measure to the advantages of a settled domicile and a more comfortable condition of life they nevertheless do yield to them surely and steadily, as is sufficiently attested by the gradual settlement of desert Arabs on the extending flanks of cultivation in Egypt. These settled Arabs still preserve habits and traditions from their tribal life, but the Cultivation will proving too strong for them and they will pass, with merely surface bubbles from their old life as we ourselves have passed, into the stream of settled folk.

I believe that Transjordania is agriculturally a r' Judea and that during the war it was the grenary of the T. ish armies in Palestine. This suggests that it is the ty of land which given an adjoining focus of good government a economic development may confidently be expected to carry those who dwell in it out of the nomadic and out of the tribal stage, if these be not artificially stereotyped and perpetuated - to the detriment alike of the people themselves and of the prospects of the economic self-dependence of Palestine. It is in any case clear that it would be handicapping the future of Palestine improperly to allow any impediment to complete economic and political unification in due course.

In winding up these notes I must ask for lenient judgment if owing to my visit to Palestine having been far too brief I gathered and have used views or information inaccurately or have discussed aspects of a complex problem that are already commonplace, or if owing to my wish to communicate my conclusions quickly I have been lacking in clarity

- 52 -

or conciseness in their presentation. That I was able in the course of five days to sum up the problem at all and to offer suggestions for its solution is due to the analogy and lessons presented in the same connection during the [?] economic development of Egypt which I have already mentioned, to my successive discharge there of the functions of Surveyor General, Chairman of the Commission on Registration of Title to Land, Under-secretary of State for Finance and Financial Adviser to Government which brought the varied aspects of the problem into the focus of a single experience, and to the striking keenness and public spirit of all the officers whom you arranged that I should meet, and who sinking any defensive attitude against an interloper, in cases when it mi[ght] have been excusable, sought with astonishing unanimity [and] single-mindedness to bring their experience and views in[me-] diately to the common vat in the hope that they might cryst[al-] lise out to some purpose. On this account and because it [is] desirable that any points that I may have misunderstood or any deductions that I have erroneously drawn should be corrected without delay, I shall esteem it a favour provided [t-] here is no impediment if these notes may be shown to the [of-] ficers, as of course to any others that you may elect, [and] that they may be invited to subject them to their unrese[rved] criticism. The officers to whom I more particularly re[fer,] taking them in the order in which I met them, are Mr. [?] Stubbs, M.C., Major J.E.F.Campbell, Mr. E.R.Sawer, Majo[r] Ley, R.E., O.B.E., Colonel C.H.F.Cox, D.S.O.,Mr. A. Ab[ram-] son, C.B.E., and Mr. R.E.H.Crosbie.

Finally, I should like to thank you and through yo[u] His Excellency the High Commissioner and your Governme[nt] generally for the excellent arrangements made to e[nable me] to assimilate a lot in a little time, for th[e] [con-]fidence shown [me] and the open field [?]

[Copy is damaged at right side.]

...se of the investigation with which I had the honour to be
requested by you to undertake.

I have the honour to be,

Your obedient servant,

(Sg.) Ernest M. Dowson,
7.12.23.

Sir Gilbert Clayton, K.B.E., C.B., C.M.G.,
    Chief Secretary,
        Government of Palestine,
            Jerusalem.

3.03

PALESTINE.

Despatch No. 1069
Reference No. Adm.351.

GOVERNMENT OFFICES,
JERUSALEM.

10th September, 1925.

Sir,

I have the honour to refer to your despatch No.1035 of the 11th August, 1925, on the subject of the Ordinance to provide for the correction of Land Registers, and to forward a revised draft which has been prepared in accordance with your instructions. Provision therefore has been made in Clause 8 of the revised draft for the collection of all fees leviable on account of transactions shown in unofficial land-books as having occurred since the 1st of January 1919 - presumably 1918 was a mistake because the Northern part of Palestine was occupied only at the end of that year.

2. I have however, reconsidered this matter in consultation with my advisers and I concur in Sir Herbert Samuel's opinion that it is inequitable to make the payment of these fees a condition of correcting the registration. Sir Ernest Dowson who studied the matter carefully while he was in this country, is in full accord with the views of this Government, and I transmit for your perusal an extract from a memorandum which he wrote in April last after he had discussed the question with your Department.

3. I shall be grateful therefore if this matter may be further considered with a view to the reinstatement of the clause which appeared in the previous draft of this

Ordinance./

The Right Honourable L.C.M.S. AMERY, P.C., M.P.,
His Majesty's Principal Secretary of State
for the Colonies.

-2-

Ordinance.

      I have the honour to be,

        Sir,

      Your most obedient,

          humble servant,

          HIGH COMMISSIONER.

Draft Ordinance to make further
provision for the correction of
the Land Registers.
==================================

BE IT ENACTED BY THE HIGH COMMISSIONER FOR PALESTINE WITH THE ADVICE OF THE ADVISORY COUNCIL THEREOF:

Short Title.

1. This Ordinance may be cited as the Correction of Land Registers Ordinance, 1925.

Definitions.

2. In this Ordinance:

"Land" includes anything attached to the earth or permanently fastened to anything attached to the earth, but does not include minerals.

"Director" means the Director of Lands.

"Official Registers" means the Land Registers of the Government of Palestine.

"Unofficial Land Books" means any books or registers other than the official registers in which a record of title to land or rights in land has been kept.

"Person" includes any corporate body.

Unofficial Land Books to be delivered to Government.

3. (1) Any person, Village Committee, or Local Council having in his or their possession any unofficial land book shall within three months from the date of this Ordinance deliver such book to the Director and shall receive an acknowledgement of its delivery.

Unofficial Land Book undelivered not to be given in evidence.

(2) No unofficial Land-Book which has not been delivered to the Director within the said period of three months shall be pleaded or given in evidence in any Court as affecting any land.

Entry in unofficial Land Book not to be given in evidence.

(3) No entry made in an unofficial land book subsequent to the date of publication of this Ordinance in the Gazette, shall be pleaded or given in evidence in any Court as affecting any land.

Restoration of Books.

(4) The Director may, subject to any regulations made hereunder, restore any unofficial land book to the person, Committee, or Council which has delivered it, provided that he receives a copy of such book.

Penalties for Possession.

(5) Any person, Village Committee, or Local Council found in possession of any such book after three months from the date of this Ordinance, save in the circumstances provided in the preceding sub-section, shall be liable to a fine not exceeding £.500.

4./

-2-

Power to apply for correction of official registers where transaction recorded in unofficial books.	4. (1) Where an unofficial land book has been delivered to the Director, any person who has an interest recorded in such book may apply to the Director for the registration of the interest in the official registers; and, notwithstanding anything in the Ordinance of the Chief Administrator dated 18th November, 1918, concerning the disposition of immovable property, or in the Transfer of Land Ordinance, 1920, and any amendment thereof, any sale, mortgage, lease, partition, or other transaction in land which, prior to the date of this Ordinance, has been recorded in an unofficial land book shall not be deemed to be null and void for the reason only that it was not recorded in the official registers. (2) The application shall be supported by such evidence relating to the interest claimed as the Director may require.
Exclusion of land which is the subject of final judgment.	5. No application under this Ordinance shall be entertained in respect of any interest in land which could have been registered in the official registers in pursuance of the final judgment of a competent Court.
Procedure on application to register.	6. (1) Every application under this Ordinance shall be published for a period of four months in such manner as may be prescribed by regulation hereunder; and the unofficial land books and any maps or plans (of the village or quarter concerned) and all documentary evidence offered in support of such application, shall be open for inspection during that period by any officer of the Department of Lands or by any person claiming an interest in the land to which the application relates. (2) If the land is registered in the official registers, notice of the application shall be served by the applicant upon the registered owner if he is in Palestine, and shall be communicated to him by registered letter if he is out of Palestine. (3) If it appears from the unofficial land books that any person other than the applicant has a recorded interest in the land, notice of the application shall be communicated to him in like manner. (4) The Director may in any appropriate case extend the period within which notice of an adverse claim may be received.

7. The Director may require any person who has a mortgage or charge recorded in the unofficial land books in respect of land which is the subject of an application to produce for his inspection any documents relating to the mortgage or charge, and if required to deliver to him copies thereof.

8./

-3-

Order for registration where no adverse claim.	8. If no adverse claim is made within four months of the publication of the application, or such extended time as the Director may prescribe, the Director may order that the interest claimed shall be registered in the official registers in the name of the applicant, on payment of all the fees leviable on account of transactions recorded in the unofficial land books as having occurred since January 1st, 1919; Provided that the High Commissioner may remit the payment of fees other than the fee that would be payable on the original registration of the interest claimed, if he is satisfied that it was not possible for the transactions recorded in the unofficial land books to have been registered at the time in the official registers.
Procedure where objection raised to registration.	9. (1) If a person having an interest registered in the official registers or the unofficial land books makes objection to the registration within the said period of four months, or any extension thereof duly made by the Director, the Director shall notify the applicant for registration and require him to refer his application within 30 days of such notification to the Land Court of the district in which the land is situate. If the applicant fails to refer his application to the Land Court within such period, no change shall be made in the registration in the official registers.
	(2) If any other person claiming an interest in the land makes objection to the registration within the same period, and notifies the Director thereof in the manner prescribed by Regulation, the Director shall require the person objecting to refer his claim forthwith to the Land Court; and if such person fails to refer the claim within 30 days, the Director shall proceed as if the objection had not been raised.
Powers of the Land Court where objection made to registration.	10. (1) Where an application is referred to the Land Court under the preceding section, the Court may, notwithstanding anything in the enactments mentioned in Section 4 hereof, have regard to all the circumstances of the case, and make such order in the matter as shall be just and equitable.
	(2) The fees payable on an action in the Land Court shall be those prescribed for a possessory action in respect of the land.
Director may retain documents.	11. Where an order has been made for registration in the official registers under this Ordinance, whether by the Director or by the Land Court, the Director may retain possession of any documents produced in support of the application for registration.

12./

-4-

Power reserved in case of a land settlement.

12. If at any time a land settlement is instituted in Palestine, the officer conducting the settlement in an area in which transactions have been recorded in the unofficial land book shall give notice to any person who has an interest recorded in the unofficial land book as well as to the owner registered in the official registers that he proposes to determine the title to the land and is prepared to receive any claim; provided that no such notice shall be given where an objection to registration under this Ordinance has been referred to a Land Court.

Regulations.

13. The High Commissioner in Executive Council may make, and when made may vary or cancel, Regulations for the purpose of giving effect to this Ordinance, and in particular, in the following matters:-

(a) As to the form of application for and objection to registration.

(b) As to the manner of the publication of the application.

(c) As to the form of notice of publication and proof of service thereof.

(d) As to the fees to be paid on an application under this Ordinance and on registration.

(e) As to the restoration of any unofficial land books when the registration has been completed.

Cornwall,
10/4/25.

x x x x x

(e) It would be inequitable to impose payment of back fees, as suggested, and in practice any attempt to do so would break down. It has to be recognised that the responsibility for the failure of people to register rights over immovable property lies primarily with the Government for providing a bad service, and that the only proper and defensible course is for Government to put its service on a sound footing, when registration would be sought and fees/follow. It was not justifiable for a State to provide a bad service and attempt to make use of it obligatory, and in fact such attempts commonly broke down as in this case.

Thus if the postal service was bad, other means of conveying letters would be devised and resorted to by the people: and there would neither be justification for, nor success in, attempting to enforce resort to the bad State service while it remained defective. The only defensible and only sensible course would be to substitute a good postal service for the bad, when the people would gladly use and pay for it.

The Government was justified in continuing an imperfect Land Registry Service faute de mieux pending improvement, and in taking fees for it when resorted to: but it required considerable discretion to pursue this course pending the substitution of a better system, and if Government attempted enforcement of back fees it was challenging a violent outcry against both the scale of its fees in relation to the service rendered, and the use to which those fees had been put by Government during recent years.

x x x x

(Sgd) ERNEST M. DOWSON.

PALESTINE
No. 1335

DOWNING STREET
5 October, 1925.

My Lord,

I have the honour to acknowledge the receipt of Your Lordship's despatch No.1069 of the 10th of September, forwarding a revised draft of the Ordinance to provide for the correction of land registers.

2. As regards the request that further consideration should be given to the proposal that the payment of back fees should be made a condition of the registration of land in regard to which transactions are shown in unofficial land books, I have to inform you that it appears to me that when the Palestine Government registers an interest in land and thereby legalise the results of a transaction which was formerly illegal by reason of its not being registered, that Government can properly claim to be paid the appropriate fee in respect of any illegal transactions which it is, in effect, thus recognising. I should for this reason have preferred to maintain Clause 6 in the form in which it appears in the revised draft but, if you strongly hold the contrary view, the Ordinance may be re-drafted to provide that only the fee payable on the original registration of the interest claimed shall be chargeab

3. The words "of the village or quarter concern should be omitted from Clause 6(1) of the draft
Ordinance

HIGH COMMISSIONER
FIELD MARSHAL
THE RIGHT HONOURABLE
LORD PLUMER, G.C.B., G.C.M.G., G.C.V.O., G.B.E.,
&c.   &c.   &c.

Ordinance, since they are otiose, and the meaning of the expression "quarter" is not clear.

4. Subject to this small amendment and to any amendment to Clause 8 which you may consider to be necessary in the light of the second paragraph of this despatch, I approve the enactment of the Ordinance.

I have the honour to be,

My Lord,

Your Lordship's most obedient

humble Servant,

(Sgd.) L. S. AMERY.

3.04

PALESTINE.

CONFIDENTIAL.

Reference No.15612/26.

GOVERNMENT OFFICES,
JERUSALEM.

8th October, 1926.

Sir,

I have the honour to forward for your information copies of (1) the report of a Committee appointed by Lord Plumer to recommend measures which could be taken in advance of systematic land settlement to replace the present system of collection of tithe, and (2) a Minority Report rendered by the Chairman of this Committee.

2. I also forward the observations by the District Commissioners on these two reports. You will observe that they are substantially in agreement with the recommendations made in the Majority Report.

3. The matter is one of vital importance to the whole agricultural population of the country and, as such, it is desirable to endeavour to elicit an expression of public opinion upon it. The need for this is increased by the fact that the recommendations in the Majority Report, if put into effect, would depend for their success principally upon public endorsement of and co-operation with the scheme proposed.

4. With these considerations in view I propose, subject to your consent, to publish the Majority and Minority Reports of the Committee with certain excisions of paragraphs relating to a reduction in the rate of tithe and cognate

questions/

The Right Honourable L.C.M.S. AMERY, P.C., M.P.,
 His Majesty's Principal Secretary of State
  for the Colonies.

- 2 -

questions. The reports would then be discussed in a series of small conferences convened by District Commissioners at which the state of public opinion as to the merits of the recommendations in the Majority Report could be fairly reliably ascertained. It would of course be made perfectly clear that these recommendations were still under consideration. I should be grateful if you would inform me by telegraph if you approve this publication.

       I have the honour to be,
        Sir,
      Your most obedient,
       humble servant,

       G.B. Symes

    OFFICER ADMINISTERING THE GOVERNMENT.

C O P Y.

480(16)4438.   26th July 1926.

Sir,

I have the honour to refer to your letter No.3347/26 of the 12th March, 1926, on the subject of the appointment and terms of reference (a copy of which is attached for facility of reference) of a Committee to consider and report what measures can be taken in advance of Land Settlement to replace the existing system of collection of tithe by the collection of revenue on an annual assessment for a term of years, and to forward three copies of the report of the Committee and a minute of dissent by the Chairman.

I have the honour to be,
Sir,
Your obedient servant,

(Sgd) W.J.Johnson
Chairman.

The Chief Secretary,
Government Offices.

C O P Y.

APPOINTMENT OF COMMITTEE.

His Excellency the High Commissioner has been pleased to appoint the undermentioned officers as a Committee:-

(i) To consider and report what measures can be advantageously taken in advance of Land Settlement to replace the existing system of collection of tithe on the products of the soil by the collection of revenue on an annual assessment for a term of years.

(ii) To recommend whether such measures shall be applied tentatively or definitely, compulsorily or optionally, to the whole country at once or by order to selected crops or areas.

(iii) To state what if any consequent increases of savings in staff or other costs of collection they envisage.

(iv) To embody their recommendations in a form that will enable the legal advisers of Government to frame legislation to give effect to the proposal made.

Chairman: W.J.Johnson, Esquire, Treasury.
Members : R.E.H.Crosbie, Esquire, M.C.
          District Administration.
       F.G.Lowick, Esquire,
          District Administration.

The Attorney General will be available for tendering legal advice to the Committee.

The Secretary to the Committee will be C.L.Horton, Esquire, Secretariat.

BY COMMAND.

(Signed) G.S.Symes,

12th March, 1926.   Chief Secretary.

C O P Y.

AVERAGE TITHE COMMITTEE.

MAJORITY REPORT.

It seems desirable at the outset of this Report to emphasise a certain peculiarity in the Terms of Reference. Most Committees of Enquiry are called upon to recommend the best solution of the given problem that they can devise, and are at liberty to design to that end elaborate machinery that may take years to perfect. The present Committee is called upon to propose an interim measure to bridge over the period till the machinery for a more comprehensive solution becomes available. In justice, therefore, any solution now offered must be compared, not with the ideal system of the future, but with the actual system of to-day. It might fairly be condemned on the ground that it was no better than the present system, or not sufficiently better to compensate the evils of change; but it cannot fairly be condemned on the ground that it is not so good as a future system not yet practicable.

2. Our Terms of Reference seem to imply acceptance of the view held by us that the best final solution of the present problem is a Land Tax; but that a fully satisfactory Land Tax cannot be introduced without an elaborate fiscal survey. Our information is that such a survey could not be completed in less than ten years. We are of opinion that this is too long a period for which to tolerate the present system, and that an effort should be made to devise a temporary system possessing as many as possible of the advantages of a Land Tax.

3. Certain of the objections to the present system are directly due to <u>the annual recurrence of assessments</u>. Under this head come the inconveniences and the actual losses arising from the inevitable delays of assessment: viz: loss of time; loss of crops by insects, by theft, by fire; loss of early high prices. Other objections are due to the <u>arbitrary nature of assessment</u>. These include the guessing of the amount of crops owned by each tithe-payer; the guessing of the price that the tithe-payer will obtain for it; the neglect of various considerations, such as the cost of production, of improvements and of transport.

4. Any form of fixed assessment will eliminate objections of the former class. It will also alleviate objections of the latter class in so far as it substitutes a single arbitrary assessment, which can be carefully controlled, for an annual series of arbitrary assessments which for sheer lack of time cannot be so carefully controlled. It is improbable that even a regular Land Tax, based on a general cadastral and fiscal survey, will entirely eliminate the arbitrary element.

5. The replacement of Tithes by a fixed assessment is open, of course, to certain objections based on loss of elasticity and the dangers of innovation. Certain sections of the population have already expressed
themselves/

- 2 -

themselves in favour of this innovation and we believe that the bulk of the remainder would soon come to appreciate it. For ourselves we are of opinion that the advantages of a fixed assessment far outweigh its disadvantages. We do not propose, however, to labour this point, as we are convinced that opposition to a fixed assessment is based not on principle but on the ground that it is impracticable. We shall endeavour to show that this is not the case.

6. The present Tithe involves two variable factors: viz: <u>the Tithe in Kind and the Redemption Price</u>. It <u>would be possible to commute only the former to a fixed assessment in kind and to leave the latter variable</u>. The obvious method of commutation would be to strike an average based on an adequate series of years. In view of the biennial olive cycle, with its major and minor year, it is desirable that the number of years should be even. The period of six complete financial years from its establishment of the Civil Government to the present time (1920/21 - 1925/26) would therefore appear to be suitable. This solution would eliminate all losses of crops at present caused by the delays of estimation and inspection, but would not eliminate the serious yearly difficulty of fixing redemption prices.

7. <u>It would be possible also to fix Redemption Prices once for all or for a selected period.</u> These prices might be based on the averages for a series of years. Since in the early years of the Palestine Government the prices of crops were abnormal, it is suggested that only the past four years (1922/23 - 1925/26) should be included in such a basis. Average market prices would not constitute a suitable basis as they obviously do not represent the prices obtained by the cultivator for his crops. The conversion at average redemption prices of average tithes in kind would give a fixed assessment, possessing the advantages, and subject to the disadvantages, already described.

8. <u>Thirdly, it would be possible to take the average for a series of years of the value of tithes in money.</u> For the reason explained in the preceding paragraph, we are of opinion that the past four years (1922/23 - 1925/26) would afford a suitable basis. The 12½% rate for the first three years would of course be adjusted to the present 10% rate. This method like the second, would give a fixed assessment, but the process of calculation would be much simpler for the Government to effect and for the people to understand.

9. At first sight it might appear that a crop average was more likely to be stable than a price average; and therefore that the best system would be to fix averages of tithes in kind but to determine redemption prices anew each year. It is probable, however, that a large crop tends to produce a low redemption price and vice versa, and that consequently the combination of the two in the money value tends to be more stable than either factor taken separately.

In any/

- 3 -

In any event, the attached Schedule A shows that the results obtained:-

(a) by converting a six years' average for Tithes in kind at a four years' average for Redemption Prices;

(b) by converting the same six years' average for Tithes in Kind at the latest Redemption Prices (1925/26);

(c) by taking a four years' average of Tithes in Money;

do not differ greatly from one another. We are therefore of opinion that the basis of the fixed assessment should be the average of Tithes in Money for the past four years (1922/23 - 1925/26).

9. a.   The necessary figures for each village in Palestine taken as a whole are available in the various Revenue Offices. If village assessments only were required, we believe that, though there would be some differences of opinion concerning the best form of average and on other point of detail, there would be no objection in principle to the scheme.

10.   The difficulty lies in distributing among the individual tithe-payers of non-Mushaa villages the amount assessed (by averaging) on the village as a whole. The owners of fruit-trees, such as oranges or olives, change little; and we believe that sufficient data usually exist for determining the average assessments of these individual owners. With cereals and other rotation crops, however, the position is different. Owing mainly to the prevalent system of agricultural "partnerships", lists of nominal tithe-payers change so much that it is impossible to trace any sequence. It is also impossible to identify any particular payment with a specific parcel of land. In Mushaa villages distribution would of course be in proportion to individual shares.

11.   Precisely the same problem arose under the tithe- farming system in Turkish times when villagers contracted for the payment of their own tithes; precisely the same problem has arisen in Syria to-day. In each case the same solution has been adopted, viz: that of allowing the villagers to effect the distribution themselves. The process is familiar to them for the ordinary purposes of village life. We are of opinion that, if such a distribution were subject to the control of the local District Officer, it would be substantially fair - and, at the lowest, as fair as the present system of estimation.

12.   It may be argued that some criterion is necessary for judging any complaints that might be lodged against such a distribution. We are of opinion that a satisfactory criterion could be found in the potential productivity of the land in terms of wheat. We are informed that this principle was adopted for the commutation of tithe in England, but we have been unable to verify this information. All land of the class now under

consideration/

- 4 -

consideration is sown in the ordinary course of crop rotation with wheat; the local cultivators habitually describe the area of any plot of land in terms of the wheat seed required to sow it and are familiar with the average yield from that amount of seed (five-fold, ten-fold etc); and any outside cultivator familiar with the conditions, could estimate both these amounts at least with as great accuracy as he could estimate the amount of grain on a threshing-floor. The attached schedule 'C' will indicate the nature of the procedure proposed.

13. The effect of this arrangement should be to attach an approximate relative valuation to each parcel of land. The parcel would often bear a local name, and could be further identified by rough measurements with ropes or rods according to local custom. The "reputed owner" of the land would then be responsible for the commuted tithe, and would provide for this liability when making arrangements with his "partners". While it is usually impossible to identify a parcel of land from the Tabu Records, no such difficulty exists in the village, where boundaries and reputed owners are familiar to all. We are advised that it would be possible to provide in legislation that such recognition of "reputed ownership" should not constitute any legal claims to the land. Apart from all other considerations, the system outlined above would have the merit of paving the way for a regular Land Tax.

14. We have examined other conceivable methods of distributing the village total among individuals. It has been suggested that, if the average tithe were determined in kind, distribution might be made in proportion to the amount of each crop grown in a given year by each individual. Reflection shows that such a system would be inequitable. For example, the average number of cultivators of sesame in a given village for the past six years might be twenty or thirty. Next year, for some reason or other, the number might drop to two or three. These two or three would then have to bear the whole weight of the commuted sesame tithe, designed to be borne by ten times the number. The result would be that, if the number of cultivators of any particular crop decreases, the remaining cultivators would gradually be driven to abandon the cultivation of it.

15. The only other method of distribution that seems at all feasible is to distribute the average tithe in proportion to werko. It is extremely difficult to obtain any accurate statistics with regard to Werko, or even to obtain figures for agricultural land separately from buildings. We are of opinion, however, that the existing assessment of Werko is so uneven that this basis would lead to grave injustice. As long as Werko only is involved, this assessment may be tolerated on the grounds that it is familiar, and that the amount to be paid is comparatively small. If Commuted Tithe were distributed on the same basis, the inequality of incidence would be increased in proportion to the greater amount to be paid, and the novelty of the system would exaggerate the grievance.

16/

- 5 -

16.   A variation of the previous suggestion would be to abandon the tithe altogether, and to substitute for it an addition to the Werko - for example, to raise it to 1c%o (1%). This variation would of course be open to the same objections as the original proposal, and would involve a greater change of principle.

17.   We therefore recommend that an Average Tithe in Money on cereals and other rotation crops should be calculated for each village, and that the total amount for each village should be distributed among the individual tithe-payers of the village in proportion to the potential productivity of their lands estimated in terms of wheat. We recommend that this distribution should be carried out in the first instance by the villagers themselves, and should then be inspected and (where necessary) revised by the local District Officer, assisted by suitable assessors. Average Tithes in Money on fruits should be calculated by Government direct for individual tithe-payers. We confine ourselves here to an enunciation of the general principles that we recommend. Questions of detail will be dealt with later.

18.   It is an axiom that a fixed assessment should be low in comparison with a fluctuating assessment. We, therefore, venture to recommend that, if our proposals should be adopted, the opportunity should be taken to make a suitable reduction in the amount that would otherwise be assessed on each village. The percentage of such a reduction we feel to be a matter for the Treasury rather than the present Committee. It would be necessary to provide for remissions of taxation in exceptional circumstances. In ordinary bad years, we are of opinion that postponement of payment should be the limit of concession.

19.   We recommend that the measures should be applied definitely and compulsorily to the whole country (and, from the nature of the measures, to all crops), at the beginning of the next financial year. Any attempt to apply them partially would lead to constant fraud, as villages which still followed the old estimation system would deposit their crops with villages that had a fixed assessment. It may be added that few villages would possess the initiative to apply for an innovation, even if they were inclined to believe in its advantages.

20.   We recommend that the individual assessments determined by Village Committees shall be revised by a Commission comprising the local District Officer and two suitable assessors who have no interest in the village concerned. It is obviously impossible to make with any accuracy an estimate of the cost of applying the scheme. However in view of our Terms of Reference we surmise that the work of revision would occupy, on an average, three days per village. Since there are some 1030 villages in Palestine and 15 Sub-Districts, the average number of villages in a Sub-District is about 69. On this basis each Sub-District would occupy one Revising Commission 3 x 69 = 137 days, or, in round figures, six months. If more commissions were appointed, the work would, of course, be completed sooner, but the total working time

would/

- 6 -

would remain unchanged. A Tithe Inspector at the present time receives £.30-40 for work occupying about two months. At the same rate of pay, a Revising Commission with two assessors would cost £.30-40 each month, or about £.200 for the whole six months required in a Sub-District. For the whole country, therefore, the cost of Revising Commissions would be about £.3,000. In addition, we consider that a local village clerk would be required for about a month to record the assessments of each Village Committee. We think it preferable that the Government should pay these clerks and we estimate the average cost per village should not exceed £.5. On this basis clerks for the whole 1030 villages would cost £.5,150. When this sum is added to the £.3,000 for Revising Commissions, the total cost would be about £.8,150, which is rather less than the budgetary figure of £.8,500 for the cost of Tithe Estimation in the year 1925-26. Even if this estimate should need to be doubled, tripled or quadrupled in the first year, the scheme would still pay its way; for in all subsequent years the whole cost of tithe estimation would be saved. Any later adjustments that might be required, arising out of sale, succession or new plantation, could be effected in the ordinary course of administrative work in the Districts.

21. It is desirable to point out that, if an Average Tithe is to be adopted, the Moslem Supreme Council will be concerned as far as Wakf Tithes are concerned. As proposals for an Average Tithe have already emanated from that quarter, it seems that no objections need be anticipated from there.

22. Special provision is required for tribal areas, where the extent of land under cultivation differs considerably from year to year, and inquiries into individual holdings are almost impracticable. A slight modification of procedure in tribal areas will, therefore, be necessary.

23. If ordinary agricultural land is converted into plantations, the Average Tithe based on its former productivity would in the ordinary course continue to be payable, though for a number of years the land in its new condition will be unproductive. To encourage enterprise among cultivators, we have provided for temporary exemption from taxation in genuine cases of this kind.

24. One class of land calls for special consideration, viz: irrigated market gardens producing vegetables. On account of the diversity of vegetables grown, the varying number of crops produced annually and the difficulty of identifying with the land the tithes assessments during the past four years, it is impossible to calculate an average tithe on these gardens. There appear to be three methods of dealing with the difficulty. It would be possible entirely to abolish the tithe on vegetables; we are of opinion that to create a class of land exempt from taxation would form an undesirable precedent. It would be possible, while maintaining the legal distinction between Mulk and Miri, to abolish the tithe and substitute Werko at Mulk rates (10%). It would be possible to regard these lands as ordinary general cultivation lands

and/

and assess in the manner suggested for such lands. We are of opinion that this last expedient would in general be the least objectionable.

25. We venture to go somewhat beyond our terms of reference, and to recommend further that the total amount of Werko assessed on the agricultural land of a village should be added to the total Average Tithe in Money and that the combined total should be distributed among individuals on the lines already proposed. Many of the fundamental Werko Registers are missing, and those that exist are inaccurate and out of date. Hence, in many villages at the present time, the total Werko assessment for the village is distributed by the villagers themselves, in the manner we have recommended for the Average Tithe. In Musha'a villages (which constitute perhaps half the number of villages in Palestine), the distribution is made in proportion to shares of Musha'a land, and, therefore, effectively, in proportion to the potential productivity of the land owned by each tax payer. In non-Musha'a villages, distribution seems to be based with a similar result on a local and fluctuating unit known as the "feedan". The great advantage of the arrangement would be that only one tithe-tax payment would have to be made by the people and collected by the Government with a resulting economy to the latter and a saving of annoyance to the former. We are of opinion also that, in many instances, the equitability of Werko payments would be substantially increased. The proposed tax might be described as Consolidated Tithe and Werko, or more shortly, as Consolidated Tax. We do not urge that consolidation should be effected immediately; but we are of opinion that it would be desirable as a further step towards the final Land Tax.

26. If an Average Tithe is introduced, it will presumably be necessary to enact that the Law of State Collections should apply to it. We suggest that the occasion would be suitable for bringing the collection law up to date. At present it is still drafted to suit the procedure of the old Turkish Regime.

27. We have thought it unnecessary at present to supplement the proposed legislation with draft administrative regulations under the proposed law. We are prepared, however, to submit such regulations if it be desired.

28. We proceed to submit our proposals in a form suitable for draft legislation.

(Sgd) R.E.H.Crosbie.
" F.G.Lowick.

Jerusalem.
29th June, 1926.

Schedule A.1.

COMPARATIVE TABLE.

Average Quantities of principal crops for six years 1920/1 to 1925/26. Metric Tons	Government & Wakf Tithe share adjusted to 10% in metric tons.	Value in £. at Av.R.P. for 4 years 1922/25 to 1925/26.	Value in £. at latest R.P. 1925/26	Average Tithe in Money on all crops for four years 22/23-25/26
		£.	£.	£.
Wheat : 85,773	8,577	84,912	128,655	
Barley : 41,322	4,132	30,164	41,320	
Lentils : 3,955	395	3,476	5,411	
Korsenneh : 7,265	726	6,316	9,293	
Beans : 4,639	464	3,944	5,939	
Peas : 1,682	168	1,462	2,184	
Water Melons : 21,509	2,151	5,378	5,162	
Sweet Melons : 522	52	411	390	
Grapes Dessert : 5,199	520	4,992	5,720	
Grapes Wine : 3,118	312	1,342	1,404	
Durrah : 25,138	2,514	18,352	23,380	
Sesame : 3,120	312	6,646	8,674	
Olives : 2,083	208	2,350	2,933	
Clive Oil : 3,529	353	19,097	19,415	
Orange and Lemons Boxes : 901,802	80,180	16,196 ~~161,196~~	18,273	
		(x) £.205,038	(x) 278,153	230,915

(x) These two totals do not include the minor crops, the tithe on which amounts roughly to £.20,000 per annum.

Schedule A.2.

Comparative Table of Tithe and Werko Assessments.

	1920-1	1921-2	1922-3	1923-4	1924-5	1925-6	Average Tithe for six years.	Average Tithe for 4 years 1922-3 to 1925-6.
	£.	£.	£.	£.	£.	£.	£.	£.
Total Assessments of Treasury and Wakfs Tithes	512,680	287,778	240,825	208,886	306,813	318,442		
Adjusted to 4/5.	410,144	230,222	192,660	167,109	245,450	318,442	260,671	230,915
Werko on Agricultural lands estimated at 4/5 of Total Werko Assessment.	114,644	118,144	128,660	134,720	141,880	151,684	151,684	151,684
	524,788	348,366	321,320	301,829	387,330	470,126	412,355	382,599

Schedule A.3.

Total Assessment of Principal Crops
(In Metric Tons).

	1920-21	1921-22	1922-23	1923-24	1924-25	1925-26	Average for six years
Wheat	78,153	72,885	87,146	86,457	92,192	100,807	85,775
Barley	31,869	61,328	35,383	26,386	32,310	40,658	41,322
Lentils	3,211	4,792	5,593	4,788	2,931	2,415	3,955
Kersenneh	4,887	7,649	7,818	9,844	7,983	5,407	7,265
Beans	2,186	4,948	7,275	6,551	4,511	2,365	4,639
Peas	3,444	2,064	781	1,070	1,296	1,438	1,682
Water Melons	16,351	18,305	19,550	20,625	24,429	29,793	21,509
Sweet Melons		132	457	527	822	670	522
Grapes Dessert	5,490	6,756	6,259	4,298	4,803	3,586	5,199
Grapes Wine	-	-	-	3,119	2,790	3,446	3,118
Durrah	30,353	14,819	23,527	16,353	33,905	31,869	25,138
Sesame	2,488	2,977	3,398	3,654	3,613	2,593	3,120
Olives	-	405	3,755	1,117	3,865	1,275	2,083
Olive Oil	6,706	594	3,297	2,984	4,901	2,692	3,529
Oranges and Lemons. (Boxes)	537,043	718,780	757,746	892,796	956,191	948,256	801,802

ANNEX B.

Detailed Proposals for Draft Legislation.

1. As from   the annual tithe in its present form shall be abolished and shall be replaced by a fixed tithe based on the average tithe in money assessed during the four financial years 1922-23 to 1925-26.

2. The average tithe shall be assessed on the village unit. The assessment shall show the amounts due in respect of (a) general cultivation lands and (b) plantations of each variety of fruit bearing tree. These amounts shall be made up of the average tithe in cash on the respective categories; provided that when, during the period on which the average tithe is based, crops have been transferred from the lands of one village to the threshing floor of another or village boundaries have been modified, the District Commissioner may cause the village assessments to be amended.

3. The amount due in respect of agricultural lands other than lands planted with fruit bearing trees shall be assessed on the principles prescribed hereafter upon the individual reputed owners of the village lands by a Committee representing them; provided that, if the reputed owners fail to elect a Committee, the District Commissioner may appoint a Committee. The assessments determined by the Committee shall be subjected to revision by a senior officer of the District Administration assisted by suitable assessors.

4. When the village lands are Musha'a, the assessments on individuals shall be proportionate to the shares held by each.

5. When the village lands are "Mufrus", the assessments on individuals shall be proportionate to the potential productivity of the land in their reputed ownership estimated in terms of wheat.

6. The amounts due in respect of lands planted with fruit bearing trees will be assessed upon the reputed owners by Government on the basis of the average tithe paid by them during the four years 1922-23 to 1925-26 in respect of each variety of plantation; provided that should the relevant records be defective, the assessment shall be determined on the average productivity by a village committee in the manner prescribed in Articles 3, 4 and 5.

7. In tribal areas the total assessment for each tribal unit shall be assessed upon individual reputed owners by a Tribal Committee in accordance with Bedouin Custom, subject to the control of the District Officer.

8. The Average Tithe shall be paid by the reputed owners of lands in accordance with the assessments made upon them. The provisions of the Ottoman Law for the Collection of Taxes of the 18th August 1909 and as amended shall apply to the Average Tithe.

- 2 -

9. The exemptions from tithe already sanctioned by law shall apply to the Average Tithe. In addition the High Commissioner may from time to time prescribe by public notice that lands planted with specified varieties of fruit trees shall be exempted from the payment of Average Tithe for such periods as may be laid down. At the end of the period for which the exemption has been granted the plantation will be assessed in the manner prescribed in the proviso to Article 6.

10. The High Commissioner may authorise the remission or postponement of payment of the Average Tithe, in the event of total or partial failure of crops.

11. The Average Tithe shall be payable in four equal instalments which shall fall due on the 15th August, 15th September, 15th October and 15th November respectively; provided that if the application of these dates shall cause hardship to owners of late maturing crops, the District Commissioner may vary these dates.

Annex C.

VILLAGE PROPORTIONATE ASSESSMENT SCHEDULE.

Average Tithe ....Village............ General Cultivation, Lands............ Sub-District

Serial No.	Cultivator	Locality	Plot	Adjoining Owners	Seed Wheat	Total Average Yield	Average Tithe Assessment	Observation

Minute of dissent.

The main recommendations of the majority report are as under:-

(1) The commutation of the tithe of the village or tribe on the basis of the average tithe revenue of the preceding four years.

(2) The apportionment of the commuted tithe among taxpayers by village or tribal committees, according to the class of land and the nature of produce, as under:

    (a) In the case of Musha' land (undivided or common land) under cereal and general crops, in proportion to the number of shares held by each.

    (b) In the case of Mafrus lands (divided land) under cereal and general crops, according to the potential productivity of the holding measured in terms of wheat.

    (c) In the case of lands planted with fruit trees, according to the average tithe of the preceding four years, or, when this is impracticable, according to the method adopted for cereal and general crops.

    (d) In the case of tribal areas, in accordance with Bedouin custom.

(3) The exemption from tax of crops at present exempted from tithe, and, in addition, of lands planted with certain varieties of fruit trees.

(4) The High Commissioner to have the power to remit or postpone collection of the tax in the event of total or partial failure of crops.

(5) The addition of the land tax (Werko) on titheable lands to the commuted tithe of the village.

2. I dissent from these recommendations for the following reasons:-

(1) The system of apportionment of a fixed land tax among villages on the basis of the average of four years' revenue from tithes is inelastic in yield and defective in distribution in that it takes no cognisance of successive changes, and alleviation by remission of tax in the event of failure of crops means a loss to Government both in bad seasons and on the average in good seasons.

(2) The system of distribution of the fixed land tax among reputed landowners or cultivators indicated in para 1 (2) preceding are more imperfect in their attempt to arrive at the true value of land as the object of taxation and to tax the agriculturist according to his ability to pay taxation and his power to carry over from a good to/bad season than the existing system of collection of tithe on the products of the soil.

(3) /

- 2 -

(3) The identification of particular holdings in villages and the registration of owners or cultivators for the purposes of distribution of the tax are impracticable in the absence of reliable data, and no suggestion is made for the collection of the tax from absentee owners or for recording changes in holdings and cultivation.

(4) The utilisation of the villager as his own assessor, subject to inspection by administrative officers, increases the facilities for speculation and general abuse.

(5) The exemption from tax of land under crops at present exempted from tithe, and lands planted with certain varieties of fruit trees, is unjustifiable from the point of view of revenue policy alone.

(6) The addition of existing assessments of Werko on titheable lands to the commuted tithe of the village is inequitable, owing to the different nature of the systems and inequalities in assessments.

(7) The change for a maximum period of ten years from the old-established and simple system of a tax on the products of the soil to a new and complicated system of a fixed annual charge on the land would have an unsettling effect on the collection of revenue and the agricultural industry itself.

3. It is true that the Mesha' system provides for the temporary partitioning of lands for the purpose of cultivation, but the considerable differences that occur in the nature of titles to shares, and the variety of methods in which partitions are made (x) render the system unadaptable for fiscal purposes; apart from this there is no reliable record of holders of shares of Mesha' lands. It must be realised, also, in the case of other lands that there is no reliable data of any sort on which to estimate the potential productivity of holdings. It is clear, therefore, that the unification of procedure for distributing the tax will be more difficult than under the existing tithe system, and that any deficiency in this respect alone may increase existing inequalities in the incidence and effects of taxation, and the opportunities for evasion. Moreover, apportionment of the tax on the basis of potential productivity is virtually a tax on unimproved values, and measurement in terms of wheat amounts to a surtax on lands cultivated with inferior crops, which convey the impression of an attempt to drive the cultivator, who is unable to work his land to its utmost capacity, to dispose of his holding. It must also be realised that in the majority of cases the burden of the tithe falls on the cultivator who is at once the producer and the chief consumer of local agricultural products: and that a proportional tax on actual yields is more within the ability of the cultivator to pay taxation than the commuted tithe distributed in a manner that has no relation to the cultivator's actual income. It is well to remember, also, that the tithe system arose out of the ruler's past proprietorship of the soil, and that any change in the system before the settlement of land policy and of the land itself may prejudice Government's interests in land.

4/

(x) See Appendix A.

- 3 -

4. I consider that there is no practical substitute for the existing tithe system in advance of Land Settlement, and that the success of any change depends mainly on a uniform and equitable assessment of land values and a rate of tax that will approximate the taxpayer's ability to pay in bad as well as in good seasons.

(Sgd) W.J.Johnson

Chairman.

Submitted by Mr. J.E.F. Campbell, O.B.E.,
District Commissioner, Jerusalem-Southern District.

NOTES ON THE TITHE COMMISSION REPORT.

The Majority Reports recommends two main changes:-

A. Commutation of Tithe to the average of the last four years.

B. Distribution of Werko on the same basis as the Commuted Tithe.

Of these A has been consistently urged by the Agricultural Department for years, and is strongly supported by the bulk of public opinion and of Administrative judgment throughout the District.

On the other hand B is a new suggestion arising out of a practical desire to simplify collection.

It is relatively unimportant. Wherever Werko is in fact distributed within the village on the same principle as that proposed for the Commuted Tithe, the addition of one tax to the other will be automatic, and collection will be simplified. In other cases, adoption of the recommendation will necessitate somewhat arbitrary changes in the incidence of werko, and will ignore the development of new properties, and changes of ownership.

I consider that it would be advisable to reject recommendation B for the present, and to concentrate on the main issue of Commutation of Tithe.

2. Opinion though overwhelmingly in favour of Commutation has wavered between (1) a crop average i.e. a fixed average in kind coupled with a variable redemption price,

and (2) a price average i.e. a fixed average in money.

The Majority Report shows that there is little difference between the total financial yield in each case, and decides in favour of (2) i.e. a price average.

At first sight the crop average seems preferable. It is more elastic and is a compromise between the varying tithe and the fixed land tax. But in practice it will add considerably to the complication of a system which should be made as simple as possible.

The same crop ripens in Jericho or Beersheba some months before it is harvested in the North. Market prices may vary considerably in the interval, so that for a given crop the Redemption Price may have to vary both chronologically and geographically. Over forty kinds of winter crops alone may occur in the same village. Again once the tithe is commuted there is no obligation for the same crops to be grown so that the application of a varying Redemption Price to a fictitious

scale/

- 2 -

scale of crops is no guarantee of equity to a given cultivator or even to a given village. The prospect of continuing the periodic controversy over Redemption Prices, is one which is not likely to be met with enthusiasm by either the public or the Administrative officer.

As the Majority Report has shown, a price average differs little, in the total burden on the tax payers, from a crop average plus a varying redemption price. It is immensely simpler. The farmer knows exactly what tax he has to pay, and the Government has corresponding accounting advantages.

I would support therefore the decision arrived at in the Majority Report in favour of a price average i.e. an Average Tithe in Money.

3.   The rest of the Majority Report suggests no fundamental change. The methods of apportioning the Commuted Tithe among tax payers of a village or tribe are all methods which are carried out to-day in some or all parts of the country. These methods are based on accurate local and common knowledge, of which judicial notice is taken every day in the Courts, and on which Land Settlement will merely superpose documentary record. Every detail of individual shares and holdings or relative productivity of lands is locally known and jealously guarded so that the chances of individual injustice are practically small.

The Majority Report has I consider demonstrated successfully that the Commuted Tithe is practicable, by utilising methods already in operation throughout the country.

4.   In regard to the reasons for dissent given in the Minority Report: (1) (a) The objection that the Commuted Tithe is inelastic in yield applies equally to the land tax which is universally admitted to be preferable to either a variable or a fixed assessment of tithe.

(b) That it takes no cognisance of successive changes and is therefore defective in distribution is obviously incorrect if changes of tithe are meant, since the vendor will see that the purchaser pays the tax. If changes of productivity are meant, the fixed tithe, like the Land Tax, will place a premium on good farming and therefore will remove the defects in distribution of a variable tithe which favours the bad farmer.

(c) That the Government will lose in the end because remission only favours the cultivator is an argument which cannot be seriously meant, as is shown by the proposals for substantial relief of the Tithe Payer in the positive recommendations of the Minority Report.

(2) The statement that the proposed systems of distribution of the fixed tithe are inferior to the existing tithe is an academic proposition which will find no support amongst those with practical experience of the losses involved to the cultivator and of the gross inaccuracies and unfairness of the present system.

(3) /

- 3 -

(3) The objection that the proposed methods of distribution are impracticable has already been discussed in para 3 above. 'Absentee owners' present no greater difficulty than fluctuating 'partners' in existing tithes, and the former already have to be dealt with in werko. Changes of ownership or cultivation have already been referred to in (B) above.

(4) Facilities for peculation and general abuse are far less in a system where a given sum is to be apportioned publicly between a large number of villagers with accurate local knowledge of mutual rights, than where a paid estimator is exposed to corrupt offers, in an estimation where the margin of error is amply sufficient to hide detection.

(5) The positive recommendations of the Minority Report propose the very exemptions which are here described as unjustifiable.

(6) As submitted in para 1 above the Majority recommendation in regard to amalgamation of Werko with Tithe is not vital to the main issue, and its consideration may well be postponed.

(7) (a) If the present Tithe system is allowed to remain it cannot be changed to a Land Tax sub-district by sub-district as the survey is completed, since villages round the border will transfer their crops to the sub-district where the tithe has been replaced by a fixed tax. On the other hand commutation of the tithe will make progressive substitution of a land tax possible. The choice therefore lies between a fixed tithe progressively changing to a land tax on the one hand, or on the other continuance of the present pernicious system until the survey is completed for the whole country, i.e. for a minimum not a maximum period of 10 years.

(b) The description of the present system as 'simple' and the proposed as 'complicated', and the fear of an unsettling effect of the latter on revenue collection and agriculture appear to have no foundation in fact, as refererence to the departments concerned will show.

5. The criticism in regard to utilising 'Masha' shares is based on an apparent misconception. The variety of origin of various systems of 'Musha' division and the constant re-division of holdings to correspond to the 'Musha' shares are equally irrelevant to the practical problem of finding a means of apportioning a fixed tithe amongst the villagers. Musha' shares which affect about the half the country completely solve the problem to that extent. There are really only two systems of holding Musha' shares, the 'sahm' system and 'zakur'. The latter is so rare as to be almost negligible. Under the former system shares are definitely and permanently known. Under the latter they are definitely known for the period of each partition. In both cases there is no difficulty in determining shares and records are found to be reliable enough to be the only basis for Werko in most Musha' villages.

6. The reference in the same paragraph of the Minority Report to the proposed basis of division, in cases of dispute on potential wheat productivity appears to miss the essence of the suggestion which is to use wheat as a proportionate means of apportioning a fixed sum and not as an absolute measure of

taxation./

- 4 -

taxation. Any other crop for the whole village would do equally for the calculation. It is therefore in no sense a tax on unimproved values nor a surtax on lands cultivated with inferior crops. The opportunities for evasion are clearly less with a fixed tithe and a registered tax payer than with shifting 'partners' and the possibilities of concealing crops. The other considerations raised have no more weight against a fixed tithe than against a Land Tax.

7. The temporary relief suggested in the constructive sections of the minority report will not affect the main problem and is open to a series of objections. Abolition of tithe on selected crops creates a class of land exempt from taxation. Estimation already costs too much. Further, expenditure will only palliate not cure the main evils of yearly assessment.

Threshing machines are practically limited to Jewish and German Colonies.

Standing crop estimation has its own difficulties especially where cultivation is widely scattered.

8. I would recommend:-

(a) immediate adoption of the Majority Report with the exception of the proposal to amalgamate Werko with Commuted Tithe;

(b) acceptance of the principle that the Commuted Tithe will be replaced by the Land Tax in each Sub-District as soon as the progress of Survey makes this possible.

C O P Y.

No.1082/2.

DISTRICT COMMISSIONER'S OFFICE
HAIFA.

August 25, 1926.

Chief Secretary,
Jerusalem.

        Subject   : Average Tithe Committee.
        Reference : Your 10622/26 of July 27th, 1926.

        I have to express the following opinions on the proposals contained in the reports:-

1.   It is submitted that the commission was appointed to report on what measures can be taken in advance of land settlement to replace the existing system of collection of tithe by the collection of revenue, based on an annual assessment for a term of years, because it was represented to His Excellency the High Commissioner that an annual estimation entails considerable loss of time and money on the cultivator, it subjects him to annually recurrent annoyance, and it involves the Government in heavy annual expenditure.

2.   Although their terms of reference suggested the alternative to an annual estimation, it is assumed that if the members of the commission had considered that the average tithe system was not a feasible proposition, they would all have reported adversely on it, and they would have sought for another solution of the problem.

3.   All the members of the commission admit that the cultivator requires relief and that his burden should be rendered less irksome. The Note of Dissent, however, states bluntly that there is no practical substitute for an annual estimation of crops. On the other hand, the signatories of the Majority Report who have had many years experience of district work, who are intimately acquainted with the customs of the cultivators, either rural or tribal, not only agree that an average tithe system is practical, but they show how it can be given effect to.

     Unlike the writer of the Note of Dissent, they have been able to acquire personal and intimate knowledge of the people, of their customs and habits, of their methods of cultivation and of annually dividing their lands for cultivation, of their intimate knowledge of the areas to which they are entitled and of the productivity of their soil, of the quantity of seed of any kind of cereal which should be sown on any particular plot, and of how jealously individuals, families and clans safeguard their rights and successfully preserve them.

4.   It is not sufficient, however, that because one member argues from theory only, and the other two base their recommendations on practical knowledge, that the views of the former may be disregarded. Both reports require to be carefully considered and their respective merits carefully weighed.

5.   It is advisable, in the first place, to discover whether the present system really entails so much hardship, loss and unnecessary expense on the cultivator as to justify a change. To do this it is necessary to consider what annual estimations involve.

6. (a) /

- 2 -

6. (a) Although estimating commissions may be appointed before reaping actually commences, many days and many weeks must of necessity elapse before they are able to commence work.

(b) No estimation can be commenced until all the inhabitants of a village have placed all of a particular crop on the threshing floors.

If estimation is made as soon as the crops of some persons are on the threshing floors, there is nothing to prevent others from placing part of their crop on the heaps which have already been estimated and thereby defraud the Treasury.

It may be argued that permission to thresh is not given until all the estimations have been inspected, and an attempted fraud will, therefore, be discovered by the inspector. This is admitted, but as it will be useless to inspect until the whole crop of a particular commodity has been estimated, delay, risks and loss will result.

(c) Neither is it possible to expedite the harvesting of the crops.

Although it may safely be assumed that the cultivator seizes the earliest opportunity to gather in his harvest, reaping can only proceed after a heavy fall of dew as the sheaves otherwise would be so dry that the grain would drop out of the ears while reaping is in progress, and still more grain would drop out while the sheaves are being transported to the threshing floors. Reaping, therefore, necessarily occupies a considerable time with each kind of cereal. Hence, annual estimation entails heavy losses because it involves unavoidable delay.

(d) The whole of a particular crop having been placed on the threshing floors, estimation is commenced. Even with the cleverest and the most careful estimator the process can only be described as guessing at the quantity of grain in a particular heap of sheaves.

I have frequently invited the village representatives, the paid estimator, the paid inspector and the District Officer, and occasionally also the Treasury expert to estimate a given heap. In not a single instance have the quantities guessed at been identical, while the percentages of differences varied from 10% to 70%.

(e) Not only is estimation merely guess work, but an estimator's guesses are deliberately increased or decreased. An evening's entertainment by the village as a whole, by a particular family or by an individual, is sufficient inducement to the estimator or to the inspector to guess moderately in favour of his host. A gift has an equally potent effect on their guessing capabilities; while on the other hand the omission of an invitation to dine, a fancied injury, or even a mere whim will result in a high estimation. It is also by no means unusual that unduly high estimations are deliberately made, in the hope that the benefactor to the Treasury will thereby have earned the right to future employment.

(f) In the Southern District it is the practice to check estimations by making a number of tests in each village. Selected heaps are threshed and the percentage of difference between the result of the tests and the quantities assessed by the estimator is applied to the particular crop of the

village/

village. Even this moderate attempt at a check is not possible in the Northern District, because, unlike those in the South, threshing floors in the North are so small and so congested that tests are not feasible.

(g) The estimation of fruit is not less guesswork than that of cereals. The unhappy estimator is unable to count or to weigh the produce of a tree. He can only walk round the tree and make a guess at what he thinks the quantity of the fruit is; and having counted, often only in a perfunctory manner, the number of trees in an orchard, and having assumed that their produce is approximately the same, he multiplies the weight guessed at of the fruit on one tree by the number of trees in the orchard; equally inaccurate is the estimation of grapes.

(h) It may be argued that if a cultivator considers that his crop has been over-estimated he can insist on a test. As this would involve immediate, long drawn out and arduous labour, and, unless he can persuade his friends or relatives to assist, expenditure also on the employment of labourers, it will be readily appreciated that he prefers to suffer in silence.

(i) Estimation having been concluded and the work inspected, the unhappy cultivator is then finally permitted to thresh. His troubles, however, are by no means over. Some time must elapse before he is informed at what figure the Government will fix the redemption price of his crops. As this is usually based on what is supposed to be the wholesale market price of the crop, no allowance is made for the time, labour and expense involved in transporting the produce to the market.

(j) An additional and by no means negligible additional expense entailed on the Arab cultivator is that incurred on entertaining, during a period of at least six months each year, the estimators, clerks, inspectors, officials and police. Attempts have been made to put a stop to this; but the law of hospitality is so much a part of the nature of the Arab that it is useless to order him to desist from providing meals; the village which omitted to do so would be looked askance at by other villages.

(k) It is, therefore, by no means a figure of speech to state that annual estimations for tithes mean that during a period of at least six months each year almost the whole of the agricultural element in the country is subject to worry, annoyance, labour, expense and loss.

7. There can be no question, therefore, that a change from the present system is imperatively necessary, and almost any substitute which would afford relief to the cultivator and which would reduce his loss to a minimum would be welcome.

8. The abolition of annual estimations would relieve District Officers for other and more important duties.

It has been suggested that those Officers have very little to do; this is entirely a misconception, and shows a disregard, or lack of knowledge, of the facts. It is perhaps not yet appreciated what additional work will devolve upon District Officers if and when they are to act as Execution Officers in civil suits.

If Land Settlement work is to be taken in hand, additional and heavy duties will devolve on District Officers.

It is/

- 4 -

It is my firm conviction that Land Settlement work will be considerably delayed and will be extremely difficult to carry out, unless District Officers are relieved of some of their duties. The substitution, for an annual estimation, of a fixed tithe would provide that relief. The alternative would appear to be the engagement of a special staff for Land Settlement work.

If annual estimations are maintained a land tax cannot easily be introduced until the Survey and Settlement of the whole country has been completed.

With the fixed tithe a land tax can be progressively adopted, as the lands of each village area are surveyed and settlement effected.

9. The recommendations in the Note of Dissent provide no solution of the problem and no practical relief to the cultivator, for, with one exception, the alleviations suggested are of little practical value.

10. Because of the nature of things, a larger number of estimators, with an increased number of estimation circles, while involving Government in additional expenditure, would result in very little saving of time. A practical knowledge of the methods of the harvesting of the small quantities grown of the crops which, it is suggested, should no longer be tithed, and which, therefore, would not need to be estimated, would show that there will be no saving of time with regard to the main crops, and the principal risk and loss is incurred with the very crops which will still be titheable and which will still, therefore, have to be estimated.

11. The extension of the system of estimating crops standing is not only unpractical but would definitely lead to extensive fraud.

It is not possible to estimate standing crops in the hilly country, and as crops on the plains ripen earlier than on the hills and would have been estimated and transported to the threshing floors before estimation of the latter can be commenced, large quantities of these would find their way at night to villages on the plains and would, thus, escape estimation.

The Note of Dissent appears to have overlooked the fact that a considerable number of villages possess lands both on the hills and on the maritime and other great plains. It is obvious, therefore, that opportunities to defraud the Treasury by the evasion of assessment would be so great as to rule out this suggestion.

12. None of the Arab villagers possess threshing machines, neither are they capable of using them. It will be some years before it will be possible to extend the system of estimating at the threshing machines in Arab villages.

13. The only recommendation which might be considered in some measure as of a practical nature is that to reduce the tithe from 10% to 8 1/3rd%. A reduction of the tithe, however, has also been recommended in the majority report, but in addition that report suggests a feasible method to avoid the annual loss of time and money and the annoyance and trouble entailed on the cultivator which annual estimations would perpetuate.

14/

- 5 -

14. It is, therefore, necessary only to consider the objections in the Note of Dissent to the recommendations made in the majority report. This will be best done by examining the recommendations in that report and to see if they provide a solution, and if the solution suggested is capable of being given effect to.

15. The Majority Report recommends two changes:- one, an immediate change, i.e. that of the commutation of the tithe to the average of the last four years, and the other, to be considered at some future date, the addition of the Werko to the amount of a fixed average tithe, the combined tax being described as a "consolidated tax".

16. Consideration of the suggestion of a consolidated tax will show that this recommendation is not a practical one. The incidence of Werko is so irregular, the values of property have altered so considerably since the country was last assessed for Werko, the original assessment and application of Werko, when introduced by the Turkish Government, was so unjust that the whole country requires to be revalued and re-assessed, and this it would be unnecessary to contemplate, as all the information required will be obtained automatically as land settlement proceeds.

17. While it might be assumed that the writers of the Majority Report have found no immediate solution for the relief of agriculture other than the average tithe system, and although they have explained the practicability of that system, and its value as a substitute for annual assessments, it must be admitted that the proposal would perpetuate for an indefinite period the payment by cultivators of a tax which has been based mainly on guess work, and would also perpetuate injustice on certain individuals because of the carelessness of estimators in the past.

On the other hand annual estimations would equally perpetuate those same disabilities.

18. Circumstances in the future are not likely to be different from those which have prevailed hitherto, and, therefore, whether annual estimations are to continue, or the average tithe system introduced, the cultivator, in the future, will pay on the average the same amount as he has paid hitherto. The change suggested would, therefore, merely definitely fix the amount of the tithe for a given number of years.

The cultivator would not be any worse off than he is at present in so far as the amount of the tithe payable is concerned, but the benefit of the system proposed is that he would be immediately relieved of annually recurrent weeks and months of labour and of vexation; and more important still, the change would immediately reduce to a minimum his loss of time and money, loss of crops by fire, theft etc. He would also be immediately relieved of an annually recurrent expenditure on entertaining estimators and officials, he would know beforehand the amount of tax due from him, and his life would not longer be as burdensome as it has been.

19. That the average tithe system is feasible, or at least desirable, is further evidenced by the fact that the Supreme Moslem Council has expressed itself in its favour. That Council has the expenditure of Waqf revenue and it might be assumed that if it considered that an average tithe would involve the Waqf Department in loss, it would not be in favour of it. Large numbers of peasant cultivators and of large land-owners have also expressed themselves in favour of the average tithe.

20/

- 6 -

20. The recommendation to take the average of an even number of years is a sound one because of the peculiar nature of the bi-annual olive cycle; equally sound and intrinsically fair is the recommendation to compute the average of the past four years only.

Because of the reasons which have been advanced, the average tithe should be fixed in money, rather than in kilos with an annually fixed redemption price.

21. That the suggestion is sound to leave to villagers the distribution of the amount to be paid by the individual, is appreciated by persons who have an intimate knowledge of the customs of the villagers. Precisely that form of distribution is resorted to every year in "Musha" villages when division of land is made for cultivation;- the same system of distribution was adopted in Turkish times when tithes were farmed out.

The tithe contractor never attempted to estimate the crops of individuals; he merely claimed a lump sum from the village, and the village elders allocated the proportions payable by individuals. Precisely the same system is in vogue today in "Musha" villages with regard to the incidence of Werko.

Everybody in the village knows the name and the situation, and what is equally important, the potential productivity of almost each square inch of land, and everybody in the village knows the proportion of land to which each individual is entitled.

22. During the past eight years I can remember only very few instances of complaints from individuals, from families, or from clans that less land had been allotted to them than they were entitled to, or that more Werko had been claimed than was due from them; and when these complaints were investigated no difficulty was experienced in arriving at the truth.

23. As an additional precaution, however, the Majority Report suggests the appointment of commissions, under the chairmanship of local District Officers, to inspect, and where necessary to revise, the schedule of distribution carried out by the villagers. Distributions, therefore, will of necessity be public, and every opportunity given to individuals to claim redress. The system of distribution suggested is, therefore, feasible and will decrease to a minimum the opportunities for peculation and abuse.

24. So intimate is the knowledge of the villagers of the areas of village lands, of their value expressed in terms of potential productivity, and of the rights of individuals to areas, that the work of Land Settlement will have to depend on that very knowledge and will largely consist in merely recording the rights claimed.

Judicial notice of this knowledge is taken in the Courts, and Land Registrars accept statements from Mukhtars and village elders on the boundaries and ownership of plots.

25. The amount payable in non-musha villages is more easily capable of distribution because of individual ownership.

26. The suggestion that the distribution of the incidence of the average tithe can be checked by the potential productivity of the soil is both valid and feasible.

The/

- 7 -

The majority report suggests that potential productivities might be expressed in terms of wheat; these might as easily be expressed in any other terms, but they are best expressed in those of wheat because all land is sown, at some time or other, in rotation with wheat.

27. There is nothing, therefore, in the objection that the percentage of the proportion payable by an individual to the total sum payable by the village, if based on the productivity in terms of wheat, amounts to a surtax of lands cultivated with inferior crops.

28. I am of the opinion that the number and dates of payment of the instalments of the tithe, as suggested in Annex B of the Majority Report, would cause hardship to cultivators. The tithe should be payable in not less than six equal monthly instalments, the first to be due on the 15th of August.

29. Mention must be made of other objections in the Note of Dissent.

The difficulty referred to in the last sentence of para 2(3) is not insuperable. Absentee landlords, if in Palestine, can be traced, and if absent, their agents can be found.

Changes of holdings will be reported annually by the villagers and will be checked by the District Officers. It will be in the interest of the village to report such changes regularly as the Mukhtars and the elders are responsible for the collection of the tithe.

The prejudice to Government interests foretold at the end of para 3 need not occur.

The average tithe system will not change Miri land to Mulk, neither will it exonerate the land owner from the law of "Mustahig Tabu" if he fails to cultivate his Miri land.

30. Recommendations:- I recommend

    (a) that Government adopt the average tithe system as proposed in the Majority Report,

    (b) that the measure be applied definitely and compulsorily to the whole Country,

    (c) that the Government reduce the percentage of the tithe from 10% to 8 1/3%,

    (d) that the suggestion of a "consolidated tax" be rejected.

(Sgd) A. Abramson,

District Commissioner.

Section 4: Memoranda and Reports on Land Survey, 1925–1946

4.01

COPY.
Mount Zion Building,
Jerusalem.

Reference No.L.S./57.   25th February, 1925.

Confidential.

The Treasurer,
Government of Palestine.

Subject : Survey and Land Settlement Estimates 1925-26.

I enclose herewith the memorandum on the Survey estimates which it was agreed I should furnish. The delay in letting you have it is due to the difficulties of communication with both Jerusalem and Jaffa while I have been on the move.

2. My figures are necessarily those which were tabled and provisionally adopted at the meeting held in your office on 9th February: subsequent modifications naturally resulted from fuller discussion with the Director of Surveys. An analysis of the changes is attached for reference.

3. I originally aimed at keeping the estimates for settlement separate from those for survey when the difference was clear, except under Beisan in which case last year's practice was repeated. I note that the modifications include a partial obliteration of this differentiation by the transfer of £E.1000 provided under the head of the two new Settlement Commissions, for Tents, equipment and travelling.

4. While I am most anxious to secure the management of Survey and Settlement in as close association as possible I am inclined to think that the change should have been in the direction of fuller rather than less differentiation, both on financial and administrative grounds. The point will, however, probably call for re-consideration next year.

5. You may think it advisable to transfer £E.100 of the £E.1000 provided for "Survey services rendered by other Governments" to some suitable item under personal emoluments, as these services may be expected to occasion a small personal fee in one or two cases (e.g. to Mr. Richards for his recent visit).

(Signed) E. Dowson.

SURVEY AND LAND SETTLEMENT ESTIMATES 1925-26.
COVERING MEMORANDUM.

This memorandum covers and is intended to be read in conjunction with the following detailed notes:

Note I. - Capital Expenditure.

Note II. - Figures - Recurrent Expenditure.

Note III.- Notes on Staff - Recurrent Expenditure.

Note IV. - Notes on other heads of Recurrent Expenditure.

I have already expressed the impossibility of making properly considered recommendations in regard to expenditure on survey and land settlement until I have terminated and digested my present enquiry: but it is evident that I must anticipate this if any progress is to be made in the forthcoming financial year.

Since the outlines of the ultimate objective are not in doubt, inability at this stage to recommend precisely the Government's future programme does not seem justification for postponing action for yet another year, if either there are defects in existing organization and equipment that can be remedied, or if an immediately useful advance can be made.

2. The accepted objective of Government is the replacement of the existing Land Registry methods inherited from the Turks by a reliable system of registration of title to land based upon a good cadastral survey consistently kept up to-date, and a clear and workable land law. The measures required to gain this objective will be discussed in my eventual report, and cannot be anticipated here: and for immediate purposes this restatement of the ultimate objective is probably sufficient.

To determine how funds can be usefully expended during the forthcoming financial year in preparation for, or advance towards, the attainment of this objective, it is advisable to review the existing organizations and see in what respects they require strengthening and to consider how they can be most advantageously employed during that year.

3. These organizations are the Survey of Palestine and the Land Registry branch of the Lands Department. My observations here are confined entirely to the latter because its expenditure is considerably the greater :

because /

- 2 -

because any necessary changes in it can be effected without, or with little, modification of existing law: and because (a) the execution of survey and settlement, and (b) the promulgation of a reformed land law, must both precede the introduction of any dependable registration of rights over land. The last condition means not only that of the two existing organizations, the Survey calls for earlier consideration, but also that no fundamental improvement can be effected in the Land Registry in the meantime. It therefore seems reasonable to concentrate immediate attention on the Survey and accept at least for a further year a repetition of current expenditure on the Land Registries.

4. Considered as an instrument for the execution of cadastral survey for purposes of land settlement, the Survey of Palestine suffers from certain outstanding weaknesses which require to be remedied before it will be in a position to discharge its functions properly, and which cannot be remedied without increased budgetary provision. These weaknesses can conveniently be considered under four heads :

(a) Inadequate Survey Framework.
(b) Defective liaison.
(c) Inability to reproduce maps.
(d) Insufficient field staff.

5 - 7. Inadequate Framework.

5. Although the country is a small country, there is still a considerable amount of work needed to complete the triangulation network over the cis-Jordan area from Beersheba northwards. While the quality of this very trying and monotonous work is high and the rate at which it is being carried on by the observers is not open to criticism, it must be recognised that until it is completed the Survey cannot move freely and execute its work reliably and economically anywhere it is required. It is most desirable therefore that every possible effort should be made to accelerate the completion of the triangulation throughout the above area. The Director is fully alive to this need and will reinforce the parties engaged upon this work to the utmost extent that staff, resources and other demands permit.

6. There is, however, another sense in which increased provision for, and increased attention to, the establishment of a reliable framework of marks on the ground is essential. It is apt to be thought that a survey is essentially a finite operation, and that an area having once been surveyed the work will stand for all time. While there are conditions in which this conception is not far from the truth: it no longer

holds,/

- 3 -

holds, even in respect of topography, when areas of economic development are concerned. And the essence of a cadastral survey for registration of title is that it shall not only constitute an accurate record of property boundaries at the time of initial survey, but also embody all future changes in such boundaries as they occur. This means that the cadastral survey must be so organized that its surveyors are incessantly moving throughout every part of the country, and so executed that these surveyors can promptly and accurately re-determine old boundaries or record new ones. To secure this it is necessary to have in the near neighbourhood of any property boundary two or more reference marks whose positions have been previously fixed. Given these conditions a surveyor can readily fix the positions of new boundaries or by a repetition of his work at a later time re-establish the position which any previously registered boundary ought to occupy, and thus authoritatively settle any uncertainties or disputes that may have arisen concerning it.

7. The Swiss authorities incline to consider the actual boundary marking of each individual property a sine qua non of any effective registration of title. But however convenient, this is not really indispensable: and it would be burdensome and costly if undertaken by the Government in Palestine. And if the conditions mentioned above are satisfied, so that the Survey can authoritatively recover any altered or disputed boundary when necessary, there is little doubt that land owners will gradually put up their own actual boundary marks for current use.

The placing and maintenance on the ground by the Survey of suitable chains of reference marks interpenetrating property holdings, as explained above, is an essential part of any cadastral survey that is not merely to be of ephemeral value: and is far more important than the making of any pictorial representation of the ground.

Failure to carry out this principle effectively has prevented the valuable work done in the neighbourhood of Beisan under the terms of the Agreement of the 19th November, 1921, from attaining the character of the permanent settlement which was intended and which it deserves. If promptly dealt with this weakness can be repaired relatively easily and at considerably less labour and cost than will be involved by the re-doing of the work de novo some years hence. Considerations of economy apart it is very desirable that any such weaknesses revealed by experience should be remedied before the confidence of the population in the permanency of the Government's work is in any way affected.

The work /

- 4 -

The work at Beisan is not an isolated instance of inadequate reference marking, but probably the importance of providing more funds for, and paying more attention to, this primary requirement of cadastral survey has been sufficiently emphasized.

8 - 13. Defective Liaison.

8. The Department of Survey has now been a number of years in existence in Palestine. It has suffered during that time from an absence of any formulation of its programme by Government, more particularly of the part it was required to take in clearing up the confusion of rights over land inherited from the Ottoman regime. This initial handicap would doubtless have been retrieved if a single organization equipped with the requisite experience and technical competence had been charged with this task, as such a service would have given a lead that would have been welcomed by Government. Unfortunately responsibility for execution appears to have hung indefinitely between two independent services one located at Jaffa, the other at Jerusalem. Both these services possessed or have acquired valuable experience within the sphere each felt to be its own: it was not to be expected that their efforts would be spontaneously unified.

In the absence of such unified effort the artillery of Survey have been shelling the hills while the infantry of the Land Registry have been independently attacking in the plains; and although useful progress has been made by each in certain directions the main battle of reducing the chaos of land rights in Palestine to order remains on the balance very much where it was seven years ago.

The introduction of common direction exercised from the capital is the only ultimate remedy; but its execution may have to be gradual and consideration of it must be reserved for my final report.

The need for at least closer liaison between the Survey and the Government, and between the Survey and the Land Registry will however be at once recognised: and this alone necessitates the location as soon as possible of the Survey Headquarters at the capital. Other considerations affecting the execution of this transfer are considered below.

9. But liaison is not only defective between the capital and Survey Headquarters at Jaffa, but also between Survey Headquarters and the field. As the Director very justly says the field parties constitute the producing part of the Department: and there is no

need /

- 5 -

need to analyse the evils of defective liaison between the producing and the controlling sides of an organisation. There appear to be three main impediments to the close and continuous association that should prevail between Survey Headquarters and the field: firstly, lack of a non-technical officer at Headquarters responsible for the management of the current administration of the service: secondly, lack of a responsible deputy charged with the regular duty of inspecting all field parties and maintaining continuous touch between them and the Director: thirdly, the immobility at present imposed on the Director and such Deputy, if nominated, by the absence of any means of getting about the country at short notice freely and unexpectedly.

10. All the three needs are appreciated by the Director. In the estimates he originally recommended the appointment of an Assistant Inspector in charge of Accounts and Stores to meet the first need. An alternative which the Director is disposed to welcome, and which I myself think on general grounds preferable, at least for the moment, has suggested itself in connection with the proposal of the Secretariat that my present office should be maintained after my departure.

I think the maintenance of this office as a central secretariat for land settlement work is to be recommended. One of my principal difficulties has been, and is, to obtain reliable information about existing affairs whether it be copies of existing legislation, the roughest statistics of land held under different tenures and classified by economic value, the approximate location of such categories of land, the names and distribution of villages throughout Palestine and the position of their boundaries, or numerous other things which should be readily available or known to anybody that is to be responsible for the planning or conduct of land settlement operations.

By steady persistence, which must sometimes be most annoying, Mr. Horton, the officer lent to me by the Secretariat, is gradually bringing together such of this information as it is possible to obtain, but the fruits of his activity will take long to gather, and it will be a pity not to garner these. It is not however desirable to set up a third organisation, however small, indefinitely related to both the Survey and the Land Registry.

11. The solution suggested and which I recommend is to second the staff of my present office, attach them to the Survey, and entrust Mr. Horton with the current administrative work of the Survey as well as his present work. He could combine the two well: and arrangements can no doubt easily be made for him to visit Jerusalem or elsewhere if necessary for Land Settlement meetings etc.

The Director /

- 6 -

12. The Director is aiming at removing the second impediment to more effective association between Headquarters and the field by promoting Mr. Giles to be his recognized lieutenant and utilizing him regularly to inspect all the field parties. (v. Note III, paragraph 1).

The third impediment can only be removed by the provision of suitable means of independent transport at the disposal of the Director. (v. Note IV, paragraph 4).

13. The first of the measures advocated above would relieve the Director of a large part of the regular routine of administration and thus enable him to absent himself more easily from Headquarters. He would then be freed for more frequent visits to the capital, to other Headquarters (e.g. Haifa), and to field parties. It is the third measure alone which will enable him and his deputy to visit even the most remote of his field parties readily at any time, see their work and inspect their arrangements personally on the spot without, or at short notice. Such inspections are vital to the well being and efficiency of a scattered service attacking a problem that is bound to present unexpected difficulties for a long time to come. Without such inspections the Director cannot know how his field parties are faring, and what they are doing and thinking: while they tend to feel cut off and to get either idle or unhappy.

14 - 17. Inability to reproduce maps.

14. While the making of an accurate miniature of property holdings, which we call a cadastral map, is of secondary importance to the making of a reliable measured record of the positions of the boundaries of such holdings in relation to fixed reference marks placed on the ground, a map is too great an economy and convenience to be dispensed with. But the value of a map is extremely limited if it is confined to a single original, or even to the few copies that can be made at some cost by tracing and sun-printing. The making of a field survey is necessarily an expensive undertaking: the multiplication of the pictorial record of it is cheap, and renders the results available to any member of the public or any branch of the service that has need of them. A Survey that does not print its maps is withholding from the public information obtained at public expense and which is daily losing its original value.

15. In the case of a purely topographical survey it is always possible to send maps out of the country to be printed, although this course is rarely to be commended because of the inconvenience it entails and the delay between survey and publication.

In the case /

- 7 -

In the case of a cadastral survey maintained for registration of title to land this course is impracticable: because the maps and registers are complementary parts of a record that may have to be consulted or amended at any moment. In short a Reproduction Office on the spot is a necessary part of the machinery of any Cadastral Survey and a most desirable part of any national Survey.

16. A Map Reproduction Office calls for certain features of orientation, arrangement and situation which make the adaptation of an existing building for the purpose difficult and uneconomical. And apart from the cost of radical initial alterations likely to be needed, such an adapted building could hardly fail to be uneconomical to run.

The situation of a Map Reproduction Office must be one that has access to a good water supply, and can be kept free from dust and from vibration. It must also be in close proximity to Survey Headquarters, if not actually in the same building. Provision for gradually increasing storage accommodation for original and published maps, for documents and registers must also not be overlooked.

17. No existing building can be expected to meet these varied requirements: and in view of the present general dependence of Government upon hired buildings, it is hardly open to question that the most economical course, both in respect of initial outlay and subsequent running cost, is to design and build special accommodation for Survey Headquarters somewhere in the vicinity of Jerusalem. Serious progress with land settlement which must include subsequent maintenance to date of maps and registers, must not be expected, until such a working base has been provided and is in use.

My accompanying Note II dealing with Capital Expenditure furnishes such indications as I can at present give of the probable cost of the accommodation needed.

Desirable as is the early transfer of the Survey Headquarters to Jerusalem it hardly seems worth while, pending the provision of the permanent quarters recommended, to dislocate the present office: even if there exists in Jerusalem any suitable building that could be rendered available for the purpose.

18. - Insufficient field staff.

18. It is impossible at this stage to state with assurance the numbers of junior field staff that will be required to execute the cadastral survey and land settlement of Palestine: but a strength of 60 surveyors may be taken as a minimum estimate. The present

strength /

strength of 30: is inadequate, and I recommend the training of additional junior field staff during the forthcoming financial year.

The senior field staff suggested in the estimates (1 Inspector, 5 Assistant Inspectors and 4 Sub-Inspectors), are sufficient to assimilate an ultimate increase of field staff to 60 or more surveyors and to meet other needs mentioned below.

For a permanent establishment the existing and proposed proportion of senior to junior staff is admittedly too high. A top heavy cadre is however inevitable during the initial years of a national survey when the foundation has to be laid, the rank and file trained and the whole organisation built up out of nothing. And although the Survey of Palestine has been in existence now for a number of years and is no longer an embryo service; it has never been put on a stable financial footing and its future organisation and functions are still awaiting definition.

19. Moreover, for some years to come and possibly until land settlement is concluded there will be a number of special pieces of work or special problems to be dealt with, which cannot be reduced to routine and will demand individual attention by senior technical officers. As in such cases delay nearly always means economic loss to the country and indirect, if not direct, loss to the State; it will be good business to accept for the present the proportion of senior staff proposed. One to two thousand pounds of expenditure per annum might be saved by reducing the proposed establishment of senior staff; but if this were done, the training of Palestinians and the general development of the service would suffer, the execution of the triangulation and other preparatory work would lag, the re-assessment of "werko" in towns and the afforestation of the country might be further retarded. On grounds of financial return to the State alone acceleration of action under the heads last mentioned, should amply justify the expenditure under discussion.

20. - Extension of Land Settlement.

20. Land Settlement of a simple character has actually been in progress for some little time at Beisan under the Agreement of the 19th November, 1921. I hope shortly to give my impressions of this work in a special note.

I am not yet satisfied that it will be practicable to expand the work of Land Settlement any further next year: but review of village and block boundaries, the determination of State land to be

reserved /

- 9 -

reserved for forests, or the re-assessment of W e r k o in some of the town areas may offer work of immediate value on which the Settlement Commissions can be tested. Subject therefore to full consideration and approval later by Government before the funds are used, I recommend provision in the forthcoming estimates for two additional Land Settlement Commissions. They are estimated on a basis of 6 months work at £E.1,500 a year each, which is the same as the Beisan Commission with some additional provision explained below.

The composition of these Commissions is a matter for subsequent recommendation: but I anticipate suggesting that they shall consist of a specially selected British officer, with a good knowledge of Arabic and of the country, as Chairman, and possibly two carefully selected Palestinians. The two Palestinian notables on the Beisan Commission are required, under the Agreement, to give their services free: but I do not think that this is really advisable. I have therefore included for budgetary purposes provision for an allowance to such notables of £E.1 a day.

There are other details which will require definition: but which cannot yet be usefully anticipated.

21. - Recurrent and Capital Expenditure.

21. It should at the outset be recognized that expenditure on survey has a dual character in countries, such as Palestine, which require it both

      (a) as a specific basis for registration of rights over immovable property, and

      (b) for general purposes.

In principle the former and all other expenses of operating such registration, should be covered by receipts from statutory fees; the latter should be met from the general revenues of the State derived from taxation.

22. In Switzerland where the expenditure is mainly of the first character, a recent report states that, registration apart, the operations of survey are needed

      (i)   as a basis for keeping the general topographical maps of the country up-to-date;

      (ii)   for construction, as a basis for schemes for railways, roads, canals, aqueducts, water supply, electric power, town planning;

(iii) /

- 10 -

(iii) in the sphere of agriculture and forest economy, as a basis for health and irrigation schemes, for forest management, for (special economic) re-arrangement of holdings;

(iv) for fiscal purposes, as a basis for equitable taxation of immovable property;

(v) for the provision of statistics of real property;

(vi) as a basis for making special maps of ways and communications, for tourists etc.

The list is not exhaustive but sufficiently illustrative of the general purposes for which a national survey is required.

23. It is difficult to estimate what the maintenance of a survey for such general purposes alone in Palestine would cost: but if allowance is made for mining and agricultural concessions, for geological maps, for forests work, and the periodic reassessment of even the present restricted land tax (werko), it will not I think be far wrong to put at £E.20,000 the annual charge that would fall on the tax payer on this account. This should keep about 20 detail surveyors in the field with all consequent expenses.

24. There has next to be considered the still more difficult problem of what is likely to be the eventual cost of maintaining after initial settlement a dependable system of Land Registration in Palestine. It was estimated that in Egypt a surveyor will be needed continuously for every six villages when the whole country is registered. There are, according to the last census return, 22 municipalities, 817 villages and 172 tribal areas in Palestine (cis-Jordan). It may, I think, be assumed that there will be many fewer transactions in Palestine than Egypt: and I will provisionally assume the future requirements here at an average of a surveyor maintained for every eighteen municipalities, villages or tribal areas. This would mean the maintenance of a staff of about 56 detail surveyors making no allowance for leave or sickness. The maintenance of 20 detail surveyors has been previously assumed available for general purposes. On the assumptions given, a total of 80 would be an underestimate for all requirements. The regular work of mapping cadastral "mutations" consequent on registered transactions will become simpler, entail

less /

- 11 -

less equipment and be otherwise cheaper as the work gets established and the Department grows. I therefore think that the cost of a national survey maintaining 80 detail field surveyors for all requirements can for purposes of this discussion be put at £E.60,000 a year.

25. The cost of the Lands Department at present is about £E.15,000 a year. This covers the combined duties of Land Registry and Conservation and Control of State Lands. The bulk is, I believe, on account of Land Registry work: but expenditure on Control of State Land is still appreciable. It is impossible at this stage to say what would be the cost of maintaining the Land Registries after Settlement in combination with the Survey: but I think £E.20,000 a year additional to Survey may be taken as an outside figure for immediate purposes.

26. On the figures given above the cost of maintaining a dependable system of Land Registration in Palestine after Settlement, may be expected to be £E.60,000 a year. As will have been realized these figures are little more than guesswork: indeed for some time to come nothing better than guesswork can be attempted. While, therefore, the figures are of no absolute value, they are of relative value for purposes of comparison with receipts, to which I will now turn.

27. The following are the numbers of, and total receipts from, registered transactions during the calendar years 1921 to 1923, as communicated to me by the Director of the Land Department.

Year	Transactions	Receipts £E.
1921	3,361	37,145
1922	5,117	35,549
1923	6,514	40,788
1924	7,113	40,191
1925	..... estimated	40,000

It will be noted that an increase of fifty per cent in the receipts from fees would be sufficient to cover the figure of £E.60,000 for expenditure given above. If a revenue of £E.40,000 per annum is obtained from fees under present conditions, a revenue of £E.60,000 per annum does not seem extravagant to expect after settlement has been completed and compulsory registration of all subsequent passage of rights over immovable property is in force.

The realization of this particular balance is not of course to be anticipated: and it is only used as an illustration of how the total operation of land registration may be expected to meet its expenses. Expenditure and receipts will both be governed by public demands and the fees taken should cover the cost of the service rendered.

28 /.

28. There is another aspect of the question which deserves consideration. At present the cost of maintaining the Land Registries is something short of £E.15,000 a year, while the receipts derived from registration total £E.40,000. On these figures it appears that the registering public are in the aggregate being required at present to pay in fees about three times the cost of the service rendered them. It is true that there are about eight surveyors paid off the Survey budget who work for, and are largely under the control of, the Lands Department. But I believe that under the Survey Fees Ordinance additional fees are charged for the work of these surveyors: but even if this is not so, the additional expenditure which they involve would not go far to redress the disparity.

29. It may be urged that at least a portion of the recurrent expenditure incurred on the Survey is a justifiable set off to the considerable annual profit in favour of Government on Land Registration fees. I think there is justification for this view; but that it is not consonant with charging Survey expenditure almost entirely to Loan Funds, while treating Registration fees as revenue which it is legitimate to apply to other purposes, as I understand has hitherto been the practice. I venture to submit that it is in principle indefensible to utilize the fees charged to members of the public for a particular service virtually as a means of undeclared taxation. Under present circumstances the Government clearly cannot consider any reduction in the scale of land registration fees; if only because they might have to raise them again in the near future on account of the cost of land settlement and survey: but I am of opinion that Government should consider whether they are justified in utilizing these fees as a source of revenue and concurrently adding to debt to carry on the cadastral survey.

30. I have earlier expressed my opinion that the maintenance in Palestine of a small national survey for general purposes is a necessary and proper charge on the general taxpayer: and I put the annual cost of such a survey at about £E.20,000 a year. This is a charge which should unquestionably be met from current annual revenue. Incidentally such a service should gradually develop receipts from sale of maps, repayment of cost of surveys for mining and other concessions etc., etc., up to possibly £E.5,000 a year: which would reduce its net cost to about £E.15,000 a year.

If in addition it is accepted that debt should not be incurred for the prosecution of the additional survey establishment needed for cadastral purposes while a considerable annual profit is being

concurrently /

- 13 -

concurrently derived from land registration fees, there will remain little justification for charging recurrent expenditure on Survey to Loan Funds at all at present.

31. Expenditure incurred on Land Settlement, so far as distinguishable from Survey, may be differently regarded as being essentially a special effort, which however long drawn out will not have to be maintained or repeated and which will yield its due return on any loan funds drawn upon. At the same time it is obviously desirable that to as large an extent as possible the extraordinary costs of Land Settlement should also be met from current revenue, so as to minimize any addition to the debt.

Similar considerations apply to such bona fide capital charges as the building and equipment of suitable Headquarters for the Survey at Jerusalem.

(Signed) E. Dowson.

SURVEY AND LAND SETTLEMENT ESTIMATES 1925-26.

NOTE I.

Capital Expenditure.

The only expenditure justly of a capital nature for which I think provision should be made in the forthcoming estimates is for the building and equipment of permanent Headquarters offices for the Survey at Jerusalem. The need for this is outlined in paragraphs 14-17 of my covering memorandum.

I have unfortunately not yet received the data I am expecting from Egypt on which to base a closer estimate and I will make good the deficiency shortly: but I put the total sum needed provisionally at £E.30,000.

Now although the construction of such a permanent Headquarters is in my opinion indispensable to the proper initiation and progress of cadastral survey and settlement, its exact site and design will require a good deal of consideration even if approval in principle to build is promptly obtained. I do not therefore think that there is any prospect of a larger sum than £E.5,000 actually being expended in this forthcoming financial year, and I suggest that provision in the 1925-26 estimates under this head be restricted to this sum.

Authority actually to incur expenditure against this item would necessarily be reserved until the whole project had been considered and approved in detail: but if the Survey are to be in suitable Headquarters at Jerusalem within the next two years, an actual start with building operations must be made during the next twelve months, and unless some definite sum is earmarked for the purpose in the estimates this start is unlikely to be made.

SURVEY AND LAND SETTLEMENT ESTIMATES 1925-26.

Comparative Statement
of
Draft estimates originally tabled, and subsequently
submitted by the Director of Surveys
(vide covering letter).

Note: There is no alteration in the
number of appointments except
that the Director of Surveys
has made provision for one
additional Grade I clerk.

		Sir E. Dowson's estimates.	Increase by Dir. of Surveys.	Decrease by Dir. of Surveys.	Dir. of Sur. estimates Dept.	Loan
	A. Pers. Emoluments.					
a	Senior Staff	6813				
	Exp. Allce. Le Ray		50			
	Exp. Allce. Gr. V.			100		
	Decrease in salary Grade IV.			50	4400	2313
b	Adm. Staff. Gr. I Clerk		312			
	Exp. Allce. "		40		1432	132
	Adm. Staff............	1212				
c	Computation Office	1356			1356	
d	Reproduction Office	3582			2502	1080
e	Field Staff	6096			3792	2304
f	Field Allces.	2250	656		1536	1370
g	Labour	7000			450	6550
h	Land Settlement	4081		548		3533
	Total Pers. Emol.	32390	1058	698	15468	17282
		32750	360		32750	

B. Other Charges /

- 2 -

	Sir E. Dowson's Estimates.	Increase by Dir. of Surveys.	Decrease by Dir. of Surveys.	Dir. of Sur. estimates Dept.	Loan
B. Other Charges.					
i: Box Cars	500				500
ii: Transp. & Trav.	4500	200		3000	1700
iii: Consumable Stores	1450			1450	
iv: Techn. Equipment.	2150				2150
v: Survey Marks	1000				1000
vi: Camp Equipment.	750				750
vii: Clothing.	200			100	100
viii: Saddlery.	100				100
ix: Office Equipment.	100			100	
x: Maps and Books.	100			100	
xi: Passages.	150				150
xii: Compensations.	100				100
xiii: Mukhtars.	250				250
xiv: Animals.	150				150
xv: Contingencies.	100			100	
xvi: Map Reproduction.	1000				1000
-: Land Settl. Tents.	1000		1000	-	-
Total	13600	200	1000	4850	7950
	12800		800	18800	

T O T A L S.

	Sir E. Dowson's Estimates.	Increase by Dir. of Surveys.	Decrease by Dir. of Surveys.	Dir. of Sur. estimates Dept.	Loan
A. Personal Emoluments	32390	1058	698	15468	17282
B. Other Charges.	13600	200	1000	4850	7950
Total	45990	1258	1698	20318	25232

440.

£E. 45550.   £E. 45550.

SURVEY AND LAND SETTLEMENT ESTIMATES.

1 9 2 5 - 2 6.

N O T E II.

Figures - Recurrent Expenditure.

Summary of Figures.

A. S U R V E Y.

1924-25.

Nos.	Cost L.E.			
		(a), (b), (c), (d) and (e), Salaries and Expatriation Allowances.		
67	13,982	95 officials costing..............£E.	19,059
	1,812	(f) Field Allowances............... "	2,250
	5,300	(g) Labour....................... "	7,000
	5,491	(h) Other Charges................. "	12,600
67	26,585		40,909

B. Land Settlement.

| 2 | 1,150 | (i), (j) and (k): 9 officials..... " | 5,081 |
| 69 | 27,735. | Grand Total: (104 officials)...... " | 45,990 |

N. B.(i). The grades referred to throughout these estimates are those indicated below with increments annually. I understand that the formation of new pensionable grades is under consideration by Government, but only in one case, when so stated, is such a new grade referred to herein or in accompanying notes.

Grade I /

- 2 -

Grade				£E.		
Grade I	–	Senior Service	–	800	– 50 –	1100
" II	–	" "	–	550	– 25 –	750
" III	–	" "	–	400	– 25 –	500
" IV	–	" "	–	300	– 20 –	400
" V	–	" "	–			
" I	–	Junior Service	–	312	– 12 –	360
" II	–	" "	–	252	– 12 –	300
" III	–	" "	–	192	– 6 –	240
" IV	–	" "	–	144	– 6 –	180
" V	–	" "	–	96	– 6 –	132

<u>N. B. (ii)</u>. A more detailed summary of the Survey staff under heads (a) Senior Staff, (b) Administrative Staff, (c) Computation Office, (d) Reproduction Office, and (e) Field Staff, is given within.

<u>N. B. (iii)</u>. The separation between settlement and survey is fictitious and cannot economically be made real. The distinction merely preserves the existing <u>status quo</u> pending decision as to future arrangements.

<u>N. B. (iv)</u>. The salary figures given are the maxima for the financial year although that figure may not be reached till late in that year.

A. SURVEY. /

- 3 -

A. Survey: (a). Senior Staff.

1924-25			1925-26	
Nos.	Cost £E.		Nos.	£E.
1	925	Director of Surveys: Grade II.... (800-50-1100)	1	1,025
	-	Expatriation Allowance		100
	650	Inspector, Grade III (550-25-750) (Mr. Giles from Gr.IV, to replace Mr. Day).	1	550
	50	Exp. Allowance.....		50
	625	Inspector, Grade III (Mr. Le Ray, special appointment without Exp.Allce. Any new appointment in this Grade at £E.550 + Exp. Allowance).		688
		Assistant Inspectors, Grade IV........(400-25-500)	6	
	450	Mr. C.J.Bishop....		475
	450	Mr. H.G.Miller....		475
	? 400	Mr. R.B.Crusher... (from Grade V)		450
	475	New appointment to fill vacancy.....		450
	500	Mr. E.J.Davies.....		500
		New appointment.....		450
	250	Exp. Allce.for same		300
		Sub-Inspectors: Grade V...........(300-20-400)	4	
	250	Mr. S.H. Lanfear..		300
	250	Mr. J.H. Mankin...		300
	250	Mr. N. Foutorian..		300
	240	(°)Mr. Holstein...... (°) now in Grade III, Junior Service. Exp. Allowances for first two being British officers....................		300 100
11	5765	.....Total.....	13	6,813

(b). Administrative Staff.

	300	Storekeeper, Gr.II, J.S. Mr. Guernstein.	1	300
	222	Chief Clerk, Gr.II, J.S. Mr. R.E.Farajallah, at present Gr.III, J.S.	1	252
1		Clerk, Grade III, J.S.	1	
3	522	... Carried Forward ...	3	552

- 4 -

1924-25.			1925-26.	
Nos.	Cost £E.		Nos.	£.E.
3	522	... Brought forward ...	3	552
2	180 177	Clerks, Grade IV, J.S. E.C. Nahas................... K. Dawoody................. }+ (transferred fr. Field) (+) one to be promoted to Grade III,J.S.).	2	192 180
	150	S. Levin...................		156
1	132	Stores clerk, Gr.V, J.S. T. Asmer...................	1	132
6	1,161	... Total ...	6	1,212

(c). Computation Office.

	240	Computer, Gr.II, J.S......... Mr. Goussinsky(now in Gr.III)	1	252
	168 162	Computers, Gr.III, J.S....... J. Shrier (now in Gr.IV)... E. Shishria " " " ...	2	192 192
	120 96	Computers, Gr.IV, J.S........ S. Jabotinsky(now in V).... D. Liebrecht " " " .... 3 new appointments.........	5	144 144 432
5	786	... Total ...	8	1,356

(d). Reproduction Office.

(i) Superintendent's Office.

		Chief Assistant, Gr.I,J.S.(to be called "Chief Draughtsmen") 1 (to be working head of Drawing office normally). (new appointment).		312
0	0	... Total ...	1	312

(ii) Drawing office.

	300 222	Draughtsmen, Gr.II,J.S. Fuad Masri (old man at max.) A. Kaplan (now in Gr.III)...	2	300 252
2	522	... Carried Forward ...	2	552

- 5 -

1924-25.			1925-26.	
Nos.	Cost £E.		Nos.	Cost £E.
2	522	... Brought Forward ...	2	552
2		Draughtsmen, Gr.III, J.S..	2	
	234	B. Ernstein............		240
	144	M. Aini (now in Gr.IV).		192
		Draughtsmen Grade IV, J.S.	4	
	144	A. Epstein............		150
	132	A. Nassibian (now in V).		144
	102	N. Azar...............		144
		New post for possible later appointment....		144
		Draughtsmen, Gr. V, J.S.	8	
	102	A. C. Nahas............		114
	102	P. Aintablian..........		114
	96	S. Krikorian...........		114
	96	E. Maminsky............		102
	60	(+) R.K. Torrosian.......		96
		(+) now Probationer.		
	60	(+) S. Ferekh "		96
	60	(+) F. Ferekh "		96
	60	(+) N. Jabagi "		96
15	1,914	... Total ...	16	2,394

(iii) <u>Photo-process office.</u>

		Photo-process worker, Gr.I, J.S. (new appointment)	1	312
-	-	Asst. Photo-process worker, Grade II, J.S.	1	252
0	0	... Total ...	2	564

<u>N.B.</u> 2 labourers will also be needed.

(iv). <u>Printing office.</u>

		Printer, Grade I, J.S. (new appointment)	1	312
0	0	... Total ...	1	312

<u>N.B.</u> 2 Apprentices to be paid off Labour item.

Summary of /

- 6 -

1924-25.			1925-26.	
Nos.	Cost £E.		Nos.	Cost £E.

Summary of Reproduction Office.

1924-25 Nos.	1924-25 Cost £E		1925-26 Nos.	1925-26 Cost £E
0	0	(i) Superintendent's office	1	312
15	1914	(ii) Drawing office..........	16	2,394
0	0	(iii) Photo-process office...	2	564
0	0	(iv) Printing office........	1	312
15	1914	... T O T A L ...	20	3,582

Survey. (e) Field Staff.

1924-25 Nos.	1924-25 Cost		1925-26 Nos.	1925-26 Cost
-		Surveyors, Grade I, J.S.	-	
2		Surveyors, Grade II, "	2	
	240	T. Alianak (now in Gr.III)..		252
	240	N. Michaelides " " " ..		252
		Surveyors, Grade III, J.S.	6	
	216	A.C. Vrachas................		222
	240	J. Rosentool................		240
	162	S. Constantinides(now in IV)		192
	180	E. Kamornik......(" " ")		192
	144	D. Kyriakos......(" " ")		192
		Post for new appointment later		192
12		Surveyors, Grade IV, J.S.	13	
	180	I. Hammash..................		180
	168	S. Toister..................		174
	162	J. Atlas....................		168
	162	M. Levin....................		168
	162	J. Giveony..................		168
	126	Y. Goldstein (now in Gr.V)..		162
	126	Y. Weinstein (" " " V)..		162
	150	L. Brown....................		156
	126	J. Hashem....(" " " V)..		144
	126	J. Amiroff...(" " " V)..		144
	132	T. Nasr......(" " " V)..		144
	126	K. Fink......(" " " V)..		144
		Post for new appointment....		144
11		Surveyors, Grade V, J.S.	27	
	108	J. Albert...................		132
	114	H. Husseini.................		132
	108	E. Rosenstein...............		132
	108	Z. Kerznerman...............		132
	108	J. Jayousy..................		132
	108	A. Abdel Hadi...............		132
	108	T. Haddad...................		132
	108	A. Aintablian...............		132
	102	W. Gotlieb..................		132
	102	C. M. Hucklesby.............		132
	114	M. Zurub....................		120
30	4,356	... Carried forward...	48	5,232

- 7 -

1924-25			1925-26	
Nos.	Cost £E.	Brought Forward	Nos.	Cost £E.
30	4,356	--do--	48	5,232
		and 16 apprentices: 8 for 1 year and 8 for 6 months to be paid £E.6 per mensem, to receive field allowance of £E.2 per mensem after six or more months, if they are satisfactorily reported on, and to be appointed at minimum of Grade or dispensed with after 12 months service...............		864
30	4,356	... T o t a l ...	48	6,096

Survey.

Summary of Staff Salaries.

11	5,740	(a)	Senior Staff...... 13 costing	........£E.	6,813
6	1,161	(b)	Administrative Staff.......... 6	.... "	1,212
5	786	(c)	Computation office.......... 8	.... "	1,356
15	1,914	(d)	Reproduction office.......... 20	.... "	3,582
30	4,356	(e)	Field Staff....... 48	.... "	6,096
67	13,957		... T o t a l .. 95		19,059

(f). Field Allowances (12 months).

832	{ 1 Inspector at £E.9 p.m..........................	£E.	108
	{ 5 Asst. Inspectors at £E.7½ p.m...................	"	450
	{ 4 Sub-Inspectors at £E.6 p.m.....................	"	288
	{ 2 Surveyors Gr.II, J.S. at £E.4...................	"	96
	{ 5 " Gr.III, J.S. at £E.4...................	"	240
980	{12 " Gr.IV, J.S. at £E.4...................	"	576
	{11 " Gr.V, J.S. at £E.3...................	"	396
	{10 Apprentices at £E.2 (4 months).................	"	96
1812	... Total ...		2,250.

Survey /

- 8 -

1924-25.			1925-26.
Nos. Cost £E.			Nos. Cost £E.

Survey. (g) L a b o u r.

1924-25 Nos.			1925-26 Cost £E
300	(i)	Headquarters	450
5000	(ii)	Field....................	6550
5300		... Total ...	7000

Survey. (h) Other Charges.

0	(i)	Purchase of Box Cars and ? motor cycles.........	500
2606	(ii)	Transport & Travelling (including maintenance and running of cars...	4500
850	(iii)	Consumable stores – Reproduction Office.... (Drawing office 850– Process office 600).	1450
250	(iv)	Technical equipment..... (e.g. instruments)	2150
350	(v)	Survey marks............	1000
250	(vi)	Camp equipment..........	750
100	(vii)	Clothing................	200
100	(viii)	Saddlery................	100
55	(ix)	Office equipment and miscellaneous..........	100
120	(x)	Purchase of maps & books	100
180	(xi)	Passages................	150
100	(xii)	Compensations & gratuities	100
250	(xiii)	Payment of Mukhtars.....	250
200	(xiv)	Purchase of animals.....	150
80	(xv)	Contingencies...........	100
–	(xvi)	Map reproduction and special assistance.....	1000
5491		.... Total	12,600

- 9 -

1924-25.		B. Land Settlement.	1925-26.	
Nos.	Cost £E.		Nos.	Cost £E.

(i). **Administrative and Statistical Office.**

? To be seconded from Secretariat.

Officer in charge, Grade III, Senior Service:

Mr. C.L. Horton (now in Grade IV, Senior Service).
✦ Expatriation Allowance.

Chief Clerk, New Grade I, Junior Service, (pensionable), (£E.290 - 10 - 340).

(Mr. A.G. Antippa.)

(j). **Beisan Settlement.**

1924-25 Nos.	1924-25 Cost £E.		1925-26 Nos.	1925-26 Cost £E.
1	644	Chairman of Commission, Gr.III, S.S. Expatriation Allowance..........	1	699
				50
1	150	Clerks Grade IV, J.S...............	2	312
	156	Field Allowances (10 months) 1 at £E.9 - 2 at £E.4................		170
	200	Labour..............................		250
2	1150		3	1481

N.B. Provision for transport, travelling and other needs for the above is included, as hitherto, in the Survey estimate proper.

(k). **Provision for two Settlement Commissions.**

		8 months...................	-	2000
		Allowance at £E.1 per working day - 4 Palestinian members		600
		Carried Forward	6	2600

- 10 -

1924-25.			1925-26.	
Nos.	Cost £E.		Nos.	Cost £E.
		... Brought Forward ...	6	2600
—	—	Tents, equipment, travelling etc., (say	—	1000
		.. Total ...	6	3600
2	1150	Total for (j) and (k):	9	5081

CONFIDENTIAL.

SURVEY AND LAND SETTLEMENT ESTIMATES 1925-26.

N O T E III.

Staff Notes.

Throughout these estimates advancement is suggested for individuals, but it is fully understood that such advancement must receive separate consideration. It is at the same time impossible to detach the position and work of individuals from a review of the organisation as a whole.

2. I have not attempted any discussion of the actual grades as I imagine these fall into a standard classification: drawn up to suit local conditions.

3. The notes that follow have been written after discussion with the Director of Surveys, but I think it will be clear when my own views differ from his. My opinions are based upon personal appreciation in the case of Messrs. Giles, Le Ray, Bishop, Miller, Crusher, Moffat and Mankin, in the Survey, and of Mr. Camp, Mr. Horton and Mr. Antippa under Land Settlement. I have unfortunately missed Mr. Lanfear upon two occasions.

I have acquired no personal knowledge of the other members of the staff and the recommendations in regard to the junior grades are those of the Director of Surveys. I am, however, generally of opinion that the expansion of the service should be accompanied by a larger measure of advancement that would be approved if it was maintained at its present size.

I should also observe in this connection that the Director of Surveys has been accustomed to recruit technical staff at a rate lower than that at which he expects ultimately to assess them. This is with a view to ensuring that the workman is worthy of his hire before he receives it. In doing so the Director has frequently found it necessary to hold out prospects of early promotion, if the candidate proves up to expectations.

4. The names suggested for appointment to the posts of Chief Draughtsman (paragraph 11), Photo-process office (paragraph 13), and Printing office (paragraph 14), from the Egyptian service, are upon Mr. Crosthwaite's recommendations and are subject to the particular people mentioned in due course severing their connection with that service, as Mr. Crosthwaite was advised they had opted to do. In

the event /

- 2 -

the event of any of them not becoming available, or not being willing to take up the proposed posts, the Surveyor General of Egypt might be able to suggest alternatives to the Director of Surveys. It will of course be appreciated that it will not be at all easy at the outset to get experienced men at moderate salaries to fill these posts, and that departures from the Egyptian service offer an exceptional opportunity in this connection. Indeed the initial establishment of an efficient reproduction office on the small scale desired will not be easy: but once it is established successfully it will be able to train its own staff for the future.

A. S U R V E Y. (a). **Senior Staff.**

5. Mr. W.H. Giles is the senior officer after the Director and should replace Mr. Day. He will then be definitely recognised as the second officer in the Department, as at present constituted, and should regularly act for the Director when the latter is absent on leave, or otherwise, for anything but a short period. Mr. Giles is an able and energetic officer who requires both a wider technical sphere, and to be brought into touch with the policy and general management of the Department. At the same time there is not room at Survey Headquarters for an Assistant Director; and it is essential that Mr. Giles should have his own duties, these being rendered compatible with keeping him in touch with Departmental policy and administration generally.

In pursuance of these aims the Director is arranging to bring Mr. Giles into Jaffa where he will be located in the field in charge of the training of young field surveyors in the neighbourhood, and in systematically inspecting all the survey parties throughout Palestine. In view of this extensive combination of duties Mr. Giles will need a good British assistant officer as is mentioned later.

6. Mr. H.G. Le Ray. I am of opinion that it is a great pity to lose this officer at the very outset of the projected effort to put registration of title to land on the basis of a reliable cadastral survey and systematic settlement. The basis of survey is applied mathematics, and I do not agree with the Director of Survey that the value of having in the service a senior British officer who is a first class mathematician will cease when the triangulation of the country has been finally adjusted. The execution of the cadastral survey in Palestine to fulfil the needs of land settlement, registration and valuation with the optimum combination of economy in its full sense, technical excellence, rapidity, adjustment to local needs, local conditions and even local prejudices will be no light achievement:

and /

- 3 -

and the factors mentioned will not be static.

The experience of twenty seven years attack of a very similar problem in Egypt is that the value of maintaining a special mathematical officer, not in executive charge of survey operations, is many times his pay. The present Director of Survey has pronounced aptitude and taste for the more scientific branches of his work, and it may be that while he himself remains in charge and is sufficiently free to look after the mathematical side himself, the services of a British Mathematical officer might be dispensed with: although I think that it is much better not to combine the directing and critical functions in this way. And in any case it is in my opinion unwise to depend upon a perpetuation of the above aptitude and taste in the Head of the service. At present the Department is a purely technical Department: it is my view that in the future the combined field of pure survey, of cadastral mapping and registration of rights over immovable property and of valuation for public requirements (e.g. taxation, expropriation etc.), should be under one direction. This may take time to bring about: but when it occurs the Head of the service will not have the time even if he has the aptitude to perform specialized functions.

And if there is not enough work in this special sphere for Mr. Le Ray, the right course is to use him more fully, not to reject him after he has proved his value and capacity. There are other scientific services which must be performed and which in a small country can be advantageously directed in association with a Mathematical office. Such are the control of weights and measures: and the collection and scientific discussion of statistics.

7. Mr. C.J. Bishop and Mr. H.G. Miller receive normal advancement within their grade. They both seem to me to be thoroughly competent officers of the type that should be permanently retained. Mr. Bishop's experience of survey of a national character is limited, but I judge him to have the energy and intelligence to remedy this handicap, and also to improve his Arabic.

8. Mr. R.B. Crusher. The Director tells me that Mr. Crusher came to Palestine on the understanding that he was to take charge of Drawing and Map Reproduction for which work he was recommended by the Director-General, Ordnance Survey, and the Colonial Office. The original field sheets embodying the results of the cadastral survey should in my opinion be photographically reproduced and I am not yet satisfied that Mr. Crusher has the necessary experience to take charge of this work. He is, however, a hardworking, keen and valuable public servant: and if he is given facilities for seeing the cadastral work photographically reproduced in Egypt, there is I hope every

prospect /

- 4 -

prospect of his making good. It is in any case right that he should be given full and sympathetic opportunity to prove his capacity.

I represented in November 1923, that Mr. Crusher was graded unduly low and understood subsequently that his advancement had been approved. I recommend that Mr. Crusher now be advanced to the middle of Grade IV, Senior Service (£E.450 per annum plus Expatriation Allowance), as from 1st April, 1925, and that he be recognised as officer in charge of Drawing and Reproduction. He should be given facilities for visiting Egypt without drawing on his own pocket and, at a later stage, the Survey of Egypt should be asked to allow officers who have specialist knowledge to visit Palestine and assist in the actual establishment of the various stages of the work.

9. <u>Mr. E.J. Davies.</u> I understand that Mr. Davies' engagement with the Government of Palestine terminated about a year ago and that the Director asked him if he was prepared to renew that engagement for a period of another year which he agreed to do. Mr. Davies is a competent surveyor personally with a good knowledge of Arabic, but the Director is of opinion that confidence cannot be placed in him to get on with a piece of work unless he is watched, and that he has neither the gift nor the inclination to train and manage Palestinians.

It is definitely undesirable to retain in Palestine any Englishman who cannot be trusted to do his work honestly unsupervised: and there is no permanent place for a man who, however competent himself, is unable to train and manage a body of Palestinians. At the same time the Director feels that so far he has no proof of the correctness of his opinion, and favours the retention of Mr. Davies for another year on specific trial. During that year he would come under regular inspection by Mr. Giles.

10. <u>New appointments to Field Assistant Inspectorships.</u>

The candidates recommended by the Director of Surveys to fill these posts are <u>Mr. Stack</u> and <u>Mr. W.S. Moffat.</u>

I have not myself met Mr. Stack but I hope, in due course, to do so. I understand he is now employed as Chief Engineer to the Municipality of Gaza and that he is a very competent surveyor, with a good knowledge of valuation and is the type of officer needed. Knowledge of valuation is important; since it will be advisable systematically to value the land during the progress of survey and settlement in preparation for possible future land tax. I, however,

understand /

- 5 -

understand from Major Ley that Mr. Stack was previously in the Department of Public Works and was dispensed with for inefficient exercise of control and laxity in financial matters. Major Ley believes that Mr. Stack was out of his depth in a class of work that was not his metier, and was in no way culpable beyond carelessness. If his impressions are correct, he hopes that Government's view of the circumstances were not such as to lead them to exclude Mr. Stack from a service in which his metier lies.

I can personally support the second recommendation. Mr. Moffat obtained his experience in the Survey of Egypt and came to Palestine because it appeared to offer a future. He was economized about eighteen months ago. While here I have received from his late associates unvarying unsolicited tribute to Mr. Moffat's character, untiring industry and knowledge of his work. Should he be appointed, the Director proposes to detail him as assistant to Mr. Giles (v. paragraph 5).

11.   Sub-Inspectors.

I am not in favour of the permanent retention of this grade for British officers nor of the engagement of any more British officers in it: and I feel strongly that material improvement and expatriation pay should be granted to Mr. Lanfear and Mr. Mankin. They are both well reported on and have hard work and a hard life.

I should not have recommended the promotion of Mr. Holstein to this Grade: but understand that he has been notified that it will be approved on probation if he opts for Palestinian nationality. If the appointment precedes such optation, I suggest that it remains strictly contingent upon it.

12.   (b). Administrative Staff.

The Director advises me that he engaged Mr. Farajallah in a grade below that at which his chief clerk was previously graded on the understanding that he would be promoted to Grade II, Junior Service, when he had proved himself. His predecessors in Grades I and II had consistently been failures.

13.   (c). Mathematical Office.

The staff of the Mathematical office appear to be underpaid having regard to the importance of their duties, and their numbers are insufficient to deal with the extension of instrumental work and area computation which must be prepared for. The Director has already lost valuable computers through their pay being scaled too low: and some material measure of general advancement in the case of the small existing nucleus seems advisable.

14. /

- 6 -

14. (d). Reproduction Office.

(i). Assistant Inspector's office.

The size of the office does not justify a second officer but provision must be made for someone to take general charge of business when the Assistant Inspector is away. The post of Chief Assistant is designed to combine the satisfaction of this need with the normal duty of Chief Draughtsman. It therefore also involves in the holder general knowledge of map reproduction. This is a second appointment that it is recommended should be made from Egypt, as there is no one in the service qualified in either capacity. A competent British officer could not be obtained at the pay and is not needed. Mr. Crosthwaite recommends the appointment of an extremely competent Armenian, Mr. Hanessian, if, as he understands, he becomes available.

15. (d). Reproduction Office.

(ii). Drawing office.

Draughtsmen Grade II, Junior Service.

Fuad Masri is an old man at the maximum.

A. Kaplan is the leading draughtsman. He is useful but not up to being in charge. He should be given substantial advancement but possibly warned thereupon that he would not be left in the leading place.

Draughtsmen Grade III, Junior Service.

M. Aini is at present in Grade IV but was originally undergraded, as nothing was known of his capacity. He was trained in Egypt and has proved both a very good draughtsman and a first class cartographical Hebrew writer, which latter is greatly needed.

Draughtsmen Grade IV, Junior Service.

A. Nassibian and N. Azar were both engaged on a low basis on the understanding that they would be promoted if they shewed that their engagement in the higher class would have been justified.

Draughtsmen Grade V, Junior Service.

Nahas, Aintablian and Krikorian are all now good draughtsmen and have had three years in the Department. A year's acceleration of advancement is recommended by the Director to enable them to reach the higher class more quickly.

The two Ferekhs have had a full year on probation and should be graded as draughtsmen.

Jabagi /

- 7 -

Jabagi will be similarly qualified half way through the financial year.

16. (d). Reproduction Office.

(iii). Photo-process office.

This is another appointment which it is extremely difficult to fill at a small salary for a modest office. Here again Mr. Crosthwaite recommends a very competent Armenian from Egypt, Mr. Kerichdjian. He has had extended experience of the work and is very well reported on.

A second man at a lower salary will be required for douglagraph reproduction after the process-work has been got going.

17. (d). Reproduction Office.

(iv). Printing office.

Similar difficulties confront an economical appointment here, and in this case Mr. Crosthwaite recommends a very experienced Italian planograph printer, Mr. de Palma, who has been for years in the Survey map-printing office in Egypt. He is a man of 50, with exceptional all round experience including the erection of printing machinery. Mr. Crosthwaite thinks that he would be the best of the four excellent bargains that he recommends.

18. (e). F i e l d S t a f f.

Surveyors Grade II, Junior Service.

Alianak and Michaelides are both good men. Indeed the Director classes the former as being fully as valuable as Holstein.

Surveyors Grade III, Junior Service.

Constantinides, Karmonik and Kyriakos are all good men who should be materially advanced. It appears that Rosentool claims the right to take private practice in addition to his public duties and to receive fees from the Courts for work done for them. Such a right seems most undesirable and the general question might perhaps be usefully looked into. Officials of the Survey should be whole time men and any fees earned by them should be paid into public receipts. Rosentool actually works for the Land Department, but I understand that both Major Ley and Mr. Stubbs are in agreement on the above point, and that the latter is taking steps in the usual way to enquire about it.

Surveyors /

- 8 -

Surveyors Grade IV, Junior Service.

Goldstein and Weinstein were both trained in the Department, and have been four years in Grade V. The Director reports that they are now among the best of the older plane table hands, are discontented that their success in improving themselves has not received more recognition, and will probably not be retained unless some material advancement can be accorded them.

Surveyors Grade V, Junior Service.

Amiroff and Hashem, Nasr and Fink, have also had four years service and are also well trained plane-tablers. Gotlieb and Hucklesby have had 3½ years and 4 years training in the Department, are very hardworking and have learnt their work well. Albert, Husseini, Rosenheim, Kezeerman, Jayousy, Abdel Hadi, Haddad and Aintablian, are well trained men who have been 2¾ years in the Department.

19.   B.   LAND SETTLEMENT.

(i) Administrative and Statistical Office.

The genesis and suggested duties of this office are stated in my covering memorandum (paragraphs 10 and 11), which should be referred to.

Here I will only deal with the staff of such office in so far as necessary from the point of view of the estimates.

Mr. C.L. Horton. Mr. Horton is well known to the Government. I can only add that during the time that he has been with me he has acquitted himself admirably. He has initiative, sense, industry and drive. He will render very useful preparatory service to Land Settlement if he carries on his present work: but I do not think, pending fuller developments, that Government will be getting full value from him unless this work can be associated with the general charge of the normal administrative work in the Survey which it is essential that some competent administrative officer should take up. I am confident that Mr. Horton would carry on these joint duties to the advantage of the public service and to the satisfaction of both the Director of Surveys and the Government.

Mr. Horton has, I understand, been at the maximum of Grade IV, Senior Service, (£E.500 per annum plus Expatriation Allowance), since 1st April, 1921. I hope that his promotion into Grade III, Senior Service, will receive the favourable consideration of Government.

Mr. A. G. Antippa /

- 9 -

Mr. A. G. Antippa has worked for me excellently and I recommend that he be retained with the office. His weakest point, naturally enough, is English stenography, but even here he is very fair. He has worked intelligently, quickly, cheerfully and hard: and he has interpreted my illegible manuscripts, full of strange words, with sense and resource. He has also co-operated intelligently in the collection and arrangement of multifarious information. I should like to add my recommendation in support of the proposal which I believe is now under consideration that Mr. Antippa should be transferred to the permanent list of Government and to suggest that this should be at the minimum of the new Grade I, Junior Service, (£E.290-10-£E.340). This will mean gain of pension rights with a slight immediate loss in salary.

20. Land Settlement. (j). Beisan Settlement.

Mr. I. N. Camp. I will not enter into the earlier vicissitudes of the Government's attempts to carry into effect the Agreement of 19th November, 1921, but there seems to be no doubt that the conversion of the original opposition and obstruction on the part of the villages to its application into the willing co-operation now existing is entirely due to the qualities of the present chairman, Mr. Camp, and it must be recognised that in him the Government has found a very successful settlement officer. He knows Arabic well and can really deal with villagers without an interpreter: he has had some legal training and is steadily making himself acquainted with Ottoman Land Law in Arabic translation, which must be its actual vehicle of approach to the Palestinian peasantry: he is courteous and sympathetic to the people and is liked by them: he is patient in arriving at a solution and knows that it is necessary to be so: he has handled a Commission composed of three Palestinians for two and a half years harmoniously and productively: and he is in consequence achieving a piece of land settlement work covering nineteen villages and five tribal areas whose success is both remarkable and encouraging. I propose to deal with the work as a whole separately. It is too slow and it is not free from more serious defects: but such defects were bound to occur in a pioneering effort; they have not been of Mr. Camp's making: and they can, I hope, all be retrieved and remedied.

I have dwelt here on the value of Mr. Camp's work because it seems to me desirable that it should be appreciated in view of the projected extension of settlement work throughout Palestine, and that Mr. Camp's engagement should be placed on a more permanent basis than I understand it is at present.

SURVEY AND LAND SETTLEMENT ESTIMATES.

NOTE IV.

Notes on other heads of Recurrent Expenditure.

In Note III I endeavoured to comment briefly on some main features of the proposals affecting staff. I now turn to consider the estimates of recurrent expenditure under other heads.

The figures in the estimates were all prepared by the Director of Surveys who can of course present detailed explanations of actual figures. The comments which follow are my own and are confined to the broad issues otherwise stated.

2. (f). <u>Field Allowances</u>.

The Director suggests the slight modification of the rates of field allowances indicated in the estimates: but is very strongly of opinion that any reduction in the field allowances of the junior staff would be disastrous to the contentment of the field staff and the output of their work. The Senior Inspector in the field, Mr. Giles, quite independently said that it was the present field allowance which in the eyes of the field staff just made the hardships of field service worth while. While I am not in a position to appraise the absolute value of salaries in Palestine, it seems to me that the existing rates of field allowances are not exaggerated as a measure between the comfort of town residence, regular office hours and four half holidays a week on the one side, and the indifferent accommodation, other hardships, separation from families, and the long hours and continuous work normal to the field on the other. I do not think the saving that would be effected by the scale of field allowances suggested by the Treasurer sufficient to justify the risk of upsetting the contentment of the producing part of a Department which in a short life has suffered considerable vicissitudes and is being asked to put up with inquisition in the present and to be ready to meet new demands in the near future. When conditions are better a reduction in the scale might be reconsidered: but I suggest that a year's notice of any reduction should be given and that it might be applied gradually as advancement is accorded.

3. (g). <u>L a b o u r</u>.

The increase in the provision for labour which covers the chainmen, staff holders and others performing minor technical duties in the field, is in proportion to the proposed expansion of the service in field surveyors.

- 2 -

4. (h.i). <u>Purchase of Box Cars and motor cycles</u>.

I have emphasized in my covering memorandum the paralysis which affects the Department through lack of means of transport, and the deterioration of staff that is bound to follow immunity from unexpected inspection. A service which by its very character above all others must be able to penetrate into any part of the country at any time cannot be properly managed unless its controlling officers have effective and independent means of transport under their own command. Government Rest Houses, whereby defective means of communication can be supplemented, do not exist. The Railway service in Palestine is, through no fault of its own, extremely bad: the public cars only keep to the main routes, cannot carry instruments, tents, or other equipment, have to be pre-arranged for, and cannot be made subservient to the work. Horses are only of value within a limited circle, and, although useful enough for local control of small parties, are useless for regular inspection by Departmental senior officers, the virtual absence of which is one of the outstanding weaknesses at present. The Director of Surveys considers that box cars are the most useful means of such transport, since inspecting officers can carry on them a tent and immediate necessities and, if necessary, be independent and camp anywhere. A box car also offers the minimum temptation to joy riding. Not that I think joy riding is to be feared, if properly represented to responsible officers.

Four box cars should I think in due course be provided; one for the use of the senior officer working in the Northern District, one similarly for the Southern District, one for Headquarters Inspectors, and one as a spare in case of breakdowns and to enable cars to be regularly withdrawn for overhaul and reconditioning, which will enormously extend both their utility and their lives. A commencement could of course be made with a lesser number. A specific senior officer should be put in charge of each car, and be responsible for it. Drivers should be part time men with other departmental duties, under the direct orders of such officers. A simple monthly return should be furnished of actual journeys made and resulting kilometres run, of consumption of fuel and other expendable stores, of any repairs necessitating payment, etc., etc. Such cars will be of little value if they form part of a general Government pool, for the very essence of the need to be met is that they shall always be available to go anywhere at any time without notice. It is disadvantageous for the drivers of such cars to be under another Department: for this introduces divided responsibility, divided discipline and unnecessary additions to Government establishment.

It is much better to have responsibility for the proper care and economical use of a car wholly

centred /

centred on a senior British official who will commonly drive and look after the car himself, than divided in a vague way between him and a Palestinian chauffeur who is under the orders of a remote Department. Under the latter conditions, discipline is also bound to be faulty: moreover, a Department such as the Survey always has already on its pay roll men (e.g. orderlies, head chainmen to Inspectors), who can be part time chauffeurs without addition to establishment, whereas if chauffeurs are members of an outside Department they must be whole time men appointed ad hoc and they will be idle more than half their time.

In addition to box cars the provision of a certain establishment of motor cycles with side cars should be considered. A motor cycle can go along almost any track in dry weather, and can either extend the range of box car inspection, or replace such car according to circumstances.

5. (h, ii). <u>Transport and Travelling</u>.

I think considerable increase is called for under this head alike on an account of expansion of field staff, the need for more inspection, and the transfer of work in appreciable measure from the plains to the hills (for triangulation and forest demarcation) that is projected in the approaching financial year.

6. (h.iii). <u>Consumable stores - Reproduction office</u>.

In 1924-25 the estimate for drawing materials was £E.850 but apparently only £E.680 worth was indented for. With a larger field staff and unknown demands I think that last year's estimate might be repeated.

Mr. Crosthwaite reports that Whatman's hand made paper, which is that hitherto purchased, is not only uneconomical but inadvisable from the point of view of reproduction. Being hand made there is nearly always a curl in it which cannot be eliminated, and if the field sheets are used for photography this interferes with correct reproduction. He advises the purchase instead of a good machine made paper such as Hollingsworths. This paper costs about £E.38 per 500 sheets against the £E.62 paid for Whatman's paper. Mr. Crosthwaite also reports that indents for consumable stores are at present made by the Department quarterly. This is both uneconomical and inconvenient. Better prices and a more constant standard of materials ought to be obtained if supplies are purchased annually: also the cost of office work, freight and handling should be less. As soon as storage accommodation is available a full two years supply of plane-table, drawing, tracing

and /

- 4 -

and printing papers should be purchased. The paper now in use is unseasoned: and shrinkage and extension of raw paper is greater than should be accepted, in view of the attendant increased difficulties and inaccuracies. Long experience in Egypt has shown that paper which has been seasoned in the country in which it is to be used becomes much less subject to such changes.

The estimate of £E.600 for consumable stores for use in photo-process and printing was supplied by Mr. Crosthwaite for a full year's regular work. The total sum cannot be spent and if a note is made of the estimated annual requirement, the provision might be halved for the current year. Some provision should I think be included as it is sincerely to be hoped that a start with reproduction can be made next year.

7. (h. iv). <u>Technical equipment.</u>

The Department is extremely short of technical equipment especially field instruments. This is the falsest economy. If there is no spare pool at Headquarters, instruments cannot be regularly brought in for cleaning, overhaul and adjustment, with the results that dirt becomes ingrained, defects become set, and damage difficult to repair. As a consequence on the one hand expensive instruments rapidly deteriorate in value and their lives are shortened: and on the other observers tend to get bad results and to become discouraged while the repetition of observations increases with the waste of effort and money that this entails. Apart from accidents, which are of course bound to occur, instruments should be periodically withdrawn from the field for cleaning and examination. For every three instruments in the field there should be at least one at Headquarters undergoing cleaning and reconditioning, or ready for issue. And what applies to field instruments applies in varying degree to office instruments.

On these grounds alone the provision of additional instruments is very necessary: but there is also an increased need to be satisfied. It is proposed in the forthcoming year to push on with the completion of the triangulation, and to train up more Palestinian surveyors in instrumental work. Greater activity in the field also means greater demands to be met at Headquarters with increased provision of office instruments also. Details of the instruments actually required with estimated cost of same will probably be called for, and can be supplied by the Director of Surveys: but reasonable modifications of these details should be subsequently allowed for reason shown. In the office there is more particularly need for a second co-ordinatograph and a pantagraph.

8. /

- 5 -

8.   (h. v).   Survey marks.

A greatly increased provision of good reference and boundary marks is probably the most important single requirement for both survey and land settlement. This has already been emphasized in my covering memorandum.

9.   (h. vi).   Camp equipment.

As with instruments so with tents, inadequate supplies mean waste. The Survey is so short of tents that it is not able even to accommodate for a week or two, a base measuring party from Egypt, who will consequently have to bring all their tents up with them. Insufficient tents and deteriorated tents also gratuitously add to the hardships of the field parties and react upon their contentment and the output and value of their work. Shortage of tents is moreover a factor in restricting inspection. The question of the type of tent to be used needs and is receiving careful consideration. Experience so far seems to show that the purchase of rot proof canvas tents from England designed for easy transport may be a real economy in spite of initially increased cost, or that alternatively the poles and the canvas might be purchased in bulk and the tents made locally. There are few things that financially repay attention more than the construction, supply and care of tentage; and the question is I suppose one affecting numerous other Departments. An increased provision of both tents and other camp equipment would in any case be necessitated by expansion of field staff: but the above considerations make it advisable to do more than satisfy this obvious need.

10.   (h. vii).   Clothing.

The Director has found the issue of two blankets and other increased supplies to chainmen and other labourers in winter to be necessary, This, combined with the proposed addition of the field staff, accounts for the large increase in the estimate under this head.

11.   (h. viii, ix, x, xi, xii, xiii, xiv). Saddlery, office equipment, purchase of maps and books, passages, compensations, payment of Mukhtars, purchase of animals.

These items seem to call for little comment. Pack and riding saddles are provided for triangulation and other travelling field parties for use with hired animals. Increased concentration in triangulation will necessitate an increase in this item.

Payment /

Payment of Mukhtars remains unaltered. The Director says that it greatly facilitates work if Mukhtars are paid. It is however also a matter for consideration whether, when land settlement really starts, village authorities should not be expected to give gratuitous assistance.

During the course of survey in Egypt it is neither the practice to pay compensation for reasonable damage nor village authorities for their services.

12. (h. xvi). Map reproduction and special assistance.

This item is to cover the cost of map printing performed by or other technical assistance rendered by the Survey of Egypt, the Royal Air Force, or the Ordnance Survey. It includes the measurement of two base lines, map printing and cost of other help by the first, the cost of air photos. that may be needed from the second, and possible map printing from the third.

SURVEY ESTIMATES 1925 - 26.

Observations on Sir E. Dowson's covering Memorandum.

(1) pp. 2 and 3, clauses 6 and 7.

Inadequate Framework.

This matter is almost wholly one of available funds. The necessities have been well studied, the essential requirements are known, and I have made arrangements for such increase in the open plains as will provide points 500 metres apart on the average.

But to attempt to go further, or to emulate what is thought necessary under wholly different conditions in Egypt or Switzerland in this matter, would, in my opinion, be to plunge into serious and uncalled for extravagance.

I do not agree with the last paragraphs of clause 7 as regards Beisan. The main trouble at Beisan has been the immense length of the Blocks of Land, enforced on us by the people, which resulted in some mistakes in demarcation on the part of a wholly inexperienced staff. These were easily remedied when discovered, and the work now stands as absolutely sound and permanent as is, humanly speaking, practicable.

pp. 4, paragraph 8.

Defective Liaison.

I do not agree with most of these arguments, except those concerning improved means of transport for inspection purposes, a really vital point, - vide also my Note (B) with Observations on Estimates.

(2) pp. 4 and 5, paragraphs 9 - 11.

The addition of an Inspector (Grade III Senior Service) to my staff who is purely an Administrative Officer is not agreed to by me. No Senior Officer of that rank who is neither a Surveyor or any kind of expert on Land is wanted by me, and I shall be all the time trying to teach him his work.

On the other hand a good British Chief Clerk who knows the Government offices and methods is very badly wanted.

p. 6, paragraph 12.

This is premature. I am not yet prepared to put forward any name for promotion to Inspector.

p. 7, paragraph 17/

- 2 -

p.7, paragraph 17.

The statement in the fourth to seventh line of paragraph 17 is surprising, and I wholly disagree with it, vide my Note (B) attached to Observations on Estimates.

It would be much against economy and convenience of work to place the Department with Reproduction Office at Jerusalem - and Reproduction would not infrequently suffer from lack of sufficient water-supply.

pp. 8 and 9, paragraph 20.

Extension of Land Settlement.

(3) In view of the fact that a legal basis for Settlement has yet to be laid I am at a loss to know upon what work the two new Settlement Commissions can be put in the ensuing season. We have and shall have no maps ready for them other than in the Gaza District, and the Department needs further time to develop its Triangulation and Training.

(4) pp. 9 to 13.

Recurrent and Capital Expenditure.

Some outlines of a Survey organisation for upkeep of the future Registration system are given in these pages.

A great scheme is being evolved, the responsibility for non-success of which might be placed upon the Director of Surveys. I therefore may be allowed at this early stage to express some apprehensions concerning what I can now see of it - from the point of view of the agricultural industry.

(i) In addition to a heavy burden of debt charges, the industry will have permanently to meet most of the cost of a great Government Department - a conservative estimate for which is given at £E.80000 per annum.

(ii) Instead of a great reduction of Registration Fees as a result of Settlement these fees will be kept at a high figure to pay for this Government Department.

(iii) It would appear that under this scheme practically all the Survey requirements of the country, Government and Public Utility, are to be catered for by the Department.

If that is the case, the profession of private land surveyor will disappear, a valuable engineering asset in this country will in due course be

lost /

- 3 -

lost, together with hope of economical adjustment of supply to demand by open competition in that sphere.

(iv) With an organisation dealing with both agricultural properties and town properties on the same basis of fees, it seems almost inevitable that the interests of the agricultural industry will be sacrificed to those of Municipalities.

(v) The country is to be perambulated by scores of Government Surveyors searching for mutations.

Yet a mutation in a country property will, say, occur once in 20 years only, and the necessity to the public for legal recognition of any change of title will sufficiently guarantee the upkeep in the Register when it occurs. Particularly would this be the case if Government fees were low and competition had free play.

(vi) When once such a large Government organisation as is foreshadowed in this Covering Memorandum has been established, I suggest that all experience shows that it is very difficult for a country to subsequently reduce it, or to prevent further growth.

(Signed) C.H. Ley

DIRECTOR OF SURVEYS.

13.3.25.

OBSERVATIONS ON SURVEY ESTIMATES 1925-26.

I submit the following explanatory observations on items of Survey Estimates for 1925-26, together with attached notes A,B,C,D, in the desire to make clear the increases asked for in relation to correct Survey Policy, as I view it.

The observations concern items taken in order from the Statement showing both Loan and Revenue Estimates.

Item.	Explanatory Observations.
1 Inspector (Loan)	Mathematical. There is no need for the Higher Mathematics in a small Cadastral Department after the completion and adjustment of the Principal Triangulation and Astronomical Work in connection therewith. The post should, I think, be abolished in October next, see Note (A) attached.
1 Inspector. (Estimates).	(New appointment). The increase in the number of scattered Field Parties and resumption of training will early necessitate the appointment of a Field Inspector. This should be by promotion from within the Department, but I desire to postpone for a short time my recommendations as to the actual selection for the post.
2 Asst. Inspectors (Loan). 3 Asst. Inspectors (Estimates).	The officers of this grade will take charge of:- 2 large-scale Topographical Parties in the Plains. 1 Chain-Survey Party in orange gardens etc. 1 Town-Survey Party. 1 Training Camp. 1 Production and Printing Office. Two vacancies in this list will have to be filled, and the names of men who, I think, are specially qualified for the posts will be forwarded as soon as possible.
4 Sub-Inspectors. (Estimates).	At present 2 of these are British Officers. But all these posts should eventually be held by Palestinians.
1 Chief Clerk Gr.I. (Estimates).	(New appointment). Additional help in the Headquarters Control Office for administration and supervision of accounts is most essential. There will shortly be 12 Field Parties rendering separate Pay Lists and cash accounts to the Office, £E.20000 worth of Instruments and Permanent Stores, and the clerical work and financial responsibility grows steadily heavier.

- 2 -

Item.	Explanatory Observations. (continued)
	I see no necessity for a purely Administrative Officer of the Senior Service for the establishment of Survey and Settlement, if a good British Chief Clerk can be provided, see Note (A) attached.- The post was agreed to in principle 3 years ago. I will submit early recommendations as regards filling it.
2 Computers Grade III. (Estimates).	(New appointments by promotion). Greater concentration upon development of the fixed-point network necessitates expansion and reorganisation of the Computation Office. It is most desirable to divide the computation of Minor Triangulation and Traverse into two sub-sections placing each under a Grade III Computer. The names of two excellent trained computers in Grade IV each having over 3 years service in the Department will be put forward.
5 Computers Grade IV. (Estimates).	(1 appointment by promotion, 3 new appointments). Expansion as indicated above will be very necessary to meet the increased work in the field. But Grade V is inadequate for qualified mathematicians - vide Note (D). A good mathematician trained at Frankfort University only recently accepted Grade V post on the understanding he would be given advancement on the first opportunity. His name will be put forward for promotion. The 3 new appointments desired are of qualified mathematicians needing no training, direct to Grade IV.
Photographer Grade I. (Estimates). Asst.Photographer Grade II. (Loan).	(New appointments). Filling of these is only thought justifiable in 1925-26 if the necessary buildings for reproduction are early provided, vide my recommendations in Note (B) attached.
1 Draftsman Grade I. (Estimates).	(New appointment). With the provision of a printer and with heavy work of arrears in the Drawing Office, an assistant in the Drawing Office to the Officer in charge of Production and Printing is essential. Appointment of a trained man from Egypt is recommended by Sir E. Dowson and will be put forward by me separately.
2 Draftsmen Grade II. (Estimates).	(One new appointment by promotion). One Gr.II man is at present in charge of scale computations of area, but another is wanted to take charge of the topographical drawing and plotting.

A superior /

- 3 -

(continued).
Explanatory Observations.

Item.	
	A superior Syrian draftsman with 15 years service in the Survey of Egypt was engaged 3 years ago on the understanding he would be given advancement at the first opportunity. The rate of increment having been recently reduced the deferment of promotion has been a grievance to him which I think should now be remedied, vide Note (B) attached.
2 Draftsmen Grade III. (Estimates).	(One change in holder). A superior Jewish draftsman with 8 years service in the Survey of Egypt recently accepted a Grade IV appointment here on the understanding he should receive promotion to fill the first vacancy occurring in the Grade above. He will be put forward for the vacancy caused by the promotion referred to in the preceding paragraph, vide also Note (D) attached.
4 Draftsmen Grade IV. (Estimates).	(Three new appointments by promotion). To all of these Note (D) applies. Two skilled men now in Grade V, one having 12 years service in the Cyprus Survey and Registry, and one a skilled architectural draftsman, accepted their posts on the understanding they would be given the first possible opportunities of promotion. A third man trained in the Department has now 2½ years service and is a good draftsman. It would be an advantage to the Department to promote the above and secure their further services by a considerably extended contract.
6 Surveyors Grade III. (Estimates).	(3 new appointments by promotion). The number of small independent Field Parties for which it is impossible to provide a Senior Service Officer will have increased to 6 by April. The responsibility of Junior Officers in charge of these for government equipment, animals, and cash for contingencies in the field is relatively heavy, and it is both inadvisable and hardly fair to expect it to be borne by officers of a grade less than III. The 3 most reliable trained men in Grade IV will be selected to fill these appointments, which are urgently required.
13 Surveyors Grade IV. (Estimates).	(One new appointment). It is now most necessary to provide for regular inspection and restoration of Survey Marks - upon the permanency of which the success of future settlement will largely depend. A beginning can be made this year with one surveyor who can be specially engaged for the work.

10 accelerations /

- 4 - (continued)

Item.	Explanatory Observations.
11 Surveyors Grade V. (Loan).	(10 accelerations in grade). With one exception the whole of these surveyors are highly trained and efficient Plane-Tablers, the survival by merit of a class of apprentices trained in the Department 3 years ago. About £E.400 has been spent upon each of these officers and their advancement with definite contract now would meet a long-felt grievance at deferment of promotion, and be much in the interests of the Department, see notes (C) and (D). The provision made allows for acceleration to the maximum of Grade V in 10 cases.
16 Probationer Surveyors.	Experience shows that the right class of probationer surveyors cannot be obtained under the conditions of this country without payment. Pay at £E.8 per month was originally found necessary, but it is probable that £E.6 per month will now suffice. A class of 8 is required in April and a second class of 8 in October next. The period of probation should be 1 year only.
Field Allowances. (Loan & Estimates).	Regulations for issue and rates of this allowance are detailed in Note (C) accompanying these observations. It is very advisable that the lowest rate of £E.2 per mensem be issued to Probationer Surveyors after 6 months service as such in the field and on recommendation of British Officers in charge of parties.
Labour Service. (Loan & Estimates).	Division of expenditure on Labour between Loan and Estimates is hardly possible in practice at the present stage, when field parties must be of composite structure and transfers are frequent. Labour at Headquarters Office has therefore been charged to Estimates and Labour with Field Parties to Loan.
LAND SETTLEMENT COMMISSIONS.	An extra clerk is an urgent necessity for the Beisan Land Agreement Commission and has been provided. Provision for two additional Commissions has been made at the special request of Sir E. Dowson. I think these premature because without a basis in law, but, in so far as they involve deflection of the energies of this Department from its present preparatory work, they will be prejudicial to ultimate progress of settlement.

- 5 -

OTHER CHARGES.
(Loan and Estimates)

(continued)

Item.	Explanatory Observations.
Transport and Travelling. (£E.4700).	The increase in number of field parties and establishment, with greater expenditure on improved inspection, also expenditure of the additional Settlement Commissions is included.
Reproduction Materials. (£E.600).	This item is intended to cover paper, chemicals, inks, and all expendible stores required in a small Photo-process and Map-printing establishment. If no building can be provided during the year for the Photo-process Office, the amount can be largely reduced, vide Note (B) attached.
Camp Equipment. (£E.750.)	A further and large increase in tentage is pressing in order to provide for increase of establishment and new field parties, including Settlement Commissions, also for replacement of a large number of unserviceable old tents by Rot-proof patterns.
Technical Equipment. (£E.2150).	The item provides for all the necessary equipment of a Photo-process Office, for 1 additional co-ordinatograph, 1 additional Angle-adding machine, 4 additional Computing machines, 10 additional Theodolites and smaller field instruments, tapes and chains to equip the increased personnel in the field.
Marks and Beacons. (£E.1000).	Arrangements are being made to more than double the number of permanent marks fixed per unit of area and to better ensure their upkeep and replacement.
Purchase of Box Cars. (£E.500).	The possibility of inspection and control of the various field parties is a matter of transport. Box-cars are the only solution seen of this very special and vital problem of survey in this country. The provision is intended to cover, if possible, purchase of 3 Box-cars and 2 Motor Cycles, the former for the Director and Inspector, the latter for the Assistant Inspectors of the Topographical Parties.

(Signed) C.H. Ley.

NOTE (A) TO ACCOMPANY OBSERVATIONS ON SURVEY ESTIMATES.
1925-26.

The Permanent Cadre of the Survey Department.

The following principles have guided me in putting forward the division of Survey Estimates for 1925-26 which shows by separate estimate the Permanent Cadre of a future Survey Department.

(1) <u>General Considerations</u>:

Palestine has suffered greatly, both directly and indirectly, from the war. Her sole clear means of recovery is the development of her agriculture. But the land is naturally poor in comparison with that of more opulent countries, e.g. the average price of ordinary agricultural land in Egypt is nearly 20 times what it is in Palestine.

Probably for at least a generation all luxuries of Government in Palestine, however admirable in the abstract or thought fitting in more fortunate countries, must be avoided.

The adaptation and improvement of existing organisations, methods, and means, are in themselves under these conditions preferable to more violent changes in pursuit of perfection which involve heavy outlay.

And least in the interests of the country would be the crystalisation during a long but temporary period of expansion of a species of unconscious vested interest in a large Government Department. That might well be thought to be both adding to the yoke of the unfortunate fellah and chastising him with scorpions.

For it is agreed that a large initial outlay spread over a number of years is necessary for the temporary operation of Land Settlement and establishment of a scientific system of Registration. And that this wave of necessary expenditure can justifiably be met by borrowing, provided future benefits to the agricultural population can be assured which will enable them both to repay such a loan and live in greater prosperity.

But if that is to be done, in addition to relief of taxation there must be large reduction of the present high Registration fees and other charges on developments and mutations of land.

And there is no prospect of such relief if to the burden of debt is to be added the charges for upkeep and for pensions of a great Department.

Fortunately /

- 2 -

Fortunately the private enterprise and genius of the people can be invoked to solve this problem, in a healthy and perfectly natural manner.

For there already exists a considerable body of private surveyors licensed by the Government to practise their profession in Palestine, and when the temporary period of expansion during initial Survey and Settlement is over a stream of trained men will pour into their ranks on contraction of the Government Department.

Thus there will be no lack of numbers and ability in the private profession, and, given economic room, competition may be trusted to adjust supply to demand. Economic room will obviously be furnished if the Government Registration Fees are reduced to cover the cost price only of pure registration and control by the Government Department which, particularly if economically organised, would be far less than the present fees.

(2) Outlines of Permanent Department.

On these lines the following rough general specification for a small permanent Government Department for all the future work of Cadastral Survey as distinct from pure Registry duties, after the main work of Settlement is completed has been arrived at and embodied in the Estimates (Revenue):-

(a) 2 Survey Districts served by a permanent field staff of 20 surveyors, 4 Sub-Inspectors, and 2 Assistant Inspectors - all, with the possible exception of the Assistant Inspectors, Palestinians. Their work will consist of the carrying out of survey revisions required for the larger mutations of private property, of plans for the development and upkeep of State Lands, of inspection of the work of the private surveyors in all ordinary mutations, and of such occasional special surveys as may be needed.

(b) A Headquarters Office including a small British control as follows:

      A Director
      One Inspector
      One Officer i/c Reproduction Office.
      One Chief Clerk and Accountant i/c
        Clerical Office.

The Reproduction Office will consist of the following Palestinian Officers:

One Chief Draftsman, one Photographer, one Printer, and 16 Draftsmen and Area Computers.

(3) /

- 3 -

(3)   Such a post-settlement Department increased as occasion demands by temporary additions and aided by the full play of private enterprise will, I think, meet all requirements of upkeep of Cadastral plans and of Special Surveys in the future in this country.

Note (B) gives my views as to the site of the Headquarters Office, and the necessity for early action as to a building programme.

(Signed) C.H. Ley.

NOTE (B) TO ACCOMPANY
OBSERVATIONS ON SURVEY ESTIMATES.
1925-26.

Site and Cost of Buildings for Survey Department.

(1)   Capital Expenditure on building Cadastral Headquarters is not included in the Estimates forwarded by me since it is almost wholly a matter of site.

Yet further delay in providing the power of Reproduction is much to be deplored, and the provision of the special staff needed has been inserted in the Estimates.

(2)   Of the two alternatives to the present site which have been mentioned in some preliminary discussions of this pressing matter - viz: Jerusalem and Haifa (Mount Carmel) - I consider the latter the superior.

The only argument in favour of Jerusalem appears to be that it is the Seat of Government, an admittedly unfortunate fact in view of the extraordinary inconvenience and uneconomy of its site as a modern capital.

(3)   It is thought that this argument is a slender one to set against the large additional expenditure, the great handicap to efficient control of a scattered Field Department, and the inconvenience and expense to the Agricultural Community in the future, involved by its acceptance.

It is relatively easy to remedy possible defects of liaison between Survey and Government if they exist. Settlement of the Policy and Organisation, with provision of the long-deferred relief on the Administrative side at Survey Headquarters, and of increased facilities for inspection, should remove all doubts in this matter.

(4)   Mount Carmel is a more convenient site for administrative and technical control than Jerusalem, and it has some advantage in being near the Headquarters of the Department of Agriculture, but it also involves heavy expenditure.

(5)   But under the considerations and conclusions of Note (A) attached it appears plain that the present site at Jaffa meets all the essential requirements in far the cheapest and readiest manner.

The existing survey building is the ex-German Consulate and will provide admirably for the future Permanent Control and Drawing Office. There is space in the compound at the back for a sufficient Photo-

process /

- 2 -

process and Printing Office, a Map-Store and, if necessary, an office for control of Land Registration. There is ample sufficient water supply and freedom from dust, vibration, etc., the site is central to the principal agricultural plains, and convenient to the public in the future as well as to the Field Organisation during the period of Settlement.

(6) The present site and building is assessed at, and can presumably be obtained for £E.5000 if purchased before August next.

The necessary additional buildings apart from a Registry Control Office are roughly estimated to cost £E.3500 - but no opportunity for study of construction recommended, it is understood by the Survey of Egypt, has yet been provided.

The Photo-process and Printing Office building could probably be completed and equipped within 6 months after approval - the building cost £E.1500.

(7) The total cost of completely housing the Department at Jerusalem or Mount Carmel would on the other hand probably exceed £E.20000.

Neither of these schemes could be much advanced in the financial year 1925-26.

(Signed) C.H. Ley.

NOTE (C) TO ACCOMPANY
OBSERVATIONS ON SURVEY ESTIMATES.
1925-26.

Field Allowances.

(1) Field Allowance has been of the utmost value in allaying the discontent of surveyors at their pay and prospects, also in providing a valuable means for maintaining discipline and efficiency in the field.

Its economy and convenience as compared with Travelling Allowance have also been considerable.

I forward therefore for approval Regulations governing the issue of this allowance which show the rates embodied in the Estimates for 1925-26.

REGULATIONS GOVERNING THE ISSUE OF FIELD ALLOWANCES.

(i) Field Allowances are issued to Survey Officers who have no fixed station and whose duties are carried out under field conditions with hours of work which are dependent upon the exigencies of work in the field.

(ii) Officers entitled to Field Allowance will not draw Travelling Allowances, nor, without special approval of the High Commissioner, are they entitled to Housing accommodation.

(iii) Field Allowance will be issued on the weekly day of rest, but pro-rata deductions will be made for absences from camp on leave exceeding one day, or for absences from camp on duty exceeding 3 days.

(iv) The High Commissioner may, on recommendation of the Director of Surveys, direct that the allowance be reduced or its issue suspended on account of bad work, low progress, or conduct to the prejudice of discipline or of the interests of the Government Service.

(v) The normal rates of Field Allowance will be :-

```
Inspector............... £E.9 per month.
Asst. Inspector......... £E.7.50  "    "
Sub-Inspector........... £E.6     "    "
Surveyor Grade I-IV..... £E.4     "    "
    "        "   V...... £E.3     "    "
Field Clerk, all grades. £E.3     "    "
Surveyor Probationer,
  after 6 months service
  as such................ £E.2
```

(Signed) C.H. Ley.

NOTE (D) TO ACCOMPANY
OBSERVATIONS ON SURVEY ESTIMATES.
1925-26.

Gradings and Pay of Technical Ranks.

(1) The Estimates provide for a number of promotions and accelerations among skilled individuals of technical grades in the Junior Service, and the following explanation is submitted for consideration:

(2) 2 surveyors, 3 draftsmen and 1 computer of Grades IV and V, together comprising a large proportion of the most skilled hands, have left the Department during the Financial Year 1924-25 owing to dissatisfaction with their pay and prospects.

I have good reason to know that other trained men are now ready to do the same the moment they can get safe opportunity.

(3) The main reason for this defection is the deferment of the prospect of promotion by the reduction of the annual increment in Grades III - V of the Junior Service from £E.12 to £E.6 per annum, with consequent locking up of individuals in their grades for 6 years in the normal course.

Young men of ambition and ability in highly specialised lines, many of them graduates of European Universities, will not remain for such a number of years in positions equal to those of lower grade clerks.

There is a market outside for them which offers an easier life with better scope and prospects, and directly they sense the power of their training they leave.

(4) At the same time, in a period of expansion, it is even more unprofitable to try to anticipate events, say, for example, by initially putting a man with some training and recommendations as an architectural draftsman directly into the grade suitable for a trained survey draftsman, or by making long-period contracts with surveyors whose ultimate suitability is problematical.

(5) Thus the practical effect of the attempt to apply a rigid universal system of grading and rates of pay to the specialised trades and professions of this Department in a period of growth is that we are often committed to training and retraining over the same ground for the

benefit /

- 2 -

benefit of others. It constitutes a disease of the organism which is extremely costly to the Government, and very damaging to its object of survey.

(6) It appears that special gradings and rates of advancement for specialised technical ranks have long been recognised as necessary in England and other countries.

Pending similar recognition in this country I urge that a reasonable number of advancements be afforded such as are provided for in these estimates.

All the cases put forward have the support of Sir Ernest Dowson.

(Signed) C.H. Ley.

4.02

GOVERNMENT OF PALESTINE

NOTE

ON THE

TECHNICAL SYSTEM

OF THE

SURVEY OF PALESTINE

JANUARY 1927

Price P. T. 10.

SURVEY OF PALESTINE.

NOTE ON THE TECHNICAL SYSTEM OF THE SURVEY.

1. Introductory Remark.

The technical system of the Survey of Palestine has been evolved to achieve a specific object in the most economical manner, and in the following brief account it has been thought well to review the main technical problems as they have in practice presented themselves, beginning at the costly business-end, and tracing back the influence of the conditions to those initial technical operations which are common to most scientific surveys.

2. Past System of Registration.

As a result of a medieval system of Land Registration succeeded by war, only a fraction of the present owners of land in Palestine are registered, and as in addition the great majority of the cultivated areas are unmapped and to a large extent featureless, and property has not been demarcated, such registrations as exist cannot as a rule be interpreted on the ground.

Post-war land registrations have been accompanied by sketch-maps, but as enforcement of permanent marking in the open lands has only recently been possible, some of this work also has become of imaginary value, tending to further confusion.

The righting of this position will, it is hoped, be effected by Settlement Commissions which will investigate and decide upon all rights, and by a Cadastral Survey which will demarcate these upon the ground and record the same upon accurate plans which can accompany new registers.

3. Objects of Survey.

The main ultimate object of the Survey has therefore been the economical production of large-scale cadastral plans correctly showing each individual parcel of land as registered.

But Registration by Land Settlement is a slow process not yet begun, present Land Registry transactions must continue and urgently need better location and control, the final cadastral operations need a large-scale topographical map and an accurate frame-work of permanent points upon which to operate, and the administrative services much need maps for general purposes.

The more immediate object of the Survey has therefore been the production of large-scale topographic plans in advance of Settlement, with the fixation in plan and upon the ground of a sufficient frame-work of permanent points to facilitate future property-demarcation, and to which the current work of the Land Registry can be hung.

— 2 —

4. Scale of Maps.

Considerations of accuracy, of the value of land, the closeness of its subdivision, and the needs of registration, have caused the 1/2500 scale to be adopted as the standard scale for all the more fertile areas of the Palestine plains.

The relatively small areas of fruit orchards and groves, which are surveyed by field-book and chain, are plotted on this scale, which is suitable also for showing on the final cadastral plans the strip properties in the open Lands — after partitioning and demarcation.

Larger scales are employed for close garden and village areas, and smaller scales for more barren or hilly areas where property is of much less value and subdivision usually less intense.

5. Topography and Cultivation System.

The open cultivated plains are as a whole almost destitute of visible features other than wadis, country roads, and camel tracks, which are usually either ill-defined or subject to seasonal changes.

So also village boundaries and internal property boundaries are known to the fellaheen but seldom visible to others. The lands in each village are held as a rule on a collective basis, and are divided into permanent cultivation blocks very roughly representing areas of different cultivable value. Each block is held by a family, a group, or by the whole village for a term of years, the members of such a group temporarily subdividing into individual strip-parcels by lot.

A main object of the Settlement by Cadastral Survey is to substitute permanent individual ownership for this system.

6. Topo-cadastral Maps by Graphic Method.

Now this open country is exceptionally suitable for Triangulation and for the Plane-Table, but unsuited for Chain-Survey, although ultimate property demarcation must be with tape or chain.

The occasional patches of close orchards around villages which are surveyed with the chain being in any case plotted on the 1/2500 scale, the scheme that has been evolved for open lands includes a graphic method on a 1/2500 sheet-system.

The principal Trig. is broken down by 3rd and 4th-Order work to so close a network that at least 3 minor Trig. Points are fixed in each 1/2500 Field Sheet. The density of these points in any locality depends upon the topography, and the average number available within the paper margins of a sheet actually works out at 5.5, giving an average distance between adjacent points of 890 metres.

But this is insufficient for rapid direct control of demarcation of properties by chain or tape, moreover the Trig. points are inconveniently sited upon topographical features independent of the cadastral requirements.

The main cadastral divisions are the village boundaries and the cultivation-blocks, and, after ascertaining these, Landmarks at a suitable distance apart which can be intersected direct from the Trig. by Plane-Table can be sited upon or near them.

— 3 —

At the same time such topographical features as exist can be put in by Plane-Table intersection, combined, when necessary, with close-range tacheometry or other graphic method, as found necessary.

The resulting preliminary map has been called a "Topo-Cadastral" one, since it shows topographic features but not the shape of the ground, and also shows with accuracy the main points and arrangement of the principal cadastral boundaries. An example on a reduced scale is given in Diagram I.

7. Precautions with Graphic Method.

The difficulties of such a graphic method lie in paper-shrinkage and errors of plotting. The unavoidable plotting error on the 1/2500 scale is about 1/2 metre on the ground, so that if an error of 1/500 is to be avoided in any controlling distance between two Landmarks, the latter must not be less than $500/\sqrt{2}$, or 350 m. apart.

It has been found that only a few of the cultivation blocks are too small to allow of such an interval and that in such cases blocks can usually be grouped together between the controlling Landmarks.

As a rule these controlling points can be placed at between 400 and 500 metres apart.

The intersections are carried out on a special Plane-Table by telescopic alidade with the finest and hardest pencils, no plottable triangle of error is allowed, nor are Landmark-intersections allowed to be inked, rubbed, pricked in, or touched up in any way in the field.

The best quality well-seasoned hand-made paper is used and fixed to the Plane-Table by a specially-devised simple method which avoids paste and allows considerable freedom for expansion or contraction. Diagram II illustrates the method.

Initial Plotting of sheet-corners and Trig. Points is done by Coradi Coordinatograph, by which also graphic coordinates of the Landmarks are microscopically obtained, corrected after careful reading of paper distortion, and recorded.

8. Accuracy of Graphic Method.

Careful tests of the accuracy of this method by tapings between Landmarks taken at random have been regularly made.

The resulting average of the 139 distances checked to-date is 445 metres and the average error of double-taping for that distance (calculated from Traverse closures on Trig. Points) is ± 0.22 metres. The average error of the distances obtained from the graphic coordinates has on this basis been calculated from differences with the taped distances and found to be ± 0.3 metres, or 1/1483 (equivalent to a probable error of ± 0.25 metres, or 1/1780) nearly.*

It is considered that this result proves that the graphic fixations of the Landmarks are adequate for the control of detail errors and for the demarcation on the ground of individual properties with the chain.

---

* The method compares well with that of Traverse in close areas. In the 56 check-tapings made between Traverse points in different but neighbouring Traverse Lines an average discrepancy of 0.25 metres between the taped and the calculated coordinate distances, in an average distance of 223 metres (1/970), was obtained. But, as might be expected from the absence of geometric control in the case of Traverse points, this result is characterised by an undue proportion of the grosser errors, an undesirable feature in a property survey.

— 4 —

Besides the low cost of the method and its automatic limitation of error, it has the great advantage of rapidly fixing the cadastral part of the frame-work without redundant points and so as most likely to be protected and maintained by the people, an important consideration in view of the curiosity of the Arab and the interval of time separating the initial from the final operations.

9. Small-scale Maps.

The production of small-scale topographic maps is subsidiary to the main object but is ultimately assured by the necessity for maps for general purposes.

The 1/2500 field sheets are being reduced to a 1/20,000 scale as a reference map for administrative purposes, which, when funds and opportunity permit, can be quickly converted into a Topographical Series by completion with approximate contours. With Trig. heights already determined at less than a kilometre apart there should be little difficulty in such conversion.

The ultimate production of a 1/100,000 general topographic map in half-degree sheets is contemplated.

10. Densities of Network

Whereas the density of the 4th-Order Triangulation is determined by the requirements of the Plane-Tablers, that of the Principal Trig. is determined by independent considerations which must be umtrammelled. And as it would clearly have been unsound to break down direct from the relatively long lines of the latter to the very short ones of the former, the question arose as to where to place a limit for intervening 3rd-Order work so as to maintain the flow of control with the proper economy.

In a well-shaped triangle internal gaps which cannot be filled by directly dependent points can be avoided by arranging to break up its sides with triangles having sides of about one-fiftn of their length, so that the necessity for the insertion of additional points and for calculation of additional junctions, with liability to multiplication of errors, is eliminated.

It appeared therefore from the geometry of the case that the average length of side of a network should be about 5 times that of the lower-order network to which it is broken down, and this ratio has on the whole been well maintained between 3rd and 4th-Order Trigs. in Palestine.

But the Principal Trig. has no superior control, its network has to cover the whole country (see Diagram III), yet its errors must not accumulate much in any direction. It therefore has to be of high-clsss nature, with well-shaped figures extended from a very accurate base-line, and the length of its sides becomes mainly dictated by the orography of the country, the atmospheric conditions, and the nature of the signals — the latter matter having an important bearing on economy. The Palestine signals were fixed iron ones of modified S. African pattern at an average distance apart only a little more than 3 times that of the 3rd-Order Sides.

Geometrically speaking, therefore, the Palestine network would here appear uneconomical.

On the other hand a possible and more perfect relationship between the side-lengths in the 3 Orders of Trig. such as 13 KM, 2.5 KM, and 0.5 KM,

— 5 —

while it might have substituted Trig. Points for graphically determined Landmarks on the maps, would, by greatly multiplying the minor Trig. points, have slowed down the whole of the Survey operations and heavily increased the total cost without justification.

Moreover, as will be seen from para. 13, it is a distinct advantage on the side of accuracy to apply a small ratio such as 3/1 to the breaking down of the Principal sides, since double values for the 3rd-Order points can be thereby obtained in adjustment.

The requirements of economy are in fact best served by putting any unavoidable additional capital expenditure in at the foundation of such a structure, where the amount required is least per unit of area covered.

11. Observations and Instruments.

Following upon these considerations, it was decided that in order to maintain a regular progression in the accumulation of error propagated through the network, the number of balanced observations with the same class of instrument should vary roughly as the square root of the average distance between the signals in each Order of Triangulation.

With side-lengths of 1, 5, and 15 KM. as originally thought possible for the 4th, 3rd, and Principal Trig., respectively, 2, 4, and 8 compete sets of balanced observations on two faces with 5-inch micrometer theodolites would therefore have been theoretically suitable, but as an 8-inch instrument was thought necessary, for the Principal Trig., the number of sets was reduced in this case to 6 — except in the case of the Base-Extension figure, where it was increased to 9.

The actual average side-lengths have worked out at 0.89, 4.20, and 13.20KM in the three cases, so that the intended relationship was fairly well maintained

12. Original Adjustment of Minor Trig.

But the most important consideration in the due control of error is the system of adjustment.

The method at first adopted in Palestine was a borrowed one, which consisted of the application of a species of arbitrary angular adjustment of the lower-order network by polygons, followed by a scale-adjustment applied to one selected chain of triangles only between a single pair of points in each higher-order controlling triangle—by means of a projection-method which resulted in approximations in both azimuth and coordinates.[*]

The points in the relatively wide spaces between these approximately adjusted chains were obtained by separate solution of the simple dependent triangles.

The method was troublesome and was proved to be insufficiently accurate for cadastral purposes in Palestine by the frequent failure of Plane-Tablers to obtain accurate intersections at Landmarks, particularly in these loosely controlled spaces.

---

[*] Vide 'The Cadastral Survey of Egypt 1892-1907' (Lyons). pp. 261, 262, 250, 281.

— 6 —

13. Later Method.

The following more complete and rigorous system, which not only has proved quite successful in meeting all the requirements of an accurate graphic method, but has resulted in an actual saving of time and labour in the Computation Office and in the Field, was substituted:—

Between each pair of points of a Principal Triangle (held as fixed) *two* 3rd-Order chains are, after separate adjustment of the triangular error in each triangle, separately adjusted so as to exactly fit the Principal side, as follows:—

The Coordinates of one terminal of a chain are calculated with reference to the other terminal on a assumed length and azimuth for one of the sides and through the shortest route.

Comparison of the resulting calculated length and azimuth of the line joining the terminals with the actual Values given by the Principal Triangulation furnishes constant corrections to the assumed scale and azimuth.

A second and complete computation for the coordinates of all the points on the corrected data is then carried out.

In the rare case of points occuring in an intervening space the mean of several values from triangles directly based upon the chains is taken.

As the average ratio of a 3rd-Order side to a Principal side was only 1/3 at least two chain-adjusetd values were obtained for a great majority of the points, from which the mean could be taken.

In the 4th-Order adjustment *one* chain between each pair of adjacent 3rd-Order points is in like manner rigorously adjusted, and points in intervening spaces are treated as before. Here, except in a few cases of junction points, two chain-adjusted values are obtained for 4th-Order points near the apices of the 3rd-Order triangles, one for point near the middle of the sides, and at least two values from dependent triangles at points in the intervening spaces.

Examples are given in Diagrams IV., V.

14. Adjustment of Principal Trig.

Owing to the early necessity for pressing forward with the maping, rigorous original ad-justment of the Principal Trig.. by the Method of Least Squares could only be applied to figures or small blocks as they became available.

Subsequent re-measurement of the principal base (points 1—2), at Imara in the South, has shown that it possesses an error of the order 1/750,000, but that the accumulated errors of the Trig. as thus adjusted result in an error at the check-base at Semakh (points 66,67) of 1/12,000. No serious error of calculated azimuth was however found at intermediate astronomical stations.

It was considered that the acceptance of such an accumulated scale-error would prove ultimately awkward for the sheet-system in the North, and that as regular mapping could not for some time be commenced in the northern District the opportunity should be seized of more rigorously re-adjusting the whole Triangulation in two large blocks on the Egyptian value for the Imara Base, which has a probable error of the order 1/2,000,000.

— 7 —

15. Accuracy of Fixed-Point Network.

The effect of the measures described in controlling the accumulation of error through the whole system can however now be fairly assessed. In the following table evidence as to the progressive propagation of error through the Minor Trig. has been derived from the discrepancies between positions of junction points from different adjusted chains, as to that of the Cadastral network of Landmarks from actual measurement, vide para (8) above, and as to that of the Principal Trig. from the theoretic rate of accumulation of its average angular error.

TABLE I.   ERRORS OF NETWORK.

Portion of Network	Average Triangular Error	Average length of a side	Average Scale-error.
Principal	± 1.4″	13.20 KM	± 1/70,000
3rd Order	± 4.9″	4.20 KM	± 1/30,000*
4th Order	± 10.0″	0.89 KM	± 1/10,000*
Graphic	—	0.45 KM	± 1/1,500*

* Includes errors transmitted from the higher order network.

16. Astronomical Observations.

Observations for Latitude and Azimuth at the Imara Base (point No. 2), checked by observations at points 31 and 73, have resulted in an almost constant difference of — 1.4″ between the Palestine and Egyptian values for latitude at a number of stations common to a triangulation carried out by the Survey of Egypt during the War.

The Imara value was considered preferable and has been adopted in the calculation of geographical coordinates.

A longitude given by the Survey of Egypt at one of these common points, being considered as accurate as any fresh determination that could at present be undertaken, has however been adopted. It is ultimately based upon a meridian at Moqattam Hill determined by a Transit of Venus Expedition in 1874.

17. Junctions with Geodetic Systems.

It is unfortunate that the valuable check upon the Palestine system that would have been afforded by the junction arranged for with the French Geodetic chain in the north has not yet been obtained owing to a delay in the latter operation.

A junction with the Egyptian Geodetic system must await the possibility of an extension through Sinai of the Principal Triangulation of Egypt.

18. The System of Coordinates.

Rectangular coordinates (Cassini's projection) with a central meridian passing through point No. 82 (Jerusalem) were decided upon. The Sheet-grid shown in Diagram III is numbered from an imaginary zero-point in the Mediterranean, each grid-square comprising 64 sheets on the 1/2500 scale.

— 8 —

The fact that a figure of the earth (Bessel's) was used for the rectangular coordinates differing from that used for the geographical coordinates (Clarke's 1866) was due to the early need for mapping and the absence of tables of constants. The anomaly does not sensibly affect Cadastral requirements but it is proposed to eliminate it in the re-adjustment now being carried out by the adoption of the same figure for all coordinates.

The systematic error due to the Projection is not included in Table I, and, on the basis of a Jerusalem Central Meridian, has been considered to have practically negligible effect in the area between the Palestine coast and the Hedjaz Railway.

19. Cost.

A de-novo survey for cadastral purposes is one for a practical economic object in which financial considerations are of the greatest importance, and the technical methods adopted have a governing influence on the cost.

A table is therefore added showing approximate figures for the cost up to date of the various sections of the work per unit of area, apart from that of preliminary training and of office work.

TABLE II.   FIELD COST.

Section of Work	Average Cost £E. per Sq. KM	Remarks.
Principal Trig.	0.58	See note
3rd-Order "	0.56	
4th-Order "	4.84	
1/2500 Topo-cadastral Mapping.		
Plane-Table (Open Lands)	10.00	Includes Landmarks
Chain Survey (Close Areas)	77.00	" Examination
Chain Survey (Very Close, requiring Traverse)	171.00	—do— —do—
1/500 Close Town Plans	913.00	—do— —do—

NOTE:— Includes base measurement, astronomical observations, reconnaissance, and cost of beacons.

The total cost of of the 1/2500 preliminary map in open village lands is therefore £E.16 per sq. KM., and in ordinary close areas £E.83 per sq. KM., on the average.

In considering these figures it should be remembered that the Survey Department is as yet immature and composed almost wholly of recently-trained and inexprienced local personnel, and that in Palestine high prices for labour and materials have ruled in the post-war period.

C. H. LEY
DIRECTOR OF SURVEYS.

JAFFA. JANUARY, 1927.

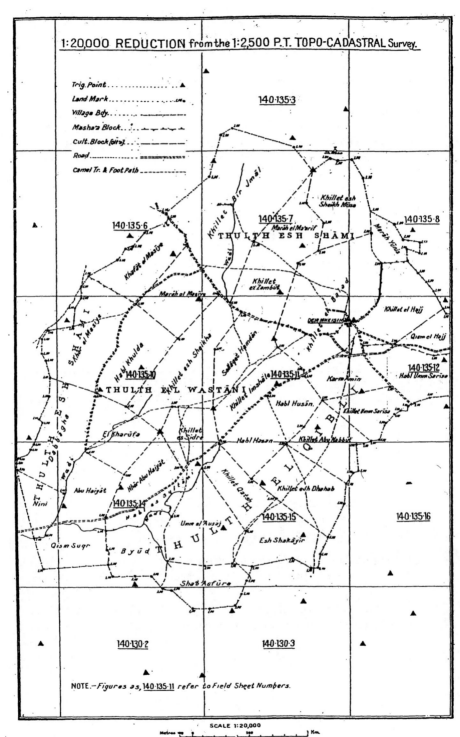

4.03

Bowyersfield,
Wrotham.
4 August 1927

My dear Shuckburgh.

In accordance with your letter of the 12th. of July last and the subsequent talk with Lord Plumer and yourself, I have interviewed and made enquiries about Mr. A.P. Mitchell with a view to his possible appointment as Survey Officer in Transjordan. I attach a brief resumé of his career. Any papers or further details that may be required can be supplied in due course if matters proceed. My own conclusions follow.

2. Mr. Mitchell is of the right age, is the right type of officer and has just the qualities and experience that are most needed to carry through to success the many-sided and difficult task for which the services of a British Survey Officer are required. His knowledge of Arabic is already very useful and should in due course become really good; his experience in the application of survey to land problems is exceptional; and he has an established record of successful supervision of several hundred Egyptian Survey Officials.

He is weak on the topographical and mathematical sides of the work, not from lack of natural capacity, but as regards the second partly owing to his education (in the scholastic sense) having been interrupted by the outbreak of war, and as regards both from lack of experience on these sides. The Survey of Egypt is a large and severely decentralised organisation, and throughout his service with it Mr. Mitchell has been almost exclusively engaged on cadastral survey, land registration and expropriation of land for public purposes.

3. The experience and qualifications that Mr. Mitchell possesses are rarer, and, having regard to the work to be done, much more valuable than the experience and qualities that he lacks. He will very rapidly make good any present poverty

[Final sentence is missing from original file copy.]

topographical experience, while it is, I think, just as well that the Survey Officer in Transjordan should be a man who has been accustomed to external mathematical control and general technical direction. Palestine and Transjordan are small and closely associated geographical areas, the surveys of which should have a united trigonometrical basis and, so far as economically possible, common technique and standards. The Survey of Palestine possesses the organisation and technical knowledge to provide this common basis and technical control; and it would be both undesirable and wasteful to establish a minor replica in Transjordan. Given good sense and a helpful spirit on both sides the necessary measure of co-operation should be readily secured without any administrative subordination. The whole of Northern Sinai was surveyed without any hitch or difficulty just before the war by an almost identical and entirely voluntary co-operation between the British War Office and the Survey of Egypt. Similar co-operation between the two halves of a common mandated territory should be even simpler and easier.

It would greatly facilitate the establishment of the necessary co-operation and give Mr. Mitchell a valuable opportunity of getting to know the officers and methods of the Survey of Palestine if he might in the event of appointment be attached to that service for a month or six weeks at the outset and see their work both in the office and in the field. I have no doubt that Major Ley would willingly arrange this and do everything possible to welcome Mr. Mitchell and enable him to get thoroughly in touch with the Survey of Palestine's work before proceeding to Transjordan.

The uncertain factor and one which cannot be decided without actual trial is Mr. Mitchell's ability to improvise to meet Transjordan's essential needs in the simplest and cheapest manner possible and in the face of a barren dearth of technical requirements, means and men at the outset. But in this respect the field has been carefully reconnoitred and the main lines upon which the problem should be attacked have been outlined.

In Egypt the principal difficulties in the way of land reform ever since the British Occupation have been preponderantly political. In the executive field reform has been planned and is so far being carried out with ample means and great thoroughness. Egypt thus provides an admirable school for similar work elsewhere for a workman who can discriminate between essentials and non-essentials and can make good elsewhere with few and crude weapons. In this respect Mr.Mitchell has still to be tested.

It is this need to make bricks without straw in Transjordan that makes the land problem there so difficult and calls for the acceptance of rude detailed methods and for a man of personal energy, resource and elasticity of mind in the post under consideration. The task is an unusually stiff one and success will depend as much upon the efforts of other officers as upon those of the Survey Officer himself. But I am confident that no better qualified candidate than Mr.Mitchell can be found; and I believe he will rise to the occasion if he is appointed. And I know from my own experience that if he is as responsive as I think he will be that he will receive the most ungrudging and sympathetic co-operation from every other officer in Transjordan.

5.   I therefore think that you cannot do better than appoint Mr.Mitchell to the post at £750 per annum on trial for a year with a view to a more permanent engagement afterwards if mutually desired. The figure is that which it was agreed in our conversation might be mentioned, but I added in reply to

Mr. Mitchell's enquiries that he could assume that otherwise the appointment would be on the regular terms of the service and would carry the allowances and other privileges usually accorded. I also said that in the event of success he might anticipate an increase in salary later.

Mr. Mitchell is married and has two young children. I have endeavoured to explain the conditions in Transjordan and he is prepared in the event of his appointment to face them; but would leave his family behind during the initial year of trial. I should add that while Mr. Mitchell is greatly attracted by the character of the work in Transjordan and very disposed to accept the engagement if offered him, he has already sought employment in England and naturally wishes to continue these enquiries in the meantime also.

Yours sincerely,
Ernest M. Dowson

RESUMÉ OF MR. MITCHELL'S CAREER.

Name: ANDREW PARK MITCHELL.

Address: 19, Mortlake Road, Kew, Surrey.

Born: 23rd. August, 1894.

Sept. 1908-July 1913: St. Paul's School. Modern side. Specialised and showed great ability in Mathematics and good capacity in all modern side subjects. School Prefect, Company Serjeant Major O.T.C., and member of School Shooting VIII., Second XV., School record for quarter mile and Challenge Cup at Annual Sports. Prominent part in school activities and excellent character (High Master).

July 1913-July 1914: London University. Matric. Sept.1913 and Intermediate for B.Sc. Engineering 1914. Athletic colours at University and for England in 1914. Education then interrupted by the War.

1914-1916: 2nd. Lieut., Lieut. and Captain Middlesex Regt.

1916-1919: Seconded to R.F.C.(pilot).

Taken prisoner 1917.

After Armistice on commission in Germany for repatriation of British prisoners of war. Demobilised September 1919.

November 1919: Selected by Egyptian Government Selection Board for E.C.Service.

1919-1927: Survey of Egypt. Detail Survey for fiscal purposes, registration of title to land, valuation and acquisition of landed property required for public purposes.

- 5 -

4.04

THE STRUCTURE AND PROCEDURE

OF

CADASTRAL SURVEY

IN

PALESTINE

(Under publication by the Palestine Government)

Survey of Palestine 1931. *All Rights Reserved.*

I. FEATURES OF THE CADASTRAL PROBLEM.

(1) Principal factors.

The reform of the land system in Palestine has involved the construction de novo of a modern 'cadastre' in a restricted area which, although it possesses many diversities, has one outstanding advantage, viz., a terrain favourable for comprehensive survey operations.

That it has been possible to make full technical use of this advantage is due to causes which, from any other aspect, would be regarded as obstacles to reform, viz., a complicated pre-existing land-code overlying ancient customs and prejudices of the people, and severe financial restriction.

The anomaly is explained by the consideration that above all other factors of the cadastral problem time has been the most important, - time to construct a close network of triangulation and to develop a technical organisation out of local elements, and time to explore the practical difficulties of Land Settlement and to evolve legal procedure to cover its operation.

Financial restriction has invited the application of scientific principle to economy of survey methods and organisation, and has thus at least tended to induce the maximum efficiency within the limits imposed.

The object of this paper is to review the technical problems which have arisen and the means and methods which have been evolved for their solution during the past 10 years, avoiding as far as possible description in detail of survey methods which are universally known.

(2) Distribution of cultivable land.

The whole of Palestine lying between the Mediterranean and the Jordan Valley Rift has an area of a little over 26000 sq.KM. or, say, 10000 square miles.

The Southern half of this area comprised by the Beersheba Sub-District is tribal land and desert, and has been omitted from the present cadastral programme.

Of the Northern half the maritime plains and the plain of Aesdraelon cover some 4170 sq.KM., the depression of the Jordan 'Ghor', including the Beisan plateau and the Lake Huleh basin, some 1260 sq.KM. Over the remaining 8860 sq.KM. stretch the limestone hills of Judea, with barren Eastern counterscarp, and, separated from these by the Valley of Jezreel, the hills of Galilee in the north.

It is estimated that of this cadastral area only 6544 sq.KM. or an area less than that of Devonshire, is cultivable, and that of this by far the most valuable portion from an agricultural point of view is to be found in the plain lands and the Beisan plateau.

- 2 -

(3) lands.

    Except for the close orchards and groves of the fruit-growing districts in the plains, which cover a relatively small area, the open, undulating, and almost featureless nature of the plain country simplifies the operations of triangulation and topographical mapping, and - wherever property is visibly defined on the ground,- those of chain-survey.

    But a main difficulty of the cadastral operations has lain in the fact that property generally is not visibly defined, and that much of it is held in shares and cultivated under a system of temporary allotments, which results in periodic change of form. The peculiarity is perhaps that of a backward and ill-watered country occupied from antiquity by a peasantry to whom little or no inducement to agricultural development has been held out.

(4) Main classes of occupied land.

    As might be expected therefore the lands of a typical Arab village of the plains exhibit stages in the slow process of settling down of pastoral folk into an agricultural community.

    Immediately around such a village will usually be found a 'Hawakir' area, i.e., an accretion of fenced orchards and gardens where more valuable crops are cultivated and protected, beyond this often exists an irregular belt of land in an intermediate stage of development, which although held in permanent parcels by individuals is partly or wholly undefined, and from thence to the village boundary frequently stretch blocks of open undefined lands held collectively by the villagers or by main sections thereof, and cultivated for cereals or used as grazing lands under a system of temporary allotments. The individually-held lands comprising the first two of these classes are generally known as Mafruz or divided lands, the temporarily-allotted but collectively-owned lands of the last class as Masha'a, or undivided lands held in shares.

    Although there are many minor varieties of these two main tenure-categories, the broad distinction between them holds that whereas in the one case parcels of land are permanent and held in permanent ownership, in the other they are held as temporarily-allotted shares and may change shape on re-distribution at periodic intervals, a fact that calls for essential variations of procedure both on the part of Survey and of Settlement.

    To appreciate the differences of Survey procedure in detail it is necessary to keep clearly in mind the distinctive characteristics of the 3 classes of land described. These will be referred to as Defined Mafruz, Undefined Mafruz, and Masha'a lands - the two former being divided lands, the two latter undefined lands.

    The heading Defined Mafruz must here include also the built-on areas of the villages themselves for which special arrangements for Survey and Settlement are made.

- 3 -

(5) The Basis of the Cadastral Structure.

But before these variations of procedure can be intelligibly described their common foundation which sets the outline and governs the technical structure must be made clear.

For the object of a cadastre is registration of land, and the product of survey is a plan, and before embarking upon cadastral survey it is necessary to ascertain the exact nature of the plan required to meet the object, to carefully consider what this plan has to show, how it should show it, how it is going to be used, what in consequence must be the broad principles of its structural design, and how these can best be given effect to in mass production.

The needs of registration and the survey implications involved will therefore first be described, but before proceeding to show the manner in which these have been worked out in the 3 types of land named, it will be advisable to review the operations of preliminary mapping found particularly essential in the case of the undefined lands.

A section briefly dealing with structural problems which present themselves at an early stage, will subsequently be added. In considering these it should not be forgotten that the striking of a due balance between the utmost economy and the accuracy required for title under the conditions has throughout had to be attempted.

II. THE REQUIREMENTS OF REGISTRATION.

(6) Definition.

The term cadastral survey being understood to mean a survey for and forming part of a cadastre, or national register of real property, it is desirable in the first instance to examine those features of the modern system of Land Registration which directly affect the structure of the Survey.

A Land Register must on the one hand describe authoritatively all primary rights of ownership, together with any secondary rights affecting these, and on the other hand must define the areas over which these rights are exercised in such manner that they can be accurately located and dealt with as physical entities upon the ground.

But accuracy is a relative term, and ownership is a human function which is subject to continual change with time, and the changes involve frequent 'mutations', or changes in the shape and area of the properties registered.   And unless a known and sufficient standard of accuracy in definition of the positions, shapes, and areas of parcels by survey is ensured and concordantly maintained, errors will accumulate and injustice may be done which will destroy confidence and lead to troublesome disputes and to neglect by the people, and the cadastre will fail in its object.

Complementary organisations, the one for investigation and registration of rights, the other for complete definition of these by survey, are therefore necessary — and these organisations must in one form or another be permanently maintained and must at all times work smoothly and in unison. This relationship alone gives to cadastral survey dynamic and economic characteristics which distinguish it from other Survey operations.

(7) The Torrens system of Registration.

The Torrens system, which is axiomatic in modern land-registration, requires that a register shall be constructed upon a basis of unchangeable units of land as opposed to a changeable basis of human ownership. The village, which as the fixed administrative unit, must remain the general Registration unit, is far too large for convenience as a working unit, and it has been necessary to sub-divide it into permanent Registration blocks of more suitable size.

In such an undertaking on a national scale a clear system of filing and indexing is necessary, books and forms must be standardised, and it is essential that, although in the case of loose-leaf Registers several blocks can be dealt with in a separate registry volume, a separate numbered folio must be provided for each parcel.

Under this system when a mutation occurs the folios affected are cancelled and fresh folios under new numbers taken up.

Although a wide expansion can be provided for in the loose-leaf system, the number of parcels in any given block is in the main determined by survey limitations to be presently described.

(8) Plans on the Block system.

Now the Survey, being the physical basis of Registration, is necessarily the part of the cadastral organisation responsible for the selection and definition of the Registration-Blocks.

These blocks are numbered in consecutive order through each village, and a plan of each to standardised dimensions, termed a Registration-Block plan, has to accompany the schedule of rights in the Register.

The parcels are consecutively numbered through each block, and if changes occur the necessary amendments and renumbering of the parts affected have to be attended to without delay.

- 5 -

It is clear that the size of the original plan-sheets cannot in such bulk operations be varied to suit the size of blocks, for they have to be available for field use on the plane-table when required, and must meet the requirements of printing, handling, and storage.

Now the actual size of the plan-sheet which has been standardised to meet these requirements is 70 cm. x 60 cm. and making allowance for the necessary headings, references, schedules of areas, etc. to be entered on the margins of a plan, and for variations in shape of the blocks, not more than $\frac{1}{4}$ of the paper area can be considered as normally available for the actual drawing.

The scales which, for reasons which will appear later, have been adopted as standards, are simple multiples of 1/10000, viz., 1/2500, 1/1250, and 1/625, and taking the limit of the available paper area as 1000 cm^2, these will provide for blocks having areas which should not exceed 625, 156 and 39 dunams respectively. The area maxima laid down are 650, 160, and 40 dunams for these scales, with the addition of the linear maxima of 1200, 600, and 300 metres respectively.

It has also been ruled that except in built-on areas the number of parcels in a block should not exceed 100, a figure which may further influence the choice of scale by affecting the minimum average paper area of a parcel in a given block.

(9) Survey on the Block System.

But property-plans on the block system necessitate property-survey on the block system.

For it is clearly unsound normally to produce large-scale Block plans by compilation from a map constructed upon a fixed sheet-grid system. If at some preliminary stage, as was done in Palestine prior to the introduction of Land Settlement, block-boundaries of any kind are surveyed on the final scale required, as part of the topography of a map constructed on a fixed sheet-grid, the sheet-lines and the block-boundaries have no relation to one another, and the former cut across the latter so that blocks will commonly fall in several different sheets. This is not only highly inconvenient but, owing to unequal climatic distortion of sheets, unsound, and attempts to compile a single Block plan on a uniform scale from parts of several distorted sheets are fraught with trouble, and result in serious subsequent complications, affecting properties not falling in one sheet.

Moreover, even in close areas where the properties are permanently if not sharply defined, it is not sound or economical to construct the chain-survey framework independently of the framework of block-controls which must subsequently be used in upkeep.

It was considered therefore that in all cases, except in close built-on areas, each Registration-Block must be surveyed independently upon the restricted basis of certain fixed points which are directly derived from the triangulation and can be plotted upon the sheet containing the plan.

(10) The triangulation.

It follows therefore that there must be a density of triangulation sufficient to provide an adequate number of basic points on each plan-sheet for development of a framework for control of the contained block. The ideal would be met if each sheet itself could contain at least 3 or 4 trig.points on commanding sites from which control-points on the block boundaries can be derived by intersection. The open nature of the country made this generally possible in the case of the standard sheets on the 1/2500 scale, each of which covers an area of about 2.5 sq.KM., and actually an average of over 5 points per sheet, resulting in an average distance between points of nearly 900 metres, has been provided in the cultivated plains.

The few and small localities requiring larger scales are those of the orchard and garden areas around villages, where visibility is usually poor. Here reliance has often to be placed upon the addition of traverse for the fixation of the necessary points.

The principles and means employed in the construction of a network of triangulation having the high density and accuracy required for this cadastral object have been described in a previous paper.*
Here it may be pointed out that nothing short of a principal framework of geodetic or high-class secondary order having relatively short-sides, adjusted en bloc, and broken down in stages in each of which the side-length and the class of instrumental work is carefully proportioned, and to each of which is applied a rigorous chain-adjustment, can be considered as satisfactory. The great labour and expense of the cadastre overshadows the relatively small initial cost of thus carrying through the principles of geodesy, and where this can be done the time spent upon it is time saved long before the initial cadastral operation is complete.

(11) Features of a Registration-Block Plan.

The main features therefore of a Registration-Block Plan are that it is independently formed to a standard scale on a sheet of standard size so disposed as to suit the particular block contained, without reference to a fixed grid or orientation, that the plan-sheet contains all the fixed points necessary for the survey or future revision of the Block, and that it is so numbered and completed that any parcel can be at once located and determined in position, shape, and area by quoting four items of the Register, viz., the names of the District and Village, and the numbers of the Block and Parcel. Fig.(1), which is a reduction of a 1/2500 Block-Plan illustrates these features, and it will be noted that two languages appear upon the plan, and that a separate schedule of areas, a north-point, and the corners of a grid-rectangle for control of sheet distortion, are inscribed upon it.

* Note on the Technical System of the Survey of Palestine 1927, paras.10-15.

Although this plan is far from perfect it fairly represents a type which exemplifies the requirements of Registration and the object of the cadastral survey, and which is the product of a direct evolution from the triangulation by a process of statics.

The active principle of this evolution is the formation of suitable self-contained blocks prior to commencement of large-scale survey operations, and the possibility of this depends upon the provision of a preliminary map on a suitable scale, and involves procedures which differ in degree according to the type of land dealt with.

III. THE TOPOCADASTRAL MAP.

(12) **Cultivation Blocks.**

It will be apparent that in undefined lands without an existing map showing at least the main topographic features, no attempt to form blocks meeting the requirements of Registration is likely to succeed.

And in the open Masha'a lands a topographic map, showing merely such visible detail as exists, would often be quite inadequate for the purpose. Something more is wanted, and this fortunately exists in the shape of recognised localities which only need discovery and marking to furnish the basis required.

For in open lands which have for long been under the plough, experience of crop-results has taught the villagers well to recognise the variations of the soil, and in the periodic re-allotment of their undivided lands, or in the conversion of these by agreement into permanent parcels, they have in most cases long since divided the lands into permanent blocks or localities having different cultivation-values.

If then these cultivation blocks (qita') are ascertained, marked, and surveyed by the mapping parties, although they themselves may be unsuitable as Registration Blocks, they provide data from which these can be formed, and which at the same time are of great value for fiscal purposes.

For they are used as a basis for formation of units by value, and for the distribution of a land tax.

(13) **Nature of topocadastral maps.**

The preliminary mapping is carried out on a medium-scale by special plane-table, using detachable sheets, a telescopic alidade, and topographic methods operating upon the triangulation network.

It shows principal topographic features, village boundaries, undefined roads, the people's cultivation-blocks, areas of uncultivated land, the boundaries between Mafruz and Masha'a lands, the nature of the cultivation, all triangulation points, and all other survey marks as fixed.

- 8 -

It defines the boundaries of the built-on sites and of the 'Hawakir' of villages, showing detached houses, wells, etc., but, beyond main divisions of these areas formed by through roads and wadis, omits all close interior detail.

These features of the map distinguish it from either purely topographic maps or from cadastral plans, and have given rise to the name 'topocadastral' as best indicating its true nature. On revision after completion of the cadastral operations the map will form a general index of Registration Blocks and of cultivation, and with the addition of contours will incidentally become a complete topographic map.

(14) **The Field-Sheet system.**

Prior to the introduction of the block system mapping on the sheet system had been carried out in certain areas on 1/2500 scale field-sheets which were reduced to the 1/20000 scale for general purposes. A standard size of sheet taking a square grid of 50 cm. sides was used for both scales, and a special plane-table, manufactured locally, employed.

For many reasons, some of which are given in para.9, this system was abandoned, and preliminary survey on the 1/10000 scale, with reduction to the 1/20000 scale for general purposes, and a method facilitating transfer to the block system for the formation of Registration Block plans, were introduced.

The square 50 cm. grid of the 1/20000 sheets covers an area of 100 sq.KM., and, with the Trig. points, is plotted from coordinates calculated on the Cassini projection based on point 82 M (Jerusalem).

Now a 1/10000 sheet of the same standard size covers 25 sq.KM. of ground, so that each of 4 topographers camped together can take up a quarter-sheet covering 6¼ sq.KM., an amount which, in view of the frequent necessity of camping at a distance, has been considered amply sufficient.

The quarter-sheet grid being 25 cm. square, could be plotted on a 50 cm. square sheet of paper which allowed of ample margins for the inclusion of sufficient Trig. points, but it rendered the introduction of a reduced size of Plane-Table board necessary in the interests of convenience and economy.

Although these modifications involved greater expenditure of paper in the overlaps of quarter-sheets, and further duplication of plotting of common points, these are found to be minor matters compared with the advantages gained in the field.

(15) Division of duties in the field.

It was early found that the survey duties of the 4 plane-tablers must be kept separate and distinct from all dealings with the villagers, and that the enquiries into village and cultivation-block boundaries, systems of tenure, land values, and local place-names, must be left to the officer in charge, assisted by a trained Arab demarcator.

These officers camp with the plane-tablers, but as in the case of cadastral parties are provided with riding transport, and work well in front of the plane-tablers fixing the necessary marks and making rough croquis for their use.

The sheet-lines as a rule lie athwart the village boundaries and cultivation blocks, and considerable experience is required on the part of the officer in charge in arranging programmes of work and moves so as to reduce delays to a minimum.

These delays are mainly due to the necessity for attendance of representatives of different villages in demarcating village boundaries, and it was found that the filling in of rough croquis of these boundaries in advance by the Trig. parties on the triangulation diagrams supplied to the mapping parties was of great assistance to the progress of the latter in this respect.

(16) **Fiscal Blocks.**

On receipt of the 1/10000 quarter-sheets from the field they are compiled by tracing into separate village maps of which sun-prints by one of the so-called 'true-to-scale' processes are made.

One print of each village is issued to the Department of the Commissioner of Lands for land-valuation purposes together with a schedule of the relative values of the cultivation blocks as assessed by the villagers ; the remaining copies are retained for the main cadastral purpose at subsequent stages.

The land-valuers investigate on the ground, group together or modify the cultivation blocks so as to form fiscal blocks, - each of which in general contains land of a certain category-value - deciding upon the boundaries of the separate blocks which enclose the built-on areas of the villages.

On return of the revised prints, the approximate areas of each fiscal block are taken out by planimeter, final prints produced and issued to the Commissioner of Lands for fiscal purposes.

(17) **Completion of Topocadastral Map.**

The 1/10000 field quarter-sheets are now reduced to the 1/20000 scale (16 quarter-sheets being required for each 1/20000 sheet) and prepared for reproduction by Douglagraph process in black and green. A print of the black plate is then made upon a canvas-backed field-sheet and issued to the contourers. On return a brown contour-plate is put down, and the map is printed and published in the 3 colours.

Consideration of these preliminary mapping operations will make prominent the three important general functions performed, viz., the provision of a basis for the introduction of the Block system for the cadastral operations, the provision of a fiscal map and data for an agricultural census, and the provision of a combined topographic map and cadastral index.

The manner in which the first of these has been applied in the 3 types of land named in para.4 will be seen in the following pages.

- 10 -

IV. PROCEDURE IN DEFINED MAFRUZ LANDS.

(18) **Nature of village 'Hawakir'.**

The important distinction for survey between the defined orchard and garden area surrounding an Arab village, and the outer undefined 'Mafruz' lands, is, in general, that as boundaries consist of hedges or walls, rapid changes are not to be feared and demarcation of parcels is restricted, and as, owing to lack of visibility, additional theodolite work and troublesome operations of chaining taking time are usually involved, the survey neither can nor need proceed rapidly, and should be carried out well in advance of Land Settlement.

Although the whole of the 'Hawakir' areas of the plains, including some extensive orchard areas at Gaza, Lydda, and Jaffa, do not amount to 10 per cent of the whole land of the plains, the sub-division in these areas is intense, thick cactus hedges often form serious obstacles, and the cost of survey is usually from 6 to 10 times that in open lands on the same scale. 3 4

(19) **Selection of Blocks.**

In Part VI rules connecting property-density with scale and size of blocks are given for the guidance of chain survey parties in Mafruz areas generally, and to apply these in the orchard areas it is necessary to make an approximate estimate of the average area of a single holding in each proposed block.

The approximate area of each block and the number of separate owners it contains are therefore required, and it becomes necessary for the Officer in charge to construct a rough plan to an approximate scale of each group of proposed blocks falling in any section into which the Hawakir is divided.

The officer is furnished with a copy of the topocadastral village map on the 1/10000 scale for this purpose, which, although showing no interior detail in the close area, shows its inner and outer boundary and the through roads or wadis which cut it up into topographical localities. It is therefore not a difficult matter after inspection on the ground to fill in these with compass sketches of the selected blocks and to roughly mensurate each area.

But the determination of the approximate number of owners needs both inspection on the ground and enquiry in the village, and care has to be taken to exclude abnormally large parcels from the calculation, vide para.63.

Any proposed block which is then found to need a larger scale than had been anticipated must, if it exceeds the maximum area laid down for that scale, be sub-divided, and the outline of the blocks in the locality revised. In this manner a croquis can be formed which will reasonably meet both the requirements of accuracy and economy.

- 11 -

(20) Block control-points in the Hawakir.

  The next point attended to is the selection, marking and fixing of points on or near the boundary of each block which, together with any useful additional interior points, will form the outer framework of chained lines of the detail survey.
  These points need not be numerous but they should if possible be visible from surrounding Trig. Points, so that they can be fixed by theodolite intersection, and neighbouring points should be capable of being made intervisible.
  In most of the hawakir areas a few additional Trig.points can usually be fixed on the flat roofs of the prominent houses, tanks, etc. commonly found in such areas, from which the control-points can be intersected if marked with 'tall-poles'. These poles are made up in sections so that when erected vertically over a point and guyed, the height from the flag to the ground is $8\frac{1}{2}$ metres, an amount sufficient to project above all ordinary fruit trees and hedges.
  Should, however, the area be considerable and so close that the intersection method cannot be used, the necessary points are fixed by traverse with steel tape and theodolite. This method is that more often required in the built-on areas and wherever the 1/625 scale is enforced.
  Although in the close areas an increased density of Trig. is normally provided, all the additional theodolite intersections and traverse work required is executed at an early stage in each group of blocks by one or more specially trained surveyors attached to the detail party.

(21) The detail survey.

  The ordinary straight-line method with field book and chain is employed - free use of the theodolite being made for tracing lines through the thicker areas. As the cuttings required through cactus hedges often involve heavy labour, considerable skill in the selection of the lines is necessary, and straight bamboos about 4 metres high for marking intermediate points are a very useful adjunct. In most cases the cactus hedges are not kept in bounds by trimming, and spread outwardly forming separate roots. It is therefore necessary to enforce the marking by reputed owners of their exact claims in a hedge, and desirable also to survey the outer roots of the hedge from chained lines on each side of it.
  The amount of chaining, offset work, and cutting, required in a close cactus-hedge area is thus liable to be large, and progress relatively slow, and, owing to the irregularity of the hedges, a lower standard of accuracy in area-measurements cannot be avoided.
  The total cost of such work, including fixation of controls and examination work, which as mentioned in para.32(v) is carried out by a separate party, roughly averages 100 mils per dunam.

- 12 -

(22) Village sites.

The difficulties met with in the built-on areas are of somewhat different nature.
For the Arab villages largely consist of irregular accretions of small mud-brick dwellings which have grown up without plan, and narrow winding alleys, often blind, form the principal means of access. Here the only available method of survey is by chain between short traverses over flat but highly irregular roofs, involving laborious ladder-work with plumbing of perpendiculars at walls, and the precaution of careful observance of Moslem customs.
The difficulty of such work can be gauged by the fact that its average cost per dunam is over 1490 mils as against 38 mils for ordinary work in the open lands, and 100 mils in the orchard areas.
But although it has been necessary for the survey to be completed and for schedules of reputed owners to be compiled in the built-on areas, the property is of such little value and so troublesome for Settlement in many cases, that the Settlement Ordinance has provided for the temporary omission of these from Settlement except in individual cases of disputed ownership.
The portions to be omitted are decided upon by Settlement Officers and form separate blocks for survey, the undisputed parcels within which are registered under the names of reputed owners.
The ownership of disputed parcels has however to be settled, and since the areas of settled parcels have to be registered, these are if possible mensurated *in situ* or, failing this, graphically obtained.
The 1/625 scale is thus generally employed for these areas, and the rules of para. 63 are applied.

(23) Urban areas.

Land Settlement has not been carried out in the townships of Palestine, and the immediate object of the survey here has been the Assessment of Urban Property Tax, which does not form strictly a part of the Cadastre.
As carried out by the Survey, however, the Town Plans form a basis for future registration, and their construction has been a valuable means of training of young surveyors.
In general the town surveys have been executed on a deliberate programme in which time has been available for the insertion of a number of additional triangulation points on prominent buildings, for cutting up of the areas by traverse, and for completion by a chain survey brought down to separate buildings and small house-blocks of street and tenement property.
On the detail survey thus produced, convenient taxation-blocks are formed by the Assessment Authority and passed to the local Assessment Commission.
The property within each house-block is then filled in, numbered in plan and on the ground by a surveyor-valuer, and valued for tax by the Commission, and the plans thus completed are reproduced by the Survey.

- 13 -

It may be added that in the older parts of such towns as Jaffa, Nablus, and Hebron - perhaps among the most ancient inhabited cities in the world - the difficulties peculiar to the Arab villages already described were found to be greatly magnified by haphazard upward expansion and reconstruction which had repeatedly taken place on constricted sites, converting narrow alleys into steep covered passages or tunnels, with small property overlapping in each plane, and so that no roof-survey was practicable.

All attempt at survey of detail in such cases had to be abandoned, leaving the skeleton plans of the parts to be used by the surveyor-valuer as indices to the location of groups of properties which could be dealt with only by numbering, recording the names of owners, and adding descriptions.

V. PROCEDURE IN UNDEFINED MAFRUZ LAND.

(24) <u>Features of undefined 'Mafruz' lands</u>.

It has been estimated that in addition to the defined areas of the village 'Hawakir' 45 per cent of the arable land in the cadastral area is held in individual ownership, but that by far the greater portion of this land is either ill-defined or wholly undefined on the ground.

In the Maritime plain much of this class of land has been absorbed from the surrounding Masha'a lands as the requirements of the village population grew, and this process has latterly been accelerated by an external stimulus.

In general, however, little of this undefined land could be precisely located from documentary evidence, - if indeed that exists, - and much of it is in a stage of transition.

(25) <u>The Cadastral problem in undefined Mafruz land</u>.

Now the essence of the technical problem in these lands is how to form blocks and to produce preliminary block-plans of the type illustrated in Fig.(1), as the basis for the investigation and settlement of rights, immediately before commencement of this investigation, and in the shortest possible time.

The latter condition is fundamental to the problem because the conditions in such lands are dynamic, all transactions and developments in a village must cease during Settlement investigations, and the Survey has to show all property claims both on paper and on the ground at the moment when the Settlement investigations begin. Attempts to combine the two operations and carry them out at one and the same time have been found merely to result in interference and delay to both, and to magnify the burden and expense of the cadastre. So that, under the conditions, the only economic procedure has appeared to be one in which Survey and Settlement

- 14 -

immediately follow each other as distinct but successive waves, and continue to do so, village by village, without delay or dislocation, on a set programme.

It was clear, however, that for the solution of the survey problem provision must be made for two essentials, viz., firstly, means of rapidly visualising and showing on a croquis with sufficient accuracy the relative position, shape, and area of selected Registration Blocks of suitable size and scale in a village, and secondly, a method of forming each individual large-scale Block plan having regard to Trig. points, so that its contained block can be separately surveyed with the chain.

(26) <u>Fixing the block controls.</u>

The first essential is provided by the 1/10000 topocadastral village map, the second, which comprises the actual process of generation of the Block Plan in undefined lands, will presently be described. But the case differs from that of the Hawakir areas, and any system which employs the theodolite and elaborate methods of calculation for the fixing of control points on the boundaries of undefined blocks, can be dismissed as impracticable under the conditions, even if it were theoretically desirable.

For since the boundaries of Blocks must run along property boundaries which require definition, the cadastral surveyor in practice has to form the Registration Blocks in the first stage of the demarcation of properties by the claimants, and immediately before the large-scale block surveys begin. Delays due to theodolite observations, taping, calculation of coordinates, and adjustments carried out in a mathematical office, could not be contemplated at such a moment ; moreover experience has shown that in a mosaic of blocks it is advisable where possible to avoid methods which involve arbitrary systems of adjustment.

On the other hand, given the means described in a previous paper,* a density of triangulation suited to the scale, and plan-sheets properly disposed, the necessary points can be fixed on the block boundaries by graphic intersection from the triangulation, and the distances between them used for control of the chain-survey, and this can be done in the required time and with the necessary accuracy.

The simple conditions for ensuring success of this operation are that the control-points should, unless special precautions are taken, not be less than 12 cm. apart on the plan, and that the Field-sheet contains the Block and all the Trig. points necessary for the intersections.

---

* Note on the Technical System of the Survey of Palestine 1927, para.7.

- 15 -

(27) Selection of Blocks.

Now although the undefined Mafruz lands are as a whole naturally of more open character, of rectilinear shape, and contain larger parcels than the closer areas of the 'Hawakir', the selection of blocks and their scales in accordance with the principles of para.63 has, owing to the absence of defined boundaries, to be made with none the less care.

As already stated, triangulation has been provided with an average density of points sufficient for plans on the 1/2500 scale. But here and there groups of small undefined Mafruz parcels are found which should be surveyed and plotted as separate blocks on the 1/1250 scale, and unless these blocks are selected by the surveyor in the first instance according to rule, suitable control-points will not have been formed for them and cannot be subsequently formed by graphic means on the 1/1250 sheets independently, owing to the absence of sufficient Trig. points on sheets of that scale.

In forming the Blocks and selecting their controls, therefore, the demarcating surveyor has to make careful investigation of the property-density before putting down the control-points, following the same general procedure as laid down for the Hawakir areas proper.

It has been seen that the preliminary village map shows certain large 'Fiscal' blocks which have been selected by the land valuers, so that the formation of Registration Blocks largely consists in cutting-up these larger blocks into suitable parts in accordance with property-density and parcel-boundaries.

(28) The scoring-diagram.

Assuming that the necessary enquiries have been made and that a croquis of a group of Registration Blocks has been formed by the demarcator in accordance with the average size of parcels (so far as this can be determined at the time), and upon the 1/10000 village map, the demarcator selects the positions of the control-points and inserts the approved pattern of control-mark.

Placing a piece of tracing-paper cut to represent a 1/2500 plan-sheet on the 1/10000 scale over each block in succession, he orients and arranges this so as best to cover not only the block and its control-points but the Trig. points required for intersection of the latter. He then pencils in the edge of the tracing-paper, and repeats the operation in succeeding blocks until a complete diagram of a group of Plan-sheets is formed, vide Fig.(2).

This is known as the 'scoring-diagram', and in forming it the demarcator treats any 1/1250 block as if it were to be drawn on the 1/2500 scale, but marks the scale upon it before forwarding to Survey Headquarters.

- 16 -

(29) Formation of 1/2500 Registration-Block Plans.

    On receipt of a scoring-diagram the plan-scorer orients and arranges each blank canvas-backed Field-Sheet under the Coordinatograph in the same manner as in the diagram, and so as to cover the Trig. points required, and, furnished with Trig. Diagrams showing the coordinates of all Trig.points in the area, plots the Trig.points on each sheet, adding a grid-rectangle approximately fitting the enclosed block, and a north point.
    The grid rectangle must be of very simple dimensions which must be marked on the plan, and it is usually divided into 4 equal parts by median lines. It is to perform the vital function of control of future sheet-distortion, but in the case of a block marked for the 1/1250 scale it is omitted at this stage pending re-plotting on a fresh sheet.
    The Plan-sheets are now eyeletted for the Plane-Table and with the scoring-diagram sent to the demarcator, who proceeds to intersect each control-point with at least 3 well-directed rays meeting in a fine pencil point. Should any two adjacent control-points be nearer together than 12 cm. in plan a double taping between them must be carried out.

(30) Formation of 1/1250 R.B.plans.

    The 1/2500 scale plan-sheets are now ready for the plotting of the chain-survey. But fresh sheets must be plotted for the 1/1250 blocks hitherto covered on the 1/2500 scale. The coordinates of the control-points of these particular sheets are therefore obtained microscopically by Coordinatograph, converted to the 1/1250 scale, and fresh sheets, disposed so as suitably to cover these and any Trig. points which may be available, plotted for the larger scale and completed with grid-rectangles and north points as before. The effect of this transference of unavoidable plotting-errors can be disregarded if the 300-metre rule*is observed, since the fractional error on the ground is unaffected.

(31) Chain survey of blocks.

    For ploughing reasons the boundaries are usually rectilinear and terminate on common straight lines, single lines along each boundary alone have to be chained, offsets are few, obstacles rare, visibility good, and a general diagram, with the chain-survey blocks already cut up and marked, pre-exists.
    Thus it has been found that the average field cost, including examination, of the chain-survey of open demarcated lands in the Palestine maritime plain having an average property density (no. of properties per sq.KM.) of 90 , by parties not having long training or experience, is about 28 mils per dunam, or about $2^s\ 5^d$ per acre.

- 17 -

But it may be added that a common source of error arises in the case of a block which has been partitioned in the past under the bad but prevalent system by which parcels run across in very long narrow strips between the side boundaries. Error here is frequently caused by the joining up of wrong marks on opposite boundaries, and relatively large errors in the areas of strips are difficult to avoid (vide para.64).

The futility of such strips for development purposes is also obvious.

(32) Summary of procedure in undefined lands.

A cadastral party, consisting of an officer in charge, a demarcator, and 3 chain surveyors, operates successively in villages according to a pre-arranged programme, and is followed as soon as possible by an examination party.

The normal procedure is as follows :-

(i)... The demarcator proceeds in advance to a village, makes the necessary arrangements with the Village Committee for supply of marks and demarcation by claimants, and ascertains the nature and density-distribution of the properties in each Mafruz fiscal block or locality.

(ii).. He then selects and lays out by groups the Registration Blocks, according to property-densities and scales required, and, having regard to property-boundaries, compiles the 1/10000 croquis and scoring-diagrams, and selects and marks the control-points.

As each group is finished he forwards its scoring diagram to Survey Headquarters, receiving it back with the scored field-sheets.

(iii).. On arrival of the main cadastral party these are handed over to the Officer in charge, who arranges for demarcation by the people, allocates one or more blocks to each chain-surveyor, intersects the control-points, completes the marking of roads and units, compiles a schedule of claimants for each Block, and returns the field-sheets, with the field-books and schedules of each group of blocks, to Survey Headquarters.

If in a block long strip-parcellation is found, a large-scale croquis showing chained frontages is made and forwarded, and further survey of the block postponed pending the receipt of instructions from the Headquarters Office.

(iv).. The officer in charge investigates any errors discovered in the plotting office, (para 59), attends to any rechainings, and as soon as the demarcator can be spared sends him on to the next village to lay out blocks in advance, as before.

- 18 -

(v)... All plans in Mafruz lands are examined prior to Settlement by a separate party. At this examination the whole of the property-mosaic is checked, and precise chaining of small dimensions for mensuration of areas carried out as described in para.65.
    Differences in the position of marks are investigated with the owners, and any disputes or additional claims recorded.

(vi).. On completion, the plans are reproduced at Survey Headquarters and issued to Settlement Officers, together with schedules of claimants, for investigation of rights. Changes made during this investigation are entered on the original Field-Sheets by a final examiner who passes them to the Area-office for evaluation of areas as described in paras.66, 67.

(vii). Final plans, complete with details as illustrated in Fig.(1),are ultimately printed and issued for confirmation and registration with the schedules of rights, from which the new registers are constructed.

VI. PARTITIONING OF UNDIVIDED LANDS.

(33) Necessity for partitioning.

    The Masha'a lands are estimated to cover about 45 per cent of the cultivable land in the country and the Masha'a system is generally regarded as the principal stumbling-block to the progress of land-development.
    The system had nevertheless some advantages in the eyes of the Arab cultivator, and in breaking it down it would be easy on the one hand to destroy these by hasty action,without facilitating and even with positive injury to future development, or on the other to become committed to operations so complicated and costly as to defeat their own object. The economic importance of partitioning, and the special nature of the problems it presents, justifies description in some detail of the somewhat difficult technique involved.

(34) General procedure.

    Partitioning is the converse problem of ordinary survey, since it involves in the first instance the conversion of share-rights into parcels of land on paper, and then the transference of these to the ground by demarcation.
    Now a principal reason why the Arab fellaheen object to partitioning on economic lines is that,even in cultivation-blocks recognised by them in the past, there are often minor variations of quality, and each share-owner naturally fears that his permanent lot will fall on stony ground.

- 19 -

The procedure laid down by Ordinance therefore allows option to the share-owners to partition any fiscal block by agreement among themselves within a specified time, and if such voluntary partitioning is approved by the Settlement Officer, the lands are dealt with by the Survey in the manner already described for divided lands. The reservation is of importance, since such voluntary partitionings frequently neglect the most elementary economic principles.

If, however, the far preferable alternative of partitioning by Government is asked for or enforced, a preliminary general scheme, based upon the fiscal block as a unit, is prepared by the Settlement Officer, and passed to the Survey Department for elaboration.

(35) **Simple and Compound Partitioning.**

Partitioning is of two main kinds, viz., simple partitioning, and compound partitioning.

Simple partitioning includes all cases in which the land in a block to be partitioned is of the same value or 'weight' throughout - so that the area-equivalent of a single share is constant throughout the block.

Compound partitioning includes all cases in which a block of land contains localities or patches having different values or 'weights', and which has to be partitioned on the basis of value.

In compound partitioning the areas of units and of parcels are normally compounded of parts having different area-equivalents.

(36) **Processes of Partitioning.**

In both simple and compound partitioning there are 3 stages which correspond to distinct survey processes, viz., Unit-Partitioning, Parcellation, and Demarcation.

By unit-partitioning is meant the planning of the framework of divisions, sub-divisions, and units of a block of land which are to be occupied by groups and sub-groups of share-owners, and the construction on paper of a concordant road-scheme providing access to all parts of such units. This is carried out in the first instance on the 1/10000 scale.

By parcellation is meant the cutting-up of the units or sub-units of land into parcels having area-values proportionate to the shares held by sections or individuals. Parcellation is carried out on the large-scale Registration-Block field-sheets upon which have been accurately drawn the outline of the units to be parcellated.

By demarcation is meant the field process of transferring the completed plans to the ground. It is carried out normally in two stages : demarcation of the unit-framework, employing survey marks, and demarcation of the parcellation, using marks supplied by owners, to whom the parcels are handed over.

At each stage the principle of sub-division, by which all parts are adjusted to fit the whole, is maintained.

- 20 -

(37) Definitions.

Further terms in use by the area-draughtsman are as follows :-

(i)... The area-equivalent (A.E.) is the metric area corresponding to a single share in Masha'a land, and the share-equivalent (S.E.) is the number of Masha'a shares corresponding to one standard dunam (1000 sq.metres).

(ii).. The direction of parcellation in any unit of land is the direction of the inter-parcel boundaries in a series of parallel adjacent parcels crossing the unit.

(iii). An open unit is an area of land, lying between roads transverse to the direction of parcellation, which can accommodate two groups of parallel adjacent parcels lying back to back, each group having a separate road-frontage.

(iv).. A closed unit is an area enclosed between a road and a fixed boundary which can accommodate one group of adjacent parallel parcels lying side by side with frontage on the road.

(v)... A variable boundary is one which is rectilinear but changes direction frequently.

(vi).. An irregular boundary is one which is not rectilinear.

(vii). The width (b) and depth (d) of a parcel are its dimensions respectively in and at right angles to the direction of parcellation.

(viii). The coefficient of shape (s) is the ratio b/d.

(38) Application of the coefficient of shape to open units.

Suppose that a group of N share-owners are to be given parcels proportionate to their share-rights in an open unit, and that the A.E. has been calculated, so that the total area NA of the unit and the average area A of a single parcel is known. Let the unit be divided by a line parallel to the roads into two sub-units containing respectively the total areas of the parcels above and below the average area A, vide HK in Fig.4.
Then the smallest parcel that can be placed in the larger sub-unit is a strip across it of area A, and if S is the maximum value of the coefficient s allowable,

$$S d^2 = A \quad \text{and} \quad b = \sqrt{SA}$$

which gives the breadth of the larger sub-unit.

- 21 -

And if P per cent of the total number of shares (or the total area) are contained in the larger sub-unit, the whole width B of the unit is given by

$$B = \frac{100}{P} \sqrt{SA}.$$

and the length L of the unit is given by

$$L = \frac{NA}{B} = \frac{PN}{100} \sqrt{\frac{A}{S}}$$

If L exceeds the limit available on the plan the group must be sub-divided as required and fresh values for A, b, P and B for separate units, to be placed side by side, determined.

In practice approximations are sufficient, and the nearest whole numbers convenient for calculation are taken.

It may here be noted that an analysis of over 700 Masha'a parcels, after excluding parcels exceeding 30 dunams (say 7 acres) in area, shows that the average area of a parcel is nearly 7.5 dunams, that nearly 35 per cent of parcels are above and 65 per cent below this average, but that these two categories of parcels take up nearly 70 and 30 per cent of the whole area respectively.

Thus in the average case

$$P = 70, \quad A = 7500, \quad \text{and, if } S = 5,$$

$$B = \frac{100}{70} \sqrt{5.7500} = 277\,m., \quad b = 194\,m., \quad B-b = 83\,m., \text{ nearly}.$$

The actual dimensions allowable in such a case would be

$$B = 290\,m., \quad b = 200\,m., \quad \text{and } B-b = 90\,m.,$$

and the <u>average</u> value of s for all parcels less than 30 dunams would lie between 2.0 and 2.5.

(39) Application to combined units.

In an open unit, S being an accepted constant, B varies as $\frac{\sqrt{A}}{P}$, so that a unit designed for any particular group of share-owners may suit a smaller or larger group in which the ratio $\frac{\sqrt{A}}{P}$ is nearly maintained.

If, then, in any group of owners a number above and below the average are so selected as when excluded to leave this ratio practically unaffected, the unit designed for the larger can be used for the smaller group with a reduction only in length L.

Now where N is considerable, it is found that if the excluded owners are selected so that the total of the shares excluded above the average holding is equal to the total excluded below the average, $\frac{\sqrt{A}}{P}$ will, over a wide range, vary very little, and B will remain nearly constant.

The fact is made use of where a fixed area has to be filled having a width greater than B, but where two open units cannot be employed.

For an open unit of width B, calculated from the values of A and P for the whole group, can first be formed on the plan and the number of shares it will hold calculated and deducted from the total owned by the group. The residue has to be divided among excluded owners, half among ownerships above and half among those below the average ownership, the distribution being reasonably spread out over the list.

This list of excluded owners can then be placed in the remaining area which may be a closed unit, and with certain provisos arranged in a suitable order so as to bring individuals into the close neighbourhood of their families in the open unit across the road.

The provisos are those embodied in (a) of para. 40, and can normally be complied with by not accepting very small owners in the excluded list, or by insetting these in the parcels of the larger ones, see part of sect.iv in the closed unit HX in Fig.3.

It is the common practice to treat large owners with parcels exceeding 30 dunams, or over 4 times the average of the group, as special cases to be placed in closed units, and to 'inset' parcels less than $\frac{1}{4}$ the average in larger parcels.

The draughtsman has to remember however that normally the removal of an exceptionally large parcel tends to affect $\sqrt{A}$ less than it does P and therefore to increase B, although b is decreased. The effect is at the expense of the shape of the small parcels.

(40) **Principles of simple partitioning.**

The principles adopted by the Survey Department in free partitioning can now be described as follows :

(a).. The best parcel for general purpose is a rectangular one having the coefficient of shape 2.0, in no case where the land is of value for intensive development should the coefficient exceed 5.0*, and in no parcel should either b or d be less than 20 metres.

(b).. In the partitioning of a block such closed or combined units as necessarily abut upon variable or irregular outer boundaries of the block should first be formed.

(c).. As far as possible the whole of the remaining interior area of the block should be cut up into rectangular open units having dimensions calculated from the share-list on the principles laid down.

In calculation of average areas, parcels of and exceeding 30 dunams should, if not frequently occurring, be excluded from the calculation, and either placed across the unit or separately provided for in closed units on outer boundaries.

* This rule is relaxed in certain forced cases

- 23 -

(d).. In an open unit where grouping by sections (or families) is required, these sections must be formed as complete strips across the unit, and adjustment should be made between individual parcel-boundaries in each section, so as to maintain a common section-front in the direction of parcellation, dislocation of transverse sub-unit boundaries being freely resorted to.
This adjustment takes precedence over a prescribed order of individuals in any section.

(e).. In a combined unit the order of sections should be manipulated so that the two parts of any original section placed in different units are brought into the close neighbourhood of one another.

(f).. Road-reservations are excluded from the area available for partitioning, and the area occupied by them should be fixed before the final area-equivalent is calculated.

(g).. In a very large unit transverse road-reservations should be placed at intervals not exceeding 600 metres.

(h).. Units containing variable or irregular boundaries are treated by graphic method with parcellation-scales.

(41) **The preliminary general scheme.**

The Settlement Officer, who is provided with a 1/10000 topocadastral plan of the fiscal blocks, furnishes the survey with :-

(i).. A share-list for each block showing the names of share-owners with the number of shares held by each, and the desired division into groups, sub-groups, sections or families, arranged in the approximate geographical order in which these are to be taken.

(ii). A croquis showing the approximate position of defined localities (if any) to which specified 'weights' or relative values are to be assigned, the approximate geographical distribution of groups and sub-groups of share-owners, and such general particulars relating to roads and directions of parcellation as may be essential.

In view of the principles already described, it is plainly desirable that this scheme should be in very general terms only, and that all conditions liable to hamper the area-draughtsman should as far as possible be avoided.

- 24 -

To take a simple example of such a scheme, in Fig.(3) ABSC represents a fiscal block on the 1/10000 scale in which all the land is of the same value, and the general scheme may require it to be divided by a North and South line (XY) into parts proportionate to the rights given in the share-list of two main groups (I and II), that each part be divided into two sub-divisions (1 and 2) proportionate to the rights of two sub-groups, a Northern and a Southern in group I, a Western and an Eastern in group II.

The directions of parcellation preferred are as follows :-

Group	Sub-group	Direction
I	1 (Northern)	N. & S.
"	2 (Southern)	E. & W.
II	1 (Western)	N. & S.
"	2 (Eastern)	E. & W.

Direct access from the intervillage road AB to Mafruz parcels M', M", M''', is desired, and road-reservations are to be 6 metres broad within ½ metre.

The share-list is arranged by family sections in the geographical order desired, but both the order of sections and of individuals is of secondary importance to the general maintenance of the grouping.

(42) Procedure.

The procedure in such a case would be as follows :-

(a).. The draughtsman, equipped with an accurate planimeter, parcellation-scales, and a Brunsviga machine, first obtains the preliminary area-equivalent by dividing the net area of the fiscal block by the total no. of Masha'a shares - and then calculates the approximate areas to be allotted to groups and sub-groups.

(b).. The block is then cut up into divisions and sub-divisions by trial and error with the planimeter, using the parcellation-scales for fine adjustment.

Thus in Fig.(3) the approximate position of XY forming Registration-Blocks I and II to be occupied by the main groups, and the sub-division boundaries LL' and EE for the sub-groups are approximately located and drawn on the 1/10000 plan.

(c).. Examination, say, of the sub-division LX shows that it should contain one open and one closed unit, but that the existence of a number of small share-parcels in the sections which could not under 40(a) span the space between M" and the irregular northern boundary, makes rearrangement of the share-list to (d)..   The approximate position of the cross-road Hhh' e between the open and closed parts of such a unit is therefore calculated as for one open unit containing the whole sub-group, using the values of P and A obtained from the share-list after deducting parcels of 30 d. and upwards, and the road is provisionally drawn in on the 1/10000 plan.

(e)..   The southern sub-division LY of Block I being obviously suitable for two open units, the roads mn and L'Y are drawn and mn adjusted so that Ln and mY are calculated to fit two divisions of the share-list of sub-group (2).

(f)..   In like manner the sub-divisions, units, and roads in Block II are arranged for, commencing with an examination of the sub-division YD and selection, say, of a small separate closed unit ED, leaving EE' for two open units.

Sub-group (2) would be conveniently provided for by a long open unit SE', and a small closed unit DS in which the direction of parcellation is north and south, contrary to that indicated in the general scheme.

(g)..   The next operation is the fixation of the area of the road-reservations. Their total length on the 1/10000 plan of the fiscal-block is measured and multiplied by the width given in the general scheme (6 metres).

This area is to be held as fixed, and must be deducted in obtaining the final net area on the large-scale plans, and if the total length of the roads on the final plans differs from that on the preliminary plans, their breadth must be altered so as to maintain the fixed area.

(h)..   The approximate position of control-points is now added as shown in the figure, and blank Registration-Block Field Sheets scored and sent to the field, as in the case of undefined Mafruz lands.

The field surveyor intersects and marks the best positions for the controls, surveys the Mafruz parcels and the outer boundary of the whole block for the large scale, and returns the Block plans with Field Books to Survey Headquarters.

(j)..   With the outer boundary surveyed and plotted on large-scale plans the whole net area available for partitioning can be accurately obtained, and by deduction of all reservations (including the fixed road-area) the true area-equivalent (A.E.) is calculated.

(k)..   The whole of the share-ownerships are then converted into parcels by application of the true A.E., and sub-divisions and units accurately drawn in on the Registration Block Field-Sheets. Parcellation can then begin.

(43) Parcellation of an open unit.

Fig.(4) represents a portion of an open unit which has been designed by the method of para.38 for a sub-group in which the average ownership (A) is 8.8 dunams and the percentage of shares (P) owned in the larger category is 70. Thus the width B of the unit is 300 metres, and for the larger sub-unit b = 210 m.

Let the two families (ii) and (iii) in the table of para.44 consisting of 9 individuals holding 54 d. and 5 individuals holding 45 d., be placed in the sections ABCD and CDEF respectively.

The actual averages of the parcels in these two sections being 6 d. and 9 d. respectively, it is clear that the unit is theoretically too wide (especially as regards b) for the first section, and the 8-dunam parcel cannot be given the width b (= 210 m.) without breach of para.40(a).

The remedy is to group it with the largest parcel of the smaller category, viz., 5 dunams, displacing the common sub-unit boundary HK, as shown in the figure, between the two parcels.

The 4 smallest parcels can then be placed between HK and BC back to back with the two remaining large parcels, and the 4-dunam parcel allowed to project into the large 15-dunam parcel along the section-front DC.

Para.40(a) can thus be complied with by all the parcels in this section, but the effect of the difference between the A and P of the section and the A and P of the whole sub-group is to stretch the smaller parcels of the section, and produce a coefficient of shape larger than the average, although allowable.

No such difficulty is encountered in the next section, where the average exceeds the average of the sub-group, the large parcel can be carried across the unit on the section-front EF, and the two smallest parcels withdrawn from HK as adjacent insets within it.

The general result in the two cases is local dislocation and interruption of the inter sub-unit boundary HK, causing some extra work for the demarcator which is unavoidable but not serious.

(44) Parcellation of a combined unit.

Suppose that in the example of para.41 the converted share-list of the first sub-group of group I (Registration-Block), there are 7 sections with 43 parcels covering 360 dunams. The sections are, if possible, to be placed generally in the order given in the following table showing the parcel areas in dunams :

- 27 -

Unit	Section							Total
	(i)	(ii)	(iii)	(iv)	(v)	(vi)	(vii)	
Combined	(35)	15*	25	17	10	(30)	21	
	18	12	11*	8	6	16	9	
	8*	8	6*	7	4	10*	4	
	5*	5*	2	6*	2	7	4	
	4	4*	1	5		5*	2	
	4	3*		3		4*		
	3*	3*				.4		
			2					
			2					
Open	26	24	28	40	22	27	40	207
Closed*	16 (35)	30	17	6		19 (30)		153
Total	77	54	45	46	22	76	40	360

and the line LL' has been provisionally drawn so that the sub-division LBXL' contains 360 dunams plus the Mafruz parcels and the road He*

After excluding the two large parcels in sections (i) and (vi) the general average A of a parcel is 7.2 dunams nearly, and the percentage P of the area held in the larger category of parcels is 64.

Thus $B = \frac{100}{64} \sqrt{5.7200} = 296.5$ m. nearly,

and the road Hhh'e, temporarily drawn in and generally parallel to LL', completes an open unit LHhh'eL' nearly of the width required.

The net area of this open unit is found on measurement to be 209 d., leaving 151 d. for the closed unit, which has to contain the two large parcels of 35 d. and 30 d.

The parcels marked with an asterisk are now selected for exclusion to the closed unit HX on the principles of para.39, their total area being 88 d., those exceeding and those less than the average covering 44 d. each.

This selection results in allotting 207 dunams to the open and 153 dunams to the closed unit, so that the road-alignment must be shifted to the south at Hh and h'e by 4.3 metres nearly.

The sections in the open unit can now be put down by successive mensuration from W. to E. on the plan, but to fill up the space South of the Mafruz parcel M', Section (vii), which has no excluded parcel, is selected for placing here, the order of sections being changed to (vii), (i), (ii)........(vi). The excluded parts of sections (i), (ii), (iii), (iv), (vi) are now formed in succession from W. to E. in the closed unit, the large parcel of

---

* LL' is adjusted to exactitude after drawing this road

Sect.(1) being placed north of the Mafruz parcel M'' to allow of better co-ordination of the parts of the remaining sections between the units.

It will be seen that in general the excluded parts of sections in the closed unit are by these means kept opposite or nearly so to their complementary parts in the open unit, thus satisfying the requirements of grouping to the utmost extent possible.

On the other hand 5 of the smallest parcels in the closed unit, or 11.5 per cent of the sub-group, have a coefficient of shape somewhat greater than the maximum laid down by para.40(a), a result which however would normally not be of sufficient importance to justify the sacrifice of further land for the sake of an additional road.

If it were otherwise, and a reselection of the excluded parcels would not satisfy the requirements, the sub-division must be cut up into 3 units instead of 2, and an additional road parallel to LL' inserted.

(45) Parcellation of irregular units.

Brief reference must now be made to the method of parcellation of units having irregular boundaries.

This is effected by dividing the unit up into a large number of very thin trapezoidal strips of equal depth and estimating the area of the small departure from the trapezoidal form at the irregular boundary in each strip.

If the depth of each strip is taken as unity, the area of the rectilinear figure formed by any number of strips, is the sum of their mean widths.

As the mean width of a trapezoidal strip is half the sum of the width of its parallel sides, a, a', the area of n complete strips is :-

$$\left\{\frac{a}{2} + a' + \ldots + a^n + \frac{a^{n+1}}{2}\right\} + \left\{d + d' + \ldots + d^n\right\}$$

where d, d', ... d^n are the small irregular departures from the trapezoidal shape.

If then $\frac{a}{2}$, a', ... $\frac{a^{n+1}}{2}$ are read on an offset scale as they are drawn, entered in a vertical column of a suitable form,* alongside d, d' ...... d^n in another column, and totals obtained by machine, the complete area is obtained in scale-units. Also by keeping the running totals of area at 10-strip intervals, any set of areas representing parcels of which the running totals have likewise been given in similar units can be quickly located and determined by successive inspection and adjustment.

(46) Parcellation scales and graticule.

The problem of rapidly drawing and reading off the values of a, a', ... and of estimating d, d' ...... has been solved by 'parcellation' scales, specially adapted for the purpose by the writer, and a tracing-paper graticule.

*See Appendix

- 29 -

The parcellation-scales consist of a set of Marquois scales having an offset scale on the bevelled edge of the triangle which exactly corresponds with that on the flat scale, i.e., is equal to the latter multiplied by the cosine of the acute angle of the boxwood triangle - vide Fig.(5). If, as indicated by the dotted lines in the figure, the scales are set to draw and read offsets from a normal line OO' at 10 divisions apart on the flat scale, the offset readings will be displaced at each corresponding move of the triangle by 10 divisions, so that no difficulty of reading offsets due to change of their zero-point will occur.

To prevent frequent resetting of the scales due to long offsets the main part of the figure under measurement is divided into numbered rectangles of simple width each 10 unit-strips in depth, as shown in the figure, and the width of each rectangle is entered in a separate column in the parcellation form and included in the summation of offsets and irregular residuals.

The tracing-paper graticule has a group of small rectangles drawn upon it of unit width and depth, which when placed over a small residual area enables this to be estimated to within a decimal point of a unit.

It should be remarked that with the scales used the normal unit of depth (10 divisions on the flat scale) is $3\frac{1}{3}$ mm. in plan, and the unit of width (1 division on the offset scale) is 0.943 mm. nearly, so that the graticule unit of area is a rectangle which on the 1/2500 scale represents 8.32 x 2.36 metres on the ground nearly, and estimation is to 2 sq.metres nearly.

The figures of area entered on the parcellation form are all in terms of this scale-unit, and their total in any given unit of land under parcellation has to be equated with the total number of shares held by the owners occupying that unit, and the resulting share-equivalent used to convert all the contained share-holdings into scale-units of which running totals are obtained before location and fine adjustment of the boundaries of the parcels in their places in the strips on the plan, can be undertaken.

(47) Advantage of the method.

The procedure would appear laborious, but when carried out by two trained men, a draughtsman drawing the unit-strips and reading out the offsets, and a booker making the entries in printed parcellation forms, and getting out totals and running-totals by machine, accurate and fairly rapid output can be obtained.

Moreover in one operation two sets of offsets can be read and booked at the same time, a great advantage where a double feature such as a wadi or a patch of land of different value has to be evaluated.

The method is in general use in the Area Office for compound partitioning and for all units having irregular or variable boundaries.

- 30 -

(48) **Simple parcellation by categories.**

Where the land is divided into blocks which can be classified with sufficient accuracy by value, the general scheme may require that each owner of shares shall be allotted one parcel in each of the categories in the ratio of his share in the village.

The requirement necessitates an adjustment of parcels between the blocks of any category to produce a whole number of parcels in each block.

Thus suppose that a total of X shares is comprised in the share-parcels x', x'', x''', ...etc., that there are 3 categories of land by value, having the areas a', a'', a''', and that these respectively contain n', n'', and n''' blocks which have been marked and surveyed.

Then, under the requirement, the owner of, say, the x''' share-parcel will be allotted the 3 parcels

$$\frac{x''' a'}{x}, \quad \frac{x''' a''}{x}, \text{ and } \frac{x''' a'''}{x}$$

The share-parcels in each category can be dealt with in any desired order block by block, but, taking the order of the notation, the parcels in the first block in the a' category would be, say,

$$\frac{x' a'}{x}, \quad \frac{x'' a'}{x}, \quad \ldots \ldots \frac{x^n a'}{x}, \text{ and } e$$

where e is the residual area, less than any remaining parcel in the category, required to exactly complete the block.

Selecting one of the larger succeeding parcels, say x^{n+2}, and dividing this into the two parts

$$e, \text{ and } \left(\frac{x^{n+2} a'}{x} - e\right),$$

its owner is allotted these as separate parcels in the first and second blocks respectively.

The second block in a' is then arranged for by the parcels

$$\left(\frac{x^{n+2} a'}{x} - e\right), \frac{x^{n+1} a'}{x}, \frac{x^{n+3} a'}{x}, \ldots \ldots \frac{x^m a'}{x}, \text{ and } e',$$

where, again, e' is a residual to be taken from one of the larger remaining parcels of the category - and so on for the remainder of the blocks.

In the n' blocks of the first category there will thus normally be formed $n'-1$ parcels in excess of the number of share-owners, and, generally, if there were N categories in the whole area there would be $n' + n'' + n''' + \ldots\ldots + n^N - N$ parcels formed in excess of the number of owners, and the same number of owners holding 2 parcels each.

In closing each block the two last owners must be selected so that neither the residuals e, e',...... nor their complementary parts, would form parcels of unsuitable size for survey and registration.

Provided that neither n', n'', ... n''' nor N are large numbers, the method is the simplest that can be adopted for land of variable quality, since simple partitioning can be adopted in each block, after deducting a percentage for the road-area found from the preliminary plan.

When the number of blocks is increased and their area reduced however, the labour of survey and the complication of road-reservations quickly become excessive.

(49) Features of compound partitioning.

The complications introduced, if localities having different cultivation-values and unrelated to the grouping of share-owners have to be taken into account, are usually formidable, and may render any exact solution or adherence to given schemes or rules impracticable.

Obviously if in the general scheme the localities were taken as the basis of the grouping of share-owners, so that each locality which contained land of a certain category of value throughout could be allotted to a complete group or sub-group of owners, no problem of compound partitioning would arise.

But agreement on such a course is often difficult to achieve and the Survey have to provide for Blocks, units, and parcels compounded of parts of localities of different value.

There are certain limits, however, beyond which such provision becomes uneconomic if not impracticable.

Thus, in land containing numerous patches of stony or marshy ground, and not capable as a whole of intensive development, it would usually be necessary to assign an average value to the whole area, to relax rules as to shape and dimensions of parcels, subject to the restriction that a series of long strips is divided into tractable sections by road-reservations at reasonable intervals. On the other hand, in poor land the greater the area given to a share-owner the less possible it often becomes for him to work it individually, a fact that tends to prevent partitioning into individual parcels and to establish the family or section as the smallest human unit to be provided for; or to induce an arrangement by which any single holder of a parcel in such land is given another parcel in better land elsewhere.

But in land to which a low value or 'weight' has been assigned, the area-equivalent of a single share, being inversely as the weight, is proportionately large, and, if also families or sections are alone to be provided for, the parcels will be relatively large, a fact that is an advantage for survey.

The problems presented to the area-draughtsman by compound partitioning are, however, of much complexity, and it is only possible here to describe by an example one of the principal methods used.

- 32 -

(50) **Example of compound partitioning.**

Let a block of land ABCDEF, Fig.(6), lying north of a road AF, contain the following localities already surveyed on the 1/10000 topocadastral map :-

Western....QBP.....area	(A),	weight	a
Central....QPDGA...	"	(B),	"	b
Wadi.......GD......	"	(D),	"	zero
Eastern....GDEF....	"	(C),	"	c

It is to be divided in proportion to value among two groups owning N and N' shares, and each group is to own a portion of the central locality (B) and one of the side localities. Each division is to be sub-divided into family parcels proportionate in value to the shares owned by the families, taken in the order given in the share-list.

A factor F has first to be determined such that

$$F \left(\frac{Aa + Bb + Cc}{m} \right) = N + N'$$

where m is the L.C.M. of a, b, c.

Then the number of shares in each locality is

$$F.\frac{Aa}{m}, \quad F.\frac{Bb}{m}, \quad F.\frac{Cc}{m},$$

and the corresponding area-equivalents of a single share are

$$\frac{m}{AF}, \quad \frac{m}{BF}, \quad \frac{m}{CF},$$

So that if the group holding N shares is given the western division they will own locality (A), holding F.Aa/m shares, and alongside it a piece of locality (B) holding N - F.Aa/m shares, and applying the area-equivalent m/BF to the latter, the area of this piece will be N.m/BF - Aa/b.

A normal central road alignment LH can now be drawn in by trial and error on the 1/10000 map cutting off this area and dividing the whole block into the two parts required, additional normal road alignments can be selected in general compliance with para.40(h), as at KJ and MN, with an extension at KP to complete an open unit, the total length and area of these accommodation-roads can be determined and fixed, approximate sites for control points chosen, and Registration-Block plans scored and sent to the field for large-scale survey of the outer boundary and boundaries of the localities and wadi, and for intersection and marking of the controls.

(51) **Compound parcellation by sections.**

After plotting of boundaries and determination of areas on the large scale, each Registration-Block is divided by parcellation scales into narrow scale-unit strips parallel to AF, using separate operations for each locality, but so that the strips are continuous over the whole width of each block, as indicated

- 33 -

Thus there will be two separate sets of parcellation-forms in the block AL, one for locality (A), the other for the remainder of the block between LH and this locality.

The running totals of area in the set for locality (A) are now multiplied by the reciprocal of the area-equivalent for (A), viz., by AF/m, using the Brunsviga machine, and similarly those of the second set by BF/m, which converts them into share-values. These figures are entered on a 3rd set of parcellation-forms and combined by addition so as to produce running-totals in terms of shares of equal value right across the block.

The family-ownerships are now taken in order, and by inspection and adjustment by calculation on the form, using intermediate running totals as required, the family boundaries are successively drawn in with accuracy.

The operation is repeated for the Registration-Block LF, with the difference that additional offsets are read at the double wadi boundary DG, and deductions of area made for the wadi as well as for the road MN at each strip.

The frontage dimensions with running totals of each family boundary along each road are now extracted for entry on the demarcation-plan.

(52) Compound individual parcels.

Now if some or all of these compound family sections have to be broken up into individual parcels a selection of a number of the smallest owners in the sections is made which can be placed as groups in a sub-unit in one or more localities of uniform value.

Thus in No.III section of Registration Block I,Fig.(6), a group of 3 small owners has been placed between xy and the central road in locality B, and a single small owner has been placed in the sub-unit between KJ and the western boundary in locality A, leaving two larger owners to occupy the compound intermediate part of the section.

The shares of the eastern group of 3 small owners are converted by use of the equivalent m/BF, and the parcels can be drawn in by calculation. The share-value of each of the unit strips crossing this group, being at the same time calculated, is deducted from that already obtained in the 3rd parcellation form for the corresponding whole unit-strip crossing the block, leaving the share-values of each unit-strip running from the extreme western boundary to xy.

The single parcel BZ on the extreme west with area equivalent m/AF being now cut off, further deductions from these unit strips are made, leaving the values of the unit-strips in the area remaining for the two large parcels, for which running totals are obtained.

- 34 -

The inter-parcel boundary wz between these large parcels can then be located by inspection and fixed with accuracy by trial and adjustment. If, as in the figure, one of these parcels must cross the road at zz', the portion to the west of the road is made a separate parcel for registration purposes, so that one large owner will have two parcels.

In the result the parcels in the two small sub-units in the extreme west and east of the section are of simple nature, but the large parcels in the central part of the section are compound.

The remaining family-sections can likewise be dealt with, and although the conditions render observance of the rules of shape impracticable, the most essential requirements may be met with reasonable economy.

But the work of compounding parcels is laborious and adds to the liability of mistakes, and multiplication of localities or categories by value greatly adds to the labour of survey and is liable to render the operations from an economic point of view impracticable.

(53) Roads and wadis.

Roads formed in partitioning for purposes of access are not regarded as involving any engineering lay-out, but merely as ways or narrow strips of land affording common access for the labour and transport animals normally employed in a village.

The road-scheme of para.50 has been formed without regard to locality-boundaries and for the purpose of splitting-up the area into tractable units which will allow of partitioning into parcels of reasonable shape. The roads are reservations which form the boundaries of units, but the wadi in this case is not, so that the actual area registered in any parcel crossing the wadi is the sum of all the areas of different weight crossed by the parcel, including that of the wadi-strip of zero weight, but excluding that of the road-strips.

The sections of wadi crossed by the parcels in such an arrangement belong to the owners, unless the wadi is a reservation.

If reserved, a wadi must be demarcated in detail, and it is desirable to 'straighten-out' the boundaries of the reservation by making them run in straight lines from point to point on the banks, which facilitate the survey operations.

Advantage also is frequently taken of the rectifying lines to set them back and to form a road-reservation of the strip lying between them and the actual edges of the wadi bank.

But the advantage for survey usually lies heavily on the side of allowing a wadi to be included in parcels which extend across it on each bank.

- 35 -

(54) **The two operations of demarcation.**

For the operations of demarcation two specially prepared prints of the final plan on linen-backed paper are prepared for Plane-Table use.
On one of these called the Partition plan, all the data necessary for demarcation on the ground of the framework of sub-divisions, units, and sub-units are entered in ink. On the other, called the Parcellation plan, all the necessary data for demarcation of the mosaic of parcels in each unit is likewise entered.
The plans are required for distinct operations in the field - for the framework has to be established as a whole with all accuracy, and marked with survey marks in the first instance; whereas the parcellation is put down unit by unit marked with local marks supplied by the people, and handed over to them piecemeal according to a programme.
To put all the dimensions required in one plan would be confusing and lead to mistakes.

(55) **The Partition Plan.**

The principle has been laid down that the framework of sub-divisions, units, and sub-units must have all the pickets in each alignment which mark the critical points and junctions of the framework lines, chained twice, once in each direction, and that proper adjustment of these is to be carried out as laid down before insertion of the survey marks.
The ordinary metric chain, 20 metres long divided to 100 links, is to be used and chainings are to be to $\frac{1}{4}$ link. It is therefore the practice for all chained distances to be given in metric links by running totals from each end along every line, so that two complementary distances have to be inserted against each point in the Partition plans by the draughtsman.
Thus, referring to Fig.(3), the points E, e, f, g, L', l, in XY and o, m, o' in LL', etc. will have two complementary figures, shown against each of them in the plan.

(56) **The Parcellation Plan.**

On the other hand in parcellation the lines are relatively short and it is neither convenient nor necessary to double-chain each line provided the closing discrepancy does not exceed 1/500 of the length of the line and is properly adjusted as laid down.
The main principle is to demarcate each unit separately, completing the establishment of each group of families and individuals in it without regard to adjoining groups.

- 36 -

The single running totals of the distances along each normal boundary in the same direction are entered by the draughtsman on the plan.
In all cases if the boundary is not a normal one, as at SC in Fig.(3), the running totals of the parcel-intercepts, obtained by division of the depths by the sine of the angle of incidence (C'CS) have to be shown on the plan.

(57) Demarcation.

The principles of demarcation do not differ from those of chain-survey, except that every chained line has to be adjusted between terminal points already determined on the ground whatever its terminal discrepancy.
As the framework is constructed by proceeding from the greater to the less, commencing with the outer lines between the fixed controls or Trig. points of the Block, each dependent line has its terminal points fixed from superior alignments.
If the distances along a line as given on the plan are then chained off and all the points so obtained adjusted proportionately so as to cancel the terminal discrepancy, the ground will, except for small accidental errors, have been divided up proportionately to the distances in plan, and actual areas proportional to shares will have been laid out.
The method of adjustment will be described in the succeeding para., but here mention should be made of a procedure commonly adopted in demarcation of parcellation with the property-owners.
Fig.(7) shows a portion of an open unit divided into family sections and sub-divided into individual parcels meeting on a common transverse sub-unit boundary.
The surveyor first chains and demarcates the sections along the outer boundaries AB, CD of the unit, fixing family pickets A1, A2, ... and D1, D2, ... by the graphic method of single adjustment described below.
The section-framework is then completed by chaining along the general alignment EF fixing the points E_1, E2 ..... and adjusting so that the pickets A, E, D and A_1, E_1, D_1, etc. are in common alignments, and that the sections and sub-sections are rectangular.
The remaining parcel-corners in the boundary alignments are then marked by chainings within AB, CD, and EF in succession, adjustments being separately made in each section.
Finally, any short departures from the common transverse alignment EF, as at O', O", ... etc. in the figure, are laid off and marked in their respective alignments or prolongations.
To prevent confusion between the pickets along the common transverse boundary EF, those belonging to the left sub-unit are marked with a bar of red paint, those belonging to the right sub-unit with a bar of white paint, and those common to both sub-units with red and white bars, on driving finally in.

- 37 -

(58) Graphic method of adjustment.

Fig.(8) shows the simple graphic method employed for adjusting pickets in a chained line, the closing discrepancy of which has been found at the terminal point.

In addition to normal examiner's equipment, including a Plane-Table, the demarcator is provided with a paged section-paper note-book known as the Field Adjustment Book.

On closing a line the demarcator plots the given distances at pickets in a page of this Book using any convenient scale, as at ABCD, and erects at D a perpendicular Dd representing the closing discrepancy on a magnified scale, and joins Ad; cutting the corresponding perpendiculars at B and C at the points b and c.

Then, except for small accidental errors of chaining, Bb and Cc represent on the same magnified scale the amounts by which the temporary pickets at B and C have to be shifted in the alignment, and can be read off on the section-paper, and used in single adjustment in parcellation.

For the double adjustment required for the partition framework, however, the chaining is repeated from D to A, a second set of temporary pickets at C, B, and A being inserted. The closing discrepancy at A is now plotted at Aa, aD and ad are joined cutting the intermediate perpendiculars at b', b" and c', c".

Now if the errors are systematic and the closing discrepancies of each chained line are of the same sign, it can be easily proved that Bb" and Cc" should represent the distances respectively between the pairs of pickets at B and C, that the true points should lie between the pairs of pickets exactly as b lies between B and b", or c between C and c", so that bb" and cc" represent the amounts by which the second set of pickets should be shifted in adjustment.

And when the closing discrepancies are of opposite sign, bb' and cc' should represent the distances between the pairs of pickets, the true points lie outside the pairs as at B and C, so that Bb' and Cc' are the amounts by which the second set should be shifted in adjustment.

If, therefore, the actual distance between, say, the two pickets at B differs materially from the theoretical distance Bb" (or bb'), this difference must be attributed to an accidental error. But, in practice, the only accidental chaining error that needs consideration is a sporadic misreading of the chain at a point, say by a multiple of 10 links, or by taking a supplementary part of 10 links such as 4 instead of 6 links. The minimum resulting error of such a misreading would thus be 2 links.

The following rule has therefore been adopted :

" If the distance between the two positions of a point as determined by fore and back chaining differs from that found graphically by 2 links or more, an accidental error in one of the chainings must be assumed which has to be discovered and corrected by rechaining to the nearest established point in the line. When corrected, proportional adjustment should be made in accordance with the principles laid down for double chaining. "

The method confers much greater reliability, and enforces the keeping by each surveyor of a systematised record of his adjustments which, - itself a valuable safeguard, - may be of great use in future upkeep.

VII. AREAS, UPKEEP, ETC.

(59) The nature of the principal errors.

In para.6 the importance of establishing and maintaining a sufficient standard of accuracy in the Cadastral Survey was alluded to, and the considerations involved and the methods adopted for meeting the requirements must now be briefly described.

The only definite figure other than its number that is registered for any parcel is its area, yet that figure is the one that it is least possible to obtain with exactitude, since in general a fractional area-error is the algebraic sum of principal fractional linear errors.

If in a cadastre separate surveys of all parcels could be made on scales suited to their magnitude using precise methods of measurement, as in the case of individual transactions, a high degree of accuracy could be ensured, but at an expenditure of time and money which would be entirely prohibitive.

Chain-survey, operating upon an accurate framework of points, is the accepted economic method of dealing comprehensively with a whole network of properties, but it cannot by itself originally ensure a high degree of accuracy of individual detail. For although in linear measurements with the chain under normal conditions a maximum fractional 'error'[*] of 1/500, corresponding to a maximum area-error of 0.4 per cent, has to be allowed, very few parcels can have all their dimensions directly chained, and many points on parcel-boundaries have to be fixed by offsets.

---

[*] The word 'error' is here used to denote the discrepancy found between the length of a line as chained and its length as predetermined by construction from the framework.

- 39 -

So that for the mensuration of areas not only has additional work in direct chaining of dimensions to be carried out by examiners, but reliance has to a considerable extent to be placed upon dimensions which are scaled off the plans and contain relatively large errors of plotting, drawing, and estimation.

These errors are practically constant for any length of line on the plan, so that their effect, for a given length of line on the ground, varies inversely as the scale of the drawing.

It becomes therefore necessary to investigate the graphic errors, and to deduce therefrom rules governing the scale of the drawing and the means to be adopted for control of the resulting area-errors, having regard to an agreed-upon general standard of accuracy.

(60) <u>The permissible error for a Registered area.</u>

Now it was considered that :-

(i)... No area, however determined, is absolutely accurate, so that any area registered is in reality a nominal one.

(ii).. If a property is defined on the ground, it exists as a real entity, whatever its nominal area, so that only if it is sold on the basis of the nominal area could the effect of any small error in the latter be felt.

(iii). While the error in a nominal area should not be large, its survival as registered in no way prevents the parties to a transaction from having an independent survey made for the purpose of agreeing as to price, should they be dissatisfied with the registered area as a basis.

(iv).. The large area-error resulting from the combination of maximum linear-errors of the same algebraic sign, will be of very rare occurrence.

(v)... The investigation does not concern parcellations of Masha'a lands, in which parcels have been formed on the basis of areas by sub-division.

In view of the average price of agricultural land and of the known density of property in many of the more extensive close areas, it was decided that probable area-errors not exceeding $\pm \frac{1}{2}$ per cent could be worked to, and that rough rules governing the selection of blocks and their scales so as not to necessitate a great amount of additional mensuration to meet this limit should be arrived at.

- 40 -

(61) Additional chaining for mensuration of areas.

Now the great majority of parcels in the divided lands are quadrilaterals not departing widely from the rectangular shape. And at examination the frontages along two opposite sides of each of these can be directly measured on the ground by the examiners with all necessary accuracy, and entered on the plan.

Fig.(9) shows 3 adjacent quadrilaterals in which the frontages a, b, c ..... and d, f, g, have been so obtained. If h, h', ... are the perpendiculars from opposite corners of each quadrilateral to the alignments of the opposite frontages, the areas of the quadrilaterals are

$$\tfrac{1}{2}(ah + dh'), \tfrac{1}{2}(bh'' + fh'''), \ldots \text{etc.}$$

If the perpendiculars h, h' ..... are then also accurately chained on the ground by the examiner these areas will be as precise as is obtainable in practice, but for the chaining the examiner should be given the distances x, y, z, ..., scaled from the corner points along the side alignments to the feet of the perpendiculars.

If h, h' ..... are scaled off the plan all the errors of plotting, drawing, and scale-reading will enter the areas, and the relative accuracy will vary with the lengths of these perpendiculars.

It is necessary therefore to determine limits for h, h'. ...... below which they must be chained and above which they may be scaled off the plan, having regard to the standard of accuracy laid down.

(62) Control of the Area-error.

If e is the constant probable error in the paper-distance as scaled between any two points on a plan, then in Fig.(9) the probable errors in the areas of the quadrilaterals are :-

$$\tfrac{1}{2} e \sqrt{a^2 + d^2}, \ \tfrac{1}{2} e \sqrt{b^2 + f^2}, \ldots \text{etc.}$$

and if the frontages a, b, ... do not greatly differ from a, f, ... respectively, these errors are roughly equivalent to :-

$$\tfrac{e}{\sqrt{2}} M, \ \tfrac{e}{\sqrt{2}} M', \ldots \text{etc.}$$

where M, M', ... are the respective means of the frontages.

And if A, A', ... are the corresponding areas of the parcels, the relative errors, expressed as percentages of these areas, are

$$\frac{100 \, e \, M}{A\sqrt{2}} \quad \frac{100 \, e \, M'}{A'\sqrt{2}} \ldots \text{etc.}$$

- 41 -

which, in parcels which are roughly rectangular, are equal approximately to :-

$$\frac{70e}{L}, \quad \frac{70e}{L'} \ldots \text{etc.}$$

where L, L', ... are the mean widths.

Also from a large number of tests it is found that e = 0.125 mm. nearly, so that 70 e = 8.75 mm. nearly.

Equating the relative errors with ½ per cent, the condition $\frac{8.75}{L} = \frac{1}{2}$ is obtained, so that L, L', ... must not exceed 2 x 8.75, or 17.5 mm. on the plan.

The rule adopted in practice is that, using the notation of para.37, every quadrilateral parcel other than a narrow strip-parcel must be mensurated from frontages (d) chained by the examiner, using values of h, h', which are graphically measured or chained according as the mean width (b) is greater or less than 20 mm. in plan.

(63) **The scale for a close property-mosaic.**

Again, in the established orchard areas around villages, where the parcels have not been formed by cutting-up of portions of the Masha'a lands into long strips, but form a rough mosaic, it has been found from a large number of measurements that the coefficient of shape (b/d) of a parcel varies between 1.0 and 6.0, that the average coefficient works out at nearly 2.0.

Applying this average coefficient to roughly rectangular parcels under the formula of the preceding para., L = 17.5 mm., and M = 8.75 mm., so that, using the 1/2500 scale, A = 43.75 x 21.875 m. = 957 sq.metres, or nearly 1 dunam.

On the average, therefore, any quadrilateral area/ parcel in an orchard surveyed by the chain and plotted on the 1/2500 scale, will, if less than 1 dunam in area, require to have both its perpendiculars h, h' (Fig.9) chained additionally.

If therefore in any block it is required to confine the additional chaining to a moderate percentage of the total number of parcels, the average area of a parcel in the block taken for calculation must be increased to several times this minimum value.

But there is usually at least one large owner in a block whose holding so greatly exceeds that of the others as to produce a false average for the purposes of this investigation.

It is the practice therefore by enquiry to deduct any holdings exceeding 4 times the average, or say 30 dunams and upwards, before taking out the final average.

The factor 4 has, on this premise, and from experience of the frequency of small parcels, been adopted in arriving at the average for the 1/2500 scale, i.e., if, after deducting parcels exceeding 30 dunams, the average area of the remaining parcels in a block is not less than 4 dunams, the 1/2500 scale is to be used. And the minimum value for the average parcel will be inversely as the square of the scale.

- 42 -

The following rules were therefore tabulated as a general guide for surveyors and plotters in the original chain survey :-

TABLE SHOWING SCALES FOR DIVIDED LANDS.

After deducting from the Block parcels exceeding	If the remaining average area of a parcel is	Use the scale	Limits		
			Block Area	Chain-reading to nearest *	Offsets maximum
30 dunams	4 dunams or greater	1/2500	650 d.	1 link	60 links
7.5 "	1 - 4 dunams	1/1250	160 d.	$\frac{1}{2}$ "	30 "
2 "	Under 1 dunam	1/625	40 d.	$\frac{1}{4}$ "	15 "

    * The maximum errors of reading will be $\frac{1}{2}$ these amounts.

(64) Method with strip-parcels.

    Hitherto the parcels occurring as part of a mosaic in the older established 'Hawakir' areas immediately surrounding a village have been considered.
    The case of the more recently-established properties of an outer zone, which have often been taken from the Masha'a lands, and often consist of long narrow strips, requires somewhat different treatment.
    Such a parcel is shown by the quadrilateral ABCD in Fig.(10), in which the sides AB, CD are relatively very long, and the two chained ends or frontages very short. If the method of para.(61) were applied to this case the perpendicular AG would have to be scaled or chained. If scaled, a large relative error may occur owing to the drawing of a long prolongation (BG) from a very short frontage (CB) ; if chained, both distances BG and AG are long and the extra chaining required with a number of parcels would be excessive. Obviously in such a case a simple alternative is to discard the chained dimensions BC and AD and chain the short end-perpendiculars CE, AF, multiplying them for area by $\frac{1}{2}$ the scaled lengths AB, CD, respectively.
    But the chaining of these short lines must be accurately carried out and the points E and F found in the exact alignments of AB produced and CD respectively, at the distances given by the plotter.
    If A, B, and C, D, are not mutually intervisible, intermediate marks M, N must be placed exactly in these alignments, an addition that is often laborious.

If, however, the parcel forms one of a series terminating on a common rectilinear boundary, it is sufficient to measure the angles FCG, ADC, to within $\frac{1}{2}$ degree on the plan and to calculate the end-perpendiculars from the formula $h = a.\sin A$ using a table of natural sines, where $\underline{a}$ is the chained frontage along either common boundary.

In practice, the plotter is guided by the rough rule that where the mean width of a parcel is over 6 times its mean breadth, it is treated as a strip-parcel in which end-perpendiculars have to be obtained by one of the above methods.

Cases of whole blocks throughout which the coefficient of shape (b/d) exceeds 20 are not infrequent, and, in some lands partitioned by the Arab, parcels over 1 KM. in length and less than 5 m. in breadth have been met with.

It is obvious that the rules for determining the scale of the drawing cannot be applied to such blocks, they may have to be cut up into smaller blocks to suit one of the larger scales, the chaining by the examiner of the end-perpendiculars must be of the most accurate order, and the whole operation becomes abnormal and uneconomic.

(65) Chainings for mensuration.

The first examination of a plotted field sheet is carried out by a surveyor of the examination party, the second examination by the officer in charge of that party. At this second examination the accurate dimensions of the parcels for the purposes of mensuration are chained and entered on the sheet.

The dimensions to be entered are the frontages (a) of all quadrilateral parcels, and the perpendiculars (h) of such of these as have a mean width (b) less than 20 mm. on the plan.

In these mensurations the chain is read by estimation to the nearest $\frac{1}{2}$ link, whatever the scale, except in very narrow strip-parcels, where readings to a decimal point of a link are made. In all cases care is taken that the terminals of perpendiculars are in the true alignments or prolongations of the sides to which they are directed.

With parcels having variable or irregular boundaries the examination is confined to checking the shape and the marking of these boundaries.

The examiner in all cases completes the marking of the framework by insertion of such additional survey landmarks at the corners of units and sub-units as are required.

(66) The evaluation of areas.

The general procedure in evaluation of areas, adopted for all divided lands, consists in the separate calculation of the area of each quadrilateral parcel, and the use of the computing-scale for variable or irregular parcels.

- 44 -

The results can only be regarded as individually precise in the cases of very large quadrilaterals or of small quadrilaterals in which all principal dimensions are chained, but in the great majority of cases they include graphically-determined dimensions of perpendiculars - which, with one important proviso, will produce a probable error not exceeding ± ½ per cent.

The proviso is that every graphic dimension must be subjected to a correction for paper contraction obtained from the grid-rectangle.

This rectangle is now universally plotted to closely fit each block, and is sub-divided into 4 equal rectangles by median lines. The draughtsman frequently checks the known lengths of the sides of one or other of these 4 rectangles against their lengths as carefully read on a graduated steel standard straight-edge, obtaining a plus or minus percentage correction to be applied to areas obtained according to the position and direction of the graphic dimension used in the calculation. If the correction is constant in a given direction over the paper, it is applied to the areas of whole groups of parcels running in that direction.

Each quadrilateral parcel has its area calculated twice independently by different draughtsmen, using a Brunsviga machine, and at each calculation factors for sheet-distortion are independently obtained.

With variable or irregular parcels the computing-scale is used, two measurements independently carried out, and factors for sheet-distortion obtained.

(67) Application of check formula.

Now a block normally contains a heterogeneous mixture of quadrilaterals and polygonic or irregular figures, and the areas of the former are obtained by mensuration and of the two latter graphically by computing-scale. Also the whole area of the block is obtained by planimeter and adjusted by equating it with its complementary part to the known area of the grid-rectangle.

Each process is carried out twice independently and the discrepancies between each pair of measurements and between their sums tested by a formula derived from that used in the Prussian cadastre for the maximum discrepancy allowable between two determinations of area, as given by Jordan[†], viz.,

$$\text{Diff. must not exceed} \quad \frac{0.3 \sqrt{A}}{2500 \times R.F.}$$

where A is the area in sq.metres and R.F. the representative fraction of the scale.

[†] Handbuch der Vermessungskunde, p.116.

- 45 -

The discrepancies between the following pairs of determinations are subjected to test by this formula, stage by stage, as follows :-

(i)... The two areas of each parcel.

(ii).. The two sums of the mensurated areas.

(iii). The two sums of the graphic areas.

(iv).. The mean planimeter area of the block and the sum of the means of the graphic and the mensurated areas within the block.

(v)... Two measurements of the Block by planimeter.

If in any of these cases the discrepancy exceeds the limit laid down, investigation is carried out and a third independent measurement made.
The mean of the values for each parcel is that finally adopted for Registration.
Thus the total area of the Block is a quantity which is used as a check but which has no significance for Registration purposes, so that if, on a mutation occurring, an error in the registered area of one or more parcels is proved to exist, the error can be corrected without affecting the registered areas of all the remaining parcels.

(68) **Machinery of maintenance.**

Unless suitable machinery for maintenance of the Register and of the property-mosaic on paper and on the ground is arranged for at an early stage in the Cadastral operations, post-settlement changes will quickly render the Cadastral record antiquated and abortive.
In Palestine the Land Registry, operating under a Land Transfer Ordinance, investigates post-Settlement changes of ownership and maintains the Register, the Survey Department maintains the plans and the marking on the ground, and both work in close coordination.
But it is not only necessary for the Survey Department to attend to the marking of each 'mutation' as it arises, since that would affect only a small percentage of the marks.
The surveyor who checks the mutation must also inspect the control-marks and Trig. points in and around the Block affected, and in addition, a periodic inspection of all marks in a village must be carried out, at which all survey marks must be restored and suitable action taken with regard to property-marks, where necessary.

(69) **Upkeep of marks.**

Now each Registration-Block plan has plotted upon it the framework of survey marks from which it has been constructed, including a number of independently situated Trig. points, some control points on or near the Block boundaries, and a number of landmarks at corners of units.

– 46 –

For maintenance of the property-mosaic the points of most immediate importance are the unit landmarks. If these remain in position any property-mark can, if lost, be immediately restored with the chain.

If the landmarks have disappeared they can be restored from the control points by the chain, and if these have disappeared they can be replaced from the Trig. points by Plane-Table intersection, some reconstruction of the chain-survey of dependent unit boundaries being necessary.

In each case the original Field-Sheet, or a re-plot by coordinatograph of the contained points on a fresh sheet, is used for the restoration.

Obviously the longer the natural life of the marks the less laborious and costly the upkeep tends to be, on the other hand true permanence is not in practice attainable, and it would be easy to waste time and money in the major initial operations in attempting it.

(70) Disadvantages of heavy marks.

It might be thought that heavy marks such as stone, iron, or reinforced posts set in concrete could alone be relied on for cadastral marks and that even property-marks should be of similar heavy pattern.

But in Palestine this is not considered to be the case, and there are in general practical difficulties attending the use of heavy marks either for control-points and landmarks, or for marking of property in the initial cadastral operation.

The experience of the Survey in the matter is as follows :-

(i)... The delay due to supply and fixing of heavy marks for controls, landmarks, or property boundaries in the plains seriously interferes with the progress of demarcation, vide paras.25, 26, at a time when speed is important.

(ii).. Apart from the great indirect cost of delay, the direct material cost of such marks is prohibitive. Initial demarcation by the people being enforced, the additional tax upon the fellaheen owners of heavy permanent marks would exceed the present burden of survey fees. And the cost of heavy control-points and landmarks alone would add largely to the cost of the survey.

(iii). A mark seldom comes to an end by natural causes, deliberate or accidental removal or displacement is its common fate. A heavy mark is almost as easily dug out as a lighter mark with foundation at the same depth, and is frequently more attractive.

- 47 -

(iv).. A control-mark or landmark should last at least 10 years if undisturbed, and in the soil and climate of the Palestine plains this life is normally attained by iron marks ¼ inch thick, properly rust-proofed.

A property-mark should last, if undisturbed, long enough to enable the property to become established by fencing or normal developments of cultivation, say 4 years.

Either period is long enough to ensure inspection by the Department.

(71) Patterns of marks.

Iron marks thoroughly treated before use with anti-rust paint have therefore been almost exclusively employed in the plains - and after experiment the patterns illustrated in Figs.(11) - (17) have been generally adopted.

The standard patterns of Minor Trig. Point in all ordinary ground are the Iron Tube Mark, Fig.(11) and the 'Dray' heavy Land-Anchor, Fig.(12). The latter is screwed into the ground by special tube spanner, grouted, and set in cement mortar. Both have been found hitherto to last very well, and their natural life is estimated to be at least 30 years.

The split and crimped Angle-Iron, Fig.(13), is used singly for unit landmarks and marks of alignment, and, in pairs at a slope rivetted or securely spiked together, for control-marks, vide Figs. (14), (15). The iron is driven by sledge hammer in to a hole jumped for a certain depth with a crowbar, when, as the pressure on the split toes increases with the depth they open out and form lugs, making it almost impossible to pull the iron out.

For harder ground the toes are pointed.

The villagers use a shorter and cheaper type of this pattern, made locally, for their property-marks.

Another type of iron control-mark adopted for light sandy soils is the chisel-edged and dogged tube shown in Fig.(16). The tube is driven in to a V-shaped excavation to a certain depth, pinned over a short cross-rod by long iron dogs driven at an angle into opposite sides of the excavation and securely locked by another rod passing through the tube and hammered over.

For hard stony ground two pointed angle-irons are used, Fig.(17), driven in at a slope and rivetted or spiked together.

All these control-marks are cheap, rapidly inserted, and difficult to extract without complete excavation.

(72) Survey of a mutation.

When a mutation occurs a revision of the particular portion of the mosaic affected is necessary, and unless a serious error of survey is discovered the areas of the parcels must be held

The Land Registry forward to the Survey Department a 'mutation-form' upon which the necessary particulars of the transaction are entered, new numbers given, and a dimensioned diagram equivalent to a Field-Book can be constructed. Usually either a portion of a property which is defined upon the ground is being sold, or the property has to be sub-divided according to certain share-rights.

In the former case a survey of the particular part is made as part of a resurvey of the property, and the area thus obtained of each part is adjusted proportionally so as to maintain the original dimensions and area of the whole, as shown on the Registration Block Plan.

In the latter case parcellation is carried out in the Area-Office on the data of the Registration-Block Plan, and the diagram is passed to the surveyor for demarcation on the ground in accordance with the principles of paras. 57, 58.

(73) Upkeep.

Now this procedure depends upon the correct definition on the ground of the original property. If the original marking has not been maintained or has been distorted it must be restored.

The surveyor executing the mutation on the ground has therefore first to investigate and check by measurement the position of the property with reference to adjoining properties and to neighbouring survey marks. The measurements must be from Unit-landmarks, or, if necessary, from control-points or Trig. points, and in all cases these points must be examined, reported-on, and if required, restored, and the report should note any deficiencies in the neighbouring property-marks.

In this manner, and apart from periodic inspections, each mutation becomes a means for local maintenance of the property-mosaic.

On completion of the work on the ground, which is done in the presence of the parties to the transaction, the survey particulars are completed and certificates added to the mutation-form, which, after the necessary amendments to Record plans have been made, is returned to the Land Registry together with a statement of the survey fees. Sun-prints of the amendment are issued to all concerned, and when in any block these become numerous a fresh edition of the Registration-Block plan is produced and issued.

(74) Correction of errors.

In order to provide for the correction of genuine errors of original survey but to discourage trivial and unnecessary charges of inaccuracy in a Registration Block Plan, it is provided under the Land Settlement and Survey Ordinances that the owner of any registered property may apply at any time for investigation by the Survey Department of the details of his property shown on the Registration Block Plan, on payment of a deposit of £P.3. If an error is proved, this sum is returned to him and the necessary authority for correction both of the Register and of the Plan is obtained.

Proof of error rests upon the results of a revision by the Survey Department of the particular properties affected, and in an ordinary transaction the cost of a challenge would only be likely to be risked in a genuine case of serious error.

The provision tends therefore generally to maintain the property mosaic as originally demarcated on the ground, and shown on the plan, and to conserve the nominal areas as registered.

It should be added however that a challenge which results in the discovery of an encroachment made since the original survey may be held to be justified, in which case the matter would if necessary be referred to the Commissioner of Lands for further action.

(75) **Further problems.**

The foregoing pages present the more immediate and outstanding technical problems of the cadastral structure in this country. But there are many minor ones, and not until the Masha'a lands have been dealt with on a greater scale, the system of upkeep has been tested and matured, and experience of Survey and Settlement in hill areas has been obtained, will it be possible to regard this structure as complete.

But its main features have been established, and have in fact taken inevitable shape from the considerations of paras. 5 and 6 in the application of simple geometric principles.

JAFFA.
October, 1930.

C. H. Ley
DIRECTOR OF SURVEYS.

Parcellation Form.

Appendix.

ARGUMENT: $A = a_1^{d^{-1}} \cdot \Sigma^n o' \pm \Sigma^n d$

Sub-District __Jaffa.__ Village __El Kheiriye.__ Block __No. 6.__ Unit __F.__

Rectangle	Line	Offsets Left and Right		Adjustment (d)			Measurements	Total Corr.	Unit-strip Areas	Gross Area	Running Total	Parcel
		Terminal (a)	Inner (a')	Σ(a')	+	−						
I	0	22.0 L 8.0 R										
	1		20.4 9.0	29.4					60			
	2		19.6 11.4	60.4	0.2				120			Parcel No.1
	3		18.4 13.4	92.2					180			
	4		17.2 16.0	125.4					240			
	5	32.6 35.6 32.6 31.3	15.2 17.4	156.7 158.0	0.2			+0.2 156.7	156.9 300	456.9	456.90	
	6		12.4 18.8	189.0		0.8	$\frac{17.08}{92.60} = 0.18$		360		473.98	5.18
	7		11.0 20.8	220.8		0.2			420			
	8		7.4 23.2	251.4					480			
	9		4.4 25.2	281.0	1.0				540			
	10	0.6 L 26.4 R 57.0	(28.5)	(309.5)	1.2	1.0		+0.2 309.5	309.7 600	909.7		
II	0	32.8 L 4.2 R										
	1		29.0 3.8	32.8					50			Parcel No.2
	2		25.4 4.8	63.0	0.2				100			
	3		21.6 5.4	90.0	0.2				150			
	4		17.4 5.2	112.6					200			
	5		13.6 5.0	131.2					250			
	6		8.8 4.8	144.8					300			
	7		7.6 4.8	157.2					350			
	8	11.2 48.2 24.1	6.4 4.8	181.3 168.4	0.2	0.2		181.3	181.3 400	581.3	1491.00	
	9		4.4 5.0	177.8			$\frac{28.11}{61.20} = 0.46$		450		1519.11	8.46
	10	1.8 L 5.2 R 45.0	(22.5)	(200.3)	0.2	0.2		+ 200.3	200.3 500	700.3	1610.00	

Measurement to External Marks

Date: __27 June 1930.__ Computed by: __M. Borouchow__ Checked by: __B. _____
Booked by: __A. Greenbrat__

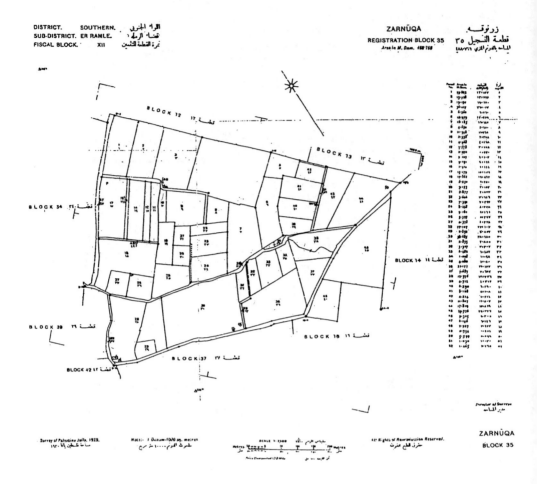

Fig. 2   TYPICAL SCORING DIAGRAM
(Scale $\frac{1}{20,000}$)

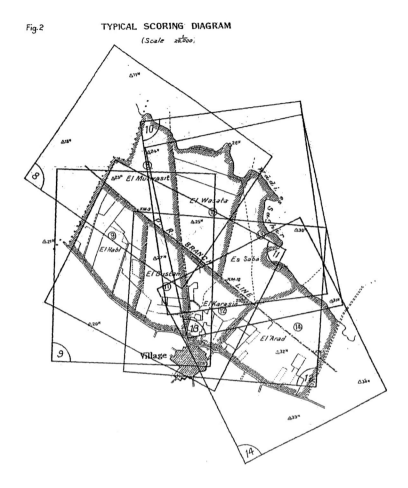

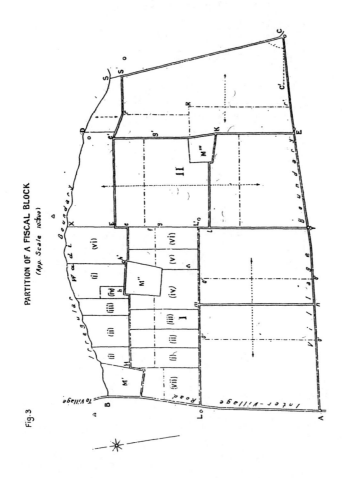

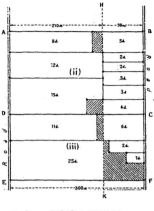

Fig. 4 PARCELLATION OF AN OPEN UNIT
(App. Scale 5000)

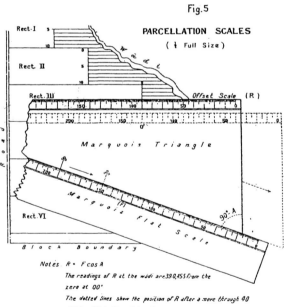

Fig. 5 PARCELLATION SCALES
(½ Full Size)

Notes. $R = F \cos A$

The readings of R at the wadi are 390,455 from the zero at 00°

The dotted lines show the position of R after a move through 40 divisions (4 depth-units) on F.

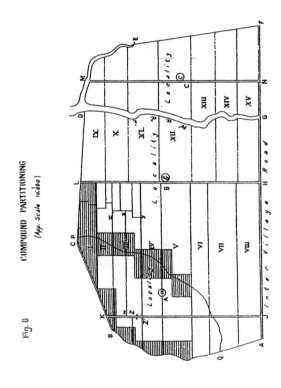

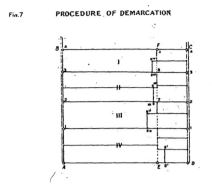

Fig. 7 PROCEDURE OF DEMARCATION

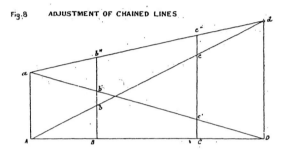

Fig. 8 ADJUSTMENT OF CHAINED LINES

MENSURATION OF QUADRILATERALS

Fig. 9

Fig. 10

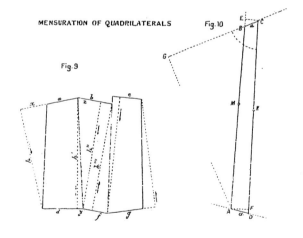

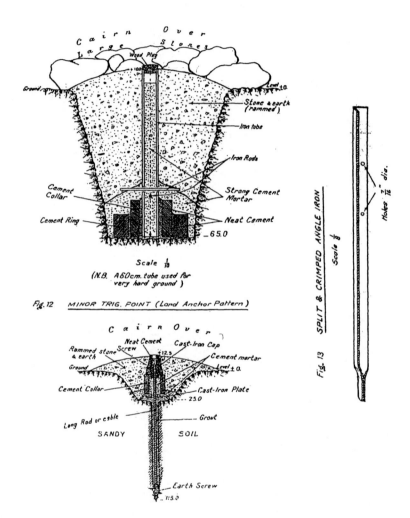

Fig. 11 MINOR TRIG. POINT (Tube Pattern)

Scale 1/10

(N.B. A 60cm. tube used for very hard ground)

Fig. 12 MINOR TRIG. POINT (Land Anchor Pattern)

Scale 1/25

Fig. 13 SPLIT & CRIMPED ANGLE IRON

Scale 1/8

Survey of Palestine Jaffa 1930.

CONTROL POINTS

Fig. 14   SPLIT ANGLE IRON MARK

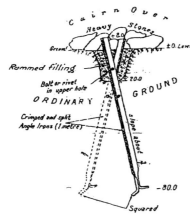

Fig. 15   SPLIT A.I. MARK (POINTED)

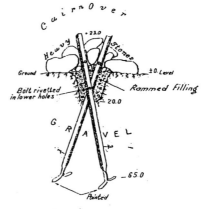

Fig. 17   POINTED A.I. MARK

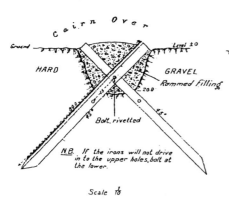

Fig. 16   DOGGED TUBE-MARK

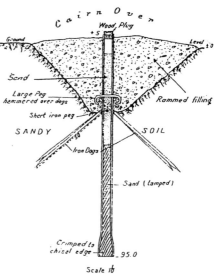

M/158/E

4.05

PALESTINE

DEPARTMENT OF SURVEYS

REPORT

for the years

1940 - 1946

Price 200 Mils

Obtainable from the Government Printer, Jerusalem, or the
Crown Agents for the Colonies, 4 Millbank, London S.W.1.

Published March, 1948.

CONTENTS

SECTION		Page
A	General	3
B	Legislation	5
C	Finance	5
D	District Survey Offices	6
E	Village development surveys	6
F	Land (Settlement of title) surveys	7
G	Town maps and plans	8
H	Triangulation and levelling	8
J	Topographical surveys	9
K	Special surveys	10
L	Headquarters sections	10

DIAGRAMS

1. Land Settlement
2. Town and Village Plans
3. Triangulation
4. Topographical Maps
5. Levelling
6. Distribution of Effective Time
7. Salaries and Cost-of-Living Allowances
8. Land Settlement Progress

TABLES

9. Appointments, etc. (First Division)
10. Appointments, etc. (Second Division)
11. Establishment
12. Sickness (officers)
13. Distribution of personnel
14. Distribution of expenditure
15. Expenditure and revenue
16. Salaries and Cost-of-Living Allowances
17. Examination for Surveyors Licences
18. Land Registration (Plans checked)
19. Land Registration (Mutations)
20. Village Development Surveys
21. Adjustment of Major Triangulation
22. Minor Triangulation and Control
23. Land Settlement Progress
24. Registration Block Plan Scales
25. Area Computing
26. Town Plans and Maps
27. Map Drawing office, plans amended
28. Printing Office output
29. Repair and Adjustment of Instruments
30. List of Publications

Department of Surveys

Report for the Years 1940 - 1946

A. GENERAL.

1. As from the 1st April 1940, the three departments, combined in 1935 to form the Department of Lands and Surveys, reverted to their former separate status. Mr. A. P. Mitchell was transferred from Transjordan to be Director of Surveys and Mr. H. G. Le Ray was promoted to Assistant Director.

2. During the seven years under review, the technical staff was increased by almost fifty per cent for the acceleration of survey for settlement of title to land and for the expansion of the map production sections of the Department. See Table 11.

At the same time a change in the percentage ratio of posts in grades I, II, and III. (Second Division) of Technical Assistants from 2:12:86 in 1940 to 3:23:74 in 1946 greatly improved the prospects of officers in the two lower grades. See Table 10.

To assist in meeting the demands of the Forces during the critical years of the war, one Royal Engineer officer and two other ranks were loaned by the Survey Directorate, M.E.F., from March 1943 to November 1945. Two British officers were seconded from the Malayan Survey Service during 1943—1944. Internal staff movements are shown in Tables 9 and 10.

3. On an average, 20 survey parties were in the field during the period under review. To carry out the expansion, referred to above, a survey school was formed early in 1942 and continued until March 1943, with an average of 9 instructors and 35 students in residence. To replace casualties due to discharges and resignations, the school was re-established on a smaller scale at Nazareth in December 1944 and continued for 17 months. Out of 880 applicants, of whom 380 were interviewed, 140 entered the schools and 90 graduated. The courses were directed mainly towards all branches of cadastral work but selected students were also instructed in triangulation, topography, and levelling.

The minimum educational standard for the first school was the School Certificate or Matriculation. Few of the applicants for the second school were up to this standard. Possessors of such a qualification prefer office jobs, which are in the same Government pay scale. This is an old problem, another aspect of which is the loss of surveyors after training to Municipalities, firms of licensed surveyors, etc., who offer higher rates of pay. There is also a small but steady demand from other Departments for trained surveyors to fill vacancies in higher-grade posts, posing the problem of either losing the Department's best men, or letting more mediocre men go and get promotion before the best men, or of blocking this avenue of advancement completely.

4. Five extensions to the Headquarters building were constructed during the last five years, bringing the total floor space up to 3000 sq. metres. The printing and stores sections are on the ground floor and all other offices on the upper floor.

5. The problem of economical surveying in the hill areas, where boundary marks are scattered, was once more taken up in 1943 and experiments continued until 1946. The following were tried:—

(i) Continued use of chain survey, with long offsets aligned by optical square;

(ii) Traverse with self-reducing tacheometer, fixing all marks instrumentally. It was found that the adjustment of the instrument soon fails in the hands of Palestinian surveyors.

(iii) Traverse with 120 m. light tapes, taking offsets to marks near the line and fixing others by intersection.

The results of the experiments were inconclusive and, owing to the shortage of supervisory officers the new methods were abandoned.

6. The organisation of labour in Palestine is making progress and the Palestine Arab Workers Society was active in recruiting Survey labourers to its membership. Representations were made by the Society for improved conditions of service. The basic pay scale for field labour of LP. $3\frac{1}{2}$ — LP. 6 monthly has remained virtually unchanged since the foundation of the Department in 1920 but now carries a large cost-of-living allowance.

7. Among the visible effects of the war was the provision of classes in First Aid and of A.R.P. shelters at Headquarters which was however not touched by the only raid on Tel Aviv. Three British officers were members of the Jaffa detachment of the Volunteer Force. One British officer and three Technical Assistants were released for military service. Two Superintendents and thirteen Technical Assistants, seconded to the Postal Censorship on the outbreak of the war, reverted to normal duties in 1940. Field parties near the Syrian frontier were evacuated at the time of the military operations there in 1941.

The inevitable shortage of supplies was felt but was not crippling. For iron boundary marks, the substitution of rock-cuts, paint-marks, cairns, and wooden pegs was not very satisfactory. Tents, clothing, chemicals, and other materials were procured locally instead of from England. Field parties ceased to hire transport locally at exorbitant prices and were moved instead by the Government Transport Agency. Eventually in 1946 the Department secured its own fleet of two trucks and two pick-ups.

The wartime rise in the cost of living (to index 258) was the cause of a strike of all Second Division officers for one week in April 1946.

Priority in filling post-war staff vacancies was given to ex-servicemen (and women) many of whom had been in No. 524 Palestine Field Survey Co. R.E. Up to the end of 1946, places had been found for thirty-eight.

8. In the course of the political disturbances in Palestine, the Jerusalem District Survey Office was destroyed by a bomb in 1944. One labourer was killed, and the equipment and a few original field records were lost.

A guard of varying strength provided by the Army or Police was placed on the Headquarters building and a floodlit barbed-wire perimeter fence set up. Several days work were lost in Jerusalem and at Headquarters by curfews and on one occasion the building was occupied by the Army for four days.

9. The incidence of sickness among officers is shown in Table 12. The rate rose during the war until in 1944 it was fifty per cent or more above normal. This was largely due to the frequent absence of a minority of officers who were unable to face up to the continual rise in the cost of living.

No member of the staff contracted smallpox, plague, or typhus, although there were several outbreaks of these diseases in the country. Inoculation of all staff against typhoid and paratyphoid was carried out every year. The number of man-days sickness attributed to malaria declined to 38 in 1946.

A severe outbreak of African Horse Sickness occurred in 1944 and one or two members of the field staff lost horses or donkeys. Restrictions were placed on movement of animals for three months while protective inoculations were being carried out.

B. LEGISLATION.

10. From December 1942 to September 1945 employment in the Department was scheduled as a War Service Occupation under the Defence Regulations. The intention of this legislation was to prevent skilled workers from resigning in order to obtain higher wages in other essential occupations during the period of labour shortage.

The sale of maps was restricted during the war. The Director was permitted to exercise his own discretion in this matter.

11. An amendment to the Survey Ordinance was published in 1946 redefining Public Surveys and validating all previous surveys carried out by the Department which were not Public Surveys within the meaning of the former definition. The amendment also made provision for deposits in advance of work for which fees are chargeable.

12. Fees for Land Settlement Surveys were abolished in 1946 as a separate charge and are now included in the revised Settlement of Title fees.

13. Survey fees for work in connection with Land Registry transactions were increased in 1940, 1943, and 1946 and are now at four times the pre-war rate.

14. Prosecutions were initiated from time to time under the Survey Ordinance for damage to marks, and convictions were secured in every case, the average fine being about LP. 2. Since there were rarely any witnesses of the act of damage, the actions were usually taken against the occupier of the land for "failing to report".

15. A booklet of Survey Legislation consolidated up-to-date was published by the Department in 1946. This comprises the Survey Ordinance, the Surveyors Rules, and the Survey (Fees) Rules.

16. The section of the Surveyors Rules dealing with examinations for licences was amended in 1942. Candidates cannot now take the practical part of the examination until they have passed the written part. This saves the examiners much time and effort. The examination fee was increased to LP. 3 but successful candidates are not required to pay for their first 3-year licence. The power of granting licences is deputed by the High Commissioner to the Director.

17. In 1945 and 1946, 26 and 28 candidates respectively entered for the annual examination for licences to practise as surveyors (about the usual pre-war number). During the seven years 1940—1946 fifty candidates passed this examination. In addition, in 1946 eleven out of seventeen suitably qualified ex-servicemen passed a special practical examination. The total number of persons entitled to licences rose from 80 to 132 but not all of these are practising. (See Table 17).

C. FINANCE.

18. The total strength of the staff increased during the seven years by nearly fifty per cent and expenditure on their basic emoluments rose in proportion. At the same time the cost of living in Palestine rose from a pre-war index of 100 to 275 in December 1946. Compensatory allowances were first paid in 1942 and in 1946 their total value far exceeded that of basic emoluments. See Diagram 7 and Table 16.

19. Total departmental expenditure in 1946—1947 of LP. 258,000 compares with LP. 35,000 in 1922—1923 and LP. 68,000 in 1940—1941.

20. Revenue (see Table 15): About half the output of sunprints (mainly of registration block plans) is for sale. The price of prints is in general 150 per cent more than pre-war and revenue from sales has trebled. The prices of printed maps have been increased mostly by only 50 per cent but sales have risen sharply and account for more revenue than sunprints. Income from survey fees has increased proportionately with the increase in fees. Total revenue in 1946 was LP. 15,657.

D. DISTRICT SURVEY OFFICES.

21. Since registration of transactions in land is compulsory in Palestine and every transaction involving a mutation (i.e. the creation of new parcels) submitted for registration must be checked on the ground, surveyors had been attached to seven of the district Land Registries since 1927. In 1943 survey personnel were detached from the Registries and eight District Survey Offices were established so as to develop closer relations with the public and other Government Departments.

The activities of the district offices comprise:—

(i) Checking on the ground of plans prepared by Licensed Surveyors for registration of land transactions.

(ii) Surveys in connection with land transactions by Government (lease, expropriation, etc.).

(iii) Restoration of boundaries.

(iv) Technical advice to the district representatives of other Government Departments.

(v) Supervision of Village Development Surveys.

22. The average strength of District Survey Office staff in recent years was 8 District Survey Officers and 23 Technical Assistants.

23. District Survey Office work is checked at Headquarters by the Land Registration Section which also deals with licensed surveyors and the organisation of Village Development Surveys. Statistics relating to these activities are given in Tables 18—20.

E. VILLAGE DEVELOPMENT SURVEYS.

24. Among post-war reconstruction schemes in Palestine the improvement of the Arab villages was given a high priority. Since an accurate plan or map is the essential basis of any kind of town or country planning, a programme for rapid surveys of village built-on and adjoining areas was drawn up in 1945.

25. There are about 1000 administrative "village" units in Palestine. Some 40 of these are "urban areas" for which town sheets or taxation plans exist. Some contain more than one built-on area, others contain none. A hundred or more built-up areas in Jewish colonies are covered by registration block plans.

26. In the financial year 1945—1946, six villages were surveyed by the staff of the Town Planning Adviser and fifteen by this Department; in 1946—1947, a further eighty-six were taken up by the Department. The objective is a hundred villages a year. Progress in surveying, drawing, and printing the plans is given in Table 20.

27. Additional triangulation has to be fixed where there are no fourth-order points. The built-on areas are surveyed by plane-table, on 1:1250 scale, and the environs on 1:2500. If the lands of the village have been settled, the block plans are revised to show all features omitted in the purely property boundary survey.

28. The average area surveyed in each village was 1650 dunums. The average area of the densely built-on nucleus (which is always excluded from Settlement of Title operations) of an Arab village is 66 dunums, within which may live 1000 or more persons.

F. LAND (SETTLEMENT OF TITLE) SURVEYS.

29. The Land (Settlement of Title) Ordinance enacted in 1928 provided for the appointment of Settlement Officers with judicial powers to investigate and settle all disputes of ownership and other rights, to partition land held in undivided shares, and to prepare schedules of rights from which new land registers are compiled, village by village. The function of the Survey Department in this procedure is to cut up the village into suitable blocks (see paragraph 32 below), demarcate and survey every parcel of land, prepare preliminary plans for the use of the Settlement Officer in his investigations and final plans incorporating his decisions with lists of areas to accompany the schedules of rights. The work is carried out village by village. At the beginning of 1940, out of a total of about 1000 village units in Palestine, 219 had been settled; by the end of 1946, the total was 473, while work was in progress or uncompleted in a further 102. The remaining villages (400 or so) are all in the hill districts of Northern Galilee, Samaria, and Jerusalem.

30. This work has absorbed the major part of the effort of this Department for the past 20 years, reaching a maximum in 1944, when the whole of the field staff (115 surveyors in 20 parties) was engaged in various stages from observation of control points to marking Settlement Officers' final amendments on the ground.

31. The efficient prosecution of Land Settlement operations depends largely on proper co-ordination of settlement and survey procedure and the elimination of unnecessary work. A great deal of thought, discussion, and experiment have been applied to these problems and new systems were introduced at intervals, notably in 1941 and 1943. The whole subject is more fully discussed in a technical paper prepared for the Conference of Commonwealth Survey Officers held in London in 1947. The various survey stages of the present system are, briefly:—

(i) Preliminary investigation by settlement staff and issue of report and diagram to guide demarcator.

(ii) Demarcation of property boundaries by surveyor-demarcators and preparation of croquis (sketch) of each block to guide surveyors.

(iii) Marking and observation of control points.

(iv) Chain survey, recorded in field books.

(v) Plotting (at Headquarters), tracing in pencil, printing and issue of preliminary plans to Settlement Officer.

At this stage there is an interval, usually of one to two years, while the Settlement work is completed.

(vi) Field examination of field sheets and execution of Settlement Officers' amendments.

(vii) Checking of field sheets and tracing with schedule of areas (at Headquarters), printing and issue of final plans to Settlement Officer for signature and passing for registration.

(viii) Preparation on scale 1:20,000 of index to blocks in village.

Progress in the various stages is shown in Diagram 8 and Table 23.

32. The average block has an area of 580 dunums and it is estimated that 20,000 will be required to cover all the village units of Palestine. At the end of 1946 over 10,000 had been surveyed and the annual average during 1940—1946 was 530. The blocks are plotted on scale 1:2500 on standard field sheets 60x70cms. (in garden areas the scale may be 1:1250 or 1:625 — see Table 24). The average area of a parcel of land is 15 dunums and there may be from one to over a hundred in one

block. They are serially numbered in the blocks and blocks are serially numbered throughout Palestine.

G. TOWN MAPS AND PLANS.

33. Urban Property Tax is levied in 40 towns and large villages. These are divided into blocks and the urban assessment plans compiled from the large-scale town surveys made by this Department. The quinquennial revision for taxation purposes is carried out by surveyor-valuers of the Land Settlement Department. There are at present 1346 plans of which 625 cover Jerusalem, Haifa, Jaffa, and Tel Aviv.

34. In 1941—1942 the original tracings were transferred from Headquarters to the District Survey Officers who keep them up-to-date by obtaining records of changes direct from the district surveyor-valuers. They also prepare the sunprints required by the various interested parties. Redrawing of worn-out tracings is done at Headquarters.

35. No town revision or extension survey was carried out during 1941—1945 except intermittently in Jerusalem. This was due to the prior claims of Land Settlement work on the field staff and of military work on the reproduction sections. Work in hand at the end of 1939 was completed in 1940. A comprehensive programme of town revision was commenced in 1946.

36. Urban development in Palestine has been rapid and frequent revision is required. At the end of 1946 the average age of town sheets was six years with a maximum of twelve years. Diagram 2 shows the places covered by town sheets or block plans.

Jerusalem and Jaffa—Tel Aviv are covered on the 1:1250 scale by 129 and 49 sheets respectively, Haifa by 47 sheets on 1:2500. These major towns are also covered by 1:10,000 scale sheets in colour. Twenty-five other towns are covered by sheets usually on 1:1250 varying from two to seventeen in number. Some of these towns are to be covered by coloured sheets on 1:5000. The first of these, Nazareth, was completed in 1946.

37. For many purposes, such as town planning, a single sheet covering an urban area on a smaller scale is more handy than a number of 1:1250 sheets or block plans. This normally involves redrawing but as an expedient direct photo-reduction can be used. Thirty-eight towns or villages have been covered by such reductions to 1:2500 or 1:5000. For town planning purposes contours have been specially surveyed for twelve of the towns.

H. TRIANGULATION AND LEVELLING.

38. No major or third-order triangulation was carried out by the Department during 1940—1946 as all the area of Palestine likely to require fourth-order triangulation for control of large-scale surveys had already been covered by the higher orders. See Diagram 3.

Army observers surveyed a chain of major triangulation in 1941 connecting the Palestine major points south of Beersheba with the Egyptian geodetic points in Sinai, thence south to the Gulf of Aqaba and north through Transjordan to close on the Palestine major net near Jericho. The area covered is mainly desert.

Details are recorded in Trig. Report No. 5, GHQ, ME, January 1942.

The computation and adjustment of part of the chain in Transjordan was done by the Computing Section of this Department for use in cadastral work. Some details are given in Table 21.

39. Fourth-order triangulation being a necessary prelude to cadastral survey, the number of observers at work rose to six in 1942 in advance of the acceleration of Land Settlement survey, but with the completion of the net in northern Palestine this number declined to one by 1945. The area still outstanding consists of the Nablus, Jerusalem, Hebron, and Beersheba Sub-Districts. The eastern and southern part of this area is largely desert and has no settled population. If a village in the area is put on the programme of Village Development Surveys (see paragraphs 24—28) some fourth-order points have to be fixed there in advance of the triangulation programme. Observations are made with a 5-inch micrometer or small Tavistock theodolite.

40. The fourth-order net is broken down at the time of chain survey by traverse or intersections to fix a sufficiency of points on to which the chain survey can be securely tied. Over 80,000 such points were fixed during 1940—1946 (see Table 22). Five-inch micrometer or vernier theodolites and 20 m. or 30 m. steel tapes are used.

41. In 1940 a 52-km. line of precise levelling from Jerusalem to Nablus was observed, subdividing an existing circuit. The new circuits had closures of 106 mm. and 23 mm. in 207 kms. and 170 kms. respectively.

The Nazareth-Beisan-Tiberias circuit remains to be closed between Nazareth and Tiberias (31 kms.). See Diagram 5.

1027 kms. of tertiary levelling were carried out during 1940—1943 in various places, mainly for Town Planning purposes.

J. TOPOGRAPHICAL SURVEYS.

42. The basic map of Palestine north of Beersheba was for half a century the Palestine Exploration Fund map of 1878 on scale 1:63,360 (one inch to a mile) with orography shown by hill shading. Most of the desert south of Beersheba (now commonly known as the Negeb) was surveyed and contoured in 1913—1914 as an extension of the military G.S.G.S. 1:125,000 Sinai series. The contoured military survey of 1917—1918 on 1:40,000, compiled largely from air-photos, extended from the desert as far north as Nablus. During 1929—1934 the whole country except Beersheba Sub-District was surveyed for fiscal purposes by this Department on 1:10,000 without contours. These fiscal maps formed the basis within that area of the present 1:20,000 and 1:100,000 series for which contours were compiled from new work (mainly at the scales of 1:20,000 and 1:50,000) and from the old 1:40,000 maps. The 1:100,000 series of 14 sheets was published during 1935—1938 and extended south to latitude 31° N (about 30 kms. south of Beersheba), the desert area west of the Dead Sea being mapped by air survey and the area south and west of Beersheba by 1:100,000 plane-table survey. A provisional compilation on 1:250,000 of the desert south of 31° N included the results of a special reconnaissance of motor tracks made in 1938. The 1:20,000 sheets published up to the end of 1939 covered only the coastal plain.

43. During 1940—1943 all topographical work had to be harnessed to military requirements. All communications (and other important features) in the 18,000 sq. kms. north of latitude 31° N were revised on one or more occasions, the surveyors using motor transport. The preparation of the 1:20,000 series (rapidly convertible by photography to the military 1:25,000 series) was sharply accelerated, the total of completed sheets rising from 45 to 126 in the four years (see Diagram 4). A further 17 were published by the end of 1946 with 13 more in hand. Some original material for the latter in the Beersheba Sub-District was supplied by an R.E. survey unit.

44. In 1942 the sheet lines of the 1:100,000 series were changed so that no sheet would be too large to print on the Army mobile presses (demy size), the number of sheets increasing from 14 to 16 with no overlaps. Of the desert south of 31° N,

three-quarters is now covered from the west and east respectively by the new Sinai and South Levant 1:100,000 Army series, leaving 2000 sq. kms. covered by the 1914 1:125,000 survey only.

45. A new edition of the 1:250,000 covering all Palestine in three sheets was produced in 1946 by compilation from all the above material.

K. SPECIAL SURVEYS.

In addition to the various systematic surveys described above, many special surveys were carried out, among which may be mentioned the following:—

46. In 1942—1943, eleven surveyors were loaned to the Army for topographical survey work in Transjordan and covered 1000 sq. kms. by plane-table on 1:50,000 scale.

47. For irrigation purposes 105 block plans covering 120 sq. kms. near Beisan, and 19 special sheets on scale 1:5000 covering 80 sq. kms. north of Lake Hula were levelled and contoured in 1942—1943. From July 1945 onwards a party of four surveyors was loaned indefinitely to the Water Commissioner for similar work.

48. Surveyors were also loaned at various times to the Departments of Forests, Town Planning, Land Settlement (for State Domain and Urban Assesement work), and to Municipalities. Many of them were eventually transferred to those Departments.

49. Large-scale contour surveys for planning purposes were made of two holy places: on 1:625 of the Haram esh Sharif (Temple Area) in Jerusalem and on 1:250 of the area in Hebron round the Mosque of Abraham beneath which is the cave of Machpelah with its tombs of the Patriarchs. The R.A.F. supplied three pairs of special large-scale photos to facilitate the latter work.

50. As a result of notes exchanged between the Governments of Palestine and Transjordan, it was agreed that Director of Surveys, Palestine, and Director of Lands and Surveys, Transjordan, should demarcate the frontier between the two countries near Aqaba.

The definition in the Order dated 1st September 1922 laid down that the frontier from the Dead Sea to the Red Sea should follow the centre of the Wadi Araba and should reach the Red Sea two miles west of Aqaba. Since this two-mile point does not coincide with the centre of the Wadi Araba it was agreed that the frontier should be traced starting from a point two miles measured along the shore from the westernmost house in Aqaba (excluding military installations of a later date) and continuing due north until the thalweg of the Wadi Araba was intersected.

One observer from each Department carried out the necessary triangulation and traverse observations and five masonry pillars were erected along a 4-km. line.

51. One surveyor was loaned in 1941 for duty with a Commission to clarify on the ground parts of the 1923 Agreement on the Palestine-Lebanon frontier.

L. HEADQUARTERS SECTIONS.

52. The distribution of staff in the Headquarters office is shown in Table 13.

The Mathematical Computing Office, in addition to computing the triangulation, traverse, and levelling mentioned in Section H, continued to carry out all triangulation computations for the Transjordan Government (e.g. 1513 points in 1946) and also prepared for the Army a trig. list for each sheet (10 km. sq.) of the 1:20,000 (Army 1:25,000) series (165 sheets). This involved converting the values of 18,200 points from the Cassini projection to the Transverse Mercator projection used by the Army.

This office is equipped with 14 electric and 5 hand calculating machines. Seven of these were acquired locally during the war and were kept fully employed.

53. The Land Settlement Plans Office deals with the office stages of all the work described in Section F and also the scoring of field sheets for Village Development Survey and for Transjordan (e.g. 136 and 429 respectively in 1946). Two Coradi co-ordinatographs are kept fully employed. Block plan tracings are amended by this section after every registered mutation (see Table 19).

54. The Area Computing Office formerly computed exact parcel areas for the preliminary large-scale block plans, dimensions for the partitioning of masha'a lands (held in common ownership) and final areas for parcels and blocks after amendment by the Settlement Officer. Schedules of areas of the various land categories, parcel by parcel, were also prepared for assessment of Rural Property Tax. Under the new system of settlement and survey introduced in 1941, preliminary areas are only issued on request and partitions are usually done entirely on the ground before being transferred to paper, while the land category schedules are prepared by settlement staff. The progress of settlement resulted in an increase in the number of applications from the public for dimensioned sketches or plans in connection with land transactions. Statistics of the above activities are given in Table 25.

The upkeep of area records for the Departments of Statistics (area of Palestine by sub-districts) and Land Settlement (area settled) occupies about 200 man-days a year.

55. The work of the Land Registration Section is dealt with in paragraph 23.

56. The Technical Archives, the yield of the two million pounds spent by the Department since 1920, now contains upwards of 60,000 documents comprising original field books and sheets, diagrams, drawings, tracings, descriptions, air-photographs, etc., stored in 96 steel presses. The plate store holds some 1500 printing plates weighing over 3 tons.

57. The Map Drawing Office produces and amends all the Town Maps and Plans (see Section G), Village Development Plans (see Section E), administrative boundary diagrams on scales from 1:10,000 to 1:250,000, reductions of registration block plans by villages to 1:10,000, and all miscellaneous large-scale compilation and drawing jobs, many of which are the result of special requests by other Departments or by Government. Three pantographs are kept fully employed in making reductions from the larger scales.

The Typing Section of this office provides all names and numerals on the above maps and plans and also on registration block plans and for many small-scale maps. The output of forms, circulars, instruction slips, etc. on the hand-operated letter-press machine rose from 22,000 copies in 1941 to 115,000 in 1946.

58. The Small-scale Drawing Section produces and revises the original drawings of the topographical maps described in Section J and the associated colour plates. The first edition of the nine-colour Motor Map, covering Palestine north of 31° N in a single sheet on the half-million scale, with three town insets on 1:40,000, was published in 1935 and proved so popular that it reached the tenth revised edition in 1939. The 1940 edition was a redrawn one and this was revised for the 1941 edition. For military purposes an edition in black, red, and blue only, without the insets, was prepared in 1942. This was frequently revised (see paragraph 43) until the end of the war allowed a new edition of the fully-coloured map to be published in 1945.

59. Second and third editions of the popular period map produced in collaboration with the Department of Antiquities, "Palestine of the Crusades" with heraldic border, were published in 1940 and 1945.

Nine maps and two charts were drawn for the Report of the Anglo-American Committee of Enquiry in 1946.

Many special drawings were made for the Army, R.A.F., and other Departments. Royal Engineer personnel assisted during 1943—1945.

60. The Printing Office, at the beginning of the war, possessed one power-driven press only, and that was a quad-crown flat-bed machine of pre-1914 vintage with a very limited output. As this could not cope with the Forces demands for maps, the R.E. Survey Directorate arranged for the installation and operation of a new double-demy Crabtree rotary offset towards the end of 1940. This unfortunately, was required elsewhere and removed in September 1941. A Leipzig quad-crown rotary was then requisitioned locally and erected by R.E. personnel early in 1942. Towards the end of 1946 the Crabtree was returned from Army Disposals and subsequently purchased. These changes in equipment, forced by circumstances, have not lightened the task of the printers.

61. Total output of the machines rose from 40,000 impressions in 1940 to 1,200,000 in 1941. It should be noted that one map may require from one to eight or more impressions. The total number of maps of one or more impressions for the Forces for the period 1941—1945 exceeded one million. In addition 130,000 sheets of co-ordinate lists were produced. Reproduction and printing were also undertaken for other Departments, public bodies, and the Survey Departments of Transjordan and Cyprus. Among the more exceptional of these may be mentioned Railway Control Charts in 4 colours, a pictorial calendar for the Soil Conservation Board, and maps to illustrate such diverse matters as locust control in the Middle East and the spread of rat plague in Haifa.

The Printing Office is also provided with ordoverax and sunprinting equipment. Statistics of output are given in Table 28.

62. An instrument and machine repair section is attached to the printing office. Its scope was greatly extended by the appointment in 1946 of a fully-trained ex-serviceman instrument mechanic. Statistics of repairs, etc., carried out are given in Table 29.

63. A Statistical Section was set up in 1940 and expanded in 1943 to include the maintenance of all non-confidential personnel records. These include all labour staff records, and records of work done, leave, sickness, transfers, etc., of officers, maintained by notifications or monthly returns sent in by all sections of the Department. From this material statistics are compiled which enable a check to be made on, e.g. the incidence of sickness, or, the cost relationships between various Departmental activities. Diagram 6 and Tables 10 to 14 are compiled from the records of this section.

64. Three handbooks of technical instructions were compiled for Departmental use: on Instrument Work, Demarcation, and Chain Survey and Examination. The originals were typed on foolscap and photo-reduced to approximately 15x32 cms. for printing and issue as booklets of a handy size.

Three other booklets were compiled for publication and printed in the same way: an official list of Road Distances, consolidated Survey Legislation, and a new edition of the descriptive Map Catalogue (see Table 30).

16th December, 1947.

A. P. MITCHELL
Director of Surveys

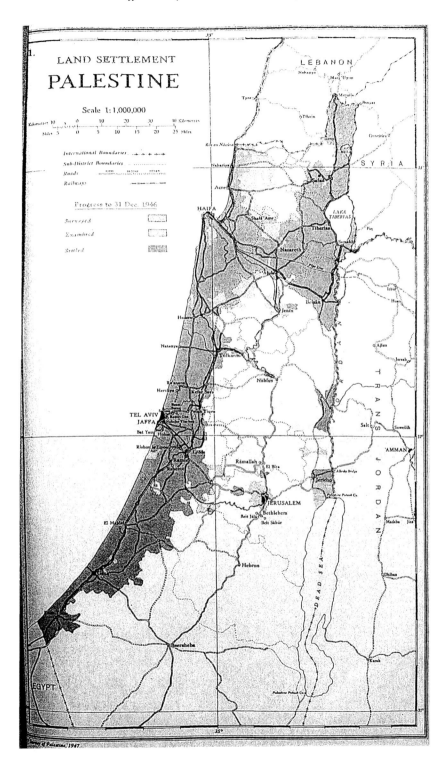

[These maps are reproduced in their original colours in the Map Box maps 3 to 7.]

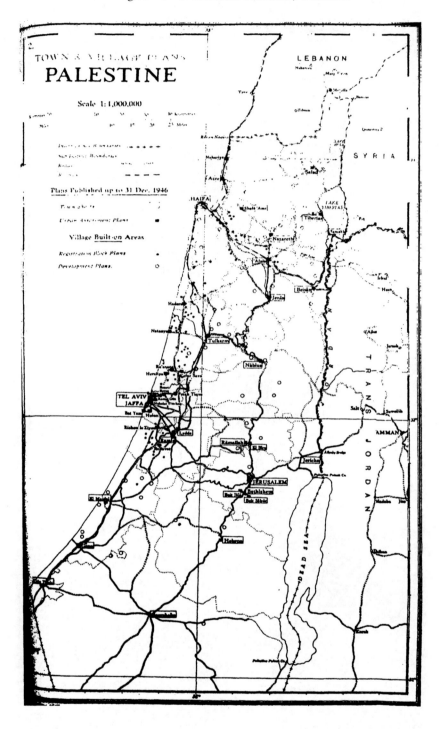

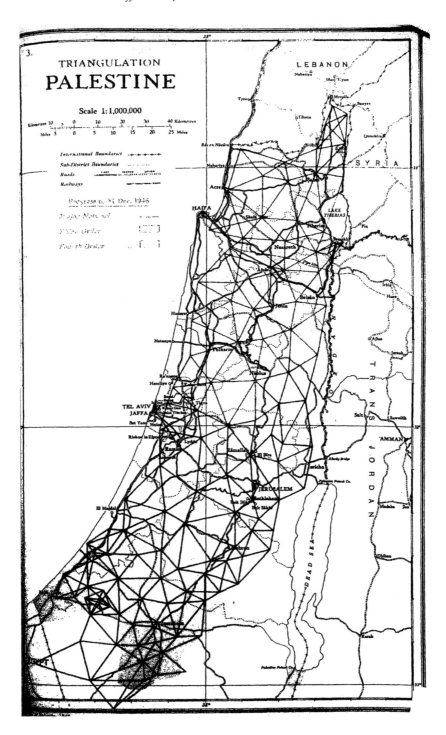

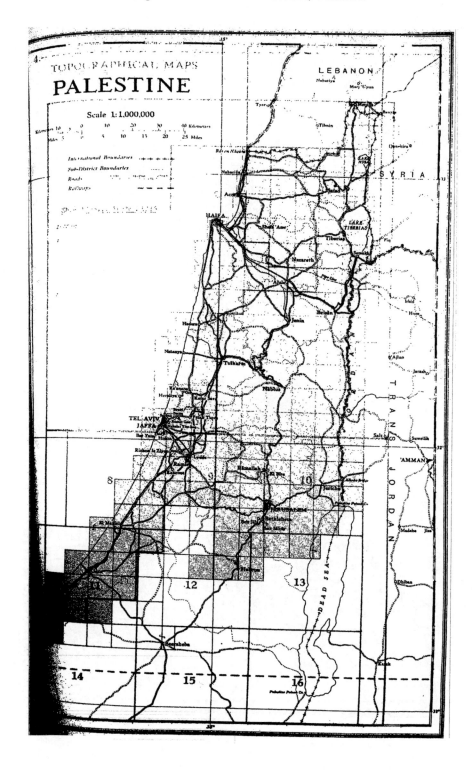

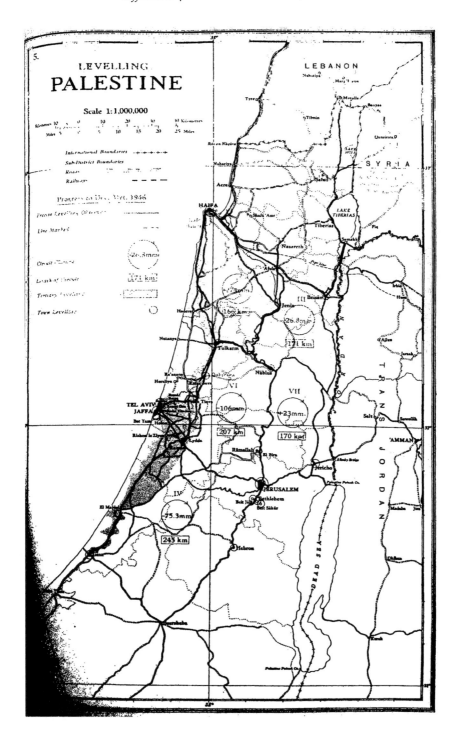

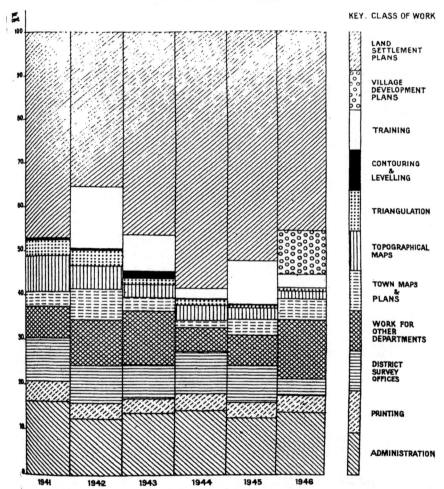

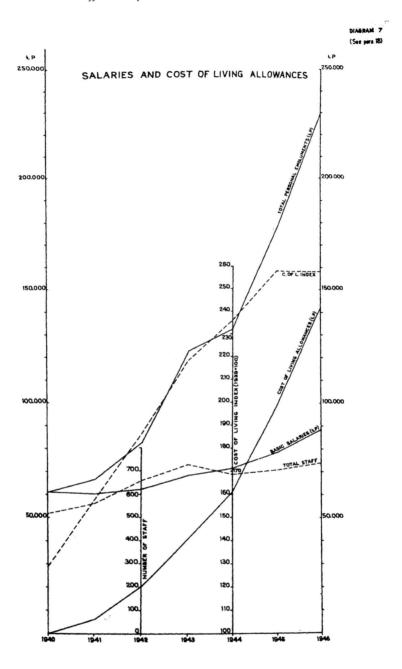

DIAGRAM 7
(See para. 18)

DIAGRAM 8
See Section F

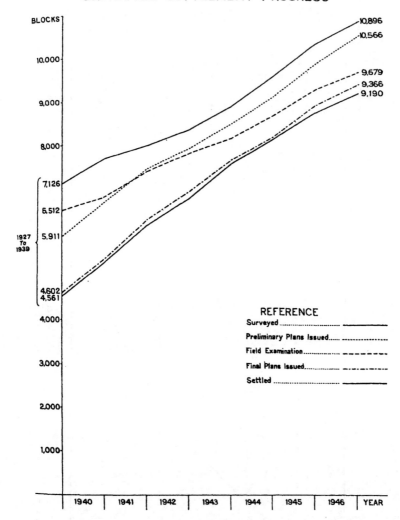

SURVEY AND SETTLEMENT PROGRESS

NOTE: Under the Old System field examination was carried out before the commencement of Settlement operations. In the new system (1941) preliminary plans are used for settlement decisions which are implemented during field examination.

TABLE 9
(*See paragraph* 2)

APPOINTMENTS, ETC. (FIRST DIVISION)

Mr. A. P. Mitchell, Director, was a member of the Committee of Enquiry into the application of the Land Transfer Regulations, in 1945.

Mr. R. B. Crusher, O.B.E., Assistant Director, who entered the Ordnance Survey in 1895 and served subsequently in Africa, Canada, Ceylon, etc., retired in 1940 after 19 years in this Department.

Mr. H. G. Le Ray was H.B.M. Government representative at discussions on the ground in 1940 concerning the position of Jebel Anaiza, the tri-junction point of the boundaries of Iraq, Transjordan, and Saudi Arabia.

Capt. J. H. Mankin, Superintendent, returned in 1945 from war service with the Royal Engineers and in 1946 was transferred, after 25 years service, to Uganda.

Mr. N. Foutorian, Superintendent, retired in 1946 after 24 years service.

Mr. B. A. McArthur-Davis, Superintendent, left in 1944 after 18 years service, on transfer to Gambia.

Mr. J. W. Loxton, Superintendent, was seconded for 19 months in 1940—1941 to the Department of Lands and Surveys, Transjordan.

Mr. S. Stollery, Superintendent, for 17 years in charge of the Printing Office, retired in 1944 after a total of 43 years Government service in the United Kingdom and Palestine.

Mr. L. W. R. Aslin was appointed to this post in 1946 after five years service with 512 Field Survey Coy. R. E.

Mr. B. Goussinsky and Mr. B. Ernstein, who both entered the Department in 1921, were promoted to be Superintendents in 1940 and 1945 respectively.

TABLE 10
(*See paragraph* 2)

APPOINTMENTS, ETC. (SECOND DIVISION)

YEAR	1940	1941	1942	1943	1944	1945	1946	Total
GRADE III								
New Appointments	7	—	58	48	9	33	36	191
Resignations	—	—	—	3	20	9	10	42
Discharges, and termination on marriage (women)	—	—	4	5	4	1	4	18
Deaths	—	—	1	—	—	—	—	1
Retirements on pension	—	—	—	—	—	—	2	2
Transfers to other Departments	—	1	3	4	7	3	2	20
Promotions to Grade II	3	1	15	15	—	5	4	43
Net increase + or decrease —	+4	—2	+35	+21	—22	+15	+14	+65
Establishment (end of year)	175	200	231	237	210	215	231	
GRADE II								
Promotions from Grade III	3	1	15	15	—	5	4	43
Transfers from other Departments	1	—	—	1	2	—	—	4
Discharges	—	—	—	—	—	1		1
Deaths	1	—	—	—	—	—	1	2
Retirements	1	—	—	—	—	1	1	3
Transfers to other Departments	—	1	1	—	1	1	—	4
Promotions to Grade I	1	—	4	1	—	1	—	7
Net increase or decrease	+1	—	+10	+15	+1	+2	+1	+30
Establishment (end of year)	27	35	43	51	70	70	73	
GRADE I								
Promotions from Grade II	1	—	4	1	—	1	—	7
Resignations	—	—	—	—	—	—	1	1
Transfers to other Departments	—	—	2	—	—	—	1	3
Promotions to First Division	1	—	—	—	—	1	—	2
Net increase or decrease	—	—	+2	+1	—	—	—2	+1
Establishment (end of year)	7	8	10	9	9	9	11	

TABLE 11
(See paragraph 2)

ESTABLISHMENT

FINANCIAL YEAR	1940/1	1941/2	1942/3	1943/4	1944/5	1945/6	1946/7
Director and Assistant Director	2	2	2	2	2	2	2
Superintendents	6	6	8	8	10	10	10
Clerks and Storekeepers	15	14	16	23	19	24	26
Technical Assistants	218	251	294	292	290	290	309
Total Officers	241	273	320	325	321	326	347
Manipulative Staff	274	274	269	269	273	273	315
Establishment	515	547	589	594	594	599	662
Casual labour (average)	—	12	70	131	90	105	74
TOTAL STRENGTH (including vacancies)	515	559	659	725	684	704	736

TABLE 12
(See paragraph 9)

SICKNESS

The following table shows the incidence of days lost ascribed to sickness (classified staff) :—

YEAR	Man-days lost		No. of officers		Days per head		(**) % of total time
	Head-quarters	Field	Head-quarters	Field	Head-quarters	Field	
(*)							
1942	1913	1107	164	112	11.6	9.9	3.5
1943	2065	2380	168	151	12.3	15.8	5.0
1944	2715	2934	154	164	17.6	17.8	5.4
1945	2690	1714	162	164	16.6	10.4	4.2
1946	2524	1245	184	150	13.7	8.6	3.6

(**) Total man-days sickness expressed as a percentage of total effective and non-effective man-days for the whole Department. Note, for comparison, that rest, holidays, and leave account for 22% of total time.

(*) Statistics prior to 1942 not complete.

TABLE 13
(See Section L, etc.)

DISTRIBUTION OF PERSONNEL

The following figures are averages for 1946 and do not include the seven First Division officers. All except 9 storekeepers and 17 clerks are rated as Technical Assistants. The totals include 26 women.

			LABOUR
HEADQUARTERS SECTIONS	Total : 176		40
Land Settlement Plans	51		
Land Registration Surveys	13		
Mathematical Computing	13		
Area Computing	15		
Mapping (large and medium scales)	29		
Mapping (small scales)	7		
Printing	10		
Technical Archives	4		
Stores and Map Sales	12		
Personnel Records and Clerical	22		
DISTRICT SURVEY OFFICES (Eight)		29	28
FIELD SURVEYORS	Total : 130		300
Land Settlement Surveys	100		
Village Development Surveys and Town Revision	25		
Levelling and Contouring	4		
Minor Triangulation	1		
TOTAL ESTABLISHMENT		335	
Unclassified Manipulative Staff			368

TABLE 14
(See paragraph 63)

DISTRIBUTION OF EXPENDITURE

YEAR	1941 £P.	1941 %	1942 £P.	1942 %	1943 £P.	1943 %	1944 £P.	1944 %	1945 £P.	1945 %	1946 £P.	1946 %
Land Settlement Plans	34,729	47.2	32,999	35.6	62,075	46.4	90,655	58.4	98,569	52.0	105,274	45.2
Training	—	—	13,018	14	10,912	8.2	3,456	2.2	18,586	9.8	6,921	3
Village Development Plans	—	—	—	—	—	—	—	—	—	—	22,879	9.8
Town Maps and Plans	2,318	3.2	6,376	6.9	4,172	3.1	2,433	1.6	6,747	3.6	11,269	4.8
Triangulation	2,634	3.6	3,209	3.5	1,846	1.4	2,015	1.3	1,259	0.7	1,667	0.7
Levelling & Contouring	360	0.5	468	0.5	2,138	1.6	458	0.3	438	0.2	278	0.1
Topographical Maps	5,966	8.1	4,692	5.1	3,933	2.9	5,215	3.4	4,969	2.6	3,935	1.7
District Survey Offices	7,035	9.6	7,813	8.4	10,165	7.6	14,764	9.5	15,830	8.3	20,170	8.7
Work for other Departments	5,188	7.1	9,393	10.1	15,863	11.9	8,224	5.3	12,675	6.7	18,981	8.2
Printing	3,326	4.5	3,238	3.5	4,273	3.2	5,761	3.7	6,591	3.5	8,979	3.8
Administration	11,950	16.2	11,486	12.4	18,328	13.7	22,116	14.3	23,945	12.6	32,449	14
TOTAL EXPENDITURE	73,506	100	92,692	100	133,705	100	155,097	100	189,609	100	232,802	100
Total man-days (effective & non-effective)	74,668		97,515		109,896		108,066		117,420		116,855	
Cost per man-day (£P. mils)	.984		.951		1.217		1.435		1.615		1.992	

Note: — Amounts include compensatory (high cost-of-living) allowances.

TABLE 15
(See Section C)

EXPENDITURE 1940/41 TO 1946/47

FINANCIAL YEAR	1940/41	1941/42	1942/43	1943/44	1944/45	1945/46	1946/47
	£P.	£P.	£P.	£P.	£P.	£P.	£P.
Personal Emoluments	60,867	59,930	62,357	67,975	71,133	77,660	87,961
Other Charges	7,148	10,143	15,798	22,088	25,397	27,890	26,755
Special Expenditure	396	798	999	—	244	900	1,699
TOTAL	68,411	70,871	79,154	90,063	96,774	106,450	116,415
Compensatory Allowance (High Cost of living)	—	5,843	19,595	54,305	60,576	98,530	142,241
GRAND TOTAL	68,411	76,714	98,749	144,368	157,350	204,980	258,656

REVENUE 1940/41 TO 1946/47

YEAR	Map Sales	Copyright Royalties	Survey Fees	Surveyors' Licences	TOTAL
	£P.	£P.	£P.	£P.	£P.
1940/41	1369	41	4,890	84	6,384
1941/42	734	19	8,318	105	9,176
1942/43	777	6	7,291	265	8,339
1943/44	1632	17	4,104	66	5,819
1944/45	6774	—	5,357	51	12,182
1945/46	5872	25	5,679	369	11,945
1946/47	6421	114	10,317	129	16,981

TABLE 16
(See paragraph 18)

SALARIES AND COST-OF-LIVING ALLOWANCES

Financial Year	Total Staff	Personal Emoluments	COST OF LIVING	
			Index *	Allowances
		£P.		£P.
1940-41	515	61,000	—	NIL
1941-42	559	60,000	—	6,000
1942-43	659	62,000	186	20,000
1943-44	725	68,000	218	54,000
1944-45	684	71,000	236	61,000
1945-46	704	78,000	258	99,000
1946-47	736	88,000	258	142,000

* At beginning of financial year.
Pre-war = 100. 1.4.47 = 281.

TABLE 17
(See paragraph 17)

EXAMINATION FOR SURVEYORS LICENCES

YEAR	Candidates	Passes	Practising (b)
1921-39	303	101	—
1940	16	4	84
1941	10	3	85
1942	11	3	86
1943	9	2	86
1944	22	8	94
1945	26	9	103
1946	28	20	—
1946(a)	17	11	132
TOTALS	442	161	

Notes: — (a) Special practical examination for ex-servicemen.
(b) Does not include Government officers who passed the examination but are not issued with licence while serving (e.g. 3 in 1946).

TABLE 18
(*See Section D*)

LAND REGISTRATION SECTION

Plans submitted for registration checked and approved.

YEAR	SETTLED AREAS		NON-SETTLED AREAS		TOTAL
	Licensed Surveyors	Survey Department (a)	Licensed Surveyors	Survey Department (a)	
1940	344	90	371	258	1063
1941	336	129	529	253	1247
1942	265	106	267	127	765
1943	368	95	358	122	943
1944	450	106	580	108	1244
1945	513	95	480	89	1177
1946	464	109	381	108	1062
TOTALS	2740	730	2966	1065	7501

The average area covered by one plan was 45 dunums. (a metric dunum is 1000 sq. m. or approximately ¼ acre).

The plans prepared by District Survey Officers (under (a) above) were:—

YEAR	1940	1941	1942	1943	1944	1945	1946	Total
For Government	236	242	126	84	89	62	55	894
For public	112	140	107	135	125	122	162	903
								1797

TABLE 19
(See Section D)

NOTIFICATIONS BY DIRECTOR OF LAND REGISTRATION CONFIRMING REGISTRATION OF MUTATIONS

YEAR	Mutations Confirmed	RUNNING TOTAL SINCE MARCH 1927		
		Confirmed	Pending	Abandoned
1940	416	4158	1153	497
1941	356	4514	1253	498
1942	362	4876	1217	542
1943	360	5236	1293	557
1944	530	5766	1303	578
1945	467	6233	1369	621
1946	434	6667	1513	631
TOTAL	2925			

The average mutation affects one or two old parcels and creates by subdivision 7—14 new parcels.

TABLE 20
(See Section E)

VILLAGE DEVELOPMENT SURVEYS
Progress to 31.12.46

Field Work begun	91	villages
Additional trig. observed	30	"
Built-on area surveyed by plane-table	55	"
Built-on area block plans revised	19	"
Adjoining area block plans revised	50	"
Adjoining area surveyed by plane-table	26	"
Field work completed	74	"
Drawn: built-on area	41	plans
adjoining area	31	"
Printed	57	plans

TABLE 21
(*See paragraph* 38)

ADJUSTMENT OF MAJOR TRIG. (NORTH TRANSJORDAN BLOCK)

The method of observation and adjustment was that of directions.

The 27 points and 69 lines of the network gave 65 condition equations, which were solved simultaneously by the method of least squares, using a modified form of the method of solution of normal equations devised by the U.S. Coast and Geodetic Survey (Doolittle method). This modified form proved to be superior to the classical one of Gauss, used in the adjustment of the Palestine Major Triangulation. Scale and orientation were fixed by the three lines 54'M-55'M-73'M-98'M of the Palestine Major Triangulation.

Rectangular Coordinates were computed on the Transverse Mercator Projection, referred to the true and false origins of the Palestine Survey. Geographicals were obtained by conversion from these rectangulars.

Excluding the time spent by the Superintendent in charge of the Computing Office in organising, forming condition equations etc., the work took about 350 man-days to complete.

Women computers, completely new to this class of work, were employed.

Errors, in seconds of arc, for 43 triangles:—

Average triangular error	1.55
Probable triangular error	1.25
P.E. of observed direction	0.5
P.E. of observed angle	0.7
P.E. of adjusted direction	0.4
P.E. of adjusted angle	0.6

TABLE 22
(*See Section H*)

MINOR TRIANGULATION AND CONTROL

YEAR	Fourth order points	Control points	Traverse points	Licensed surveyors points
1940	752	1494	5,428	—
1941	402	582	5,816	—
1942	1070	991	6,302	—
1943	537	1998	7,704	2587
1944	723	2070	11,872	2016
1945	498(a)	1194	13,626	3371
1946	796(b)	391	12,382	1514
TOTALS	4778	8720	63,135	9488

(a) Includes 31 points for Village Development
(b) Includes 358 points for Village Development
(i.e. in advance of main net-work).

Levelling	Precise	Tertiary
Kilometers run	52	1027
Bench Marks fixed	25	1861

TABLE 23
(See Section F)

LAND SETTLEMENT PROGRESS (BLOCKS).

YEAR	(a) Blocks surveyed	(b) Preliminary Plans	(c) Field Examination	(d) Final Plans	(e) Blocks settled	(f) Not completed
1927-39	7126	5911	6512	4602	4561	2565
1940	536	766	273	757	738	2363
1941	288	738	586	873	832	1819
1942	356	454	395	620	612	1563
1943	550	571	355	746	821	1292
1944	721	645	512	554	575	1438
1945	771	797	624	731	606	1603
1946	548	684	422	483	445	1706
TOTALS	10,896	10,566	9679	9366	*9190	1706

Note: — See Table 24 for statistics of block sizes.
* The total area settled is 5140 sq. kms.
(a) Includes blocks surveyed by licensed surveyors and accepted.
(b) Traced and prints issued to Settlement Officers. Includes plans traced of blocks surveyed under "1941" system for which no preliminaries were printed.
(c) Plotted field sheets examined in field.
(d) Traces amended and prints issued to Settlement Officers.
(e) Schedules of Rights published.
(f) Difference between (a) and (e).

TABLE 24
(See Section F)

REGISTRATION BLOCK PLAN SCALES

(Figures cover the 7 years 1940—1946)

SCALE	1:5000(*)	1:2500	1:1250	1:625
No. of blocks	371	2,102	680	14
Percentage of blocks	12	66	22	(0.4)
No. of parcels	2,012	74,575	41,074	918
Parcels per block	5	35	60	66
Area (dunums)	344,445	1,567,050	126,850	733
Percentage of area	17	77	6	(0.04)
Area of block	928	745	186	52
Area of parcel	171	21	3	0.8

(*) The maximum ground size and precision of survey of these blocks is as for 1:2500 but, containing little detail, they can be plotted in groups on one field sheet on the smaller scale.

TABLE 25
(See paragraph 54)

AREA COMPUTING

YEAR	Preliminary		Final		Amendment	Land Category Schedules	Applications for Dimensions
	Blocks	Parcels	Blocks	Parcels	Parcels		
1940	512	18,419	782	28,900	7,950	1310	567
1941	409	13,225	891	32,655	9,320	531	531
1942	135	5,626	563	18,267	500	458	592
1943	39	1,230	778	24,307	396	219	817
1944	53	705	579	24,054	298	234	967
1945	105	3,877	681	25,012	145	180	1036
1946	101	4,155	512	25,723	75	43	971
TOTALS	1354	47,237	4786	178,918	18,684	2975	5481

Area (dunums) 638.818   2,829,940

Note effect of introduction of new system in 1942.

TABLE 26
(*See Section C*)

TOWN PLANS AND MAPS

YEAR	PLANS (1:1250 etc.)				MAPS (1:10,000)
	New Survey (dunums)	Field Revision (dunums)	Drawing (Plans)	Office Revision (Plans)	Sheets compiled
1940	} 32,500	7,750	5	11	—
1941		—	—	—	—
1942		—	—	—	—
1943	—	—	2	—	1
1944	250	—	18	16	6
1945	—	—	40	19	3
1946	—	90,290	28	58	3
TOTALS	32,750	98,040	93	104	13

TABLE 27
(*See paragraph 57*)

MAP DRAWING OFFICE

Plans amended due to changes in administrative boundaries. (Block plans of settled villages, 1:10,000 fiscal map of other villages)

YEAR	VILLAGES	
	Settled	Others
1940	—	—
1941	—	56
1942	221	378
1943	—	198
1944	8	20
1945	—	—
1946	—	3

In addition the following had to be amended accordingly:—
1 : 20,000 Series Maps.
1 : 100,000 Series overprints (boundaries)
1 : 150,00 ⎱ Index to Villages
1 : 250,00 ⎰ and Settlements

TABLE 28
(*See paragraph 60*)

PRINTING OFFICE

YEAR	Machines (Impressions)	Handpress (proofs)	Ordoverax Process	Sunprints
1940	39,855	1264	4440	16,725
1941	1,195,400	1777	5558	18,817
1942	642,644	2867	5555	10,650
1943	265,553	2101	3656	13,365
1944	780,000	3793	—	15,160
1945	760,000	6960	2000	20,901
1946	451,258	6667	680	24,656

PLATE-MAKING

YEAR	Photography (negatives)	Helio Process	Douglagraph process	Total plates	Plates grained
(*)					
1942	200	142	486	628	800
1943	228	224	486	710	1120
1944	284	284	678	962	1513
1945	272	234	873	1007	1180
1946	380	248	646	904	2301

(*) = Statistics prior to 1942 not complete.

TABLE 29
(See paragraph 62)

REPAIR AND ADJUSTMENT OF INSTRUMENTS ETC.

YEAR	1940	1941	1942	1943	1944	1945	1946
Theodolites and Levels	49	32	29	41	36	19	31
Theodolites and Levels, bubbles for	*	*	*	*	*	*	28
Plane tables	*	*	*	*	*	*	17
Tripods	27	*	*	19	22	16	51
Abney Levels, field glasses, Prismatic and trough compasses, telescopic alidades	69	100	86	87	79	86	45
Calculating machines and typewriters	*	*	38	49	74	85	70
Drawing Instruments	*	*	51	36	100	107	104
Tapes and chains (including standardising)	*	*	122	160	104	225	211
Printing machinery	*	*	*	*	*	*	19
Electric apparatus and wiring	*	*	*	*	*	*	21
Miscellaneous repairs	*	*	*	36	45	62	45

* = not recorded.

Note: — Major repairs requiring the use of machinery such as lathes, etc., were carried out in a local precision workshop and are not included in the above.

TABLE 30

SURVEY OF PALESTINE
PUBLICATIONS AS AT 1ST DECEMBER 1947

Orders for Survey of Palestine publications may be made at the Survey Department, Tel Aviv (P.O. Box 676, Jaffa), or at the District Survey Offices at Jerusalem, Haifa, Tel Aviv, Jaffa, Gaza, Tiberias, and Tulkarm, or at authorised booksellers. The London agents are E.W. Stanford, Ltd., and Sifton, Praed & Co., Ltd.

Note: No agents discount for sunprints. 1000 mils = one pound sterling.

PLANS OF VILLAGES AND SETTLEMENTS	SCALE	PRICE (Each sheet, mils)
Registration Block Plans	1:2500 or 1:1250	250 (sunprint)
Registration Block Plans (Reduction)	1:10,000	250
Registration Block Plans (Index)	1:20,000	50 (sunprint)
Development Plans (Built on area)	1:1250	250
Development Plans (Adjoining area)	1:2500	250
TOWN PLANS AND MAPS		
Urban Assessment Block Plans	1:1250	250 (sunprint)
Urban Assessment Block Plans (Index)	1:20,000 or 1:10,000	50 (sunprint)
Town Sheets	1:2500 or 1:1250	200
Town Sheets (Index)	1:10,000	50
Towns Maps :—		
Jerusalem (1 sheet)	1:5000	200
Jerusalem (1 sheet)	1:10,000	200
Jerusalem & Suburbs (6 sheets)	1:10,000	200
Jerusalem & Suburbs (1 sheet)	1:10,000	300 (linen 350)
Jaffa—Tel Aviv (*) (2 sheets)	1:10,000	200
Haifa (*) (4 sheets)	1:10,000	200
Nazareth (1 sheet)	1:5000	200
Ramle (2 sheets)	1:2500	200
Block and Sheet Index overprint (for * only)	1:10,000	250
Town Planning Areas :—		
Jerusalem	1:10,000	250
Jerusalem, Block Index overprint	1:10,000	300
Tel Aviv	1:12,500	200
Jaffa	1:12,500	200
GENERAL MAPS		
Topocadastral Series (150 sheets)	1:20,000	200 (linen 240)
Central Judaea	1:50,000	200
Topographical Series (16 sheets)	1:100,000	200 (folded 250)
Topographical Series (3 sheets)	1:250,000	150 (linen 200)
Topographical Series (Administrative Divisions)	1:250,000	150 (linen 200)
Motor Map (linen)	1:500,000	150 (folded 200)
General Map, Palestine	1:750,000	150
Index to Villages & Settlements (3 sheets)	1:150,000	250
Index to Villages & Settlements (1 sheet)	1:250,000	250
Index to Villages & Settlements (Land Transfer Zones)	1:250,000	250

(see over)

TABLE 30 (cont.)

SPECIAL MAPS	SCALE	PRICE (Each sheet, mils)
Palestine of the Old Testament (linen)	1:500,000	150 (folded 200)
Palestine of the Crusades (linen)	1:350,000	250
Palestine of the Crusades (folded with gazetteer)	1:350,000	375
Palestine of the Crusades (gazetteer)	booklet	100
Jerusalem Old City	1:2500	150 (folded 200)
Haram esh Sharif (Temple Area) English & Arabic	1:625	500
Geological Map — North Sheet	1:250,000	out of print
Geological Map — South Palestine (sheet 3)	1:250,000	500
Hula Contour Survey (19 sheets)	1:5000	200
Rainfall	1:500,000	200

U.N.S.C.O.P. MAPS 1947		
Jewish Land with Transfer Zones	1:250,000	200
Progress of Land Settlement	1:250,000	200
Population	1:250,000	200
Rainfall	1:750,000	150
Land Classification	1:1,000,000	100
Forest Lands	1:250,000	250
State Domain	1:250,000	250
Administrative Divisions	1:750,000	100
Climatic Elements	diagrams	100
Folder containing above plus General Map	—	1000 (£P. 1.)

OTHER PUBLICATIONS		
Road Distances for Palestine	booklet	100
Survey Legislation (consolidated)	booklet	100
Descriptive Map Catalogue, with indexes	booklet	50
Licensed Surveyors Examination	set of papers	250
Town Triangulation & Traverse Diagrams (Jerusalem 7, Haifa 12, Jaffa, Tel Aviv)	1:10,000	150

PALESTINE

DEPARTMENT OF SURVEYS

SUPPLEMENT

to the

"REPORT for the years 1940-1946"

to cover the period

JANUARY 1947 – MARCH 1948

DEPARTMENT OF SURVEYS

Supplement to "Report for 1940-1946" for the period up to 31.3.48.

1. The impact of political events in Palestine was increasingly felt by the Department as the year 1947 progressed. At the beginning of February British wives and children were evacuated from Palestine ("Operation Polly") while British officers were escorted to and from their offices. Martial Law was enforced in "Elephant Area" (including Tel Aviv) from 2 to 17 March during which period Headquarters was cut off from all communication with the field and other offices of the Department. The Headquarters building in Tel Aviv was guarded by British Army detachments from February until November.

2. Following the visit of UNSCOP (U.N. Special Committee) to Palestine, there were disturbances on the Jaffa - Tel Aviv border and the Arab staff were unable to come to work from 15 to 19 August. Tension in Tel Aviv then relaxed and the archives which had been evacuated to a security zone in August 1946 were returned in October, 1947.

3. Finally the disturbances following the UNO Vote for Partition on 29 November resulted in a stoppage of all intercourse between the Jewish and Arab populations in the Jaffa - Tel Aviv area with the result that no Arab staff could approach the office. As it was out of the question to transfer the whole Department to Jerusalem, steps were taken to obtain possession of part of the former R.A.F. Station at Ramle (20 kms. from Jaffa) and to transfer the Arab personnel with the appropriate office equipment, stores, and records. Although at variance with official 'non-implementation' policy, the division of the land (settlement of title) plans and associated field books, etc., was made in accordance with the UNO partition boundary. The alternatives were to leave all such records at Tel Aviv or move them all to Ramle.

4. Routine technical work virtually ceased for two months while the division was organised. Transport across 'no-mans-land' was arranged but as soon as the removal began the office was twice raided by Jewish extremists who took away a large quantity of printed maps, office machines, instruments, etc. The Army was therefore called in to remove immediately the Arab records under escort. Subsequently there were further thefts, including those of two vehicles while on the road, and it became necessary for the two remaining British officers to leave Tel Aviv. At Ramle, the R.A.F. Station was invaded by hundreds of Arab looters during the temporary withdrawal of armed guards. In spite of all these difficulties the office there began to function in February 1948.

5. Field work was less seriously affected as most of the surveyors were Arabs and working in Arab areas. The mixed staff of the District Survey Offices at Jerusalem, Haifa, and Tiberias continued to work together as far as local conditions permitted. Documents and maps were stolen by Arab raiders from the Haifa office in January 1948 and from the Nazareth office in March.

6. Following the upward revision of salary scales of Second Division officers in 1946, those of the First Division and of the manipulative services were revised in 1947 (with effect from 1946), the maximum of the new basic salary scale for field labourers becoming LP.12 per mensem. The cost-of-living index had risen to 285 by the end of 1947.

7. The local Arabic press took some interest in staff problems early in the year and published reports of meetings or interviews on four occasions.

Steps were taken to establish a departmental joint consultative committee of nine members for the discussion of internal staff problems and submission of recommendations to the Director. The constitution was approved by Government but the electoral committee was unable to meet.

8. Mr. J. W. Loxton represented the Department at the Conference of Commonwealth Survey Officers in London in August when a paper on "Surveys for Settlement of Title and Registration of Rights to land in Palestine" was presented and discussed.

9. Mr. T. Haddad and Mr. M. Kaminsky, who entered the Department in 1922 and 1924 respectively, were promoted Superintendents with effect from 1 April 1947.

The appointment to Palestine of a British Superintendent under training at the R.E. Survey Training Centre in England was cancelled by the Colonial Office in view of the impending withdrawal of British administration.

10. There were 35 candidates at the annual examination for Surveyors Licences held in May 1947, of whom 18 were successful.

Government survey officers with long service, faced with the prospect of abolition of office, applied for licences towards the end of the year. Steps were therefore taken to enact an amendment to the Survey Ordinance giving the Director discretion to grant licences without an examination to suitably qualified officers.

11. The number of plans for registration checked by District Survey Offices increased sharply during the year, the total being about 50 per cent more than in 1946.

There was also a sudden rise in the public demand for maps and plans from December onwards but owing to depleted stocks (see paragraph 4), sales had to be restricted after January.

12. The programme of surveys of village sites for development plans was continued at the rate of a hundred a year until December when field work had to be abandoned in several villages.

The number of surveyors engaged in Settlement of Title surveys continued to decline. In December, work in the Jerusalem area was abandoned. Chain survey parties continued in the Jenin Sub-District and examination parties in parts of Galilee until the end of March 1948.

- 3 -

13. Fourth order triangulation for Development Surveys was carried out round several more villages during 1947 and for Settlement of Title Surveys in the Jerusalem District until February 1948.

Observations of magnetic variation with the Connolly Compass were recommenced during the triangulation west of Jerusalem.

Observations were started in November to close the precise levelling circuit between Nazareth and Tiberias (31 kms.) which had been marked in 1937.

The party of surveyors loaned to the Water Commissioner completed its field work in November and was broken up.

Three surveyors were loaned in December for three months to Army Disposals (Fixed Assets) for area computing work.

14. Town revision was carried on throughout 1947. In several towns revised sheets or new extension sheets of the existing series of large scale plans were published, while El Faluja was covered for the first time by two sheets on 1:2500. A new two-sheet plan of Ramle on 1:2500, showing roads, contours, and cultivation in colours was published and new similarly coloured plans of Gaza (2 sheets), Lydda (4), Safad (2), and Ramallah and El Bira (3) were in an advanced state of preparation.

15. Other publications during 1947 :-

(a) 10 new sheets of the 1:20,000 series in the vicinity of and north of Beersheba.

(b) A new general map (layered) on scale 1:750,000 covering the whole of Palestine in one sheet.

(c) A Geological edition of sheet 3 of the 1:250,000 series covering the area from $31°$ N southwards to the Gulf of 'Aqaba, compiled by the Government Geologist.

(d) Revised editions of the Motor Map (1:500,000), seven sheets of the 1:100,000 series, the Old Testament map, the Old City of Jerusalem, and several other maps.

(e) The set of maps and diagrams prepared for the Anglo-American Committee in 1946 was brought up to date for UNSCOP and published.

(f) A new general map, layered, covering Palestine in one sheet on 1:500,000 was in course of preparation. (The Motor Map on this scale does not cover the southern desert).

16. A power-driven Furnival Quad Crown proving and duplicating press and a Crossland guillotine were acquired from Army Disposals and installed in the Printing Office early in 1947.

The ordoverax table and a sunprinting frame were removed to Ramle in January 1948.

A. P. Mitchell

31st March, 1948.   DIRECTOR OF SURVEYS.